THE INDOMITABLE MR COTHAM

ST GREGORY'S CHURCH, CHELTENHAM.

THE INDOMITABLE
MR COTHAM

Missioner, Convict Chaplain and Monk

Joanna Vials

GRACEWING

First published in England in 2019
by
Gracewing
2 Southern Avenue
Leominster
Herefordshire HR6 0QF
United Kingdom
www.gracewing.co.uk

No part of this publication may be reproduced, stored in a
retrieval system, or transmitted in any form or by any means,
electronic, mechanical, photocopying, recording or otherwise,
without the written permission of the publisher.

The right of Joanna Vials to be identified
as the author of this work has been asserted in accordance
with the Copyright, Designs and Patents Act 1988.

© 2019 Joanna Vials

ISBN 978 085244 928 8

Typeset by Gracewing

Cover design by Bernardita Peña Hurtado

Front cover: Hobart Town on the River Derwent, Van Diemen's Land by
Edward Duncan

To Chris, my companion along the way

CONTENTS

Acknowledgments..xi

Abbreviations..xiii

Illustrations..xiv

Foreword by Rt Revd Abbot Geoffrey Scott OSB..........xv

Introduction..xix

PART ONE: 'ENGLAND SEEMED HARDLY LARGE ENOUGH'..1

1 'I was known there by the name of Little Larry'..........3

2 Alma Mater..11

3 'The Most Neglected Portion of the Catholic World'..21

4 'You may calculate upon no little trouble with him'....29

5 A miserable state of affairs..49

6 Hobart and Richmond, 1835–1838..............................57

7 Launceston, 1838–1844..67

8 'Ce Jeune Prètre Parle le Francais'................................83

9 Widening Horizons...95

10 Teetotal Society..105

11 Lawrence and Sarah Cotham in Van Diemen's Land....119

12 New Regimes..127

13 Taking up the Reins...137

14 In his own words...153

15 HMS Anson..161

16 Quid prodest?..173

17 Fr Cotham's Oratory...191

18 Convict Chaplains in the Sole Gaol of England........199

19 'When You Destroy Hope in Man You Destroy Everything'...219

20 Congenial Pursuits..231

21 Interlude: Visit to Port Phillip, 1846.......................241

22 'The Sure Prospect'—Loosening the Ties................251

23 'Called To Go On Board'..263

PART TWO 'THERE CAME A MAN OF INDOMITABLE ENERGY'..269

24 Return to England..271

25 'Cheltenham, resort of the good and the gay'...........285

26 'I consider it is time we should bestir ourselves in good earnest.'..303

27 'Numerous but Poor'..321

28 Appeals and Tenders..333

29 Co-Worker and Friend...347

30 'A Ceremonial of a Very Gorgeous Character'.........357

31 'Cum Illo Benè'..371

32 School Report: Making Good Progress.....................381

33 'Much yet remains to be done.'................................393

34 'I hope you will withstand their rascality.'...............409

35 Celebrating the Divine Service.................................419

36 The Congregation of the Daughters of the Cross of Liège...433

37 Reluctant Guarantor and Landlord..........................453

38 Family Business and Financial Acumen....................463

39 Indefatigable?..485

40 Looking Beyond St Gregory's...................................503

41 Resignation from the Cheltenham Mission..............511

42 Leaving Douai Again..521

43 The Final Mission..531

44 Enforced Quiet..537

45 The Spolia of Ambrose Cotham's Life........................543

Appendix A: The Letter of March 1836..........................557

Appendix B: Cotham's Companions: After Australia and
Cheltenham..563

Appendix C: The Family Left Behind............................569

Bibliography..577

Index of Personal Names.......................................585

ACKNOWLEDGEMENTS

MY THANKS EXTEND over both hemispheres, as did Fr Cotham's labours. I am grateful to those at a distance who took an interest in Fr Cotham's mission in Van Diemen's Land and recognised him as one of their own: Brian Andrews, Heritage Officer, Archdiocese of Hobart, Tasmania; Dr Prudence Francis and Dr Nicholas Brodie, who searched for Fr Cotham's trail in the Hobart Archdiocesan Archives; the late Fr Terry Southerwood, a pioneer in his own right; Janet Phippard for material on her convict ancestor James O'Keefe; the inspirational Dr Dianne Snowden AM and her co-workers who have given identities to formerly forgotten women and orphans.

In England, knowledge of Fr Cotham was generously shared with me by members of the English Benedictine Congregation. The Rt Revd Geoffrey Scott OSB, Abbot of Douai Abbey, opened the abbey's archives to me and offered a Foreword before publication was assured; Revd Fr Alban Hood, the monastic community, and former archivist Alison Day also welcomed my visits to Douai Abbey. Revd Fr Anselm Cramer OSB diligently searched the archives of Ampleforth Abbey for signs of Fr Cotham, as did Steve Parsons at Downside Abbey and Brenda Warde at Belmont Abbey.

In the diocese of Clifton, archivist Revd Canon Dr Anthony Harding and assistant archivist Gill Hogarth joined me in looking for early records of St Gregory's Parish. David Knight at Stonyhurst College and Mary Allen at Farm Street, London, found the important Cotham family connections with the Jesuit order.

In Gloucestershire, Fr Cotham was introduced to the Cheltenham Local History Society, which gave me opportunities to talk about and display my research. Kate Greenaway at the Cheltenham Ladies College; staff at Gloucestershire Archives, and Cheltenham Local History Library perpetuated the reputation of archivists for patient interest in the minutiae of their enquirer's current knotty piece of study. Independent local historians Richard Barton and the late Revd Brian Torode were unfailingly kind, encouraging. and knowledgeable; David Drinkwater and Mike Grindley added their distinctive input to journalistic resources.

The editorial support of David McConkey came at an opportune time and has been invaluable; his sharp eye, acute ear, and ecclesiastical erudition have been an asset to the text.

Finally, the parish of St Gregory the Great, Cheltenham has allowed me to explore, develop and evaluate the contribution of its little-known founding father. Canon Bosco Macdonald and Fr David Mills, Fr Frank Wainwright, and Fr David McDonald, diocesan successors to the Benedictines, have worked valiantly to maintain and enhance the work begun by Fr Cotham in the church and among the people of Cheltenham.

Tom Longford and Revd Dr Paul Haffner of Gracewing have guided the work to published completion with a light hand and a steadying belief that it has been a worthwhile undertaking.

My husband Chris Bentall accompanied me in all aspects of the research. He now knows Fr Cotham as well as anybody, since the reverend gentleman has been our houseguest for a number of years and Chris has never tired of his company.

ABBREVIATIONS

AAA	Ampleforth Abbey Archives
CDA	Clifton Diocesan Archives
DA	Douai Abbey Archives
DAA	Downside Abbey Archives
GRO	Gloucestershire Record Office
HAA	Hobart Archdiocesan Archives, Tasmania

Australian newspaper extracts are from www.trove.nla.gov.au

References to *The Tablet* are taken from www.archive.thetablet.co.uk unless stated otherwise.

All quotations relating to the correspondence and papers of James Ambrose Cotham OSB are from DA IV.C.XI or DA VIII.A.Cotham, Douai Abbey Archives, unless noted otherwise.

ILLUSTRATIONS

1. Catholic Church of St Gregory the Great, Cheltenham, opened 1857. Engraving from a watercolour by the architect Charles Hansom, 1853. [Gloucestershire Archives]   Frontispiece

2. Cotham's Journal, Hobart, March 1846. [DAA]..................163

3. Cotham's Journal, Hobart, June 1846. [DAA]......................184

4. Fr James Ambrose Cotham OSB, carte de visite c 1860. [DAA]...269

5. The Catholic Chapel, 1845. From *George Rowe's Illustrated Cheltenham Guide 1845*. This is the only known image of the first Catholic chapel in Cheltenham. [Out of copyright].......290

6. Dr George Ford Copeland, the largest donor of St Gregory's and Fr Cotham's local link with the Oxford Movement. [Richard Barton Collection, now in the author's possession]................353

7. Fr William Cotham SJ, 1806-1895, Fr James Cotham's elder brother. [Farm St Archives]...464

8. Mary St, Gympie, Queensland, 1868. The hometown of Fr Cotham's younger brother Lawrence Cotham and his family. [Gympie Regional Library]...473

9. The Douai community, 1874/75. Fr Cotham seated third from left; Prior Anselm O'Gorman, centre; Fr Austin O'Neill, third from right; Fr Wilfrid Raynal, back row, far right. [DAA].....514

10. Fr Cotham's grave, Belmont Abbey. [Author's collection]....550

11. James Cotham (Fr Cotham's great nephew from Queensland) seated on the ground, with the novitiate group, 1887/88, Douai. [DAA]...574

FOREWORD

A BIOGRAPHY OF THE English Benedictine monk and missioner, James Ambrose Cotham (1810–1883) reflects a shift in historical studies of the English Catholic clergy. With his story, we have moved beyond the thoroughly ploughed furrows of accounts dealing with English Catholic leaders and heroes and descend to the lower echelons of the ordinary parish clergy. This has been possible partly because of recent discoveries of archival resources which have here been fully exploited with enthusiasm by Joanna Vials in her meticulous research.

James Cotham belonged to the aspiring Catholic professional class in Lancashire which was to benefit from Catholic Emancipation granted in 1829, the year he was clothed as 'Ambrose' in the Benedictine habit at St Edmund's priory in Douai. His family ties remained strong throughout his life. As a monk, he was a typical example of the rugged idiosyncratic and independent Benedictine missionary, a type which had produced martyrs in the seventeenth century. In the nineteenth century such characters found it an easy transition from working in an England experiencing rapid industrialisation to labouring abroad among convicts without hope. Australia was not virgin territory to be exposed to the gospel; it was far closer to what monks like Cotham had already known in England, where Catholics had lived as exiles for centuries. Being exiles in the southern antipodes held few surprises for them.

Within a year of his ordination, Cotham sailed in 1835 for Australia with Bede Polding, his fellow monk, who had been appointed Vicar Apostolic of New Holland in eastern Australia the previous year. Ambrose Cotham belonged to the missionary enterprise of the first half of the nineteenth century which was a dominating feature of the pontificate of Pope Gregory XVI (1831–1846), and Cotham was an ultramontane by inclination.

Despite the return to the pope of the papal states in 1815 following the downfall of Napoleon, the papacy had lost much influence, especially in Europe, and so began to search for new territories fit for evangelisation. Australia was distinctive in that through the transportation of convicts into the colony there was already a sizable, but fairly nominal, Christian body present when Cotham landed in Van Diemen's Land (later Tasmania) as a member of the early English Benedictine Australian mission. It was for his work in Van Diemen's Land between 1835 and 1851 in prisons, asylums, orphanages, and prison hulks that Cotham is principally remembered. He had left before transportation finally ended in the colony in 1853.

Cotham is unusual in that he had a second career on the English mission between 1851 and his death in 1883. In this he closely paralleled Bernard Ullathorne (1806–1889), his fellow Benedictine who left Australia in 1840 where he had been Vicar-General since 1833. Ullathorne returned to England in 1841 to work on the Benedictine mission in Coventry until he became Vicar Apostolic of the Western District in 1846. Cotham made his mark in Cheltenham, a Benedictine mission which he administered from 1852 until 1873, and where he erected the magnificent church of St Gregory the Great which when completed outshone all other places of worship in that increasingly fashionable spa town. Ullathorne's church in Coventry and Cotham's in Cheltenham were both designed by Charles Hansom. Sometimes by design, and sometimes by coincidence, the English Benedictines were drawn to spas like Cheltenham, where they were responsible, as in Bath whose church was also designed by Charles Hansom, for building grand churches. In Australia, Cotham had been militant in his campaigns for the temperance movement, organising societies, processions, and supporting the Independent Order of Rechabites, although his brother, Lawrence, also an immigrant in Van Diemen's Land, owned a public house. In Coventry, Ullathorne borrowed temperance sermons he had written in New South Wales, which he believed had similarities with Coventry. His most

Foreword xvii

famous temperance sermon, *The Drunkard*, was preached in Australia and England. In Cheltenham, Cotham had to contend with the fiercely anti-Catholic Dean Francis Close, although both were strong advocates of temperance.

After Cheltenham and as he grew older, Cotham's life became more unsettled. He hardly spent more than two years in each of his six abodes in England and on the continent before his death at St Michael's Priory, Belmont, on 1 May 1883. Belmont was by this time the perfect type of a neo-medieval monastery, gothic and romantic, resembling architecturally the church Cotham had erected in Cheltenham. But the reformed monastic conventual life which Belmont's walls now sheltered had little appeal for the old retired missionary. It is not surprising that with such a strong character, Cotham contributed to the folklore of his community at St Edmund's, Douai, and to giving a strong symbol of the presence of the Catholic Church in England through his vision realised in St Gregory the Great Church in Cheltenham.

Abbot Geoffrey Scott OSB
Douai Abbey, Woolhampton

INTRODUCTION

'Men speak too much about the world. Each one of us here, let the world go how it will, and be victorious or not victorious, has he not a life of his own to lead? One Life; a little gleam of Time between two eternities; no second chance to us for evermore!'

Thomas Carlyle, Lecture 5: 'The Hero as Man of Letters', May 1840.

IDWAY THROUGH JAMES Ambrose Cotham's life Thomas Carlyle delivered a series of lectures in which he proposed that 'the history of what man has accomplished in the world, is at bottom the History of Great Men who have worked here' and the 'bewildering, inextricable jungle of confusions, delusions, falsehoods and absurdities' thrown up by a philosophical utilitarianism could only be solved by a new Hero to stand alongside those of former epochs: Odin, Mahomet, Dante, Shakespeare, Cromwell, and Napoleon.[1] Cotham was neither a Hero nor a hero, but his 'little gleam of time' was not insignificant to the world or to his neighbours closer to hand. A guiding principle from boyhood was obedience to others: once he accepted life as a Benedictine monk, which both suited and vexed his personality, his major life choices were made for him, to serve others' objectives. At times the structures restrained and restricted him but within them he was also given opportunities to lead collaborative initiatives in 'the world, go how it will' that were small instances of major shifts in society.

When I compiled a small guidebook for the Catholic church of St Gregory the Great in Cheltenham—a church designed to stand prominently in the town as a challenge to the Established tradition—I was puzzled by the obscurity of the priest who spearheaded its expansion for twenty years. There is no mention of his name anywhere in the church; there is no plaque beside the memorial stained glass windows of St James and St Ambrose. However, once I began searching it was relatively easy to trace his life story, from Lancashire, to Douai in northern France, to Tasmania, to Cheltenham, Somerset and finally Herefordshire, as he lived through significant political, social, and church developments. A *carte de visite* portrait photograph c. 1860 shows a man who fits the description of him in contemporary Cheltenham newspapers: energetic, zealous, and indefatigable and this could be said of him throughout his life.

James Cotham grew to adulthood when the proud memory of religious defiance was being replaced by expectations arising from reform and emancipation. The British Government found it expedient to incorporate elements of the Catholic Church into its global expansionism so Cotham, as a chaplain employed by the Colonial Office, was drawn into the disputed system of convict transportation to Australia as well as the transformation of Van Diemen's Land into Tasmania. He returned to England in mid-life, wiser to the ways of ecclesial and national governance, having acquired a self-reliance and readiness to work with all manner of men and women demanded by life in a penal colony at 'this utmost extremity of the earth'.[2]

Cheltenham in 1852, when Fr Cotham became the Catholic missioner, was a town of visitors and newcomers: fashionable, impoverished, or aspirational. Its celebrated Regency facades, then as now, have utilitarian, unlovely rear elevations. Tangent Alley, along which George III walked from the Royal Old Wells to the Parish Church in 1788, shares a boundary wall with St Gregory's church and is a scruffy alley like any other alleyway. Cotham's task was to provide for the Irish immigrants and the rising professional middle class; this he achieved by harnessing the wealth and abilities of the latter for the education and care of the former. Since a considerable number of converts from Anglicanism formed the Catholic professional class in Cheltenham, Cotham was also able

Introduction   xxi

to meet their desire for, and willingness to pay and work for, a handsome Gothic Revival church to replace the old chapel.

After two decades of raising funds and successive phases of building Ambrose Cotham, approaching old age, wanted one more fresh opportunity. When his proposal to go to Australia was rejected he took himself off for a tour of Europe before asking for a small mission in Somerset. Despite ill health he could not resist another building project, completed after he had retired to St Michael's and All Angels Priory, Belmont near Hereford.

Ambrose Cotham led the building teams for three churches and one new mission: St John's, Richmond and St Joseph's, Launceston in Tasmania, and St Gregory the Great, Cheltenham and St Luke's, Wincanton in England. Yet the names of his immediate successors are better known in those churches: Fr Dunne, Dean Butler, Fr Wilkinson, and the Carmelite Friars. Fr Cotham was a building missioner whose priority was to provide a fitting place of worship. For this he had to collaborate closely with congregations and committees for people of diverse nationalities, classes, and moralities. His successors—most of whom stayed in their new missions for the majority of their lifetimes—made the churches their own, improving, developing, and beautifying but also defining a different clergy-laity relationship which has marked the Catholic Church since 1850.

The first nine months in Van Diemen's Land, from early August 1835 to the end of April 1836, were probably the most intense of his whole life: the physical, emotional, and mental experiences are documented; these were the crucible for his spiritual development. That time of his early manhood, in his mid-twenties, is mirrored in the final year of his active ministry more than forty years later; the one hundred and twenty-five miles on horseback across Van Diemen's Land is replaced by a five mile drive with a horse and gig in Somerset and the country road is no longer dangerous. When he was minister to a small congregation in Wincanton without a proper church he formed a committee—including once again a southern European immigrant as at Launceston in Van Diemen's Land, and a convert as at Cheltenham—provoking indignation in the local press. The opening Mass of the new mission was celebrated by his elder brother, a Jesuit, who was also to retire and then return to active ministry ten years later. If events in Bonham and Wincanton echo the Tasmanian experiences from forty-five years earlier it would be a sad reflection on his life if he was merely repeating himself, becoming a dusty legend of his own making, but they reveal a mind that stayed fresh.

Whilst it is true that Ambrose Cotham was a thorough-going missioner he was no less a Benedictine monk, in the mould of the English Benedictine Congregation. His closest priest associates—in authority, for retreats, and for socialising—were his Benedictine confrères but life in a monastic community chafed him, especially when his own ageing and illness restricted his activity as he lived at close quarters with others and followed a fixed *horarium*. He was at Belmont when 'young monks used to look with amazement on the attire of aged Capitular or Mission Fathers, who would appear with a scapular thrown over their ordinary clothes and wearing a top hat'.[3] Yet he loved the place as much as he loved his own family, which was very much. Despite arousing adverse comment he saw his duty towards his family as compatible with obedience to his vows and his religious superiors and not as a compromise to his personal integrity. His final weeks were not altogether peaceful: apart from physical pain, his disposal of money to family and religious communities was censured by his Prior and he was pressured to change his Will. He refused.

Twenty years after his death his memory was still alive and his reputation, then, was bright, even allowing for hyperbole; the *Downside Review* in 1902 spoke of 'D. Ambrose Cotham, a distinguished son of St Edmund's, whose services to Cheltenham can never be forgotten'.[4] Since then his services to Cheltenham have been largely forgotten and reading the archive material referring to him led me to wonder if he had been deliberately

Introduction xxiii

overlooked because of disapproval from his Benedictine community and Congregation; there were certainly acerbic references to him in letters written by his contemporaries in the Order. Nothing scandalous has come to light and when his confrères' opinions of him were judgemental it was usually because money was the issue.

If there is no reason why his memory should be left obscure I believe there is something to be gained in recalling his life and work. Judith Champ has written about a false norm by which the Catholic Church since 1950 has measured itself. The programme of church building to serve growing parishes which followed the Emancipation Act of 1829 and the restoration of the Catholic hierarchy in 1850 was followed by a long period of maintenance underpinned by the expectation that growth must inevitably continue.[5] Champ argues that apart from exceptional circumstances—such as the large-scale immigration of Irish Catholics and priests, and the conditions created by the Second World War—growth was not an inherent feature of the twentieth-century Catholic Church in England. The aberration is found not in the slowing down since 1950 but in the explosive expansionist period in the mid-nineteenth century. By looking back to that period, to the age when 'riding missioners' experimentally became leaders for highly visible congregations and their church buildings, we may find a model of church which speaks to post-Vatican II circumstances. Disparate groups of lay people, often new to church or Catholicism, were supported by instruction, administration of the sacraments, and exhortation, but were called to exercise the privileges of emancipation wherever they found themselves:

> This, I would say ... if I had a right to do so, to the Catholics of England generally. Let each stand on his own ground; let each approve himself in his own neighbourhood; if each portion is defended, the whole is secured ... care not for popular opinion, cultivate local.[6]

The necessities of earlier centuries when priests were not on hand daily to manage religious observance were replaced by the end of the century by a conscious effort to overlap all areas of life with corresponding church activity. Leadership became concentrated in clerical hands and lay voices were muted again, though they were no longer confined to the secluded estate or obscure mission of post-Reformation Catholic society.

During his lifetime Fr Ambrose Cotham was variously an itinerant pastor to a scattered flock, an evangeliser among a largely disaffected population, a church builder and administrator—raising funds, overseeing construction, and managing men and women involved in diverse roles—and both subordinate to authority and a figure of authority as a monk and a priest. When his lifelong attachment to his natural family and his concern with finances is added to the mix, it is worthwhile asking if and how he kept to a singular purpose through life, coming to the end with his integrity intact. A word applied to him by his contemporaries was *simple*, in its best senses, but his life was also one of rich complexity. James Ambrose Cotham did not achieve high office and his name has little prominence in written histories. Perhaps this book is Cotham's second chance to show how women and men—not Heroes—make the world a closer reality to what they believe it can and should be.

7 December 2018
Feast of St Ambrose of Milan

Notes

[1] T. Carlyle, *On Heroes, Hero-Worship, and the Heroic as History*. Edited by D. Sorenson and B. Kinser (New Haven and London: Press, 2013), p. 148.

[2] This classical phrase—*ultima thule*—was used by Cotham at a public meeting (*Hobarton Guardian*, 22 March 1848), p. 2, as well as by early explorers of the Antarctic.

[3] B. Whelan OSB, *The Annals of the English Congregation of the Black Monks of St Benedict (1850–1900)*, private publication, 1942, 2nd edition, reissued 1971, Vol. 1, p. 107.

[4] *Downside Review*, New Series Vol. 2 (Vol. 31), April–July–December 1902 (Weston Super Mare: The Mendip Press Limited), p. 278.

[5] J. Champ, *The Secular Priesthood in England and Wales: History, Mission and Identity* (Oscott Publications, 2016).

[6] J. H. Newman, *Lectures on the Present Position of Catholics in England addressed to the Brothers of the Oratory in the Summer of 1851*, 'Lecture 9: Duties of Catholics Towards the Protestant View'; www.newmanreader.org.

PART ONE
'England seemed hardly large enough'

1 'I WAS KNOWN THERE BY THE NAME OF LITTLE LARRY'

WITH HINDSIGHT IT can be seen which revolution, piece of legislation, or push for colonial expansion has influenced a person's life. But on the birth day of a baby for a very brief moment the world is as big as its parents' eyes. Very soon the world expands to family, neighbourhood, and—in the early nineteenth century—church. The influences become reciprocal, relationships are formed, and a separate identity emerges into an evolving social landscape. Choosing any particular point for stepping into history—as if there really is a before and after defined by that point—is a useful convention for a historian. For the individual who attaches his or her name to that date and place, it is not merely a metaphorical device but the beginning of a coherent sense of self, belonging, and potential.

James Cotham was born on 12 February 1810, in the hamlet of Orford, in Warrington, Lancashire. His father Lawrence Cotham, surgeon and man-midwife in Liverpool,[1] belonged to the professional middle class of Catholics which was established and accepted in the north-west of England to a degree not found throughout the country. He married Isabella Hall in St Elphin's Church, Warrington in October 1805, with Hamer Gaskell, a professional soldier, and Isabella's sister Mary Ann Pollard, as witnesses.[2] Warrington was Isabella's home town and St Elphin's was the Anglican parish church where all marriages were solemnized by law, irrespective of the couple's denomination. In eight years of marriage Lawrence and Isabella had four children: William born in 1806, Mary Ann in 1808, James in 1810, and Lawrence in 1812. James and Lawrence junior were born in Orford but all four children were baptised in Liverpool: William and Mary Ann at the Benedictine mission of St Peter's Priory,

Seel Street, James and Lawrence at St Anthony's Chapel, by its emigré founder, Fr Jean Baptiste Antoinet Gerardot. The godparents indicate the Cothams' social circle: William's godfather was James Irenaeus Rowe, Liverpool gentleman and tax assessor, and his godmother was Mary Ann Pollard; Mary Ann's and Lawrence's godfathers were Fr James Calderbank OSB and Fr Raphael Platt respectively, and for James the sponsors were John and Alice Swarbreck. These were people close to the family and their names recur in James' life, sometimes surprisingly so.

The Cothams provided a strong religious and family background. As one of the most Catholic counties in the country, Lancashire was proud of its recusant history, with local networks supporting each other in keeping alive a religious allegiance that at the turn of the nineteenth century was only just beginning to emerge from centuries of persecution. These characteristics are found in James Cotham's family which counted Blessed Thomas Cottam SJ, hung, drawn, and quartered at Tyburn in 1592, as a direct ancestor. Among James Cotham's loose papers is a hand drawn copy of the coat of arms for the Cottams of Cottam (or Knoll) Hall, Dilworth. The link is tenuous but he believed it to be real and significant, and he personalised the sketch for himself as a second son, intending it to be used as a bookplate.[3] Nearer in time were the Cothams of Bannister Hey, Windle, and Hardshaw; the smallness of the locality concentrated the occurrence of the family name so that this corner of Lancashire was truly Cotham country.

When Lawrence Cotham died in 1813[4] in his early thirties his widow Isabella was left with the four young children, probably only the eldest having begun his formal education. Help from the extended family may have led to the two oldest boys eventually going to Stonyhurst College. Two Cotham brothers from another branch of the family—the Cothams of Hardshaw Hall—joined the school in April 1802 and left in mid-1809. The younger of the two, William, was born at Hardshaw Hall in 1791 and at the age of 19 he entered the Jesuit novitiate immediately from school. He

'I Was Known There by the Name of Little Larry'   5

was ordained at Ushaw in December 1818 and spent time on the missions at Wigan and Hereford before his final profession at Stonyhurst, on 2 February 1831.[5] The elder boy, Lawrence, inherited Hardshaw Hall as a minor in 1797. After he died in 1819 his widow, Winifred Maria formerly Tuohy, née West, and her infant son spent years in the law courts before securing the inheritance to the Hardshaw estate.[6] The legacy was eventually put to one of its intended purposes: the building of St Mary's Catholic Church, Lowe House, in 1857. Although not directly affecting the young James Cotham, the proximity of this tradition, and the wranglings that went with it, gave him early familiarisation with the realities of holding a religious faith not only in a world of secular values but one at odds with the established Church of England. For Catholics of that period the establishment of *place*, both for worship and fellowship, was of paramount importance. Establishing that place, though, unavoidably necessitated the mastery of the subtle arts of negotiation to counter discrimination and legal disbarment. The practice of discretion and tact, stopping short of compromise, served to establish and to advance the standing of Catholics in society.

Considering the complexity of the family line and the duplication of names it is not surprising that the sons of Dr Cotham of Liverpool were able to claim a close connection to Hardshaw Hall without quite explaining where they stood in relation to it. What is certain is that when James Cotham went to Stonyhurst College in 1823 his Cotham namesakes were known and perhaps to avoid confusion he and his brother were known as Big Larry and Little Larry.[7]

The obituary of James' brother, Fr William Cotham SJ, junior (1806-1895), begins with an inaccuracy which is surprising given the detailed reminiscences which follow about his early career. Perhaps, having lost their father at a young age, his children preferred an embellished memory of him.

> Fr William Cotham was born at Liverpool on 30 August 1806, the younger of the two sons of Squire Lawrence

Cotham of Hardshaw Hall, St Helens, who was in the medical profession. When a boy of thirteen he was sent to Stonyhurst and after passing through the seven different classes he joined the novitiate at Mont Rouge in 1826 at the age of twenty, leaving it after to complete the two years in Avignon. He then studied logic at Hodder for a year, as he himself stated, and wound up with a year's Philosophy in "Shirk". In 1830 he taught for a short time in one of the earliest schools established by the restored Society in England, that in Marylebone Road, London.[8]

The start of William's schooling at Stonyhurst coincided with the remarriage of his mother in 1819 to Richard Shepherd, a saddler in Warrington, strongly Catholic and comfortably prosperous. They had two sons together, John and Thomas; the four Cotham siblings, and the surviving step-brother Thomas, kept in touch all their lives and through their legacies after death. Family support was one of the most important elements in James' life and he was never without close contact with one or other of his brothers for personal encouragement, practical help, or plain enjoyment.

James went to Stonyhurst at the age of 13, overlapping with his brother William from 1823 to 1826. There is no doubt that the period was a happy one for him, remembered above all for the friendships he made and valued for the rest of his life. The Jesuit approach to education prepared him and his brother for the rigours of life in particularly strenuous missions. As penalties against practising Catholics were systematically relaxed by the Toleration Acts of 1778 and 1791, and were to be largely removed by the 1829 Emancipation Act, the route to English university education was theoretically opened to Catholics. However, the opportunity was blocked by the reluctance of Church leaders to endorse the secular education of Catholic youth. Nor were religious orders keen to support the foundation of a Catholic University which, if based on the model of the diocesan New College at Oscott, would erode the prestige of colleges such as Stonyhurst, Ampleforth, and Downside, making them less attrac-

'I Was Known There by the Name of Little Larry' 7

tive to wealthy patronage. Catholic education in Catholic hands was a primary aim throughout the nineteenth century and beyond.

What could not have been foreseen in the first quarter of the nineteenth century was the influence exerted by converts to Catholicism as a consequence of the Oxford Movement. The school curricula disparagingly described by the Revd William Petre in his pamphlet on *The Problem of Catholic Liberal Education* in 1877 would not, in the 1820s, have seemed such a poor preparation for the future which faced the students at Stonyhurst. He criticised a system of

> unbending discipline, excessive surveillance [and] denial of all leisure [leading to] contracted mental power or a coarseness of character fitted for the reclamation of land in Australia or New Zealand [rather] than for competition with the cultivation, refinement, knowledge and mental grasp, the scholarship of ... our Protestant fellow-subjects.[9]

His assessment did an injustice to the group of cousins Charles Clifford, Henry Petre, William Vavasour, and Frederick Weld, who played a significant part in the colonisation of New Zealand in the 1840s, as landowners, legislators, and contributors to social development. Twenty years after their schooldays together at Stonyhurst, Charles Clifford replied to a letter from James Cotham 'with a great deal of pleasure' and as an 'old friend and schoolfellow' in the Antipodes. If there was narrowness in the school regime there was some compensation in the strength of friendship bonds it fostered.

Stonyhurst College had relocated to Lancashire from St Omer, northern France, in 1794. By the 1820s it had grown to house two hundred students and fifty clergy. After receiving basic education in reading and writing at Hodder, the nearby preparatory school, boys progressed to the College where they might stay for the full six-year course, passing through the classes known as Abecedarians, Figuritians, Grammar, Syntax, Poets, and Rhetoricians. To the basics of reading and writing were added the duties of religion and morality, elocution, French, arithmetic, and geography. As

8 *The Indomitable Mr Cotham*

the students advanced their curriculum was supplemented by history, algebra, geometry, logic, natural philosophy (biology), chemistry, and higher mathematics. To accommodate the rigorous timetable the boys rose at 5:30 a.m., attended chapel at 6 a.m., and followed a closely regimented day until bedtime at 8:30 p.m. Corporal punishment was employed to reinforce discipline. The concentration on a classical education nevertheless left room for the cultivation of music, drawing, and dancing for those with a taste for it, and the tutors encouraged 'modern' interests such as electricity, mechanics, herbiculture, and agriculture.

For this privileged education for a boy his parents paid up to fifty guineas per annum.[10] In 1829 three Curr brothers—Edward, William, and Richard—arrived from Van Diemen's Land to spend eight years at Stonyhurst. Two more brothers joined them in 1833 so the regimen was obviously considered satisfactory by their wealthy colonialist parents, although the three elder boys also spent a year at St Edmunds, Douai from August 1837, to perfect their French.[11] Although Edward and Elizabeth Curr had found Hobart a rough posting when they first arrived in March 1826, later moving to the northern coast to establish the Van Diemen's Land Company, nothing about them suggests they would have allowed an education for their sons which led to 'contracted mental powers' or 'coarseness of character' as appropriate preparation for life in Australia.

Notes

[1]   Addresses given for him are 11 Ranelagh Street, Liverpool, *1805 Holden's Triennial Directory*, Vol. 2, and 69 Mount Pleasant, *Gore's Liverpool Directory 1807.*

[2]   Isabella's father, James Hall, was a surgeon in Whalley, Cheshire when he married Mary Ann Wharton of Longridge in 1777.

[3]   The device is drawn on each side of a small piece of paper with the explanations, '*Cotham. Gules. A chevron between three crescents Argent. On the chevron a crescent for difference of second son, Azure*' and on the

'I Was Known There by the Name of Little Larry'   9

reverse '*Ex libris Jacobi Cotham in ord: S. B. Dom: Ambrosii, Duacensis (MDLVI)*'

[4] *The Monthly Magazine*, Vol. 35, No. 3, April 1813, p. 272; 'Deaths: Mr. L. Cotham, surgeon, late of Elliot Hall, Liverpool.' He was buried in the old Catholic Cemetery of St Helens (DA; letter from Joseph Galvin, 29 February 1988).

[5] After a period of administrative work at Stonyhurst, Fr William Cotham senior was sent to Jamaica which, with the neighbouring islands of British West Indies, was put in the charge of the English Province of the Society of Jesus in 1835. In 1848 he received a member of the governing Council and district judge into the church but more commonly he encountered poverty, disease, and sectarian prejudice. Fr Cotham SJ died in Kingston, Jamaica in November 1860. 'One gets the impression that he was a dependable, good, mediocre man, rather colourless, quiet, unassertive. He and Father Dupeyron arrived at Kingston December 4, 1837.' K. Wirtenberger, 'The Jesuits in Jamaica' (1942). Master's Theses. Paper 426. http://ecommons.luc.edu/luc_theses/426; p. 50. [Accessed online 27.7.2017]

[6] William Penketh Cotham II (1817–1846), son of Lawrence and Winifred, (and great nephew of William Penketh Cotham I, 1700–1797) married Anna Taylor in July 1840; his inheritance was left to Anna Maria Isabella Cotham (1812–1888), daughter of William Cotham of Springfield, Eccleston. She married Thomas Walmsley (a younger son of Charles Walmsley of Westwood, Ince and Elizabeth Jeffrys) and their younger son, Alfred Angelo, adopted the name Walmsley-Cotham.

[7] DA IV.C.XI, unposted note, Cotham to Fr Thomas Ignatius Sisk, October 1853.

[8] *Letters and Notices,* No. XCIX, April 1895, House Journal of the British Province of the Society of Jesus, obituary, p. 131.

[9] Quoted in Professor V. A. McClelland, '"School or Cloister?" An English Educational Dilemma 1794–1880', English Benedictine Congregation History Commission Symposium, 1997, privately published paper, p. 7.

[10] P. Fitzgerald, *Stonyhurst Memories; or, Six Years At School* (London: Richard Bentley & Son, 1895), Ch. 4, pp. 54–74 for the daily regime in the mid-1840s. David Knight, archivist at Stonyhurst College, says the prospectus had 'changed very little' since the mid-1820s (pc, 1 June 2017).

[11] S. Furphy, *Edward M. Curr and the Tide of History* (Canberra: ANU Press, 2013), pp. 16–17 for a description of conditions at Stonyhurst College for the Curr brothers.

2 ALMA MATER

ONE OF THE unintended and lesser consequences of the French Revolution and the ensuing Reign of Terror (1789–1793) was a realignment of sympathies in England for Catholics who survived the bloodshed. As refugees from mob violence and social catastrophe, having forfeited property, livelihood, and status, they were welcomed into England. Hundreds of exiled French priests swelled the numbers of the relatively few English-born priests, and when they offered lessons in French or music to support themselves they found a niche in English society. For the English Benedictine Congregation[1] one consequence of the upheavals was the removal of their houses from France. The English Benedictine monasteries at Douai and Dieulouard—St Gregory's and St Laurence's—relocated to Acton Burnell (and later to Downside) and Ampleforth, respectively, and the nuns of Our Lady of Consolation at Cambrai moved successively to Woolton, Abbot's Salford, Callow End, Worcestershire and Wass, Lancashire.

After periods of imprisonment and dispersal lasting nearly thirty years, the three surviving members of St Edmund's Monastery, Paris, having settled in England, were entitled, but unwilling, to resume their rights of succession to the Paris house when the French government was once again well-disposed towards religious educational establishments. The Gregorian community briefly considered returning to Douai in 1816 but, having acquired property at Downside, decided against another disruption. Dr Richard Marsh, a monk of St Laurence's, Ampleforth (and former prior of Dieulouard) was chosen to revive religious life at Douai in 1818. He was not able to draw on what remained of the Edmundian community from Paris—men who were too old, ill, or settled into English missions—so his companion for the first three years was a newly professed monk of Ampleforth,

Matthew Charles Fairclough. The two men brought four boys as the nucleus of the college: Edward Glassbrook, Edward Hall, Felix Larkin, and John Marsh.

In contrast to Stonyhurst College, St Edmund's was a much smaller and homelier environment when James Cotham went there in 1826 at the same time that his elder brother entered the Jesuit novitiate. James took with him his younger brother Lawrence, 14, who had just completed a year at Sedgeley Park, Staffordshire, noted for the commercial, rather than classical, education it offered to boys from middle class families. For the first twelve years the yearly intake at Douai averaged between six and eight boys, half of whom went on to become novices in the community or, less frequently, were eventually ordained as secular priests. The families of a few boys lived in northern France or Belgium but the majority of boys came from the north of England, very often as pairs of siblings known to Benedictine clergy in their neighbourhood. The two younger Cotham brothers, James and Lawrence, fitted this typical profile of the Douai student: neither gentry nor impoverished, academically solid rather than sparkling, and robust enough to cope with the rather primitive conditions of the establishment. Laurence Burgess, Prior of Ampleforth, expressed the rivalry engendered by Dr Marsh's choice of St Edmund's over St Laurence's when he sarcastically described the rough-and-ready college as 'a colony of Lancashire Blacksmiths and Joiners'[2] but the missioners it produced were fit for purpose when faced with rugged conditions. In a centenary essay Dom Cuthbert Doyle described the environment to which Dr Marsh introduced his founding students:

> The great college stood before them in a sad state of dilapidation; and in the centre of the quadrangle there was a pile of ashes, cinders and scoriæ from the furnaces of M. Barruel who, in 1811, had rented the building and manufactured his beetroot sugar among the pillars of the beautiful colonnade which generation after generation of Douai boys for some inexplicable reason were accustomed

Alma Mater 13

to call the 'Piazza'. If we may believe those who saw this pile of rubbish, it rose as high as the windows in the first storey, and occupied about one-third of the space in front of the college.[3]

William Bernard Collier, one of the first boys and then one of the first teachers at St Edmunds, looked back over a period of sixty years and vividly remembered the French occupants who shared the college buildings with the English newcomers and made no concessions to them:

> One half of the ground floor was let out for carpenters and blacksmiths, the blacksmiths had a blazing fire, when they needed one, in the boys' playground. The underground cellar was let out to a brewer whose carts and horses used to come into what is now the garden behind the house, to bring in or carry out the barrels of beer as they liked.[4]

In due course the squatting families, small traders, livestock, and detritus were cleared away, although not entirely. Doyle recorded an anecdote from James Cotham about one of the remaining pigs which the boys would attempt to use as war-horse: 'The nose of this gentleman was very much *retroussé*; his ears were like the ears of an elephant; his back was curved; and his movements were as nimble as those of a greyhound.'[5]

Dr Marsh already had over twenty years of educational experience in England, beginning with a school at Scholes, near St Helens, Lancashire for boys aged seven to fourteen where they were 'taught the principles of Religion and Morality, Reading, Writing, Grammar … French, Latin, Greek, Mathematics, Geography, Algebra'. Marsh moved his school to Vernon Hall, Parbold, and Ampleforth with mixed fortunes before taking on the challenge of Douai in 1818. As part of the French government's compensation for confiscated Catholic property, grants were available to Douai as an educational establishment so making it attractive to English bishops insofar as the curriculum suited the requirements of a minor seminary. The school presented itself as appropriate to church or secular scholars, to English students wanting to perfect their French or French students learning English. The judgement of a later Abbot who said Douai was 'not academic, not adventurous and not monastic'[6] indicates the problems of casting a net too widely, but the growth in numbers and the steady flow of new members for the expanding mission seemed to justify the approach taken at that period.[7]

Dr Collier made two comments which initially seem at odds with each other: 'Gloomy beginnings are sometimes the forerunners of success. Look at Douai: If you had seen what I had seen of its beginnings, you would indeed have foretold a great fiasco.' Forebodings may have weighed on hard-pressed superiors but Collier's other reminiscence that Douai was called the 'Botany Bay of monks,' for 'unruly and dissatisfied monks were sent there: they gave no end of trouble'[8] suggests an atmosphere anything but gloomy or despondent, although it certainly lacked the military discipline he admiringly associated with St Ignatius Loyola's Jesuits. Collier's own duties were recorded in 1828 by Francis Appleton, a former schoolboy promoted to schoolmaster on joining the novitiate in 1826, bringing the monastic community to six:

> We are employed in the following manner ... Mr Collier has the affairs of the house to manage and our divinity schools to hear and Gruarts, a French student of philosophy, to hear. Besides this he teaches French to an English gentleman in the town and perhaps several others ... Father Marsh too is well occupied; he has to attend the churches in the town and at home to manage three youngsters who are just commencing their studies. Glassbrook has a little French man under him, to whom he teaches Latin and English. He has two others in the town to attend to. Br Bede Swale teaches the class that follows mine and Br Ignatius Greenough the one that succeeds his in order. Thus we are all labouring from morning until night without a moment's respite ... we cannot expect to

Alma Mater 15

receive any assistance from the students we are bringing up, until three years have lapsed.[9]

The schoolmaster-monks did not wear habits until later in the century and priests were addressed as 'Mister' rather than 'Father'. The dress of Fr Charles Fairclough, which became anachronistic during his lifetime, was standard for a clerical gentleman in the 1820s: a swallow-tailed coat with high collar and broad white neck-cloth, straight trousers, and tall silk hat. Lay masters were not employed in any number until much later in the century, in order to keep costs down rather than as a matter of principle, as the demand for priests to be sent on the mission was always the most pressing need. Francis Appleton went on to describe the impact on his studies of the pressure to share the teaching load:

> We three that were last professed ... began our course of theology on the 17th November [1827]. After we had finished the prolegomena we began the treatise De Deo. Bailly is the author we study. The plan which Mr Collier has adopted in teaching us is to make us learn the author by heart and afterward to fix our lessons with our seniors by making an analysis of them ... As for my private studies I am obliged to lay all these aside. There are many things I should like to apply to but time will not permit. However, to perfect myself in English I generally continue to write a short sermon every month and if I have any time remaining I employ it either in reading ecclesiastical history or in learning by heart a portion of the old Scripture.[10]

Six years later Francis Appleton was writing as Prior and described how bread and milk was 'not limited morning and evening and for dinner there is a good soup, a good joint of meat and vegetables ... corporal punishment is seldom or never had recourse to. The students are ruled with mildness and condescension'.[11] He evidently believed in maintaining a healthy balance between mind and body, and good relationships between boys and masters.

To offset any academic shortcomings Douai encouraged a strong sense of history, of community, and of active service. The students of the English Benedictine Congregation educated at St Edmund's, Ampleforth, and Downside were destined for 'the mission', a term indicative of how English Catholics had in a sense become foreigners in their own country even when they had escaped expulsion and exile. Since the re-establishment of the English Benedictine Congregation in the seventeenth century every monk took an innovative fourth vow (in addition to stability, conversion of life, and obedience) to be ready to go on the mission if sent. The purpose of the mission was twofold: priestly ministry to the faithful, principally by celebrating Mass and the sacraments for Catholics in England adhering to a proscribed religion, and working towards the conversion of Protestant England to the Catholic faith, mainly through contact with individuals and families.

From 1620 to 1890, for the purposes of the Benedictine mission, England was divided into the North Province of York, and the South Province of Canterbury, each governed by a Provincial elected at General Chapter and responsible for the monks in his province who were thus no longer under the immediate jurisdiction of the superiors of their own monasteries. Parallel with this Benedictine form of governance, and in the absence of diocesan bishops before 1850, the country was divided into four districts (increased to eight in 1840) administered by Vicars Apostolic who had authority over the secular priests and who were directly responsible to Rome. The arrangement frequently produced competitive clashes between the superiors of religious orders and the Vicars Apostolic, or between the orders themselves vying for territory.

As penalties were gradually relaxed in a series of reforms from 1778, Catholics were increasingly served from urban mission centres with purpose built churches, coinciding with the demographic changes of industrialisation. In the rural areas the private chapels of landed gentry remained the meeting place for clusters

Alma Mater 17

of Catholic families well into the nineteenth century.[12] Except in the larger cities, priests usually worked alone, using their own initiative when in a remote location. English Benedictine monks were allowed to manage their own financial affairs, known as their *peculium*, a custom surviving from hazardous penal times, when monks were allowed to retain, out of necessity, any inheritance or gifts which might be given to them. In settled circumstances the custom became increasingly obsolete, and was superseded by renewed emphasis on the monastic vow of poverty, eventually being abolished by the end of the nineteenth century.

However, the tradition of English Benedictines being responsible for keeping themselves safe from the risks of destitution or even death was part of the monastic formation for the Douai novices; even after material circumstances became less uncertain the English Benedictines guarded their prerogative of pecuniary independence. James Cotham used his private income to supplement the revenues of his congregations, as was his right, but he also provoked disapproval, evidenced by the acrimonious correspondence in the last weeks of his life, as he made detailed provision for the dispersal of a considerable fortune.

Lawrence Cotham was at Douai for two years and left to become an apprentice pharmacist-druggist, thus preparing for the first of his various—and usually successful—commercial enterprises.[13] James joined St Edmund's novitiate on 18 May 1829 and was given the name Ambrose; he made his profession a year later on 21 May.[14] During this time he came to know well his Benedictine confrères William Bernard Collier and Edward Anselm Glassbrook, both of whom, in their very different ways, supported his efforts in later life. Much more significant to his own future at this point was the business, sometimes frenetic, of providing prelates and priests for vacant sees and missions in the expanding British Empire.

Contact with the school at Douai continued when Thomas and John Shepherd (known as the Warrington Shepherds to distinguish them from Thomas (Maurus) Shepherd of Liverpool) joined in 1833. In the earliest account books for St Edmunds, Douai, there is evidence that the Cothams were at least comfortably prosperous, especially after Isabella Cotham's marriage to Richard Shepherd. The pensions for the two boys—£30 annually for each—were paid promptly in advance, half-yearly, with a few pounds added for extras, until 1836.[15]

Notes

[1] Following the dissolution of the monasteries in England and Wales, 1535–1540, religious life could be followed only in a continental European monastery. Between 1607 and 1633 English and Welsh monks and nuns were drawn together to form the English Benedictine Congregation, according to the Papal Bull, *Plantata*, 1634. This document not only outlined the status and constitutions of the Congregation, but also, by enjoining its members to take a missionary oath, it defined the Congregation's identity as both missionary and monastic.

[2] A. Hood OSB, *From Repatriation to Revival* (Farnborough: St Michael's Abbey Press, 2014), p. 34. Prior Burgess to Fr John Turner, 8 August 1826.

[3] F. C. Doyle OSB (Ed.), *Tercentenary of St Edmund's Monastery* (London: R. & T. Washbourne Ltd, 1917), p. 42.

[4] DA VII.A.3.f; Dr Bernard Collier to Abbot President Anselm O'Gorman, 1 August 1887.

[5] F. C. Doyle OSB (Ed.), *Tercentenary of St Edmund's Monastery* (London: R. & T. Washbourne Ltd, 1917), p. 44.

[6] A. Hood OSB, Chapter 3, 'Douai 1818–1903', p. 4, quoting Abbot Gregory Freeman in G. Scott OSB, et al, *Douai 1903, Woolhampton 2003: A Centenary History* (Stanbrook Abbey Press, 2003). www.douaiabbey.org.uk /files/HistCHAP3b.pdf [Accessed online 27.7.2017]

[7] Material for the section on education at Douai in the 1820s is taken from A. Hood OSB, *From Repatriation to Revival* (Farnborough: St Michael's Abbey Press, 2014), Chapter 6, and A. Hood OSB, Chapter 3, 'Douai 1818–1903' in G. Scott OSB et al, *Douai 1903, Woolhampton 2003: A Centenary History* (Stanbrook Abbey Press, 2003); www.douaiabbey.org.uk /files/HistCHAP3b.pdf [Accessed online 27.7.2017]

[8] DA VII.A.3.f; Collier to O'Gorman, 7 July, and 1 August 1887.

[9] A. Hood OSB, Chapter 3, 'Douai 1818–1903', p. 14, *Douai 1903, Woolhampton 2003: A Centenary History* (Stanbrook Abbey Press, 2003). www.douaiabbey.org.uk/files/HistCHAP3b.pdf [Accessed online 27.7.2017]

Alma Mater

19

[10] A. Hood OSB, *From Repatriation to Revival* (Farnborough: St Michael's Abbey Press, 2014), p. 144.

[11] *Ibid.*, p. 172 and 170.

[12] A distant relative of James Cotham, the Revd Seth Eccles DD (1800–1884) spent the whole of his priestly life in Weston Underwood, Buckinghamshire under the patronage of the Throckmorton family, an increasingly rare and anachronistic experience as the century progressed.

[13] *Preston Chronicle*, 12 January 1833, p. 1. Advertisement: 'L. Cotham, 124 Fishergate. Shop taken from Mr T.W. Fallowfield.' As Fallowfield's was an established pharmacist-druggist firm in Preston it is quite likely that Lawrence Cotham had served his apprenticeship there before leasing or taking ownership of one of Fallowfield's premises.

[14] From this point I shall refer to Cotham by his name in religion, Ambrose, except where it is more natural to use the name by which his family knew him. He used his given name, James, in correspondence throughout his life, and it is the name used in newspapers, government documents, etc.

[15] DA VII.A.2.8.

3 'THE MOST NEGLECTED PORTION OF THE CATHOLIC WORLD'[1]

FROM 1815 THE Catholic vicariate of New Holland—Australia—had been under the jurisdiction of the bishop of Port Louis, Mauritius, in the Indian Ocean. The growth of the colony and its vast distance from Mauritius made the presence of a local bishop imperative for the good ordering of the infant church. Fr William Bernard Ullathorne OSB, acting as Vicar General in Sydney in 1833 for Bishop Morris in Mauritius, strongly reiterated the petition of Catholics in the penal colony to Bishop Bramston in London: that nothing less than episcopal authority in situ, not exercised from thousands of miles away in Mauritius, could manage the complexities of a constantly evolving mix of military, free, and transported convict populations. Ullathorne had only three priests working with him in New South Wales: Frs McEncroe, Dowling, and Therry. Van Diemen's Land was under the sole care of Fr Philip Conolly, who was himself in dispute with his Catholic flock. The intricate, and at times contradictory, negotiations about New Holland were brought to a head by Ullathorne's report. Opinions were canvassed from Bishop Bramston and Fr John Augustine Birdsall, President of the English Benedictine Congregation and rector of the Cheltenham mission, in England, Fr Thomas Brown in Rome, and the London offices of the Governor of New Holland and the Colonial Secretary on behalf of the Australian colony. President Birdsall was in favour of the scheme to create a new diocese and backed his secretary, Bede Polding, as the man to realise it.

John Bede Polding OSB (1794–1877), a gifted monk of Downside, was nominated as bishop for Mauritius in 1829 and for

Madras in 1832 but refused both, with much painful indecision since the prospect threw his mind into 'a state of the utmost agitation worked up to a phrensy almost by the dread of the dangers to be encountered; above all by a sense of my own weakness and vacillation of which I have given in this business most abundant proof'.[2] He committed his future to Downside after refusing the bishopric of Madras, 'and never, no never, would I think of leaving'.[3] He was greatly valued in facing down the danger posed by the schemes of Bishop Peter Augustine Baines, including the contentious Prior Park venture near Bath, which threatened to destabilise the nascent colleges of Ampleforth and Downside. Nevertheless, when the pressing needs of a third British colony—New Holland, with centres of government administration in Sydney and Hobart—could no longer be ignored, Polding did not refuse the opportunity offered to him, especially as it had long been his own preferred mission field. Although Downside protested against losing Polding, a key member of their community, Birdsall was adamant he should go and, furthermore, be ambitious on behalf of the Benedictine Order for 'it is absolutely necessary that New South Wales be made a District for itself; a new Seminary and a new Monastery must there be established: the provinces of our Congregation must be increased'.[4]

English priests were positively sought after by the British Government for work in the colony. Religious establishments were considered a regulating influence over the large convict population and an inducement to free settlers who wanted to develop a civilised society. Even when the government acknowledged that Irish priests would be the most numerous national group, positions of leadership were given to English men. Dr Bramston, Bishop of London and Vicar Apostolic, and his predecessor before 1827, Bishop Poynter, hoped the recently-repatriated Benedictines could supply the resources for both levels of pastorate.[5] Hence, comparatively young Benedictine priests such as Ullathorne and Polding were given seniority over

'The Most Neglected Portion of the Catholic World' 23

longer serving secular Irish missionaries, leaving them to resolve the consequent strained relationships among themselves.

When the very junior Ambrose Cotham was brought to Downside by Polding's close friend Fr William Dunstan Scott in August 1831[6] to finish his theological training before ordination, it seems unlikely that he could have foreseen the possibility of accompanying Polding to Australia. Speaking fifty years later in Cheltenham Fr Aloysius Wilkinson interpreted Cotham's motivation thus:

> England seemed hardly large enough for the zealous ardour, the overflowing spirit and the indomitable energy of the young priest, so he requested to be sent to Australia, where there was but one Bishop, a Benedictine Bishop ... His request was complied with.[7]

The initiative almost certainly did not come from Cotham, nor was a request from him likely to carry weight, whatever the strength of his ardour and energy. Catholic priests were in very short supply everywhere and one wonders why Cotham was chosen to be spared from the English mission, unless he did indeed badger his superiors into submission, or was too boisterous to be sent anywhere except Australia. More positively, his robust health and sanguine temperament would be advantageous. He seems not to have been one of Polding's favourites even in the preparatory stages of the Australian mission so it is unlikely he was seen as a potential candidate for future preferment.

The appointment of Polding to the new See was appropriate given the role he had played at Downside. He was remembered as 'for many years ... the mainstay of almost every department of college and monastery. On him, as a counsellor and friend, many, especially among the younger members of the community and the elder boys, relied'. One of these, Br Charles Davis, wrote at the time:

> His loss will be felt greatly by our entire community; but, perhaps, no individual member of the College will experi-

ence it more than I shall. He has been my spiritual director and my fast and best of friends ... I assure you that were it the will of my superiors I would with pleasure accompany him to New Holland.[8]

A petition was sent to Rome asking that Polding's appointment be reconsidered since Downside had need of him as 'the column and mainstay' of the community since on him 'the entire studies of the College depend, and [he] fills so admirably many of the offices of the house'.[9] The Holy See unsurprisingly chose not to reconsider the appointment of an ideal candidate.

Polding, the Benedictine novice master at Downside in the 1820s, had been fascinated by stories of Botany Bay and transported convicts[10] since boyhood and he had dreamed of the Australian Catholic Church being a Benedictine foundation. Although he inspired personal loyalty from his novices, from the outset the difficulty of recruiting fully-fledged Benedictine priests was apparent. Although the British Government was prepared to pay for four priests to go out in 1835, Polding was able to persuade only one mature priest, Fr Corcoran, an Irish Dominican, to join him.[11] Perhaps the addition of Ambrose Cotham was an act of reluctant desperation, there being no other alternative. The third priest, Clement Fisher, was a very late arrival to the party, joining them in Liverpool shortly before embarkation on the advice of his doctor: not as strange as it may now seem as it was well attested that many emigrants benefitted from the sea air and healthy regime of a long sea voyage. Fr Fisher was given a grant of only £100 while the student Br Bede Sumner was granted £150 although he was not ordained to the priesthood until May 1836. It seems Polding wanted to take full advantage of the money on offer (four priests at £150 each) by naming Sumner, along with Cotham, as priests, before either had been ordained. Fortunately, the Colonial Secretary, the Earl of Aberdeen, took Polding's word in the matter, and passed on the information unchecked to Governor Bourke in New South Wales. In fact, Polding had secured only three ordained men, including himself, until Fr Fisher's unplanned late arrival.[12]

The other members of the party included just three Benedictine students (counting Sumner). The most junior man was Benedict Spencer, an uncertain prospect from the outset; Joseph Bede Sumner and Henry Gregory Gregory had both undertaken their early monastic education at Douai before joining Ambrose Cotham at Downside to make their religious profession. Sumner came from Samborne, Warwickshire, from a well-established Catholic family; having been ordained sub-deacon in 1835 at the age of 34 before leaving Downside, Sumner was one of the more mature men but Polding was never able to place his confidence in 'poor Bede' who had humiliating episodes of drunkenness. The withholding of friendship from a superior who was noted for warmth of feeling towards others has left Sumner as an 'outsider' in the subsequent narrative of their shared history.[13] Instead, Polding formed his greatest attachment to Gregory.

Henry Gregory Gregory was known to Cotham from their Douai school days. He was from Charlton Kings, near Cheltenham, and his family had been received into the church by Fr Birdsall in the 1820s. Henry had joined Birdsall's short-lived monastery in Broadway, Worcestershire and was professed there as a monk of the community of St Denis and St Aiden (a continuation of Birdsall's exiled community of Lamspringe in Westphalia) before going on to Douai and Downside.

Bishop Polding did not shirk the necessary business of raising funds, from individuals and from church congregations. A small number of people shared his enthusiasm for Australia and pledged regular subscriptions. The diverse group—including Lady Stanley, Miss Floris, and the family of John Gorman who was going out as a potential postulant—were drawn together by the personal charisma of Bede Polding. Mrs Sarah Neve, who had made herself a particular patron of the Benedictines in south west England, took as much interest in the removal to New South Wales as if she had been going, which she says she would have done if she had been twenty or thirty years younger (she was then 68). Writing from Cheltenham on 23 May 1835[14] she tells Polding she is busy marking some of her books *N.S.W.M*[ission], intending them for the episcopal library, but on condition 'that they are never to be lent out but to careful persons and that for missionary purposes'. Going further she proposed sending him some unwanted trinkets and ornaments which he could sell, 'understanding as I do, and I hope rightly, that there are rich convicts, who have plenty of money, and deny themselves no one luxury'. Even the furniture earmarked for the mission of Chipping Sodbury, founded by her endowment, she is prepared to ship out to him if it is worth the carriage costs. Sarah Neve, the widow of an Anglican clergyman and heiress to her sister's French fortune, had converted to Catholicism and was enjoying the excitement her financial independence gave her to go on the missions vicariously.

Notes

[1]   Fr J. McEncroe to Archbishop Murray of Dublin, 2 November 1832, quoted in H. N. Birt OSB, *Benedictine Pioneers in Australia* (London: Herbert and Daniel, 2 Vols, 1911), Vol. 1, p. 223.

[2]   F. O'Donoghue, *The Bishop of Botany Bay: The Life of John Bede Polding, Australia's First Catholic Archbishop* (Sydney: Angus and Robertson Publishers, 1982), p. 15. Polding to Thomas Brown, 12 October 1832.

[3]   *Ibid.*, p. 15.

[4]   *Ibid.*, p. 18, Birdsall to Prior George Turner of Downside, 3 March 1834.

[5]   *Ibid.*, Chapter 1, for an overview of this period.

[6]   Downside Abbey Guest Book, Southerwood Collection, HAA. Cotham returned to Douai for the summer in June 1832, the fare costing £3; DA VII.A.2.8.

[7]   *Cheltenham Examiner*, 9 May 1883, p. 8.

[8]   'Memoirs of Distinguished Gregorians. No. II: The Most Reverend John Bede Polding, DD, OSB', *Downside Review*, April 1881, pp. 166–167. Davis did in due course go to Australia, as Bishop of Maitland, at a time when Polding's reputation and personal relationships had come under criticism due to the perceived partisanship he allowed to develop amongst his clergy.

'The Most Neglected Portion of the Catholic World'

9   *Ibid.*, p. 167.

10   The First Fleet of three ships landed at Botany Bay in 1788. In total about 160,000 convicts were transported to Australia, the last of whom went to Western Australia in 1868.

11   Clergy Returns, 31 October 1829, list Fr G. D. Corcoran, age 30, as an Irish Dominican born in Loughrea.

12   *Catholic Magazine and Review*, Vol. 2, p. 444. 'London: Rev. Wm Riddell, Rev. Clement Fisher and Rev. Thomas Hawarden, late students of the English College Rome, arrived in London 13 June 1832.' Fisher belonged to the Northern Province and was priest at St Anthony's, Scotland Road, Liverpool, 1833.

13   Despite Polding's coolness, Bede Sumner became titular Dean of St Mary's Cathedral, Sydney. The nuns of Jamberoo Abbey (formerly at Subiaco, Sydney) hold him in greater affection and keep his anniversary in their necrology: 'October 17 [1871]: Fr. Bede Sumner. Fr. Bede lived at our monastery in the last years of his life. He freed our community from debt in 1864, and was therefore our most generous benefactor of the early decades of our history.' www.jamberooabbey.org.au/_uploads/rsfil/002477_fdab.pdf [Accessed online 27.7.2017]

14   H. N. Birt OSB, *Benedictine Pioneers in Australia* (London: Herbert and Daniel, 2 Vols, 1911), Vol. 1, pp. 258–260.

4 'YOU MAY CALCULATE UPON NO LITTLE TROUBLE WITH HIM'

AMBROSE COTHAM WAS ordained at Prior Park near Bath on 20 December 1834, hurried on six months before completing his seminary training, in readiness for joining the Australian pioneer band which Bishop Polding hoped would be leaving by the first available convict ship in January 1835.[1] There was no ceremonial attached to his ordination. Bishop Polding had travelled to Prior Park, to consult with Bishop Baines (on President Birdsall's behalf) about serious administrative and property difficulties the Benedictines had amongst themselves concerning Bath, Ampleforth, and Prior Park. Finding Bishop Baines away from home, Polding took the opportunity of presenting Cotham to Dr Brindle for ordination later in the week by which time Baines should have returned.[2]

The prematurely ordained Fr Cotham was not abashed or subservient. He questioned Bishop Polding about his rights over handling money, a query touching on Polding's new dual status as a diocesan bishop as well as Benedictine superior; the men going out with him were under his authority in his capacity as Bishop which, in this instance, superseded the Benedictines' obedience to the superior of their home monastery or the Abbot President. Polding, not their monastic superiors, would be able to recall them to England if he wished. The Bishop turned to the Abbot President for advice about an individual's financial arrangements and Birdsall was clearly not impressed by the new man's perceived impertinence. He wrote back to Polding telling him to impress on 'Mr Cotham and on Mr Everyone' that they were going out as Polding's subjects. 'It is no other than a suspicious symptom in Mr Cotham to be speaking about Canon Law; if his duties and his rights are to be determined or were

30 *The Indomitable Mr Cotham*

discussed by Canon Law you may calculate upon no little trouble with him'.[3] It was a clear warning to Bishop Polding not to let Cotham get above himself in the experimental situation on which they were embarking. As he did not have access to private money at this time it is most likely that he was simply curious about a point of law—his simplicity and curiosity were character traits other people remarked on in later life—but his question brought against him a charge of mischief-making. Ambrose Cotham had been inauspiciously singled out before the missioners had set sail.

The party of ten, about half the total number of passengers on board with general cargo, left Brunswick Docks, Liverpool, destination Hobart, on the sailing ship *Oriental* on 27 March 1835[4] after an enthusiastic send-off by the local Catholic population. Polding later recounted how as the ship 'moved down the Mersey, a number of Irishmen working at the docks gave them three hearty cheers'.[5] The *Oriental* was much smaller than the anticipated convict ship, having a crew of thirty-three and nineteen passengers (only two of whom were expected to disembark in Hobart); the cabin passengers formed a party of ten gentlemen and one lady around the dining table. The sailing route took them via Buenos Aires and the Cape of Good Hope, early on encountering a great storm in the Bay of Biscay when the passengers feared for their survival. For anyone experiencing sea sickness the recommended treatment was a 'recumbent position and a glass of brandy with Cayenne pepper'.[6]

During the four months on board the ecclesiastics formed a little floating monastic community; Bishop Polding organised them in a regular pattern of prayer, reading, and lectures on Moral Theology, which Mr Harding piously noted in his Diary:

> On Sundays, prayers in the Bishop's cabin, read out of Garden of the Soul, the Venite Exultemus sung and played on the piano, terminating with a meditation and an instruction by the Bishop, always 'veramente bella e propria alla nostra situazione.'[7] In the evening the Compline and Litany of the BVM were sung with accompaniment. Also the

> Blessed Sacrament was kept in Fr Fisher's cabin as long as
> he lived (about two months) where we met for night prayers,
> and afterwards in the Oratory which was made up.[8]

The emphasis in their preparation was on the work they were to do with the convict population; this was the ministry that inspired Polding and in which he engaged most successfully. Unfortunately for him, the necessities of administration and decision-making—not his strong points by his own admission—diverted his energies away from the personal contacts where he excelled.

On occasion the little group collapsed in laughter which Polding enjoyed as much as anyone and related in a letter home to Fr Barber on 3 May:

> I was giving the blessing at Prime on Easter Sunday, and
> just as I said the word *disponet* [*send down*] the ship gave
> a lurch and seated me on the floor of my cabin. Bede was
> thrown to the side opposite to that on which he was sitting,
> and no sooner there than another lurch sent him back to
> his first position.[9]

On the evening of 13 May a large flaming meteor appeared, passing near the ship and causing consternation, before splitting in two and vanishing. Six weeks into the voyage Polding wrote

> the weather is extremely hot—the thermometer stands at
> 85°F in the shade. We enjoy nevertheless a breeze which
> is very refreshing. I cannot say I am much incommoded
> by the heat, but poor Bede Sumner is quite in a melting
> mood, & Mr Cotham is not much better.[10]

At this point they were all still in good health and united amongst themselves. However, soon after this letter Fr Clement Fisher died and was given a burial at sea of impressive solemnity.

As well as illness there was a more colourful danger, as noted in Harding's diary for 21 April: 'Stations and duties assigned in case of attack by pirates. Dr Polding's in cockpit with surgeon to attend the wounded.'[11] Among the passengers was Sizar Elliott who celebrated his 21st birthday during the voyage and was going to work in his uncle's store in Launceston. In his brief memoir, *Fifty Years of Colonial Life*,[12] Elliott recalled his companions on board the *Oriental*, 'an old East Indiaman, teak built ... in the China trade' which carried four guns and a quantity of small arms. The passengers formed themselves into 'a happy family' but also had a duty to make themselves into 'a defensive body against pirates' and were regularly drilled for this on Saturdays. All the men and boys were assigned to stations under the direction of an experienced sailor under the command of Captain Allen. To either side of him stood the navigator at the helm, and the surgeon and Bishop Polding in the cockpit. Elliott was on the mizzen top as part of the third gun emplacement, Spencer and Kenny had small arms on the forecastle and the other ecclesiastics were on the fourth gun with small arms, except for Mr Gregory who, curiously, was placed on the quarter deck apparently without task or arms. That Gregory also shared the Bishop's cabin, except when he was deputed to nurse the dying Fisher, suggests how early the seeds of discontent and murmurings of favouritism were sown.

Fr Cotham celebrated his first Mass at sea on 11 June, nearly three months after leaving Liverpool. Perhaps the delay was to 'put right' the fact that he had been ordained before formally completing his studies; on the 29th Polding celebrated the first anniversary of his episcopal ordination. Sizar Elliott attended the services held in the Bishop's 'room', conducted in English, with an extempore sermon from Polding and piano accompaniment for the hymns provided by Benedict Spencer. He recalled the Bishop as 'a most social and kindly man; he joined in whist parties and invited us to his cabin once a week for a social evening, singing and music ... He was fond of a bit of quiet fun and amusement' helped along by the jorum of punch in his cabin. Polding's understanding of community life, appreciating the importance of recreation from daily routine, is evident.

The approach to Hobart along the River Derwent on 6 August was a memorable introduction to the colony: 'smooth as glass were the waters of the majestic river and not a leaf stirred on its thickly wooded banks, nor did a cloud float on the rich, blue expanse of the heavens, not a breath of wind to stir the sails.'[13] As was customary the docking of the ship in an Australian port was announced in the local press under shipping news:

> Aug. 7.—Arrived the ship *Oriental*, 517 tons, Captain Allen, from Liverpool the 27th March, with a general cargo. Passengers, Mr. Elliott, Mr. Roberts. For Sydney, the Right Reverend Doctor Polding, Rev. Mr. Corcoran, Rev. Mr. Cotham, Rev. Mr. Gregory, Rev. Mr. Spencer, Mr. Sumner, Mr. Kenny, Mr. Harding, Mr. Curtoys, Mr. Smith, Mrs. Curtoys, Mrs. Gibbs, Caroline M'Candlish, James Steward, E. Coffee, J. Gorman.[14]

Sizar Elliott, as a Canadian, was happy to see snow on the top of Mount Wellington overlooking Hobart but it was the beginning of cultural adjustment for the newcomers who had sailed from an English spring into an Australian mid-winter. The day after docking Bishop Polding visited a group of condemned men due for execution: his mission had begun as he wished to continue it.

The ship was warmly greeted by the Catholic population, some of whom had been petitioning Bishop Bramston in London for new blood in the clergy. The welcome was led by John Cassidy, who 'had served in the 23rd Fusiliers, then the 4th Veterans Battalion, and through the 102nd, 73rd and 46th regiments. His recommendation from Governor Macquarie resulted in his initial land grant'[15] and he became one of the very few wealthy Catholics in Van Diemen's Land in this period. Cassidy was a major benefactor to the second generation of Catholic evangelisation in the Hobart region, as well as forming a familial bond with Fr Cotham. Bishop Polding's group spent a month ashore; on 23 August he celebrated Mass at the homestead of John Cassidy's fine property Woodburn, acquired in 1833, a little to the north-east of Richmond, some fifteen miles inland from Hobart. Bishop Polding symbolically laid the first stone of the new church of St John's at Richmond, with adjacent burying ground, on four acres of land given by John Cassidy. Cassidy donated £200 of the £535 which was raised immediately when subscriptions were invited.[16] When donations came from non-Catholics it was assumed to be not from ecumenical feeling but from a desire 'to see the rising generation of colonists educated in their duty to God and their fellow men',[17] that, of course, also being the reason for government assistance to the Catholic chaplains.

After one month the whole party departed for Sydney, except for Fr Cotham and John Kenny, a student-catechist left behind for six months to help with setting up a school in Hobart.[18] In the passenger arrivals list printed in the *Colonial Times* the party was listed 'all for Sydney', apart from Mr Elliot and Mr Roberts, so it appears none of Polding's party was originally destined for Van Diemen's Land. The decision to leave two men behind was Polding's response—intended as a temporary measure—to the fractious situation surrounding the incumbent priest Fr Philip Conolly and the demand for prompt action to resolve it from a section of the Catholic population and from the Lieutenant-Governor George Arthur, with whom Polding had several meetings during his month on the island. Cotham's own account, written up in January 1852, is that he 'received an appointment as Chaplain in New South Wales under Earl Grey's administration in 1834, and arrived in Van Diemen's Land in August of the following year, where I was detained at the request of the then Lieutenant-Governor Col. Geo. Arthur'.[19] The expectation locally and in Sydney was that 'the talented' Fr Ullathorne, the Vicar General, would be stationed in the colony immediately after the Bishop's arrival in Sydney, or at the latest after his formal installation in October.[20]

However, having failed to persuade Fr Conolly to sail with him to Sydney, to be replaced by Fr Ullathorne, Polding created a new problem by leaving Cotham to assist Fr Conolly while also giving him the injunction that he was not under Conolly's jurisdiction; the ambivalence of his position, hasty preparation, and Polding's evident lack of respect for his own Vicar General on the island

'You May Calculate upon no Little Trouble with Him' 35

marked an abrupt end to the congenial quasi-monastic life Cotham had shared for nearly six months with his bishop and companions. On a positive note, Cotham was based at Richmond, where the plans for a new church would not directly clash with Fr Conolly's claims in Hobart. Bishop Polding was hopeful he could work around the status quo and keep the two priests apart.

Although it was a daunting prospect to be left behind in Van Diemen's Land there was, nevertheless, a personal welcome waiting for Fr Cotham from his enterprising younger brother Lawrence. He had sold his pharmacy business in Preston by the time he was 22 and made his own way out to Australia. He cleverly announced his arrival in Hobart by placing an advertisement in the local press with two companions; if Captain Ellis possessed all the fine qualities they listed, they were the sort of men to recognise and appreciate them:

> WE, the Undersigned Cabin Passengers, per brig Bachelor, thus publicly express our grateful acknowledgements to Captain Ellis, for the kindness and attention we have invariably received at his hands, throughout the whole of our passage from Liverpool. Though it does not enter our province, to speak of the qualities requisite to form a seaman, we can testify, from experience, to the high character he bears in England, as a gentleman possessing in an eminent degree, activity, vigilance, and the highest nautical science and skill.
>
> W. CROMPTON, H. JAMIESON, L. COTHAM
>
> April 21, 1835[21]

Lawrence sailed from England at the time his brothers were being ordained. Presumably he intended to sail to Sydney with James when they rendezvoused in Van Diemen's Land. There were other friends who had preceded Fr Cotham from Lancashire. One of his contemporaries from Stonyhurst, a 25-year-old colonial surgeon and free settler John Pearson Rowe, had apparently waited for the arrival of the new clergyman to conduct the wedding ceremony with his 16-year-old fiancée Mary Lowe. She was the daughter of a former convict, George Lowe, who had become a successful businessman and wealthy trader and he, too, had waited for the newly appointed priest to conduct his daughter's marriage before selling up and relocating most of his family to Sydney.[22] The couple were married on 8 September 1835, in Hobart, in a Catholic ceremony with Fr Cotham officiating, surely his first solo public duty following the departure of Polding two days earlier. Later in September Rowe appeared in the Supreme Court of Van Diemen's Land accused by Fr Conolly of causing 'a false, scandalous, and malicious libel' to be published in the Morning Star, on 23 January 1835.[23] For this Rowe was fined £70. Rowe's choice of Fr Cotham to celebrate his marriage sprang from bitter partisanship among Hobart's Catholics and was an act calculated to set the two priests at odds with each other and for the self-appointed 'Roman Catholic Committee' to claim Cotham as their man.

The Committee had summoned Fr Conolly to a meeting in January 1834, to hear resolutions censuring his lack of action in providing religious instruction and education, and his unacceptable 'deportment to his flock'. His only supporters on this occasion had been Protestants.[24] The Committee, headed by James Hackett, an affluent, opinionated distiller from Cork, and John Rowe, followed up their censure of Fr Conolly by raising a subscription to pay for the education of Catholic children, money which under their care would 'avoid the fate which befell [sic] former subscriptions' raised under the priest's authority.[25] However, when the Committee tried to suggest, by way of a congratulatory note of welcome in the press, that they expected and hoped Vicar General Ullathorne in New South Wales would champion their cause, Ullathorne immediately placed his own notice to the effect that having read certain statements in the newspaper 'tending to identify me with an association of individuals calling themselves "the Roman Catholic Committee" I hasten to express my surprise and utter astonishment, as I have not, in

'You May Calculate upon no Little Trouble with Him'   37

any manner, hitherto recognized or communicated with any such "Committee" or other Association'.[26] Privately, however, Ullathorne shared their dismay about Fr Conolly.

An early friend who proved to be steadfastly loyal to Fr Cotham and to the Catholic community was Dr Edward Swarbreck Hall, who had emigrated from Liverpool with his wife in 1833. Hall was to become a leading lay person in Tasmania's Catholic Church and a noted epidemiologist, but he did not have a smooth passage in either vocation. Towards the end of his life he reminisced about his first days in Hobart. His memoir supports observations made by Ullathorne and Polding about the state of Fr Conolly's chapel although his tone is less judgemental. After disembarking with his wife Mary:

> ... we proceeded to attend Mass at the rude, barn-like building which then served for the only Catholic place of worship on the island. It was built of brick, unceiled, unplastered, and floored with loose warped boards, which would fly up by a careless tread on their extremities; their edges were very sharp to the knees of the worshippers, and only a few forms to sit upon.

They were soon spotted as newcomers by Fr Conolly and after affably chatting with him he went to prepare for Mass, some soldiers having arrived:

> At that time there were two regiments in Hobart Town, the 21st and the 66th, and many of them were Catholics. The chapel was densely crowded, and the service and accessories altogether of a rude and primitive character, and when Father Conolly thrust his way among the people with an old hat to make the collection after the offertory, my better half, who had been accustomed only to the decorous and solemn services of England was astounded. After Mass we were invited into the vestry, which was also Father Conolly's sitting room, his rude dwelling being only a lean-to against the chapel.

Hall continues:

> Next day we were surprised with the visit from a Catholic gentleman who had held an appointment in the large charitable institution of our native town [Liverpool] to which I was one of the honorary medical officers. I was not aware that he was in this part of the world ... He was Mr J. P. Rowe.[27]

Hall dutifully came to welcome Bishop Polding's party but paid heavily for it as an advertisement in the *Colonial Times* showed:

> Twenty Shillings Reward. LOST, a Pocket-case of Surgical Instruments, with the owner's name (E. S. Hall) in gilt letters inside, whoever has found the same, and will bring it to Mr E. S. Hall, Surgeon, Baghdad, or to Mr Cassidy, Richmond will receive the above reward.[28]

Despite these few familiar faces the young priest was left to find his own way in what was essentially a penal settlement containing thousands of convicts, a few hundred free settlers, and one other Catholic priest with an ambiguous reputation. Cotham was expected to cover hundreds of miles on horseback in unfamiliar territory, have no fixed home or church buildings and no one to advise him. He had no experience of life on the mission in England; even the shipboard routine with Polding had been an intensified, almost idealised, model of monastic community life with a strong spiritual leader and clear demarcations of status between the priests, the students, and the young aspirant, John Gorman.

The British Government had sanctioned their mission by awarding grants of £150 for 'Outfit and Passage'[29] to the four clerics: Polding, Cotham, Corcoran, and Sumner, and £100 to the catechists (as the non-ordained men were styled) and the deceased Fr Fisher who, having joined the party in Liverpool on the point of departure, was taken on as a catechist. The same amounts were awarded as annual stipends. John Gorman's father paid for his son's passage, the hope being that he would join Polding's new monastery, when it was built, as a novice. In recognition of his episcopal status Bishop Polding's travel allowance and stipend was raised to £200 on condition that Ullathorne

'You May Calculate upon no Little Trouble with Him'   39

would move to Van Diemen's Land as soon as convenient after Polding's arrival in New South Wales, because the government was not prepared to support two Catholic clergymen on a higher stipend in one colony.[30] Polding's reluctance to adhere to this arrangement and lose Ullathorne's assistance was to cause Cotham considerable anguish.

The Catholic community in Van Diemen's Land had petitioned the authorities in England via Bishop Bramston to provide a replacement for Fr Conolly. Not only was Cotham an answer to their petition, he had on his side a ready-made contingent of lay-people eager to promote their religion. These free settlers and former convicts had knowledge and experience that Cotham lacked; they were enterprising people, often running more than one line of business, and the English class system of aristocracy, gentry, trade, and labourer, although not entirely absent, did not define them. The well-regarded citizen was the one who improved the prosperity and living standards of the whole community through personal involvement and advocacy with the governing bodies. Fr Cotham had neither a sole patron to support him (and to demand his loyalty) nor exceptionally wealthy families to provide funds, but the Catholic community did not expect or want that either. If Fr Cotham would cooperate with them (and in his position he could hardly do otherwise) they would give him the authority and respect due to his office and do much of the work for him. Cotham found the early months intolerably difficult in some respects, but he did not complain about his congregations.

The construction of church buildings, which was such a feature of Catholic life in England from the 1840s onwards, began necessarily earlier in the Australian colonies, lacking as they did the household chapels in the countryside or the remnants of urban recusant chapels. Bishop Polding symbolically laid a foundation stone during his short time in Hobart, but the real work began after he left. A public meeting was held on 21 September 1835, chaired by Fr Cotham, for the Catholic community of Richmond and its environs at the Lennox Arms Inn 'for the purpose of adopting measures for the erection of a Catholic church in that town.'[31] The land donated for the church by John Cassidy, to the east of the Coal River, on an elevated position, was tactfully at a distance from Fr Conolly's chapel, so the location was eminently suitable for a newcomer.

St John's, Richmond was the first of four places of worship Cotham provided for his congregations, and in each he seems to have worked harmoniously with the working party, following a similar pattern. Preparations for the Richmond meeting had been thorough, to judge from the resolutions arising. Five committee members were chosen: John Cassidy, R. Troy, R. Gavin, S. M'Cullock and Andrew Counsell, Cassidy taking the office of Treasurer and William Stynes acting as Secretary. A detailed resolution followed regarding the terms of subscriptions, essential for qualifying for a Government grant:

> That subscribers to the amount of £5 and under, shall give acceptances to the treasurer, for the purpose contemplated, (the erection of a church for the Catholic community), at three months; the said bills to be dated 1st Oct. 1835, and fall due on the 4th of January 1836. And in like manner, subscribers above £5, and under £10, shall give acceptances for the said purpose, at three and six months, viz.—one half of the subscription to be paid on bills falling due on the 4th of January 1836, and the other on the 4th April 1836. In like manner, subscribers above £10 and under £20, in three instalments, at such like periods. As also, subscribers of and above £20 at four periods, 3, 6, 9 and 12 months, viz.—the 4th of January 1836, 4th of April 1836, 4th of July 1836, and the 4th of October 1836.[32]

With the hope that funds would be forthcoming the committee was charged with advertising for tenders to erect the church, plans for which could be seen at Mr Cassidy's house, or at the Lennox Arms Inn, Richmond. These plans were part of a small portfolio by Henry Edmund Goodridge (c. 1800–1863), a Bath architect who had

'You May Calculate upon no Little Trouble with Him' 41

worked on an extension to Downside Priory in 1823 while Polding was Prefect with responsibility for buildings. Goodridge's Romantic Gothick design for a chapel and generous accommodation satisfied the monastic community, so he was an obvious choice for Polding ten years later. All the designs in the Australian portfolio were for small rectangular Gothic boxes with Early English detail and pinnacled buttresses at the corners. St John's, Richmond, measured 50 ft 6 in. long by 19 ft wide. The proportions were modest but identifiably ecclesiastical features graced it with four windows along each side with wooden Y-tracery and a three-light Early English window on the west façade which was completed by a panelled entrance door and a bell-cote surmounted by a cross at the apex of the west gable.[33]

Meanwhile, since local subscriptions had rapidly raised £700, Fr Cotham and Mr Cassidy would 'wait upon his Excellency the Governor, to solicit the assistance of government towards the erection of the intended church' according to policy in the colony. Finally, a resolution was passed 'that the thanks of the meeting be given to the Protestant gentlemen of Richmond and the neighbourhood, for the noble and generous manner in which they have come forward in support of this object'.[34] Cotham made his request on 9 October for £500 to complete the new church, emphasising the benefits for the military and convict population of the district. Lieutenant-Governor Arthur was disposed to recommend the request to Whitehall, alongside applications from the Wesleyans in Launceston and the Independent Chapel in Hobart:

> The Roman Catholics have hitherto been a very inconsiderable body in this Community, possessing one very rude chapel in Hobart Town and a school in connection with it. The arrival of Dr Polding, however, has excited a degree of energy which has given them a more influential appearance, and has had the effect of recalling some persons, who had been in the habit of attending the Established Church.[35]

The good Catholics who had been energised by a visit from their bishop were not privy to the minutes of Arthur's Executive Council which added another incentive to build:

> With respect to the application of the Roman Catholics of Richmond, it is in the knowledge of the Council that the population in that neighbourhood and in the vicinity of Sorell, comprising as it does many families of that persuasion who settled there at the period of the first establishment of the Colony, have enjoyed but few opportunities of receiving instruction, and that drunkenness and its attendant vices are therefore comparatively prevalent.[36]

With the first round of subscriptions pocketed in early 1836 John Cassidy advertised for tenders for the building work, particulars to be supplied by himself or the Revd J Cotham of Hobart Town[37] and two months later he was again placing a notice in the press asking subscribers to keep their payments up to date into the Derwent Bank as the contractor, Mr Buscombe, would need to be paid very shortly 'the Chapel being rapidly advancing'.[38] The choice of James Kestall Buscombe was a sound one; he had opened the Lennox Arms Inn in 1827 and built his own stone windmill, a prominent Richmond landmark, between 1829 and 1831.

Whilst Cotham had able support from an influential portion of his congregation he had to work with, or around, the foibles of the other priest on the island, Fr Philip Conolly, who had come out from Northern Ireland with Fr John Joseph Therry[39] in 1820. Conolly had received even less support than Cotham in his ministry which, in the first years, was mainly with convicts. Although he had tried to obtain government money for church building little had been forthcoming. He enjoyed, however, a positive reputation as the convicts' priest. He was able to speak Gaelic with the Irish prisoners who had no English language and for more than ten years he worked single handedly. As chaplain he had secured land for church purposes at Launceston, Pittwater, and Hobart, but he claimed that one portion of the land in Hobart had been a personal grant. This was the chief cause,

'You May Calculate upon no Little Trouble with Him' 43

among lesser complaints, of contention with the local Catholic population and by the time Bishop Polding arrived he seems to have become rather eccentric and perhaps no longer had the energy to adapt to the changing nature of Tasmanian society.

Dean John Kenny, the former catechist, charitably remembered Conolly as a man 'of no small ability and attainment, but he had grown rather antiquated in his manner on account of being so long by himself'.[40] Dr Swarbreck Hall, who frequently received the priest as his guest, found him sensible and warm hearted despite his many peculiarities. Nevertheless, Conolly did not fit into the Benedictine vision of Australia's Catholic future. He had become close friends with the veteran Church of England minister, Revd Mr Knopwood, and the two were said to be drinking partners. The unwelcome fact that Fr Conolly was the senior priest, experienced and already established on the island, was a difficulty Bishop Polding, Fr Cotham's superior many miles away, left the younger man to manage as best he could.

The growing number of Catholic free settlers wanted civic society to develop in ways that were more obviously respectable, with efficient education for their children, and which could give the rising generation opportunities for occupations unrelated to convictism. Fr Conolly belonged to Van Diemen's Land's origins as a penal colony; the next generation of settlers wanted a priest who could minister to them and would understand and share their aspirations. An anti-Conolly clique, 'The Friends of Roman Catholicism', petitioned Rome for the pioneer priest's removal, to be replaced by 'an exemplary divine who will be qualified to teach our children'. It is true that the condition of his chapel in Hobart— a small hut—was damned by Fr Ullathorne in 1833 when he came as Vicar General to New South Wales, and he remembered the shock all his life. 'The altar was covered with dirt and dust, the Chalice was on the altar dirty and black, and the Sanctuary was the receptacle of old books, clothes and household utensils.'[41] It was all so far removed from what Bishop Polding was already achieving in New South Wales. The laying of the foundation stone at St Patrick's, Parramatta, on 17 March 1836 was an early opportunity for Bishop Polding to bring home to all observers that a new era of Catholic advancement had arrived.

With such a speedy and efficient beginning to the erection of St John's, Richmond (now the oldest church in Australia still in use although remodelled according to A. W. N. Pugin's designs in 1859), the enthusiastic newcomer was making friends among the local Catholic population in Richmond and in Launceston, one hundred and twenty five miles away to the north. But the bright start soon clouded over and the early months of Fr Cotham's ministry nearly broke him. In March 1836, before he had a chance to read about the impressive ceremonial Polding had managed to put together at Parramatta, he sent a heartfelt, angry, and desperate letter to the Bishop who, he felt, had abandoned him.

Notes

[1] *The Tasmanian (Hobart Town)*, 22 May 1835, p. 6.
[2] DAA 1.139, letter from Polding to Birdsall, 20 December 1834. James' elder brother William was ordained at Stonyhurst by Dr Penswick on 20 December 1834; *Letters and Notices*, No. XCIX, 1895, House Journal of the British Province of the Society of Jesus, obituary, p. 132.
[3] DAA; Birdsall to Polding, 17 March 1834, *Records and Letters* by A. Allanson OSB. www.plantata.org.uk [Accessed online, 24.10.2013]
[4] *Colonial Times* (Hobart), 11 August 1835, p. 4.
[5] P. F. Moran, *History of the Catholic Church in Australasia* (Sydney: Oceanic Publishing Company, 1896), p. 185.
[6] J. Clay, *Maconochie's Experiment, How one man's extraordinary vision saved transported convicts from degradation and despair*, (London: John Murray, 2001), p. 53.
[7] 'truly beautiful and appropriate to our circumstances'
[8] H. N. Birt OSB, *Benedictine Pioneers in Australia* (London: Herbert and Daniel, 2 Vols, 1911), Vol. 1, p. 255.
[9] *Ibid.*, p. 254.
[10] *Ibid.*, pp. 236ff.
[11] *Ibid.*, p. 255.
[12] S. Elliott JP, *Fifty Years of Colonial Life* (Melbourne: T. Smith and

'You May Calculate upon no Little Trouble with Him' 45

Company, 1887), pp. 21–25. Elliott (1809–1901) wrote the account of his 'long and eventful life' in 1886, from his birth in Essex, his childhood in New Brunswick, Canada, through to his successful business enterprises in Sydney and Melbourne.

[13] P. F. Moran, *History of the Catholic Church in Australasia* (Sydney: Oceanic Publishing Company, 1896), p. 186, quoting an unnamed member of the missionary party.

[14] *Colonial Times* (Hobart), 11 August 1835, p. 4.

[15] P. MacFie, '*Silent Impact: The Irish Inheritance of Richmond & the Coal River Valley 1840–1970*' (2000), reprint of paper published in Irish-Australian Studies, R. Davis (Ed.), 8th Irish Australian Conference, (Crossing Press, 1995) pp. 486 and 489. Quoted by Brian Andrews, 'Pugin's Australian Works—St John the Evangelist's Church, Richmond (Part 1)' *Newsletter*; Pugin Foundation No. 28, January 2009. www.thepuginsociety.co.uk/uploads/2/0/5/6/20562880/newsletter_28. pdf [Accessed online 27.7.2017]

[16] *The Hobart Town Courier,* 28 August 1835, p. 4.

[17] *Ibid.,* p. 4.

[18] The second priest, from Ireland, Fr Corcoran died a year after arriving when his gig was overturned by a pothole and he was thrown out. Br Benedict Spencer never settled and became a mischief maker, disturbing the young boy accompanying them, John Gorman, so both had to be sent home. Fr Henry Gregory became the Bishop's Vicar General but following complaints from Sydney he was recalled to England by Rome in 1861. Frs Sumner and Kenny both spent the rest of their lives in Australia.

[19] DA VIII.A.Cotham; journal copy of a letter written 27 January 1852 to the Colonial Secretary asking for an extended leave of absence.

[20] *The Hobart Town Courier,* 7 August 1835, p. 2, and 9 October 1835, p. 4.

[21] *Colonial Times* (Hobart), 21 April 1835, p. 3.

[22] 'Family tradition has the story that Mary was told by a maid "If you peep around the parlour door, you'll see your father talking with the man you are going to marry"'. One of Lowe's conditions of the marriage was that Rowe would give his daughter an education. On 19 November 1839 George Lowe's wife Honora née Ahern died in Hobart, aged 44, and was buried in the Catholic cemetery at St Mary's, Hobart. There is no evidence that Honora had practised as a Catholic after leaving Ireland in 1814; she was married in the Church of England and all her children were baptised there. However, two of her children had since married Catholics. Mary's husband, John Pearson Rowe, was a committed Catholic and he may have encouraged his mother-in-law to reconcile with her faith towards the end of her life. The following year, George Lowe was listed amongst subscrib-

46   *The Indomitable Mr Cotham*

ers to St Mary's Church, Mt Carmel, Hobart Town: 'G. Lowe £1. 6s'; in comparison, John Cassidy donated £50 and Lawrence Cotham, £10; *The Courier* (Hobart), 27 Nov 1840, p. 3. Unfortunately, the newspaper announcement of the marriage named the celebrant as 'Rev. Laurence Cotham'; the younger brother had evidently made his name known in the short time he had been in Hobart; *The True Colonist and Van Diemen's Land Political Despatch, and Commercial and Agricultural Advertiser,* 11 September 1835, p. 8. See www.rosfamilyhistory.esco.net.au for biographies of the Rowe and Lowe families. [Accessed online 19.9.2017]

23   *Colonial Times* (Hobart), 25 September 1835, p. 7, and *The Tasmanian* (Hobart Town), 30 September 1835, p. 5.

24   *Colonial Times* (Hobart), 28 January 1834, pp. 4–5.

25   *Trumpeter General* (Hobart), 4 February 1834, p. 2.

26   *Colonial Times* (Hobart), *20 May 1834, p. 7,* and *The True Colonist and Van Diemen's Political Despatch, and Commercial and Agricultural Advertiser* (Hobart), 20 May 1834, p. 4. James Hackett, described as an entrepreneur and democrat, became disillusioned with the frustrations of Van Diemen's Land and returned to Ireland with his family in 1841; he died in 1847 while giving assistance during a typhoid epidemic. Lawrence Cotham, at least in his first months in Hobart, added his name to Hackett's party, see 'Letter to the Editor of *The True Colonist'*, *The Tasmanian* (Hobart Town), 28 August 1835, p. 7.

27   E. F. Haynes, *Edward Swarbreck Hall—Medical Scientist and Social Reformer in Colonial Tasmania,* (MA Thesis, UNTAS, 1976), pp. 6–7, quoting from 'The Catholic Church in Tasmania, No III, Collections and Recollections, Reminiscences of Catholicity in Tasmania (By an old resident)', *The Catholic Standard,* May 1879. www.eprints.utas.edu.au /15766/2/1Haynes_whole_thesis.pdf [Accessed online 27.7.2017]

28   *Colonial Times* (Hobart), 1 September 1835, p. 3, and 8 September 1835, p. 3.

29   *The Sydney Monitor,* 24 July 1837, p. 3. Report of monies paid out on colonial business 1833 to 1835.

30   Despatch from the Earl of Aberdeen, Downing Street, London, to Governor Sir Richard Bourke, KCB, Government House, Sydney; 20 February 1835. Bourke's governing Council agreed to raise the stipend for Bishop Polding to £500 for the discharge of his duties with 'requisite efficiency'. The correspondence, Bourke to Lord Glenelg, 4 October 1835, again referred to the condition attached to the higher stipend being awarded 'only in the event of Mr Ullathorne's removal to Van Diemen's Land'. *Historical Records of Australia,* Series 1, Volume 18 (Sydney: The Library Committee of the Commonwealth Parliament, 1923);www.

'You May Calculate upon no Little Trouble with Him' 47

archive.org/stream/historicalrecord00v18aust; p. 131 [Accessed online 27.7.2017]

31 *The Hobart Town Courier*, 16 October 1835, p. 1.

32 *Ibid.*, p. 1.

33 B. Andrews, 'Pugin's Australian Works—St John the Evangelist's Church, Richmond (Part 1)', *Newsletter* Pugin Foundation No. 28 (January 2009). I am greatly indebted to Brian Andrews for his contribution in making widely available his knowledge of the richness of Tasmanian ecclesiastical architecture and furnishings.

34 *The Hobart Town Courier*, 16 October 1835, p.1.

35 *Historical Records of Australia*; www. archive.org/stream/historicalrecord 00v18aust; pp. 489- 490.

36 *Ibid.*, p. 494.

37 *Colonial Times* (Hobart), 5 January 1836, p. 1.

38 *Ibid.*, 29 March 1836, p. 3.

39 C. Dowd OP, *Rome in Australia: The Papacy and Conflict in the Australian Catholic Missions, 1834–1884* (Leiden: Boston, 2008), p. 116. 'Born in Cork, 1790, Therry attended St Patrick's College, Carlow and was ordained to the priesthood 1815. He combined energetic, single-minded, and compassionate service of his people with an argumentative, obstinate, and unpredictable stance towards superiors, whether ecclesiastical or civil. As a side-line to priestly ministry he was also a highly successful, wealthy businessman.'

40 H. N. Birt OSB, *Benedictine Pioneers in Australia* (London: Herbert and Daniel, 2 Vols, 1911), Vol. 1, p. 86.

41 L. Madigan (Ed.), *The Devil is a Jackass; William Bernard Ullathorne 1806–1889* (Leominster: Gracewing, 1995), p. 68.

5 A MISERABLE STATE OF AFFAIRS

AMBROSE COTHAM'S LETTER,[1] a reply to one just received from Polding, starts quite buoyantly, describing 'a rather tedious but somewhat romantic journey' he had made to reach Launceston. He had been lost from six in the morning until four thirty in the afternoon 'without food, save a little grass which I chewed to moisten my mouth, the heat being great and my thirst almost intolerable'. After walking through bush for fifty miles, pulling his horse after him, he came to a cart road and found a shepherd's hut. He was now writing from an inn in Launceston 'without any of kindred feeling around me' and missing his college friends. He describes his routine, and complains that the necessity of dividing his time between Hobart and Launceston means that he cannot be committed to either place properly. He would prefer to concentrate his efforts in Launceston but the people of Hobart will not accept Fr Conolly's services and Fr Conolly has not helped in getting government grants for church building.

The mention of Conolly quickly causes Cotham's mood to change; he feels that 'without one friend to assist or console me I am nearly distracted, nearly mad'. Mr Kenny has done well in his work with the schoolchildren and that has been 'a subject of the greatest consolation, it has been indeed the only beam of sunshine amidst the darkness that surrounded me'. But John Kenny had got his release from Van Diemen's Land in March and had returned to the Bishop's company in Sydney to continue his training as a priest. In any case, the Scotsman, six years Cotham's junior, had probably not been personally very helpful to Cotham; fifty years later Kenny was remembered for his dourness by Catholics in Australia, and was respected rather than loved by his parishioners. As for the Bishop, Cotham had been daily expecting to hear from him about future arrangements for the colony but he has heard 'nothing to the point'. Conolly still remained in place and there was no sign of Fr Ullathorne's arrival, or any extra help, as promised by the Bishop.

There follows a tirade against Fr Conolly. He complains of his drinking habits and calls his behaviour towards other people unchristian and disgusting, although between the two priests there is 'the civility of policy without much love on either side'. One wonders if Fr Conolly might have been of greater help to the younger priest if he had been encouraged to recount some of his experiences, but Fr Cotham could not bring himself to see beyond appearances and he lacked the maturity to understand how the man could have reached this state of demoralisation. His seniority in religion and in age—he was born in 1786—did not deter Cotham. Instead, 'I have an opinion of Mr Conolly which I never had of any man yet—it is indescribable. Entre nous, I really sometimes have taken him to have dealings with his Satanic Majesty ... indeed, I do not know what to think of him.' The long journey to Launceston had, in fact, given him plenty of time to think about the predicament in which he had been left.

From the Bishop's letter alluded to it seems he wanted to believe Cotham was settling in nicely but Cotham tells him plainly

> if someone does not come down from Sydney [to replace Conolly] within two months I cannot in conscience remain in the Colony ... I must candidly tell your Lordship that nothing on earth would induce me to remain here much longer, as circumstances are at present ... Nothing but the miserable state of affairs here could make me write to you as I have done. I have not any means of attending my own religious duties and cannot therefore minister with the same effect to the salvation of others.

In this letter Cotham reveals how much he feared for his life, his sanity, and even his soul: everything he had known and relied on he was now separated from 'by an immeasurable ocean'. His problems were an inconvenience to Bishop Polding, who was

A Miserable State of Affairs

busy laying foundation stones for new churches and celebrating confirmations. The bishop celebrated his first Easter in Sydney but in light of Cotham's impassioned letter he could not put off the journey to Van Diemen's Land any longer. He hurriedly made provisional arrangements for his absence:

> On Sunday next, I hold my first Ordinations; Mr Sumner and Gregory, Deacons, Mr Spencer, Subdeacon. On Thursday after, Mr Sumner, Priest. I could wish to defer this, but I cannot. I must go to Hobart Town, and I am obliged to ordain him to keep things in their places ... I have decided on sending Mr Ullathorne to beat up and select recruits [in England]. How I shall manage without him I scarcely know. Providence will aid. He is most useful to me. His intelligence, aptitude for business, and zeal, render him a most valuable coadjutor. He has certainly great merit for what he did previous to my arrival.[2]

Bishop Polding and Fr Ullathorne sailed for Hobart on 11 May 1836, with the sad outcome of Fr Conolly's suspension and the promise of a new Vicar General from the Bishop's sparse clerical resources. Had someone of Ullathorne's stature, even at this early stage in his ecclesiastical career, been appointed in the island, Cotham's subsequent personal and pastoral development would surely have been different. As it was, he was to have three superiors in his first ten years of ministry, all of whom were in varying ways problematic to the Bishop, and none of whom were well suited to guide a young priest.

The *Sydney Herald*[3] gave a full report of what it understood took place when the two senior prelates arrived from Sydney. On his arrival from England the previous August, Polding had proposed to Conolly 'as a means of tranquillity, and to prevent the continuance of the unfortunate dissention so long existing between that clergyman and his congregation' that Conolly should remove to New South Wales and Ullathorne take his place as Vicar General (a stipulation already made by the Colonial Office on grounds of cost). Conolly refused to give up his position as the 'original' Vicar General of the Colony, claiming furthermore that the existing chapel and its ground were his own private property, properly registered in the Survey Office. Polding, after a 'very careful investigation' of his claims and those of the congregation, sided with the congregation and brought Ullathorne with him to replace Conolly. Conolly was given the equally unwelcome alternatives of continuing to serve in the Colony, but under Ullathorne's authority, or of going elsewhere. Since Conolly disdained both alternatives, Polding, realising that he could not force Conolly to hand over the proprietorship of St Virgil's Chapel, poor place though it was, took the drastic step of putting both the chapel and Conolly under an interdict: divine worship was not to be held at St Virgil's, nor was Fr Conolly to officiate there. Ullathorne read out the decree in St Virgil's Chapel in the presence of Conolly and his congregation; Fr Conolly immediately walked out.

When Ullathorne was installed as Vicar General the following Sunday at a Mass held at Bellevue House 'the whole congregation, to a man' turned out to hear him; their attendance probably was occasioned more by a desire to hear further dramatic announcements than by their wholesale desertion of their priest. Conolly preferred a charge against Bishop Polding that the Bishop's actions had caused Conolly to lose £1,000; Polding was placed under house arrest. Naturally, the good gentlemen of the congregation were incensed at such proceedings and protested to Lieutenant-Governor Arthur who, on the advice of the Attorney General Mr Stephen, ordered Polding to be liberated (apparently after only twenty-four hours spent indoors). The Bishop hastily departed for Sydney, leaving Ullathorne and Cotham as the only properly sanctioned Catholic functionaries on the island. In the words of the *Sydney Herald*,

> however well-disposed Colonel Arthur may be towards Mr Conolly, yet his Excellency cannot with any propriety continue to pay from the Colonial Chest the stipend of £151 a year to Mr Conolly, if that part of the prison

population, being Catholics, who attended to hear Mr Conolly should attend to hear the Rev Messrs Ullathorne and Cotham.[4]

Polding had probably not thought about the consequences of an immediate cessation of income for Conolly and it is even more doubtful that the majority of the convict population, even if free to choose their place of worship, would desert a priest who had a long connection with them, in favour of the newcomers brought in at the request of respectable, aspiring free settlers. Additional material from *The Tasmanian* was appended to the *Sydney Herald*'s account of the affairs of the day:

> The Bishop felt exceedingly the indignity thus offered to him, and his flock, assembled on the instant, when the following resolutions were unanimously passed.
>
> Catholic Meeting, Mr. Riechenberg in the chair;
>
> Resolved—That having learned that the Right Rev. Dr. Polding has been pleased to suspend the sacerdotal functions of the Rev. Mr. Conolly, that we most heartily concur in the propriety of that proceeding.
>
> Resolved—That as the Right Rev. Dr. Polding has been grossly insulted by Mr. Conolly, who has this day caused a writ to be served upon him by the hands of a sheriff's bailiff, we do immediately claim the protection of the Government for the head of our church in this island.
>
> A deputation forthwith proceeded to Government House, and His Excellency was pleased to promise to afford the Catholics all the protection in his power.
>
> On Sunday, Dr. Polding addressed his flock, to whom he retained thanks for their obedience to his orders, and their deportment to Mr. Conolly during his absence. He also stated that having received both sympathy and protection from the Governor, he called upon the Catholics to signify to his Excellency their sense thereof accordingly.

When Cotham wrote his letter from Launceston in March he could not have conceived the course of events that would follow. That Conolly should be reprimanded and removed to New South Wales might have been in his mind, but that he had been in large measure responsible for the imprisonment of his Bishop, a public demonstration to the Crown office, a priest and chapel put under interdict, and discussion in the press about ecclesiastical in-fighting must have been unnerving. His personal distress had unintentionally served the purposes of a faction in the Catholic population: if Cotham had felt in September 1835 that he had been badly served by Bishop Polding, now in March 1836 Cotham's letter to his bishop had, arguably, agitated Polding into taking precipitate action against the hapless Conolly, humiliating him and removing him from his position and from his livelihood. But Conolly, as Cotham readily admitted, had never behaved in a provocative or insulting manner towards him. It is unlikely that Polding had time to sympathise with Cotham's troubles even if he had a mind to, and when Polding returned to Sydney it is unlikely Cotham would have wanted to go with him, however unlikely it was that he would be invited to join his Benedictine confrères.

On his return to Sydney, without Ullathorne, Bishop Polding wrote to President Birdsall:

> If any of my confrères are willing to join me ... they must be of the <u>right sort</u>—zealous, laborious Missioners, no love for self nor pelf. How necessary it is to be careful in choosing clergymen for these colonies! They live so continually in the eye of the public, their conduct must be spotless or Religion vitally suffers: every trifling incident respecting them spreads through the country. With those who accompanied me I have every reason to be satisfied, save one. Him I wish again in France.[5]

Ironically, the 'one'—presumably Cotham—was not the man who was to give him most trouble in those first years. Although Fr Ullathorne said that he would not have allowed Br Benedict Spencer to disembark on arrival, remembering him as a wayward

A Miserable State of Affairs 55

student at Downside, Polding ordained him sub-deacon by way of encouraging him by 'giving strong motives to a manly line of conduct ... I am determined he shall have a fair trial and for this purpose, I shall send him to Port Macquarie; the resort of all the invalids and what are called the Gentleman Convicts.'[6]

Towards Cotham, who was struggling to follow a manly line of conduct without encouragement, there was no sympathy. There is no record of what Ambrose Cotham thought of Bishop Polding's attitude towards him. Ullathorne, after many dealings with Polding over a twenty-five year period, expressed his opinion bluntly in 1859, and there is no reason to think Cotham would have disagreed:

> While the Archbishop supported me in secret, before the public he did not show me any co-operation or help. This was what ruined my health ... in short he could never treat those who had been his novices or disciples otherwise than if they were still novices or scholars. Moreover I knew that the great fear that he had of public opinion would lead him to abandon others in difficulties, at the same time that he would want to be followed in everything. This is only a sketch of a story too long to tell further.[7]

The appointment of Ullathorne in Van Diemen's Land was short-lived and was probably made only to unseat Conolly.[8] Before they left Sydney Bishop Polding already had plans for him to sail for England, which he promptly did, embarking on the *Eldon*,

> with a view to return shortly with an adequate supply of duly qualified clergymen for the care and instruction of the members of the Roman Catholic church in these Colonies. Meantime, it is understood, that the Rev. Mr. Watkins will be sent down from Sydney to supply, as far as his single means can, the wants of the people in this Colony.[9]

Notes

[1] H. N. Birt OSB, *Benedictine Pioneers in Australia* (London: Herbert and Daniel, 2 Vols, 1911), Cotham to Polding, 12 March 1836, Vol. 1, pp. 101–105. See Appendix A for the full text of the letter.

[2] *Ibid.*, Polding to Heptonstall, 1 May 1836, Vol. 1, p. 291.

[3] *Sydney Herald*, 4 July 1836, p. 2.

[4] *Ibid.*, p. 2.

[5] H. N. Birt, *Benedictine Pioneers in Australia* (London: Herbert and Daniel, 2 Vols, 1911), Vol. 1, p. 293.Polding to Birdsall, 7 June 1836, from Bishop's House, Sydney.

[6] *Ibid.*, p. 293.

[7] J. Champ, *William Bernard Ullathorne 1806–1889, A Different Kind of Monk* (Leominster: Gracewing, 2006), p. 256.

[8] Fr Conolly lived on, in broken health, until 9 August 1839, when he died leaving memories of a plain, blunt, honest, and kindly pastor. He was buried in St. Mary's Cathedral, Hobart. His death was mischievously announced by the *Sydney Gazette and New South Wales Advertiser*, 13 August 1839, p. 2; 'Mr Conolly, the Roman Catholic priest who, for the last four years has held Dr Polding and the whole Catholic clergy at bay, is no more.' This was unfair to Fr Therry who had remained friendly to Conolly. However, Fr Cotham was not sent for from Launceston to join Fr Therry and Fr Butler to make up sufficient clergy numbers to celebrate High Mass for his funeral. Instead, a large number of Protestant clergy of different denominations followed the hearse, including the Episcopalian Revd William Bedford who had administered the last rites to Fr Conolly.

[9] *Sydney Herald*, 4 July 1836, p. 2, citing *Bent's News*.

6 HOBART & RICHMOND, 1835–1838

SINCE ITS SETTLEMENT in 1804, Hobart and its environs had been populated by convicts and their guards, government officials, and settlers, both free and emancipated. The general trend of development was towards establishing a civil society amid the inescapable trappings of a penal settlement. The early, shameful treatment of the indigenous aboriginal population had resulted in their almost complete elimination as a group, threatening or otherwise, by 1830. When Charles Darwin visited Hobart Town in February 1836 as part of the *Beagle* expedition he was satisfied, though not overwhelmed, by what he saw of the town and Derwent estuary.

> The bases of these mountains, following the edges of the bay, are cleared & cultivated; the bright yellow fields of corn, & dark green ones of potato crops appear very luxuriant ... In the morning I walked on shore—The streets are fine and broad, but the houses rather scattered: the shops appeared good. The town stands at the base of Mt. Wellington, a mountain 3100 ft high [*sic*], but of very little picturesque beauty: from this source however it receives a good supply of water, a thing much wanted in Sydney ... Comparing this town to Sydney, I was chiefly struck by the comparative fewness of large houses, either built or building—I should think this must indicate that fewer people are gaining large fortunes. The growth however of small houses has been most abundant, & the vast number of little red brick dwellings scattered on the hill behind the town, sadly destroys its picturesque appearance ... The inhabitants for this year are 13,826 inhabitants, in the whole of Tasmania 36,505.[1]

Hobart's location on the wide estuary of the River Derwent, twenty miles inland, provided a harbour that was one of the best and most secure in the world at that time. Until the Bass Strait between Van Diemen's Land and South Australia was charted it was a necessary port of call for international shipping: for passenger travel, commerce, exploration, and for England's convict transportation system. By 1835 the town covered one square mile, its long, wide streets arranged in grid formation fronted by stores, government offices, civic institutions, and the first generation of churches. The Hobart Rivulet ran through the centre of the town towards the estuary. The appearance of the town was surprisingly pleasant and well ordered on first acquaintance, although the progress of infrastructure lagged behind its growth in population and the ubiquitous public houses, grog shops, and alcohol stores belied its respectable façade. Lady Jane Franklin, who arrived in 1837 as wife of Lieutenant-Governor Sir John Franklin, wrote that everyone 'makes an involuntary shudder at the bare thought of being side by side in the street with convicts. Yet the feeling of security and the knowledge of good order and vigilance soon dissipate this feeling'.[2]

Cotham was fortunate in being placed in Richmond, about fifteen miles distance from Hobart, for his first experience of Van Diemen's Land; and despite his early difficulties the country had much to please him. Exploration of the Coal River area began in 1803, followed in the next two decades by land grants, the construction of roads, the official naming of the township in 1824 by Lieutenant-Governor Sorell, and the opening to traffic of the convict-built bridge in 1825. It remained an outstation until 1827 when it became the centre of one of the ten newly-formed police districts set up by Sorell's successor George Arthur.[3] Although Richmond's continued growth relied on its importance as a convict station and a military post, within ten years of its official establishment it had the appearance of a well-ordered English village. Several roads led into and out of the town, and town services expanded with businesses including blacksmiths, wheel-

Hobart & Richmond, 1835–1838

wrights, saddlers, stockyards, tanneries, a market place, a pound, brick and lime kilns, as well as general stores. The fertile countryside was a centre for arable farming, mainly wheat, and livestock grazing supported markets and rural industries. By 1835 the Richmond area had Van Diemen's Land's largest district population, and it was the third largest township in the colony after Hobart and Launceston. The danger posed by gangs of bushrangers had markedly declined; the infamous 'Black Line' policy, and George Robinson's more benign, though unsuccessful, efforts to resettle Aboriginal people to Flinders Island, had removed not only the native islanders but also the tensions between them and incoming settlers.[4]

Most residential buildings were of a simple and uniform design, built from brick or stone with the occasional prominent house denoting its owner's wealth, such as that of G. W. Gunning Esq., J.P., whose estate included a fine racecourse.

> The English picturesque qualities of Richmond were found in the combination of simple Georgian buildings constructed from the local, warm coloured stone, the small size of the village, the proximity of farmhouses, the valley setting with sparse tree cover and the focus on the Bridge.[5]

There was, however, a preponderance of inns and Fr Cotham had familiarity with them, as did the whole population; his brother Lawrence successfully managed and owned the Richmond Hotel for a number of years. But the colony also had serious problems with alcohol misuse, beginning with the official use of alcohol as a legitimate form of currency. Cotham had occasion to act in individual cases of drunkenness and in time became a leading member of the temperance movement in Catholic circles. He was not inclined to total abstention himself but in the circumstances of the period this was a position often strongly advocated as the only remedy for endemic alcohol abuse.

The establishment of the town naturally included planning for religious buildings and in due course the Anglican and Roman

Catholic Churches formed the major landmarks at the southern and northern ends of the town. Each denomination was allocated some twenty acres of land for a church and necessary facilities, half-an-acre being designated as a burial ground. It was not until 3 February 1834 that Lieutenant-Governor Arthur laid the foundation stone for St Luke's Anglican Church, consecrated by Bishop Broughton on 19 May 1838. The construction of the Roman Catholic Church took longer, blamed by some Catholics on Fr Conolly's reluctance to act.

Cotham may not have been able fully to appreciate his natural environment during his first year but in later journal entries he writes of swimming and of picnics in the hills; moreover his fondness for long walks never left him. While Bishop Polding used a gig occasionally to travel to mission stations, both because of long distances and excessive heat, Fr Cotham seems mostly to have ridden horseback, even when lashing rain rather than heat made travel a misery. His journal includes many references to his horse and its welfare.

The new Vicar General arrived in Hobart in August 1836. Fr James Watkins, a Welshman from Monmouth, had freelanced his way to Sydney from London in 1835 after a dispute with Bishop Bramston had resulted in his removal from his mission in London in 1833.[6] He was Polding's exact contemporary: born in 1794 and ordained priest at the same ceremony in 1819 at Old Hall College, Ware, by Bishop Poynter. Later histories of the Tasmanian church during this period barely mention Fr Watkins, although his presence is noted, without adverse comment, in the local newspapers of the time. He took on Fr Conolly's disputed claim to ownership of the land granted for the Catholic chapel and burial ground in Hobart and secured the decision (for the second time) of the Commissioners for Grants of Land that Conolly did not have a valid claim; those seven acres were granted to Watkins. Even in the local press there was agreement that the matter needed resolving:

Hobart & Richmond, 1835–1838

> We [the Editor] confess that the Roman Catholics have just grounds for complaint. The service on Sunday last was performed in a large room at the back of the "George and Dragon," on Langlow's Hill. The greater portion of the congregation, including the military, could not find room in-doors, but were obliged to stand outside in the scorching sun, while those within were almost suffocated with heat.[7]

In September 1836 work began on the foundations of the New Church in Richmond. Looking for a carpenter in April 1837, Cotham tried to arrange for convict James Powell to be assigned to him but the request was refused; Powell was a house carpenter belonging to a loan-gang, and not available for a long assignment. As often happened, the convicts with useful skills were most in demand for private and government work and might be hired out ahead of men who had been longer in the system but were less valuable as employees. The nave was completed first and the church was opened on 31 December 1837. There seems little doubt from a newspaper account of the occasion that the accomplished dignity of the proceedings was a new and unexpected Catholic phenomenon. Fr Watkins, despite his failings, was cultured and musical, and his experience supplied for Cotham's lack. On the other hand, Cotham was already a confident preacher and he would have carefully prepared his 'extemporaneous discourse'; his themes—religious education and the building of churches—were to become favourites with him.

> In pursuance of the advertisement announcing the opening of this unique and classic edifice for divine worship on Sunday [31 Dec], a highly respectable and numerous assembly of gentry arrived at eleven o'clock, to witness this most solemn and imposing ceremony. Nothing could equal the surprise of the audience at finding a most efficient choir contributing to the solemnity of the scene. The well played clarinet of that professor of music, Mr. Reichenberg, aided by the skill on the piano of a talented young gentleman, a son of Francis Smith, Esq. with the delicate taste displayed by a lady, who accompanied that instrument, in incompa-

rable style, and also by the skill of Mr Solicitor Wynne, from Hobart Town, contributed to excite feelings of religious fervour and enchantment amongst the entire audience. The Vicar General sang the high Mass with great ability. An extemporaneous discourse on the benefits of the extension of religious instruction, and the erection of houses to the glory of God, was delivered by the Rev. Mr Cotham, and met with general approbation. The liberality of the subscription which then took place set the impress of approval beyond the region of doubt. It was delightful to witness practical Christianity so fully exemplified—Dissenters from the form of worship of the Catholics lending their unpurchased and unpurchaseable ability to sing the praises of God, and it were well if equal liberality characterised the government of this colony, when its notions would vanish, and Christian unanimity prevail. A sumptuous repast was prepared by Mr Cassidy for his friends of the choir and others, when the health and prosperity of the worthy host, (to whose instrumentality the erection of the Catholic Church was mainly due) was drank [sic] in the warmest manner by the guests, who returned to Hobart Town in the evening, delighted with their day's pilgrimage to Richmond.[8]

The *Eucalyptus globulus* (Blue Gum) trees still standing on St John's hill and in St Luke's Anglican cemetery were probably planted around the time of the construction of the church or shortly afterwards, since by the 1880s they were higher than the nave of the Church. From its elevated position St John's had wide-ranging views; its burial ground situated to the rear of the church is located in a dramatic position on a steep escarpment overlooking the eastern bank of the Coal River. This, the earliest of Fr Cotham's mission churches, is characteristic of his lifelong preference to be in an open environment, enjoying fine air and far reaching views from a high vantage point.

A few months after the opening of the church Fr Watkins bought a painting for it. His taste was again considered an exem-

Hobart & Richmond, 1835–1838 63

plar to others and he gave Cotham his first experience of seeing a church building constructed and furnished from start to finish:

> We have been favoured, through the kindness of the Rev. Mr. Watkins, with a view of two splendid Paintings, recently arrived from England. The subjects are, 'The Adoration of the Magi at the Birth of Our Saviour,' and 'The Resurrection'... The first, which, we are happy to say, has been purchased for an Altar Piece for the New Catholic Chapel at Richmond and has been conveyed thither, is a painting of great beauty of design, and brilliancy of execution; admirably suited to a small building. The other, which is at present in the Argyle Rooms [Hobart's temporary place of worship], the only place used as a Catholic place of worship, is necessarily upon a larger scale, but of no less beauty or brilliancy ... They are the work of Mather Brown, an artist of considerable eminence as an Historical painter. The price is so moderate—only £65—that we cannot for a moment suppose The Resurrection will be allowed to leave the Colony. The inhabitants of Richmond have shown a good example in the purchase of one ... let us of Hobart Town follow that example, and purchase the other; it would amply adorn any religious edifice in the Colony.[9]

Gradually Cotham gathered the support of the Catholic settlers, including his younger brother Lawrence. By 1837 he was established as the licensee of the Richmond Hotel on Henry Street in premises built and owned by John Cassidy whose own farming enterprises were thriving in this period. Funds were available, with persistent requests, from government grants which were equally available in principle to all denominations which raised sufficient congregational subscriptions, although in practise they were rarely paid punctually to Catholic missions. The same was true of Cotham's allowance, both for himself and the 'forage' allowance for his horse.

Fr Watkins' appointment to Hobart had been a stop-gap arrangement. He had not come to Australia with a mandate from the Colonial Office, receiving no assistance for his passage from

England and no allowance until Ullathorne managed to arrange something for him. From August 1835 until Fr Therry came in April 1838 Fr Cotham was the only government-appointed colonial chaplain ministering to 6,000 Catholics spread across 26,000 square miles. Watkins himself was unhappy with his lot and he was not to be relied on. Even after the Court of Claims had ruled in Polding's favour in October 1837 that Conolly did not have a claim on church property in Hobart, Polding wrote:

> The pleasure I have in this information is much embittered by the desire expressed by Mr Watkins to relinquish his present situation. The Congregation at Hobart Town present probably the slightest attraction of any earthly kind to a Clergyman. He has to cultivate a long neglected, ungrateful soil.[10]

Despite his successes, Watkins did not enjoy Polding's confidence. In April 1838 the Bishop sent Fr Therry to Hobart; he went reluctantly, and as he believed temporarily, as a 'Visitor' while Watkins remained officially in post as Vicar General. When the visit inevitably became protracted due to 'unexpected difficulties' Therry deployed the unusual situation of three priests working in the colony by sending Watkins to Richmond, leaving Cotham free at last to develop the Launceston district.[11] Polding acknowledged he was making a compromise of quantity over quality when he wrote to Therry in July 1838 that 'even the very circumstances of Mr Watkins officiating as chief clergyman in VDL has excited rumours in England not creditable to my jurisdiction. That he should desist from missionary duty is absolutely necessary'.[12] The *Colonial Times* reported that 'three more clergy are to arrive; therefore the Catholics of the district will be well provided for'.[13] As usual, the expectation was far ahead of its realisation.

By then Cotham had faced one of the severest tests of his life and his vocation. He had come through not only with his confidence restored but with an experience of his own and others' personal despair that deepened his capacity to empathise and minister in truly desperate situations. Notwithstanding the

Hobart & Richmond, 1835–1838   65

presence of his brother Lawrence, he was probably never so lonely again as he had been during his first nine months in Van Diemen's Land, nor placed alone among such uncongenial colleagues as during the first three years after ordination. The essential solitariness of family life, monastic life, and mission life had bitten deeply into his soul.

Notes

[1]   R. D. Keynes (Ed.), *Charles Darwin's Beagle Diary* (Cambridge: Cambridge University Press, 2001), pp. 209–10.

[2]   K. McGoogan. *Lady Franklin's Revenge* (London: Bantam Press, 2006), p. 154.

[3]   *Richmond Bridge: Conservation Management Plan Department of Infrastructure, Energy and Resources* (January 2010), p. 76. 'In 1831, the population of the Richmond district was 2,800, comprising 1,700 free settlers and 1,100 convicts. Some emancipists took up land in the Richmond area. However the size of their grants was often too small to make a success from farming. At least one-fifth, but more likely more than half of those granted land before 1824, were emancipated convicts'. *Ibid.*, p. 66. www.transport.tas.gov.au/__data/assets/pdf_file/0010/109567/39593_Richmond_Bridge_CMP_Final_Report_-_Jan_2010_Part1of2.pdf [Accessed online 27.7.2017]

[4]   Fr Cotham is unlikely to have had personal contact with any Aboriginal people. Among his personal papers is a newspaper cutting (from *The Weekly Register of Politics, Facts and General Literature* (Sydney), 8 February 1845 of an article, 'Native Customs' by Edward Stone Parker (1802–1865), Assistant Protector of Aboriginals at the Loddon River, Port Phillip, settlement, and a Methodist preacher. Stone's administration from 1841 to 1848 was humane and respectful of Aboriginal culture and spirituality and he made careful anthropological observations of people living in the settlement.

[5]   *Richmond Bridge: Conservation Management Plan Department of Infrastructure, Energy and Resource* (January 2010), p. 23.http://www.transport.tas.gov.au/__data/assets/pdf_file/0010/109567/39593_Richmond_Bridge_CMP_Final_Report_-_Jan_2010_Part1of2.pdf [Accessed online 27.7.2017]

[6]   F. O'Donoghue, *The Bishop of Botany Bay: The Life of John Bede Polding, Australia's First Catholic Archbishop* (Sydney: Angus and Robertson Publishers, 1982), p. 39. Various branches of the Watkins family emigrated to Australia in the 1840s; see 'Watkins Family Papers c. 1810–1965' held

66   *The Indomitable Mr Cotham*

in the State Library of NSW. After returning to the mainland Fr Watkins was sent to various missions in New South Wales and Victoria. By 1861 he was living in retirement in Abergavenny, South Wales. He died on 11 January 1869.

[7] *The Hobart Town Courier*, 23 February 1838, p. 3.

[8] *The True Colonist* (Tasmania), 5 January 1838, p. 5.

[9] *Colonial Times* (Hobart), 22 May 1838, p. 6. Both paintings remain in the churches for which they were bought and have been restored since 2008.

[10] Sr M. X. Compton *et al.* (Eds.), *The letters of John Bede Polding OSB, 1844–60 Volume 1* (Sydney: Sisters of the Good Samaritan, 1994), p. 89. Polding to J. O'Sullivan, 16 October 1837.

[11] E. M. O'Brien, *Life and Letters of Archpriest John Joseph Therry* (Sydney: Angus and Robertson, 1922), Vol. 2, pp. 196–197.

[12] F. O'Donoghue, *The Bishop of Botany Bay: The Life of John Bede Polding, Australia's First Catholic Archbishop* (Sydney: Angus and Robertson Publishers, 1982), quoting a letter of Polding to Therry, 12 July 1838, p. 57. O'Donoghue says Watkins had a drinking problem (p. 75).

[13] *Colonial Times* (Hobart), 29 May 1838, p. 7.

7 LAUNCESTON, 1838–1844

As EARLY AS March 1836 Cotham lamented the fact he was not able to meet the expectations of the Launceston Catholics because of the unresolved dispute with Fr Conolly. The arrival of Fr Watkins in August 1836 eased his duties in Hobart, but it was not until Fr Therry came in 1838 that he had a sound model of priesthood close at hand. Describing the changes he had made in Hobart by June 1838, Fr Therry wrote, 'two Masses were celebrated in the morning, Rosary in the evening, and commenced the enrolment of many Catholics desirous of becoming members of the Sacred Heart Society, the Sodality of the Blessed Virgin Mary, and the confraternity of St Joseph for the avoidance of strong drink'.[1] Though brief, it was a valuable piece of training before Fr Cotham officially left Richmond on 2 June 1838 to start life as an independent missioner in Launceston, just as his arrival presented the township with its first opportunity to develop a visible Catholic community. His character matured along with his confidence. 'Everywhere he was a welcome guest as he had a particularly courteous and gentlemanly manner and yet very simple-minded.'[2] The reputation for simplicity stayed with him, alongside tenacity and self-belief.

The two Launceston newspapers carried prominent reports of the progress towards the establishment of a church and school:

> Roman Catholic Meeting. At a Public Meeting of the Roman Catholics of Launceston, and the neighbourhood, held on the 25th instant, the following resolutions were proposed, seconded, and unanimously adopted. 1st. — That the Catholics of this Town, and its neighbourhood, deeply regret the inconvenience they suffer, for the want of a place of worship in which they may assemble to worship God after the manner of their fathers, and where their children may be instructed in the duties of their

religion. 2nd. — That subscriptions be immediately entered into, and that a list for subscribers be left at the Tamar Bank, and at the Stationery Warehouse, where the friends of benevolence who may feel disposed to assist their fellows Christians in so laudable an undertaking, are requested to deposit the amount of their subscription. 3rd. — That the Rev. James Cotham be requested to apply to His Excellency the Lieutenant-Governor, for pecuniary assistance on the part of Government, towards the support of a school-master, and the paying the rent of a building, which may serve as a temporary place of worship and school, until such time as the proposed building be finished. 4th.—That these resolutions be twice published in the Launceston papers.

J. COTHAM, Chairman.

25th March, 1838.[3]

The proposals provoked some sardonic and ambiguous editorial remarks concerning the request for 'pecuniary assistance':

for although we do not profess to be minutely conversant with the doctrines of Catholicity, yet we have repeatedly heard them assert their decided antipathy to anything connected with Church and State. The Catholics ought, therefore, to bear in mind, that by receiving pecuniary assistance from the Government, it (the Government) reserves to itself particular rights of interference, which we imagine would not accord with the spirit of voluntaryism upon which the Catholic Church prides itself of being supported. Be this as it may, we sincerely hope that they may obtain their object, for, by the last religious census it would appear, that there are a great many more Catholics in this town than could have been anticipated. We feel persuaded too, that however much some of our readers may feel disposed to raise the cry of 'No Popery,' that, whoever may be selected as minister, relying as he must upon his congregation for support, will not be suffered to indulge with impunity in such, we had almost said,

Launceston, 1838–1844

immoral acts, as those which degrade the character of the worthy minister of the Church as by law established.[4]

As in Richmond, a local Catholic, Antonio Martini, provided the first place of worship, a long, one-storey wooden building standing next to his hotel on the corner of Tamar and Cameron Streets. It was rented for £60 a year and an average of sixty people attended weekly. Martini was born in Spain and he had joined the British Militia to protect Portugal against Napoleon's invading army. In 1810 he was court martialled for desertion and transported to New South Wales. Having received his ticket-of-leave in 1823, towards the end of his fourteen-year sentence, he moved to Launceston and when he was finally a free man in 1825 he was able to build on his town allotments of land. One dwelling place was converted to a hotel, the Sawyer's Arms, in 1834, Martini being in the timber trade at the time. The purpose-built wooden structure next door erected in 1838 served as the Catholic chapel for four years. Although Martini was in his late fifties, he had been married only three years to Mary O'Mara before his young wife died in 1836, leaving him with two infant children.[5]

The plot of land chosen for the permanent church of St Joseph's was centrally located in Margaret Street but was in a poorly drained area, having been obtained from the government in exchange for land granted to Fr Conolly in a higher but less accessible position. This town allotment, at the foot of Cataract Hill, had been earmarked for military barracks which were not built, having become surplus to requirements. Major Ryan, in charge of the military presence in Launceston, helped Fr Therry to secure the site; permission for the exchange was given on 4 June 1838, two days after Fr Cotham began the first permanent mission in the township. At the laying of the foundation stone on 19 March 1839, Fr Therry shared the occasion with Major Ryan (not a Catholic), each man making gracious addresses to the other in a spirit of ecumenism.[6]

The town Fr Cotham worked in has been described as 'the Launceston of the struggle to end transportation, in its brief heyday

70   *The Indomitable Mr Cotham*

before the discovery of gold in Victoria ended its aspiration to be the great entrepôt of Bass Strait'.[7] When it was founded in 1806 there was uncertainty about the best location for a new settlement in the vicinity of the Tamar River. The journey to Hobart at that time was a hazardous ride of eight or nine days through unmapped territory, which was gradually eased by nearly forty years of road building, by convict gangs, through the midland districts. The turning point for its fortunes was the development of regular shipping across the Bass Strait to Port Phillip in the 1830s. Unfairly depriving the indigenous population of their land rights—John Batman (1801–1839) acquired 500,000 acres in exchange for blankets, tools, and mirrors—vast areas of grazing land were made available for the sheep farmers of northern Van Diemen's Land. The farmers passed through Launceston with their flocks, onto Launceston-built ships for the twenty hour journey to the mainland, having stocked up on supplies from the town's tradesmen. Launceston was no longer the distant relation of Hobart but the enterprising landlord of Port Phillip.

The infrastructure of Launceston was slower to develop. In 1842 it was still 'a small straggling town of four to five thousand inhabitants ... with unformed streets and footpaths, lighted at night by only public-house oil lamps, and dependent for its water supply on carts'.[8] Nevertheless, as a consequence of the relative wealth and confidence of this brief period a number of Nonconformist chapels were quickly built. The proposal to replace the Independent Chapel in Frederick Street with a larger building for its rapidly expanding congregation prompted the *Launceston Advertiser* to enumerate the town's accumulated blessings in terms of religion and education:

> In addition to this intended [Independent] chapel, there is a handsome church being erected for the Catholics, on the square at the foot of the Cataract Hill. The Wesleyan Chapel, Patterson-street, the Independent Chapel, Tamar-street, and the Chapel in Frederick-street, the Baptist Chapel in York-Street, and the Catholic Chapel in Cam-

Launceston, 1838–1844 71

eron-street, have all been built within the last four or five years, and principally by public subscription.[9]

The Catholic congregation reflected Launceston's state of flux set against the background of penal colonial life. Twenty people were involved in receiving, and soliciting 'if not inconvenient',[10] subscriptions for the new church. In Launceston, as well as Martini, Antonio Peregalli, James Gerrard, and Arthur Haynes were the collectors. Fifteen others were dispersed in the outlying districts: Norfolk Plains, Springs, White Hills, Strathmore, Jacob's Sugar Loaf, Avoca, Perth, Campbell Town, and Oatlands, all served from Launceston; James William Cowell was the Honorary Secretary for the fund-raising group.[11]

Peregalli, like Martini, came to the colony as a convict, with a life sentence for larceny against the person. He married in 1835 soon after receiving his ticket-of-leave and began his rise to prosperity. In 1842 he sold up his considerable stock in Launceston and resettled in Melbourne; at the time of his second marriage in 1853 he was a 'gentleman'. Both men died in their late eighties, remembered in their obituaries as among the 'oldest residents' of the colony. Arthur Haynes, having arrived as a free emigrant from Ireland, was titled one of the 'oldest colonists' when he died in 1887. His wealth came from a succession of farming properties around Launceston, with an episode of insolvency in 1844 when he tried storekeeping in the town. A more successful trader was James Cowell, also a former larcenist, who had been transported in 1831. Ten years later he was able to sell his Elizabeth Street store, with its complete stock-in-trade, 'comprising every useful article in the Earthenware, Slop, Provision, and Grocery line'.[12] He married his wife Catherine Pender in 1837 when she was apparently only 12. After the couple migrated to Melbourne in 1841 Cowell followed his father-in-law, a pioneer publican, into the hotel business; he had considerable success with the Royal Oak Hotel, but died relatively young in 1850, followed by his wife in 1853.

Such were the early supporters of the new church in Launceston: men who valued opportunity above stability and for whom permanency was an alien concept. They were mostly a few years older than James Cotham and were still expecting to change the direction of their lives to follow their fortunes. Building churches and schools was for them a necessity for social progress, especially because of the role these institutions would play in fostering civic respectability and in providing for the education of young families. Nevertheless, economic mobility remained the priority for these men as they considered the best means to obtain their families' prosperity. Doubtless Cotham was aware of the conditional nature of the loyalty of his congregation.

Some three hundred subscribers gave at least ten shillings to the building fund—lesser amounts were not itemised—and Cotham kept a press cutting recording the names among his personal papers.[13] The list details a preponderance of Irish names, the largest amounts being subscribed by James Keane (£200), M. Murphy (£101 15s.) and Michael Dugan (£101). Peregalli gave £60, and Martini £6. In the period between 1835 and 1843 the congregation raised nearly £1,400 from subscriptions, and pew rents brought in a further £74. Other sums were lent at the high rate of ten per cent per annum interest, except for Mr Monaghan who loaned his £125 without interest. The government grant amounted to £639; Fr Cotham formally noted that at the end of his tenure, in December 1843, 'the sums advanced by me and borrowed on my credit, or the liabilities for which I am personally and individually responsible ... amount to five hundred and sixty three pounds sterling'. He calculated his outright donation as £220 13s. 3d.

The architect-builder who successfully tendered for the contract to construct St Joseph's was Robert de Little. He emigrated from England with his parents' family in 1830, moving to Launceston in 1832 where he was a merchant in building supplies as well as being a builder and carpenter providing architectural designs and specifications. The scope of his work, encompassing private

Launceston, 1838–1844

houses, businesses, schools, and churches, reflects the immature state of the built environment for anything other than state-funded institutions. The primary considerations governing the external appearance of St Joseph's were the space available, the number of seats required, and the funds that could be raised in a short time. The characteristics of a Catholic place of worship would be evidenced by the requirements for the celebration of the liturgy, above all. Nevertheless, St Joseph's was a not inconsiderable building. De Little's contract was for £2,600, to include the tower; the interior gallery cost an extra £100. The arrangement of seating reflected the customary observance of class difference: sixteen best quality cedar pews cost £76, a further sixteen simpler cedar pews cost £36, and thirty plain forms cost £20.

Fr Therry's involvement with St Joseph's, Launceston, was without the acrimony that bedevilled the church building programme in Hobart. Having obtained the church site for St Joseph's he did his best to secure Ambrose Cotham's salary, albeit with limited success. The Governor's reasoning was that 'salaries are confined to ministers whose churches have been erected for their congregations'[14] and no provision was made for clergymen without permanent churches, even when they were actively engaged in erecting a new church. Cotham wrote many letters stating his dire need for funds, and there was even a petition from two hundred local Catholics, but he waited several years for a resolution. An early letter to Fr Therry ended, 'I have not one shilling in my house or I would pay the postage of this letter'.[15] Fr Therry subsidised the junior priest from his own allowance and Cotham kept a record of loans he received; the relationship between the two men seems to have been one of mutual support and respect for the hard work each undertook. Although the Colonial Government acknowledged the fairness of paying £250 per annum, on the grounds of its own financial hardship it allowed only £60, rising to £150 for a period until this ceased in August 1842. Even the forage allowance for Cotham's horse was discontinued in June 1842. Despite the difficulties caused by personal poverty, Cotham was getting to grips with managing his first sole mission. It was easy for Thomas Anstey to be condescending about St Joseph's Church—'the new church at Launceston will, I fear, be built of bricks, but this I will do everything in my power to prevent'[16]—but in the circumstances the design was appropriate; only a few years would pass before Anstey's dreamed-of stone Gothic churches would become a reality on the island.

While the modestly handsome brick church was being constructed Cotham was provided with a cottage owned by Therry but as it was inconveniently situated outside the town Cotham asked for correspondence to be sent to Martini instead, or to James Cowell, Secretary to the Committee.[17] For greater convenience Cotham made up a room at the end of the temporary chapel which served him as parlour, dining room, and bedroom, and as a meeting room for the choir. The written building accounts for St Joseph's cover only two sides of foolscap paper, detailed but untidily set out. As an early attempt at book-keeping by Fr Cotham they are just about adequate; record-keeping was a skill which he developed during his ministry, for church, family, and personal accounts. In time Cotham became meticulous in keeping accurate records and taught at least one seminarian how to do it properly.

The date for the solemn opening and consecration of St Joseph's—All Saints, 1 November 1842—was repeatedly advertised in Launceston newspapers from August until late October, with the firm expectation that Bishop Polding would preside. In fact, Polding was in Europe, engaged in the complicated negotiations for appointing a bishop to the new diocese of Hobart. In his absence there possibly was no official opening ceremony; usage alone defined the change in status. Until September marriages were conducted in 'the Catholic Chapel, Launceston'; the following month a couple were married in 'the Catholic Church' and from mid-November 1842 marriage registers referred to 'St Joseph's Church'.[18]

Launceston, 1838–1844 75

After completion, the church was used most frequently, apart from religious services, for meetings of the St Joseph's Total Abstinence Society. These usually filled the church to capacity. Fund-raising performances of Oratorios and Grand Music Festivals were a popular form of cultural entertainment in the colony. The St Cecilia's Day concert held at St Joseph's, Hobart, on 22 November 1842 met with a mixed reaction. Between two and three hundred people attended, although notable Catholics were absent, and the performances were fair but not outstanding, despite the loan of members of a regimental band for the evening.[19] The Grand Oratorio held in St Joseph's, Launceston in April 1843 was more ambitious, employing the professional singers John and Elizabeth Bushelle (who gave their services free of charge to offset the debt on the building) to sing excerpts from *Messiah*. With men from the Sacred Choral Society and distinguished amateur singers they were accompanied by 'all the instrumental talent of Launceston, strengthened ... by the excellent band of H.M. 96th regiment'.[20] John Bushelle was Bishop Polding's protegé, a ticket-of-leave convict who had taken charge of the St Mary's choir in Sydney when Br Benedict Spencer was dismissed. John and his wife Elizabeth were given permission to make an extended tour of Van Diemen's Land, their concerts meeting with considerable acclaim until John unexpectedly died in July 1843. The announcement of his death included only a discreet reference to his personal history which 'under a prudent restraint in his earlier days' might have allowed him to attain even higher musical honours.[21]

While based solely in Launceston (at least until Fr Watkins returned to Sydney without a replacement) Cotham still had an extensive area to cover around the northern part of the island, visiting Campbell Town, Deloraine, and Circular Head to say Mass at the homes of Catholic families and to minister to the convict stations, staying at the military barracks in Ross for want of separate accommodation in that small township.

The vital collaboration between priest and people is exemplified by Dr Swarbreck Hall's role in providing services to supplement what a single clergyman could achieve. Cotham was long a regular visitor to the Halls, having used their home in Bothwell as a Mass centre when he was based in Richmond. Hall's living quarters and government salary in Westbury near Launceston, where the family moved in August 1843, were just about adequate for his expanding family, but they were an improvement on the domestic constraints and low income in their previous homes in Brighton and Bothwell. In an agitated letter concerning financial matters written a month after moving in, Dr Hall says the family is nevertheless 'well and hearty and somewhat more comfortable in our quarters, though still chairless' and much 'carving and patching' had been necessary to make six rolls of papers stretch round the small living room. His major piece of personal news is briefly dealt with: 'Our <u>Son</u> became a member of the Catholic Church on Saturday last, the Rev[d] Mr Cotham having to visit a case in the hospital.' This son, Latham, was born after five daughters, one already deceased, but he lived only eighteen months.[22] In Westbury hospital, Hall prepared a large ward where Cotham was able to celebrate Mass once a month, for which the doctor was reproved by the Hiring Depot superintendent and commended by the Comptroller General, with customary ambivalence. On the other three Sundays of the month, Hall conducted a service himself, reading prayers and sermons, and he occasionally officiated at burials when no priest was available.[23]

The Connell home near Ross was a gathering place for the few Catholics in the district and Mass was celebrated in their house first by Fr Conolly and then Fr Cotham. For families with the stamina and temperament to endure hardship in their early years, it was possible to acquire wealth and status in one generation. John and Maria Connell arrived in Hobart from Cork in 1820. The couple attended Fr Conolly's first Mass at Curr's Store in Hobart in 1821, and they were present when the primitive chapel of St Virgil's opened in 1822, when less than a dozen civilian

Launceston, 1838–1844 77

Catholics attended regularly. Moving north when they obtained a land grant near Ross, they faced down challenges from the wilderness and bushrangers to establish a prosperous farm at Glen Connell within twenty years.

The contact with a Benedictine priest prompted Daniel Connell's parents to send him to St Mary's Seminary in Sydney when it opened in 1838, the island still being without the opportunity for a senior Catholic education. Boys such as 13-year-old Daniel, born locally and aspiring to monastic life, were exactly the material Bishop Polding needed to supplement the few students he had been able to bring with him from England. The relative merits of employing Benedictine or Irish clergy for Australia were already actively debated but the Lancashire Benedictines, Cotham and Polding, were able to attract and nurture Daniel without stifling his Irish identity: he chose to be known through his long priestly life as Dom Daniel Vincent Maurus O'Connell.

By early 1839 Cotham was once again riding the one hundred and twenty-five miles between Launceston and Hobart to share duties with Fr Therry. The long-awaited increase in clergy numbers arrived in the person of Fr Thomas Butler on 31 March 1839, three months after he landed in Sydney as one of the group of Irish clergy recruited by Ullathorne.[24] Thomas Butler was to spend the rest of his life in Tasmania and became Bishop Willson's most trusted advisor from the mid-1840s and his preferred episcopal successor but on Butler's arrival Fr Cotham saw only a young man—his exact contemporary—ready for service, and he fairly fell on him with relief. The recollection remained vivid for Butler:

> Dean Butler used to narrate the great surprise he gave Father Cotham on Easter Sunday 1839, when he walked into the room where Father Cotham was hearing confessions in Argyle-street, Hobart, that morning before 8 o'clock Mass and announced himself. The greeting he met with was most overpowering, for never was a more welcome Easter gift

78   *The Indomitable Mr Cotham*

> received by any one than was this arrival, an assistant priest
> at such an hour and on such a day by the overworked Father
> Cotham, who had on this occasion exchanged places with
> Father Therry then in Launceston.[25]

In his end of year report to Fr Therry for 1843, Cotham outlined his duties and the state of the church he was leaving. He attended the Female House of Correction daily to lead prayers and to deliver a brief homily to the eighty Catholic prisoners; additionally he regularly visited the outdoor probation gangs in Westbury and Deloraine. In the course of his tenure he had administered ninety-eight baptisms, for which he received a total of only £3 in fees, and he had solemnized forty-eight marriages, for which £21 in fees had been received. For burials there was no charge at all since 'the people are very very poor'. In light of the amount raised for church building it seems the congregation valued the property above the services rendered in it. The expenditure over the seven year period was in the region of £3,100, for church building, maintenance, and furnishing. Everything from £27 for Gothic railings round the sanctuary to £10 for a brick drain around the church is itemised in the accounts. Despite the poor reputation Fr Therry had as a financial manager it seems he mentored Fr Cotham well in his first mission and the younger man formed a friendship with Therry even as he was later drawn into criticism against him out of loyalty to his bishop. It was an early instance of a senior Irish priest having authority over a junior Benedictine and there is no hint of animosity between them as they worked together in their challenging mission field.

The Catholics of Launceston appreciated Fr Cotham's efforts on their behalf. They wrote 'surreptitiously' to the Vicar General asking him to order Cotham to be 'less reckless in his health in the discharge of his heavy duties'.[26] A letter written in 1856, after Cotham had returned to England, shows how attachments were formed on either side of the altar rails. The correspondent, Robert McCarthy, addresses Fr Cotham respectfully but freely, as

Launceston, 1838–1844 79

someone on comfortable terms with his approachable pastor, confident that his news will interest him.

Tasmania, Launceston Hotel

20 September 1856

Revd and dear sir, You will probably feel some surprise at hearing from one whom you have not seen now for some years but from the fact of my former friendship in years gone by, the days of my boyhood and the pleasing recollections of those happy days I enjoyed under your hospitable roof when residing on the 'Windmill Hill' at the time I held a situation in the Police Office here, formed in my mind feelings of no ordinary nature and which I ever will feel great pleasure in pondering over—permit me therefore now to convey the happiness and pleasure I felt in hearing through Father Butler the other day, of your excellent health and vocation in your native land and I need scarcely add the delight and pleasure my wife heard the same intelligence—whom, by the bye you must first know was Mrs Porter of the Cocked Hat—we have now been married some months and keeping the Launceston Hotel formerly kept by Mrs Kitson her daughter, but who died about three years back, we are as happy as happy can be, and I need not tell you, how fortunate I feel myself in being united to one so good and so amiable.

Oft and oft our conversation turns upon yourself and usually terminates with the expression of 'poor Father Cotham' indeed the only wish we all express is that you were once more back among us, as loved and endeared were you to all that had the pleasure of your acquaintance. I cannot express to you with what feelings of attachment and regard Mrs McCarthy always refers to you and speaks so often of your kind visits to her at the Cocked Hat, those of her Family that are living are all well, and her son John Porter has now a little family rising about him. You will I have no doubt feel some surprise at this union of mine, but I can assure you sincerely that I was alone actuated by feelings of admiration and respect for the one who is now my better half, her devotion to her religion and her mild and amiable practises led me in toto to solicit her hand at any risk, and happy we both are, this she particularly wishes me to inform you.

The change in the congregation is very great since you left, only here and there an odd member of yours and the Church is much dilapidated owing I believe in the first instance to the badness of the foundation, trade and business altogether is exceedingly dull just now in the Colony. In conclusion permit me to associate Mrs McCarthy's kind wishes with my own for your welfare and blessing in your native land, and may Almighty God long continue you his favours and blessings is the sincere wish of yours most sincerely, Revd and dear sir,

Robert McCarthy[27]

'Poor Father Cotham' was in his early thirties when the McCarthys knew him but in their remembrance of him he seems older: mature as a pastor and able to shoulder a heavy workload relying on his own resourcefulness.

Notes

[1]   E. M. O'Brien, *Life and Letters of Archpriest John Joseph Therry* (Sydney: Angus and Robertson, 1922), Vol. 2, p. 201.

[2]   *The Catholic Standard*, August 1883, p. 129. It is worth comparing this opinion with the observation made in the obituary of Fr William Cotham SJ: 'He was as blunt, straightforward, and guileless as a child.' in *Letters and Notices*, No. XCIX, 1895, House Journal of the British Province of the Society of Jesus, p. 136.

[3]   *Launceston Advertiser*, 19 April 1838, p. 1, and *The Cornwall Chronicle* (Launceston), 31 March 1838, p. 51.

[4]   *The Cornwall Chronicle* (Launceston), 7 April 1838, p. 1.

[5]   Launceston History Society Inc., *Newsletter*, No. 104, October 2007, p. 6.

[6]   *The Cornwall Chronicle* (Launceston), 23 March 1839, p. 2.

[7]   E. Ratcliff, 'Here I Raise My Ebenezer: Two Transient Architects in Van Diemen's Land and Tasmania'. Tasmanian Historical Research Associa-

Launceston, 1838–1844   81

tion, *Papers & Proceedings*, Vol. 54 No. 2, August 2007, p. 87.

[8]   *Launceston Examiner*, Jubilee edition, 19 March 1892, p. 1.

[9]   *Launceston Advertiser*, 15 April 1841, p. 3.

[10] *The Cornwall Chronicle* (Launceston), 4 May 1839, p. 4.

[11] *Launceston Advertiser*, 9 May 1839, p. 4.

[12] *Ibid.*, 7 January 1841, p. 1.

[13] The same list appeared twice in *The Cornwall Chronicle* (Launceston); 30 November, p. 3, and 4 December 1844, p. 3. See W. T. Southerwood, *New Standard*, July 1988, pp. 9–10, 'Benedictine was first P.P. in Launceston' for an account of the building of St Joseph's, Launceston.

[14] E. M. O'Brien, *Life and Letters of Archpriest John Joseph Therry* (Sydney: Angus and Robertson, 1922), Vol. 2, p. 197.

[15] *Ibid.*, p. 197.

[16] *The Tablet*, 5 December 1840, p. 4.

[17] *The Cornwall Chronicle* (Launceston), 30 March 1839, p. 3.

[18] The ambiguous information about the opening of St Joseph's was kindly elucidated for me by Dr Nicholas Brodie.

[19] *The Austral-Asiatic Review, Tasmanian and Australian Advertiser (Hobart)*, 25 November 1842, p. 2.

[20] *Launceston Examiner*, 5 April 1843, p. 5.

[21] *The Teetotal Advocate* (Launceston), 24 July 1843, p. 3.

[22] Hall to John Clark, 27 September 1843; Royal Society of Tasmania, University of Tasmania Library Special and Rare Materials Collection, RS.8/B23. Another son, Leventhorpe Michael, was born on 29 September 1846 and survived.

[23] E. F. Haynes, MA Thesis, *Edward Swarbreck Hall—Medical Scientist and Social Reformer in Colonial Tasmania* (UNTAS, 1976), p. 87.

[24] W.T Southerwood, 'A Neglected Giant among the Men of '38: Fr Thomas Butler' in *The Australasian Catholic Record* (2015), pp. 16–26.

[25] *The Catholic Standard*, August 1883, p. 129.

[26] W. T. Southerwood, 'Benedictine was the first PP in Launceston' in *New Standard*, July 1988, pp. 9–10.

[27] Elizabeth McCarthy was over 50 and widowed at the time of her marriage to Robert McCarthy. It was his first marriage and he was probably some years younger than his capable wife. Soon after writing, the McCarthys transferred to a larger hotel in Launceston but were insolvent by the end of the decade. Happily the marriage lasted nearly twenty years until her death in 1875, when it was noted that she was 'a colonist of 71 years' standing,' *Launceston Examiner*, 21 September 1875, p. 2.

8 'CE JEUNE PRÈTRE PARLE LE FRANCAIS'

THE REMOTENESS OF Australia and length of sailing time might have led emigrants and convicts to expect profound isolation from events in Europe and elsewhere. In fact, Australian provincial newspapers carried full reports of international affairs and a port such as Hobart attracted many foreign ships. In early 1840 Fr Cotham was called upon to work closely with a French expeditionary force. Although it was for a very short period he received a letter of warm friendship from one of the French officers which he kept to the end of his life.[1]

Between the 1820s and 1840s a number of national expeditionary parties landed at various points on the Antarctic ice shelf, going on to the further challenge of reaching the South Magnetic Pole.[2] When two French 10-gun corvettes, the *Astrolabe* and *Zélée*, put into Hobart on 12 December 1839 they excited curiosity and sympathy, as well as patriotic rivalry. Captain Jules Dumont D'Urville had sailed from Java and Sumatra for Hobart on 18 October with a crew that had contracted twenty cases of dysentery during the short time they had spent ashore. Le Guillou, surgeon from the *Zélée*, wanted to turn back to Mauritius and home, but D'Urville needed both ships in order to continue the exploration to which he was committed by royal command. Le Guillou described the situation:

> Men are lying on pallets or in hammocks, some unable to move because of excruciating intestinal pain and frequent bowel movements; others are sleepless because of anxiety, lack of space to stretch out, physical discomfort or the foul air; some are kept awake by the moans of their neighbours and their death rattles.[3]

By the time the two corvettes arrived in Hobart eighteen men had been lost, others were desperately ill, and the ships scarcely habitable.

The expedition was welcomed generously into Hobart; Lieutenant-Governor Sir John Franklin, a navy man and expert navigator, took a personal interest in the party. Large and airy premises were leased in the town and turned into temporary hospital quarters in the charge of the Chief Surgeon and ship's naturalist, Jacques Hombron, with assistance from three of the crew. Civic functions were arranged for the officers by Franklin's staff but D'Urville was too unwell, and unwilling, to enjoy such gatherings. He preferred to focus on continuing his expedition especially when informed by Franklin that the veteran British navigator James Ross was berthed at Sydney waiting for the earliest opportunity to sail south. D'Urville himself planned to make an exploratory journey as far south as necessary to determine the latitude of the ice shelf. He recognised, however, that his men needed some diversion from their recent ordeal and on their first Sunday in Hobart—'it is well known with what respect the English observe this holy day of rest'—he allowed them ashore. 'But I soon saw that despite the impaired state of their health, their freedom to roam the streets at will could be more harmful than beneficial, because of the numerous grog shops in town to which our sailors paid too frequent visits.'[4] It took less than forty-eight hours for the sick sailors to be drawn into the infamous alcohol culture of Van Diemen's Land.

D'Urville allowed the corvettes a mere three weeks in port to put ashore the sick, repaint the ships inside and out as a way of cleaning them, make repairs, and take on provisions, and this exhaustive programme was undertaken by a crew depleted in numbers and health. His plan was for the *Astrolabe* to make landfall either in the Auckland Islands or New Zealand after its return from the far south and await a rendezvous with the *Zélée* which would make a detour to Hobart to pick up the recovered sick crew members. After pleading from the *Zélée's* captain,

'Ce Jeune Prêtre parle le Francais'   85

Jacquinot, for the two vessels not to be separated, it was agreed both ships would return to Hobart in mid-February.

In D'Urville's posthumously published account of this, his last expedition,[5] there are extensive supplementary notes by Jacques Hombron. He describes how Simon, the 52-year-old first mate, regretted that he had not lived to reach 60 and enjoy some years of retirement with his family after a life spent at sea. He was the first seaman in the hospital to whom Fr Therry administered the last rites. Twenty-six-year-old Ernest Auguste Goupil, the expedition's talented chief illustrator, had been chronically ill with dysentery for over two months. His commandant described him affectionately: '... a friend to all of us ... full of talent and promise, ignorant of the sea, ignorant of the terrible dangers of a campaign like ours ... his proven courage, his sweetness, his boundless cheerfulness, could not save him. Poor Goupil!'[6] Fr Therry ministered to Goupil on 29 December and received his final wishes (Goupil either spoke English or Therry had the services of an interpreter from among the crew); he died in the early hours of 1 January 1840.

Although the expedition could not delay its departure for Goupil's funeral, the English military authorities decided to give the young artist—who ranked as an infantry lieutenant—a funeral with military honours. M. Hombron tactfully chose a coffin appropriate to Goupil's rank and to local custom: suitably ornate but not offensively ostentatious. The funeral itself on 4 January was solemn and impressive but it took place without a priest. Perhaps the late hour—four o'clock—was chosen to allow every chance for Fr Cotham to arrive from Launceston in time. Instead, a detachment of fifty armed and fifty unarmed soldiers under the command of Major Butler accompanied the cortège led by a military band and followed by civil and military officials and townsmen. Cotham would have regretted being absent as he enjoyed a good procession. However, the dignity of this occasion was marred by the previous day's thunderstorm; the *Colonial Times* took it as an opportunity to make a point to the Department of Public Works:

> The upper ends of Melville, Brisbane and Argyle streets
> are in a state of nature, impassable by animals of burden
> in the best weather, and scarcely so by foot passengers in
> wet weather. This circumstance was pitifully manifested
> on Saturday last when the French officer was interred in
> the Roman Catholic Burying ground ... in the public
> performance of the last duty to our fellow creatures,
> moderately good access should at least be made more
> easily available.[7]

During the few days it took to make the arrangements Fr Therry travelled to Launceston, as 'he is wretched not to be able to help, without the assistance of an interpreter, those among us who are in danger of death. He has gone to look for his nephew, Mr Cothain [sic]; this young priest speaks French; the reverend Vicar intends him to be our chaplain.'[8] The absence of a priest from Hobart posed a dilemma for the funeral organisers; it was hardly likely that Fr Cotham would arrive in less than four days but the funeral could not be delayed at the height of mid-summer. Although he arrived the day after the funeral (5 January) Cotham was in time to give the last rites to the *Zélée's* master carpenter, Couteleng, who was still able to respond to him; he died early on 7 January.

Captain D'Urville recruited a few French and English sailors in Hobart, despite his opinion of them as deserters from French whalers or vagabonds reluctant to sail to the Antarctic. He had also found a good, if high priced, supply of provisions in Hobart. Lieutenant-Governor Franklin, at his own request, was allowed to inspect the corvettes and was genuinely impressed by what he saw of the ships and the scientific instruments.[9] In the temporary hospital M. Hombron, the *Astrolabe's* chief surgeon, and one semi-invalid officer, M. Demas, were left in charge of the sick seamen. One of Hombron's first duties when left in charge was to write a letter to the editors of the *Colonial Times* and *The True Colonist* 'expressing the high consideration and grateful acknowledgement to the Authorities and Public of Hobart-town not only

'*Ce Jeune Prètre parle le Francais*'

for their attentions during the previous month but especially at the funeral of Ernest Goupil'.[10]

On the day after Goupil's funeral Hombron felt unable to decline an invitation from Deputy Commissioner and meterologist Lamprière to visit the Coal Mines penal station he administered at Port Arthur, on the Tasman Peninsula. Hombron's junior assistant Demas was eager for the trip; his convalescence was progressing well and whenever the weather permitted went horse riding in the neighbourhood. Despite his reluctance for the outing Hombron found the Port Arthur regime for convicts and delinquent children interesting, based as it was on moral improvement through ordered labour and training in useful trades. The theme of moral improvement was continued when a gift of Bibles and pious reading material, in French, was brought to the temporary hospital for the sailors' benefit by a Protestant missionary. Hombron checked the contents for anything which might disturb their Catholic faith but was edified to find the material soundly orthodox; furthermore, the sailors appreciated the diversion and asked him to write a letter of thanks on their behalf.

Hombron was sensitive to the personal solicitude shown by Sir John and Lady Franklin, both noted for their Christian rectitude. When he was invited to dine with them on the day following the outing to Port Arthur he enjoyed their company and kindness; Demas used his state of health as a reason to make his apologies on this occasion. Evidently Demas returned for a longer stay in Port Arthur as in his notes Hombron wrote: 'M. Demas owes the good health in which we are happy to see him today to his visit to Port Arthur; so thanks must be given to the kind hospitality of M. Lamprière.'[11] In fact, Demas would probably have stayed longer and travelled more widely in Van Diemen's Land if time had allowed; for him at least the interlude in port had been a happy one.

In the consideration given to the French expeditionary remnant, genuine and heartfelt though it undoubtedly was, there is also a sense of the denominational rivalry which marked most church related business. After missing the actual funeral, Fr Cotham celebrated a Requiem Mass on 12 January for the repose of the soul of Ernest Goupil; as well as the seamen well enough to go to the church, parishioners and ladies of the choir took part. The captains of two French whaling ships recently put into Hobart were also invited: M. Roster of the *Nancy* and M. Longuet of the *Mississipi*. After the Mass the surplus from a collection made by the expeditionary officers for the memorial stone was handed over by Hombron to be given to the Catholic poor of Hobart. This occasion, less formal and more familiar to the French invalids, seems to have forged feelings of friendship between the Chief Surgeon and Fr Cotham.

In his log book Hombron noted the effect of the weather on the fluctuations in health of the seamen who remained in a precarious position. When they had arrived in early December the fine weather had helped young Goupil to make a temporary recovery; the onset of colder, wet weather at the end of December had hastened his decline. With a naturalist's observation, Hombron noted the basic temperateness of the island's weather patterns in summer and winter. But he would have preferred the changes in temperature to have been less marked. He believed dysentery in particular reacted to climatic changes, although it was an illness with a range of complex causes and characteristics. The only intervention he recorded as a form of treatment is the use of arrowroot. In the letter of appreciation sent to two local newspapers Hombron appended a brief biography of Ernest Goupil in which he claimed there was a direct link between the young man's fatal illness and 'the effect of different climates and sudden changes of temperature'. The week of Goupil's death was an extreme example of Hobart's climate:

> The weather during the last week has been of a most changeable description. On Wednesday, Thursday, and Friday, the heat was excessive, but on the evening of the last mentioned day, a thunder storm broke over the town, with a most refreshing and abundant shower. Since then,

'Ce Jeune Prêtre parle le Francais'

> the weather has been showery and much cooler, indeed
> early this morning it was actually cold. We are glad to find
> that the scorching heat has not, in any important degree,
> injured the crops for, fortunately, it was not accompanied
> by that bane to vegetation, the hot wind or Sirocco.[12]

On this point Hombron and Fr Cotham were in agreement and Hombron shared Cotham's exasperation expressed by his reiterations of *Rain! rain! rain!* in his journal.

The last two seamen to die in the first week of February were Bernard and Baudoin; they were accompanied to their burial in the Catholic cemetery by the captains and sailors of eight French whaling ships then in port. The remaining invalids were by then all able to take exercise so Hombron spent two days with them putting in order the French graves gathered into one corner of the Catholic cemetery, placing on each mound of earth an inscribed cross.

D'Urville did not reach as far south as he had hoped and because men on board the corvettes were again ill and dying from dysentery both ships turned back for Hobart, making landfall once more on 17 February. While they were at sea three further crew members had died and two were critically ill. Sir John Franklin arranged more dinners and receptions, as well as the scientifically useful task of sending D'Urville's report on his achievements thus far back to France via the *Calcutta*, to avoid being pre-empted by any report of success by James Ross. D'Urville allowed his expedition members eight days to prepare for their final departure on 26 February.

As part of his own preparations Hombron completed his personal correspondence, including a letter to Fr Cotham who had returned to Launceston before the beginning of February. In an informal letter addressed to 'mon cher ami' he tells Cotham how his hopes for the recovery of two invalids came to nothing as their improvement could not be maintained. In these 'nouvelles souffrances' [further sufferings] they had been supported by Fr Therry and Mr Reichenberg. There still remained a dozen men in the hospital but these were doing well. As for himself, he had hardly been out of his quarters except to get necessary supplies from Temple House, a clothing and general store in Davey Street.

Hombron says he has also written to the people he had been introduced to in Richmond by Fr Cotham, not forgetting 'Monsieur Votre Frère' who had taken much trouble in taking Hombron and his men back and forth to Hobart-town. Demas had asked to be remembered to Cotham, promising to return to Fr Therry two books Cotham had lent him. At the time of writing Demas was on a visit to Port Arthur; he wanted to call on Cotham in Launceston but Hombron thought he would not have sufficient time to make such a long journey. Hombron closes his letter with expressions of appreciation for the kindness shown to him and to their 'pauvres Camarades d'infortune' [poor unfortunate comrades] and he hopes Cotham will visit France one day so Hombron can better demonstrate his gratitude.

The two French ships called a halt to their polar explorations and returned to D'Urville's preferred waters in the Pacific and East Indies before finally arriving in Toulon in November 1840. The three months spent in Hobart had been a brief episode in their two-and-a-half-year voyage but it had been particularly intense, for the French and for those who were involved in their plight.

It seems Jacques Hombron's farewell letter crossed with a return journey to Hobart by Fr Cotham. He may have been recalled specifically to be present at a public execution which took place on 16 February 1840. As the four condemned men were attended by a number of clergymen during the night before the executions, as was customary, in all likelihood Cotham was there, too. He certainly mounted the scaffold with them at 8 o'clock the following morning.

Fr Cotham attended public executions on at least two recorded occasions in his capacity as colonial chaplain. Of the four criminals hanged in 1840, convicted among them of three murders, two were attended by the Anglican minister, the Revd

'Ce Jeune Prêtre parle le Francais' 91

Mr Bedford and two by Cotham. Of Bedford's two men, Davis 'continued in fervent prayer' while Pettit 'appeared totally indifferent'. Likewise, one of Cotham's charges, Martin, 'seemed quite indifferent to his awful situation'; the other, Riley, had tried, unsuccessfully, to implicate others in his crime, possibly to prevent his death by being required to witness against someone else. The drama of the occasion was heightened by the night-long vigil of ministers and by the 'large concourse of spectators' in the morning. Nevertheless, the *Colonial Times* concluded: 'It is happily some time since a public execution took place in this town, and we earnestly hope few (if any) more will ever take place, to disgrace a land of Christian civilisation.'[13]

However, another execution attended by Fr Cotham took place only one year later, in Launceston. The trial of William Watson and Patrick Wallace was notable for several reasons; it was the first case in Van Diemen's Land to be tried by a civilian jury following the abolition of military juries, and it was felt that civilians, being less accustomed to the task, were more attentive to the proceedings. Watson and Wallace, who had previous convictions, were accused of armed burglary and although they had not murdered their victims they had inflicted 'bodily fear' on them. There was a plea to Governor-General Gipps in Sydney to exercise leniency but the sentence of the trial judge was not overturned. Patrick Wallace distinguished himself by writing, apparently unaided, an eloquent letter addressed to his fellow prisoners under the prompting of his 'inward monitor'. The *Launceston Courier* printed the letter in full, impressed as much by its correct grammar and spelling as by its penitent sentiments.

On the scaffold the two men conducted themselves with 'a tone of repentant piety' and the newspaper regretted the failure of pleas for clemency made on their behalf. 'Yet, there is this consolation as far as regards the unfortunate beings themselves; that the sincerity of their repentance will procure from a Higher Power that mercy and forgiveness which was denied to them by man.'[14] The newspaper report repeated claims of Wallace being a Catholic but the executioner, 25 year-old Solomon Blay, believed he had had a Protestant upbringing and, in his experience, it was not unusual for a condemned man to prefer a Catholic priest to attend his last days, presumably for the hope offered by confession, repentance, and the possibility of heaven after purgatory. Whatever had passed between Fr Cotham and Wallace before the execution, it took place calmly and without the horror of a botched job on Blay's part.[15] Executed criminals were often young men in their twenties—Pettit had been only 19—as were the crew of the French expeditionary ships. Cotham himself had only just turned 30 but was already called on by Fr Therry to carry out the full range of clerical duties expected of a colonial chaplain.

Notes

[1] DA VIII.A.Cotham, letter dated 13 February 1840; catalogued as 'letter in French, signature indecipherable'.

[2] James Weddell and James Clark Ross for Britain and Charles Wilkes for the United States were the main rivals to French expeditions.

[3] J. Dunmore, *From Venus to Antartica: The Life of Dumont D'Urville* (Auckland: Exisle Publishing, 2007), pp. 288ff.

[4] H. Rosenman (Ed.), *An Account in Two Volumes of Two Voyages to the South Seas by Captain (later Rear-admiral) Jules S-C Dumont D'Urville of the French Navy to Australia, New Zealand, Oceania, 1826–1829, in the Corvette Astrolabe and to the Straits of Magellan, Chile, Oceania, South East Asia, Australia, Antarctica, New Zealand and Torres Strait, 1837–1840, in the Corvettes Astrolabe and Zélée: Astrolabe and Zélée, 1837–1840*, (Melbourne University Press, 1987), p. 448.

[5] D'Urville, his wife and their only surviving child were burnt to death in 1842 following a train derailment.

[6] M. J. Dumont-Durville, *Voyage au pole sud et dans l'Océanie sur les corvettes l'Astrolabe et la Zélée*, (Paris: Gide et Co, 1846), p. 92: 'notre ami a tous ... plein de talent et d'avenir, ignorant de la mer, ignorant des terrible hasards d'une campagne comme la nôtre ... son courage à l'épreuve de tout, sa douce, son intarissable gaieté ne l'ont pas préservé. Pauvre Goupil!' Jacques Hombron's account is taken from Note 4 by M.

'Ce Jeune Prètre parle le Francais'

Hombron pp. 254–265. www.archive.org/details/voyageaupolesude 21842dumo [Accessed online 27.7.2017]

[7] *Colonial Times* (Hobart), 7 January 1840, p. 7.

[8] *Voyage au pole sud*, p. 255: 'il est désolé de ne pouvoir assister, sans le secours d'un interprète, ceux d'entre nous qui sont en danger de mort. Il va chercher son neveu, M. Cothain [*sic*]; ce jeune prêtre parle le francais; M. le vicaire nous le destine pour aumônier.'

[9] After Sir John Franklin (1786–1847) was removed from office in Van Diemen's Land in 1843 he led an 1845 expedition attempting to navigate a North West Passage in the Canadian Arctic. The circumstances of the expedition's fate remained a debated mystery for the next one hundred and fifty years.

[10] *Colonial Times* (Hobart), 14 January 1840, p. 7, and *The True Colonist* (Hobart Town), 10 January 1840, p. 7.

[11] *Voyage au pole sud,* p. 264: 'M Demas doit, à son voyage à Port Arthur, la belle santé que nous sommes heureux de lui voir aujourd'hui; grâce donc soit rendue à l'aimable hopitalité de M. Lamprière'

[12] *Colonial Times* (Hobart), 7 January 1840, p. 7.

[13] *Colonial Times* (Hobart), 18 February 1840, p. 7.

[14] *Launceston Courier*, 1 February 1841, p. 2.

[15] S. Harris, *Solomon's Noose: The True Story of Her Majesty's Hangman of Hobart* (Melbourne: Melbourne Books, 2015). Online preview version, no page given [Accessed 27.7.2017]

9 WIDENING HORIZONS

AMONG THE FEW comparatively wealthy Catholics in Van Diemen's Land the imperious Edward Curr, a 'proud, tough and uncompromising' father of fifteen, stood out.[1] After establishing his stores company at Circular Head on the north coast he eventually constructed a twenty-four room mansion-cum-manor house there for his family and servants. Curr was able to send his sons Edward, William, and Richard to England for their education, firstly to Stonyhurst for eight years and then for a 'finishing' year at St Edmunds's, Douai in 1837 (two younger sons and two daughters were also educated in England). But this was an exceptional arrangement; more practically aspirational Catholics were keen to establish local educational facilities and Catholic organisations.

Those who travelled to England for an education often brought back more than was expected. For a brief period the self-appointed political and cultural leader of Catholics in Van Diemen's Land was Thomas Chisholm Anstey (1816–1873), the second son of the distinguished pastoralist Thomas Anstey who had emigrated from England in 1823. Anstey senior amassed an estate of 20,000 acres at Anstey Barton and as a devout Anglican patronised the establishment of churches in his neighbourhood. His three younger sons converted to Catholicism under the influence of the Oxford Movement while in England furthering their education. Thomas Chisholm returned to Hobart in 1839 for a short while, during which he introduced branches of the Van Diemen's Land Auxiliary Catholic Institutes, affiliated to the Catholic Institute of Great Britain. As one of the speakers at the Mechanics Institute in Hobart in 1840,

> Mr. T. C. Anstey delivered, to a full audience, a very pleasing lecture 'On the Importance of the Antiquities of our Native

96 *The Indomitable Mr Cotham*

Country'. The learned gentleman dwelt with happy effect upon the value of nationality, as the only means by which feelings of patriotism to our own country and justice to others could be acquired. The study of history was strongly inculcated, particularly that of remote periods.[2]

He also constituted himself the infant *Tablet*'s own correspondent from Van Diemen's Land. He gave his appraisal, dated 28 April 1840:

I have called to-day upon our vicar-general, M. Therry, and made his acquaintance. Things look better than they did. The ancient prejudices of our old governor, Sir John Franklin, have considerably softened down, and he entertains at last a tolerable opinion of Catholics. The bishop [Polding] will be here in a month or two to lay the foundation stone of our grand new church (a stone one), the shell of which is to cost £3,000. It will be dedicated to our blessed Lady. In the meanwhile we are building, for a few hundreds of pounds, a brick chapel, in another quarter of the town, the exterior of which will, they say, be finished in two months from its commencement. This will be lucky for the temporary wants of all the congregation, as at present we have mass in a public assembly room, over a public house of no very good repute, the lease of which will have expired somewhere about the same time as that of the completion of the little brick chapel aforesaid (to be dedicated, by the way, in honour of St. Joseph) ... M. Therry is alone in Hobarton. He tells me that he has never known a community so easily convertible to good, if there were a priest here able to devote his whole time to the missionary life ... For deplorably ignorant are the people of Van Diemen's Land, in general, of even the first and simplest and most general principles of Christianity; and yet as earnest to seek for the truth, and embrace it when found, as they are ignorant ... As soon as the *Lady of the Lake* arrives with my library, &c., containing, inter alia, the tracts and blank forms sent out by the Catholic Institute, a meeting is to be summoned of all our Hobarton Catholics

Widening Horizons 97

> in the chapel, with M. Therry for chairman, and myself for
> chief speaker and propounder ... I heard from [Mr Therry]
> that besides his subscription to the Launceston Catholic
> church last year, my father has recently subscribed towards
> the church fund of Hobarton £25; the Chief Justice, Sir
> John Lewis Pedder, has given 10/-, &c. &c. It is cheering
> to know that the respectable Protestants show such warm
> feeling towards our church's altars, despite the fearful
> scandals of the last few years ... The Rev. Mr. Butler, a
> priest from Kilkenny, is at Richmond; the only other priest
> in the island, besides M. Therry, is the Rev. Mr. Cotham,
> at Launceston, a Downside [*sic*] monk'.[3]

Included in Anstey's full report is his belief that Fr Therry
proposed gifting twenty acres from private property he owned
near Sydney for the site of a college 'for the various islands of the
Southern Ocean',[4] to be under the jurisdiction of Bishop Pom-
pallier, Vicar Apostolic of Oceania, based in New Zealand. In the
proposals, sent to France via Captain D'Urville of the *Astrolabe*
in early 1840, Therry suggested that four Jesuit priests, with lay
brothers, should be sent from France with the probability that
they 'would soon be joined by other members of that most
illustrious order from England'. Anstey cannot have been ignorant of the tensions between Bishop Polding and Therry, nor the
former's possible anxieties concerning a move to Sydney by a
band of Jesuit fathers, even if destined for Oceania. In light of the
great need for educational advancement in the southern hemi-
sphere it was difficult to be patient and share Polding's aspiration
for Benedictine supremacy.

Anstey ended his report with a modest reference to his own call
to the Bar and forthcoming meetings with senior members of the
Van Diemen's Land Judiciary. He successfully practised his legal
profession but after only three months as commissioner of insolvent estates he was dismissed for eccentric conduct. Returning
once more to England he became professor of law and jurispru-
dence at the Catholic College at Prior Park, publishing, among

much else, *A Guide to the Laws of England Affecting Roman Catholics* (London, 1842). His youngest brother, Henry Frampton Anstey (1822–1862) spent most of his adult life in Van Diemen's Land, filling posts in the judiciary and legislature. He and Thomas Chisolm both received papal knighthoods, demonstrating the influence of converts in raising the profile of colonial Catholicism in Rome, and bringing Roman prestige to an infant church.

The Catholic Institute was duly propounded and founded in Richmond with Fr Thomas Butler as President, Lawrence Cotham as secretary and John Cassidy once again taking on the treasurer's role. In October 1841 the Launceston Branch of the Van Diemen's Land Auxiliary Catholic Institute was formed comprising a general committee of all members present at the opening meeting, a select committee of eight members who would meet once a month, and quarterly to audit accounts, the officers to be Fr Therry, President, Fr Cotham, Vice-President, Mr J. W. Hay, Honorary Secretary, and Mr James Gerrard, Treasurer for the branch.[5] The right ordering of the gathering was clearly as important as the content of the lectures in raising the tone of Catholic meetings.

The first of three visits to the mainland was made by Cotham in 1841 and duly reported in Adelaide on Friday 9 February:

> THE CATHOLICS of South Australia are informed that the Rev. Mr Cotham, of Launceston, has just arrived, and that Mass will be celebrated on Sunday next, at the late Auction Rooms of Mr Neale, Franklin-street. Morning service will commence at 11 o'clock, and evening at 6.[6]

The purpose of Fr Cotham's visit was to offer support to the newly-appointed resident priest, Fr William Benson, who was to arrive shortly, after sailing from Sydney on 14 February. Although it was Bishop Polding's avowed policy not to place a missioner more than one day's journey away from another, and to place two together in the interior regions, this policy was not adhered to in Fr Benson's case. The town of Adelaide was only four years old

Widening Horizons 99

when Fr Ullathorne had visited in 1840 and the small Catholic community was centred around the home of Mr and Mrs Phillips, two of the original 1836 settlers, and it was there that Ullathorne celebrated the first Mass in the province. In the absence of an ordained priest, William Gerard Phillips, Polding's contemporary at Downside, was in every way a pastor to the few Catholics in Adelaide.

> He opened his house to them on Sundays, recited the holy Rosary and other prayers, and read a chapter or two of a spiritual book; he also visited the sick, baptised children in danger of death, and even attended on the scaffold an unfortunate man.[7]

Bishop Polding had raised their hopes when he wrote to them excusing himself for not being able to visit personally:

> I feel my conscience alleviated in [Fr Ullathorne's] going to perform his pastoral duties amongst the distant portion of my flock. You will give me credit for the preference I have made in your regard to give you this opportunity of enjoying the benefits and consolation of religion. I have deferred a visit I have long promised to V.D. Land, yet in this I have only imitated the conduct of the good Shepherd, who left the ninety and nine in the fold to look after the sheep far away ... Soon ... I expect to hear of the selection of the clergymen to minister to your wants. In some few months they will be amongst you; the sojourn of the Vicar-General will render the privation tolerable.[8]

Ullathorne noted the Evangelical and Presbyterian spirit of the town:

> It soon became obvious that the Catholics were few in number, the Government unfavourable, and as there was no convict settlement there was no ground for obtaining Government assistance towards supporting a priest ... Nothing could be done for South Australia for the present, but to visit it from time to time.[9]

In fact, Benson's appointment came much sooner than might have been wise or realistic, but at least he had a sympathetic supporter in Fr Cotham, fifteen years his junior, to give him a brief introduction to mission life. In Sydney, the *Australasian Chronicle* glossed over the precariousness of the venture, heralding it as the start of a rapid expansion:

> CHURCH OF AUSTRALIA. WE have to congratulate the Catholic community upon the arrival of a valuable addition to our ecclesiastical establishment, in the person of the Reverend Mr Benson. Mr Benson is destined for South Australia, and our brethren in that province will be proud to learn that their pastor is a disciple of the illustrious and immortal Milner of happy memory. Another clergyman is daily expected to join Mr Benson, in his new mission, and several others were about to embark for New South Wales. The Very Rev. Vicar General [Ullathorne] has received the invoice of the new organ for St Mary's; it occupies sixteen immense packing cases.[10]

It would have been a familiar scenario to Cotham: silence on the crucial matter of funds, the promise of additional helpers daily expected, and in Sydney grand schemes going ahead at the Cathedral.

William Benson eventually arrived from Sydney on 2 March, having taken two weeks at sea to travel the eight hundred miles, leaving him in no doubt as to the remoteness of his mission. The *Australasian Chronicle* looked forward to seeing speedy action:

> By a private letter from an esteemed correspondent, dated Adelaide, March 16th, we learn with pleasure that the Rev. W. Benson had arrived safely at Adelaide, and is diligently occupied in preparing for the erection of a neat and beautiful church in the most conspicuous part of the town, a plan and description of which we are promised in due time. The arrival of Mr Johnson, with further missionary supplies, from England, was daily expected.[11]

Widening Horizons 101

Cotham's stay was relatively brief; having left Launceston on 2 February, he was back by 25 March, relieving Fr Butler who had travelled from Richmond on alternate Sundays to celebrate Mass. A letter written on 9 March expressed the Adelaide congregation's gratitude. 'Your coming amongst us so unexpectedly and the kind, able and affectionate manner in which you have performed your ministerial duties call upon us for our warmest gratitude.'[12] Fr Benson had just three weeks to learn the basics of buying property and finding money to maintain himself, before being left alone. A letter to the Governor's Office in July sounded all the familiar difficulties; the congratulations offered to the Catholics on the occasions of visits from Ullathorne and Cotham came at a price for Fr Benson when he discovered the resources promised to him had to be expended on their fleeting presence:

> Sir, I received your letter of yesterday, and if in my letter anything is omitted that the Governor wishes to know please state it, for I am anxious to give every information in my power on the present subject. It is a fact that ten or twelve acres of land in or near Adelaide was given to our body by Messrs Wright and Co., Bankers. In consequence of their bankruptcy all that is lost. Before I left Sydney I was informed that the Catholics were procuring subscriptions towards building a church. On my arrival here I found that the amount collected did not exceed £160, the whole of which has been expended *viz.* more than £100 expenses for Dr. Ullathorne's visit to this place from Sydney—and the Rev. Cotham's from Launceston more than £40—so that I have no funds for a prospective building. I would barely get a decent livelihood from my congregation. It was only in consequence of hearing that Capt. Holmes' house would be very cheap and suit me very well for a house of divine worship that I ventured to propose the purchase of it to our people, who are nearly all mechanics under diminished wages and complaining of the scarcity of money—under these disadvantages I have appealed to His Excellency. I intend to solicit assistance

generally to enable us to accomplish an object of so much importance to our body.

The amount for the house will be £220 and £50 more will make the property freehold. The house is 40 ft. x 20 ft., the land 75 x 50 with a small cottage included. Messrs Smart and Wilson have kindly undertaken to furnish the writings gratis. The property will be placed in the hands of Trustees viz. Rt Rev. Dr Polding, Rev. W. Benson and three other resident Catholics.

I trust we shall be able to pay £100 in ten days from this time and the Assurance Company will advance the rest on the mortgage on the premises at £20 per cent., which I hope to be able to pay off in two years. I feel greatly obliged by the interest which His Excellency has taken in this affair.[13]

Cotham's own experience of similar difficulties had developed in him a capacity for empathy with the struggles of others which he had lacked in the first months of his ministry. After returning to Launceston he sent his impressions to Therry. The Catholics of Adelaide were 'poor but very good ... most of the emigrants having recently arrived, and there not being sufficient employment for them.'[14] He wrote encouragingly and sent money to Fr Benson. Thanking him for the gift of £5 Fr Benson replied in October 1841, 'I assure you I feel and appreciate your charity ... It was really wanted—and I hope God will reward you.' Nevertheless, the absence of hard cash from his poor congregation, who were themselves often paid by store vouchers, made business difficult, even if they meant well: 'I sometimes get a rupee instead of half a crown, or half a doz. eggs or half lb butter or some Tea'.[15] It was nearly three years before Fr Benson saw another priest. His efforts at public speaking were not successful due to his nervous, hesitant manner; he was remembered as 'a quiet, delicate gentleman [who] scarcely ever left the city. He hired a wooden building which stood near the corner of Topham and Waymouth streets, and lived in a small slab hut in the rear of his temporary chapel'.[16] Leaving the township was a problem because he could neither

Widening Horizons 103

ride a horse nor afford to hire a gig; he supplemented his income by doing small carpentry jobs. His health completely gave way during the heat of January 1843 and he returned to Sydney the following April before leaving for England.[17] His successor, Fr Edmund Mahony, was similarly overburdened and complained that 'he has bottled his sins till every bin is full, and he cries out lustily for help'.[18] Eventually he was joined by Francis Murphy, later appointed Bishop of Adelaide in 1844, who was greatly helped by the generous patronage of William Leigh of Woodchester, Gloucestershire.

Notes

[1]   S. Furphy, *Edward M. Curr and the tide of History* (Canberra: ANU Press, 2013), p. 6.

[2]   *Australasian Chronicle* (Sydney), 13 August 1840, p. 2; report taken from the *Hobart Advertiser*.

[3]   *The Tablet*, 31 October 1840, p. 4.

[4]   *Ibid.*, p. 4.

[5]   *Ibid.*, 30 April 1842, p. 6.

[6]   *Southern Australian*, 9 February 1841, p. 2.

[7]   N. Turner, *A Social History of Catholics in Australia* (North Blackburn: Collins Dove, 1992), Vol. 1, p. 99.

[8]   B. Condon, *Letters and Documents in 19th Century Australian Catholic History*, Polding to Mr and Mrs Phillips of Adelaide (delivered by W. Ullathorne), 20 May 1840.www.library.unisa.edu.au/condon/ CatholicLetters/ [Accessed online 27.7.2017]

[9]   L. Madigan (Ed.), *The Devil is a Jackass; William Bernard Ullathorne 1806–1889* (Leominster: Gracewing, 1995), p. 187.

[10] *Australasian Chronicle* (Sydney), 23 January 1841, p. 2.

[11] *Ibid.*, 8 April 1841, p. 2.

[12] Southerwood Collection, HAA, Tasmania.

[13] Benson to A. M. Munday, Secretary to Governor Grey, 14 July 1841. Adelaide Archdiocesan Archives copy of South Australian Archives GRG 787/1841, no. 436. Condon, *Letters and Documents*.

[14] N. Turner, *A Social History of Catholics in Australia* (North Blackburn: Collins Dove, 1992), Vol. 1, p. 100.

[15] Benson to Cotham, 7 October 1841. Condon, *Letters and Documents*.

16   J. W. Bull, *Early Experiences of Colonial Life in South Australia* (Adelaide: Printed at the Advertiser, Chronicle, and Express Offices, 1878), pp. 184–185. www.archive.org/details/earlyexperience00bullgoog [Accessed online 27.7.2017]

17   Fr Benson recovered his health and died in Wolverhampton in 1868 aged 73.

18   Polding to Heptonstall, 13 July 1844; quoted in F. O'Donoghue, *The Bishop of Botany Bay; The Life of John Bede Polding, Australia's First Catholic Archbishop* (Sydney: Angus and Robertson Publishers, 1982), p. 73.

10 TEETOTAL SOCIETY

THE FLOURISHING OF teetotal societies in Van Diemen's Land in the 1840s was a late corrective to the almost privileged role given to alcohol from the earliest days of Australian settlement. Rum was issued or sold at a reduced price to military officers, soldiers, free settlers, and convicts with an abandon not used elsewhere in the colonies. In 1792, four years after the landing of the First Fleet at Botany Bay, 2,319 gallons of rum were dispatched to New South Wales by the English Colonial Secretary: a quota of half-a-gallon per head (military, free, or convict) per annum. The practice of an annual issue to the military continued after the settlement of Van Diemen's Land in 1804 and prisoners were often rewarded with spirits for doing extra work apart from their allotted punishment.

To address the problems caused by drunken prisoners, the British Government issued a General Order in 1804 stating that no more than half-a-pint of ale was to be given to a prisoner on any one day. Rum from Bengal, Mauritius, and the West Indies was imported into Van Diemen's Land in such quantities, and commanded such a demand, that in the absence of an adequate cash currency it became a convenient method of trade and barter, and public celebrations to mark occasions such as the Monarch's birthday involved heavy consumption by everybody. Soldiers selling their allowances to licensed publicans were able to undercut importers and there was plenty available for sly-grog shops, in both instances cheating the government of revenue from duty. The hierarchy of colonial life was measured by the annual quota of gallons: by 1815 magistrates, civil, and military officers were allowed fifty gallons, head constables, school masters, and gaolers, twenty gallons, subordinate clerks and constables, ten gallons and licensed publicans, thirty gallons per year from the government stores.

By 1840 Van Diemen's Land was trying to free itself from alcohol use as a characteristic of its penal identity since the entrenchment of the excessive use of alcohol, in structural and personal life, was taken to be one of the most visible signs of the 'moral degradation' associated with convictism. The relative scarcity of women in the population as a whole, and the absence of domestic comfort, effectively drove men to congregate in the profusion of inns, hotels, and sly-grog shops which often masqueraded as coffee shops or confectioners. It was estimated in 1854 that Hobart alone had one hundred and eighty public houses, one for every one hundred and twenty-seven inhabitants; one in twenty-three houses was a public house, making publicans the largest commercial group on the island.[1]

The visit of the Quakers George Walker and James Backhouse in 1832 can be considered the foundation of an organised temperance movement in the colony and the Society of Friends was perhaps the earliest group to work in a concerted way against the evils of excessive drinking. It advocated total abstinence as the only 'ground of safety' for the suppression of intemperance and the reform of 'the drinking usages' of society.[2] Therefore the form of the pledge taken by absolutists covered social as well as individual circumstances. When various independent organisations united themselves in 1836 under the auspices of the Tasmanian Temperance Society the Quaker pledge was adopted:

> We, the undersigned, do agree that we will not use intoxicating liquors as a beverage, nor traffic in them: that we will not provide them as an article of entertainment, or for persons in our employment, and that, in all suitable ways, we will discountenance their use throughout the community.

Not surprisingly the various Christian denominations taken together comprised the backbone of the movement, although they held differing views on the means to be employed. The non-conformist and evangelical churches held the strictest line of total abstinence while the Catholic Church advocated moderation

Teetotal Society 107

rather than abstention as a norm. Cultural influences informed this stance: both the close associations between the Catholic Church and European countries as well as the fact that most Catholics in the colony had Irish roots, coming as they generally did from the convict and ex-convict strata. Catholic congregations formed their own temperance societies but as the goal was moral improvement, without doctrinal complications, happily they were not in competition with Protestant or secular groups on this issue. Crime, domestic degradation, and excessive alcohol intake—at least as reported in the island's newspapers—seemed inseparable and therefore it was the duty of Christians of all persuasions to ally themselves in the attempt to ameliorate this particular evil in society. The Quakers, at least, graciously acknowledged this: 'And most happy are we to acknowledge the efforts of some Roman Catholic brethren to introduce into this country the pledge of Father Mathew, as a man well deserving the regard which millions of Catholics and Protestants cherish for him.'[3]

The cause of the temperance movement was one that Fr Cotham made very closely his own. As the growth of Catholic involvement coincided with his ministry in Launceston he was able, as a priest working within his own mission, to shape his response according to his own style of leadership. The pioneering work began by Fr Theobald Mathew (1790–1856) in Cork in 1838 provided the inspiration for the Catholic movements in Australia although not all of them adopted outright the practice of taking Fr Mathew's Pledge made once in a person's lifetime to abstain totally from all alcoholic drink. In Ireland the movement may have enrolled as many as three million people, half the adult population, at its height in the early 1840s. The effects of 'taking the pledge' in such numbers is credited with a substantial fall in serious crime in Ireland during this same period; Fr Mathew also held rallies with great success in the industrial centres of Liverpool, Manchester, and London in 1844.

The first public meeting of St. Joseph's branch of Father Mathew's Total Abstinence Society was held on 22 November

1842 in the evening in the nave of the new Catholic Church, a temporary screen having been raised to divide the nave from the transept. The Revd J. Cotham, President of the Society, was in the chair. Although notice of the meeting had been advertised in the press only on the preceding day the chapel was surprisingly full and the meeting went off 'with great spirit and decorum'.[4] Fr Cotham described 'the course of the drunkard from his first commencement as a moderate drinker until the finish of his career' advising those who felt themselves liable to be carried away by temptation to adopt the safe course of total abstinence.

> The Rev. gentleman completely riveted the attention of his audience by the earnestness and eloquence of the address, and the only feeling existent in the mind of any person present, whether friendly or inimical to teetotalism, must have been that of entire concurrence in the justice of his observations.

The invitation to Isaac Sherwin, a Wesleyan Methodist, philanthropist, and President of the Tasmanian Teetotal Society, to be present and to address the meeting gave added authority to the new Catholic society:

> He remarked upon the catholicity of teetotalism, which comprised in its followers members of all denominations. The vice of drunkenness was also generally prevalent, and no one sect could reproach another for being more addicted to this vice than themselves ... He congratulated the society on being presided over by a minister; he believed that in New South Wales all the catholic ministers were teetotallers, and he need not remind them of the extraordinary success attendant upon the labours of Father Mathew.

If Isaac Sherwin brought personal integrity and the respectability of his position to the proceedings (he was also a banker, merchant, and irrigationist), the next speaker, Patrick Carolan, a former publican, spoke candidly from his own experience. He was well known in Launceston and as a trophy of teetotalism he

Teetotal Society

was a hero of the meeting. He narrated at considerable length the circumstances which led to his impoverishment, and traced them all to the vice of intoxication, saying that if he had continued the same as he was in 1825, avoiding the 'foolish speculations undertaken in moments of inebriation', he might now have been driving through the streets of the town in his carriage and four, whereas now 'he could not drive an ass!' Carolan strongly urged the necessity of total abstinence; his experience had taught him that a confident resolution to drink moderately could not be trusted to prevent ultimate addiction to drunkenness.

When a private of the 51st regiment stepped forward to join the society Cotham took the opportunity to counter the absolutist position. He thought it best, in the early days of the society, that members should join for twelve months only, for if they kept the pledge for that length of time they would have no difficulty in renewing it for a longer period or even for a lifetime. The pledge adopted by St Joseph's Society differed from the Tasmanian pledge, inasmuch as only those who signed must abstain, while they were not prohibited from offering certain drinks to others.

The meeting allowed a free exchange of opinions: Messrs Smith and Tyson urged the benefits gained by joining the total abstinence societies while Mr J. W. Bell commended the Catholic pledge, 'as persons in his situation were compelled to touch and called upon to sell intoxicating drinks, but who, nevertheless, might refrain from their use'. Fr Cotham and Sherwin debated the relative merits of different forms of the pledge but far from being rivals, the societies agreed to meet on alternate Tuesdays to accommodate each other. The press remarked on the lack of even a 'scintillation' of the violence which all too often character-ised teetotal meetings, noting the display of a 'unity of purpose and harmony of feeling ... exceedingly gratifying to all lovers of the cause'. No less gratifying was the sight of Mr Byron, Chief District Constable, bringing several of his constables forward to be introduced to Fr Cotham prior to taking the pledge.

The dangers of immoderate enthusiasm among the followers of teetotalism was fully recognised at the time and discussed at length in the newspapers, accepting the reality that the momentum needed to bring people into the temperance movement might not mature into a settled persistence in sobriety. Following the inaugural meeting the *Launceston Examiner* took up the cudgels in support of St Joseph's moderate approach, neatly accusing *The Advocate* of 'an admirable specimen of jesuitism'.

> The 'Tasmanian pledge', as it is called, supposes that fermented drinks are poison, and forbids a totalist to offer or sell them. Mr. Cotham dissents from this opinion, and therefore shapes his formula accordingly. He considers that habitual abuse may require a certain check, and what cannot be used with discretion, ought to be abandoned ... If those beverages are not poison, Mr. Cotham's course is clear. He forbids a temptation which is irresistible, but does not curse a gift which God has bestowed, and the use of which he has permitted. If fermented drinks are poison, they ought to be driven from every house — much more from every Christian temple ... The Advocate wonders that we oppose total abstinence. We never opposed it. We should be glad were it adopted by every drunkard in the island. It is at once the proper penalty and cure of excess. We have opposed the manner in which it has been enforced ... We do not profess to approve of pledges. They are often made without thought, and violated without remorse. They are administered on the spur of the moment, without a preparatory abstinence, or any security for their fulfilment ... In a word, we esteem abstinence better than drunkenness, but that nothing can be superior to sobriety and temperance.[5]

At the second meeting a fortnight later on 6 December Fr Cotham opened the evening by stating two of the guiding principles for the Society: 'that no religious subject ought to be introduced, or extracts made from the Bible ... and that no personal allusions would be allowed.'[6] Mr Smith, of Elizabeth Street, read an address

Teetotal Society 111

from the Liverpool Society to Fr Mathew, thereby avoiding trespass against the first principle but a Mr Moore had to be rebuked by Fr Cotham for alleging he had been sent an anonymous letter by someone in the room whom he now publicly challenged to confront him. Sherwin sympathised with Moore's hurt feelings as a teetotaller, and quickly moved the discussion on to happier matters: the teetotal festival which would take place on Wednesday 27 December.

The teetotal demonstration was covered at great length in the press as a novelty, certainly, but also as the presage of a sea change in social morals and behaviour. A full account[7] is worth studying as an example of the critical changes emerging in the colony:

TEETOTAL DEMONSTRATION

We are bound to record the all but unanimous gratification which the demonstration produced amongst the inhabitants of Launceston. The town has never been in such a state of pleasing excitement within the memory of its oldest inhabitants; and such a display as the procession afforded has never been witnessed in the colony. From morning till night the streets presented a scene of unusual bustle and briskness. Hundreds of people came from the country on purpose to witness the proceedings, and the windows of the houses where the procession passed were crowded with spectators. The teetotallers assembled in the Horticultural Gardens about 12 o'clock, none but those who wore medals being permitted to join in the procession.

Normal life in Van Diemen's Land was not without 'bustle and briskness' especially in the sea ports, the penal establishments, and commercial establishments, but excitement was too often associated with crime, extreme punishments, and disorderly behaviour. The opportunities for pleasurable excitement affording unanimous gratification were infrequent because entertainments were inclined to deteriorate in propriety the longer they were fuelled by alcoholic intake. A repeated motif in this demonstration is the care taken to maintain order:

112 *The Indomitable Mr Cotham*

> After being arranged in proper order, the band played the national anthem, when every male Teetotaller in the procession, in proof of loyalty to his sovereign, removed his hat and remained uncovered till the anthem was concluded. Thousands of people were collected outside the gates of the gardens, but not a taunt or jeer was heard—a feeling of utter astonishment being created. A few of the greatest trophies of teetotalism led the van, wearing sashes and rosettes, followed by the Society's grand banner of rich blue silk, supported on two poles, and exceedingly handsome in design and masterly in execution. The band was well organised, and the best that ever paraded the streets of Launceston.

That the first burst of music—the English national anthem, no less—passed without ribaldry or political jeering was a cause for astonishment. The demonstration began on literally the right note.

> Next came the president's flag of crimson silk, upon which was inscribed in letters of gold, — 'Peace on earth, and good will toward man.' The next banner contained the pledge written at length, surrounded by fancy scroll work, and at the bottom was a design containing the flags of all nations united together, signifying the universality of the cause, and unity of its members. The space between the flags in the procession was filled up by teetotallers, walking three abreast, many of whom wore sashes, and nearly all exhibited a blue rosette. A number of boys and girls, carrying small banners of all shapes and colours, inscribed with useful moral maxims, &c. made up the next division of the procession. Then followed the females' flag of white silk, with the words, 'Industry and Perseverance' on one side and 'Domestic Comfort' on the other in letters of green and gold.

The banners carried messages of universality and domesticity, the colours, designs, and the intricacy lifting the inscriptions into noble proclamations above the mundane realities behind industry and domestic comfort. That women and children were able to

Teetotal Society   113

march with the men was a demonstration of the family cohesion
which was a cause and a consequence of the desire, at least, for
greater sobriety and a more civilised society:

> The cordwainers' and St Crispin's arms were neatly exe-
> cuted on a banner of pink silk, and followed by the
> shoemakers, each wearing a rosette. The St Joseph's
> Society came next in order, headed by a splendid flag of
> green silk, on one side of which was a rich and appropriate
> design, executed with great taste, and on the other an
> excellent full sized portrait of Father Mathew, holding in
> his hand a scroll containing the pledge. The members of
> the society following this flag were preceded by the Rev.
> Mr Cotham, their President, and wore sashes, ribbons and
> rosettes to match the colour of their banner. The Longford
> Branch Society had a handsome red silk flag, with the
> name of the branch in large gold letters. The flag of the
> Perth Society was of pink silk, having also its title on both
> sides, in letters of gold upon a blue and green ribbon. The
> carpenters and joiners followed a splendid flag of green
> silk, containing on one side a chaste and elegant design
> comprising the arms of the carpenters, joiners and cabinet
> makers, worked into one, and made colonial by the addi-
> tion of a kangaroo and emu as supporters. On the other
> side was a large circle, in the centre of which were two
> hands united, in token of friendship, surrounded by 'Unity
> and Concord' in gold letters. The press of the *Advocate*
> was fixed in a cart, surmounted by a blue canopy, printing
> an address to the public, which was distributed amongst
> them as the procession proceeded through the streets. The
> rear was brought up by the saddlers, whose banner was of
> a particularly chaste description. The ground work was of
> blue silk, surrounded by a border of rich yellow silk fringe.
> The design, executed on both sides, consisted of the
> saddlers' arms, the supporters to which, being two wild
> horses, had a beautiful effect.

In a society which boasted inn-keeping as a primary occupation,
it would have seemed astonishing (again) not to have seen it

114   *The Indomitable Mr Cotham*

represented at all. Instead, the 'respectable' trades paraded almost as if they had the status of European medieval guilds; however, the woodworkers' banner was proudly colonial and antipodean, with the kangaroo and emu standing sentinel on either side of the carpenters' arms.

> The procession paraded through the town without any disturbance, accompanied by an immense number of spectators. Such a body has never been collected in our streets before; it was altogether by far the most lively and animating scene we have witnessed, and reminded us of an election day at home, minus the effects of alcohol. Upon returning to the gardens the gates were thrown open to the public upon payment of two shillings, and a very large number paid for admission. The booth was the most capacious ever erected here, being capable of accommo-dating nine hundred persons. At tea time every seat was occupied, and numbers had to wait outside until others retired from the tables. Whilst the band remained in the gardens, the members of the Harmonic Society were stationed on a platform in the booth and entertained the company by playing a variety of sacred music. After tea the assembly was addressed by a variety of speakers …

The visual spectacle of the procession had obviously involved considerable expense, expertise, and logistical arrangement. The parade was an end in itself, a demonstration not only that such numbers could come together without descending into disorder but that women and children were safe among menfolk who were identified by their lawful professions. The taking of tea in a large tent should have been an anti-climax but in this context it was wholly appropriate. Nevertheless, it had the importance of something beyond a mere tea-party; the newspaper report likened the gathering to 'an election day at home', as the parade voted with its feet to step aside, in principle at least, from the power of alcohol. The speeches are not reported, for lack of space, but

Teetotal Society

probably also because they could not match the impression on the senses made by the scenes of the day:

> The bitterest enemy of teetotalism cannot say that he ever witnessed such gratifying scenes before in this colony; or that the interests of society would not be promoted by their more frequent repetition. The proceedings were uninterrupted by any casualties or disturbances; nor was there any attempt at opposition, if we except that of a publican, who mounted a cask upon a cart, together with an effigy of Guy Fawkes, and sent it about town. At any rate, it was universally agreed, that the association of Guy Fawkes and alcohol was appropriate and the teetotallers very properly judged of the spirits by the company they were in, and recommended them to be burnt together. Between sixty and seventy persons signed the pledge during the day.

The demonstrators could afford to be condescendingly gracious to the opposition from this sole protester with his traditional guy as an accomplice, joining in the fun and reducing the publican's professional annoyance to mere child's play.

The following year the second annual festival of the Tasmanian Teetotal Society was reported again, with the arrangements similar to those of the previous year. The banner for St Joseph's Society was described in greater detail: it was made of green silk, bordered with white; on the one side appeared a shield, divided into three compartments, in which were represented a figure casting from him the shackles of slavery, a bee-hive, and in golden letters 'I. H. S.' On the reverse side of the flag was drawn a faithful portrait of Father Mathew, represented in the act of administering the pledge. This banner was followed by the Revd Cotham, R.C.C., and the members of the society, three abreast, wearing sashes and rosettes of green, to correspond with the flag.[8] The three compartments are interesting for the breadth of their allusion. The abolition of slavery is put alongside the abolition of alcoholism as a humanitarian cause; it may also contain a reference to St Gregory's encounter with Anglo-Saxon slave

116 *The Indomitable Mr Cotham*

children in the Roman markets as the impetus for the Benedictine mission to England. A beehive naturally symbolises harmonious industry but it is also the emblem for St Ambrose, Cotham's patron saint. The letters IHS—abbreviation for the name Jesus— highlight the religious and Catholic faith of the majority of the Society members.

The Tasmanian Teetotal Society did not have to invent the elements of their demonstration. These followed the format of similar celebrations in England reported by the Australian press. A nice example of ecumenism was reported from the Bath Abstinence Association annual meeting.

> The Rev T Spencer had been asked if it would be any objection to him if a Roman Catholic Priest were in the same carriage [in the procession]? He replied no; if the Pope himself were in the carriage he should have no objection to join him, for he understood the Pope wore Father Mathew's teetotal medal; and if he came to their meeting as a teetotaller, he should not enquire what were his religious principles.[9]

Fr Cotham preached moderation in drinking except for those who were addicted to it. For himself, it seems he followed the way of temperance but not absolute sobriety, and knew what it was to go too far occasionally. After a gruelling round of duties during Christmas 1846 he allowed himself to spend New Year's Eve with Mr Loughnan, not returning home until 11 p.m. The following day, 1 January 1847, his journal reveals that he is 'indisposed' and spends the day indoors reading quietly. January 2 sees him back at his duties. Bishop Willson took a firmer line and preferred total abstention or at the very least strict moderation, using alcohol only on medical advice or to observe social custom. His concession that a priest could drink alone if he was wet and cold after attending priestly duties[10] must have been a dispensation often invoked by the rain-averse Cotham. Ten years later in Cheltenham Cotham is still checking his occasional over indulgence; having recom-

Teetotal Society 117

menced his journal on 12 February 1859, his 49th birthday, he makes the firm statement: *'Risolutu benè viviendi et nil bibendi'.*[11]

Fr Cotham's temperance activities show him in a leadership role alongside men of different denominations, backgrounds, and moralities. In the same month as Bishop Robert Willson's long awaited arrival, in May 1844, to tackle myriad challenges in the new Catholic diocese of Hobart, Cotham was enjoying, it seems, an afternoon with the Rechabites in Launceston, to celebrate their first anniversary. The meeting was held 'at their Tent (the Star of Tasmania) at brother Stoneham's'. After a procession to the chapel, for a service he would not have attended, the assembly returned to the Tent for 'a sumptuous dinner'. The usual toasts were made in due order and after royalty and government came the Revds Messrs Price, Cotham and Turner and Mr Nichols, President of the Teetotal Society. The 'neat speaches' made in response, with vocal music, Rechabite and other, enlivened proceedings until 10 o'clock at night.[12]

The proximity to alcohol, its imbibers and its purveyors, was inescapable in the colony and Cotham was pragmatic in his approach. The letter he received from the McCarthys in 1856 indicates the acceptability of inn-keeping as a trade and a social necessity. Cotham had his own principles to expound without alienating those who thought differently. In Launceston he was able to work independently of immediate oversight from the Vicar General in Hobart, and certainly from Bishop Polding in Sydney. In the space of seven years and by the age of 33 he had clearly grown in confidence in his ministerial role in a socially evolving colony.

Notes

[1]   Kym Roberts' website describing The Bush Inn, New Norfolk (Australia's oldest continuously licensed hotel) has provided much background information for this section. www.stors.tas.gov.au/au-7-0095-00680 [Accessed online 27.7.2017]

[2]   *The Friend*, Vol. I, Number VII, 27 July 1843 Edition 01.

118 *The Indomitable Mr Cotham*

[3] *Ibid.*

[4] *Launceston Courier*, 28 November 1842, p. 4, and *Launceston Examiner*, 26 November 1842, p. 3, for accounts of this inaugural meeting.

[5] *Launceston Examiner*, 3 December 1842, p. 3.

[6] *Ibid.*, 7 December 1842, p. 4.

[7] *Launceston Advertiser*, 29 December 1842, p. 2.

[8] *Launceston Examiner*, 6 January 1844, p. 7.

[9] *Launceston Courier*, 2 January 1843, p. 3.

[10] W. T. Southerwood, *The Convicts' Friend: Bishop R. W. Willson* (George Town, Tasmania, Stella Maris Books, 1989), p. 278.

[11] Resolved to live well and drink nothing.

[12] *Launceston Advertiser*, 23 May 1844, p. 2.

11 LAWRENCE AND SARAH COTHAM IN VAN DIEMEN'S LAND

IN THE ABSENCE of any correspondence, or journals for the period before 1845, there is no direct evidence for the state of James' relationship with his brother Lawrence. However, where records exist they show the two men having regular dealings with one another. Opposition to temperance—apart from inveterate inebriates—is generally supposed to have come from licensed publicans, of whom Lawrence Cotham was one. As for many others, inn-keeping was only one of his businesses and in his case he made it a respectable route to relative wealth. Lawrence's career was wholly secular but at no point, to the very end of their lives, was there ever a cooling in the relationship between the two brothers despite the miles separating them. Although Lawrence had qualified as a pharmacist before leaving England, and had premises to lease or sell, he seems not to have tried this profession in Van Diemen's Land. There was a surplus of medically trained men on the island in the 1830s competing for posts in the Government medical service or as private practitioners since working one's passage as a ship's surgeon was a popular way to travel to Australia. The advertisements in Britain exaggerated the prospects for physicians and surgeons hoping to practise among a basically healthy and scattered population. Apothecaries such as Lawrence were far down the list of useful professionals. In any case, when Lawrence turned his hand to commercial enterprises he usually prospered and his true metier seems to have been that of entrepreneur.

After a brief period at Kilmore Park in the midlands Oatlands District, Lawrence moved south to his permanent Tasmanian home in Richmond. He married Sarah Cassidy early in 1836 and his first son was born in December, but died in infancy. A notice of the transfer of a prisoner's assignment to Lawrence from John Cassidy in May 1837[1] signals the beginning of his rise to prosperity. Whether it was Lawrence or Cassidy who initiated the shrewd move of forming a business partnership, or whether John's daughter Sarah was the catalyst for it, it proved profitable for both men. Eventually the younger man outstripped the old colonist in wealth but he never matched him in having such a high profile as a supporter of the Catholic Church. The proximity of his Benedictine brother, and the deep piety of his Cassidy in-laws, fostered a sincere practice of religious duties in the family, but Lawrence's combative personality thrived on exploration, risk-taking, and confrontation. James Cotham supported his brother and his family throughout their lives but it is doubtful that he was able to restrain him when his mind was set, or his temper roused.

The predominance of public houses continued for a number of years after Lawrence Cotham joined the trade in the mid-1830s, despite growing calls for the reform of morals and behaviour associated with the prevalent alcohol culture. The revenue from the rising numbers of licensed public houses saved the government from financial embarrassment. By 1844 the three hundred inns, hotels, and public houses in Van Diemen's Land raised £7,500 per annum from the £25 license fee. Additionally, conservative estimates of the revenue from duties on spirits sold in pubs put the sum at £55,000.[2] One of John Cassidy's ventures was the building of the Richmond Hotel in about 1830 for which Lawrence Cotham was granted a license as landlord in October 1837 and 1838. This was not his first license; in December 1837 he was advertising for a tenant to replace him at the Commercial Hotel, Hobart:

> THE attention of the present proprietor being engrossed in other pursuits, begs to offer, for any term of years, and at such rent as may be agreed upon, those new, substantial, commodious and eligible premises,

Lawrence and Sarah Cotham in Van Diemen's Land 121

THE COMMERCIAL HOTEL,
with capacious cellarage, stabling, coach house, and a very productive garden.

The Good-Will of the business, including that profitable auxiliary, the Tap, is invaluable, but will nevertheless be sacrificed to the in-coming tenant without any consideration. The Stock of Wines, Spirits, &c. may be taken at a valuation, and though not very extensive, is extremely choice.

It may be superfluous to point out any greater inducement to an obliging and industrious man, than to say, Mr Buscombe has already accumulated a fortune as an inn-keeper in this wealthy and populous township.

N. B. For terms and further particulars, apply to Mr L. Cotham, on the premises.[3]

The 'other pursuits' were the tenancy and eventual ownership of the Richmond Hotel. Only one week later Lawrence was again advertising:

Richmond Hotel L. COTHAM has the pleasure to announce to the public generally, that he has commenced business at RICHMOND as an Innkeeper, and Wholesale & Retail Wine & Spirit Merchant; and has recently enlarged the house and premises known as the RICH-MOND HOTEL by building additional rooms, capacious coach-houses, stables, &c., and fitted up the whole establishment in a very superior manner, paying throughout the strictest regard to the comfort and convenience of his guests. He has also exercised the utmost care in the selection of Wines, Spirits, Malt Liquors, etc. The present stock, however, has been chosen expressly for the RACES consisting of every luxurious beverage procurable in the colony. If L.C. can possibly procure to himself public patronage in this undertaking by engaging none but attentive and obliging servants, by keeping well aired beds, wholesome provender for horses, together with the very best CATERING and COOKING and his personal super-intendence of the whole, he cannot fail of success.

Dec. 28 1837.[4]

This was to be an altogether grander enterprise: respectable, aimed at the higher end of the market and, possibly, above reproach from his temperance-preaching brother. Lawrence held the tenancy until at least 1848. By that point John Cassidy had succumbed to financial catastrophe during the period of deep economic depression in Van Diemen's Land; Lawrence had diversified his business interests and did not suffer the same losses. Nevertheless, Lawrence fell foul of an occupational hazard of inn tenancy, namely the eagerness of a cash-strapped constabulary to fine landlords for contravention of licensing laws.

> Central to this branch of revenue were the police, many of whom spent much time watching for breaches or entrapping publicans into breaching the various restrictions imposed on their trade as to who they could serve and when. That the police received half of the fine was a powerful incentive to exert themselves against publicans.[5]

So in March 1838 the respectable Lawrence Cotham was in the police courts for breach of the Quarter Sessions Act and was fined £1 and costs.[6] Lawrence, never slow to extend his business interests, was licensee of two other public houses, Restdown Inn at Restdown Ferry (1852) and the Richmond Hill Hotel (1858) before he left the island.

A natural extension of Lawrence's inn-keeping business was the development of a successful, and frequently advertised, coaching service based in Richmond. On one occasion the editor supplemented Lawrence's advertisement: 'From the celebrity of the cattle kept by Mr. C., and comfortable coaches kept by him, as well as the good things kept at his hotel, in Richmond, we are in no doubt he will meet with that public patronage to which he is entitled'.[7] The extent of his farming interests is clear from the auction held when Lawrence decided to end his career as a farmer in 1847 and concentrate on the coaching business:

MESSRS. LOWES & MACMICHAEL WILL SELL BY PUBLIC AUCTION,
On MONDAY, 5th April, commencing at 11 o'clock,
By instructions from the proprietor, L. COTHAM, Esq.
removed from his farm for the convenience of sale, in consequence of his retiring from agricultural pursuits,
At the Richmond Hotel,
TWELVE PAIRS OF VERY EXCELLENT WORKING BULLOCKS
Twelve superior well-bred dairy cows; Three cart and plough horses; Six gig and saddle horses
A celebrated gig mare, by Sir Raymond; A quantity of pigs; A capital 4-horse threshing machine, with winnowing machine attached ...
And the usual variety of farming implements and other effects.[8]

Lawrence was as successful as a coaching proprietor as he had been as a grazier. In July 1851 a Launceston newspaper noted approvingly

the launching of a new mail coach, built by Mr Fraser for Mr Lawrence Cotham of Richmond, which is intended to be run as the mail coach; it is neatly embellished with gold paint, and varnish, and is the best looking coach in Hobart Town. The general increase of coaches ... on the main and cross roads of this island may be considered as an indication of the prosperity of the community.[9]

However, Lawrence's ambitions were not satisfied even by this recognition of his superiority. Only three months later he was selling twenty horses and vehicles, 'the proprietor leaving the township [Richmond]'[10] and in early 1852 he decamped to Ballarat in the Victorian goldfields with his 11-year-old son Lawrence junior at a time when it seemed most of the male population of the island was gripped by gold fever. The Cothams banked thirty-two ounces of gold in Geelong in December before returning home, although they may have bought it rather than prospected personally for it; however, father and son stored away their first-hand experience of the gold-rush for a later opportunity. Until the end of his life Lawrence was looking for new projects, and in the last he may have invited his brother James to join him.

Lawrence had a particular interest in horseflesh. Horse breeding was a serious business in the colony and Lawrence was soon on the itinerary of stallions such as Young Sam 'the property of Mr John Espie, Bagdad [who] will commence travelling on the 18th instant, and serve mares this season at £3.3s. each, and 5/- groomage, by bill at 3 months from 1st February, 1839'.[11] He shared his interest with his father-in-law who provided a new course on his property where 'the Galloway Race was won by Mr Cotham's Billy-go-by-them; but we are sorry to say Billy died on the course in a few minutes after winning—and not pressed in the race'.[12] Despite these occasional losses, Lawrence's stature increased until he became treasurer and secretary of the Richmond Races in 1851.

Ambrose Cotham's journal entries suggest he also had a close interest in horses but without the entertainment factor. He notes how his horse fared during his travels: sometimes the horse went hungry for twenty-four hours or had to leap down into a ferry over choppy waters. The horse was essential for his mission work even though riding carried the danger of falls with the horse coming down on top of the rider. In middle age Ambrose preferred to take his exercise on foot as long as the weather was dry.

In that staple of provincial newspapers, the accounts of court proceedings, Lawrence Cotham provided regular material, both as plaintiff and defendant. Cases of trespass, damaged goods offered for auction, and threats of assault—usually with insults and sticks being brandished by both parties—were commonplace and though deplored for interfering with business and lowering the tone of society there is bemusement rather than strong disapproval even when 'a very respectable person' such as Lawrence Cotham is the victim:

Lawrence and Sarah Cotham in Van Diemen's Land

> Is it not too bad and really a serious inconvenience and a wrong to Mr Cotham that he has been placed at the bar of the police office, for a charge of assault, dated so far back as the 18th July, and emanating from a person [Mr Thorneloe] in such an unfortunate state of mental excitement. For the defendant too it happened at a peculiarly unfortunate time, just when the ploughing match and meeting at Sorell was being celebrated, when conveyances on the Richmond road are so much in requisition, the proprietor of the regular vehicle is called off, as well as the driver, to appear at the police office and answer a fantastic charge disproved by the complainant's own witnesses![13]

Van Diemen's Land was not a place for settlers of delicate constitutions and sensibilities. The tension between achieving material prosperity and cultural improvement, while being neither coarsened nor disillusioned by the struggle, was at the heart of the colonial agenda for society and church. Happily, Fr Cotham shared in the life of the people around him without finding himself in the defendant's dock. In 1842, however, his name did appear in the Police reports column of the *Launceston Examiner*:

> The existing sentence of transportation of James Smith (ticket-of-leave) was extended two years for stealing one pair of spectacles, the property of the Rev. J. Cotham, and to be removed to Port Arthur, he having threatened to shoot him.[14]

Of far greater personal significance for James Cotham than Lawrence's commercial enterprises was his brother's marriage to Sarah Cassidy. Of their ten children, three died in infancy and were buried in St John's churchyard, Richmond. James knew all but the youngest of these children while he was in Van Diemen's Land: Marianne Eleanor, born 1839; Isabella, 1840; Lawrence Leopold, 1841; William, 1843; Sarah, 1844; Eleanor, 1846; and Hugh, 1851. His involvement with them lasted throughout his life to an extraordinary degree and though it caused resentment among some of his Benedictine confrères it seems Cotham himself was more than happy to be an uncle-benefactor, together with his elder brother William, to their extended antipodean family.

Notes

[1] 12 May 1837; Prisoner 676 F. Parkin, *Persian*. Francis Parkin (30) and George Parkin (20) were sentenced to death for aggravated burglary, commuted to transportation for life, at Nottingham in March 1830.

[2] S. Petrow, *After Arthur: Policing in Van Diemen's Land 1837–1846*, Paper presented at the History of Crime, Policing and Punishment Conference convened by the Australian Institute of Criminology in conjunction with Charles Sturt University and held in Canberra, 9–10 December 1999, p. 20, citing *Colonial Times* (Hobart), 10 September 1844, p. 2. www.aic.gov.au/media_library/conferences/hcpp/petrow.pdf [Accessed online 27.7.2017]

[3] *The Hobart Town Courier,* 22 December 1837, p. 3.

[4] *Ibid.,* 29 December 1837, p. 3.

[5] S. Petrow, *After Arthur: Policing in Van Diemen's Land 1837–1846*, p. 20.

[6] *The Hobart Town Courier,* 2 March 1838, p. 4.

[7] *Hobarton Guardian, or, True Friend of Tasmania*, 28 August 1847, p. 2.

[8] *The Courier* (Hobart), 20 March 1847, p. 3.

[9] *The Cornwall Chronicle* (Launceston), 26 July 1851, p. 468.

[10] *Colonial Times* (Hobart), 24 October 1851, p. 3.

[11] *The Hobart Town Courier,* 5 October 1838, p. 1.

[12] *Colonial Times* (Hobart), 8 January 1850, p. 3.

[13] *Hobarton Guardian, or, True Friend of Tasmania*, 20 September 1848, p. 3.

[14] *Launceston Examiner,* 26 October 1842, p. 5.

12 NEW REGIMES

B Y THE VERY nature of Tasmanian[1] society and political structure until 1843 all church ministers were *de facto* chaplains to convicts, to the military personnel, and to free settlers. The system of assignment necessitated the integration of convicted persons with their assigned civilian 'masters and mistresses'. It was tacitly accepted that as convicts moved through the process towards emancipation, via a spent sentence or pardon, the reasons for their advent on the island would not be referred to if they were able to pass into respectable employment and marriage. Thus, the first decade of Cotham's career took place in an environment of relative equilibrium; Catholics and Protestants observed their customary separate spheres of influence, the former not discriminated against by law although often having to press their claims in practice.

Transportation to New South Wales ended in 1840 when that state gained the coveted status of a settlement rather than a convict colony. Conversely, in Tasmania the population was incensed that it was to become the dumping ground for up to 5,000 new convicts annually, not including the 'desperadoes' nearing the end of their sentences on far-away Norfolk Island, one thousand miles east of Sydney in the Pacific Ocean. All this was to be inflicted on them without a corresponding increase in revenue to maintain the extra persons or suitable staff to superintend them, while the withdrawal of cheap labour from assigned convicts threatened the growth of the economy. The island was brought to the point of bankruptcy, financial and administrative, as its whole *raison d'être* as a penal colony was undermined by calls from free settlers for a new political administration.

The introduction of the probation system[2] was regarded as a self-serving initiative by a British political establishment that gave no heed to the aspirations of free settlers. The negatively critical report issued by Sir William Molesworth, head of the Transportation Commission from 1837 to 1838 (to which Ullathorne added his testimony) was part of the evidence brought against transportation as a whole, as was the distaste for an assignment system which seemed to share the immorality of narrowly-defined slave ownership, illegal in the British Empire since 1833. In reality, assignment covered a wide range of experience: for many convicts it was the beginning of opportunities unavailable in Britain to rise above poverty and servitude, rural or industrial. In many cases there were abuses by masters little better than criminals themselves, but it was also the case that many men and women convicted of petty crimes found themselves in a position of respectability within a short time of receiving their ticket-of-leave.

> Probation's first years, between 1840 and 1843, saw a state of fluidity that caused great confusion amongst those administering the fledgling system ... The confusion in these early years illustrates how unprepared both the colony and the Home Government were for the requirements of the new system. The funds necessary for the massive building program were slow to materialise, resulting in poor-quality stations that fell far short of the system's lofty aims. The colony's commissary and staffing capabilities were vastly overstretched, resulting in poor levels of superintendence.[3]

The task of implementing the flawed Molesworth Report—strong on moral tone, weak on practical solutions—fell to Sir John Franklin and his successor as Lieutenant-Governor, Eardley-Wilmot. Both men advocated the role of religious chaplains as integral to the discipline of the prisoners; the probation system was intended to be a dynamic one through which a male convict with a life sentence would pass from preliminary detention on Norfolk Island to probationary labour gangs in Tasmania, successively gaining a probationary pass, ticket-of-leave, and finally a pardon or a spent conviction. Male prisoners with a lesser sentence would begin their sentence at a probation station and all female

New Regimes 129

prisoners would be assessed at a Factory or Hiring Station before serving their sentence outside the institution as far as their behaviour and hiring circumstances allowed. For this process to work the prisoners had to be incentivised to believe in a future for themselves outside criminality through remorse, reparation, and rehabilitation. The roles of teacher, catechist, and minister of religion were central to a moral programme which was part of the pragmatic need to deal with crime and criminals; Franklin and his wife Jane were personally committed to this scheme of administration but hard reality undermined its implementation.

The change in Cotham's career coincided with the establishment of a separate Catholic diocese of Hobart and the arrival of a new Lieutenant-Governor in 1843 to replace Franklin: Sir John Eardley Eardley-Wilmot. The latter had a relatively short, troubled tenure and in his own words he was the 'Victim of the most extraordinary conspiracy that ever succeeded in defaming the character of a Public Servant ... subjected to the condemnation of a Minister of the Crown, founded on anonymous information and unauthenticated representations'.[4] The state of the island and the task he faced in the penal department almost made inevitable the failure of his period in office which ended controversially and was followed almost immediately by his death in 1847; with two other Catholic priests, Fr Cotham was to the forefront of the funeral cortege.[5] As a Religious Instructor (the title was settled on as a compromise to sidestep the clash between civil and ecclesiastical jurisdiction of ordained ministers of religion) Cotham experienced the ambivalence of working for two masters: the first, his highly respected and competent Bishop, and the other, a government minister saddled with an unpopular remit and insufficient resources. If Cotham was nearly broken as a young missioner by isolation and conflicting demands, in his second period in Tasmania he was almost worn out by overwork, an unrelenting routine, and ambivalence about the value of his role.

The arrival in 1844 of Bishop Robert William Willson from Nottingham to be Tasmania's first Catholic bishop was of great personal significance for Cotham. It was his first experience—nearly ten years after ordination—of being under the close supervision and guidance of a proficient bishop with substantial background knowledge. Moreover, Willson's Catholic upbringing was distinctly different from Cotham's early education and companionship among Jesuits and Benedictines. With the establishment of a Tasmanian hierarchy and, finally, a steady increase in the number of priests, the initiatives taken by the congregational laity were brought into a parochial system. If this sometimes weakened the bond between a priest and his congregation, for Cotham it also introduced him to the advantages of strong links between a diocesan bishop and fellow clergy. As the pioneering age closed the latitude allowed for personal idiosyncrasies such as Fr Conolly's and the wayward individualism of Fr Therry and Fr Watkins would be checked by closer scrutiny and discipline. As Ullathorne later reminisced:

> one thing I had long striven to impress on [Polding's] mind, and that was the importance of obtaining a second Bishop for Van Diemen's Land ... During my absence in England he had sent Father Therry to Hobart Town, and that with authority as Vicar-General, there being only two other priests on the island. This removed a difficulty from New South Wales, but created a serious state of things in that island ... I repeated on every fitting occasion that Van Diemen's Land was 'the sore point on the episcopal conscience.'[6]

Cotham would have seconded Ullathorne's assessment and Bishop Willson soon came to the same conclusion. His arrival marked the beginning of a parish system and someone on the island with immediate authority and responsibility for the spiritual needs of Catholics. But it was also another step away from the realisation of Bede Polding's dream for a majority Benedictine influence in the Antipodes. There were simply not enough Benedictine—or secular—priests available in England to spare and increasingly the Church in Australia became dominated by Irish missionaries and an Irish hierarchy. For Ambrose Cotham

New Regimes   131

it was a crucial development: on the one hand he found himself part of a system which might limit his personal influence while providing a stronger organisational framework in which to act, while on the other hand his immediate allegiance was to a secular bishop whose own relationship with the Benedictine archbishop would be strained. While Polding ensured that in Sydney 'the religious habit is worn with as much publicity as in the home itself whenever the novices visit the hospitals and asylums'[7] Cotham continued to wear his woollen hose and silk fronts at all times.

There is nothing to suggest Bishop Willson found Cotham, fifteen years his junior and a relative stranger to the effects of English post-1829 Catholic Emancipation, wayward in his discipline or divided in his loyalty. For Cotham, the change afforded him a practical training in working as a Benedictine monk under the authority of a diocesan bishop. The distance from Sydney, Willson's own stance towards Polding, and pressure of work meant the debate on monastic versus secular episcopal governance engaging the mission in England in the 1840s did not figure largely for the sole monk in Tasmania.

Bishop Willson (1794–1866) was 50 when he arrived in Tasmania on 11 May 1844, a relatively mature age which reflected his experience. He had not started his studies for the priesthood at Oscott College until he was 22, after a few years spent working on a farm, and he was 30 when he was ordained. The eighteen years he spent in Nottingham gave him skills in two quite different spheres. As the son of a builder and brother of a talented architect, Fr Willson took an intelligent interest in the building of St Barnabas' Church which later became the impressive cathedral church of the newly-formed diocese of Nottingham. His personal friendship with the church's architect, Augustus Pugin, led directly to a transfer of Gothic principles to Tasmania in the 1840s, giving the fledgling diocese of Hobart an immense injection of ecclesiastical capital at its outset. Pugin's practical generosity and belief in the revival of pre-Reformation principles of architecture and liturgy provided an enduring legacy to

Tasmania through Bishop Willson. The quality of the vestments was not stinted. 'All were of silk with woven silk braids and were embellished with raised silk and metal thread embroidery on silk velvet in the bright heraldic colours typical of Pugin's work.'[8] Fr Cotham gained direct knowledge of the trend in England for Benedictines to favour Gothic theories when building new churches and monasteries in the second half of the nineteenth century, knowledge which he was able to apply so confidently a decade later.

The second area of expertise in which Willson became outstanding concerned the care of prisoners and the mentally afflicted. He informed himself and civic leaders on how to obtain the best results from the built environment and methods of supervision for restrained persons. In England he was part of a movement spanning architecture, prison reform, and therapeutic treatment of the insane, even gaining a license to lodge mentally ill persons in his own home. In Tasmania he found very little had been done in any of these fields in an integrated fashion and he applied himself with characteristic firmness, reporting back to Parliament about the appallingly brutal conditions of the 'hell holes' of Norfolk Island which, in large part, he was responsible for mitigating and finally abolishing. His appointment coincided with a movement towards prison reform in England and he was not alone in advocating the moral reform of criminals rather than punishment for its own sake, but a lack of political will in London to meet the cost of adequate resources, and a disregard for Tasmania's aspirations for self-determination, meant the high ideals were never realistically achievable.

The appointment of two bishops in Tasmania within two years, the Anglican Bishop Francis Russell Nixon in 1843 and Bishop Willson the following year, led to a lengthy and tiresome correspondence in the colonial press until the end of 1845. In brief, the Lord Bishop of Tasmania, Nixon, objected to the ecclesiastical title used by Willson, Bishop of Hobart. The argument was resolved only by the adjudication of the Colonial

New Regimes 133

Secretary, Lord Stanley, that Bishop Willson was 'to dispense with the title Hobartonian, and to be content with the appellation of the Right Revd Dr Willson'.[9] Although the decision went in favour of Nixon, it was frequently noted that Willson was the more emollient man, even when chiding Nixon for 'engaging in religious strife and allowing the religion of Christ to degenerate into a "tinkling cymbal" at a time when thousands of their respective flocks were festering in misery and crying for spiritual aid and consolation'.[10] Bishop Nixon's series of Lent lectures in 1844, directed against particular Catholic practices such as the invocation of saints and the use of images, backfired on him when one of his own clergy, the veteran Revd Mr William Bedford, objected to St David's Cathedral being used as the venue for the lectures. Clergy of both denominations were unaccustomed to close scrutiny from a local bishop and some, such as Bedford, gave up their independent ways reluctantly. The indignation felt by Cotham at the slight to his Bishop simmered until 1846 when he found a public occasion to speak out on his behalf.

The first ten years of Bishop Willson's tenure were necessarily spent dealing mainly with the penal system which was reaching breaking point in Tasmania prior to the end of transportation in 1853. On his arrival in May 1844 convicts still formed the majority of the Catholic population on the island which had become the sole destination for transported convicts from the British Isles, their percentage of the population as a whole even increasing by the end of the decade. Willson found some 3,000 Catholics in over thirty penal institutions scattered around the island, the men employed on public works in gangs (but not always in chains); repeat offenders were incarcerated in the brutal institutions on Norfolk Island and at Port Arthur. Separated from the men, convicted women were held in probation factories and the children caught up as collateral dependents were housed alongside the women or in orphanages. Of the 36,000 convicts sent to Tasmania during the final decade of transportation nearly 12,000 were Irish Catholics.[11] As chaplains to this dispersed penal

134 *The Indomitable Mr Cotham*

population Willson found three priests working out of their small churches in Hobart, Richmond, and Launceston, which were the hubs for a scattered civilian congregation. Bishop Willson brought four missioners with him: a small enough number but in the circumstances providing a greater impetus than anything achieved in the colony by Archbishop Polding in the preceding decade. William Hall was appointed Vicar General and was respected as such although he seems not to have been a man to inspire great affection initially. George Hunter and Br James Luke Levermore OC were still in training for the priesthood and with Fr William Bond were destined for posts in the penal department.

Notes

[1] The change of name from Van Diemen's Land to Tasmania was officially made in 1853 when the colony obtained self-government from New South Wales. However, the term 'Tasmania' had become increasingly popular since the 1820s, for example in Godwin's *Emigrants Guide to Van Diemen's Land, more properly called Tasmania* (1823) and noted by Charles Darwin in 1836. It is appropriate, therefore, to use this name from this point to reflect the developing identity of the colony and the process of distancing itself from its convict history, especially through the use of language. See A. Alexander, *Tasmania's Convicts: How Felons built a Free Society* (Crows Nest NSW: Allen and Unwin, 2010), for a full treatment of this subject.

[2] See www.parliament.tas.gov.au/php/BecomingTasmania; ©Parliament of Tasmania, 2005, '*Becoming a Penal Colony*' for a summary of the penal system: '• Stage one—Temporary incarceration in an English penitentiary, with some hard labour • Stage two—Transportation to VDL with a hard labour in a probation gang • Stage three—Potential to earn a Probation Pass to wholly or partly work for one's self • Stage four—Earn a Ticket-of-Leave or self-sufficiency before pardon or emancipation'.

[3] R. Tuffin, *Tasmanian Research and Historical Association, Papers and Proceedings* Vol. 54 No. 2 (August 2007). 'The Evolution of Convict Labour Management in Van Diemen's Land: Placing the "Penal Peninsula" in a Colonial Context', p. 73.

[4] CO280/196 (AJCP 545) Eardley-Wilmot to Secretary of State for the Colonies, 30 October 1846. Quoted in L. C. Mickleborough, '*Victim of an*

New Regimes 135

'*Extraordinary Conspiracy*'? *Sir John Eardley Eardley-Wilmot Lieutenant Governor of Van Diemen's Land 1843-46*' PhD Thesis (University of Tasmania, 2011), p. 1.

[5] *The Courier* (Hobart), 13 February 1847, p. 3.

[6] L. Madigan (Ed.), *The Devil is a Jackass*; *William Bernard Ullathorne 1806–1889* (Leominster: Gracewing, 1995), p. 206.

[7] A. Hood OSB, *From Repatriation to Revival* (Farnborough: St Michael's Abbey Press, 2014), p. 51.

[8] B. Andrews, 'Heritage Treasures', Hobart Cathedral Website, 2016.

[9] *The Melbourne Courier*, 3 October 1845, p. 2.

[10] Quoted in L. C. Mickleborough, '*Victim of an 'Extraordinary Conspiracy'? Sir John Eardley Eardley-Wilmot Lieutenant Governor of Van Diemen's Land 1843-46*' PhD Thesis (University of Tasmania, 2011), p. 206.

[11] *Ibid.*, p. 212, citing official correspondence from Willson.

13 TAKING UP THE REINS

ISHOP WILLSON'S ARRIVAL, or rather the arrival of Fr Hall as his preferred Vicar General, caused some grumblings. A letter from a correspondent calling himself *Hibernicus*[1] expressed faint praise for the benign remarks directed to Fr Therry by the Revd Mr Hall at the Sunday service following his arrival the previous evening. As 'a comparative stranger', he pointed out, Hall could not know the full extent of Therry's contribution, and 'it is to be hoped the Bishop will use his influence to retain the services of the Vicar General, more especially as the number of clergymen is unexpectedly small'. Hibernicus was mistaken: Therry was no longer Vicar General, the Bishop's influence would be bent on removing him from further disservice, and the clergymen, though small in number (newspaper reports had led to the expectation of a party of thirteen), would be stamped in the Bishop's reforming mould. Furthermore, Therry showed no inclination to return to 'the land of his adoption' on the mainland even when the Colonial Secretary's Office ratified the change in Fr Therry's role a month later. The repercussions from this early confusion concerning Fr Therry's status overshadowed Bishop Willson's episcopacy for the next decade.

Of the three priests already on the island—Therry, Thomas Butler (who had come out with Ullathorne in 1838) and Cotham—Ambrose Cotham was the one most eligible for appointment to the new, full-time, post of Religious Instructor in the Penal Department, in December 1844. The ending of transportation to New South Wales and the redirection of all convict ships to Tasmania caused a major, though temporary, reversal of the trend towards a predominantly civil rather than convict society. As part of the restructuring of the system Cotham received a Government salary solely for work with convicts and kept a detailed timetable of his duties, the aim of which was to imple-

138   *The Indomitable Mr Cotham*

ment, in Bishop Willson's phrase, an 'efficient system of moral culture'[2] into a regime intended to reform and rehabilitate convicts. Cotham kept up his journal entries with uncharacteristic regularity during 1846 and 1847, either at the behest of his bishop or his paymasters.

Bishop Willson's first major ecclesiastical duties in Australia took him to Sydney. Archbishop Polding had been the presiding prelate at his episcopal ordination in Nottingham in October 1842 and he was frustrated by the delay before Willson arrived in the colony. The appointment of Francis Murphy to the see of Adelaide had also been made in 1842 and Polding was awaiting Willson's arrival before ordaining Murphy to the episcopate on 8 September 1844. Having acquired his two suffragan bishops Polding convened the inaugural Australian Provincial Synod which took place over 11, 12 and 13 September 1844. It introduced Cotham to policies which were specific to Australia but would also provide him with pastoral guidelines when his circumstances altered. The synod

> was called to promote Catholic unity and solidarity in a hostile sectarian environment, as well as to deal with internal organizational issues. Attended by the bishops of Sydney, Hobart and Adelaide and 33 priests of the colony, it was the first Catholic synod held with public solemnity in the British Dominions since the Reformation ... In regulating clerical life this synod recognized the itinerant, missionary nature of the Australian priesthood and, contrary to the Irish practice of distinguishing between parish priests and curates, determined that all priests in Australia should be of equal status, an egalitarian stance that both reflected and significantly influenced clerical life ... It also insisted on the celebration of the Eucharist being the central feature of the Australian mission, together with communion. It instructed travelling priests to always carry the consecrated host, to encourage frequent communion, and to promote individual confession before communion ... This synod also emphasised the sanctity of marriage,

Taking up the Reins 139

> and urged compassion and tact where marriages had been contracted without a priest. But no mention of mixed marriages between Catholics and non-Catholics was made, for although Polding was opposed to them, his principal concern was that Catholics living in de facto liaisons should convert them into marriages. He preferred a mixed marriage to no marriage at all.[3]

After only three months in Tasmania Bishop Willson did not have much choice of companion from his fledgling diocesan team. Hall had seniority as Vicar General but Cotham had much greater first-hand knowledge of the local situation. He, therefore, accompanied the Bishop to Sydney in mid-August, variously described as canon or consulting theologian to Bishop Willson and Synodal witness to the diocese of Hobart Town. The Synod was convened at St Mary's Cathedral, and Cotham had his first sight of what Polding had accomplished on the mainland while he toiled in obscurity in Tasmania. During his visit Bishop Willson laid the foundation stone of a new mortuary chapel in the Catholic burial ground at Parramatta, attended by Frs Gregory, Coffey (Dean of Windsor and also one of Willson's consulting theologians), and Cotham; it was one of the few occasions when Cotham took part in the life of the diocese of Sydney, although Polding was not present.[4]

Apart from Archbishop Polding, Cotham met other senior members of the new hierarchy: Francis Murphy, the newly consecrated Bishop of Adelaide, John McEncroe, James Goold, and Patrick Geoghegan. He also reacquainted himself with some of his former companions: Henry Gregory Gregory, Prior of the Cathedral and Secretary to the Synod; Bede Sumner, Procurator General to the Benedictine Mission; and William Benson, relieved of Adelaide and acting as Synodal witness for the Sydney Deanery. He also met for the first time some of the later Benedictine arrivals to the Australian mission such as Vincent Dowling. Together with members of the Franciscan and Augustinian Orders, and an increasing number of Irish priests, the clerical

140   *The Indomitable Mr Cotham*

mix would have given Cotham the intellectual stimulus and variety he had lacked in his religious life in Tasmania, in addition to underlining how far Polding's missionary team had moved from its Benedictine inception. Despite evidence to the contrary, he would have heard first-hand of the Archbishop's tenacious hopes for a strengthened Benedictine presence in Australia, from which he had been largely excluded for the past nine years. Soon after the Synod, Polding outlined the purpose behind St Mary's Seminary:

> We shall in our Institute come as near to the form of the Benedictine Institute as it existed in England and Wales before the Reformation, blending as it did in perfect harmony Episcopal authority with the Abbatial and producing missionaries who more zealously fulfilled their duties from the habitual renunciation of all things, the consequences of their monastic profession.[5]

The reality for Cotham, of his own and others' practise of habitual renunciation, was little different whether its motivation came from the profession of monastic vows or through obedience to the demands made by a diocesan bishop. Zealous commitment to the mission was not the prerogative of Benedictines.

Ambrose Cotham was not a man to be abashed by his surroundings but on one occasion at least in Sydney he would have felt especially confident. The 'usual weekly meeting of the St Patrick's Total Abstinence Society' was held in the saloon of Sydney's Royal Hotel, the largest meeting hall in the colony, chaired by its president, Fr John McEncroe.[6] Archbishop Polding and Bishop Willson were to be the honoured guests, but Cotham was there as a speaker, in his capacity as president of St Joseph's Teetotal Society in Launceston. On this occasion Cotham spoke of the benefits of total abstinence from alcohol, especially among the working classes. He was some way into 'a happy eulogium on the great founder of temperance, and on the majestic and wide-spreading triumph of total abstinence' when the 'revered dignitaries' arrived to claim the limelight. Both prelates spoke to

Taking up the Reins 141

the enthusiastic gathering, Bishop Willson's words being notably less triumphalist than the previous speakers' when he recalled meeting Fr Mathew who was called to restore to the inhabitants of Ireland 'comparative happiness and contentment' by means of abstention from alcohol. Bishop Willson's tone was altogether more emollient than Cotham was accustomed to hearing:

> He would beg to make one remark to those who had received the grace of total abstinence, and it was that they should not look down with scorn or censure on their fellow creatures, who may not have the moral courage to take the pledge, but that they should by kindness, good example, and Christian advice endeavour to dissuade their fellow men from the paths of intemperance, and thus by degrees, and with the blessing of God, induce them to adopt the total abstinence principle.[7]

The speech was a fine example of how the Bishop characteristically sought to temper a call to the highest standards with pragmatism and a gentle approach.

After the edification of a unified display of loyalty from the Synod's participants, Archbishop Polding and Vicar General McEncroe sailed for Hobart on 17 September with Bishop Willson and Fr Cotham to face a more hostile assembly. Willson blamed Polding for the lack of resolution regarding the debts on property that he had found on his arrival in Tasmania. Willson had been led to believe that he would arrive in Hobart free of any encumbrance from Fr Therry or diocesan debts; he was misled on both counts. The debt on church property was in the region of £3,000 and Therry refused to hand over the accounts or the title deeds until Willson accepted responsibility for the debt. The negotiations were fractious and prolonged. Polding remembered this particular occasion well and with lasting indignation:

> To my great astonishment on 27 September, between two and three in the afternoon, Your Lordship came to my room and very distinctly gave me to understand that as Archbishop I had no right to interfere in the temporal

concerns of your diocese ... that you had advisors on whose opinion and judgement you would rather act than mine—and much more of the same purpose. I made a note of this protest. It is signed by Mr McEncroe and myself.[8]

A measure of the divisiveness caused by Therry in Willson's bishopric is the Testimonial presented to Fr Therry while Willson was away in Sydney. It was apparently agreed upon at a meeting in July 1844, chaired by Joseph Reichenberg, but the collection of monies took some time. The testimonial spoke of the signatories' 'fullest and most entire approval' of Therry's conduct as a private individual and in the performance of public office, as a friend, a neighbour and a member of society.[9] They also hoped that if Fr Therry left Tasmania it would be for promotion elsewhere in the Church, a sentiment repeated in other sections of the press although never fulfilled.

The disputed matters in the diocese were patched up, temporarily, although Therry remained on the island; when called upon to speak up the junior clergy backed their bishop, an implicit criticism of the Archbishop's handling of the situation. The background dissension caused by Fr Therry had been constant since Cotham's arrival in 1835; it was something he, Ullathorne, and Archbishop Polding had learned to live with, but Bishop Willson was not prepared to tolerate the anomalous situation though it must have seemed an infuriating, and anachronistic, waste of his time and energy.

After the confrontations with Willson during a stay of just over a week, Polding and McEncroe travelled north to Launceston to make a long overdue pastoral visit to Cotham's mission. On the way they called on Edward Swarbreck Hall to discuss the hopes he had for the establishment of a new mission at Westbury and they could not fail to be impressed by the sincerity and integrity the doctor brought to all his enterprises. In Launceston yet another temperance meeting was attended, presided over by Fr Cotham: the regularity of the meetings was clearly one of the strengths of the movement. After Fr McEncroe reported on the

Taking up the Reins 143

New South Wales situation, two examples of the particular characteristics of the Tasmanian movement were given: Isaac Sherwin, the Wesleyan Methodist, spoke of the importance of teetotalism to morals and economics, and the Revd Mr Price emphasised the peaceful nature of the cause which fostered meeting on common ground. The Launceston Catholic congregation presented an appreciative Address to the Archbishop before he embarked for the next stage of his pastoral tour.

Following the departure of Archbishop Polding and his Vicar General, Cotham received a brief letter from McEncroe from Melbourne, asking him to forward the Archbishop's 'rochette'[10] which had been left behind. He and Polding crossed the Bass Strait to Port Phillip, for the Archbishop's first visit to the expanding city of Melbourne. There they had intercepted Bishop Francis Murphy en route to his see at Adelaide. Polding's itinerary took him to Geelong, Port Fairy, and Portland Bay, undertaking first-hand the mission work (*sans* rochet) he was so committed to. The *Geelong Advertiser*[11] praised him as 'the nearest approach to the character of a perfect and blameless christian'. In his letter McEncroe cordially asked Cotham how his plans for building a school and Temperance Hall were progressing; after being subjected to Bishop Willson's ire, it was satisfying to correspond with an apparently compliant priest who was doing exactly what was expected of him. With episcopal encouragement behind him, Cotham opened a building subscription fund at St Joseph's, Launceston before the end of the year, his final act as pastor of the Catholics in the northern district for whom he had worked hard and travelled many miles to serve since his earliest days in Tasmania.

In his first full year in office, Bishop Willson wrote over fifty letters to the convict department as it impacted on his Church's ministry to Catholic convicts. Most pressing was the need for more clergy and catechists, but there were also complaints about poor buildings and accommodation for prisoners, and requests for an adequate amount of Catholic religious literature as a resource for religious instruction and improvement. In February

1845 Willson applied for six additional priests and extra religious instructors to attend the spiritual needs of convicts in probation stations, the Coal Mines, and at Launceston. As William Willson was himself only the sixth priest to work full time in Tasmania since 1804 he immediately grasped the need for an exponential expansion in all areas of the mission, free and convict. The demand for religious instruction throughout the decade underlines the basic level at which pastoral ministry was undertaken. In Tasmania the opportunity for mission to Aboriginal people had been lost; the thousands of Irish convicts who came into the island after 1840 presented a non-native population in need of education, cultural preparation, and religious training to fit them for the fluid society which they had become part of under duress.

Nevertheless, progress was dogged by history. Archbishop Polding followed up his unsatisfactory visit to Hobart by dispatching Henry Gregory in April 1845 to attempt mediation between the two senior men, Willson and Therry. Instead of reconciliation, Gregory angered Willson by suggesting the *impasse* would be resolved if the Bishop gave up his mitre. His lack of diplomacy, amounting to impudence, earned him Willson's abiding dislike, and he joined his voice to others who were later to call for the removal from power of Gregory, Polding's favourite son. Gregory travelled on the schooner *Waterlily* with Fr Bede Sumner; the latter's two-week stay would have pleased Cotham greatly as the two Benedictines shared opinions about their respective bishops. Meanwhile Fr Gregory was engaged in antagonising Bishop Willson, his reluctant host, until his departure in June.[12]

The two antagonists, Willson and Therry, met with Mr W. Offor who did his best to understand Therry's muddled accounts in consultation with Solicitor General Fleming. He came up with the sum of £1,000 as a compromise solution to the disputed debt, a sum which would leave Therry out of pocket, he claimed, but which he was willing to accept. A group, Catholic and Protestant, calling themselves The Friends of the Revd Mr J. J. Therry, met on 28 August with a view to taking steps, in conjunction with a

Taking up the Reins 145

similar group in Sydney, 'to raise a fund for assisting to liquidate the debts due on St Joseph's Church'.[13] Therry read a letter to the meeting, written that day by Bishop Willson, expressly forbidding him to solicit subscriptions 'under any plea whatsoever' for St Joseph's, and the meeting agreed to suspend fundraising until Therry could question the Bishop further.[14] Offor's letter was also read to the meeting. It was not the end of the matter.

> Willson's attitude towards the Sydney Benedictine leadership had been permanently soured, convinced as he was that his ordeal would have been terminated much earlier had Polding kept his promises ... [and] he was firmly of the opinion that Gregory lacked prudence, judgement, diplomacy and other qualities needed for a role of leadership.[15]

Nearly eighteen months after his arrival in the colony Bishop Willson found it necessary to issue a Pastoral Letter on 8 October 1845 concerning the pecuniary affairs of St Joseph's, Hobart, following a meeting with the Catholic clergy the preceding day. It was couched in a 'quiet, amiable spirit'[16] but was unbending in its refusal to let Therry escape censure altogether. Regarding the £3,000 of liabilities outstanding on the church, £1,000 of which was the disputed personal liability of Fr Therry, even the Solicitor General, Mr Fleming, who had been asked to advise the church authorities, found the documents 'too confused to furnish data sufficiently distinct for him to give his opinion'.[17] In public, Bishop Willson allowed that Fr Therry 'had fallen into errors of judgement in this business especially from the very imperfect system of keeping accounts' and his integrity could not be impugned;[18] in private his attitude towards Therry was less lenient. When Fr Cotham embarked on his own major building project ten years later his system of record keeping was meticulous and he avoided any suggestion of mismanagement; no one embroiled in the Therry affair could fail to learn lessons from it. Cotham's journal entries make no comment about Archbishop Polding but the atmosphere in Bishop Willson's household was reminiscent of his own time of trial and frustration almost ten years earlier. In 1836 he had been obliged to turn to and trust his own judgement and conscience, risking unknown consequences, when he challenged Polding's failure to act. In 1845, Cotham stood behind Willson, a far weightier opponent to Polding, but he was still ambivalent about the fairness of the treatment accorded to Therry.

Following his appointment as Religious Instructor for the Convict Department at the end of December 1844 Cotham moved to the Bishop's residence in Hobart in February 1845 and became part of his household, resuming a communal lifestyle after a decade of being a lone missioner. Until 1847 the Bishop used the presbytery at the back of St Joseph's church; Fr Therry owned an extensive property nearby which he shared with his brother and sister.[19] Bishop Willson replaced Fr Therry as the senior prelate at the 'second church' in Hobart, St Joseph's, which he used as his pro-Cathedral while the 'first church', St Mary's, was very slowly completed.

On the feast of St Luke, 18 October 1844, Br Luke Levermore OC was ordained to the priesthood, on his 47th birthday, by the Bishop. He stayed in Hobart at the beginning of his convict duties before moving to a difficult posting at Darlington Station on Maria Island. In Sydney one of Archbishop Polding's priorities had been the establishment of a school and seminary, but only one priest—Fr Thomas Butler—had subsequently been sent from Sydney to augment the Tasmanian clergy and Daniel O'Connell had been lost to Sydney. Fr Levermore was, therefore, the first Catholic priest to be ordained in Tasmania, for Tasmania. Fr Butler was transferred to Launceston in place of Cotham and Fr William Dunne[20] came out from Sydney to take over in Richmond. The memory of these two priests, Cotham's contemporaries, has somewhat overshadowed the achievement of Cotham during his pioneer years in Richmond and Launceston. But this was not foreseeable in 1844 when the two Irish priests began their long tenure in their respective parishes. They became justifiably invaluable to Bishop Willson (and later to his successor) in the

Taking up the Reins 147

decades when references to convictism, and those associated with it, were avoided as Tasmania shaped a new identity.

It would seem that Ambrose Cotham enjoyed his new company and the responsibility he had for teaching and mentoring the junior men. His knowledge of local customs supplemented Willson's experience and a variety of duties were devolved to him for the first two years as the convict chaplaincy became embedded in the probation system. Among a dozen small sheets of loose-leaf papers Cotham had written brief guidelines of the sort delivered at novices' daily lessons or conferences. For the first time in many years he was able to put himself back into a quasi-monastic routine, this time as teacher rather than pupil. So the following subjects were discussed:

> The children must not receive instruction in the houses of the Priests, but in the churches. Great evils may result from a contrary practice. Liguori would not allow women to go to the house of any ecclesiastic whatsoever to be instructed, never one alone!!

> Charity must be regulated: if I have not enough to give to my own poor, how can I give to others?

> One of my chief thoughts in reference to the church and the priests attached to it is to introduce among us an ecclesiastical community life. Immense advantages will easily result from such a manner of living. It would be wise therefore to draw up a few constitutions, which we may immediately begin to observe with unanimous contentment. Meditation and little hours—Mass. As to the service of the house, to wait at table—each one for one day, for some time they serve in the kitchen week by week—to read at table, week and week about, 2 thirds of the meal, the other third to be spent in proposing some moral doubt or case of conscience. As to the service of the church, all to take part in sweeping it every other day—after dinner to sing Vespers.

If, indeed, he did propose the above to his brethren in the Bishop's household, it would have been welcomed by Brother Luke, who seems to have been a meek soul, and taken up with enthusiasm by George Hunter as something akin to proper seminary life as practised in England or on the Continent. Cotham had lived as a solitary missioner for ten years; it had not turned him against the merits of a life in common, and he knew that a formal framework supported rather than constricted individuals' efforts to form a harmonious group.

Ambrose Cotham probably accompanied the Vicar General, William Hall, on his tour of the midland districts in February 1845 where their 'mild and imposing manner' impressed the *Cornwall Chronicle*.[21] Hall took his turn with the unenviable task of attending executions, even on New Year's Day, 1845. The press report is sober and emphasises the propriety, speed, and lack of drama attending the hanging of the two men, one Catholic and the other Protestant, convicted of attempted murder at Port Arthur convict station. 'The crowd was not very great, consisting primarily of workmen going to their breakfast; we did not observe one female among the spectators.'[22] The police formed a cordon around the few onlookers to prevent any unseemly interruption, and it is their presence that most impresses the reporter: 'a finer, or, indeed, smarter body of Police we never saw, even in England'.[23] Even an execution could be turned into an occasion for reminding the populace that Tasmania could leave behind its shameful past.

The tension caused by the aspirations of civil society and the necessities arising from the probation system is caught in the report concerning the Penitentiary Chapel used for parochial services in the Anglican Trinity parish. From February 1845 it was put at the disposal of the Church of England convict chaplain for morning and evening services and the Catholic chaplain for the intervening times on Sundays, the general public being excluded.[24] Trinity parish itself had been raising subscriptions for its own church building since 1841 and it was still unfinished: giving priority to convicts over free civilians in this circumstance was particularly galling, and moreover Catholic convicts were being permitted to take the place of Anglican worshippers. Nor

Taking up the Reins 149

was this an isolated example of divergence between the claims of colonial and convict populations. The Report for 1844 of the Finance Committee on the Revenue and Expenditure of the Colonial Department covered all departments under the Colonial Office's remit. This included the courts, constabulary, and gaols but not convict establishments. However, it reported:

> The Gaols of the Colony are in want of repairs in every case, and in many of enlargement; and on looking to this item of expense, we fear that it must be considerably increased rather than diminished.
>
> The expense of Religious Instruction is one-sixth part of the Revenue; and at the present moment is out of all proportion to the want of the free portion of the community, and the very limited means of the Colony. But, though the aggregate expense is large the salary of the individual cannot be alleged to be more than men of education, expected to fill a certain rank, are entitled to receive. Living as we do among a Convict population, we cannot recommend the reduction of the salaries of Religious Instructors ... But we venture to urge the propriety of refusing all fresh applications for assistance under the Church Act; and also to call attention to the circumstance of the Clergy, particularly the Roman Catholics and the Wesleyans, performing much duty that is expressly convict, while they are paid wholly out of Colonial funds. For instance, all the Roman Catholic Clergy paid from the Colonial chest are far more engaged in attending on the Convicts at the Penitentiaries, Hospitals, and Probation Stations than they are in giving spiritual aid to the free. So too of the Wesleyans, to whom is allowed £500 a year, and to whom the Home Government contributes nothing. It is no doubt contemplated in the Convict Estimates to provide all religious instruction for the Convicts; but in practice it is impossible for the colony to refuse its aid, even more liberally than its limited means will justify. To do otherwise would be a reproach.[25]

On the one hand the Finance Committee lamented, but could not openly criticise, the gentlemanly manner in which the large number of Protestant ministers expected to be maintained. For the most part they saw their time in Tasmania as limited to ten years or less and, expecting to be at a disadvantage when they returned to the British Isles having lost contact with the network of patronage for livings, they were not prepared to take a lesser salary. Instead the Committee aimed criticism at the vanishingly small number of Catholic and Wesleyan Methodist ministers who, having been appointed by the Colonial Office in London, found themselves devoting an increasing amount of their time to the convict institutions under the post-assignment regime in addition to their civilian duties. The role of Religious Instructor was an integral part of convict discipline and could not be skimped if the Probation system was to be safely sustained, as explained at the outset in 1843:

> An officer, entitled Comptroller of Convicts, to be appointed to the charge of the probation parties, and at his suggestion alone are relaxations to be granted to any member of them. The estimated number in those gangs will be about 8000. These will be divided into gangs from 250 to 300, employed on works of public utility; they will be placed in such vicinity that they shall be under the efficient control of a single superintendent, but not so near that they can communicate together.

> Subordinate to the controller for the administration of the gangs, will be the ministers of religion—Church of England, Roman-Catholic, or Wesleyan—liable to suspension at the will of the controller, subject to the governor's decision. An overseer, and subordinates for each gang. The controller will establish rules subject to the governor's approval. Weekly returns will be made to the controller by the minister of religion and overseer, in which shall be comprised the good or bad conduct of each man, these shall be reduced to a system of numerical rotation, and from them shall be compiled such a character as will, at once, show

Taking up the Reins 151

how far he may be entitled to the indulgence of the crown, or enhanced rigour of punishment. To further this object contemporaneous records are to be kept.[26]

Religious instructors, teachers, and overseers were, at the very least, 'persons employed in the convict department',[27] and at worst, convict guards, a role inevitably compromising the clergy's primary role as pastor. They were further separated from parochial clergy by drawing an enhanced salary from the Convict Department of the Colonial Office. The very term 'religious instructor' signalled a serious point of contention which had been strenuously debated by Bishop Nixon on behalf of all denominations. Since the chaplains for convicts were exclusively under the Colonial Office's civil jurisdiction, Nixon refused to take any responsibility for them, even in church matters, rather than share it. Lieutenant-Governor Eardley-Wilmot therefore devised the title 'religious instructor' so that ordination would not be seen as a necessary qualification for the post. As a compromise, Archdeacon Marriott was appointed superintendent of convict chaplains acting under the Bishop's authority. Bishop Willson took no part in these arguments between established Church and State, and 'pursued a more yielding course'[28] towards the *fait accompli* of civil jurisdiction over Catholic convict chaplains. Neither did his reputation suffer on account of his perceived mildness of manner but instead won him a measure of tolerance leading to respect.

Notes

[1] *Colonial Times* (Hobart), 21 May 1844, p. 3.
[2] W. T. Southerwood, 'Pioneer of Justice' in *The Catholic Leader* 29 October 2006, catholicleader.com.au/news/pioneer_of_justice_42267 [Accessed online 27.7.2017]
[3] P. J. Wilkinson, 'Catholic Synods in Australia, 1844–2011'. http://v2catholic.com/bloggers/pwilkinson/2011/Synods [Accessed online 27.7.2017]
[4] *Morning Chronicle* (Sydney), 28 August 1844, p. 2.
[5] O. Thorpe CP, *The First Mission to the Australian Aborigines* (Sydney:

150   *The Indomitable Mr Cotham*

Pellegrini and Co, 1950), p. 193. Polding to William Leigh, 7 January 1845.

[6] Among other impressive details of John McEncroe's life is his personal struggle against alcoholism, eventually successfully overcome.

[7] *Morning Chronicle* (Sydney), 28 August 1844, p. 2.

[8] Polding to Willson, 4 October 1848. Cited in F. O'Donoghue, *The Bishop of Botany Bay; The Life of John Bede Polding, Australia's First Catholic Archbishop* (Sydney: Angus and Robertson Publishers, 1982), p. 74.

[9] *Colonial Times* (Hobart), 24 September 1844, p. 2.

[10] A rochet is a white vestment similar to a surplice, distinguished by more closely fitting sleeves. It is usually reserved for bishops and other prelates.

[11] *Geelong Advertiser*, 24 October 1844, p. 2.

[12] *Morning Chronicle* (Sydney), 19 April 1845, p. 3, 14 May 1845, p. 3, and *The Observer* (Hobart), 19 June 1845, p. 2, for shipping intelligence.

[13] *The Observer* (Hobart), 5 September 1845, p. 1.

[14] *Colonial Times* (Hobart), 2 September 1845, p. 3.

[15] C. Dowd OP, *Rome in Australia: The Papacy and Conflict in the Australian Catholic Missions, 1834–1884* (Leiden: Boston, Brill, 2008), p. 211.

[16] *The Cornwall Chronicle* (Launceston), 1 November 1845, p. 295.

[17] *Ibid.*, p. 295.

[18] *Ibid.*, 29 November 1845, p. 377.

[19] Between 1847 and 1872 the official residence of the Catholic Bishop of Hobart was 218 Macquarie Street, also known as Stephenville, being the former home of Alfred Stephen, Solicitor General for Tasmania, for whom it was built in 1825. It was leased to the government from 1840 for five years and used as the Queen's School to early 1844. The listed house is now part of the campus of the Collegiate College, 212–218 Macquarie Street.

[20] William John Dunne, 1814–1883, was born near Kilkenny, Ireland. Having been recruited by Bishop Polding he completed his studies in England and was ordained in Sydney by Polding in 1843.

[21] *Colonial Times* (Hobart), 11 February 1845, p. 3, citing *The Cornwall Chronicle* (Launceston).

[22] *Ibid.*, p. 3.

[23] *Launceston Advertiser*, 3 January 1845, p. 2.

[24] *The Courier* (Hobart), 25 February 1845, p. 3.

[25] *Ibid.*, 6 March 1845, p. 2.

[26] *The Cornwall Chronicle* (Launceston), 10 June 1843, p. 2.

[27] *Ibid.*, p. 2.

[28] *The Courier* (Hobart), 16 September 1846, p. 2.

14 IN HIS OWN WORDS

By his own admission Ambrose Cotham was not the best of diarists; he restarted his narrative a number of times and then quickly lost interest:

1868—January 13—Commenced this journal in this old book because in a few days I shall as usual get tired of it have nothing to enter and discontinue it—but at least it is well to enter the Masses for whom said.

The most complete series of entries was made in 1846, when every month is accounted for except October when he was away from Tasmania. The page starts with a flourish, *Journal for the Year 1846*, but the first entry suggests it is a continuation rather than a completely fresh beginning: 'Prevented from boarding the Anson on account of the stormy weather'. And so it continues for the year with regular references to the weather, especially when raining, without explanatory notes about the places referred to, and often giving the briefest of entries about what he was doing. That he kept up the journal for a whole year suggests he was following instructions from the Bishop or the Comptroller General to keep a record, in effect his timesheet, of his engagements. The period of his career as convict chaplain is covered by his own journal in one notebook as follows:

- 1 January—10 September 1846;
- a page of expenses for November and December 1846; followed by
- single entries on two pages: 'Tu 18: The Works of William Ellery Channing DD, complete in one volume, Glasgow, Richard Griffin and Co, 1840' and 'Sermon on Sunday Schools by Tim Neve DD; On Fasting by the same author'; followed by

- the opening page for 1 January 1868, quoted above, and the rest of January 1868 (this includes a page heading 'October', crossed through, obviously prepared in advance for October 1846); followed by
- December 1846; January 1847; evidence of torn-out pages; a fragment of a (?) sermon; March 11—April 13; followed by
- 20—28 October 1848; followed by
- 13—28 January 1851.

His routine as he recorded it gives an insight into the volume and variety of work he was tasked to do and it is evident that his responsibilities far exceeded those he received when he was appointed. In a letter to the Comptroller General in February 1849 he made the point that his duties on appointment had been confined to the *Anson* and the Queen's Orphan School, although he also took responsibility for the convicts' General Hospital, with its male and female wards on different sites. Twelve months after his appointment it is clear he was already doing much more than these three duties. Inevitably he was called on by Bishop Willson to support and, to a considerable extent, set up the system of Catholic chaplaincy to the probation regime into which later chaplains were inducted as they arrived on the island or completed their training. His account of the service conducted on 5 January 1846 at Port Arthur reads like a training manual for a junior clergyman. The entries for January 1846 are characteristic of the whole year: sociable occasions merit a mention, as does his brother Lawrence's company for part of the ferry journey to Port Arthur on 2 January. The state of the weather and petty expenses are usually noted, as well as concern for his horse and his own occasional indisposition.

In His Own Words   155

Journal for the Year 1846

January

Thurs 1: Prevented from boarding the Anson on account of the stormy weather. The Revd. Mr Bond in town from Monday last. Wishes me to supply at P. Arthur.

Fri 2: Attended the G. Hospital

Left Hobart at 4o'c for Port Arthur on the Pony. Lawrence accop. Kangaroo Point: Rough sea: Horses to jump 4ft into the Boat: reached the Carlton 1st Ferry. Small boat: swum the horse. Awful weather: the Night at Dawson's Inn. B.T. off [Divine Office]. B. & Horse 6/7½d &c 1/- People civil Ferry 2/6 & 6d.

Satur 3: Started at 7o'c. Breakfast at Maginnis.[1] Reached the Sounds, Kennedy's at 12o'c. Men 2/- Reached Port Arthur at 5o'c. Rain: Wet through: Mr O.Halloran [catechist] dined with me: off B[ed].

Sun 4: Prayers at the Hospital with O.Halloran: First Mass at Point Puer: Ser: &c

Returned to P.A. for Service at 11o'c.

Vest in Alb and Stole and go into the Pulpit and on knees and say 'Come Holy Ghost &c', then rise up and sing 'Let us adore' then kneel down and say Pater, Ave, Credo, Confiteor, acts of Faith, Hope, Charity &c and the Scriptural Litany Page 293. Then sit down whilst the Choir sing—after the Choir finishes say prayer before Mass as in Garden of the Soul Page 291. Then go from Pulpit and say Mass.

After Mass go from Pulpit in Alb and Stole and say Te Deum', p301, Prayers for the dead and sick, p296 then the Choir again sing—

After the Choir has finished say Prayer before Sermon & then read Epistle and Gospel, and work away at them like thunder and bricks.

Evening Prayers in Pulpit in Stole and Surplice.

'Come Holy Ghost' & then Choir sings, after that on knees Pater, Ave, &c and Litany p321: then the Choir sings again. After that seated say seven Penitential Psalms or Psalms for Sundays and Holy days, the Choir always singing 'Glory be to the Father'—and then Litany of the Saints; after which the Choir again sing—then say Prayer before Sermon, then speak as soft as you like or as hard as you please. Prayer in conclusion.

On Week Days

Morning Prayers at ¼ to 5o'c in the yard for about 8 minutes—& in the evening at ½ p 6o/c. Visit the Cells and Hospital at whatever hour you please. Visit the School or Chain Gang at 11o/c. Prayers. Some instruction or entertaining History. On Friday night immediately after Evening Prayers go to School for Confessions.

Mon 5: Prayers at ¼ to 5. 11o/c Prayers to Chain Gang till 12o/c. Card at Mr Champs. Lieutenant—and Ensign Cumberland called. Dined at Mr. Champs.

Tues 6: Prayers &c. Horse not fed during 24 Hours, no bed. Sick call from Wedge Bay Soldiers wife Mrs White.

Wed 7: Journey to Wedge Bay. Ad. com. to Soldiers wife, stopped at Mr J. I. White whose wife is a convert: he is the Protestant Catechist.

Thurs 8: Walk with Mr. W. after dinner returned to Port. A. visited sick &c &c

Fri 9 The usual duties P[reached] Chrisostoms works &c

Satur 10

Sun 11: The same as the 4th

Mon 12

Tues 13

Weds 14

In His Own Words

Thurs 15: Sick call signalized from Wedge Bay at 7o'c

Fri 16: Journey to Wedge Bay. Ad. All the Sac[raments] to man in Hospital. Started for the Mines at 11o'c arrived at ½p 1o'c. Visited Mr Boyle, Capt Young's Lady, Mr Bachelor. Solitary cells. Dined at 6o'c at Wedge Bay. Evening with Captain Biggar and the Doctor of the Station. rain. sore throat.

Satur 17: Called on Mr Wigmor[e] the Superintendent. Vin. Reached P.A. by 12o'c. Rain. Wet through P.W.N. Mr O.Halloran dined with me, and stopped the night.

Sun 18: Not well. Service as on the 4th.

Mon 19: Prayers &c Medicine. Signal from Superintendent Wedge Bay to inter the Body of—[*sic*]

Tues 20: Started for Wedge Bay at ½p5o'c. Rain. Rain. Preached to the assembled Catholics over the Body. Funeral Service &c. Returned to Port Arthur, the Revd. Mr Keating[2] arrived per Steamer. Dinn[er] Father Bond arrived at 8o'c. Wet. Much rain.

Wed 21: Rain. Ride to Point Puer.

Thurs 22: Rain. Pleasant evening with Keating and Bond.

Fri 23: Left Port Arthur at 12o'c. Kennedys at 3. Maginnis at 7. Pt T. of B. Mutton Bird Feathers [? badly cleaned mutton bird feathers in the pillows]. Bad Inn. 11/.

~~Dodge's Ferry Kangaroo Point at 11o'c~~

Satur 24: Dogs [Dodges] Ferry; Kangaroo Point 11o'c Hobart at 2o'c. Conf. &c

Sun 25 Celebrated Divine Service and preached at the Female Assignment Depot. Brickfields, at the Q.O. School, & Anson.

Mon 26: G. Hospital

Tues 29: Service at the Female Ass. Depot Brickfields

Wed 28: D. S. &c at the Queen's Orphan School & Anson.

Thurs 29: Attended the General Hospital

Fri 30: Service at O. School & H.M.S. Anson

Satur 31: Religious Instruction on board the Anson

Fr Cotham's journal entries are usually a little fuller at the beginning of the year, before he loses interest. He may have made the colourful entry on 4 January to be used for instruction with Br Luke Levermore OC and George Hunter, but he also followed the routine himself since the entry for Sundays 11 and 18 January reads 'The same as the 4th'. When he is back in Hobart on Sunday 25th there is no further mention of this schema. There is more than a hint in the entry written at Port Arthur that Cotham enjoyed the opportunity afforded by preaching for using his voice as an instrument when playing with language. He recognised that words and style of delivery are both important in conveying the meaning—intellectual and emotional—of the content, and his efforts were noted approvingly more than once in local newspapers. Bishop Willson personally attended to his students' training for ordination, using Cotham to supplement their education and act as mentor to men who were either not much younger than himself or considerably older. It was a duty he probably enjoyed, as he enjoyed all social occasions.

Since Cotham was officially chaplain only to the *Anson* and the Queen's Orphan School, although he also served the General, Male and Female, Hospitals in Hobart, the entry for January 1846 should have been atypical, mentioning as it does the stations on the Tasman Peninsula at Port Arthur, Puer Point, and the Coal Mines, but in February he was again away from Hobart travelling to Darlington Point Station on Maria Island off the west coast, and later to the Insane Asylum inland at New Norfolk. Although these journeys undoubtedly added to his workload and involved hard travelling they provided a variety of company and changes of scene. Weeks such as these told on his physical strength and health; the weeks that saw him confined to the routines of Hobart drained him emotionally and mentally.

In His Own Words 159

Sun 15 [February]: Divine Service and preached at Richmond [on the way back from Spring Bay] and at the Anson.

Mon 16: Indisposed.

Tues 17: D.S. [Divine Service] R.I. [Religious Instruction] at F. Assig. D. Brickfields [the Female Assignment Depot at Brickfields housed the Female Convict Hospital]. Attended the Gen/Male Hospital.

Wed 18: D.S. & R.I. at Anson and O. School.

Thurs 19: S. & R.I. at F.A.D. Brickfields. Attended Hospital.

Fri 20: D.S. & R.I. at Anson and Queen's Orphan School.

Satur 21: Attended the General Hospital.

Sun 22: Celebrated and preached at the Anson, at Orphan School, and the F.A. Depot Brickfields.

Mon 23: Sick call to New Norfolk Hospital. Visited the Asylum and Invalid Station; celebrated D.S. &c &c. Returned to Hobart.

Tues 24: Attended G./M./Hospital

Weds 25: Celebrated at the Anson. Engaged in Investigation from 9 till 4o'c.

Thurs 26: Engaged on an investigation on board the Anson from 9 till 4o'c.

Fri 27: 9 till 2o'c on Investigation at the Anson; Service &c at the Queen's O. School.

Satur 28: Went in carriage with Mrs and Miss Garrett on board the Anson. From 9 till 3o'c engaged in investigation on Board the Anson. Attended G. Hospital.

There were many occasions for investigations into serious matters at penal institutions but the following month Fr Cotham was engaged in one which was petty and time consuming but unavoidable.

Notes

[1]   Fr Patrick Maginnis was ordained in Sydney in September 1843. After a period as convict chaplain he went to the mission at Yass.

[2]   Fr Jerome Keating OSB, from Ireland, and Fr Hall VG travelled to Sydney on 5 February 1846; if Keating had been considering a move to Tasmania to join the convict department this visit did not persuade him.

15 HMS ANSON

THE NUMBER OF male convicts undergoing assessment and hard labour in gangs before earning their ticket-of-leave necessitated a dramatic increase in the provision of secure accommodation available to the probation system. For female convicts the system meant being assessed, segregated into one of three categories, and prepared for hire for outside work if appropriate, usually after a period of six months' close observation and training. In the women's hiring depots there was a relentless through flow of new arrivals from the first stages, together with the return of repeat offenders or failed hirings. Existing stations were expanded, mothballed stations such as Darlington Point were brought back into service and many new stations were built, all using convict hard labour as part of the punishment regime.

The Cascades Women's Factory near Hobart was sited in a cold valley at the base of Mount Wellington, out of sight but not inconveniently distant from the town. During its course of operation as a Female Factory from 1828 to 1856 it was enlarged and developed but never overcame its notorious reputation. It was chronically overcrowded, holding five hundred women in 1842—more than double its capacity—and press of sheer numbers undermined its purpose. There was a lack of industry, despite the substantial amount of labour used to service its own infrastructure and that of nearby penal institutions. The separation of the three classes of prisoner—crime, probation, and assignable, differentiated in part by the clothing and diet allotted to each class—was inadequately practised despite being a core principle of the system.

Disease was prevalent and in the nurseries the infant mortality rate, consequent on a high birth rate, was estimated in 1838 to be one in four. Despite numerous enquiries little was done to alleviate conditions until Dr Edward Swarbreck Hall demonstrated, by epidemiological rigour, the effects of meagre diet, restricted space, foul air, and poor hygiene in the 1850s. The factories were intended to be self-sufficient institutions where various workshops would produce saleable goods or services, chiefly needlework or laundering, and women would learn household skills by working in the hospital, nursery, laundry, and cook houses. Hard labour 'at the washtub' was a particularly harsh form of punishment, intended to be a means of moral reform when coupled with education and spiritual instruction. The women were housed in dormitories or solitary punishment cells and guards and other staff lived on site. Space was also allocated for general education and religious instruction and the ideal was for a designated chapel to be available for regular divine worship.

Following reports to the British Government in 1842 of serious overcrowding in the women's factories, it was decided in 1843 that a large house of correction should be built near Hobart to address the failings. However, political and financial reluctance to commit to the plans downgraded proposals for a purpose-built institution to the temporary use of a prison hulk taken out from Gravesend. Thus, HMS *Anson*, formerly a naval quarantine ship and then a transport vessel, sailed from Gravesend in September 1843, carrying five hundred male prisoners and over three hundred crew and soldiers.[1] On arrival in Hobart Town on 4 February 1844 the *Anson* was refitted as a prison hulk, with four 'wards' on each of the three decks; the existing rigging and stores were sold for £12,000. After two months the ship received its complement of approximately five hundred women transportees from the convict ships *Woodbridge* and the *Angelina*, and was towed out of sight and moored in Prince of Wales Bay on the River Derwent,[2] a site insisted on by Dr and Mrs Bowden, Superintendent and Matron, in preference to the less suitable Oyster Cove chosen by the Convict Department.

Cotham's Journal, Hobart, March 1846.

The senior staff for the *Anson* were recruited in 1843 and arrrived in Hobart in December 1843 on the *Woodbridge*, just a few weeks after the *Anson*. The choice of staff, in particular the matron Phillipa Bull Bowden *née* Powell, was confirmation that the proposed new institution was intended to be a model reformatory in the probation system. Mrs Bowden had been employed at Hanwell Pauper Lunatic Asylum, Middlesex. The first Medical Superindent of Hanwell (1831 to 1838), Dr Sir William Ellis, introduced his own Therapy of Employment whereby inmates were encouraged to follow their existing trade or skill, or be otherwise employed, to bring structure into their lives, restore their self-respect, and strengthen the links with the patient's life before illness. The third Medical Superintendent, and later Visiting Physician (1839 to 1852), Dr John Connolly, built on Ellis's practise of occupational therapy by abolishing the use of all mechanical restraints to restrain violent behaviour. More humane methods of restraint—protective clothing, padded rooms, seclusion, and sedatives—were used for even the most behaviourally disturbed patients. Phillipa Bowden was highly commended by Dr Connolly as his Assistant and Matron of the Asylum and she was more highly qualified for the work than her husband, Edward Bowden, whom she married in 1841. In addition, she had connections with Elizabeth Fry, the British Society for Promoting the Reformation of Female Prisoners, and the British Ladies' Committee, all of which, justifiably, gave her opinions added weight.

Dr Bowden and Mrs Bowden were appointed Superintendent and Matron of the *Anson* with a joint salary of £500, supplemented by Dr Bowden's salary of £300 for his role as Medical Inspector. Bowden's 14 year-old daughter Amelia accompanied them but she did not relish the work or lifestyle and eloped at the age of eighteen. The Bowdens were also able to take a core staff from Hanwell: the chaplain the Revd Mr George Giles, who travelled with his wife and two young daughters; male and female nurses and wardens; and a housekeeper. Some of the staff went as married couples: George and Sarah Hislet, Edward and Sarah Pearce, John and Eliza Serviss, and Robert and Sarah Wright. With the addition of the three Richardson sisters, Elizabeth, Mary, and Sarah and three Holdich sisters, Jane, Martha, and Susannah/Sarah, the staff formed a close-knit group. Rather than lose their daughters, the Holdich parents, Matthew and Catherine, decided in their mid-sixties to take their chances in Tasmania and emigrated with the *Anson* group; the change seems to have done them no harm. Most of the original staff worked on the

HMS Anson 165

Anson until it was taken out of service in 1849, having seen nearly four thousand women, from twenty-five ships, pass through the six-month probationary period before onward movement to the Cascades, Brickfields, Launceston, or Ross Hiring Factories. The subsequent lives of the staff in Tasmania and elsewhere indicate their choice of employment had been a good move for the most part and in no way restricted their opportunities.

Ambrose Cotham was an integral member of the staff although he was not resident on board, unlike the Anglican chaplain George Giles who had family quarters on the ship. Giles might have wondered if the conditions were responsible for the death of his 10-year-old daughter Anna Martha a year later.[3] On a return visit to England, when the *Anson* had been operational for two years, Bishop Willson spoke at a meeting, in his customary mild manner, about government ambivalence towards the floating reformatory, an ambivalence that he believed compromised its efficiency:

> The female part of the convicts, who certainly claim our strongest sympathies, are not placed up and down the country, but are first detained in a ship. There is a 74-gun vessel, the Anson, which was sent four years since, to save the expense of building a penitentiary. That ship has contained as many as between 500 and 600 females at once and I am shocked to say that their ages were from 15 to 80. Here was a task of difficulty to perform, to fit them, in a moderate time, to be good members of society, for many of them, as you may suppose, had been very, very unfortunate. The government was anxious to reform them. The expenses of the ship have been great indeed; not perhaps too great, but I mention this to show you that government have done all they can for this unfortunate class. Probably, when they have obtained their liberty, they have succeeded as well as might have been calculated upon. Any breach of discipline in that land is very severely punished.[4]

166 *The Indomitable Mr Cotham*

It was the Bowdens who had to deal directly with the lack of official support. In their reports to the Comptroller General and to the Parliamentary Committee it is clear that they were dedicated to the principle of moral reformation, and the priority of this principle distinguished the regime of the *Anson* from the punitive practices found at the Cascades Female Factory and Brickfields Depot since 'reformation and punishment cannot be allowed to mix; a distinct chain of feeling is set up by each process; one all hope; the other all recklessness, and in the jostle reformation is damaged'.[5]

Bishop Willson and the Bowdens shared the same approach towards the treatment of women convicts and there is nothing to suggest that Fr Cotham was not in full agreement with them. Certainly he shared their frustration at the carping attitude of the Convict Department. Within six months of beginning their work the Bowdens invited visitors from the public to inspect the *Anson*; a favourable report was published, commenting on the cleanliness, health and industriousness of the women 'as far as the very limited means at Mrs Bowden's command will allow'.[6] The impressive appearances were surpassed by the female convicts' demeanour.

> We remarked with great satisfaction the subdued, respectful, and throughout proper deportment of the women, exhibiting a very striking contrast with what we have been too long accustomed to in similar establishments in this country ... We only lament that one so well fitted for her sphere of duty, and actuated by principles so high, and distinguished by energy so great, should not find everything favourable to her permanent success.[7]

Impressive though the Bowdens were in their principled professionalism Fr Cotham's duties were irksome at times and his relationship with the superintendent could be strained. In March 1846 his journal mentions the companions who sometimes accompanied him to the Orphan School and the *Anson*: Mrs Montgomery, the Catholic catechist (about whom little is known except that she was the widow of a Captain Montgomery), and

HMS Anson
167

Mrs Garrett and her daughters, the family of Robert Stocker Garrett, deceased Assistant Colonial Surgeon, and relatives of the Revd Mr James Garrett, an outspoken Presbyterian minister in the colony. Ladies such as these were a vital resource in working with such a large number of women. What they lacked in formal training was more than compensated for by their own life experiences; for widows such as Mesdames Montgomery and Garrett service in the convict department offered them an opportunity to earn a living and accrue a pension. No doubt Fr Cotham knew their circumstances but in line with Tasmanian social etiquette he would not have alluded to it. It is more likely that he enjoyed the company of the beautiful Maria Henrietta Garrett and teased her younger sister Elizabeth.

Cotham's journal for 1 March noted Mrs Montgomery's absence from Divine Service on board the *Anson*, and although she accompanied the Garrett ladies to the Orphan School on the 4th she did not go with Fr Cotham to the *Anson*. On the 7th Cotham called on the Comptroller General's office and saw Mr Nairn, Acting Comptroller General, about the report he had prepared concerning an incident on board the *Anson*. Mrs Montgomery again declined joining the chaplain for Sunday service on the 8th but on the 11th he 'sent Mrs Montg. in Gig to Anson' while he 'rode the Pony'. He also 'took down Mrs Montgomery's statement and wrote to Dr Boden [*sic*] for an apology for myself'. The following day he noted baldly 'Dr Boden returned my letter with the old cover' letting his action speak for him. Fr Cotham did not have time until the following Tuesday, 17 March, to send Mrs Montgomery's 'complaint of assault against Dr Boden' to the Comptroller General. Cotham noted no details or opinions about the trouble; for the next week he continued his duties as well as buying a hat, razors and Rimmel's shaving soap, and a supply of books.

On Tuesday 24 March, Fr Cotham

> went on board the Anson to an investigation on my complaint, and of Mrs Montgomery's for an assault and

168 *The Indomitable Mr Cotham*

> battery, against Ed. Bowden MD the Superintendent. Dr
> Bowden called me a lyer [*sic*] or said that what I stated 'was
> false' and afterwards confirmed in his evidence that very
> statement; remained on board from 10 till 6o'c, 8 hours.
> Wearied out!

The allegation of assault and battery seems to have been overtaken by Fr Cotham's personal indignation and he was losing
patience with the *Anson*. In retaliation he may have been deliberately needled by the staff. On the following Sunday he went to
celebrate as usual:

> Mass at the Anson: Interrupted at the beginning of Prayers
> by noise. Mrs Montg. went to down [*sic*] to stay the noise.
> Inconvenienced during Mass by Miss Susan Holdich
> reading or talking loud. This continued the whole time
> until the end of service.

Susannah Holdich was the Assistant Superintendent, one of Mrs
Bowden's handpicked staff, and such disrespectful behaviour
suggests the complaints incident had upset everybody's equilibrium. But Fr Cotham was not deterred and took with him fifty
catechisms and seven copies of *The Garden of the Soul*, however
much the *Anson* seemed anything but a bed of roses. Finally on 6
April he received a letter from Lieutenant-Governor Eardley-
Wilmot 'requiring Mr Boden to make an apology' which was made
by letter a week later. While this was going on between the two
gentlemen, Fr Cotham was attending the *Anson* for the women to
make their Easter duties during Lent; on Holy Saturday, 11 April,
he heard thirty-two Confessions between nine o'clock and midday
after which he was in the confessional at St Joseph's until 11 p.m.
The 'Bowden affair' ran its course: another letter was sent to the
Comptroller General's office on 16 April and one to Mr Champ
(another short-term Acting Comptroller General) the following
day. Finally, after Easter, on Wednesday 29th Cotham was able to
write 'Satisfactory note to Dr Bowden in reply to his Apology. Con.
at the Anson. Left card with Dr B.' Had it all been worthwhile? The

final entry suggests Cotham was back on cordial terms with Dr Boden/Bowden. Unfortunately there remains the cryptic comment made on Good Friday, 10 April: 'Ser[mon] ad multos populous. Prayers and Preached at the Anson. Mr Murray at Orphan School … Mrs Montg. valde inebr[iatum]'.[8]

Remarkably there were only two recorded deaths of women on the *Anson*: Mary Murphy, who died on 9 January 1846 while Fr Cotham was away at Port Arthur; and Fanny Doherty from Londonderry on 26 March 1846. Inquests into both deaths were held on the *Anson*, Fanny's inquest being dealt with by Dr Bowden while he was also answering questions about his treatment of Mrs Montgomery. Dr Bowden's testimony at the inquest reflects his humane approach to the inmates:

> Fanny Doherty … had been here about four months, her age was about twenty seven, she died on the twenty sixth instant of dysentery. She was admitted first into the Hospital on the eleventh of January the first time and was under my charge. She was discharged convalescent on the sixth of February. She was readmitted on the tenth of the same month suffering the same symptoms … She was of consumptive habit and was occasionally better but ultimately weakening under the dysentery. I saw her daily whilst in Hospital, she had everything necessary and proper for her.

Margaret Power, the hospital warder on the *Anson* who had come out with the Bowdens in 1843, corroborated the doctor's evidence.

> I knew the deceased Fanny Doherty, she has been under my charge with the intermission of three or four days since the eleventh of January last; during that period she was attended by Dr Bowden, he saw her once every day and latterly twice. I never heard her make any complaint during her illness, she had everything she could wish for. We are not restricted in any way in the Hospital here under the direction of the Doctor, the patients obtain all they wish.

At Mary Murphy's inquest Bowden testified that 'The Government allows every sort of medical comfort on board. I am not under any restriction as to what I give', although the government might have wished he was not so generous with their funds. Evidence was also taken from Margaret Newman, 'a Prisoner of the Crown and nurse'. The verdict given on Fanny was that she died 'by the Visitation of God in a natural way'.[9] On the 26th when, as Cotham noted, 'Heavy rain continued', he made a 'Sick Call to Anson: omnia sacram. to Fanny Doherty. T. & conver[n] with Ct. Cotterell and Lady', Captain Cotterell being the Commandant of the *Anson*.[10] Then it was onto the ferry again for the ride back into Hobart.

Looking at Fr Cotham's journal for the six weeks of Lent in 1846 suggests that his energies must have been fully occupied with his institutional duties and the added complication of 'the Bowden affair'. But this was not the case; Cotham's focus was on the totality of his pastoral ministry which gave him enough satisfaction to compensate for the hard grind of convict duties. Beyond the extra hours given to hearing confessions during Holy Week Cotham worked on an important sermon he had been asked to deliver by Bishop Willson, which he finished two days before it was preached. He had the satisfaction of seeing it reported at length in the Hobart press.

After the high point of Easter, Cotham returned to his routine visits to the Orphan School, the *Anson*, and the hospital wards. On 29 April Bishop Willson left Hobart for his first visit to Norfolk Island, taking Mr Murray with him. After he returned on 19 June he was determined that nothing less than a journey to England, to the seat of government, would enable him to convey his distress and disgust at what he had found in that penal station.[11]

Notes

1. The 1742-ton Anson was built in 1812 near Hull. Measuring 175 ft 6 in. (deck), 144 ft 6 in. (keel) by a beam of 48 ft 4 in. (53.6 m x 44.0 m 14.73 m) and a hull depth of 22 ft (6.7 m).

2. B. Williams, 'The archaeological potential of colonial prison hulks: The Tasmanian case study' *Bulletin of the Australasian Institute for Maritime Archaeology* 29 (2005), pp. 77–86.

3. *The Cornwall Chronicle* (Launceston), 8 March 1845, p. 2.

4. *The Courier* (Hobart), 28 July 1847, p. 4, report of a meeting held on 16 February 1847 in the Exchange Rooms, Nottingham, England.

5. *Launceston Examiner,* 16 November 1850, p. 3. Mrs Bowden's response, *'Upon Reports in the Blue Books laid upon the table of the House of Lords', March 1849,* was reported as part of the *Examiner*'s extensive account (pp. 3-5) of the British Government's half-hearted commitment to the *Anson* experiment.

6. *The Courier* (Hobart), 29 October 1844, p. 2.

7. *Ibid.,* p. 2.

8. 'Sermon to many people ... Mrs Montgomery extremely drunk.'

9. J. Kavanagh and D. Snowden, *Van Diemen's Women: A History of Transportation to Tasmania* (Dublin: The History Press, 2015). The lives of these two women, who arrived from Ireland on 3 December 1845 on board the *Tasmania* (2), are considered in detail in this book. TAHO, SC195/1/17 Inquest No. 1384 (10 January 1846) Mary Murphy; TAHO, SC195/1/17 Inquest No. 1410 (26 March 1846) Fanny Doherty.

10. See *Colonial Times* (Hobart), 30 April 1844, p. 7, for a testimonial to Captain Cotterell on his removal from the post of Superintendent at Jericho Probation Station to commandership of the *Anson*.

11. Bishop Willson's visit to Europe coincided with that of Archbishop Polding. Both men were scouting for additional clergy for their dioceses. They shared lodgings at the English College in Rome in 1857 and made a tentative reconciliation but the Therry business was not settled until 1858 when Bishop Murphy of Adelaide mediated between the three parties.

16 QUID PRODEST?

Queen's Orphan School

THE PURPOSE OF Hobart's Orphan School changed radically during the nineteenth century but exteriorly it remained immediately recognisable and daunting. At the end of a long avenue of oak trees with two stone guardhouses at its entrance a double-storeyed building stood on either side of St John's Anglican Church, one each for girls and boys. Built initially for orphaned or abandoned children of free settlers, military personnel, aboriginals, or convicts, it gradually catered mainly for the children of convicts, especially after the arrival of Lieutenant-Governor Franklin in 1837. Children had sometimes travelled out with a parent on a convict ship before being separated or had been genuinely orphaned after arrival. Following Franklin's example, and always mindful of costs and public opinion, Lieutenant-Governor Eardley-Wilmot decided that as 'the Orphan School had become an asylum for lodging, clothing, maintaining and educating the children of convicts'[1] control should pass to the Convict Department in 1844. Neglected, abandoned, or illegitimate children of non-convicts were still taken in until 1847, at the expense of the colonial government, but the Orphan School had effectively become part of the penal system rather than a place of protection for children in need.

As Vicar General from 1838 Fr Therry had been able to address the long-standing neglect of the religious education of the Catholic children in the Orphan School, stemming from the period when Catholics were few in number. Coinciding with Therry's appointment, the Revd Mr Thomas James Ewing became Superintendent of the Orphan School and reinforced the view that as children of convicts were *de facto* children of the state they must be brought up in the established religion. Therry argued his case for a separate Catholic orphanage, even one partly funded by Catholics, without success, and he was hampered and criticised for personally helping in individual cases of destitute or dying children. The recall of Franklin signalled a change in policy, though one founded on economy rather than religious tolerance. Eardley-Wilmot reduced the budget faced by the colonial government from its estimated cost for 1845 of nearly £6,000 to an actual cost of £1,700 by formally putting the Orphan School under the control of the Convict Department and paying separately to the colonial government for the smaller proportion of free children.

The regime of the Orphan School reflected its status as part of the convict system, even to the appointment of Captain Charles O'Hara Booth as Superintendent, transferred from his post of Superintendent at the boys' reformatory, Point Puer, in 1844. Ewing remained Chaplain at St John's and also Protestant chaplain to the Orphan School despite reports of scandalously immoral behaviour on his part. However, the change in status necessitated the appointment of a Catholic chaplain in order to provide separate religious instruction and services of worship for Catholics, as was done in all penal establishments; the segregation even went so far as separate dormitories along denominational lines. As one of his last acts as Vicar General Fr Therry had recommended the appointment of a 'Catholic Lady' as school mistress at the Orphan Schools in May 1844 but Eardley-Wilmot considered the best arrangement was for a 'properly qualified person'[2] to visit the School daily. The following year Bishop Willson (taking advice from Cotham) recommended Miss Quin as school mistress to the Catholic girls and she was appointed at the same time that Mrs Montgomery was appointed Female Catechist, on Bishop Willson's recommendation, as 'properly qualified for the situation' on the *Anson*. Salaries for both women were paid from colonial funds.[3] Catherine Anastasia Quin had, at least, had some teaching experience while still a pupil in Ireland; her brother James Michael Quin, appointed assistant

Quid Prodest? 175

teacher in the Male Orphan School at the same time, had been a clerk. However, both Quins stayed in their posts until 1866, joining a mainly untrained staff of teachers who lived with the children and supervised them full-time.[4] The master of the Male School, Mr Dickenson, had also been an office clerk, coming to the school in his mid-fifties. With his wife as Matron and a family of seven children of their own the Male Orphanage School provided them with a home as well as their livelihood.[5]

The opening for an ordained Catholic clergyman for the Orphan School posed a problem for the recently arrived Bishop Willson: he did not have one available. His proposal for a layman, Mr Boyle, to read daily prayers and to give moral instruction on Wednesdays and Fridays 'until I can be prepared to lay before you such alterations in the different establishments, as may be deemed advisable' was recommended by the Comptroller General to the Lieutenant-Governor and accepted. Mr Boyle was to receive the same rate of pay as a clergyman, £50 per annum.[6] It was six months before Ambrose Cotham was free to leave Launceston to take up duties at the Orphan School under the auspices of the Convict Department.

Children were kept at the School until the age of fourteen, after which they were apprenticed, unless they had been 'fostered' at a younger age to someone who guaranteed to continue their education and training. While on a visit to Port Phillip in the autumn of 1846 Fr Cotham made the acquaintance of Fr Richard Walsh, an experienced convict chaplain himself at Geelong.[7] The two letters from Fr Walsh are self-explanatory:

> 26th December 1846
>
> My dear Father Cotham
>
> I have to acknowledge your letter the 20th inst. [Writes about bedding sent by Fr Hall and books he would like Cotham to send.]
> My dear Father C., I hope you will have the kindness to select a good and proper boy at the Orphan School for me

and send him by the *David*. I am going to part with my present boy, and I shall take every care that the boy you will send will be properly treated; he can be at school every day from eleven until 2 o'clock. If you could select a docile and mild boy it would be great pleasure to me to have him bound to myself.

Your friends Capt and Mrs Fyans would feel much obliged to you if you would select a good girl for them age from thirteen to fourteen, they will receive either Prot. or Catholic and you know and I am sure she will be well treated. There is a Catholic friend of mine who went with me to Portland Bay, as a guide, he is indeed a very good Catholic and he begs of me to get a girl for him. I am sure she will be well treated. His name is Mr John Fitzgerald. I will not again trouble you in such business, I know it will be troublesome to you.

I see the Very Rev. P. B. Geoghegan has again visited Melbourne. I think he was sorry to leave, but he was his own tormentor, every little thing even the slightest annoyed him and made him miserable himself and not very pleasing to others. Our present Vicar [Therry] is going on very quietly, he is cautious at present and in great anxiety about Hobart Town, can things ever be arranged; he paid me a visit since you left, he likes Geelong very much. My little Church is going on very well. I hope God will prosper the work. When shall we have the pleasure of seeing you, I hope soon.

Believe me to be my dear Father Cotham, Yours very sincerely R Walsh.

[written in the margin, crossways:]

I now enclose a draft for £3.0.0 pounds, I hope you will send me the books per *David*. I trust to you not forget to send me the Boy, also the girl for Mrs Fyans and one for Fitzgerald. Mr McShane will take care of them, pray let me know in your letter if there be any thing objectionable in making these applications. Yours for ever and a day.

Quid Prodest? 177

Geelong 10th March 1847

My dear Father Cotham,

I should have returned you many thanks by the last *David*, but I was from home on very disagreeable business as you will acknowledge, that is <u>begging</u> for my little church but succeeded very well, and we are still going on rapidly with the building. When you will again give us the pleasure of a visit we will have a better church to receive you.

The boy William Butler arrived in good order, and though as you say he is not very bright yet he will improve by time, and I think he will be a good boy and will give him every opportunity to be so.

Maria Murphy is a very good girl and is daily improving and I hope she will be useful to herself and others in after life. She has a time for teaching and she is likely to do good for herself and others.

Margaret the other girl is doing very well and her mistress is very well pleased with her and she is in a very good place, at least these girls are well provided for and I am sure they do not regret the change.

Captain and Mrs Fyans expected you would send a girl to them this time. I hope you will endeavour to send a good girl to them this time per *David*.

I am well aware it must be troublesome to you to send these girls, and it is improper for me to add one load more to your many labours. I know you have much to do in Hobart Town—but as you are personally acquainted with Capt and Mrs Fyans and as they admire you so much the trouble will be an agreeable one. I fear that if you were in this Colony they would not care about others. The old Capt. says, That Father Cotham is a very nice [*sic*]. I wish he was in this Colony &c &c &c &c

We have meetings and counter meetings here about labour, the introduction of convicts &c &c, the people in general are against convicts on any terms but they may speak. We must have labour from some quarter whether free or bond, we cannot get servants here, and the few we have it is impossible to speak to them; in fact we are the servants and they the masters. Would you know a good old woman who would be likely to be a good housekeeper for me. She should be advanced in years, say from forty to fifty, not less. She should be a person who does not drink and good in every other respect. If you could meet a person according to your own tastes and whom you think will do well I would receive such a person. The wages would be from fifteen to sixteen or even a little better, if the person was good and humble, and inclined to continence so, if you know of such an old woman, she could come by the *David*, and I would engage her, I will not make a permanent engagement until I hear from you. There is one thing, she would not have much to do but she should be steady. Now I am giving you trouble enough but if you want any thing on my side of the water I will repay you with interest.

Believe me to say in J.C.

Yours, R Walsh

William Butler, the mild and docile boy picked out by Cotham, had come to Tasmania with his widowed mother Margaret Butler and 2-year-old sister Mary Ann on board the convict transport ship *Tasmania* (2) leaving four siblings behind in Ireland. He was admitted to the Male Orphan School on 9 December 1845 and his sister was taken from her mother in May 1846 to the Female Orphan School. Fr Walsh's letters reflect a commonplace ambivalence towards convictism, when a mixture of compassion, convenience, and economy was focused on the uses and abuses of the system.[8]

Little William Butler, and Maria Murphy who was sent to Julia Reily,[9] stood in great need of a protector and they were not disappointed. Captain Foster Fyans (1790–1870) was usually in a position to bestow favours and judgements on others but it seems the labour shortage was a problem even to him, or perhaps Fr Walsh wanted to put him in his debt. After a long military career, including a term as acting commandant at Norfolk Island in 1833, Fyans settled in the Port Phillip district of Victoria and was a

Quid Prodest? 179

prominent public servant in the judiciary and as a land commissioner. He had no close links with the Catholic Church having been brought up as an Irish Anglican. In 1843 he married Elizabeth Cane, sixteen years his junior, and they settled in Geelong. It was with this couple that Fr Cotham had made such a favourable impression. Although Fyans had a mixed reputation, as a martinet, eccentric in later life but also fair in his dealings, Cotham could appreciate the wisdom of his attitude towards convicts:

> I was always of opinion that mitigation to the deserving tended to good, and feel not sorry to acknowledge that I was instrumental to mitigating to a great extent seventy convicts [of Moreton Bay station], and well pleased often I have been in meeting some of these men doing well in the world as respectable citizens, and only in one solitary instance I failed in my hope.[10]

Cotham would have wanted to oblige young Mrs Fyans as she started married life with this formidable character.

Fr Cotham received a letter from James Quin eight years after leaving the Orphan School. It suggests they had a genuine friendship that grew out of the experience of sharing hardship, with the orphans and on behalf of the orphans. It also gave him news of rebuilding and expansion that could hardly have been expected to happen in such a short space of time.

> Queen's Orphan School, New Town, Tasmania.
>
> 4th April 1859
>
> My Dear Father Cotham
> I avail myself of this opportunity of writing to you and I flatter myself that you will be glad to hear how myself and sister have been getting on for the last eight years. My sister and I are still at the Orphan Schools, which we owe to your kind exertion. We have had many difficulties to encounter as there have been many changes in so long a period. Mr Low and Mrs Smyth are still in the Schools, persons who have caused us a great deal of annoyance since the decease

of Capt Booth in 1851. Your old friend A. B. Jones [Algernon Burdett Jones] is Capt B's successor, thank goodness we have braved all opposition for the last fourteen years. A fact which is most singular is that the Catholic children have still a majority. At present the Schools occupy a large amount of public interest being likely to be given over from the Imperial to the Colonial Government, goodness only knows what will be our fate then, however we are entitled to fourteen years pension, notwithstanding all these little difficulties we are well and happy thank God.

The Revd W. Downing your successor only remained two months at the Schools and was succeeded by the Rev. H. Magorian, who was removed at the end of two years, who was succeeded by your old friend the Rev. G. Hunter, who has been with us now nearly seven years; he has had our little Oratory decorated and beautified that you would scarcely know it if it were possible for you to see it.

He has also built a very handsome church at O'Meara's Bridge, on part of Mr Loughnan's land which was a gift from His Lady. It was opened on Shrove-Tuesday at which was made a very handsome collection, and Mass is celebrated every other Sunday at 9 a.m., so you can judge from this that our much esteemed and respected Chaplain is kept fully occupied, though I won't say, such severe duty, as fell to your lot when you had to visit the *Anson*. Mr Henry Hunter is married to Miss Celia Robertson, Mrs Loughnan's daughter.

St Joseph's Church [Hobart] has been altered and decorated since you left, and the old debt has been settled by the late lamented Bishop Murphy, Father Therry paying the disputed £1000, with the interest due to Mr Regan which amounted to nearly £900—the fifteen hundred due on the Church is nearly paid off. There has been built a Temperance Hall on the ground at the back of the Hospital which you selected years ago; it is a handsome stone building and will seat six hundred people; it is quite payed for.

Father Hall I am told leaves for home on the May mail.

Quid Prodest? 181

Father Bond is conducting a Catholic seminary in the old Macquarie Hotel. Father Butler is still in Launceston who is collecting to rebuild his church which is falling, the foundation having sunk. Father Maguire is located in Port Arthur. The Richmond Church has been rebuilt and Fr Dunn[e] is still the resident priest. Mr and Mrs Cassidy are well and John is a fine young man. Pat is at Carlow College [Ireland].[11]
... My sister unites in kindest wishes to you hoping that you are well and enjoying all the blessing of this life. You can never be better than we wish you to be. [cross hatched] We often have a chat relative to your kindness of past years which will never be forgotten by us and pray that you will remember old friends in your prayers.
I remain yours ever faithfully and sincerely,

James Michael Quin.

Brickfields Hiring Depot

The positions of Chaplain to the *Anson* and the Queen's Orphan School were Fr Cotham's official appointments but as Bishop Willson's envoy, and one of few available priests, he ministered to a number of other key institutions associated with the penal system. A nice distinction was made for the Brickfields Hiring Depot: 'The building in the Brickfields, however, is not used as a Penitentiary, or Factory within the spirit and meaning of the Act, neither as a place of punishment, but merely as a Depot for the accommodation of Female Pass Holders awaiting service.'[12] The premises in North Hobart were not too distant to be inconvenient to people wanting to hire a woman for service, for which she would receive a wage. Initially about two hundred women were transferred from the overcrowded Cascades Factory, but the Brickfields site was expanded in May 1843 with a view to its being run as an adjunct to the proposed new penitentiary, or to the 'temporary' accommodation used instead at the *Anson*.

182   *The Indomitable Mr Cotham*

At the hiring depot women who had passed through the assessment and moral improvement programme of the *Anson* would be housed before being taken into service, or after being returned from an expired or unsatisfactory contract of service, always with a view towards eventual freedom and social usefulness. In practise this meant that it did not benefit from a comprehensive regime such as the Bowdens supervised at the *Anson*. In fact it was hotly debated whether the Visiting Magistrates charged with reporting on conditions in penal institutions had any right to inspect the Brickfields. Its role was strictly defined:

> the Factory at the Brickfields tho' used heretofore as a Prison or House of Correction & therefore under the Visiting Magistrates according to the Act, yet that it is no longer used as a Gaol or House of Correction, though still called 'Factory' but is a mere Building used for the convenience of the *Anson* & part of that Penitentiary, in order to receive the inmates of the *Anson* when discharged from or changing their service, until again hired instead of the inconvenience of sending such persons on board the *Anson* again, & that it is neither a Prison nor a House of Correction, nor a receptacle for any Prisoners under any other sentence than the one they had received in England.[13]

The report made by magistrates William Watchorn and William Carter stands nevertheless as a vivid account of what Fr Cotham might have found on any given day in late 1844:

> On the 3rd August they again visited the Brickfields Factory & were induced to go at an early hour, from information they had received of the general irregularity & bad conduct of that prison. It was about ½ past 9. The Prisoners were just commencing Breakfast. There was a total absence of all order & regularity, & the noise & confusion from Talk & Clatter were beyond description … In the sleeping apartment the night clothes & bedding had not at that hour of the morning (past 9) been removed to the open air. The floors were covered with expectoration. Tobacco ashes showed certain tokens of persons

Quid Prodest? 183

having smoked there during the night or morning. On asking the Superintendent for an explanation of these things, he answered (to the effect) he could not help it, he could do nothing with them (the female Prisoners). The Comptroller General knew of their smoking & sanctioned it, they were not there he (the Comptroller General) said for punishment & had a right to smoke if they pleased.

Daily prayers are not read in this Factory.
The Women do not work! They have no employment, a state of absolute Idleness, of itself sufficient to engender vice & counteract reformation. The practise of Tobacco smoking (most strangely encouraged here) for females & more especially for young ones is filthy & disgusting. A habit which not only stupefies the faculties but renders the female mind callous to reproof & shame.
The Visiting Magistrates conceive the whole system is one of great mismanagement dangerous to the community & destructive of any hope that might otherwise be entertained of the moral reformation of any of the Class.
The Visiting Magistrates could not but contrast the difference of appearance & behaviour of the prisoners at this Establishment with those of the Cascade Factory. At the latter every Female was modestly & becomingly drest their behaviour quiet and respectful. At the former place there were women in Groups of 3 or 4 seated on the Ground not deigning to get up on the appearance of Visitors or the Superintendent & only acknowledging their presence by a loud laugh or a bold stare, many with their dresses loose & immodest, their language generally loud & impudent & their whole behaviour with few exceptions more like the unrestricted libertine of the pavé than Females undergoing a process of moral reformation.[14]

Cotham's Journal, Hobart, June 1846

Given this poorly administered system it is hardly surprising if the civil population who wanted to hire skilled or well-behaved probation pass-holders into service found a way of circumventing officialdom to 'snap up' women recommended by subordinate staff (Superintendent Williams was exempted from blame on this occasion).[15] Inevitably, some unskilled or less attractive women

Quid Prodest? 185

found themselves always at the back of the queue: the pass-holder system for women had changed little from the assignment system.

The details for the Brickfields from the census of 1843, during the superintendence of Mr Brooks, indicate the breakdown of the 179 women housed there on the night of 31 December 1842:[16]

- 136 single females aged 14 to under 21 years
- 136 single females aged 21 to under 45 years
- 19 single females aged 45 to under 60 years
- 179 single females in Government employment
- 72 single females Church of England
- 16 single females Church of Scotland
- 3 single females Wesleyan Methodist
- 88 single females Roman Catholic

Although numbers fluctuated during the decade (for example, in September 1845 there were two hundred and twenty six women available for hire) the spread of ages and religious affiliation remained fairly constant.

The Colonial Hospital

Fr Cotham made almost daily visits to the hospitalised sick. A free service had been provided for convicts and settlers as early as 1804 and a purpose built hospital was completed in 1820. It was known by various names: the government, colonial, or convict hospital, and Fr Cotham's journal entries reflect this usage. Over time, like the Orphan School, it became associated with the convicts and paupers; anyone who could afford to do so would use a private establishment or hire a nurse in their own home. The Invalid Depot in New Norfolk was opened in 1827 with mentally ill patients being admitted in the early 1830s. The general cases were gradually moved elsewhere until by 1848 New Norfolk was solely a Lunatic Asylum for the whole of Tasmania, with the exception of violent convicts who were taken to the Asylum at Port Arthur. A coroner's inquest held in 1840 high-

186 *The Indomitable Mr Cotham*

lighted a local problem at New Norfolk but easily replicated across the system:

> It also came out in evidence, that the man had been removed from the hospital before he was convalescent, because the hospital was too crowded. He was therefore removed merely as a matter of convenience. This is a very economical way of stowing the sick, certainly, sending a man still dangerously ill, amongst a body of 700, but especially into the convalescent ward of the Prisoners' Barracks. We should have thought that instead of this, another temporary hospital would have been taken, at any rent. But here comes in again, the pounds, shillings, and pence calculations, even in cases of life and death.
>
> Again—there is no surgeon resident inside the hospital walls, neither is there any regulation as to his residing in the immediate vicinity. On the night in question, the person in charge of the man when he died did not even know where the Surgeon lived. This was stated in evidence, we are not distorting the facts … To the Principal Superintendent, Mr. W. Gunn, every praise is due for the promptitude and humanity which he displayed on this occasion; they add another honourable testimonial to the great interest and concern which he evinces for the welfare and comfort of the unfortunate beings placed under his charge.[17]

Cotham made an overnight visit to New Norfolk in April 1846 to take the funeral service for John McKenna, cordially drinking 'T. with Dr Brooks' in the evening. Cotham's days of long horse rides were over by now; he could afford fourteen shillings to take the coach to get there and return by steamer. Unlike the Bowdens' positive management of public relations at the *Anson*, New Norfolk Asylum was a secretive place; the lack of visitors added to the idea that conditions behind the walls were bad. It was regarded as a place of imprisonment rather than treatment for the mentally sick. Twelve years later Bishop Willson used his

Quid Prodest? 187

position on the Board of Commissioners of the Asylum to force through changes.[18]

Establishments such as the *Anson*, Brickfields Depot, Cascades Factory, children's nursery, and (male) Prisoners' Barracks all had their own wards for medical cases, while surgical cases—the majority of them limb amputations—were treated at the General Hospital in Liverpool Street, Hobart. Thus, a typical entry by Cotham, for Sunday 21 June 1846, reads: 'Mass at the Anson. Rain! Rain. Prayers at the Orphan School, Hospital, and Brickfields.' The frequent repetition of 'Rain!' is supplemented on Wednesday 23rd by 'Lumbago'. After a year of following this routine Cotham wrote a report to the Comptroller General in July 1847 giving as his opinion that duties at the *Anson* and Orphan School required his full time attention. In January 1849 he reiterated his comments with a schedule of his weekly visits for the Convict Department, which he still considered as too onerous, but by this time he was settled on the idea of taking leave of absence and returning to England.

Cotham's primary duties were to celebrate Divine Service (that is, the Mass) and the sacraments, to provide religious instruction by teaching and providing suitable reading material, and to promote moral improvement by individual attention to the men, women, and children he encountered. He took his duties further by making the lives of the inmates more pleasant in little ways. He bought lollipops for the children at the Orphan School during Easter week and apples for the *Anson*. On Sunday 28 June 1846 he noted, 'Took Alice Burgess' daughter on board the Anson'. In all likelihood Alice was the daughter of Esther Burgess, a widow, who, with her eldest daughter Mary, was one of five Carlow women transported for seven years on the *Tasmania* (2) for stealing potatoes. The family arrived in December 1845 and were separated. Esther, Mary, and toddler Robert went to the *Anson*, while three girls and one boy were taken to the Orphan School. In May 1846 Robert briefly joined his siblings and 14-year-old Elizabeth was apprenticed to Charles Pulfrey of Hobart on 14

188   *The Indomitable Mr Cotham*

July. Alice might have been taken to the *Anson* for her own benefit or for her mother's; in any case it was a kind act for a clergyman to do on a busy Sunday. When little Robert Burgess died at the Orphan School four months later, Fr Cotham was away from the colony and not able to help mother or children.

Cotham also did what he could do to help Mrs Bowden find work for the women on the *Anson*, taking (and paying for) his personal laundry to be washed on board: two shillings for a dozen pieces of laundry, a halfpenny for a collar. On 7 April 1846 he took six collars for washing; on 23 May he had twice as many pieces of laundry and twenty-six collars, presumably collecting them up from his house companions. At the Cascades Factory, where heavy laundry was done for the colonial hospitals and other government institutions, three months hard labour at the washtub was meted out as punishment but on the *Anson* learning useful laundering skills was considered part of the reformatory system. The purchase of 'Beeds 5d for 5 dozen' to a total of £1 (in other words four gross) and whip cord for a shilling (1 June 1846) might have been an experiment in making rosary beads, a suitable employment for Catholic women on the *Anson*.

Cotham added a two-word remark to his journal for Sunday, 5 April 1846. Perhaps the day had been particularly frustrating, or perhaps he reveals a habitual frame of mind usually kept hidden. 'Preached &c &c at Brickfields; at the Queen's O. School; and on board the Anson. Quid prodest?[19]

Notes

[1]   S. Dean, *'Our Children, Our Orphans'*. BA Thesis (University of Tasmania, 2000), p. 25. http://eprints.utas.edu.au/11740/ [Accessed online 27.7.2017]

[2]   L. C. Mickleborough, *'Victim of an 'Extraordinary Conspiracy'? Sir John Eardley Eardley-Wilmot Lieutenant Governor of Van Diemen's Land 1843–46'* PhD Thesis (University of Tasmania, 2011), p. 200. http://eprints.utas.edu.au/11740/ [Accessed online 27.7.2017]

[3]   The details of these appointments are taken from Mickleborough, *Victim;*

Quid Prodest? 189

CA6/WIL 1C 19/1 Colonial Correspondence, Catholic Church Archives, Forster to Therry, 17 May 1844; CA6/WIL 1B 57/89 Convict Correspondence Catholic Church Archives, Comptroller General to Willson, 7 August 1845; CA6/WIL 1B 57/91 Convict Correspondence Catholic Church Archives, Comptroller General to Willson, 17 August 1845; TAHO CSO20/ 1/17 Willson to Eardley-Wilmot 7 August 1845, p. 91 and Bicheno's Memo 14 August 1845, p. 94 for Montgomery; TAHO CSO20/ 1/17 Willson to Eardley-Wilmot 17 August 1845, p. 186 and Bicheno's Memo 21 August 1845, p. 186. See also CA6/WIL 1B 59/99 Nairne to Willson, 11 September 1845. Miss Quin's salary was £60 per annum.

4   Friends of the Orphan Schools and St. John's Precinct New Town Tasmania, Issue 3 Newsletter, May 2009, 'The Story of Sidney Quinn Davis' Box'. http://www.orphanschool.org.au/downloads/Newsletter_issue_3_May [Accessed 27.7.2017]

5   J. Purtscher, 'Suffer Little Children', 5 June 2008, Friends of the Orphan Schools.www.orphanschool.org.au/suffer.php [Accessed online 27.7.2017]

6   TAHO, CSO 22/112 No 2385. Item 1467/2; 29 June and 6 July 1844. Cited by Friends of the Orphan Schools.www.orphanschool.org.au/ CSO_22_112–2385.php [Accessed online 27.7.2017]

7   Fr Richard Walsh, ordained in Sydney by Polding, was sent to join Fr Patrick B Geoghegan OSF in Port Phillip in August 1839 as his first assistant. After quarrelling with Geoghegan (not the only assistant to find him difficult to work with) Walsh went as chaplain to Norfolk Island in 1840. Fr Walsh laid the foundation stone for St. Mary's Church, Geelong in August 1846. Fr Walsh died on 18 July 1868, aged 52, in his niece's home in Ireland where he had gone to regain his health. Fr Patrick B Geoghegan, OSF was recruited in Ireland by Fr Ullathorne in 1837 and accompanied him to New South Wales before being sent as the first Catholic missionary to Victoria. He was consecrated Bishop of Adelaide in September 1859 following the death of Bishop Francis Murphy.

8   William Butler has been identified as her forebear by Dianne Snowden. See, among many other works by Snowden, 'These Unfortunate Females', *Irish Journal, Carlow Past and Present* http://www.rootsweb.ancestry.com /~irlcar2/convicts_burgess_2.htm [Accessed online 27.7.2017]

9   Researchtasmania.com.au/documents/biographies/MURPHY_Eleanor.pdf [Accessed online 27.7.2017].

10   P. L. Brown, 'Fyans, Foster (1790–1870)', Australian Dictionary of Biography, National Centre of Biography, Australian National University, http://adb.anu.edu.au/biography/fyans-foster-2075/text2595, published first in hardcopy 1966 [Accessed online 27.7.2017]

11   Hugh and Harriet Cassidy were brother-in-law and sister-in-law to

Lawrence Cotham. Their son Patrick Augustine returned from Ireland in 1862; his elder brother was called James Ambrose, not John. Carlow College was where Fr Therry trained.

12 Reply to the Visiting Magistrates, William Watchorn and William Carter (appointed in 1844 to visit the houses of correction in Hobart on a regular basis and report on their findings) by Lieutenant-Governor Eardley-Wilmot, 12 October 1844. (TAHO, GO33/52 pp.172–194). Female Convicts Research Centre: http://www.femaleconvicts.org.au/index.php/cwp/13 [Accessed online 27.7.2017]

13 *Ibid.*

14 *Ibid.* Report of the Visiting Magistrates, 7 October 1844.

15 *Colonial Times and Tasmanian* (Hobart), 6 June 1848, p. 3.

16 FCRC; http://www.femaleconvicts.org.au/index.php/cwp/13 [Accessed online 27.7.2017]

17 *Colonial Times* (Hobart), 9 June 1840, p. 4.

18 *Colonial Times and Tasmanian* (Hobart), Editorial, 10 December 1847, pp. 2–3. Bishop Willson was to bring his expertise to bear in challenging conditions at the Asylum. In 1858 Willson was appointed to the Board of Commissioners placed in charge of New Norfolk and he began the task of seeking major improvements through a series of letters to the Colonial Secretary. 'New Norfolk', he wrote, 'resembled nothing more than a prison. Gloomy ill ventilated dark cells, prison walled yards, swarms of vermin in the wooden buildings, no classification at all with the noisy and offensive mixed with the delicate and tranquil, the congenital idiot with the recently admitted, the imbecile with the neat in habits.' S. Piddock, *A Space of Their Own: The Archaeology of Nineteenth Century Lunatic Asylums* (Sydney: Springer, 2007), p. 188.

19 The Latin *quid prodest* means: 'What good does it do?'

17 FR COTHAM'S ORATORY

O N GOOD FRIDAY, 10 April 1846 Fr Cotham delivered a 'Ser. ad multos populos' before going on to lead prayers and preach at the *Anson*.[1] The Good Friday sermon is a fine example of Cotham's fluency and lack of restraint even when working with solid material. In its context it is a piece of ecclesiastical politics, inoffensive to sincere churchgoers but with a sting for Bishop Willson's antagonists. During Lent the previous year the press had published Bishop Nixon's series of anti-Catholic sermons delivered in St David's Cathedral. Now it reported Cotham's rebuttal, on behalf of his own bishop, contrasting 'the most mild and truly gentlemanly manner, yet with great strength and power' with which he spoke out against 'the coarse and illiberal charges' made by the Protestant bishop against Catholic doctrine and practice. But he did not abuse the solemnity of Good Friday to make his case. Fr Cotham linked the proper worship owed to God, aided by the use of symbolic imagery, to the easily appreciated human feelings aroused by bereavement when the 'tenderest influences of affection [are] awakened and impressed on the memory, by contemplating a picture, a lock of the hair, or some other symbol of the dear departed'. And so he moved on to the focus of the day: the passion and death of Jesus.

The orthodox subject matter is addressed 'with extreme feeling and eloquence', appropriate to the homely examples he gives; overall the impression is of a man in control of his argument, confident in a large arena, and using all his abilities, 'where the energies of his mind were aided by the freedom of his body' towards one aim. While the newspaper report overstated the case by comparing Cotham's oratory with that of St Paul or John Knox (and the latter reference is a side comment on the dispute in Hobart against alleged 'Puseyite' Anglicans such as

Bishop Nixon), the sermon demonstrates the man at work as much as any physical activity does.

> On Good Friday, after the usual services of the day, at St Joseph's Cathedral, the Rev. Mr. Cotham, chaplain to the Lord Bishop of Hobart Town , delivered a truly eloquent discourse to a highly respectable congregation, amongst whom were several Protestant families, crowded to the utmost capacity of the Cathedral. The subject, of course, was appropriate to the sanctity of the day; but in the course of discussing it, Mr. Cotham took occasion to comment, and although in the most mild and truly gentlemanly manner, yet with great strength and power, upon the coarse and illiberal charges which had been made (Bishop Nixon was supposed to be referred to) against what was so unfoundedly called Catholic idolatry. The reverend chaplain stated in the most distinct manner, that the Catholic doctrine expressly excluded all worship, direct and indirect, of any being or substance, or the representation of any, either image, painting, or other symbol, other than of the Supreme Being, under one of the three persons of 'the blessed Trinity,' (as the able writer of the excellent letter in our last, signed 'A Presbyterian', so truly decorously expresses himself). All other Divine worship, of every sort and description, the reverend chaplain, in his address from the altar to his crowded congregation, most emphatically and distinctly denied.

> He referred to the practice amongst Catholics of showing the strongest marks of respect and affection to symbolical representations of the Deity under the second person of the Holy Trinity; and 'who is there,' asked Mr. Cotham, only expressing himself in very elegant language and with strong marks of deep emotion, 'who, having suffered the calamity of losing a beloved parent, consort, or child, snatched away by the unsparing hand of death, has not felt the tenderest influences of affection awakened and impressed on the memory, by contemplating a picture, a lock of the hair, or some other symbol of the dear

Fr Cotham's Oratory 193

departed? It is with such feelings that we contemplate the representations of the blessed Saviour, and all connected with the great sacrifice of our Redemption. Are those who so cruelly calumniate us plunged in the depths of such brutal ignorance? or do they suppose that we, in this advanced state of the human intellect, are so plunged, as to imagine that a piece of ivory, be it ever so beautifully curved, or a pictorial representation, be it ever so splendidly painted, can be the objects of Divine worship?'

The reverend chaplain then proceeded with extreme feeling and eloquence to inveigh in the strongest terms against the abomination of idolatry, a sin denounced by the Deity himself in his express commandment, to which the precepts and practice of no Church enacted and paid more religious obedience than did the Catholic. It is to be hoped that, after the solemn declaration, delivered literally ex cathedra, from the very altar itself, by the Bishop's chaplain, and therefore to be taken as coming from the colonial head of the Catholic Church himself, in the presence of an immense congregation, will have the effect of putting down the base calumnies in which a clergy, who ought to be incapable of such a violation of truth—saying nothing of that first of Christian virtues, charity—have been too prone ungenerously to indulge. There can be no doubt that a preacher, addressing his hearers from an open space, where action can add its influence to eloquence, possesses many advantages over one confined in a close box. Thus it was that the great Raphael represents St. Paul delivering his splendid oration from a raised dais in an open vestibule, and thus it was that one of the effective masters of the art of influencing the passions, the celebrated John Knox, was enabled to influence a whole nation, proverbially strongly intellectually gifted with the principles of an almost organic religious reform invariably addressing the people from an open space, where the energies of his mind were aided by the freedom of his body. And this advantageous position gave the reverend Catholic chaplain great advantages of which he seemed well to

194 *The Indomitable Mr Cotham*

understand the use, on the occasion which we have very feebly and inadequately reported.[2]

It is fascinating to apply his elder brother William's obituary to the younger man. They were ordained simultaneously and, given their quite separate seminary training, they did not share formation in homiletics or an opportunity to hear one another's preaching. Both brothers enjoyed the occasion to preach but from Fr William's obituary it would seem that he became something of a caricature of himself in old age:

> Fr [William] Cotham was nowhere more at home than in the pulpit, he was very assiduous as a writer of sermons, and with previous care and effort could preach powerfully and to the purpose. He not unusually carried on a running colloquy with his congregation and even with the priest seated at the altar should any difficulty occur connected with either the notices or with the services ... He had splendid lungs and a most stentorian voice, and he quite revelled in their possession ... it is undoubted that he had considerable power of declamation and did credit to his master of elocution, Father Brigham of whom he was so proud, while he had a good knowledge of music and a very correct ear.[3]

However, there is no hint of ridiculousness in his younger brother's preaching style. On this occasion Fr Ambrose had sufficient pride or vanity to want his brothers to know of his success in preaching. Two weeks later in his journal for 14 May he notes: 'Letters to Thomas [Shepherd]: sent Col. Times & Tas. 24th April 1846 on service on good Friday', dispatched by the *Aden*. It is the only reference he makes to writing home.

The eminence of the models he used for preaching, John Chrysostom from the fourth century, Bossuet from the seventeenth century, Massillon and Alphonsus de Liguori from the eighteenth century, show Cotham striving for excellence of effect, intellectual and emotional. The weakness of his congregations' educational and cultural attainments did not deter him from giving them an enriching experience within the grasp of their understand-

Fr Cotham's Oratory 195

ing. He loved word play, and spoke French fluently and used Italian phrases freely, so the general impression is of a man who was not afraid of being never less than personally expressive and, if he could attain it, eloquently persuasive of others.

The Universal Church, 1848

It is difficult to appreciate the consciousness of distance, in time and space, experienced by emigrants to Australia: on the one hand they were resigned to the strong possibility—and the reality for the majority—of never seeing their country or family of origin again. On the other hand, journeys back and forth were made with apparent ease when necessity arose: Ullathorne made the return journey twice in less than a decade and Bishop Willson spent two of his first four years either on board ship or back in England. The newspapers, too, mitigated the isolation of Australians who could choose to respond as if tumultuous events in Europe were taking place almost within earshot, buttressing their self-belief against the perception in England that theirs was a barely civilised, ramshackle society.

The Austrian aggression against the papacy in 1848 was one instance when the Catholics of Tasmania came together in solidarity with their European spiritual leaders. On a very wet evening in March 1848, Fr William Hall VG convened a meeting in Hobart of the resident Catholic clergy—Cotham, Hunter, and Odilo Woolfrey—and interested laymen and women. Four resolutions of loyalty to Pope Pius IX and objections to Austria's actions were passed and two rousing addresses were given by Fr Cotham and Fr Woolfrey. The latter focused on the Pope's role as the champion of genuine Christian liberty which ensured the proper ordering of the common good. 'That people enjoys true liberty, when the powers that are of God, and vested in the rightful rulers, are exercised for their good and benefit, and not for the private interest or to gratify the selfish views and caprices of the ruler.'[4] Fr Cotham's stirring address, greeted with loud cheering, was constructed around a sustained metaphor of the power of moving water, as if the emotions he aroused could be carried by their fervour to the papal throne itself. Cotham's eloquence came from his ability to evoke the grandeur of the natural world rather than an intellectual exposition of the issues, and the theme of unity is one to which he often returned.

> Perhaps, ladies and gentlemen, it may appear somewhat strange to some that we, a mere handful of men, of humblest resources, and at this utmost extremity of the earth, should deem ourselves of sufficient importance to forward expressions of sympathy to the great Spiritual Father of the majority of the Christian world—the Supreme Pastor of two hundred millions of men, comprising the great—the good—the learned, of almost every civilised nation under heaven. But we trust in so doing we are not presumptuous. For as a broad and majestic river that sweeps along in increasing strength, carrying on its waters the arts of peace and happiness from people to people, is composed of various streams, and even the smallest streamlet contributes to swell the moving mass of waters, and as the greater the distance the stream has flowed before its junction with the moving deluge, the greater is its depth at that junction, so we, by forwarding our sympathy over sixteen thousand miles of ocean, would testify how deep is the stream of affection which rolls in our hearts towards the religion of our fathers, and how dear to us is our Chief Pastor, the great, the enlightened and good, Pope Pius IX. Assemblies of sympathy have been called together in every nation of the Christian world, to cheer and encourage the heart of our most truly Father, in his noble efforts to uphold the interests of patriotism, virtue, and national liberty. The feeling of devotedness and admiration for that great Prince outstrips all the motives of sympathy amongst men of different countries; it flees over mountains, and seas, and oceans, and puts into the mouths of nations, one deep and heartfelt outburst of profoundest sympathy and admiration, and by raising our

Fr Cotham's Oratory

voices thus, by the winds of the press, our sympathies will be wafted to the foot of the Papal throne. It would be unworthy of us to remain silent. This is a glorious cause, a cause which has elicited the sympathy not only of Catholics, but of all right minds and honest men of all persuasions throughout the world. All the great principals for which patriots in all ages have fought and bled, are at stake in the struggle between Pope Pius IX, and the despot of Austria. To Catholics this cause was of the utmost importance; not only in a political, but in a religious, point of view. On the contest now going on in Italy, depended the question, whether the Head of the Church should be a free Prince, or subject to foreign dominion. If then we be lovers of liberty—if we hold patriotism—if we detest tyranny and oppression—if we be faithful children of the common parent of Christendom we shall unite with the Christian world in execrating the conduct of Austria, and professing our sympathy, with the great advocate of liberal institutions, Pope Pius IX, the greatest and most illustrious of all living men.[5]

Catholics in Hobart were at one with their European coreligionists in holding that 'the Rome of the early Christian martyrs was becoming identified with the Rome of contemporary martyrdom. The Pope as victim, as persecuted father of an ungrateful family, as spiritual hero, came to predominate in the imagination.'[6] Fr Cotham could not resist an opportunity to appeal to the imagination of his listeners.

Notes

[1] The *Sermo ad multos populos* is literally a sermon addressed to many people.

[2] *Colonial Times and Tasmanian,* 24 April 1846, p. 3.

[3] House Journal of the British Province of the Society of Jesus, *Letters and Notices,* No. XCIX, April 1895, p. 137.

[4] *Hobarton Guardian,* 22 March 1848, p. 2.

[5] *Ibid.,* p. 2.

[6] J. Champ, *The English Pilgrimage to Rome: A Dwelling for the Soul* (Leominster: Gracewing, 2000), p. 190.

18 CONVICT CHAPLAINS IN THE SOLE GAOL OF ENGLAND

A MBROSE COTHAM HAD not only his own round of duties; he also worked alongside Bishop Willson in training the church students. When the Bishop returned to Europe, between September 1846 and April 1848, Cotham had charge of the junior men for nearly two years. His journal gives brief insights into the mix of activities he undertook with them. His senior companion was Fr William Hall, a Londoner who had volunteered for the mission. He was appointed as Vicar General before leaving England, an appointment insisted on by Willson who had no intention of retaining Therry in that position. At 38-years-old William Hall was not the oldest of the newcomers but his role and demeanour set him apart. Whilst he was devoted to the Bishop and served him well as an able, hardworking administrator and mission priest, he was not particularly liked by his fellow clergy, being rather severe. However, he mellowed over time to become respected and appreciated in the diocese.

Far more congenial to Ambrose Cotham were the two junior men who had come out with the Bishop in 1844, Br Luke Levermore and George Hunter, usually referred to simply as 'George'. They were joined for two months by Fr Murray,[1] one of the students (though already nearly sixty years-old) recruited by Archbishop Polding in 1842. In his capacity as keeper of the petty cash for the Bishop's household Cotham lent Murray money for a dressing gown, comb, and toothbrushes; Cotham was fastidious about such things for himself as befitted a gentleman. Fr Murray took his turn preaching at the Orphan Schools and went with the Bishop, Cotham, and George to Richmond during Easter Week. After a taste of convict duty in Tasmania he sailed for Norfolk Island with Bishop Willson at the end of April. During a particularly violent period in that particularly harsh establishment Murray was joined by Fr Bond, who had gone out in September 1846, to 'attend in their last moments' nine Catholic prisoners who, with three Protestant convicts, were condemned to death for the murder of a constable during a prison riot.[2] Fr Bond returned to Tasmania early in 1847 leaving Fr Murray as the sole Catholic chaplain on Norfolk Island. In the returns made to Parliament by Comptroller General James Hampton in 1848 it was noted that Fr Murray's 'advanced age and growing infirmities ... render it urgently necessary to transfer him at once to some less laborious sphere of duty' away from the 'ultra penal establishment ... of generally extremely vicious and ignorant men'.[3]

George Hunter was spared the rigours of Norfolk Island, as was Fr Cotham who never visited that remote outpost. In September 1846 George was accredited as a catechist by the government and continued his studies under Cotham until ordination in March 1850, still only 24-years-old, the same age as Cotham was at ordination. He spent time in Launceston with Fr Butler and accompanied Cotham on a visit to Chigwell and the influential Mr Loughnan in May 1846. Cotham encouraged his companions to share his own love of long walks. On Monday 8 June he took a 'Prom with George and John Mason to Val Umbrosa. Visited four men living in trees'. One shilling was spent either on alms for the tree dwellers or for refreshments. There is an impression in the journal that Cotham liked to enliven the routine, even if it meant making much out of little. On Thursday 7 January 1847 he noted, 'Arranged with Mr Cox to ascend the Mountain of Wellington' and on the following Saturday he 'ascended Mount Wellington in company with W Norbert Woolfry [sic], G Hunter, Mr Cox and Murray Burgess. Returned at 8o'c'. The picnic had required a box of Lucifers, tea, ½lb sugar, 2lbs bread, six twists (of tobacco), butter, mutton, and salt, and the eau de cologne which he found indispensable. A tea pot, two pannikins and an iron spoon, knife, and fork completed the kit for which he paid his housekeeper Alice eight shillings. George

Convict Chaplains in the Sole Gaol of England 201

Hunter was treated with affection by Fr Ambrose, as the youngest member of the Bishop's diocesan team as well as a family friend and protégé of the Bishop.[4]

Fr William Peter Bond

The name of William Peter Bond, one of the earliest convict chaplains working alongside Cotham, weaves throughout the surviving Tasmanian journal. It appears in the first entry on 1 January 1846 when, having come to Hobart a few days earlier, Bond asked Cotham to supply for him at Port Arthur. The following day Cotham set off on horseback at 4 o'clock in the afternoon in 'awful weather' for the twenty-four hour journey to Port Arthur. Arriving on the evening of 3 January, 'wet through', he nevertheless entertained Mr O'Halloran, the catechist, to supper in Fr Bond's house. Company would have been a restorative to him as much as a hot meal.

The Catholic chaplaincy at Port Arthur had come about as a result of convict unrest in August 1843. When the Wesleyan Methodist chaplain was replaced by a Church of England minister the Catholic prisoners refused to attend religious services. Superintendent Captain Booth recommended that a Catholic chaplain be appointed as soon as possible and a house be provided for him. The building was easier to supply than manpower; Mr O'Halloran was sent as Catechist in January 1844 and Fr Bond eventually arrived later in the year, his first appointment in Tasmania. According to Fr Cotham's journal for 1846 Fr Bond travelled to and from Port Arthur fairly frequently, keeping in touch with diocesan affairs and the Therry business, joining Fr Cotham and Fr Dunne in Hobart (and probably the Bishop and Fr Hall) in retreat in August, as well as spending four months on Norfolk Island.

Ambrose Cotham had spent most of the first ten years after his ordination with older priests. William Peter Bond was eighteen months junior to Cotham and had been ordained three months after him following studies at the English College, Lisbon.

His father, William Vincent Bond, was listed as a gardener in the 1851 census but his lack of a profession was not a disadvantage to his large family. He and his wife Nancy converted to Catholicism in 1806, as a recently-married young couple. They were noted for their piety and the number of their children who became priests or nuns. In the latter cause they were supported by the patronage of old English Catholic families. The Bond home in St Mawgams, Cornwall, was probably on the estate of the Arundells who gave property and land to settle the Carmelite community from Antwerp at Lanherne. Two of the Bond daughters became choir sisters there (and two were Franciscan nuns elsewhere) and it is likely the Arundell family provided their dowry. The boys enjoyed a good education: William, the eldest, went to Sedgeley Park before Lisbon, four younger sons joined the Society of Jesus, and one became a secular priest. Neither of the two boys who were contemporaries with the Warrington Shepherds at Douai from 1833 to 1836 decided to join the Benedictine Order: James Isidore went to St Mary's College, Oscott from Prior Park, while John Isidore entered the Society of Jesus at Stonyhurst. The latter died on the mission in Calcutta in March 1844 while his eldest brother William was en route to Tasmania. Thus Ambrose Cotham and William Bond shared links with Douai and Stonyhurst through their respective brothers. Connections such as these were not uncommon in the Catholic community before 1850. Lawrence Cotham had a similar education to the Bond brothers but his choice of career made him a relative outsider in adult life. Although this was no hindrance to intimacy with his brothers, his close relationship with James Ambrose was a source of friction between Cotham and his Benedictine confrères.

Fr Bond's ten years of ministry in England after ordination introduced him to a Catholic environment with which Ambrose Cotham was unfamiliar from his childhood in Lancashire. After ordination Bond served in Swansea and Marnhull before being appointed to Chideock, Dorset. There he was pastor to the local

Catholic community living on the estate of Sir Humphrey Weld to whom Bond was chaplain. Chideock was, and is, proud of the four Chideock Martyrs who died as a result of religious persecutions in the sixteenth century during the Arundells' ownership of the estate. William Bond succeeded Fr Tilbury who had held the appointment for nearly four decades; in the four years Bond was in Chideock he made an impression on the Weld family that was remembered more than forty years later.

While Fr Bond was making friends who would smooth his return to England when he chose to return, Fr Cotham's prickly relationship with Archbishop Polding in his first years of priesthood may have blighted his reputation with some of his Benedictine confrères when he returned to Europe. Among lay people in Tasmania, however, he was fondly remembered during his lifetime and appreciated for his dedication on their behalf. Bond was a welcome addition to the Catholic life of Hobart. Considered 'talented and zealous'[5] in England and 'warm hearted, cheerful and unaffected'[6] in Tasmania he had the intelligence and temperament to be an asset to the new diocese, although Cotham's welcome was probably less effusive than the one given to Thomas Butler during the wilderness years.

Fr Bond's first chaplaincy at Port Arthur was at one of the most challenging locations in the colony. It was designated as a place of secondary punishment in 1833, along with Sarah Island and Maria Island. Its position on the Tasman peninsula, easy to guard while giving cheaper access than the island stations, led to its development as the largest penal settlement in the colonies. Its purpose was to exact severe punishment on convicts who had reoffended or were guilty of particularly heinous crimes. It also provided separate accommodation for so-called gentlemen convicts and political prisoners, considered a particular danger because of their ability to foment unrest among less sophisticated inmates. The prisoners' barracks were repeatedly enlarged and adapted to provide solitary cells for the 'silent punishment' of all classes of problematic convicts.

The introduction of the probation system in 1840, whereby all newly arrived convicts had to spend a period on a work gang before becoming eligible for a probation pass, boosted the population on the Tasman Peninsula. It hosted a number of different stations within the Port Arthur infrastructure, until the convict population reached 3,500. With plentiful natural resources, a large workforce, many of them skilled, and a good harbour, Port Arthur was not only self-supporting but also a significant contributor to the Tasmanian economy and unpopular when it undercut depressed civilian enterprises. The arduous primary employment of timber getting diversified into an astonishing range of industries: shoe making, blacksmithing, tailoring, and construction trades. All were used to provide convict necessities and consumer goods: the blacksmiths produced and fitted leg-irons as well as forging kettles and candlesticks for domestic use. The construction of a flour mill and granary between 1842 and 1845, in what had become an intensively industrialized township, exemplified Port Arthur's role as a place of punishment by hard labour; men were employed on the tread-wheel in preference to using other, mechanical, means of generating energy. Like the convicts who were forced to live there, the staff who worked alongside them could not escape from the penitentiary's boundaries unless they left the peninsula. Fr Bond had the luxury of separate accommodation but not surprisingly he made the most of opportunities to ride over to Hobart.

In order to deal with the undesirable consequences of housing young male offenders, aged between ten and fourteen, with adult convicts, a separate establishment was built alongside the Port Arthur prison complex. Port Puer was accessible only by boat, and was served by Port Arthur's Catholic chaplain. From 1834 to 1849 Point Puer operated with the ambivalence characteristic of the whole convict system. The acknowledgement that boys should be given the opportunity to reform their lives and learn useful trades was tempered by the reality that most of them were already suffering the consequences of deprivation and criminal associations from a very young age. Captain O'Hara Booth initiated a regime of strict discipline and severe punishment in which little account was taken of social circumstances for which the boys were not to blame. Booth was later transferred to the Queen's Orphan School and Fr Cotham was able to speak to him, in May 1846, about his concerns for Point Puer boys who were being transferred to Hobart New Town penitentiary, having had first-hand experience of the boys' station during his January visit to Port Arthur.

Fr James Luke Levermore OC

Unlike his companion George Hunter, Luke Levermore was not so young when he sailed for Tasmania, and he had turned 46 by the time he was ordained in 1844. As an non-ordained Cistercian monk of Mount St Bernard, Leicestershire, he was not an obvious choice for one of Bishop Willson's recruits. He joined the party as a catechist at short notice in place of a diocesan priest who dropped out and whose passage had been paid for. Although he did not have much time to prepare himself for this specific mission, he was a devout and experienced monk who had already been part of the foundation of Mount St Bernard's. After a period of serious ill-health in 1845 he gradually became proficient in a number of convict chaplaincy roles, remaining in Hobart and carrying out duties alongside Fr Cotham for the convict department and Fr Hall for the colonial department.[7] An unfortunate incident in May 1846 gives an insight into the dual nature of Tasmanian society and highlights how clergymen had to dance to the paymaster's tune even in strictly pastoral matters.

The distinction between colonial and convict departments was clearly understood by everyone, but if it created an opportunity to lambast 'unfeeling' churchmen the opportunity was not missed. In late April 1846 the botched funeral arrangements for Mrs Greenhatch caused her grieving widower to trundle his cart carrying her body, accompanied by grieving friends, 'bad and inclement as the day was, and almost impassible as were the streets leading to the cemetery,' around the neighbourhood looking for a priest bury her. *The Colonial Times*[8] carried an indignant account titled *Extraordinary Occurrence* of the poor man's troubles, followed the week after by a letter to the Editor from Fr Hall, who had been out of town with the Bishop at the time. After detailing the various unsuccessful alternative arrangements made with the undertaker to accommodate the funeral with Fr Levermore's duties at the Colonial Hospital and the Cascades Factory, Fr Hall made some general points:

> First—The Rev. Mr Levermore has nothing to do with colonial duties; he undertook this duty out of kindness to me.
>
> Second—The day and hour had been several times changed by the undertaker, much to the inconvenience of the Rev. Mr. Levermore, who had been detained a long time on the ground the previous day.
>
> Third—It is not correct that the Rev. Mr. Levermore arrived on the ground precisely at 2 o'clock, and left immediately, or that the corpse arrived at ten minutes past 2 o'clock.
>
> Fourth—The Rev. Mr. Cotham was not asked to bury the corpse, or if he were, he did not hear the request; but even so, Mr. Cotham's duties are convict, and they must be attended to first.
>
> I have examined the case well, and find that the fault was entirely with the undertaker, who several times changed the hour, and at last did not keep the time appointed. If truth had been stated by your informant, I should not have troubled you with these remarks.[9]

Fr Cotham, passing by on horseback, had apparently been begged by the undertaker to bury the corpse but he had 'refused to do so, as he was urgently required at the Orphan School'. Local newspaper journalism has, of necessity, to make much of the doings of big fish in little ponds, but the incident provides an insight into the effect of general policies on everyday routines and attitudes, when the pastoral needs of people competed with the official duties owed to the government by a hard-pressed handful of clergy.

Having acquired experience in Hobart Fr Levermore was assigned to the demanding post of chaplain to Darlington Probation Station on Maria Island, off the east coast of Tasmania. While Port Arthur prospered economically due to its relative closeness to Hobart, its harbour facilities, and the range of trades practised by the inmates, Maria Island was characterised by its remoteness and difficulty of access. It was reopened for use as a probation station in 1842; by the time of Fr Cotham's reconnaissance visit in February 1846 the convict population had peaked at nearly five hundred. The focus at Darlington was on progressing—or demoting—men through four classes: the best behaved, the tolerably good, the indifferent and, fourthly, the chain-gang and crime-class. Class status was marked by differences in work, food, living conditions, privileges, or solitary confinement as deemed appropriate to each man's behaviour. A regime of constant surveillance was needed to make these assessments. Oppressive vigilance by means of all-night lighting, boarded-up bunks to enforce separation, and solitary cells for fourth class prisoners, were used as punitive measures. Apart from a preoccupation with preventing 'unnatural' night-time activities, convicts' daily routines were strictly adhered to, including school and church attendance as part of the moral rehabilitation of prisoners.

Unlike stations on the Tasman Peninsula, Darlington Station was a compact environment where convicts, civilians, and military personnel lived closely together and there was no escape physically or psychologically from the suspicions of watchful guards. The senior assistant superintendent, James Boyd, wrote at length on conditions at Darlington Station to the Comptroller General in December 1846, and the *Launceston Examiner* found his account 'so methodically arranged and clearly expressed' that it was printed in full without comment. Boyd claimed to 'have heard the most disgusting evidence on this subject [unnatural crimes, that is to say homosexual practices]; in fact, so much so, that I have been perfectly shocked at the horrible depravity exhibited by the convicts'.[10] As lurid reports came in from other stations (the Coal Mines in particular) the probation system generally became morally discredited, adding to the growing distaste for transportation in England and Australia.

Fr Cotham's five-day visit to Maria Island was made two weeks after his locum duty at Port Arthur and with hardly a break in his normal routine in Hobart, although he did allow himself a day in Richmond on the way home, and was 'indisposed' on his first day back in Hobart. At the end of the month he wrote up a few notes about Darlington Station, probably in preparation for a permanent chaplain being sent out:

> Mon 9 [February] Journey overland to Spring Bay. Sailed in the evening in Government boat to Darlington, Maria Island. Boatmen were insubordinate to coxswain.

> Tues 10 Journey to Long Point to attend convicts ill of dysentery. Attended Hospital &c &c. Celebrated Divine Service, and preached to the Catholic convicts of the Station and returned to Darlington.

> Wed 11. Celebrated divine service and preached to convicts at the Darlington Station. Visited men in solitary cells. Attended Hospital &c &c.

> Thur 12 Sailed to Spring Bay township in Government Boat. Service and Religious Instruction for the Military stationed at Spring Bay.

> Fri 13 Journey homewards as far as Richmond. [Doubtless to visit Lawrence's family and celebrate his own 36th birthday on 12th February.]

> Sat 14 Med: Visited Mrs Rose sick of Dropsy.

> Sun 15 Divine Service and preached at Richmond and at the Anson.

Mon 16 Indisposed.

Memo. At Maria Island

John Marabella Italian good cook confict [*sic*]: house St [servant?] &c

Thomas Stapleton who read for the Sick. Farmer. At Long Point Mr Evans Superintendent 64 Catholics, 300 Men. Mr Bright C.C.E Brough B.C. Stephen Sadler 2nd Class without any trial sent to Separate Treatment and lost his promotion by sole Authority of Mr Lapham Superintendent. Mason Hospital Attendant at Long Point Prison and Protestant. Attentive and humane.

The Men in Solitary not let out to D. Service on Sundays

At 5o'c Prayers. From 10 to 1o'c Hospital and Solitary Cells. At 6o'c Prayers. From six to eight separate treatment cells.

Long Point every other Sunday and the Sick sometimes twice a week

Sunday from 11o'c till ½ past 12o'c.

Hospital and Solitary cells till 3

Prayers from 3 to 4o'c.

A vessel every week from Lucas' to Maria Isd.

In July 1847 Fr Levermore wrote a heartfelt reply to a 'sweet and consoling letter' he had received from Fr Cotham. He was struggling on Maria Island with loneliness and feelings of being unequal to his task. In his 'very great need' he resorts to many underlinings in his letter, as if to hammer home to himself the pastoral skills he needed to learn. Having unburdened his soul to Fr Cotham his mind turns to people and places he wants to hear about and his letter ends in a reassuringly cheerful tone. The letter is different in every way to Cotham's letter written to Bishop Polding in 1836, when he was the 'one poor and far away.' Cotham had received no encouragement, no advice on how to take his difficulties into his prayer life, and no sense of being part of the wider mission. Levermore's writing suggests he had a deep empathy with the convicts located on Maria Island, especially as its superintendent, Mr Lapham, adhered to the 'new' practice of separate cells and enforced silence to subdue his charges, imposing on men who had few intellectual resources what they dreaded more than physical hardship: psychological and emotional isolation. Living closely alongside them, the pious Fr Luke was certainly brought to his knees and wept for his sorry condition, consoled by memories and resolving to do better.

H.W.G.

Revd & very dear Father Cotham

Your sweet and consoling letter was most welcome. A letter from my spiritual Father will be welcome at any time that he thinks to write to one poor and far away. I thank you very humbly in our Lord for your spiritual advice, your words of consolation & peace, it is true there have been some difficulties, some disagreeables in this new mission. Pray for me that I may do as you advise, bear them patiently, and that has been a great deal, but you carry me further & advise much more to a poor weak nature, yea to embrace them with joy and affection these latter must be for the great—good—& fervent, for the saints and perfect, but for me it is a great thing to bow my neck in humble submission to the Eternal God, and to endure what I cannot well avoid. Some times I feel in my mind a will & desire to be lifted up above all earthly & [indecipherable] affections and presently I am brought down to utter a complaint but as if you would have me not only good & perfect but you attempt to carry up to consummate perfection by advising the praying God to prolong our troubles, if you my ever dear Father can say with St Paul not only so but we Glory in tribulation knowing that tribulation worketh patience & patience trust and trust Hope, and Hope confoundeth not, certainly I must congratulate with you my dear Father, but then you have been long in the vineyard of our Lord and I am only a new workman. Moreover an unskilful workman, one who has yet to learn the first rudiments of what it is to be a good vine dresser, one who has yet very great need of understanding how to prune, to lop off, to tye & prop up, to dig about and manure with the Divine Word of the Eternal Herald, to train and lead on in all virtues, to be a prop to the lame & the Blind, in fine a Physician to cure or to prescribe remedies for all sorts of complaints, wounds and evils. Pray therefore for me that I may be perfect in all the above Science, that so I may honour Almighty God and benefit my neigbour, in fine save my own Soul.

One thought that often comforts me in all difficulties—namely—that invariably through life after any trial and tribulation a blessing followed more or less according to the affliction proceeding, that has been through every change of scenery in life. As to this time I cannot say what is a covering(?), if any thing, but only I have found myself in great tribulation, so that if only that I have been humble and patient perhaps the great good God will also this time give a blessing, if so blessed be his Divine and ever holy name for ever and if I am not worthy of any special blessing even so may his divine and ever blessed name be for ever praised and loved, Amen.

I thank Almighty God that you have satisfaction among your orphan school children, the more when you see them approach piously the Holy Table, 17 at the feast of Sts Peter and Paul must have comforted your paternal heart, no doubt but Mr & Miss Quinn [sic] are a great support to your labours among them. Will you please give them my compliments, and to Mrs Gazard my kind regards. I hope they are all well. I am glad also that all goes on peaceably at the Anson. I hope they are civil to you and give no annoyance.

You did not tell me that you had a good Lady Religious instructor at the *Anson*, but some one reported it to me. I am obliged to hear that there is news from our Beloved

Bishop personally. You promise & Mr Hall also that by next boat I shall have his Letter, that the almighty Lord may prosper him. My dear Father I have been informed that you have had a trip to Port Phillip, have you seen Fr Therry. Was he not expected over to this Colony? Was your passage pleasant? You have not stated any thing about these things.

I am delighted to learn that you have at length some holy souls come to Hobart Town, the good nuns from Sydney. We are in great hopes that Almighty God will bless them and by his sacred blessing and enable them to do great good. Are they not the first nuns that have ever landed upon the soil of Vandiemens Land. May many follow to the cause of the Eternal God and his Church. Please present kind regards to them, say that I wish them very many blessings.

May the most just, the most high, the great and Eternal God, give you his sacred and holy Grace to do his ever holy Will in all things unto the bright day of Eternity is the humble prayer of your devoted servant and fellow labourer in the vineyard of our Lord,

J L Levermore[11]

Referred to as Brother Luke before his ordination in Hobart, Levermore had completed his monastic training before leaving Mount St Bernard, and had a mature faith life to sustain him. It seems from his reply to Fr Ambrose that his mentor (although twelve years junior in age) encouraged him with counsels of perfection such as both would have heard in the novitiate. The reflection on the parable of the vinedresser is sustained and verses from Scripture are readily incorporated into Fr Luke's personal narrative; despite the lack of community life the individual monk took responsibility for maintaining practices of monastic observance such as *lectio divina* and the recitation of the Divine Office. Faithful adherence to these duties was instilled into the novices'

Convict Chaplains in the Sole Gaol of England 213

training since self-discipline would be the norm when they were assigned to a mission outside the monastery.

Fr Cotham's journal contains many abbreviated references to the Divine Office, a cycle of psalms, readings, and prayers said at frequent intervals during waking hours. For all monks and priests handling a heavy working schedule alone there is the problem of fitting everything into the time available. An anecdote probably told by Cotham against himself was published after his death:

> He was so absent at times that when riding through the bush he would give the reins to his horse and attend so earnestly to his prayers and Divine Office that he paid no attention to the course taken by his horse till forcibly reminded of earthly affairs by being brought in contact with a tree.[12]

'The good nuns from Sydney' referred to in Levermore's letter were three Sisters of Charity who had arrived in Hobart more than two years after a subscription for their passage, foundation, and support had been launched by Bishop Willson in April 1845.[13] The intention at that point had been for five or six Sisters to live in a small cottage fitted up for their requirements and to take up positions at the *Anson* and Orphan School subsequently filled by lay catechists. As it happened, the three who eventually arrived took over the house at the rear of St Joseph's Church and the Bishop's household moved elsewhere. The first religious sisters had been brought to Sydney by Ullathorne in 1838 and, beginning at the Female Factory at Parramatta, had developed their ministry to women convicts. In Hobart they followed the same pattern of visits to the Female Factory and hospitals as well as starting St Joseph's School adjacent to their premises in Harrington Street. There is no reference to them at all in Fr Cotham's journal nor, it seems, in his correspondence. The arrival of the Sisters of Charity may well have been his first encounter with female religious but there is no evidence about his response to them. However, in later years he valued their contribution to church life and in person was characteristically chivalrous and practical towards them.

The Woolfrey Brothers

Luke Levermore had not expected to be long on his own in Tasmania. Two other monks from Mount St Bernard, brothers William Odilo Woolfrey OC, Prior of Mount St Bernard, and Henry Norbert Woolfrey OC, intended joining Bishop Willson in his new diocese, although they did not travel with him in 1844. They may have stayed behind in England to raise funds for their own project of establishing a Cistercian monastery in Tasmania. A foundation Cistercian community, including the Woolfreys, had come from Mount Melleray in Ireland to Mount St Bernard in the English East Midlands in 1835. Mount Melleray itself had a distinguished heritage of displacement from Brittany to Lulworth in Dorset, birthplace of the Woolfreys; a new house in the antipodes was eminently possible for such experienced foundation missioners. They were accompanied by William Xavier Johnson, a professed lay brother and also a founding member of Mount St Bernard, and perhaps intended as another catechist for Willson.

The status of Br Johnson caused some confusion as he was variously described at the time as a postulant or a priest, but a letter by Archbishop Polding makes it clear that he was ordained in Sydney and there is no indication that he spent much time in Tasmania. Nevertheless the monks' arrival in Tasmania in October 1846 was announced as 'an accession of three priests by the *Calcutta*'.[14] Twenty-five years later Abbot John Bartholomew Anderson of Mount St Bernard corrected some errors made in Fr Norbert's Australian obituary notices. 'In the May of 1846 he left [Hornby Castle] for Australia. His main object was to establish a colony of Cistercians in that far-off country. But, again, local wants were allowed by him to take precedence of personal projects.'[15] The matter of precedence of projects was to be the

Convict Chaplains in the Sole Gaol of England 215

cause of tensions between the Woolfreys and their bishops on both sides of the Bass Straits although it must have been clear to all that the over-riding incentive for four middle-aged men to leave their monastery was to spread the Cistercian charism in its integrity.

Mention of the Woolfreys is sporadic in Cotham's journal but it is not unreasonable to think there would have been a special bond with them as fellow monks. He was absent when they landed in Hobart but soon after his return from Port Phillip he notes £2 spent on a pyx for Fr Norbert and in December the loan of £1 to 'Fr O Dillon'; the spelling of Odilo's name consistently defeated him. On 4 January 1847 'Fr Norbert and George returned from Southport [convict station]' where George had gone two days earlier and the following day Fr Norbert accompanied Cotham to the *Anson* for prayers. The following week he makes the curious entry 'Drawing card for collars Father O Dillon—1/6d' and a few days later four shillings for Fr O Dillon's envelopes; at the end of January there is a cryptic entry regarding a 'journey with Father O Dillon to the back of the Orphan School. Stephen Madden's &c &c'. Fr Norbert had accompanied the climbing party to Mount Wellington in the meantime so it seems the two brothers were pursuing their own interests, Norbert being the more robust of the two. There is also a *Red Ruled Book* for Mr Johnston [*sic*], possibly the postulant. Gradually the Woolfreys found their places on the Bishop's team: Fr Odilo remained in Hobart, assisting Fr Cotham and George Hunter while Fr Norbert was stationed at Southport, on the south coast.

In August 1847 Messrs Cotham and Woolfrey are listed as buying an allotment of land—Lot 17 for £425—at an auction of Mr D. Lord's extensive estate.[16] The following month Fr Odilo who 'recently laboured under severe indisposition, has removed to some distance from Hobart Town and the Rev Mr Cottham [sic] has gone to reside with him in order to be nearer to his duties among the outstations'.[17] Twelve months later the two priests were sharing a house in Davey Street where there was a 'daring

216 *The Indomitable Mr Cotham*

attempt' at burglary, the second in three weeks, doubtless being targeted by the burglar as clerical gentlemen known to have access to relatively substantial funds.[18] The housing arrangement may have been made to reduce pressure on the Bishop's residence, and it was common for convict chaplains to have their own accommodation. Living with Fr Odilo, taking the opportunity to recite the Divine Office in common, joining 'Fr O Dillon' on a journey to the River Ouse district in October 1848, probably on another reconnaissance trip for a monastic foundation, were reminders to Ambrose Cotham of his own monastic calling, distancing him from diocesan and convict concerns. As fresh manpower arrived from England, Cotham's wish to take leave of absence from Tasmania seemed a realistic possibility.

Notes

[1]   Thomas Joseph Malachy Murray OSB, born c. 1785 Ireland, died 1853 Wollongong.

[2]   *The Courier* (Hobart), 31 October 1846, p. 2.

[3]   Accounts and Papers, Volume 43, Session February 1849 (Great Britain Parliament; House of Commons and Command; H.M. Stationery Office, 1849); 'Convict Discipline and Transportation', pp. 199–200. Mr Elliot, the only Protestant religious instructor on Norfolk Island after the departure of the unsuitable Revd Mr Ison was 'a layman, in bad health, and quite unequal to all the duties that have devolved upon him.' Hampton nevertheless commended the zealous endeavours of these two overburdened men.

[4]   Walter and Thomasina Hunter were friends of the Bishop during his time in Nottingham, and after Willson's visit to England in the mid-1840s they decided to emigrate to New South Wales with their younger son, Henry, and three daughters. The Hunter parents were dead by 1851. Henry Hunter brought his sisters to Tasmania and, encouraged by Bishop Willson, followed his father's profession as an architect. He was extremely successful in his business life and in positions of civic influence. As a leading Catholic layman he joined Bishop Willson as a commissioner of the New Norfolk Asylum and was leader of St Joseph's Choir for over thirty years; he also contributed to Hobart's civic and cultural development for nearly forty years.

Convict Chaplains in the Sole Gaol of England

5   G. Oliver, *Collections Illustrating the History of the Catholic Religion* [in South West England] (London: Dolman, 1857), p. 243.

6   *The Hobart Town Daily Mercury*, 4 April 1860, p. 3.

7   W. T. Southerwood, 'The Land That I Will Show You' in *Tjurunga*, No. 8, December 1974, pp. 77–92.

8   *Colonial Times (Hobart)*, 29 May 1846, p. 3.

9   *Ibid.*, 5 June 1846, p. 3.

10 *Launceston Examiner*, 30 December 1846, p. 7

11 DA VIII.A.Cotham; Levermore to Cotham, 16 July 1847.

12 *The Catholic Standard* (August 1883), p. 129, 'The Church in Tasmania: Collections and Recollections'.

13 *The Cornwall Chronicle* (Launceston), 5 April 1845, p. 2.

14 *Launceston Advertiser*, 26 October 1846, p. 3.

15 *Freeman's Journal* (Sydney), 24 August 1872, p. 10.

16 *Colonial Times* (Hobart), 13 August 1847, p. 3.

17 *Sydney Chronicle*, 30 September 1847, p. 3.

18 *Hobarton Guardian*, 8 November 1848, p. 3.

19 'WHEN YOU DESTROY HOPE IN MAN YOU DESTROY EVERYTHING'

AMBROSE COTHAM WAS conscious of his social standing, and kept within its parameters, but the men and women around him were not so circumscribed. Those who came to the colony as free emigrants or became emancipists had opportunities for change not available in the old country. Nevertheless, variables such as their own attitude, providence (or chance), and personal contacts made the outcomes unpredictable. Mobility through society applied to working class emigrants especially; scarcity of labour, of women, of incriminating information about the past, provided openings missing from English society. On 16 February 1847 Bishop Willson addressed an audience[1] in Nottingham during his first return visit to England, offering a constructive account of the government's probation system whereby a convict could, given a favourable wind, progress through the system's classifications. Significantly, he declared that, 'When you destroy hope in a man you destroy everything'. Willson believed that giving grounds for hope in a better future was one of the essential tasks of a humane penal system.

A Coded Language

'Friday 14 Peter Hughes the Coachman droped [sic] dead this morning at ½ past 6 oC.' This unadorned diary entry by Fr Cotham in August 1846 illustrates a peculiarly Tasmanian worldview of the period, one which Cotham and the other clergy imbibed. If they had questioned it too deeply they would have found themselves uncomfortably at odds with their social envi-

220 *The Indomitable Mr Cotham*

ronment, but happily the Gospel they preached supported a belief in the possibility of personal conversion. The entry is significant for what it does not say. Why should Fr Cotham not say simply that Peter Hughes, the Bishop's coachman, dropped dead; what more could he have said? The death was shockingly sudden for a youngish man used to out-door work with horses and an inquest was held. In *The Cornwall Chronicle*[2] the inquest report followed items about the Jewish Rabbi and the Anglican Bishop, so the connection with Bishop Willson gave Peter Hughes a prominence in death he would not otherwise have had. The witnesses in the coroner's court filled in the details about Peter Hughes:

> On Friday last [14th August], an inquest was held at Mr Dudgeon's Tavern, before A. B. Jones, Esq., Coroner, on the body of Peter Hughes, aged 33, a pass-holder in the service of Dr Willson, the Roman Catholic Bishop. From the evidence adduced, it appeared that the deceased had formerly led a very bad life, having been in the bush with Jackey Jackey, but since his servitude with the Bishop, he had become an altered man, and in the Bishop's own words, perfectly reformed, being sober, attentive, and in every respect steady and well-conducted; two of his fellow-servants deposed to the fact of his occasionally having complained of illness, for which he declined having medical advice, observing that there was nothing of consequence the matter with him; the pain would soon wear away, as it was only the effect of the heavy floggings he had received; all the witnesses stated that the deceased had not been drinking. Dr Crowther, who made the post mortem examination, stated that the immediate cause of death was the bursting of an aneurism of the heart, which was also much thickened; all the other viscera were perfectly healthy. A verdict to this effect was accordingly returned.[3]

The facts of Peter's life, as well as his death, were plainly stated; the edifying testimony from the Bishop suggests Peter was an exceptional case, a criminal reformed by particular attention, but

'When You Destroy Hope in Man You Destroy Everything'   221

his circumstances were not extraordinary; they were such as Tasmania was built upon.

Fr William Ullathorne had written about convict colonies in the bleakest of terms:

> Fifty thousand souls are festering in bondage ... We have taken a vast portion of God's earth and have made it a cess-pool ... we have poured down scum upon scum, and dregs upon dregs, of the offscourings of mankind, and, as these harden and become consistent together, we are building up with them a nation of crime.[4]

Ullathorne was deliberately stirring up public opinion to support reform of the convict system, and the Molesworth Inquiry of 1838 took up the challenge to the British Government to address a state of immorality that included not only the 'unnatural crime' of homosexuality 'but a range of activities including rape, murder, bestiality, drunkenness, the corruption of young children by convict servants, and anything involving violence'.[5] An outcome of the Molesworth Inquiry was the concentration of convicts in Tasmania under the new probation system, essentially a way of cleansing mainland Australia and managing the swollen numbers in Tasmania. The reputation in Britain of the island colony naturally suffered as a result, its identity being synonymous with depravity and moral danger. The perspective of Tasmanians themselves was different. They knew from experience that the development and economy of the colony had been possible not only from the forced labour of chain gangs (a relatively rare form of convict labour) but by the trades and skills the convicts brought with them. Standards of domestic life were raised not only by the assignment of women convicts to work as servants but by those women eventually taking their place as home builders in their own right.

Tasmanians knew how convictism worked not only by the experience of living alongside those who been transported but by themselves being former transportees, or married to them, or in business partnership with them. Their lived experience gave the lie to the notion of a criminal class of people who were bound

222   *The Indomitable Mr Cotham*

to follow a life of crime wherever they were and whatever their circumstances. In the interests of social cohesion it was pragmatic to avoid inflammatory language: to call a person a convict was worse than calling them a blackguard, and a code of language was deployed which endeavoured to mask the truth from visitors from abroad as well as from potential partners. The blind English traveller James Holman was sensitive to the power of words:

> In speaking of them the word *prisoner* is invariably substituted for *convict* by all classes ... the latter term being considered by them so exceedingly opprobrious that its application is highly offensive, and never forgiven.[6]

The 'very bad life' mentioned in the inquest report on Hughes referred to the years he had spent in Australia since his transportation, and the pain he suffered as a result of punishment is given as an example of his stoicism; there is no allusion to the reasons why he came to be transported in the first place.

Peter Hughes was born in Manchester in 1813 and his first offence was that for which he was transported: stealing iron in the street. The sentence of fourteen years reflected the fact that no violence was done against another person. He was 19 at the time and his accomplice was 22-year-old Jonathan Hope. Both men were convicted at Liverpool Quarter Sessions on 9 July 1832; by the 27th they were at Woolwich on board the hulk *Justitia*, awaiting transportation.[7] The gaoler's report noted that Hughes was 'extremely well conducted' and Hope was 'orderly' among many men who were of 'bad character' or worse. The men were separated for the four month voyage to Australia; Hope sailed in November on the *Surrey*, arriving in Tasmania in March 1833; Hughes was one of two hundred and thirty-six men on the *Mangles* which sailed on 8 December and docked in Sydney Cove in April 1833. For the purposes of identification Hughes was closely observed on board ship: he was of average build, five and a half feet tall and stocky, with a dark, ruddy, freckled complexion, dark brown hair and grey eyes. He was not marked by disease,

'When You Destroy Hope in Man You Destroy Everything' 223

scars or tattoos; as a hackney coachman he was probably a healthy looking young man, used to being outdoors; he could read but not write, and he was a Catholic.

Given the same sentence for the same crime, the outcome for the two young men was very different. Peter Hughes evidently made bad connections, as he moved from Sydney Cove to Parramatta to Darlinghurst. At some point he came into contact with the infamous William Westwood, known as Jackey Jackey or 'the gentleman bushranger', and probably spent time with him during Westwood's seven months on the run between 1840 and 1841. Like Westwood, Peter Hughes received a sentence of transportation for life at Berrima, and both were transferred to Tasmania in 1842.[8] Hughes was able to avoid trouble for long enough to gain a probationary pass as Bishop Willson's coachman, where he was able to work with his employer rather than rebel against him. In the whole colony he could not have found a more supportive master, nor a household so disposed to see him succeed in reforming his life. It was not the crimes of his past life which killed him but the hard punishment to which he had been subjected and which ultimately cut short the restitution he might have made.

Jonathan Hope avoided the pitfalls of bad company and being assigned to the constabulary his good behaviour was noted in the right places. Newspapers reported the changes in status for convicts, whether it was a change of assignment or the award of a probationary pass, by listing their names and the ship they had arrived on. The log book recording pardons gave each man a brief individual citation, almost congratulatory in tone; thus, in 1843

> John Harden (convicted 1818) For good conduct, there being only three offences being recorded against him in the last eleven years.

> William Harris (1825) Having been in the colony so long and his conduct having considerably improved.

Jonathan Hope (1832) For special services in the Police Department of the Colony and being well recommended by the Chief Police Magistrate.[9]

As a free man Jonathan chose to leave Tasmania; he married Amelia Smith in the Wellington district of New South Wales in 1850 and spent the rest of his life there, working as a police constable apart from a short period spent at the gold diggings in Wellington. His name appears in the Police Gazette as a victim of crime in November 1863 after he reported the loss of clothing from his tent. Unlike Peter Hughes he did not suffer lasting harm from harsh punishment. After the death of his wife he became a resident in the Liverpool Asylum for the Destitute where he lived for eleven years until his death in 1895. The entry in the Asylum log book is coded, but only to outsiders, 'Came to Australia by ship *Surrey* in 1833'.

'It Depends Upon Your Own Exertions'

Only a few of the many letters he received remain among Fr Cotham's papers. There are none from his family and we have only hints of what he might have written to them, as in the memoranda he made for himself in his journal for 21 March 1846: 'Attended G. Hospital. Wrote to Lawrence that his bill for £70 would be due April 3rd, sent the letter by F. Livermore', followed by a further 'letter to Law—dr £70'.

Despite distance and complicated lines of communication people went to considerable lengths to stay in touch (although Post Offices printed long columns of names of those whose letters awaited collection). After Fr Keating visited Port Arthur during Cotham's supply visit in January 1846 and the priests spent an evening together, it was no coincidence that Cotham received a letter from Joseph William Hay, the former Secretary of the Launceston Catholic Institute, in April. Keating was Hay's parish priest in Penrith, New South Wales and news of Fr Cotham put

'When You Destroy Hope in Man You Destroy Everything' 225

an idea into Joseph's head. His letter is an example of how not to curry favour:

> Penrith, 8th April 1846
>
> Revd & Dear Sir
>
> I know not what excuse to offer for not writing to you before this but I have been really so tossed about the world … with every exertion and economy we are barely able to keep house …
>
> I wish you would be kind enough to speak to Mr Rowe concerning the money which he honestly owes me for *Tablets* supplied. I sent him the bill more than once. It amounts to £6.13.6d, a copy of which is enclosed … besides which I was obliged to borrow £5 from my brother-in-law to pay marriage licence &c. You will perhaps say why get married when so badly off? But my answer is, that no school would be allowed to be conducted by a single man having children of both sexes attending; besides which we live every bit as cheaply if not cheaper than I did or could have done when single. … Just on the morning that I left Launceston, O'Meara stopped my box of beautiful books 197 in number … for a claim which he said he had on me.
>
> I was glad to hear from Revd Keating who is our parish priest that Mr Quin and his sister were doing well at the Orphan School in H. Town, please to remember me kindly to them both … Many a night have I watered my pillow with my tears for the loss of my property & goods, especially my poor dear father's gold watch, his last parting gift to me, which, under present circumstances, I <u>fear</u> I shall never be able to redeem. I wish you would be so good as to lend me your old silver watch until such time as I could redeem my gold one. You might send it by the Capt of the *Louisa* to care of Very Revd Dr Gregory St Mary's Sydney. I lose a great deal in the course of my duty for the want of a watch. I suppose it would be useless for me to ask you to send my own—I would remit you the £25 after my arrival in Valparaiso … Sometimes I think of entering an action

> against Girard for swindling me out of my property, but
> then where is the money to come from? Please send me a
> long letter in return.

Hay is so 'greatly distressed for a little money' that he will take whatever Dr Rowe sees fit to pay for his outstanding subscriptions for *The Tablet* and he will settle for £4 or £5 only if he cannot get the whole £9 owing to him. Hay had left Launceston in a hurry, having given up his partnership with Stephen Skitter in a wholesale butchery business to clear his debts. In New South Wales he had reverted to more suitable work as a schoolmaster; the small Catholic school in Penrith was his second posting and though the salary was higher than in the first—£40 instead of £30—it was still paltry for a man of his expectations. Family connections and reputation were important to him, well-educated and cultured as he was, and he wanted his appearance to be equally impressive. So if Fr Cotham could lend him his old silver watch until he can redeem his own gold watch from the pawnbroker he would be most grateful.

Joseph was trying to get what he could to make a poor situation less irksome but he probably realised, having reached the age of twenty-eight, that he did not have the enterprising skills needed to become a rich man in Australia. He had already formulated an alternative plan, 'I have written a long letter to my cousin in Valparaiso and hope ere long to remove out of this country altogether', a course of action suggesting the loan of a silver watch was likely to become a permanent gift.

There is no record of Cotham's reply, but almost certainly it was not a long one nor did he part with his silver watch, although he forwarded a letter from a Mr Hay to Mr McDonagh at Lydney in May. Although Australia was an opportunity for many people, bond or free, to do well in life, success was not a foregone conclusion, and neither education nor good contacts would necessarily make the path smooth. Lawrence Cotham was helped considerably by his Cassidy father-in-law and loans from his brother's chaplaincy salary but self-pity or presumption would have turned Fr Ambrose against helping him. One of his notebook jottings, probably his own comment on a passage he read, expresses his opinion:

> vol 7 Making small provision for young men is hardly justifiable; and is of all things the most prejudicial to themselves. They think what they have much larger than what it is, and make no exertion.

> The young should never hear any language but this; You have your own way to make, and it depends upon your own exertions whether you starve or not.

'I am in a pretty fair way of doing'

A young man who did exert himself was Peter Dawson, who seems to have made Ambrose Cotham's acquaintance by chance. He came out, with his brother Edward, on the *Bachelor* in 1835 as a steerage passenger. The long voyage and few passengers, about thirty in all, including a dozen children, unsurprisingly brought him and Lawrence Cotham together. As a fellow Catholic he settled in among the Hobart congregation, subscribing the middling sum of £5 to St Mary's building fund. In 1840 he decided to try his prospects in Victoria. The letter he sent to Fr Cotham soon after his arrival is written in a clear hand, and its formality does not stifle his optimistic outlook. If the reference to his new wife comes from the head rather than the heart it was no less likely to bode well for their future prosperity.

> Melbourne

> 7th February 1841

> Reverend & dear Sir

> Your enclosed note of the 28th December I received upon the 18th ultimo. Indeed you cannot imagine how happy I was to hear from my dear friends, I mean to write directly to my friends. I have also to inform you that my brother Edward arrived here on last Monday from Sydney so we both intend writing Home in a day or two.

228 *The Indomitable Mr Cotham*

Dear Sir, I see you are still anxious for my welfare as you have always been and thank God I am happy to inform you that I am doing well. I have got a most respectable and industrious wife, <u>a woman of superior education</u>. She follows the dressmaking and <u>earns</u> a good deal in the week. I live with a Messrs Chisholm & Co, Linen drapers etc, whose <u>friendship</u> I have gained, and has told me if I <u>conduct</u> myself as well as I have done hitherto he would give me a share in a business. My hours are from 9 o'clock in the morning till 9 o'clock at night but one hour for dinner and one for tea. As I board at home, my salary is <u>£150</u> per annum and he has promised to raise it still higher; he told me he could not think of parting with me when I was about to leave him and go to a Messrs Manton, the Merchants and Ship owners so I consented to stop. I have a few boarders who pay me 25/- per week, so now dear sir, I am in a pretty fair way of doing.

I should be happy to hear from you oftener and I would have written you ere now but least [*sic*] you might find it too much presumption in me. I shall send you a piece of Port Phillips' papers by the same post and I should be happy to see you some day or other in this beautiful country, but certainly trade is very dull at present owing to want of money, but the crops are beautiful and abundant; labour is still very high notwithstanding the flow of emigrants for the last two months; we had emigrants to the amount of 10 or 12 hundred souls. More are daily expected. The Parish Priest the Very Revd Mr Geoghehan is my greatest friend.

I fear I am trespassing too much upon your precious time with my scribbling so I shall conclude with wishing you may be long a zealous preacher of the Gospel of Christ and long a worthy pastor of your Holy flock is the ardent prayer of your most obedient Humble Servant, Peter Dawson

His profitable wife was Anna Elizabeth née O'Dell from Tipperary. She had come out to Victoria as an assisted emigrant in 1839,

'*When You Destroy Hope in Man You Destroy Everything*'   229

aged 24, one of forty-one single women on the *Westminster*, most of whom could read and write. Peter knew the worth of his wife and his own good fortune in marrying her. His employer, John Moffat Chisholm, had arrived not long before, in 1838, and had set up in business as a merchant and married Miss Osbourne before the year was out. Although not particularly wealthy, the smallness of Port Phillip's community enabled him to become one of its leading lights, in no way hampered by insolvency on various occasions in the 1840s.

Peter does not complain about his long working hours, but the strength of the labour market was such that employers were forced to reduce the shop opening hours, closing at 8 p.m. except on Saturdays. For their part, a dozen small business men were willing to band together to accept the liability for the debts, amounting to £10,000, of Mr W. Rucker, which bankrupted all of them in turn. Nevertheless, Peter Dawson was set up in a shop and although he disappears from Fr Cotham's life there is no reason to suppose he and his wife did not continue to do well in 'this beautiful country'.

Notes

[1]   *The Courier* (Hobart) 28 July 1847, p. 4.

[2]   *The Cornwall Chronicle* (Launceston), 15 August 1846, p. 623.

[3]   *Colonial Times* (Hobart), 18 August 1846, p. 3.

[4]   W. Ullathorne, *The Catholic Mission in Australia* 1837; quoted by A. Alexander, *Tasmania's Convicts; How Felons Built A Free Society* (Crows Nest NSW: Allen and Unwin, 2010), p. 123.

[5]   A. Alexander, *Tasmania's Convicts; How Felons Built A Free Society* (Crows Nest NSW: Allen and Unwin, 2010), p. 124.

[6]   J. Holman, *A Voyage Round the World, Including Travels in Africa, Asia, America etc From MDCCCXXVII to MDCCCXXXII Vol. IV* (London: Smith, Elder and Co, Cornhill, 1835), p. 395, following a visit to the Cascades Female Factory in early March 1831.

[7]   Ancestry.com provides details of the convict records of Peter Hughes and Jonathan Hope.

[8] Despite being allowed to leave Port Arthur, for displaying brave conduct, to serve six months' probation at Glenorchy in 1845, Westwood was not able to profit from the opportunity. He was tried for armed robbery and sentenced to life imprisonment on Norfolk Island. In 1846 he led an insurrection of prisoners resulting in the death of four prison staff. He was hanged with eleven other convicts in October 1846; this was the mass execution at which Fr Bond was present.

[9] Ancestry.com; 'NSW and Tasmania, Australia, Convict Pardons and Tickets of Leave, 1834–1859'.

20 CONGENIAL PURSUITS

MBROSE COTHAM FOUND activity and companionship energising and worth noting in his fragmentary journal. He saw his enterprising brother Lawrence ('Law') in Richmond or Hobart fairly frequently, sometimes with the object of lending money to him or trying to get it repaid. Lawrence was his family and the young nephews and nieces were well known to their uncle James. The Cassidy in-laws were model church stalwarts: John was

> a most charitable man and a great benefactor to the Catholic church, of which he was a worthy member, having kindly given the valuable land on which the Richmond church, school rooms, sexton's house, grave yard &c., now occupy, as well as large sums of money, from time to time, to complete the same, and it is only just to add that, the deceased was never known to refuse aid to deserving objects, no matter what their creed or country,

and his wife Eleanor

> ever united a constant attention to her domestic affairs to an ardent love of God, and an anxious desire for the salvation of her soul. To prayer she devoted the hours that business allowed for leisure, and was always observant to all her religious duties. Charitable, humble, retiring, her 'life was hidden with Christ in God'.[1]

As Irish farming people they may not have reminded the Cotham brothers of their own Lancashire parents but in their own way they were the foundation of solid virtues and strong ties.

More to Ambrose's social taste was a man like Murray Burgess who had joined the clerical climbing party on Mount Wellington in January 1847. He was remembered as 'a ripe Shakesperian scholar, an admirable elocutionist, theatrical critic, and friend of old-time actors' but when Cotham knew him he was a cultured young man just beginning a distinguished career in public service, on the way to becoming 'a noted conversationalist' and a companion for visits to the Van Diemen's Land Mechanics Institute. Bishop Willson may have had hopes of drawing him into the priesthood but Murray married Emma Ross in 1849 and together they had a family of twelve children.[2]

A painstaking, and yet pleasurable, duty for Cotham was the purchasing, supplying, and arranging of books, the single most frequently noted activity in his journals. Thus, on Wednesday 18 March 1846:

> Lent the Bishop to pay Wallace £5.12/-
> Pious Biography for Young Men 2/6
> Lessons on the Principles of Morality or the Learned Man of the Village   2/6
> The Portable Key of Heaven (4 copies)   3/8
> Popular Instructions on the Commandments and Sacraments by Liguori   3/-
> Fr Rowland   2/-
> Spirit of Liguori 2/-
> Lenten Monitor, totalling 19/8   4/-
> £8.1/8
> Rain pm. Ride to Anson to visit sick Woman. Lent Life of St Stephen to School Master at O.S.

Similar volumes of Catholic doctrine and devotion were readily available in Hobart from John Moore, printer and publisher of the *Hobarton Guardian, or True Friend of Tasmania* at his premises at 11 Macquarie Street.[3] After being 'wearied out!' with Mrs Montgomery's business on the *Anson* on the 24th Cotham had another long day on the 25th as he spent the evening 'till late, tired!' going over Fr Butler's church and private accounts. Fr Cotham then 'wrote letter to Lawrence dr. Pecuniaries' before finally going to bed at 2 a.m. As the heavy rain continued on the following day Fr Butler took the coach to his parish in Launceston, while Cotham stayed indoors 'removing the Derby books

Congenial Pursuits 233

from Long Room to the Room below' before being called out to the dying Fanny Doherty on the *Anson*. There was more arranging of the Long Room the next day. That evening he 'returned to sleep at the Bishop's', possibly in the book-free Long Room. After yet another session in the Long Room, and four shillings and sixpence spent on 'Lead and Cedar F Polished; Paper Holder' the rearrangement of books was finished.

On Sunday 29 March, Cotham

Took to the Anson Catechisms 50
Derby Garden of Soul   12
7th Monthly Weekly Instructor 1
Vol 1st, 7th [instalment]

On Monday 13 April he returned to his ongoing pastoral and personal concerns:

Arranged books. Ser[mon] on education. Lawrence called and borrowed the £5 he had before returned

and the following day,

Received from Mr Dunne for books £0.13.0.

There is no complaint about the book work, and ten years later after a session arranging bookcases in Cheltenham the contented remark, 'all is well' summed up the day.

The interest in books was more than a personal hobby; a concern for education was part of a convict chaplain's duty. Returns to the Convict Department recorded not only the numbers of those who could read and write on arrival but the number of those who had learnt since then. As another measure of efficiency, the proportion of convicts who could recite the Lord's Prayer was recorded; the figure was almost always one hundred per cent although some stations admitted there was one incorrigible person out of five hundred who could not recite it from memory. The use of religious tracts had an obvious connection with the aim of subduing and improving the behaviour and language of convicts, but the place of books in the system is more nuanced than simple pedagogy and exhortation.[4]

The probation system entailed the confinement and segregation of convicts, therefore what to do with them when they were not working was a crucial part of maintaining discipline in a rigorous routine. Standing Orders issued in 1841 emphasised the punitive aspect of the probation system as always paramount while allowing for aids to the convict's reformation of life:

> The Superintendent will issue the Books in his charge, at discretion, to the best conducted Convicts of each class, on Saturday and Sunday afternoons; taking great care that they are returned to him through his Assistants on each evening in a proper state. So, upon days upon which the usual labour cannot be performed, owing to the state of the weather; and on these days, in addition to the Saturday afternoons, such Convicts as are desirous of obtaining instruction in reading will be allowed to attend in a hut set apart for that purpose. Upon all these occasions the Superintendent will read a moral lecture and an evening prayer to the Convicts in the Gang.[5]

An instruction of 1843 put the management of station libraries under the religious instructors' care as part of the nucleus of moral improvement formed by the religious instructor and schoolmaster with their chapel, classroom, and library. Alexander Maconochie, commandant of Norfolk Island from 1840 to 1844, requested not only religious and moral books but also 'works of practical instruction' on topics such as gardening, agriculture, cottage architecture, brewing, and baking. He considered *Robinson Crusoe* an example that taught 'energy, hopefulness in difficulty, regard and affection' and he recommended novels by Walter Scott, Maria Edgeworth, and Jane Austen.[6] The provision of reading material would rely very much on the commitment of the person responsible for supplying it, including their persuasiveness in procuring donations from sympathetic supporters in

Congenial Pursuits 235

the neighbourhood. It is likely that Fr Cotham's own literary leanings impacted directly on his convict charges.

It would be a mistake, however, to put convict reading on a par with the instructive or leisurely pursuits enjoyed by literate free persons. Within the penal system, the enforcement of silence while convicts communally listened to a reader or read alone was primarily a disciplinary measure. Convicts were prevented from interacting with one another even when they were in close proximity. (When ordinary measures failed solitary confinement was the next stage of controlling unruly behaviour or language, or the use of the loathsome tube-gag.) Though the reading matter might be instructive or entertaining it was to be listened to in strict silence, without movement or interruption. An extreme form of the 'silent system' was officially adopted between 1846 and 1848 but was soon discredited due to the lack of appreciable benefits. However, throughout this decade surveillance and separation, aimed particularly at preventing depraved sexual activity, exploitation, and corruption among prisoners, were underpinning principles.[7] The 'contamination' could also move in the other direction, so that what was a pleasure to the religious instructor— his books, his hymn singing—became associated with coercive control of vicious habits. It would be easy to overlook the mental and physical adjustments needed every time Fr Cotham and his co-workers stepped into and out of the penal environments.

Fr Cotham was fortunate in having his salary, averaging £22 per month, to use against the pervasiveness of convictism in his everyday life. His journal records his duties but not his feelings as he went about them. His simple financial accounts could be read as evidence of dandyism or self-indulgence if they were part of a broader picture of such character traits. Read in the context of his duties they are hints about his coping strategies. The most regular personal item to appear is snuff (on one occasion Cuba snuff), a modest ounce or two each week, costing one shilling per ounce. When his snuff-box was stolen from an open window, it was not such a minor incident to him and was duly recorded in his journal.[8] If supplies were precarious he bought in bulk: from Mr White's 1lb of snuff for eight shillings and sixpence on 28 July 1846. Taking snuff was a lifelong habit; in 1876 his Douai account for it amounted to six francs and thirty centimes. In this particular habit Cotham ran contrary to his bishop who found the effect sickening as when twenty priests gathered together in one room, were 'snuffing, spitting, hawking, blowing snouts' while he was conducting their spiritual retreat in 1862.[9] The uncouth behaviour sounds unlike Cotham, but Bishop Willson may have had to make allowances for him as a man set in his ways after years without close supervision.

Ironically, tobacco was a bugbear throughout the convict system. Men, and women, were allowed a small ration that inevitably became a form of currency. James O'Keefe, serving ten years for thieving in Cheltenham, was a master at procurement and 'having tobacco improperly in his possession'. On Norfolk Island his punishment was one month hard labour in chains, in Port Arthur a mere four days in solitary confinement.[10]

Having cleared his airways by snuff, the bad smells assailing them were countered by essential oil of lavender, 6d., Eau de cologne, 5s., or a smelling bottle, 4s. To keep a smart appearance— vital for a gentleman's morale—he used Odonto powder, 3s. 6d., Rimmels Shaving cream, 2s., and an occasional hair cut for one shilling. His health was boosted by six dozen 101 Pills, 6s., two dozen Rhubarb and blue Pills, 1s. 6d., a two ounce canister of Sundifoot, 2s., and a bottle of olive oil, 2s. 6d.; twice he bought morphia costing 2s. for himself. Finally, the outer man was presented in well-soled boots, £2 16s. 6d. paid to John O'Donnell between September 1845 and May 1846; in the spring (August and September) of 1846 his new clothes for travelling with the Bishop and prior to his visit to Port Phillip were almost entirely woollen: one lambswool shirt, a pair of Angola braces, five pairs of Shetland Wool hose, three pairs of wool sox [sic], and one pair worsted hose; gloves and a silk front completed the turn-out.

Congenial Pursuits 237

Some items of expenditure were not for himself. Treats were taken regularly to the *Anson:* lollipops for the children, apples and peppermints for the women, and sixpence for the old woman who held his horse while he conducted prayers at the Brickfields Depot on Sunday afternoon. Besides the fares for the ferry or occasional coach he would tip the men an extra shilling. Fr Cotham was careful with his money but he enjoyed being at liberty to spend it and make life a little more pleasant for everyone, himself included.

A single entry, for Friday 10 July 1846, records fifteen shillings spent for 'Music at the M. Institute'. There was a regular programme of talks given at the Mechanics' Institutes of Hobart and Launceston, usually on a scientific, geological, or historical topic. Clergymen were frequent speakers, but Cotham does not seem to have been a regular attender. However, in June and July of 1846 much was made in the local newspapers of the tour to the mainland and Tasmania by violinist Leopold Ravac and his accompanist Julius Imberg, both originally from Germany.

> On Thursday evening, this distinguished Violinist will give his <u>last</u> Concert in Hobart Town, at the Mechanics' Institution ... We are sure that those who have heard him, will be happy to hear him again; and we cannot doubt that those who have not yet enjoyed the privilege, will avail themselves of the last opportunity that may occur for years of listening to so accomplished an artiste.[11]

Their repertoire included their own adaptations of excerpts from Rossini, Bériot, Bellini, and Donizetti, much of it stirring and colourful. However, the *Colonial Times*, and presumably the 'genteel audience', preferred otherwise:

> To our taste, however, his adagio performances are the most pleasing and delightful, breathing, as they do, the very soul of melancholy and pathos, and thus constituting the very poetry of music. The audience was perfectly entranced ...[12]

238   *The Indomitable Mr Cotham*

A taste for music that induced a sense of 'pensive luxury' and 'dreamy ecstasy' is easy to ridicule but in the circumstances of Tasmania in 1846 it is understandable, and forgivable, if people, having paid their five shillings (too much, thought the Launceston press) should want to be taken away from 'a life of noisy riot, of filth, indecency and profaneness', the natural consequence a system which operated by 'herding in numbers and in idleness men whose former lives are evidence of their demoralization, and whose latter condition neither imposes a restraint on bad passions, nor affords assistance to good dispositions'.[13] The audience at the Mechanics Institute needed to know that their lives were the antithesis of the majority.

Fr Cotham did not need to pay to hear good music. George Hunter's brother Henry was able to build on the sound musical footing given to the Catholic Church in Hobart by Joseph Reichenberg. The unlikely career of this latter gentleman had taken him from his birthplace in Naples to Sydney after he joined the 40th Foot Regiment and became its bandmaster. Once discharged from the army he settled in Hobart in 1825 as a music teacher, credited with conducting the first reported musical concert in Hobart in 1826. He was a stalwart for the small Catholic congregation in many ways, including musically. He founded St Joseph's choir and was the first organist of that church, as well as composing pieces for it. His generosity extended to the Jewish congregation at the opening of their first synagogue in 1845. From one young man's memory of a similar ceremony in Europe, Reichenberg was able to construct a five-part harmonization which he taught to the cantors, learning a little Hebrew himself to be able to fit words to music.[14] Tutored by Henry Hunter, Reichenberg's daughter Jane

> had an excellent training in the high-class sacred music which was so well rendered by the small, but efficient choir of St. Joseph's Church, as to earn some fame for it even beyond Tasmania, and the young organist became a

Congenial Pursuits 239

proficient exponent of the church music of Mozart, Haydn, Gounod, and other masters.[15]

The opportunity for hearing a range of music, well-performed, was another experience for Cotham to store away for later use in a more judgemental environment.

Notes

[1] Obituaries for John Cassidy and Eleanor Cassidy, *Hobarton Guardian*, 12 July 1851, p. 3, and 15 January 1850, p. 2 respectively.

[2] *Sydney Morning Herald*, 24 July 1906, p. 6, obituary. 'Mr Murray Burgess [1824–1906], one of Hobart's old notabilities … had been a clerk in the Medical Department [17 May 1844], secretary to the Board of Education [July 1855], and Inspector of Schools [1863], which position he retained until 1872. Subsequently he was Secretary to the Tasmanian Education Department.'

[3] 'Portable' refers to the book, not the Key; Dr Milner's (1752–1826) compendium remained a sound staple of Catholic devotion for at least another century. St Alphonsus de Liguori (1696–1787) taught a method that aimed to make the practice of mental prayer simple and clear, within easy reach of everyone. See, for example, J Moore's advertisement in *Hobarton Guardian, or True Friend of Tasmania*, 8 September 1847, p. 4, for books available to the public.

[4] See K. Adkins, *Standing Orders for the Regulation of the Probation System of Convict Labour in Van Diemen's Land*, (Hobart: James Barnard, Government Printer, 1841), 6, quoted in 'Convict Probation Station Libraries in Colonial Tasmania' *Script & Print* 34:2 (UTAS: online 2010), pp. 87–92, © 2010 BSANZ [ISSN 1834–9013], p. 87. In this brief, fascinating, introduction to the topic works cited by Adkins include *Historical Records of Australia*, ser. 1, vol. xx (February 1839–September 1840) (Commonwealth Parliament, Government Printer, 1924), pp. 535–37; I. Brand, *The Convict Probation System: Van Diemen's Land 1839–1854* (Hobart: Blubber Head Press, 1990), p. 28; *Regulations for the Religious and Moral Instruction of Convicts in Van Diemen's Land*, 1 December 1843, reproduced in Brand, *Convict Probation System*, pp. 240–41.

[5] *Ibid., Standing Orders 14–15.*

[6] *Ibid.*, p. 92.

[7] See C. Gilchrist, 'A life of noisy riot, of filth, indecency and profaneness': the convict voice and the bourgeois imagination' in *Journal of the Royal*

240 *The Indomitable Mr Cotham*

Australian Historical Society (June 2006).

[8] 24 October 1848.

[9] W. T. Southerwood, *The Convicts' Friend: Bishop R. W. Willson* (George Town, Tasmania: Stella Maris Books, 1989), p. 278.

[10] Conduct Record Card: references Con 33/1/79; Con 17–1-2 pp. 170–171; Con 30–1-2 p.319. Transcribed by Port Arthur Historic Site Management Authority and kindly forwarded to the author by Janet Phippard.

[11] *The Courier* (Hobart), 1 July 1846, p. 2.

[12] *Colonial Times* (Hobart), 26 June 1846, p. 3; see also *The Cornwall Chronicle* (Launceston), 20 June 1846, p. 469.

[13] *Launceston Examiner*, 24 October 1846, p. 6, 'The State of Van Diemen's Land'.

[14] *Colonial Times* (Hobart), 11 July 1845, p. 3.

[15] *The Mercury* (Hobart), 1 September 1923, p. 15; report on the occasion of achieving fifty-five years as organist at St Joseph's Church, Hobart.

21 INTERLUDE: VISIT TO PORT PHILLIP, 1846

THE THIRD, AND final, period Cotham spent away from Tasmania concerned Fr Therry's removal from the island although this was not the sole reason for his short visit to Port Phillip. On 8 September 1846 he accompanied Bishop Willson for seven miles down the Derwent River as the Bishop embarked on a voyage to England. Protracted farewells were not uncommon when all parties were aware of the dangers from attack, storms, or illness at sea. Bishop Willson was fully aware of Cotham's wish to take his own leave of absence in England; it was one of the reasons given by him to the Colonial Office when he sought permission to recruit new clergymen for his diocese. A week after the Bishop's departure Cotham wrote to the government requesting leave of absence and delivered the letter to the Comptroller General the following day. He knew nothing could be done until the Bishop's return so, perhaps as a fillip to his spirits, it had been arranged that he should have a short time away from his duties. There are two instances in his journal, in August and December, when Cotham makes a note of having bought morphia for two shillings so it seems he was suffering more than usually from pain or ill health. Ten days after the Bishop sailed he drew out nearly £40 in gold and cash, spending some of it on a hat, gloves, and silk front for himself and a rug for the journey.

Although dubbed in the local newspapers the 'Father of the Australian Catholic Church' and as such an apparent candidate for advancement as far as the laity were concerned, Therry had been a constant thorn in the side of Ullathorne, Polding, and Willson. Within weeks of Archbishop Polding's arrival in Sydney in 1835 Fr Ullathorne had helped him extricate church papers

242 *The Indomitable Mr Cotham*

from Therry's tenacious hold. Ullathorne tried to be fair to everyone when he wrote, 'He [Therry] was sent to Hobart Town after I left the Colony, which put things into a long confusion and very much embarrassed Dr Willson after he became the first Bishop of that See. Still, he was always a good and pious man.'[1] In July 1846 the tortuous and divisive issue of property rights for St Joseph's Church, Hobart was tackled once more, with strong words and feelings. Frs Dunne, Butler, and Bond came from their respective postings at Richmond, Launceston, and Port Arthur to attend a meeting between the Bishop and Fr Therry. Messrs Alcock and Regan of St Joseph's church committee visited later in the day. Cotham tersely summed up the day's outcome: 'Blow up with Ep[Episcopus/Bishop]' although his official record dated 23 July, and printed three years later, was more circumspect:

> The memorandum drawn up by the Catholic Clergymen and Mr. Therry was no more than an alteration of a section of the previous agreement, proposed by Captain Swanston. It was afterwards agreed by Mr. Therry and the Clergymen assembled, that the application for a mortgage should not be made, and this proviso in the agreement was rescinded. Mr. Therry and the Clergymen assembled mentioned several times, and it was distinctly understood by all, that no advantage was to be taken of any incompleteness in the document, that the matter was to be submitted to the respective solicitors, and a formal document drawn up by them.[2]

In some sections of the press[3] Bishop Willson was accused of harassment and 'exceedingly reprehensible' conduct towards the venerable Therry, who was still being credited with many worthy achievements, even as mundane as getting the local roads levelled and metalled by his 'untiring exertions'.[4] The heated dispute—the origins of which grew more convoluted over time—touched on matters of ecclesiastical governance and authority, property, and money. Cotham had been aware of its beginnings in 1839; the memoranda and resolutions made in July 1846 were revisited in detail in the Hobart press reporting on

Interlude: Visit to Port Phillip, 1846 243

> a Meeting of Lay Members of the Catholic Community,
> held in St. Joseph's School Room, 13th July, 1849, con-
> vened by the Church wardens, in pursuance of a requisi-
> tion from some Members of the Community, for the
> purpose of removing certain allegations publicly made
> against the Right Reverend the Bishop; J. M. Loughnan,
> Esq., Churchwarden, in the Chair.'[5]

Cotham might have reflected on the transition he had made from solitary missioner to diocesan clergyman and wondered which was the more vexing.

In September 1846 Fr Therry sailed for Sydney and celebrated Mass there as a respected visitor, while pleading poverty and collecting money to pay off the debts on St Joseph's and com-plaining of harshly unfair treatment from Willson. Later in the month he was on board ship again, bound for Melbourne, to replace Fr Geoghegan who sailed for Europe on 6 October. A report in Adelaide's *South Australian* in early December (taken from the *Port Phillip Herald* of 12 October) catches the intricacies of Catholic episcopal appointments for Australia in this period; what it does not bring out is the reluctance of some of the parties named to be nominated, and the reluctance on the part of others to let them go.

> The following from the Port Phillip Herald of October
> 12th, will probably be interesting to our Roman Catholic
> friends:
>
> CATHOLIC BISHOP. 'Coming events cast their shadows
> before;' and we can already foresee the not distant advent
> to our shores of a Catholic Bishop. Separation [that is to say
> a division of the archdiocese] is decided on. An Episcopalian
> Bishop is ere this nominated to Australia Felix. The eve of
> such an occurrence in the see of Rome is at hand. The
> Archbishop of Sydney, and the Bishops of Adelaide and
> Hobart Town, have proceeded to Europe upon matters of
> moment to the Church which they represent. Their almost
> simultaneous arrival at the City of the Pontiff will decide

the appointment of a Bishop of Melbourne. At present it is impossible to conjecture upon whom the mitre will descend. Several high and honourable ecclesiastics are spoken of. Amongst them we may mention Dr. Ullathorne, Very Rev. Mr. Geoghegan, Rev. Mr. M'Encroe, Dean of Sydney; Very Rev. Mr. Therry, Father of the Australian Catholic Church, and the Rev. Dr. Gregory, the present locum tenens of the Archbishop of Sydney. Dr. Ullathorne, in consequence of his recent appointment as successor to Dr. Bankes in the North West of England will not in all probability again leave his native land. Dr. Gregory has not yet attained that seniority which would entitle him to fill so responsible a position. The matter then rests between the Rev. Mr. Geoghegan and Mr. M'Encroe; the latter gentleman, who is highly esteemed, may be the new Bishop; but the former has strong and peculiar claims upon the Court of Rome. He it was who, combating impediments of no trifling nature, stemming torrents of embarrassments of which but few are aware, toiled day and night in establishing here the faith, of which he is a minister. That success beamed upon his efforts, the church which now raises its form in Lonsdale-street, is the most striking monument. By his example and edifying discourses he exalted the position of his spiritual charge in no inconsiderable degree. His claims, therefore, in an infant colony, where all that has been done is the work of his own hand, are paramount, and will no doubt receive due attention in the proper quarter.

It is not altogether improbable that the Right Rev. Dr. Murphy, Bishop of Adelaide, may be translated to Melbourne; in which case, even South Australia will have to receive the new appointee. At all events a decision will be come to ere long in the matter; and as far as this province is concerned it will be a circumstance of no ordinary importance.[6]

While Archbishop Polding was negotiating in England and Rome for more recruits, both episcopal and parochial, but preferably Benedictine in both cases, Fr Therry was joined in Port Phillip by

Interlude: Visit to Port Phillip, 1846   245

Cotham who sailed from Hobart on 18 September, arriving on 24 September.[7] For a brief period Melbourne was supplied with four Catholic priests: Therry and Cotham, Richard Walsh in nearby Geelong, and John Kavanagh who came to act as curate to Therry. Presumably Cotham was sent as a companion, however briefly, for Therry with whom he remained on cordial terms, taking him to the *Anson* (while Bishop Willson was away) since Therry had an abiding interest in convict welfare. His acrimonious departure from Tasmania was a painful and public exhibition of divided loyalties. Although Cotham, together with the other Tasmanian priests, wrote memoranda in favour of Bishop Willson's case against Therry, in private Cotham was less accepting of Willson's behaviour. Whereas in his journal he had tersely noted, 'Blow up with Ep.', only two weeks later he wrote 'Ep. vult prohibere audire et absol[vere] Dom. Therry. Non habet potestatem.'[8]

Fr Therry's concerns did not overshadow the visit. A new scene and audience gave Fr Cotham the opportunity to attend one of his many Temperance events. 'On the [5th October] the Father Mathew Society proceeded, in processional array, to lay the foundation stone of a Temperance Hall. The Rev. Mr. Cotham delivered an interesting address on the occasion, and about £20 was collected.'[9]

By December Cotham was back at his normal convict duties in Hobart. His journal for that month gives the unvarying daily round of duties without a break: divine service or prayers at the *Anson*, the Brickfields, Queen's Orphan Schools, New Norfolk Hospital, Male and Female Hospitals and Asylum until 25 December. On Christmas Day the entry reads: 'Mass and Communion to children and Mr and Miss Quin his sister 8o/c at O. School. Deacon and preached on the Temple in public worship. Preached at the *Anson* at 3o/c. Benediction Mr H[unter] preached. Paid Ferry 8/9; men 2/-'. Normal duties were resumed until the 30th, when he noted that Mr Bond had returned from Norfolk Island and accompanied him to divine service at the Orphan School.

246 *The Indomitable Mr Cotham*

New Year's Eve began with divine service at the Brickfields, after which he drove with Fr Bond to Chigwell, where they dined with Mr Nelson. On his return he stopped at Mr Loughnan's house at O'Brien's Bridge, Glenorchy, where the retired army captain lived with his wife and young children. Although John Michael Loughnan (1806–1875) was a near contemporary in age to Fr Cotham, he was quite different in temperament: 'intensely Catholic ... of a retiring disposition, and in rather delicate health'.[10] Although he was not interested in wider political matters he was active on behalf of the local church and chaired meetings to discuss the Therry business; his moderately expressed opinions would have been valued by the clergy. Cotham spent the evening with this generous young family before returning to town at 11 o'clock.

On Friday 1 January 1847 he is, unsurprisingly, 'Indisposed' so heard, rather than celebrated, Mass at 11 o'clock. The weather was 'Rain! Rain!' and he passed the day reading the life of an ex-dissenter. Cotham observed in a letter written to the Colonial Office in London in 1852 that 'the situation of a Clergyman to Convicts, continued in one unvarying round for many years, is peculiarly depressive', and this from a resilient man whose natural attitude was one of ebullience and who made the most of opportunities for diversion and refreshment. The sentiment was expressed plaintively in one of his notebook jottings: 'Padre mio, I am not a bird that I should be satisfied with this scanty allowance', of consolation in this instance rather than financial recompense.

Bishop Willson was absent in Europe from September 1846 to April 1848, his formal duties being taken on by William Hall VG. Archbishop Polding also went to Europe in 1847, in part to recruit men (and on this occasion, women) for the Australian mission. In January 1848 he landed at Sydney with Sr Mary Magdelen LeClerc and Sr Mary Scholastica Gregory, two Benedictine nuns brought over to found a convent, as well as Fr Ruggiero Emmanuelet from Sicily, Fr Magganotto coming to join his Italian Passionist colleagues, and a French Benedictine from

Interlude: Visit to Port Phillip, 1846 247

Solesmes, Fr Jean Gorbeillon. Among the non-ordained men were three Benedictine students: the Caldwell brothers, Edmund and Bernard from Downside, and Br Edmund Moore from Ampleforth. Polding was not long in regretting his choice of men but his Co-Adjutor Bishop Charles Davis summed up the situation in St Mary's monastery even sooner. Writing home to Prior Wilson at Downside in the month of the newcomers' arrival his judgement was that

> Entre nous, the good Archbishop made a slip in the last importation of labourers. Father Peter the Passionist is a failure. Father Gourbellion the French Benedictine is little better—one of the Caldwells is gone off to Dr Murphy [in Adelaide] ... Brother Edmund Moore will, I fear, never have health and strength to be of much use, his appearance is very delicate.[11]

While Edmund Caldwell went to be of service to Bishop Murphy, being ordained by him in 1849 and spending two years in charge of the mission at Willunga, his younger brother Bernard and Edmund Moore were testing Polding's forbearance to the limit in Sydney. Although Bishop Davis tried to counter the authoritarianism of Polding and Henry Gregory by administering a more consistent regime in their absence, when he fell ill the Archbishop clashed with the two newcomers without his tactful mediation. Polding was appalled by the way they criticised their superiors,

> in a manner altogether strange in our young people. What is the Archbishop? He is but a man. What are other superiors? They are but men, and so forth—and then my dress—my manners—all a lump of affectation, and so forth ... [not] that reverential love and forbearance of judgement as regards Superiors which has prevailed amongst us.[12]

Moore was a reformer, and 'change and amelioration in the Reformer's dictionary are synonymous'; Caldwell was dismissed as no more than 'a pious fool'.[13] To Bishop Serra in Western Australia, Polding admitted he had endured a 'very bitter and

248 *The Indomitable Mr Cotham*

expensive experience' but 'I am about to dismiss two ... the last importation of those brought with me have disturbed almost to destruction the peace and well-being of my infant community'.[14] Bernard Caldwell and Edmund Moore were sent back to England in May 1849; to mitigate the adverse reports they carried home Polding himself solicited letters testifying to the good order and discipline at St Mary's which he forwarded to President Barber.

The sorry episode epitomised the tensions evident in Sydney, between missionary endeavours and monastic discipline, which were to resurface during the soul-searching of the English Benedictine Congregation two decades later in England. Polding's response to the newcomers, in contrast to Davis's more sympathetic effort to understand their viewpoint, also echoes his apparent attitude to Cotham some thirteen years earlier. He also had displayed 'a manner altogether strange in our young people' by his forthright demand to be listened to; Polding then could not afford to lose a man so soon from the problematic district of Van Diemen's Land, but Cotham was never allowed to disturb the well-being of St Mary's Monastery, nor to take any part in the Benedictine project in New South Wales. Nothing less than a distance of one thousand miles enabled the two men to work in the same mission field, barely acknowledging one another's existence in their letters and diaries.

Notes

[1]   L. Madigan (Ed.), *The Devil is a Jackass*; *William Bernard Ullathorne 1806–1889* (Leominster: Gracewing, 1995), p. 130.
[2]   *Colonial Times* (Hobart), 20 July 1849, p. 2.
[3]   *Geelong Advertiser and Squatters Advocate*, 29 August 1846, p. 2.
[4]   *The Observer* (Hobart), 24 February 1846, p. 3.
[5]   *Colonial Times* (Hobart), 20 July 1849, p. 2.
[6]   *South Australian*, 1 December 1846, p. 8.
[7]   *The Courier* (Hobart), 23 September 1846, p. 2, and *Sydney Morning Herald*, 7 October 1846, p. 2.
[8]   'The bishop wishes to prohibit the hearing [of confession] and absolving

Interlude: Visit to Port Phillip, 1846   249

of Father Therry. He does not have that power.' DA VIII.A.Cotham; Cotham journal, 1 and 18 July 1846. On this point he was in agreement with Archbishop Polding who wrote a bitter letter to Willson two years later: '... the powers of the Church appear to have been exercised to an extent I have not known within my personal experience. To be denied the liberty of performing any sacerdotal function in any circumstance, and this for months; to be denied the Sacrament of Penance, all the Priests of the Diocese being directed not to absolve him - what is this but suspension, but the severest portion of Excommunication? If innocent, is there not injustice in depriving a Priest of the exercise of his functions, if guilty how is he to be brought to a sense of his guiltiness otherwise than by the Sacrament of Penance? Are not these prohibitions calculated to exacerbate? And let the position Mr Therry once held in the Missions of Van Diemen's Land be considered. Will not there be many who will look upon him as an ill used man?' B. Condon, *Letters and Documents in 19th Century Australian Catholic History*, Polding to Willson and Hobart Clergy, 14 October 1848; http://www.library.unisa.edu.au/condon/ CatholicLetters/ [Accessed online 27.7.2017]

[9]   *The Courier* (Hobart), 17 October 1846, p. 4.

[10] *The Advocate* (Melbourne), 25 September 1875, p. 9, obituary.

[11] F. O'Donoghue, *The Bishop of Botany Bay: The Life of John Bede Polding, Australia's First Archbishop* (Sydney: Angus and Robertson Publishers, 1982), p. 95, Bishop Davis to Prior Wilson 28 February 1849.

[12] *Ibid.*, Polding to President Barber, 21 May 1849, p. 96.

[13] *Ibid.*, 25 September 1849, p 96.

[14] *Ibid.*, Polding to Serra, 22 May 1849, p. 96.

22 'THE SURE PROSPECT'— LOOSENING THE TIES

T HE TIDE OF convicts arriving in Tasmania peaked in 1846, but there was at last an appreciable increase in the number of Catholic clergy. In 1848 a return sent to the British Government showing the number of chaplains ministering to free and convict Catholics indicated the disproportionate amount of official support given to the two sections of society. The three main centres of civilian population—Hobart Town, Launceston, and Richmond—and their surrounding districts were served respectively by the veteran Very Revd Fr William Hall, Fr William Dunne, and Fr Thomas Butler. The combined Catholic population on the island according to the 1847 census was 6,577, with four hundred and twenty-four baptisms during that year. Although eligible for grants from the colonial department the three churches depended heavily on pew rents, fees, and Sunday collections for financial support. The convict department employed rather more clergymen: in Hobart Town Cotham was assisted by Fr Odilo Woolfrey OC and the newly ordained Fr George Hunter; Oatlands had Fr William Bond; Maria Island, Fr James Luke Levermore OC; Port Arthur, Fr Andrew Maguire; Southport, Fr Norbert Woolfrey OC, and Fr Hugh Magorian was at the Coal Mines. The chaplains attended the Catholic officers and their families and the 'free sick' in their locality if necessary.[1]

In 1847, before most of the new men came into post, Bishop Willson was afraid that he was going to lose Cotham who felt he could not continue to carry so many duties;[2] Willson wrote asking him to stay longer due to pressing demand for his services. Cotham was relieved of some of his duties and managed to stay almost three years more before taking six month's leave of absence in England. Although only 39, Cotham was a veteran in

Tasmania but he seems not to have been considered for preferment. Bishop Willson successfully brought back a number of recruits in 1848, and it seemed these would be his favourites for diocesan appointments and promotion rather than the Benedictine who, in any case, stood in a special relationship of subjection to Archbishop Polding.

Close contact with the Woolfreys reminded Cotham of his own monastic identity and may have been an unsettling factor but there would have been no request from him to join St Mary's Monastery in Sydney, nor would he have received an invitation. More demoralising to him would have been the process of dismantling the *Anson* without its long awaited permanent replacement. The vessel's eventual breaking-up in 1850 was preceded by official reports designed to denigrate its usefulness to the convict system and question its beneficial influence on the women who had spent time on board. There is no record of Fr Cotham's reaction to the concerted efforts by Comptroller General Hampton to rid himself of the *Anson*, but Philippa Bowden, Superintendent after the death of her husband, wrote vigorously in support of the late Dr Bowden and their shared efforts. In this she included the Protestant and Catholic chaplains, and her staff, as able collaborators. It was inevitable, therefore, that they were implicated in Hampton's damning assessment, made as early as July 1847 following his only official visit in March of that year, that 'I entertain the strongest general impression that the experiment is a total failure, as far as regards the real improvement of the female prisoner'.[3]

It is clear from the correspondence between Comptroller General Hampton and the Colonial Office in London that he had no faith in the *Anson* as an integral part of the female penal system. The very existence of such a system at all was an affront to society and it was difficult to talk of it in similar terms to those used for the male convict population; the vocabulary used was more lurid and more unforgiving as convict women were deemed to be further removed from what was natural for their sex than

'The Sure Prospect'— Loosening the Ties 253

were male convicts. For men there was a greater range of transgression, from petty misdemeanours descending to the lowest forms of 'unnatural vice', especially troubling to penal legislators in England in the 1840s. In women, all wrongdoing was closer to being an unnatural vice, transforming them from criminals into 'uncontrollable viragos'[4] unless they were closely monitored and disciplined. The regime followed by the *Anson* was, in the main, praised by the Tasmanian press in proportion to its vilification in London. Whereas it was believed men in gangs were hardened by the experience of close association, women in a structured environment of discipline, classification, instruction, and employment were considered to be amenable to the inculcation of improved morals and practical skills.

Dr Edmund Bowden died aged 46, on board the *Anson* in September 1847. His wife took over as Superintendent for a short while until the Revd Mr Giles was appointed as Acting Superintendent in early 1848 so she could return to England on leave of absence. Despite her 'impaired health and spirits'[5] following her bereavement, and fears for her brother's life in England, she might have delayed her departure if she had known that in her absence decisions about the future of the reformatory would be made without consulting or notifying her. Fr Cotham cannot have been unaware of moves to abandon the *Anson*—it may have been a contributory factor in his asking for leave of absence in 1847—so it seems strange that in his report to Comptroller General Hampton in February 1849 he asked to be relieved of his duties at the Male Hospital and Brickfields Hiring Depot 'that in order to do justice to those two very important establishments [the *Anson* and the Orphan School], my attention should be devoted exclusively to them'. He might have known that his remarks would be considered just the sort of maudlin sentimentality Hampton despised in the prison system, but he made them anyway and Bishop Willson would not have gainsaid him:

> When it is considered that the Roman Catholic Convicts
> at the *Anson* number from three to four hundred;—that

on their arrival, with few exceptions, they have never been instructed in religious duties, are ignorant of the first principles of moral law, and unacquainted even with the commandments;—that they differ materially from a fixed and permanent congregation, so far as the labours of the clergyman is concerned, and they receive instructions for six months only, and are succeeded by another mass of ignorance;—and, that, moreover, these women may hereafter exert no inconsiderable influence, as domestics, and the mothers of families, over the future well being of this rising colony:—from these considerations, it appears to me very desirable that more of my time should be dedicated to that important establishment.[6]

The deployment of ten Roman Catholic chaplains for the Tasmanian convict establishments, including Norfolk Island, was forecast for May 1849. Despite the loss of the *Anson* three chaplains were still allocated to the Hobart stations so Cotham would not have been made redundant by the changes. He may have had no heart for work other than at his two designated establishments, especially without the principles and structure provided by the *Anson*. By the time Mrs Bowden's refutations of Hampton's criticisms were published in November 1850, Cotham had shaken the dust of convictism from his feet. He received no address of appreciation from the convict department for the work he had done but he may have taken some comfort from the columns of the *Launceston Examiner*, appropriating the sentiments to himself:

Never before did individuals bring to a task assigned them higher qualifications, or purer motives, than Dr. and Mrs. Bowden. But because they were zealous and earnest, their services were unsuited to this meridian of sham and cant, where corruption, not reformation, had been and is, the end of the hypocritical phantasies played off in the face of high heaven, under the misnomer of penal discipline.[7]

'The Sure Prospect'— Loosening the Ties

And he would not have disagreed with Philippa Bowden's own conclusions, appended to the editorial:

> Whatever good has been effected by the institution of the *Anson*, there is no doubt much more might have been accomplished but for the general apathy and indifference which hung around me like a shroud; every one can appreciate the distinction between official formality and cordial help, and I have felt such bitterly.[8]

However, by the time these remarks were printed the *Anson* had already been brought up from Risdon to Hobart harbour in July 1849 and was in due course broken up and its salvaged parts auctioned off.

For the junior members of the *Anson* team the experience had been more positive, and they remained on the staff from 1844 to 1849. The three Holdich sisters married soon afterwards. Martha married Thomas Abbot in 1849 and was able to provide the wedding venue for her sister Susannah, when she married Robert Harcourt in 1850 and Jane, who married James Allan Learmonth in 1852. The move to Australia had done no harm to their father Matthew who died in 1857 aged 80. Robert Harcourt and his brother James were store owners in Hobart and agents for their father's brass foundry business in Birmingham. Nevertheless, on the strength of Susannah's career Robert sold his share of the business to James and the couple moved to Victoria and established Hanbury Retreat House for the Insane. Robert, formerly in the fancy, furnishing, and heavy ironmongery trade, was now a Proprietor and Superintendent, and not abashed to advertise himself as 'a gentleman well known in England for his experience in the treatment of mental and nervous diseases'.[9] His wife was prudently installed as Matron. The private asylum for upper and middle class patients was based on the Hanwell system:

> Mr. Harcourt's object will be to keep patients under no more restraint than is absolutely needed, and to have them so managed that all appearance of surveillance is so far as

possible dispensed with ... Music, gardening, and such light amusements as tend to divert the mind from gloomy fancies will be provided for the inmates, and, in fact, they will be treated as visitors to a private house—all the obnoxious forms which tend to impress them with a sense of being inmates of an asylum will be done away with.[10]

The experimental asylum was not a success and the family returned to England in 1862, with an extra son, Philip, born during the voyage. The naming of their daughter, Phillipa Edmund, was a lasting tribute to the close relationship between Susannah and the Bowdens. In England, Harcourt returned to the brass foundry business but was able to retire comfortably as a gentleman to Dorset, where his widowed sister-in-law Jane Learmonth also settled.

John Serviss remained in the prison service, being promoted from gatekeeper to senior warder at the Cascades House of Correction, as recorded in his obituary notice.[11] When he died in October 1887, aged 80, he left £1,565 to his wife Eliza who died six years later aged 84. Convictism had gone, and prison warder-ship became a civil service; working for both provided the Servisses with an enviable pension in old age.

Finally, an innocuous family notice epitomises the opportunities that existed in Tasmania for men and women who had spent convictions or had worked within the convict system:

> On Wednesday, the 11th inst [July 1849], at St. John's Church, New Town, by the Rev. T. J. Ewing, Stephen Aldhouse B.C.L to Miss Elizabeth Richardson, many years housekeeper of the *Anson* female penitentiary.[12]

Elizabeth was 46, her husband three years older. He was also known as 'S. Aldous, *John Renwick*', having been transported for seven years in 1842 for bigamy. His case, heard at the Old Bailey, and involving an educated, well-connected, reverend gentleman with two wives, was widely reported in England and in Tasmania. However, after two years hard labour he moved through the

'The Sure Prospect'— Loosening the Ties

system and by the time he received his conditional pardon in February 1847 he had already advertised the establishment of his private grammar school in Hobart. His academic credentials— second master at King's School, Rochester and headmaster at All Hallows, London, with various classical publications to his name—now superseded the *John Renwick* association. The Hobart school flourished financially, so that by the time the Revd Mr and Mrs Aldhouse retired to England in 1854 they had a very handsomely furnished four-bedroomed house to dispose of by auction.

The Aldhouses lived in London until the Revd Mr Aldhouse's death in 1867, after which Elizabeth retired to her home village of Leire, Leicestershire, able to live independently on a legacy of £1,500 and her government pension. Like Ambrose Cotham she could have told many stories—a near fatal attack on her husband in 1853 resulted in his assailant's execution and more publicity— but she probably valued her respectability too much to break the Tasmanian code of oblique language.

Cotham did not have the liberty to reinvent himself, and he was constrained in the risks he could take with the future. He had covered thousands of miles on horseback and learnt how to work in the most depraved conditions, negotiating with government officials and encouraging free settlers to build up their Catholic identity and establish their place in the developing colony. Just as Fr Conolly was a man out of time by 1835, Cotham was perhaps too closely identified with Tasmania's convict history by 1849. Cotham needed a changed environment in which he could exercise new initiatives. Such a new environment was offered by the Catholic Church in England on the eve of the restoration of the Catholic hierarchy. If Archbishop Polding and Bishop Willson felt able to take long leaves of absence from their duties, neither was Cotham indispensable, especially as the call for the end of transportation to the colony seemed bound to succeed sooner rather than later.

However, there is a strange absence of attention given to Fr Cotham's departure from Tasmania. It was customary, even to the point of over-dramatising the event, to present a testimonial of appreciation to a departing dignitary or clergyman from his post or from the island. Bishop Willson received several for his visit to England only two years after his arrival. For Ambrose Cotham there is not even a brief newspaper advertisement until the publication of the shipping departures in January 1851.

His decision to leave was not an impetuous move. Bishop Willson had cited it as one justification for asking to take five clergymen with him when he returned to Tasmania from his first visit to England; the Colonial Secretary Earl Grey communicated this to Lieutenant-Governor Denison in a despatch dated 28 October 1847[13] and Bishop Willson referred to it again in a letter to Archbishop Polding written in September 1850[14] regarding the need for a second 'efficient' priest on Norfolk Island to take the place of Fr Ryan. Polding proposed handing over spiritual jurisdiction of the penal settlement to Willson, with £50 per annum, if Willson could supply the priest. Willson acknowledged the continuing difficulties on Norfolk Island and said he would 'joyfully' send a priest 'for the sake of that most pitiable class, perhaps on earth, of our fellow beings' but 'with the sure prospect of losing Mr Cotham next January I am totally at loss to do so at present.' Bishop Willson was clear about the need to send a priest fitted for that 'peculiar mission' but it is doubtful if Cotham, at that stage of his career, could have taken on the challenges of Norfolk Island or, indeed, if he was willing to move to any new convict posting.

Coinciding with Cotham's firm intention to leave, for a temporary period at least, was the departure of Fr Norbert Woolfrey OC. He received a purse of £22 12s. 6d. from friends and congregation delivered by a 'deputation' of Messrs M'Carthy, Murphy, and A'Herne whose covering letter expressed their disgruntlement with the hard-pressed Bishop Willson:

'The Sure Prospect'— Loosening the Ties

> ... our sorrow is the more, when we know ample provision would have been made by a vastly growing district, desirous of securing the service of so revered a Pastor, had it pleased our Bishop to have sanctioned the wished-for arrangement of a people, now by his decision left unprovided, and without spiritual aid.[15]

Woolfrey subsequently said he had asked the sentence to be omitted from publication but as his response was printed directly below it looked as if he agreed with the deputation. In fact, he and Odilo both left Tasmania in 1851 and by 1852 were in the Macdonald River district of New South Wales, with recently ordained Fr William Xavier Johnson OC, hoping to make a Cistercian foundation at Kincumber. The new foundation did not materialise, but they never gave up trying to fulfil their original intentions.

In the light of Bishop Willson's difficulties with clergy recruitment and retention—had Cotham ever known the situation to be otherwise?—he may have chosen to keep a low profile when making his own arrangements. If that was his reasoning, he was exhibiting more than ordinary tact, for he was not usually afraid of making his presence felt. Bishop Willson still felt woefully short of priests to meet the demands of convict and civilian needs (although the former had passed their peak). In 1848 there were eight in the convict department; the 1849 deployment reckoned on ten to cover all stations, and in 1850 Cotham and the Woolfreys were making plans to leave. The major shift, however, in the clergy constituency was already well under way with the predominance of Irish priests in the Australian mission. Cotham's position as a solitary Benedictine, with little prospect of further monastic assistance from Sydney or England, may have been a major influence in his decision to return to England.[16]

Although there is apparently no formal testimonial to mark his departure, a letter appeared in the *Hobart Guardian* dated 1 September 1849, signed L.S.D. It challenged two letters from 'John' printed in the *Britannia*. A rancorous exchange of correspondence in the *Britannia* had picked over the saga of Fr Therry's mortgage and the debt it incurred for Bishop Willson. It was a piece of mischief making by the proprietor John Morgan, an Orangeman in politics, to take the side of Mr Therry and foment discord among the Catholic community. It is ironic that the letter by L.S.D. is the single tribute that appeared as Fr Cotham neared the end of his Tasmanian ministry. Taken on its own, it is a warm acknowledgement of Fr Cotham's achievements and he was happy to keep it among his papers; at the time of its publication he probably groaned to see his name in print in the context of a vitriolic correspondence. Nevertheless, L.S.D.'s reply to 'John', who, he implies, is John Joseph Therry writing on his own behalf and admitting only to 'over zeal and imprudence' is not only a defence of Bishop Willson but an unsolicited tribute to his junior co-worker.

> Surely Mr Therry was not the first or only labourer, up to the Bishop's arrival, in the vineyard of the Church of Tasmania! Surely some credit is due to that unpresuming predecessor, who built the first Catholic church in Van Diemen's Land, which every body knows was that at Richmond! Surely that worthy Priest's subsequent labours in the erection of another church in the Northern capital, entitles him to some share of the gratitude of the Catholics of Van Diemen's Land. True, he pursued the even tenor of his way, without noise, strife, parade or contention; and, true it is, that ably aided, by his equally zealous, equally humble, equally discreet, and equally beloved successor [Fr Butler] in both missions—those churches are now, and have been for years, free from all debt, and a source of pride and comfort to their congregations! Thus has heaven truly smiled on their peaceful and loving labours!

1 September 1849, L.S.D.[17]

Notes

1.   T. Kelsh, *Recollections of the Rt Rev Robert Willson* (Hobart: Davies Bros, 1882), 'Bishop Willson, accompanied by the Reverend Fathers Hall and Bond, Brother Luke Levermore, and Mr George Hunter, an ecclesiastical student, set sail ... from London at the end of January, 1844.', p. 28 and 62. Frs Maguire and Magorian sailed out with Bishop Willson in April 1848.

2.   Accounts and Papers, Volume 43, Session July 1849 (Great Britain Parliament; House of Commons and Command; H.M. Stationery Office, 1849); 'Convict Discipline and Transportation', p. 51.

3.   *Launceston Examiner,* 16 November 1850, p. 4.

4.   *Ibid.,* p. 3.

5.   *Ibid.,* p. 4.

6.   DA VIII.A.Cotham, Statement of duties to Comptroller General, 27 February 1849.

7.   *Launceston Examiner,* 16 November 1850, p. 4.

8.   *Ibid.,* p. 5.

9.   *Colonial Times* (Hobart), 8 October 1856, p. 2.

10.   *Ibid.,* p. 2.

11.   *The Mercury* (Hobart), 27 October 1887, p. 1.

12.   *The Cornwall Chronicle* (Launceston), 14 July 1849, p. 718.

13.   Accounts and Papers, Volume 43, Session July 1849 (Great Britain Parliament; House of Commons and Command; H.M. Stationery Office, 1849), p. 51.

14.   HAA, CA.6/WIL.301; Willson to Polding, 2 September 1850.

15.   *Colonial Times* (Hobart), August 1849, p. 3.

16.   Cardinal Moran's verdict on Archbishop Polding's overall ambition for Australia was gloomy in the extreme: 'His seminary failed, his college failed, his religious community failed, the Monastic Cathedral failed, his long cherished scheme of setting the seal of the Benedictine Order on the whole Australian Church melted away like an idle dream.' P. F. Moran, *History of the Catholic Church in Australasia* (Sydney: Oceanic Publishing Company, 1896), p. 449. Ambrose Cotham had no such grandiose dreams but he must have realised he would remain an isolated monk if he stayed in Tasmania.

17.   *The Guardian* (Hobart), 8 September 1849, p. 2.

23 'CALLED TO GO ON BOARD'

F R COTHAM WROTE an uncharacteristically personal account of his last days in Hobart in mid-January 1851. Mr Cassidy gave him a cash gift and he drank champagne with Mr Fitzgerald. He made final arrangements for the disposal of his horse Bob and the gig (both unpaid for) and gave Captain Innes McPherson letters for Father Provincial, in case of his death during the voyage. His brother Lawrence accompanied him to the boat with his wife and five children ('Law, Sarah, Larry, M Ann, Bella, William and Ellin'). On the day of departure Cotham was driven to the wharf by Fr Hall and accompanied on board the *Australasia* by Frs Butler, Dunne, Downing, and Maguire, and a fiddler, who all intended to sail as far as the lighthouse but as the sea was rough they were advised to disembark. His 'Reverend Friends ... embracing me bade me farewell!!!' and he set off on a squally sea for England.

Besides the general cargo and mail, there were only eight cabin passengers on board, and none in steerage. Mrs Butler was the only lady, accompanying her husband; Mr George Roope belonged to the family of Lavington Roope, merchant and businessman, and a regular long-distance traveller; Mr C. G. Stevens, another businessman and importer, was accompanied by his young son; Dr LeGrand, a Senior Superintendent Medical Officer for convict ships had arrived only the previous November, and was going home without duties; Mr Hulmes and Revd Mr J Cotham completed the company.[1] Cotham began a brief log book on Thursday 16 January, noting his sea sickness for the first two days, the speed of the boat (between seven and nine knots) and the weather (variable). He 'forgot the day' on the 24th and the last entry was made on 28 January. He had noted that Roope had 'bad eyes' and Stevens was 'very intelligent'; he found 'all agreeable' to him during the first month.

Although few in number the passengers had plenty of table talk to occupy them. In the ship's mail bag was a copy of 'printed lists of the contributions to the Exhibition of the Industry of all Nations, to be held in London, 1851 … [with] the numbers of the articles, name, and description, whence and by whom forwarded, by whom produced or manufactured'[2] drawn up by the Standing Committee for selecting the Tasmanian contributions, one of whom was Lavington Roope. Included in the great variety of natural and manufactured items destined for the Great Exhibition at Crystal Palace, many not unique to Tasmania, were a few of peculiar significance, both in time and place:

> … thirteen necklaces worn by the aborigines of Tasmania, were sent by Mr Milligan, a number of knitted socks, shawls, &c were sent from the Queen's Orphan School, gloves made of opossum fur trim from Mrs McKenzie, of Blue Hills Bothwell, Mrs Stieglitz of Killymoon and Mrs E Tooth; a stockman's pair of ankle boots were forwarded from Mr C. Ward of Collins-street.[3]

None of it, however, was intended to be quaint or merely ornamental. The Standing Committee, in calling for contributions, reminded the citizens of Tasmania that this was an opportunity for them to show themselves as a vital and mature part of the modern civilised world. The colony that prided itself on natural resources surely hoped rather than believed that the attitude on the other side of world was one of equality, where the centre of empire viewed colonial assets as so much fuel for its industrial programme:

> The spirit of generous rivalry which pervades Europe, and has stirred the civilised world, must find an echo at the Antipodes. Great Britain, confident in the vast and varied resources of an empire on which the sun never sets, and in the possession of machinery, engineering skill, and artisanship all but omnipotent, has challenged the world to competition. Let us not think that we bring a feeble or inefficient contingent to the aid of our mighty Fatherland.

'Called to Go on Board' 265

> We have corn, wool, and oil, for man's necessities and his
> comfort,—we have have coal and iron to give him power
> and command,—we have timber (not to be surpassed in
> the world) for shipbuilding and for ornamental purposes;
> at once elements of national strength, and a guarantee for
> advancement in commerce, civilisation, and refinement.[4]

While they were debating the choice of materials sent to represent Tasmania abroad the ship's company would undoubtedly raise the question of whether it was time for Tasmania's status as a convict island to be revoked. On this subject Stevens had plenty to say. In May 1850 he had sold his share of the business of Stevens and Harcourt to his partner (Robert Harcourt, husband of Susannah Holdich), perhaps in order to become a full time campaigner for the Anti-Transportation League. The journey to England had been intended by him for several months, Stevens having first gone to Sydney in October 1850 en route to London, although he returned home before eventually sailing from Hobart again. The Committee of the Anti-Transportation League in Sydney had been so impressed by Stevens' letter in the *Sydney Morning Press* that they made fifteen hundred copies for circulation:

> The public demonstration at Sydney was to be held in the
> open air. The hustings were to accommodate 300 persons—all the ministers of religion, including the Protestant
> and Roman Catholic Bishops, had notified their intention
> to be present. Thus the victorious progress of the popular
> cause will not want the sanction of religion. That banner
> is always triumphant which the clergy bless. But for us the
> League is the grand idea.[5]

Although the call for reform was intensifying by 1851, especially with the formation of the Australasian League for the Prevention of Transportation that year, the arguments were still vociferously contested in the Tasmanian press. As a Religious Instructor for the Penal Department Fr Cotham had first-hand knowledge of the efficacy, or otherwise, of the variations that had been tried by the

British Government; he knew, too, the impact of convicts and former convicts on civil life. During their early years in the colony he and his brother Lawrence had used assigned convict labour until this was replaced in 1840 by the probation system and he had taken a particular interest in the children caught up in the system.

Dr LeGrand was both an insider and an outsider in the matter of transportation to Tasmania, but on this particular voyage his presence had an added piquancy. In November 1850 he was responsible for the safe passage of William Cuffay, a prominent Chartist convicted of treason in 1848 for his part in the Orange Tree Plot in London to lead an armed uprising against the government. Cuffay was born in San Domingo (St Kitts), son of a former Black slave and an English mother. When the family moved to England William Cuffay, working as a tailor, became a campaigner for universal suffrage and the rights of workers. He was elected to the national executive of the National Charter Association in 1842 and later that year voted president of the London Chartists. After a life of militant activism against injustice he was transported to Tasmania at the age of 60.[6]

The tangles of Empire and industry, workers' rights and the shadow of racism and slavery, and the making of a Christian society from a population—free, emancipist, and convict—'tainted' by immorality and crime gave plenty of material for debate by these strong-minded and strong-willed passengers who were not onlookers but fully engaged participants in the web that made up colonial life.

Notes

[1]   *The Courier* (Hobart), 11 January 1851, p. 2, and *Launceston Examiner*, 18 January 1851, p. 3.

[2]   *The Courier* (Hobart), 15 January, p. 2.

[3]   *Ibid.*, p. 2.

'Called to Go on Board' 267

4   *Ibid.*, 7 September 1850, p. 2.

5   *Ibid.*, 2 October 1850, p. 2.

6   Although Cuffay and two fellow Chartists, Lacey and Fay, were sentenced to twenty-one years, three years later all political prisoners in Tasmania were pardoned. Cuffay decided to remain and was joined by his wife in 1853. He carried on his trade as a tailor and again became involved in radical politics and trade union issues. He played an important role in persuading the authorities to amend the Master and Servant Law in the colony before dying in poverty in July 1870.

PART TWO

'There came a man of indomitable energy'

24 RETURN TO ENGLAND

THE *AUSTRALASIA* BERTHED at Gravesend on Sunday 4 May 1851, 'a bitterly cold day' as Queen Victoria noted in her journal.[1] Whether Fr Cotham was well rested by the voyage home, or made restless by it, he soon set off on the first of his tours around the country and abroad. The absence of any mention of the newly opened Great Exhibition in London, during the two weeks he spent in the capital after disembarking, is a strange omission for a man of his curiosity. He may have shared the ambivalence towards it from some church quarters. Evangelical Protestants deplored the emphasis on man-made artefacts that detracted from honour due to God the Creator. Catholics were wary of British jingoism, especially so soon after the furore of 1850, while Ireland, still reeling from the famine years, had an additional cause for antipathy. Queen Victoria visited the Exhibition almost daily during May and wrote enthusiastically and meticulously in her journal about the great variety of exhibits. She was only quietly impressed by those from the antipodes and Fr Cotham perhaps agreed that they were not the best representation of the continent he had just left. The sovereign moved through the galleries: 'Next went to South Australia and New Zealand, where the exhibits consist chiefly of raw products—but very valuable ones, such as beautiful specimens of wood etc'.[2] It was only 7 May and the consignment from Tasmania had not yet been installed.

Cotham had made his own plans before arriving. By 1850 almost 6,000 miles of railway tracks had been laid, connecting the majority of main cities,[3] and Cotham took full advantage. The convenience of railway travel, and the timetables to access it, would have been a marvel to him if only for the opportunity to keep dry. Characteristically, his journal frequently recorded rain but rarely fine weather. From May to the end of November he visited St Edmunds, Douai twice, as might be expected, but stayed only three full days on the first occasion before going to Paris for ten days. Two days after leaving St Edmunds he wrote to Fr Prior Burchall who was not 'at home' when he had visited the college. Anxious though he was to meet his Prior, Cotham was not going to disrupt his own itinerary, only promising to be punctual if the Prior could coordinate his own arrangements with his.

> Hotel des Missions Etrangeurs
>
> 28th May 1851
>
> My dear Father Prior,
>
> I received your note dated from Roubaix last night. I am sorry it will not be in my power to meet you and our old and well beloved Confrere Father Hoole at Liverpool so soon as Saturday next. Much to Father Greenough's and my disappointment Weld Blundell Esqr and Lady had just set out for Orleons, and will not return till Friday next. As Mr Blundell is a gentleman well known here in Paris he may be good enough to introduce me to Mon Choiselat-Gallien tresoeur de la Propagation de la Foi [tresaurer of the Propagation of the Faith], hence I do not expect to be able to leave Paris before the middle of next week. It would give me great pleasure to meet you either at Douai about the 3rd or 4th June or in London about the 5th or 6th of June or in Coventry at Mr Heptonstall's on Pentecost Monday or in Liverpool about the 10th or the 11th. You have only to mention any day about these times and I will be punctual.
>
> Fr Greenough is waiting so I have no more to say.
>
> Ever, my dear Father Prior,
>
> Yours most sincerely in J.C.
>
> James Cotham[4]

The spare time in Paris was spent sight-seeing until he left for London on 5 June where he changed his plans and went to Ireland for the last two weeks in June. On his return the correspondence with Prior Burchall is resumed:

Return to England 273

No 11 Charles Street, Manchester Square

London 28th June 1851

My dear Father Prior

I was sorry to hear by Father Heptonstall that you had been ill. I hope you have quite recovered. I am living at McShane's opposite the Spanish Chapel. Dr Gregory is with me.

If I knew by what train you would come up to London I would meet you at the station.

Perhaps I may take a 5^s trip to Coventry and return with you to London. This however is only an idea, a passing thought, not a fixed intention.

Should it not be convenient for you to meet me at Spanish Place I shall be glad to meet you at any place you may appoint. I have not called on Mr Bullen since my return from Paris, but intend to call on Monday. I go to Birmingham on Tuesday by the train which leaves London at one o'c in the afternoon. I shall not stop at Coventry on my way, notwithstanding the love and affection I bear Father Sutton to whom Ambrose, the monk from Van Diemen's, sendeth greeting in the Lord.

Ever, my dear Father Prior,

your humble Confrere, James Cotham[5]

Dr Gregory—his junior companion Henry Gregory at Downside, fellow passenger on the *Oriental* in 1835, and now Archbishop Polding's right hand man in Sydney—had quietly sailed from Sydney in mid-March and went with Cotham to the Treasury at the end of the June. What else they shared is not recorded. Gregory was on his way to Rome to defend Archbishop Polding against critics of his regime. Although brief, these two letters are significant. The names of monks—confrères—he had not seen for nearly twenty years are used with familiar affection; time and distance had not made them remote, nor was Cotham awkward

274   *The Indomitable Mr Cotham*

in their company. And his travels, whether local or global, are consciously made in a missionary spirit. His play on words, echoing St Paul, could be read as pompous self-preening except that the rest of the letter is almost banal, with its precise detail of a five shilling fare to Coventry. The simplicity of mind, through which 'only an idea, a passing thought, not a fixed intention' passes without stopping, is guilelessly shown to his reader.

In July he resumed his carefully arranged itinerary of visits in the English Midlands to places that were not in existence when he left in 1835. The venues had personal associations not noted in his journal: the Cistercian monks' monastery at Mount St Bernard, Leicestershire, and the convent of the Rosminian Sisters of Providence in Loughborough where Bishop Willson's sister was a nun; Mount St Mary, Spinkhill, Derbyshire, a Jesuit boarding school; and St Mary's College, Oscott, the nexus for so many of the new developments in the English Catholic Church, and seminary where John Fitzgerald was training for the Hobart diocese. Also in Birmingham on Sunday 6 July he preached at St Chad's Cathedral, William Ullathorne's diocesan seat since 1850. The existence of these prestigious institutions was a direct consequence of the two late eighteenth century Toleration Acts for religious freedom, the 1829 Emancipation Act, and the re-establishment of the Catholic hierarchy in England and Wales in 1850, together with substantial patronage from wealthy converts. Catholicism had come out of the shadows, sometimes provoking opposition and riots, elsewhere becoming almost fashionable; it was a manifestation more impressive than anything Cotham might have seen at the Crystal Palace.

On 7 July, Fr Cotham 'left for Warrington', his home town. For almost the next five weeks, apart from a few days revisiting the Midlands to call at the Benedictine missions, he travelled around Lancashire visiting Wigan, St Helen's, Preston, and Ormskirk, and celebrating Mass at St Anthony's and St Augustine's in Liverpool where he and his siblings had been baptised. Above all in Lanca-shire he spent time with his Jesuit brother William, priest at Wigan

Return to England 275

since 1847. They dined with their sister Mary Ann Maguire and her husband at Appleton and went to Stonyhurst together for a Prize Day, where Fr James Cotham's mission is recorded in the guest list as 'Australia'. The frequent overnight visits to Warrington were spent with his half-brother Thomas Shepherd, 28-years-old and becoming a successful solicitor. Although the two Shepherd brothers were barely known to their older half-brothers the four of them had Douai in common. Isabella and Richard Shepherd, and their eldest son John, had all died by 1848, so the Cothams were Thomas's closest family. He lived in Warrington all his life as a bachelor, not far from the Maguires, and took an interest in his extended Australian step family.

Thomas accompanied Cotham to Liverpool on 1 August and may have travelled with him as he visited one or two places each day, immersing himself in Lancashire life. On 11 August he sailed for Dublin, and although he does not mention it he was part of a large exodus of Catholic clergy making their way to a Grand Meeting at the Rotunda on the 19th. Although he stayed in various places—naturally—he says he was 'quartered at Drumcondra' on the 15th, suggesting the almost barracks-like accommodation required for hundreds of priests attending the inaugural meeting of the Catholic Defence Association in Ireland. The spur for the meeting was the passing of the Ecclesiastical Titles Act in July 1851, itself a reaction to the perceived 'Papal Aggression' of the restoration of the Catholic hierarchy the previous year, and an opportunity for the Irish hierarchy—who attended in strength—to press for independent Irish political activity at home.

The meeting was led by Archbishop Paul Cullen (of Armagh since 1849, and of Dublin from 1852); although the Associations were a short-lived phenomenon in England and Ireland, and the Act was ignored before being repealed twenty years later without having been enforced, the event was a show of clerical solidarity and strength against Protestant vitriol and a marker of Cullen's ascendency. Cotham came with a particular acuity: Archbishop

Cullen had already established his ascendency over Archbishop Polding in the matter of filling most of the new sees of Australia with Irish candidates, and the vital source of priests was the missionary college of All Hallows, Dublin, most likely Cotham's quarters during his first week in Ireland. Bishop Ullathorne was the senior English prelate to attend and he declared himself at once prepared to go to gaol—signal for tremendous cheering, and waving of hats and handkerchiefs—rather than submit to this new penal law. For the hundreds of clergy present it was a thrilling reminder of glorious martyrdom, and Ullathorne, like Cotham, had no qualms about the Irish stage on which it took place.

After the crowding of Dublin, Cotham took the whole of September for a tour of Ireland, working his way down the east coast—Wicklow, Limerick, and Kilkenny, with a detour to Carlow College—before going across to the south west hills and seaside towns of Killarney, Kenmare, Bantry, and Cork. If he travelled alone he did not travel as a silent or solitary passenger. Returning from Ireland he spent a week in the north west of England and a week in London, before the second visit to Douai. Again it was only a short visit, of two full days, then onwards to Paris, by rail to Marseilles and boat to Genoa. The whole of November was spent in Rome where he 'ascended St Peter's Dome' and was impressed by the Dominican library containing 240,000 volumes. An excursion to Subiaco, site of St Benedict's first monastery, at the end of the month preceded a brief tour of Naples, complete with the ascent of Mount Vesuvius on 11 December. He boarded a boat again on 12 December for Marseilles, the quickest and safest way to reach Florence, and thence to Paris. His step-brother Thomas was with him for the Italian tour; he and Fr Cotham made a gift of two hundred francs to Douai on 18 November (noted as a cheque for ten pounds sterling by Cotham), and paid three francs for laundry. Thomas may well have been a companion for most of the summer, though he never replaced William in James' affections. Although they would not have made the

Return to England 277

distinction, the step-brothers were travelling mainly as cultural tourists rather than as pilgrims.

They returned to England in mid-December and as James Cotham was in Warrington in January 1852 it is likely he spent Christmas with his family. The Cothams' sister, Mary Ann, married Thomas Maguire, a chemical manufacturer of varying success, in 1838. Together they had three children: Nicholas (1840), James (1844), and Emily (1848). Ten years after this visit, small sums of money were sent to Nicholas Hall, a medical student at King's College, by Cotham. Nicholas probably changed his name to Hall when he inherited from his maternal great-grandfather, James Hall, at the same time as his Cotham uncles. The younger son, James, apparently died young. He was a dental student at the time of his mother's death and the family were staying with Nicholas, by then a medical practitioner, when Mary Ann died in 1871. Her two Cotham brothers took a particular interest in their niece Emily's shaky financial affairs; Nicholas, having become a fully-fledged surgeon, emigrated to Australia and lost contact with the family.

The visits to Mary Ann may have provided a reason why Fr Cotham, for all his love of family and Lancashire, opted to stay in the south west. Despite the name, Appleton was not a pleasant place to live being at the heart of alkali manufacturing in the area. It was one of the villages subsumed into the town of Widnes, and Widnes was considered one of the ugliest and dirtiest towns of the industrial north:

> Their especial ugliness is, however, never more marked than when the spring is making beautiful every nook and corner of England, for the spring never comes hither. It never comes because, neither at Widnes nor St. Helens, is there any place in which it can manifest itself. The foul gases which, belched forth night and day from the many factories, rot the clothes, the teeth, and, in the end, the bodies of the workers, have killed every tree and every blade of grass for miles around.[6]

278 *The Indomitable Mr Cotham*

Contrast this with assessments of the Tasmanian environment, made one hundred and fifty years apart. 'Perhaps the most salubrious and congenial climate of any in the known world for an European constitution. It has been ascertained by the thermometer to be similar to that of the south of France' and 'the air of Tasmania was to that of England as cream to skimmed milk'[7] while a scientific measurement 'in 1970, [at] the Cape Grim Baseline Air Pollution Station judged the air here [NW top of the island] "the clearest ever measured on earth"'.[8] For someone who took every opportunity to walk miles, and who at the end of his life is said to have preferred the solitude of a church tower to the crowding of communal living, urban life in Lancashire would have been scarcely tolerable. Nor would Cotham have been proud of such sensitivity. His own brother William boasted that he had routinely been sent to the fever cases of Liverpool on account of his strong constitution which his Jesuit superiors believed would protect him from contamination during the cholera outbreaks of the 1850s.

After his return to England Fr Cotham was in regular contact with William, who seems to have been even more energetic and gregarious than his two younger brothers. After ordination in 1831, as one of nine newly ordained Jesuits, William became chaplain to Lord Clifford of Ugbrooke and was missioner for Chudleigh in Devon for ten years. A long article in *The Tablet* in November 1845,[9] written to the Editor by Clifford, reported a confrontation in Devon between Fr William Cotham and a proponent of the British Reformation Society who claimed to have stolen a consecrated Host for propaganda purposes. Fr James in Tasmania was able to read this long article, either in *The Tablet* or in the *Sydney Morning Chronicle*[10] where it appeared on 2 May 1846.

Bigotry in England in the 1840s escalated into outbreaks of sectarian violence after the restoration of the Catholic hierarchy in England and Wales in the autumn of 1850. Fr Glassbrook's chapel in Cheltenham was attacked during a riot, although compensation for the damage was paid out of public funds as a

Return to England 279

sign of civic disapproval. However, the Catholic Church also took opportunities to display its loyalty to crown and country and Fr William's convivial nature found an outlet in local celebrations for national occasions:

> The children of the Catholic school at St. Nicholas Chapel, in Exeter, have been regaled with roast beef and plum-pudding in honour of the birth of the Prince of Wales, at the school-room, in the Mint. The feast was got up by a benevolent lady of the congregation, Miss Benson, who not only *founded* it, but—aided by Mrs. Fanshawe, the excellent pastor, the Rev. G. Oliver, and the Rev. W. Cotham, of Ugbrooke—waited on the little happy group.[11]

In January 1852 Ambrose Cotham wrote from Warrington to the Secretary of State for the Colonies, Earl Grey, asking for a further six months extension of his leave of absence.[12] As grounds for his request Cotham provided a summary of his life during the past seventeen years. Although it was written to plead his case (which was granted) and may therefore have been exaggerated it is probably not too far from the truth; at this point Cotham did not want to be assessed as permanently unfit for service. He describes how he attended the spiritual wants of 'bond and free, but principally bond, scattered over more than half the island'. The poor state of the roads and the long distances necessitated 'much travelling on horse-back, occasionally as much as two hundred and fifty miles in the week, and the bodily and mental labour which these numerous duties involved affected my health—more especially injurious I received from horses on two occasions falling upon me'. Within a fortnight Cotham's leave of absence was extended for a further six months on a half-salary of £100 per annum.

Cotham was appointed to the mission in Cheltenham in July 1852 while still officially attached to the Colonial service. He asked again for an extension on his leave of absence in December 1852 'pending the result of future Government legislation respecting transportation'. Not unreasonably the Colonial Office informed Cotham on 23 December that his services as convict

280 *The Indomitable Mr Cotham*

chaplain could be dispensed with altogether with the cessation of transportation. Fr Cotham accepted the decision without appeal but wrote on 4 February 1853 about his right to a retiring pension as an officer of the Convict Department. After fourteen months of correspondence between the Colonial Office in London and the Convict Department in Hobart, Cotham was allowed £57 10s. pension per annum, the maximum entitlement. If he had been eager to return to Tasmania doubtless Bishop Willson would have found him a position in the diocese. For those who did stay on as chaplains in the convict department the work load dramatically decreased after 1850 and with their government salaries they were financially better off than their diocesan colleagues. The prospect evidently held no appeal for Cotham.

There are a number of possible explanations for the extended leave of absence negotiations: he may have been genuinely undecided about returning and wanted to restore his health as much as possible before making his decision; by extending his period of government service he may have intended to accrue a greater pension; or having left in a state of burn-out (his leave having been delayed by two years) possibly he could not face going back even with the end of transportation in view. Cotham had noted the 'peculiarly depressive' effect of repetitive work without obvious signs of achievement or change: the work done with convicts had to be started from scratch with each new batch of arrivals or repeated with reoffenders. The working conditions were unsavoury: hours spent in a fetid atmosphere with sullen, demoralised, or recalcitrant men and women and hapless children, with journeys on horseback or by ferry to reach them and return home. These were the lesser evils; the more sickening cruelties and depravities were not written or spoken about with outsiders although their existence enveloped Tasmanian society like a putrid miasma. Cotham had learnt hard lessons similar to those which informed Bishop Ullathorne's later life:

> Australia taught him a great deal about the need for order
> and authority in the organisation of clergy as missioners,

Return to England 281

but also about the strain of solitary missionary life on the spirit and energy of a priest, and the need for deep inner spiritual and psychological resources in situations which bred isolation and depression.[13]

One of Cotham's companions on the *Oriental* in 1835 was John Aloysius Harding, a member of the Trelawny family of Cornwall. Harding spent five years from 1837 to 1842 as a lay catechist on the notorious Norfolk Island convict station. After a period in Sydney as Polding's secretary he returned to England in 1846, his physical and nervous health still completely shattered. The cause of his breakdown, scandalously, was his treatment by the island Superintendent. His successor Fr Richard Walsh, having himself become seriously ill on the island, wrote:

> Norfolk Island at present is in a very unsettled state. Captain Maconochie is sending Mr. Harding off the Island for writing an article in the *Chronicle* about the taking of the Brig [by mutinous convicts]. He has endeavoured to injure him in every way and even exposed his life to the fury of prisoners by circulating among them that Mr. Harding was their enemy and that he was writing against them. I hope he will pay for this, as Mr. Harding is to take an action against him. Rev. Mr. McEncroe is returning to Sydney by the same Barque and I fear he will not come back as he is disgusted with the old Captain's management of the prisoners, so that I am left alone to do the best I can.[14]

Revd Fr Walsh did manage very well for four years and afterwards expressed the almost inexpressible experience in the simple comment 'there were some good, and some very bad'.[15]

Harding's physician in England, Dr Jonathan Couch, a naturalist himself, advised an early form of occupational therapy for Harding; through it he not only recovered his health but became notable for his close observations of rooks and for his expertise in photography. The ingredients in Harding's convalescence—a return to a supportive family in Cornwall, outdoor pursuits, and a fulfilling occupation away from the harsher machinations of

282   *The Indomitable Mr Cotham*

societal systems—allowed him to regain not only his health but his enthusiasm for life.[16] Whether by instinct or advice Fr Cotham also tried to introduce therapeutic features into his pastoral routine, though these might have been viewed by some as the indulgence of a naturally sociable temperament.

In the space of eighteen months Fr Cotham seems to have taken every opportunity not only to reacquaint himself with the people and places he had left behind but to learn about the new circumstances of the Catholic Church since emancipation and restoration of the hierarchy. Bishop Ullathorne of Birmingham had used his Australian experience—fraught with financial and personnel difficulties—to advise Rome in the matter of erecting entirely new structures of government and administration in the English dioceses. Birmingham was also the setting for St Mary's College at Old Oscott on the city outskirts, a departure from the traditional form of monastic education which once dominated the choices for higher education; Fr John Henry Newman had chosen the city for the innovative Congregation of the Oratory. Fr Cotham was familiar with these developments from a distance and he lost no time in gaining some personal experience of them. His itinerary following his return to England suggests he was also immediately considering places of education for his brother Lawrence's sons, a plan likely to have been discussed before his departure from Tasmania. It was a preoccupation for the rest of his life.

Notes

1   C. H. Gibbs-Smith, *The Great Exhibition of 1851: A Commemorative Album* (London: HMSO, 1950), p. 18.
2   *Ibid.,* p. 18.
3   J. Simmons, *The Victorian Railway* (London: Thames & Hudson, 1995), p. 76.
4   AAA RB-262–150; Cotham to Revd R. Burchall, 28 May 1851. Richard Placid Burchall was Prior at St Edmunds, Douai from 1841 to 1854 and President of the English Benedictine Congregation between 1854 and 1883.
5   AAA RB-262–163, Cotham to Burchall, 28 June 1851.

Return to England 283

6   R. H. Sherard, *The White Slaves of England, Being True Pictures of Certain Social Conditions in the Kingdom of England In the Year 1897* (London: James Bowden, 1897), p. 47.

7   N. Shakespeare, *In Tasmania* (London: The Harvill Press, 2004), p. 228, quoting from *Godwin's Emigrant Guide to Van Diemen's Land*, 1823, and *A Home in the colonies: Edward Braddon's Letters to India from North West Tasmania 1878.*

8   *Ibid.*, p. 229.

9   *The Tablet*, 1 November 1845, p. 6.

10 *Sydney Morning Chronicle*, 2 May 1846, p. 4.

11 *Western Times* quoted in *The Tablet*, 15 January 1842, p. 5.

12 Cotham made copies of the correspondence with the Colonial Office, January 1852-March 1854, concerning his leave of absence and subsequent retirement, in one of his notebooks.

13 J. Champ, *William Bernard Ullathorne 1806–1889, A Different Kind of Monk* (Leominster: Gracewing, 2006), p. 393.

14 B. Condon, *Letters and Documents in 19th Century Australian Catholic History*, Walsh to Geoghegan, 21 September 1842; http://www.library.unisa.edu.au/condon/CatholicLetters. [Accessed online 27.7.2017]

15 *Freeman's Journal* (Sydney), 17 April 1861, p. 5.

16 Known as Lewis Harding (1806–1893), he is remembered especially in Polperro, Cornwall as a rookist and early photographer.

25 'CHELTENHAM, RESORT OF THE GOOD AND THE GAY'

THE 42 YEAR-OLD priest who came to Cheltenham in July 1852, with his official status still undecided, had 'a sturdy figure, high complexion and white hair, heralded by a corresponding strength and exercise of voice',[1] despite his plea to the government that 'the length of the voyage, [his] state of bodily health, [and] advancing years' would involve 'uselessly expended' money should he return to Tasmania.[2] Having travelled overnight from Douai on Tuesday 5 July, he stayed only until the 8th before going to Warrington and preaching there on Sunday. While in Lancashire he visited his family, dentist, and tailor coming back on Saturday 17 July. The journal entry for the day is assured and brisk: 'Arrived at Cheltenham 4o'c a.m, in charge of the Mission. Rev. James Kendal left at 9 a.m.'.

Book-keeping entries immediately follow; the school's debt stood at seven pounds and threepence, and he took stock of the quantities and prices of candles, wine, oil, and coals in hand. One of the first tradesmen he met, to buy coal, was David Gregory, a brother of Henry Gregory Gregory. The Gregorys were parishioners but were not prominent in church affairs; few small shopkeepers were until later. Fr Cotham also bought four surplices at half price, presumably from Fr Kendal. From the outset we see his drive for getting on with the job; his ability to work independently; and his attention to detail, especially financial. He was a man in charge of his mission from the outset. It drew almost all its congregants from the borough of Cheltenham, although its boundaries were defined 'by the old rule of meeting neighbouring missions halfway', Gloucester being the closest, and Chipping Norton the most distant (seven miles and twenty miles respectively).[3] Fr Cotham estimated the number of Catholics to be about

1300, out of a town population which fluctuated between 35,000 and 44,000 according to the season.[4]

Cotham's journal until the end of November does not indicate if he considered the appointment temporary or long term; the entries concern mission and household accounts, Masses said, and payments to the organ blower and gardener. There is nothing about his opinions or plans, and the correspondence with the Colonial Office was about leave of absence and not resignation until late December. Until the end of the year Revd James Basil Duck OSB assisted him in the parish. Fr Cotham administered his first baptism in Cheltenham on 1 August and all those in the parish thereafter until mid-1854 with the exception of three celebrated in August, September, and December by Fr Duck, and one in January 1853 by Fr Glassbrook. As soon as Cotham's resignation from the Colonial service was certain Fr Duck moved to Studley, to carry forward plans for a Catholic church with patronage from the Throckmorton family at nearby Coughton Court.

It would be a misconception to think that Cotham came to Cheltenham ill-prepared or shocked by an unfamiliar culture. Not only had he travelled widely during his period of leave, he had first-hand knowledge of Catholic diocesan life in Tasmania that was legally sanctioned, and, at least in part, government funded. His Australian journal shows him to be worldly-wise: he was at ease with the spiritual work of a pastor, confessor, and teacher but he found no difficulty in negotiating astutely with landowners, bank officials, and builders. His younger brother Lawrence became something of an entrepreneur and landowner before taking his family to Queensland. Finding himself once again in pioneer country, he bought shares in a gold mine and opened a pharmacy, regularly helped by investments in foreign stocks and shipments of supplies sent out from England by Fr Cotham. There is nothing to suggest Cotham was daunted by the mission he had been given in Cheltenham. On the contrary, from January 1853 he acted resolutely with an eye to the future and he carried others with him.

'Cheltenham, Resort of the Good and the Gay' 287

During his twenty years in Cheltenham Fr Cotham had good support from his assistant priests, especially Fr Blount and Fr Wilkinson, but for eighteen months, from January 1853, he was mostly on his own. In answer to his request to be allowed to minister alone Bishop Burgess of Clifton wrote in strong terms; 'It is killing a priest by inches to do two duties' on a Sunday and as instruction cannot be given adequately at both Masses the lax will prefer the first, shorter, service before 'going off jaunting'. For the Cheltenham congregation to plead poverty and inability to keep two priests 'of such moderate habits' was not acceptable. Fr Cotham was reluctantly given permission to remain alone for a further four months 'during the bad weather' after which the congregation 'must be told to come forward with means for keeping two priests or lose the convenience of two Masses'.[5]

In a fund-raising appeal sent out in October 1853 it was stated that the pastor had worked single-handedly specifically in order to husband the resources of the mission. Clearly working alone was not a new situation for Fr Cotham, and he may even have welcomed the chance to work independently at the beginning, but from July 1854 he always had at least one assistant priest with whom, for the most part, he worked collaboratively and whose company he enjoyed. However, at this point Cotham apparently had no wish, or did not see the need, for 'a full choir of habited missionary monks' to take up residence alongside the church. Later he would have heard of Bishop Ullathorne's foresighted vision of a different style of Benedictine clergy life, and at the end of his life he may have come to share that view to some extent:

> If, on the mission, and especially in important towns, we could only live in community, and with as much community life as the circumstances of a mission would allow of, we should not only ourselves have the kind of life which is natural and proper to us, but that the spirit of our Holy Order would become understood, and fit and generous minds would be drawn towards us and towards our state of life.[6]

Cheltenham might have seemed uncannily familiar to Fr Cotham from a brief glimpse offered by the *Cheltenham Looker-On* in July 1852:

> The Town Commissioners, at their meeting yesterday, issued an order directing that for the space of twenty-one days from the present date all dogs shall be confined from eight o'clock in the morning to eight o'clock at night ... The hot weather of the past fortnight fully justifies this interference, and we hope, now this order has issued, that the authorites will see that it is enforced.[7]

Heat and the nuisance caused by dogs roaming loose in the streets was nothing new. However, what would have passed for unremarkable normality in Hobart was an affront to the image Cheltenham still wanted to portray, although that image was considerably faded by the mid-century.

> Our Departure Lists for the last three or four weeks, have exhibited Cheltenham under a strangely altered phase to that which, a few years ago, it presented at a corresponding period of the Season. Then we had a long array of arrivals to announce with comparatively few departures—now the reverse takes place, and, for the first three months of Summer, the number of families who leave for change of air and upon expeditions of pleasure, very far exceeds that of those who, with the same objects in view, or for the benefit of our Spas, come to us from other places ... But the result [which railways and steam have introduced] has been in part also hastened by the change which, during the last ten or fifteen years, has taken place in the character and appearance of Cheltenham itself—which, though still confessedly the most beautiful town in Europe, has lost those peculiarly summer attractions which caused it to be the resort of thousands who ... came hither to luxuriate in the enjoyment of our Garden Walks and Promenades, and to participate in amusement congenial to such scenes. These have nearly all disappeared: 'Vistas of over-arching green' have been supplanted by parallelograms of brick

'Cheltenham, Resort of the Good and the Gay' 289

and mortar, and by rows of shops where weary hearts and aching heads may be seen struggling for existence behind plate-glass windows and French-polished counters.[8]

Cheltenham was a comparatively 'new town' having chosen its identity as one of the watering-places of England in the 1750s, and receiving its seal of royal approval by the visit in 1788 of George III and his entourage. From this foundation based on the vanities of a very small elite the town literally blossomed with the promenades, assemblies, and fashionable pastimes provided for its visitors. Servicing the open air, avowedly healthy pursuits, of walking between the wells to take the waters, was an expanding class of hotel and lodging-house keepers, employing the usual domestic staff. Visitors and working people were housed in the terraces, crescents, and large establishments built by investors in stone and mortar; tradespeople provided food and transport— wheelchair conveyors were in demand—and women were able to manage or support businesses such as millinery, language teaching, or the provision of specialised garments: corsets, trusses, and the like. The medical profession was well-represented in the town although opportunities for recreation, frivolous or earnest, were considered equally salubrious for the well-being of visitors.

The location of the old Catholic Chapel on the corner of Somerset Place (north) and St James Square (west) epitomised the town's mix of identities. Somerset Place was part of Manchester Walk, an inconveniently narrow passage out of the town centre. It faced the corner of Ambrose Street, running into the Lower High Street to the north, and Knapp Road on the west, leading to the old, unused workhouse and open fields beyond. The Quaker Meeting House was on the eastern side of Tangent Alley, the boundary of the Chapel and its garden. Across the road, the dignified Baptist Chapel, built in 1823, stood at the head of St James Square, a prestigious housing development that was never completed and is still not a square.

The Catholic Chapel, 1845.

When Revd John Birdsall obtained the site for the Chapel in 1809 it was on the edge of the town and from his windows looking west he saw cows in the fields. This open land of about twenty acres was developed by the enterprising Jessop Brothers; greenhouses, flower beds, and aviary gardens were connected by gravel walks to encourage the public to indulge in two of Cheltenham's finest entertainments: promenading and shopping. At its most ambitious the Jessops' Collection, 'calculated to interest the naturalist, and amuse and instruct the young' included Golden Eagles and storks among a score of other varieties of birds, and poultry, kangaroos, monkeys, American bull frogs, and an assortment of fish. 'The Gardens are laid out with spacious walks for the accommodation of wheel-chairs, and a MAZE has been constructed for the further amusement of visitors.' This was the extent of the gardens in 1860, after half the original acreage had been taken over by the construction of the terminus of the Great Western Station, and catastrophic flooding in 1855 had almost ruined the Jessops.[9] In the mid-1850s a French Vice Consul used

'Cheltenham, Resort of the Good and the Gay'

premises just across the road from what would be the south porch entrance of a new Catholic church.[10] The activity around St James Square was enough to satisfy even Fr Cotham's curiosity.

Places of worship were not peripheral to the amenities for health of body, mind, and soul. Two or three minutes walk from the Catholic Chapel, the medieval parish church of St Mary, lying just behind the High Street, with its churchyard and small school room in a roof space, kept its pre-eminence due to its antiquity and the remarkable presence of Revd Francis Close from 1826 to 1856. The Evangelical churchmanship of the Revd Mr Close left its mark beyond the confines of theology and liturgy as he forcefully gave his opinion on matters of education, entertainment, and civic life. He provided the benchmark against which other Anglican churches in the town were pronounced High or Low, tantamount to being a judgement on their Christian orthodoxy and their loyalty to the Crown. Close's greatest disgust was for the High Church movement within the Church of England, and although demonstrations against ritualist churchmen occurred in Bristol, Bath and Frome in the diocese of Clifton,[11] the effect of Close's preaching was felt most directly by the Catholics of Cheltenham. In the second quarter of the nineteenth century two religious forces collided in Cheltenham as the consequences of Catholic emancipation from civil limitations, and the career of Revd Francis Close, confronted one another.

It was Close's custom to preach annually on 5 November against the teaching of the Catholic Church, publishing his sermon under a title such as *The Errors of Romanism, the Perversion of Truth*.[12] The topic was endlessly debated, for example as a course of Lent lectures by Close's ally, the Revd Archibald Boyd of Christ Church, and though there could be no doubt that Boyd's focus on 'the real character of Popery' was to reveal what he thought were its fallacies, the moderate-sounding series entitled 'The distinctive Differences between the Church of England and the Church of Rome' was presented as 'a valuable and important course of theological instruction'.[13] John Henry

Newman regarded Cheltenham as 'a sort of headquarters against the [Oxford] Movement, and hard words were current', but he was 'much amused' at the idea of his close friend Anne Mozley choosing to visit Cheltenham during the first week of November 1842. He would have enjoyed, too, the satirical writing in the *British Critic*, then under Thomas Mozley's editorship:

> The last anniversary of the Gunpowder Plot seems to have been celebrated at Cheltenham with unusual éclat. Amongst other suitable entertainments of the fulminating, cracking, or phizzing description, the enterprising and spirited minister of the parish church [Francis Close], ever alive to the just claims of innocent recreation, exhibited a sort of polemical 'jack-in-the-box' or 'volcano,' which went off remarkably well ... Some over-fastidious people may probably think the pulpit of that sacred and venerable edifice was not the most appropriate place for an amusement ... But in Cheltenham, the resort of the good and the gay, where the Church and the world so harmoniously combine, where luxury smooths the path of devotion, and the votaries of fashion are enabled to present their offerings on the shrine of genuine piety, such a scruple we are sure is misplaced. The 'performance' was repeated a few days later at the annual meeting of the District Association for the Propagation of the Gospel at the lecture room on the Promenade, where the Secretary assured the assembly that no converts from Christians of other denominations would be admitted, the presence of Baptists at a meeting in Calcutta having 'necessarily caused much strife'.[14]

Francis Close was easy to lampoon as an opponent of Sunday railway travel, horse racing, the theatre, and tobacco. He had to overcome his repugnance to the influential involvement of the Catholic Church in the temperance movement, and his own fears that eliminating alchohol altogether from his diet would be harmful to his health, before eventually becoming founder and first President of the Church of England Total Abstinence Society in 1862. However, his thundering presence was a valuable

'*Cheltenham, Resort of the Good and the Gay*' 293

counterweight to Cheltenham's flightier aspects; alongside other opponents to the Oxford Movement, his uncompromising Evangelicanism brought the Church of England back into vital confrontation with the challenges of Victorian society.

The Revd Mr Close's sermons were unapologetically polemical and, on occasion, literally inflammatory. Following the reintroduction of the Catholic hierarchy in 1850 the customary 5 November commemorative sermon was followed by two so-called Great Protestant Meetings in Cheltenham. The return of Catholic bishops to take direct responsibility for dioceses of the Catholic Church in England, in place of oversight being vested in English delegates in Rome, was seen as a presumptuous encroachment by the Pope on the authority of the monarchy and an attempt to enslave the nation. Mr Close called on the first meeting[15] to oppose Romish apostasy that 'attempts to crush the human intellect, shuts up men and women in convents and nunneries, interferes with the charities of life [and] breaks into the bosoms of families'. In identifying the Tractarian writings as instrumental in causing many Anglicans to convert to Catholicism he called for unified opposition against Anglo-Catholics and Roman Catholics. The Revd Mr Calder maintained England was justified in 'thrusting out the Roman intruders from the country'. The danger from the presence of English Catholic bishops in their own dioceses in England stretched across 'the full enjoyment of the liberties of the English nation'. A loyal address to the Queen was prepared asking her to take measures to 'frustrate the machinations of the Roman Pontiff.'[16]

The installation of Cardinal Wiseman at Westminster was expected imminently and to maintain momentum a second Great Meeting, on 21 November, was convened for the purpose of making and hearing further addresses which included Mr Close reading a direct translation from the Latin of an allegedly original document written by Archbishop Cranmer. The high tone of his intervention was lost on the general populace who, catching only the enthusiasm of the occasion, decided on direct action in the form of a Guy Fawkes-style demonstration. An effigy, supposedly of either Pope Pius IX or Cardinal Wiseman, was prepared and exhibited in a shop window in the High Street. At 10 o'clock on the evening of the 21st a crowd broke into the shop, stole the effigy, and after parading it up and down the High Street, moved the short distance to the Catholic Chapel where the effigy was burned. The demonstration ended with the mob breaking every window in the chapel.

Although the *Cheltenham Looker-On* mildly deplored events which 'the respectable and right-thinking portion of our population'[17] lamented, other publications reported more colourfully the clashes between the demonstrators and excited Irish residents from the nearby streets which must have been seriously disturbing for Fr Glassbrook, lodged next to the chapel. Fortunately he was not a man of delicate constitution and he successfully sued the town commissioners for compensation, claiming they had been negligent in preventing the unrest.

Cheltenham was not unusual in its experience of anti-Catholic feeling at this period, although its façade of gentility, the vehemence of Mr Close's rhetoric, and the inarticulate anger felt by the disenfranchised Irish immigrants, gave a particular piquancy to its expression. This was the last gross display of anti-Catholic feeling in the town but the lively memory of it sustained the self-identity of Catholics as a faithful remnant always on the cusp of martyrdom as it faithfully trod in the footsteps of its heroic forefathers and mothers. The rhetoric employed by Fr Cotham in 1848, in defence of the papacy, was echoed in his exhortations to his Cheltenham parishioners to support his ambitious schemes.

If Cheltenham had lost its magnetic summer powers it still prided itself on being pre-eminent as a town for winter residence, at least among those still able to afford and enjoy its pleasures. The *Cheltenham Looker-On*, a weekly Saturday publication for high society, acknowledged in passing the convulsing effects of changes in social and political enonomy in England and on the Continent but still promoted 'the cheerfulness, good order and

'Cheltenham, Resort of the Good and the Gay'

regularity' of the townscape, 'the facilities of intercommunication', and below national average rental costs as reassuringly accessible together with the 'commingling of families of recognised station and affluence' in private festivities.[18] The large scale fêtes, galas, and summer balls were replaced by domestic card parties and select dinner parties. The insular, self-serving emphasis on gaiety and pleasure, without even a pretence of benefits to health, is not attractive, but in truth it did not apply to the majority of Cheltenham townspeople. They did not need a 'constant succession of amusements' to keep themselves occupied, unless it was to provide work in the service of those families of recognised station.

Revd Fr Birdsall had acknowledged as early as 1809 that

> on the part of the townspeople no opposition has been experienced; indeed they were all well aware that it was for the benefit of the town that there should be a Catholic Chapel ... [Cheltenham's] prosperity was necessarily connected with every improvement by which conveniences and recommendations of the various visitors might be promoted and so inducement be held out to them to prolong their stay.[19]

The modest chapel provided by Fr Birdsall was remembered as

> a poor and small brick building, and yet it was considered at the time it was raised as a very great improvement on what had gone before, which was nothing better than a garret or something of that kind. That little chapel was considered handsome in its day.[20]

It depended on patronage from wealthy visitors, including a significant number of Irish gentry such as the Earl of Kenmare, Lord Castlerosse, and their sister Lady Charlotte Gould. As Birdsall expanded the chapel, gifts of plate, vestments, and furnishings were provided by the old families of Weld, Hornyold, Turville, and Vavasour. When English visitors were able to visit the Continent more freely after 1815 the drop in numbers coming to Cheltenham was compensated for by an increase in French visitors who brought the *éclat* of nobility: the Duke and Duchess of Angouleme, the Comte d'Artois, and the Comte de Jarnac. Fr James Calderbank OSB had inspected Cheltenham in 1806, considered it an unprofitable town for a Benedictine mission, and promptly returned to Bath. Fr Birdsall, on the other hand, was able to bring personal money and pensions with him and saw the possibilities Cheltenham offered. He was not immune from enjoying the flattery of being greeted as an old acquaintance when he attended a levée given by the exiled French King in Bath.

The Catholic congregation, like the rest of Cheltenham, could look back on the days when royalty passed through the streets, and even down Tangent Alley, bestowing a glow which coloured the town's identity for decades. Even in the days when the Catholic Chapel resembled a modest non-conformist building from the outside, the quality of its musical performance accompanied on a Bevington organ brought up from London was notable:

> An excellent selection of music was given last Sunday at the Catholic Chapel, Somerset Place, comprising parts of Mozart's beautiful Mass in C, and Handel's 'Lord, remember David' which was sung there for the first time, as was also Pio Cianchettini's celebrated 'Benedictus', for three voices, by Miss Sullivan, Mr Sapio, and that excellent amateur, Mr ***. We have had, and more than once, the pleasure of mentioning Miss Sullivan, as an excellent musician and a very pleasing vocalist; on this occasion we must add that she not only realized our expectations, but even surpassed them. As for our friend Sapio—he is <u>always</u> in his glory in sacred music, and this we think the greatest compliment that can be paid to a vocalist.[21]

Between the two proven Christian traditions, the fluid Oxford Movement was taking shape by distinguishing itself from Protestant Evangelicalism and recusant Roman Catholicism alike. By 1852, when Fr Cotham arrived to carry forward the benefits of emancipation and its consequences, support from former adherents of Anglicanism and Anglo-Catholicism was more than a match for the followers of Francis Close's churchmanship. Nevertheless, Cheltenham's leading high society publication maintained its anti-Catholic stance for decades to come, publishing caustic comment and pseudo-information to keep alive the animosity which had become entrenched during Mr Close's curacy.

> Cardinal Wiseman has been preaching on the 'Conversion of England' lately at Rome. Among other topics, his Eminence congratulated the Roman Catholics on the schisms among the various dissenting bodies in England, and especially on the difference of opinion in the Church of England on the subject of baptismal regeneration, which he considered betokened the speedy dissolution of that establishment, adding, that more converts had been made to the Roman Catholic Church in England during the last ten years than in three hundred previously.[22]

The presence and influence of converts, especially from wealthy backgrounds, became a feature of Cheltenham's Catholic mission, but shortly before Fr Cotham's arrival Daniel Evans, a convert and a draper in the High Street, wrote a letter to Bishop Hendren of Clifton which is remarkable for its astute articulation of the laity's assessment of the state of their town and church. Hendren was the first bishop of Clifton, but overwhelmed by the state of affairs he found in the new diocese he resigned in 1851. However, notice seems to have been taken of Evans' comments as Cotham's appointment as missioner was a fitting response.

At a meeting with the Bishop, Evans had been asked to form a congregational committee to advise and act for the benefit of the mission, in collaboration with Fr Glassbrook. Evans failed to establish a committee so he submitted 'the leading facts of our temporal and general position' for the Bishop's consideration.

> Our Chapel is encumbered with a heavy debt for the interest of which the Benedictine Body of course are responsible. Our Bench Rents, Offertory, and donations if any, are

fluctuating in amount, and are inadequate to the due support of the mission, if the interest of the debt were paid in full.

We have a Boy's and Girl's School, supported hitherto by the direct exertions and influence of a Gentleman and Lady whose further services, owing to circumstances cannot be safely calculated on any longer. We require a new school room so badly, that had not the Revd Mr Glassbrook rented a large room in the locality of the Chapel the refusal must have been given to very many.

There has been for some time a general opinion that the proceeds of the mission ought not to be applied to the payment of interest on a debt which there appears no probability of ever being paid, and also that it was contracted by the majority who are not now living or residing amongst us. It is thought that the amount now raised from the services before named would support a mission and form a reserve fund to help build a new Church, or that a larger sum could be raised were a new Church built to pay the interest, were capital borrowed to build, and support the mission likewise. This is what no person can dispute to be essentially necessary. Our chapel only affords room for renting in the Body and Gallery together for 260 persons. We have room under the Gallery for about 100 persons which is appropriated for free seats if that number is represented by fresh persons at the second Mass. This shews accommodation for 460 persons. The petition to her Majesty expressing loyalty &c from the Catholics here contained more than 1000 signatures uniting the heads and members of families, the correctness of which I can testify having personally with others witnessed the signing.

When the Revd Mr Dowding resided here there was a complaint from many that we required two priests and that our Religion required to be carried out with more ceremonial, and a subscription was entered into for that purpose and a second priest not being appointed the money was left to Mr Dowding's disposal who very justly and kindly returned it to those who wished it, and the residue was devoted to the repairs and alterations of the chapel and other public purposes. When the Revd Mr Glassbrook succeeded the Revd Mr Dowding in the Mission he commenced with great zeal what had been desired, a second priest was sent to us, the Gass [*sic*] was introduced, and the Evening Service established, which is estimated more especially by our poor.

There are now complaints forwarded to the [Benedictine] provincial that our present clergy are not eloquent preachers, unfitted for the present crisis, and the class of persons (Protestants) who often come to our chapel. I do not take on myself to suggest anything or to offer an opinion for your Lordship's guidance but were our present clergy removed we should not be the appointers of others. I think the most dissatisfied amongst us can bring no charge against our present clergy either in zeal, morals, or doctrine. What is termed an eloquent preacher and clever controversialist might attract but not edify so much as simplicity of preaching and kindness and goodwill to all.

I believe I mentioned to your Lordship that the formation of a committee was prevented by an order from the Provincial and also that our evening service was ordered to be discontinued in the same way without any reason being stated. This morning the Revd Mr Glassbrook received a letter from his superior intimating that he is to be removed to the northern district without assigning any reason for such a step being taken ... For the sake of extending Religion may I entreat your Lordship to use your influence to further such measures as may tend to make us more satisfied with the spiritual advantages we now possess and I have no doubt we shall then as a consequence be more united in carrying out those matters which appear to be so necessary.

In submission to your Lordship there appears one of two things required; our clergy to be established permanently independent of the caprice of the [Benedictine] congregation, or, if the superiors of the Benedictine Body still continue to cripple the extension of Religion by allowing that to interfere, the population and intelligence of Cheltenham warrant the establishing of a Mission which could act with more freedom and correspond with the requirements of the age.

Although I would wish my remarks to be of a general character I cannot refrain from alluding to this removal as bearing hard on an individual who has gained the good opinion of so many without the pale of the church, and who has expended a considerable sum from his private means for the temporal benefit of the mission, and has also invested some money in house property here which his absence may lessen in its value to him.

If my letter should appear disrespectful or intrusive in any way I must beg your Lordship's indulgence as neither is intended.[23]

The successors to the formidable Fr Birdsall had been, almost inevitably, weaker characters by comparison, but worse, they had been frequently moved. Three assistant priests—Frs Levy, Lynass, and Basil Duck—had been appointed within little more than a year, between 1851 and 1852. The Benedictines, as a body, were blamed for not keeping up with 'the requirements of the age', while religious orders and diocesan bishops were hard pressed to provide priests to meet the demands emancipation had generated. Furthermore, the particular character of Cheltenham, as a stronghold of Evangelical Protestantism with many visiting Protestants who expected to sample the different types of worship on offer, needed a strong preacher who would make an immediate impact and hold his own among the competition. Evans speculates that the Benedictines might not be able to hold onto Cheltenham in its entirety if the mission split into two.

Daniel Evans knew what Cheltenham Catholics wanted: an eloquent advocate for the faith, long term commitment, financial stability, with new schools and a bigger, more impressive church. They were disenchanted with the Benedictine province, and probably had unrealistic expectations from the new diocesan

'Cheltenham, Resort of the Good and the Gay'

administration, but they were alert to the signs of the times. When Fr Provincial Heptonstall appointed Cotham he must have hoped that, even without previous experience of an English mission, he possessed sufficient self-confidence to adapt to his ambitious congregation and keep Cheltenham safe for the Benedictine Congregation.

Notes

[1] House Journal of the of the Society of Jesus, *Letters and Notices*, No. XCIX, 1895, p. 130.The description of his brother William can safely be applied to James Ambrose as their similarity was striking.

[2] Letter to Colonial Office, 2 December 1852.

[3] CDA, Cheltenham Box, Parish Visitation Report, 1858–59.

[4] The Religious Census taken in 1851 shows Cheltenham had seven Anglican churches and about twenty non-Anglican places of worship (depending on where parish boundaries are drawn). Of the 23,000 sittings available in Cheltenham churches and chapels, only 360 were available at the Catholic Chapel. Four Anglican churches in the town exceeded 1,000 adult attendances on Sunday mornings, and non-Anglican attendance varied between 30 and 800. See A. Munden, 'The Religious Census in Cheltenham in 1851' in *Cheltenham Local History Society*, Journal 21, 2005, pp. 36–50, for a full analysis of the census returns.

[5] Bishop Burgess to Cotham, 15 January 1853.

[6] Bishop Ullathorne to President Burchall OSB, 20 July 1874, quoted in A. Hood OSB, *From Repatriation to Revival* (Farnborough: St Michael's Abbey Press, 2014), p. 117.

[7] *Cheltenham Looker-On*, 24 July 1852, pp. 481–482.

[8] *Ibid.*, 4 July 1846, p. 424.

[9] *Cheltenham Examiner*, 5 December 1860, p. 3, and *Cheltenham Looker-On*, 4 August 1855, p. 583. The construction of 'a more commodious and accessible' passenger station abutting the road along the west side of St Gregory's was not debated until 1872; see *Cheltenham Looker-On*, 27 April 1872, p. 266.

[10] Cheltenham Old Town Survey 1855–57. Compact disc issued by Cheltenham Local History Society and Gloucestershire Record Office, 2011.

[11] J. A. Harding, *Clifford of Clifton (1823–1893): England's Youngest Catholic Bishop* (Diocese of Clifton, 2011), pp. 316–317.

[12] *Cheltenham Looker-On*, 4 December 1847, p. 784.

13 *Ibid.*, 1 March 1851, p. 139.

14 www.newman.reader.org/works/letters_diaries, Newman to T. Mozley, 9 November 1842; Vol. IX, p. 147, and footnote 5 citing *The British Critic*, Number 33, January 1843, p. 291.

15 *Cheltenham Looker-On*, 16 November 1850, 'The Protestant Meeting', p. 724.

16 *Ibid.*, 'Great Protestant Meeting', p. 733.

17 *Ibid.*, 23 November 1850, p. 741.

18 *Ibid.*, 2 October 1847, p. 360.

19 Richard Barton Collection now in author's possession. Copy of Birdsall's diary; the original is held in Downside Abbey Archives.

20 *Cheltenham Examiner*, 14 November 1877, p. 3. Recollection by Bishop Collier.

21 *Cheltenham Looker-On*, 13 April 1839, p. 231.

22 *Ibid.*, 10 December 1853, p. 838.

23 CDA Cheltenham Box, Daniel Evans to Bishop Hendren, 2 March 1851.

26 'I CONSIDER IT IS TIME WE SHOULD BESTIR OURSELVES IN GOOD EARNEST.'

IN ONE IMPORTANT respect Fr Cotham was well informed by his time in Tasmania: he was acquainted with the Gothic Revival style of architecture and furnishing so favoured by the wave of church building after 1850. When Bishop Willson was given responsibility for the Catholics of Tasmania his good friend Augustus Pugin had arranged with John Hardman to do everything they could to provide a total outfitting for his infant diocese. Willson shared Pugin's belief that 'architecture is the barometer of faith ... the revival or decline of true Ecclesiastical architecture is commensurate with that of the true faith' and was delighted to be one of the two bishops who had 'departed across the ocean to the antipodes, carrying the seeds of Christian design to grow and flourish in the New World.'[1] As a consequence, Fr Cotham was familiar not only with the architectural scaled models and stone exemplars of details such as piscinas, sacrariums, holy water stoups, and gable crosses sent for local craftsmen to work from, but he would have worn one of the forty silk chasubles and used the chalice and paten designed principally for convict service.[2]

However, Cheltenham did not have the personal services of Augustus Pugin, nor his wealthy patrons, anachronisms by 1853 in any case. The high point of Romantic Catholicism, linked to medievalism and the taste for picturesque ruins left behind by Reformation and Puritan purges, had passed by the 1840s. The subsequent moral quest to make real the ideals of the Catholic Church, as understood by Pugin, Ambrose de Lisle Phillips, and the Earl of Shrewsbury, by unifying faith, history, and buildings

304   *The Indomitable Mr Cotham*

through the medium of architecture, had lost its main protagonists. Rosemary Hill emphasises the volatility of the 1820s and 1830s.

> These years saw the the worst civil unrest in English history. Religious division brought fears of social disintegration. The spectre of revolution was not far from anyone's mind ... Catholic Emancipation challenged the position of the established church and millenarianism was so widespread that 'prophecy became a normal intellectual activity ... in England'.[3]

The restoration of the Catholic hierarchy in 1850 reignited the polemical fireworks briefly, especially in Evangelical towns such as Cheltenham, but in fact the stabilising presence of a pragmatic diocesan structure in England outweighed the annoyance caused by flamboyant displays of devotion. Anti-Catholic feeling did not go away but the Catholic community became a less simplistic target to vilify as it diversified.

Charles Hansom's career had been enormously boosted by his involvement as a member of William Ullathorne's congregation in Coventry. Their collaboration on St Osburg's, completed in 1845, not only made Hansom the Benedictines' favourite architect for the next two decades, but also introduced a selection of his designs to mainland Australia, via Ullathorne and Polding (Bishop Willson, of course, having his own personal connection with A. W. N. Pugin). The almost inevitable choice of Hansom as architect for Cheltenham's new Catholic church, with the firms of Hardman, Farmer, and Boulton supplying craftsmanship, gave Cotham the opportunity to erect 'a magnificent Church', especially given the enthusiasm of sufficiently affluent members of his congregation. His financial backers varied in their adherence to the high Gothic philosophy. James de Lacy Towle and Robert Biddulph Phillips were able to commission churches themselves as an expression of their own faith. Phillips went so far as to restore a pre-reformation chapel and incorporate it into the new convent he built for his daughter and her sisters in religion. For others, Gothic was the fashion of the time—as it was for non-

'I consider it is Time we should bestir ourselves in Good Earnest.'   305

conformists and Anglicans—and it is unlikely they were swayed by treatises such as Pugin's *Contrasts*. The building of churches for the worship of God was a frequent topic for Fr Cotham's homilies but there is nothing to suggest aesthetics played much part. It is more likely he shared his brother William's robust views of the time 'When our old cath'lic fathers lived a long time ago.'[4] As for the mechanics of church building, far from representing an abrupt break with his Tasmanian experience, Cheltenham was a natural, and confident, development of it.

In early January 1853 Fr Cotham was ready to plan in earnest. Fifteen years later, in January 1868, his notes outlining the course of events and decisions taken were copied out as Memoranda giving 'a little history of why and how we first began this Building of St Gregory's'. He began with the facts concerning the school: as of 31 December 1852, sixty-seven girls attended lessons in two small rooms, 15 ft by 12 ft, over the vestries. The sixty-five boys who attended fared even worse, being accommodated in an old carpenter's workshop with a brick floor and a small window 'not made to open', without a playground or 'ordinary conveniences'. In order to discuss this state of affairs Fr Cotham convened a meeting of all chapel seat holders who paid pew rent. As a shrewd priest he made a particular appeal to the women of the church, and to encourage everybody to a friendly rivalry he alluded, surely not for the last time, to his experience far away:

> I am aware that ladies form part of our congregation as well as gentlemen and I shall be glad if they will be present at our meeting after Mass. Indeed I may say that the Ladies form the most zealous portion, the corner stone, of our congregation. At the call of Religion and of Charity they are always the first and most zealous … I feel assured that the Catholics here as well as in other parts of the world, when their object is to glorify and honour God … will forget their minor differences and concentrate their energies to accomplish the end in view … this I trust will be the case with us.

As well as the later Memoranda, his rough speaking notes for the inaugural meeting show his line of reasoning and persuasion. 'The object we have in view in meeting is to take into consideration the most efficient means of providing School accommodation for the poor children of our Congregation.' The provision of Catholic elementary schools had been given the highest priority by the bishops attending the Provincial Council of Westminster in 1852. To this end Cotham offered two proposals: either to convert the present chapel into school rooms and erect the nave and aisles only 'of what may ultimately when completed be formed into a magnificent Church', or to keep the existing chapel for some years longer and build against the chapel walls 'at small expense Schools which would serve our purpose for some years'. An estimate for the latter, complete with two water closets, was given as £155. This proposal was considered but 'the effort to obtain means ... was ineffectual'. The relatively modest option did not appeal to the seat holders; perhaps the prospect of beginning to build 'a magnificent church' had caught their imaginations as doubtless Fr Cotham hoped it would.

On 24 January a second, public, meeting of the whole congregation was held and those assembled were evidently ready to take decisive action, particularly in the matter of erecting a new church. Again Fr Cotham's own notes provide a commentary to the more orderly account of the Memoranda. In the first place it was proposed to find a more spacious site than the chapel garden to begin work on the nave and aisles. Secondly, a General Committee, comprising 'the most energetic and influential' among the congregation should be formed to determine the site and plans of the building. The wording of the third proposal, put forward by Cotham himself and seconded by Mr G. A. Williams, is stamped with the force of the missioner's own personality:

> That the urgent necessity of immediately erecting the nave and aisles of a Church upon a site hereafter to be found and converting our present Chapel into schools, demanding as it does the prompt and strenuous exertions of every member

> of the Congregation, this meeting hereby pledges itself, as a matter of the strictest religious duty to promote the above object by the most active zeal and persevering efforts.

In Cotham's working notes there is an undated piece which clearly suggests there was a confrontation of wills at this early point in the negotiations. The passage reads very much like reported speech from two or more speakers, but there is little indication of who said what to whom. The antagonist is not named; however one person present at the meeting of the 24th January who seems not to have played any further active role was Hon. Swinburne Berkeley and he may have been the competitor for Fr Cotham's role. The notes are a curious mixture of caution and confidence; the first speaker was nervous about an 'injudicious' and hastily conceived scheme involving a dangerously large financial outlay in uncertain times for an unspecified building.

> New Church
>
> My duty is a simple one, to lay a few facts before you, which, though patent to all, are not the less important. I may premise by observing that I, in common with many others, look upon the building of a Church or any other work of the kind, at the present time, as most injudicious and injurious schemes for the Catholic Community here that could by any possibility be contemplated, particularly where due regard is had to the present political state of the times and of the money market. Money is very scarce, at Gurney's the best names in the city have to give 5¼ per cent; and the Union Bank, as well as Gurney's will give 4 per cent for money deposited at call. Labour, too, as well as materials, are now exceedingly dear. It may be argued that this unsettled state of things will not last. I will not enter into that question, beyond giving my belief that we are on the eve of a great political crisis, which will involve this country in continual warfare. I therefore think that we ought to pause before paying £750 more for a building (estimated at £3000) than we should have to do at the former market price of labour and materials. The South Western and other

Railways have given up the design of extending their lines on account of the unsettled state of things.

The gloomy political prognostications of the speaker, urging caution until the bank rate was in their favour, seemed to pre-empt the investigations and decision of the Committee.

> In reply to Mr N. I beg to say he was misinformed in respect to the matter on which that part of his statement was made. The information he had received in that respect was erroneous. I will not venture to anticipate that decision.
>
> I accept at once the explanation made by [*sic*] I must say that the warmth of the gent. is quite uncalled for, and the manner in which he gave expression to it unbecoming the position which he at present holds. It is fruitless to vent indignation when none is needed. I can assure him I had not the slightest intention of doing so, and I cannot think the feeling of the meeting at all joins in the somewhat singular demonstration of wasted wrath he has made. I consider union as the Keystone of our projected building, and it appears to me that we cannot look too closely at that Keystone as it has to bear a very important superstructure. I for my part must [*sic*] on that Keystone is sound before I should consider myself justified in commencing the superstructure.

Any righteous cause for indignation on the part of 'the gent' is played down. The gentleman evidently retracted his comments, not wanting to play the role of autocrat in the meeting.

> We must all approve of the spirit of considerate kindness which has dictated the reply of that most respectable gentleman.
>
> I think the pew holders of this congregation will hardly consent that Mr N is so far to put himself forward as the autocrat of our chapel …
>
> 'that may be all very fine, but I can't conceive it just that that income which a man enjoys for his life upon secured capital, and may give to his heirs, shall pay the same as mine, which

> I may lose by a casualty or by a stroke of paralysis tomorrow, leaving my children to the care of the parish.'

The final paragraph, in speech marks, may have come from another member of the congregation or it may have been Cotham's own evaluation of the relative moral worth of contributions made out of secured capital compared with those from more precarious earnings and the weight they afforded to the contributor's opinions. The comparison is interesting in the light of his own financial dealings during the course of the next twenty years, when his earned money, largely his government pension, was gradually superseded by 'income ... from secured capital.' The strong appeal to 'union as the Keystone' sounds like vintage Cotham rhetoric, and he was prepared to assert his personal authority as the safeguard of unity, the only ground for secure progress. He was not about to forget the lessons learnt from his Tasmanian experience as a junior witness to his Bishop's wrangles with an uncooperative clergyman church builder.

The meeting concluded with a vote of thanks, proposed by Mr Caffieri and seconded by Hon. Swinburne Berkeley to Mr Wybault for presiding over the meeting. The General Committee was duly formed from among those who had proposed and seconded the motions at the meeting: Messrs Hector Caffieri, James de Lacy Towle, George Arthur Williams and Patrick Robert Wybault Esq. Mlle Sophie Tiesset had also spoken but she either declined or was not offered a place on the committee. Nevertheless, for thirty years until her death in 1884 she fulfilled to the letter Fr Cotham's strictures on the duty which had now been given to every member of the congregation. The astute Daniel Evans was not on this committee, but he remained active in church matters.

The First Committee: The Most Energetic & Influential

Hector Caffieri, P. R. Wybault, G. A. Williams, James de Lacy Towle and Sophie Tiesset (an honorary and honoured member

310 *The Indomitable Mr Cotham*

of any church gathering): these names recur frequently not only in relation to the early management of the New Church but also in the affairs of the town. Their owners were neither grandees of the town nor the labourers but were representative—though not exhaustively—of the middling sort who increasingly made up Cheltenham society as the century progressed. The *Cheltenham Looker-On* reflected on the changing patterns with some ambivalence as it reviewed 1853.

> From a state of acute depression the town has attained a condition of prosperity as unexpected as it has been almost unparalleled. The value of its property has increased, upon a fair average, full twenty per cent, and houses and mansions which had been unoccupied for years, have, within the last six months, found tenants ... the place is, at the present time, much fuller than it was ever known to be in any winter or summer of its past existence. As a consequence of this its trade has improved, and the entire mass of its population has undergone a corresponding elevation.[5]

While the *Looker-On* attributed the rise in numbers and prosperity to 'a succession of refined and elegant entertainments' the revival was more likely to be a consequence of the expanding middle class of trades and professions which had succeeded the booming years of Cheltenham as a pleasure town. The development of St Gregory's was affected by the rise in land and property prices but it was more than recompensed by the contribution of its home-grown congregation.

However, to speak of 'home-grown' in relation to Cheltenham's population has needed qualification since the spa waters were developed in the mid eighteenth century. Of the five energetic and influential people representing the congregation, only George Arthur Williams could be called a Cheltonian and his family came to the Catholic faith through his grandmother who was not received into the church until 1822 when she was 79. Williams began in business as a bookseller, stationer, and printer in 1815, aged 21. During his lifetime he became an expert in antiquarian

'I consider it is Time we should bestir ourselves in Good Earnest.' 311

books but his interest in all aspects of public life and modernisation was probably unequalled in Cheltenham and his interest was matched by practical involvement. He was invariably found at meetings and on committees, whether as a member of the Board of Guardians overseeing the Parish Workhouse, or a Town Improvement Commissioner, or lobbying for the advancement of the Gloucester and Dean Forest Railway in 1844 and the Cheltenham and Southampton Railway in 1845. He was a man of trade himself and advocated shorter working hours, with shops closing at seven in winter and eight in summer, for tradesmen's employees. During the severe winter of 1849–1850 he subscribed to provide work for the unemployed poor who were also provided with food, firing, clothes, and soup kitchens. He also acted as trustee for the 8 year-old orphan son of Pio Cianchettini, once a distinguished composer and pianist in Cheltenham who died in penury in 1851. For this particular case the subscription fund was supported mainly by the clergy and congregation of St Gregory's but Williams's Library was always open to receive subscriptions for the day's good cause and his name was always on the list with a modest one pound or one guinea. In 1865 a dinner was held in his honour at the Queen's Hotel, acknowledging his half century as a respected tradesman in Cheltenham.

Williams knew how to position himself: his 'circulating' English and Foreign Library, the largest in Cheltenham and 'famous for sixty years far beyond the limits of the town',[6] was located in the High Street at the corner of the Assembly Rooms. He was happy (or at least willing) to sit alongside the Revd Mr Close, an Evangelical, or Colonel Berkeley, Master of the Berkeley Hunt, who chose the Library as the rendezvous for hunt members when out of the saddle. Williams himself was a supporter of hunting, horseracing and boxing.[7] 'In politics a Liberal; in religion a Roman Catholic, he observed towards those who differed from him in either, a deference and courtesy which disarmed opposition and secured him many friends.'[8] Fr Cotham could ask for no better channel of communication for knowing what was afoot in

Cheltenham or how to negotiate with town commissioners, clergymen, and local politicians of all stripes. Williams was reputed to have been 'chosen in 1847 high bailiff of the borough, being the first Catholic who had attained that honour since the days of Queen Elizabeth'[9] but the title is difficult to verify. He died in 1880, his wife and only one son surviving him; his eldest son had committed suicide two years previously having 'suffered from mental depression since he was invalided home from Australia as a result of sunstroke, several years ago'.[10]

Until the late 1860s, when the family moved away, Hector Caffieri's name was seen almost as regularly in print as that of Williams, partly because of his appearances in subscription lists to good causes but mainly due to advertising his prosperous trade as a wine merchant. Caffieri was born in Bath but his father, formerly a 'Bonopartist' soldier, was a peripatetic language teacher around the Stroud area at the time of Hector's birth in 1816. Nicholas Caffieri continued his teaching when he settled in Cheltenham as well as establishing himself in business with his son as wine merchants in Portland Place and Montpellier Walk, the latter near the offices of the *Cheltenham Looker-On*. One of the earliest windows in the New Church, in the Lady Chapel, was installed in memory of the elder Caffieris, the only window with a dedication as an integral part of the design. Caffieri had dual nationality through his mother, Marie le Feuvre from Jersey, and his own wife Mary Clowes was a merchant's daughter from London. He maintained close links with his home in Boulogne, however, as did his eldest son, another Hector. After education at Downside and a false start as an apprentice merchant seaman Hector E. P. Caffieri chose art over trade and became an accomplished water colourist, favouring English landscapes and Breton seascapes. The Caffieri family was a happy example of integration, advancement, and contribution to society through sound education and business acumen. Caffieri's liberality was not confined to church matters. In a graciously worded advertisement the tone of a gentleman, as well as a tradesman, is distinctly heard:

> If the Lady, who, on Tuesday last, obtained Change for a
> £5 Note, at Mr Caffieri's, Montpellier Walk, giving a Note
> of larger amount to the attendant—who received the same
> in mistake—will apply <u>personally</u> as above, the mistake
> shall be rectified.[11]

If the lady was not English, and unfamiliar with English notes and coins, Caffieri's sympathy would have been doubly assured.

Patrick Robert Wybault's Catholic Irish heritage no doubt gave him a special understanding of the plight of the mass of poor Catholic emigrants from Ireland who flocked to England in the 1840s, although his career and wealth protected him from their tribulations. His early career was in the British Army serving on the staff of the Duke of Wellington in the Peninsula Wars (1809–1814) and of Sir George Prevost in Canada (1815–1819), becoming Assistant Commissary General by the end of his service, and acquiring a land grant in Frontenac. This seems to have been the end of his professional career in the army. In 1821 he married Amelia Anne Macklin at Versailles and after his 'beloved' wife's death in 1842 he moved from Hampshire to Cheltenham where he lived two doors from his brother Joseph (a colonel in the commissariat) and his young family.

Patrick's second marriage in 1846 began with a double ceremony, the first being celebrated (one imagines quietly) at the Roman Catholic Chapel, Cheltenham before the wedding party proceeded to the Parish Church at Charlton Kings, home of the bride's family. Wybault was 56; his wife Frances Maria Best was 43, the daughter of Sir John Ryecroft Best, a former plantation owner in the Caribbean owning one hundred and fifty slaves. As Best and his wife subscribed £1 to the church building fund it may be surmised that they was neither strongly enamoured nor antagonistic towards their son-in-law's faith. When Frances died ten years later she left effects of less than £100 but it is likely that some of Patrick Wybault's estate of £14,000 at his death came from his wife's marriage settlement.[12] Patrick was childless from both marriages; after Frances' death a niece lived with him,

314   *The Indomitable Mr Cotham*

sharing their large house with a young butler and housekeeper
and their infant son in Lansdown Crescent, an area popular with
retired army and East India Company personnel.

Wybault's donations to the building funds were considerable:
£80 to the general fund, £185 to the Tower fund, and £100
towards the Spire, although he did not see the last of these
projects completed before his death in 1867. Contributions to
public subscriptions indicate an individual's concerns: we see
Hector Caffieri and Mlle Tiesset on the list for sending relief
following flood inundations in France (June 1855), Wybault
supporting the formation of a Volunteer Rifle Corps (June 1859),
and Fr Cotham contributing for the relief of flood damage in
Cheltenham, particularly ruinous for his neighbour Jessops'
Nurseries in St James Square, in August 1855. The reporting of
news was often supplemented by a working committee's plan to
raise funds for the people adversely affected by war, natural
disaster, or social deprivation. To have one's name appear in print
was an announcement of a well-informed conscience prompted
to action by a sufficient amount of wealth. Committee members
and subscribers to the New Church building fund were not so
different although they were motivated by their additional—some
might say, alien—loyalty to the Catholic faith.

James de Lacy Towle was less prominent in local public affairs
but immersed himself in promoting the growth of Catholic life
in England. His personality is shadowy and perhaps his most
valuable gift to the committee was his personal friendship and
legal advice to Fr Cotham. Cotham's journal is very sparse for the
1850s but among the few entries for 1856 and 1858 he includes
walks and tea with de Lacy Towle, a fellow Lancastrian ten years
his junior with an enthusiasm for literature and the printed word.
He was received into the Catholic Church in the early 1850s and
admitted to practise as an attorney in 1851; thereafter he divided
his time, and his legal practice, between London and Cheltenham
until 1865.[13] At a time when periodicals were thriving he became
the proprietor of *The Weekly Register* (formerly *The Catholic*

'I consider it is Time we should bestir ourselves in Good Earnest.' 315

Standard) and produced a three-penny paper similar in content to *The Tablet*, priced at sixpence, but favouring Liberals and Nationalists in its political stance; he may have been acting for Cardinal Manning in this venture although it would certainly have been congenial to him. After his marriage to Martha Lingard in 1862, concelebrated by Fr Glassbrook in Kent, the childless couple's focus switched to the capital where he supported Cardinal Manning with financial help towards church and convent building. His own lasting memorial, St James' Catholic Church in Twickenham, was not opened until 1885 and consecrated in 1887, a year before his death, but while in Cheltenham he shared Fr Cotham's aspirations and trials.[14]

The named Committee members were representative of Cheltenham's male middle-class population having experience of public office, trade, military service, and the professions. Sophie Tiesset moved among them with an assurance and acceptance that can only be explained by her personal qualities. She was not wealthy, nor a property owner but always a lodger; she was not British; she was not married nor a daughter whose father was well-known. Like Hector Caffieri, her name appeared regularly in the *Cheltenham Looker-On* as she advertised her services as an educator; she gave modestly to public subscriptions and, in Father Wilkinson's time, took her turn on the bazaar stalls. Sophie Tiesset's career as a teacher exemplified developments in education and her own self-confidence. In 1836

> Mdlle Tiesset was induced by the late Lady Darling, Lady Ford, and other leaders of society of that day, to leave Boulogne ... the powerful introduction of her friends and her exceptional talent as a teacher soon procured for her a wide circle of pupils, and both as a teacher herself, and as the author of one or two useful works for the guidance of others engaged in tuition, she occupied a distinguished position in her profession.[15]

She was always more than a teacher of young ladies about to enter society. Her arrival in Cheltenham coincided with the period when Samuel Wilderspin, a pioneer of infant schools, was based in the town. Her first lodgings were at his home and headquarters in Alpha House, Alstone on the outskirts of Cheltenham. In his book *On the Importance of Educating the Infant Poor*, published in 1823, Wilderspin claimed a teacher had to become childlike himself if he was to be successful as an educator of children. Sophie Tiesset combined a deceptively simple approach to learning with an astute understanding of how it was best accomplished. In her own textbooks, such as *The Little French Instructor*, still in print, she 'deserted the long trodden paths of theory' and proposed a modern system of becoming familiar with conversation 'from imitation only' before tackling the intricacies of grammar. She summed up her educational philosophy very simply: 'Why should we not in this, as in everything else, follow as much as possible the course of nature' in allowing scope for the ingenuity of the pupil.[16] By 1858 her curriculum had expanded to a course in Chronology, promising to render 'this usually difficult and uninteresting study both easy and amusing' while still covering all the principal events of Ancient History.[17]

Sophie Tiesset and her younger brother Casimir both found employment at the Cheltenham College Institution for the Education of Young Ladies (the Cheltenham Ladies College) when it opened its doors at Cambray House in February 1854 with eighty-two pupils and a staff of ten, three of whom were visiting teachers.[18] In the words of its Education Committee in 1857, the aims of the College were 'to give sound instruction without sacrificing accomplishments, to develop the intellect without making female pedants, to combine efficiency with economy ... through the education of the faculties of the mind by slow, steady and judicious training.'[19] When Miss Annie Proctor resigned after four years as Lady Principal, Miss Dorothea Beale was appointed. Despite the consolidation of the school's results and reputation outside Cheltenham, there was a lack of support in the town for 'advanced' education of a 'more public character'[20] than was thought proper for a Ladies establishment.

'I consider it is Time we should bestir ourselves in Good Earnest.' 317

The appointment of Roman Catholics onto the staff caused critical comment; a headmistress of one of the private academies deplored the dangers arising from 'new things': 'yet large numbers say three hundred girls together must be an evil and five to be employed in it as Professors are Roman Catholics'.[21] Miss Beale was able to steer a steady course amid the religious tensions of this period which led at times to stormy confrontations in the public life of the town. She had a deeply held Christian faith, with discreet leanings towards Anglo-Catholicism, which enabled her to respect the differing church affiliations among her members of staff and fend off factional criticisms. The Revd Francis Close had been a founding member of the board, as he was for the Boys College in 1841, but the Ladies College was never drawn into the Evangelical church tradition, nor to any other Anglican movement. For Fr Cotham the natural course for Catholic parents was to send their children to Catholic schools, if necessary boarding them away from home; nevertheless, to have among his congregation highly competent teachers at prestigious establishments in the town was doubtless gratifying.

Sophie Tiesset was remembered as 'a lady of very kindly disposition. Many a poor girl struggling to qualify herself as a teacher found in Mdlle Tiesset a ready instructress and a generous friend'.[22] This probably refers to the help, and perhaps leadership, she gave to the night school provided by Catholic ladies to poor girls, and to the pupil teachers employed at St Gregory's School. She needed to support herself and did so by conventional means but she, and Casimir, were essentially educationalists as well as teachers. Addressing a meeting of the Cheltenham Literary and Philosophical Institute Casimir spoke of 'the importance of recognising religious and moral influences in co-operation with the very earliest attempts at mental training' and advocated a holistic approach of carefully attending to 'the different faculties as they severally and successively became developed' rather than trying to impart mere knowledge.[23] Though couched in different language to what he was accus-

318 *The Indomitable Mr Cotham*

tomed to as a Religious Instructor in the convict penal system, Fr Cotham would have recognised and approved the Tiessets' high regard for the calling of educators to expand the powers of the mind, even the infant mind.

Notes

[1] *The Tablet*, 2 September 1848, p. 3.

[2] B. Andrews, '"Solemn Chancels and Cross Crowned Spires": Pugin's Antipodean Vision and its Implementation' in *Ecclesiology Abroad: Studies in Victorian Architecture and Design*, Vol. 4, Chapter 2 (London: The Victorian Society, 2012).

[3] R. Hill, 'The Ivi'd Ruins of Forlorn Grace Dieu: Catholics, Romantics and late Georgian Gothic' in M. Hall (Ed.), *Gothic Architecture and its Meanings 1550-1830* (Reading: Spire Books Ltd, 2002), pp. 159–184.

[4] Revd William Cotham SJ attended the annual meeting of the Broughton Club for which he wrote a club song, performed by him with great gusto each year. Given the closeness of the two brothers we must imagine Fr Ambrose Cotham OSB in a duet:
Now join in hearty chorus as I sing my hearty rhyme
And you shall hear how things went on in good old cath'lic time;
When England was a merry land her sons were brave and free
And English men kept company with mirth and jollity;
And thus we passed a merry time as ev'ry one may know
When our old cath'lic fathers lived a long time ago,
When our old cath'lic fathers lived a long time ago.

[5] *Cheltenham Looker-On*, 31 December 1853, p. 913.

[6] G. Hart, *A History of Cheltenham* (Gloucester: Alan Sutton, 1981, 2nd impression), p. 181.

[7] *Cheltenham Mercury*, 20 June 1885, p. 2; 'At one time pugilism was all the go in Cheltenham ... G. A. Williams ... then a spruce fellow in frock coat and white ducks with his inevitable bouquet in buttonhole ... and others of the stalwart and muscular school, went in a large party to Worcester to see Spring and Langham fight.'

[8] *Cheltenham Looker-On*, 17 July 1880, p. 459, obituary. In almost any edition of the *Looker-On* until the late 1860s there is a reference to G. A. Williams, always addressed as Mr rather than Esq. in this publication.

[9] *The Tablet*, 6 June 1857; Richard Barton Collection now in the author's possession. No page number.

[10] *Cheltenham Examiner*, 3 July 1878, p. 8.

'I consider it is Time we should bestir ourselves in Good Earnest.'   319

11   *Cheltenham Looker-On*, 1 January 1859, p. 17.

12   Ryecroft Best received £30,000 compensation after the abolition of slavery in the British Empire in 1834. The number of slaves in which Cheltenham residents had an interest in 1831 was approximately 10,000, while the town itself had a population of 23,000. The social and economic make-up of the Catholic population in Cheltenham precluded a significant presence in this trade, although it was not entirely absent, as shown by the Wybault/Best marriage and the first marriage of a later convert George Copeland. See E. Miller, 'Plantocrats and Rentiers: Cheltenham's Slave-owners' in *Cheltenham Local History Society*, Journal 34, 2018, pp. 57 and 64–65.

13   Richard Barton Collection now in the author's possession. Details of de Lacy Towle's legal career, 1851 to 1885, were supplied by Miss B. McNeill, Librarian and Keeper of the Records for the Middle Temple, London, in correspondence dated 2 April 1984.

14   *The Tablet*, 18 August 1888, p. 34, obituary. James de Lacy Towle also took special interest in the development of the Catholic College of Higher Studies at Strawberry Hill, becoming a lay member of the Senate in 1874.

15   *Cheltenham Mercury*, 3 January 1885, p. 2, obituary.

16   S. Tiesset, *The Little French Instructor, or French Taught by Conversation and Familiar Correspondence* (London: Whittaker & Co, 1845), p. 4.

17   *Cheltenham Looker-On*, 4 September 1858, p. 876.

18   Council Minutes, 22 October 1853; they were appointed 'as professors of French at a fixed salary of £200 per annum.' Information kindly provided by Kate Greenaway, Assistant Archivist at Cheltenham Ladies College, 2015. Casimir Tiesset became a naturalised British citizen in May 1853, perhaps to improve his employment prospects. He and his family subsequently emigrated to Chicago, only to lose everything in the Great Fire of 1871. The family relocated to Newcastle-upon-Tyne where Casimir died in April 1879.

19   A. K. Clarke, *1853–1979 A History of the Cheltenham Ladies College* (Saxmundham: John Catt Ltd, 1979, 3rd edition), pp. 26-27.

20   *Ibid.*, citing the Fifth Annual Report, p. 37.

21   G. Avery, *Cheltenham Ladies: A History of The Cheltenham Ladies College* (London: James & James, 2003), p. 14.

22   *Cheltenham Mercury*, 3 January 1885, p. 2, obituary.

23   *Cheltenham Looker-On*, 15 November 1845, p. 5. 'A Lecture on Intellectual Culture'. Casimir Tiesset sat on the Council of the Cheltenham Literary and Philosophical Institute between 1848 and 1852.

27 'NUMEROUS BUT POOR'

F ROM THE OUTSET the few, energetic, committee members—whatever their personal aspirations to see themselves worshipping in a fine building—worked on behalf of the 'poorest of the poor', in large part made up of the Irish immigrant portion of the congregation. The Catholic mission had provided a school for the children of poor Catholics since Lady Vavasour made funds available for Fr Birdsall to provide two rooms above the vestry in 1827. Thirty years later there were forty boys and thirty-five girls being taught by a school master and mistress, a fraction of the school age children in the town who were nominally Catholic. The provision of places had not changed to meet the influx of Irish immigrants following the potato famine years of the mid to late 1840s. The newspapers reported their presence with mixed feelings: between sixty and one hundred vagrants were daily receiving relief from the parish, but when these 'unfortunates' reappeared a few days later and claimed to be newcomers, they received little sympathy. However, the pathos of inquests held on children who had died on the roadside while their families trundled through the neighbourhood was unavoidable. The well-known rhyme from the early spa years had ceased to be amusing by the middle of the century, even to someone who enjoyed simple rhymes as much as Fr Cotham:

> The Churchyard's so small, and the Irish so many,
> They ought to be pickled and sent to Kilkenny![1]

The return of a Catholic hierarchy had enabled a national Poor School Committee to organise a diocesan system of school inspectors to raise the standard of religious instruction, and thereby of education generally, as the same teachers provided both. Thomas Allies, Secretary of the Committee from 1853 to 1890, was one of the most influential lay leaders of the period, shaping and directing the educational policy of the hierarchy. His guiding principles were threefold: there could be no sound education without religion; as is the teacher so is the child; as is the trainer so is the teacher. 'This was said at a time when only one Catholic child in three was in a Catholic school, when most of those attending were under 8, and when only a third even of these attended for more than a year.'[2] Fr Cotham's committee would have had varying levels of interest in and knowledge of schools but nobody in Cheltenham could have been unaware of the large number of children wandering the streets and living within a few hundred yards of the Chapel but unaccounted for educationally or sacramentally.

Cheltenham lacked the intense industrialisation that is usually supposed to be an attraction for impoverished incomers, but its building and service industries were still expanding in the mid-century and in the returns of the 1851 census it was deemed the only 'principal town' in Gloucestershire. The modestly wealthy, educated populace that Cheltenham boasted needed residential homes, superior lodging houses, colleges, schools, and all the associated commercial premises to cater for the comfortable lifestyle this rising class enjoyed. Additionally there was the traditional seasonal agricultural work from the rural surroundings, and railway expansion. For families seeking health and culture from their environment the town combined an attractive bustling economy set in the rural Cotswolds. And yet, Cheltenham was a smallish town and the poorer parts were never far from sight or smell. The presence of unruly, unschooled children in the town persisted throughout the late nineteenth century but enormous efforts were made towards providing a greater range of school opportunities.

In the official report from Horace Mann to the Registrar General on education, derived from the 1851 census, he noted, 'no feature of our educational advancement in the present century is more remarkable than this,—the great extent to which whatever progress, satisfactory or otherwise, has been achieved,

'Numerous but Poor' 323

is owing to denominational activity or rivalry'.[3] The Roman Catholics stood fourth among the denominational day schools (behind the Church of England, Congregationalists, and Wesleyan Methodists, and just ahead of the Baptists who did not support denominational education on principle). The numbers reflected the importance of Sunday Schools in contributing towards general education; reading and writing were practised in the Sunday classes around biblical and devotional themes. The Catholic day schools numbered 339 with 41,000 pupils, with 232 Sunday Schools; Church of England schools had 929,474 pupils in 10,500 schools with similar numbers attending Sunday Schools. The census estimated the Catholic population of England and Wales to be at least one million, of whom Irish-born residents numbered in excess of half the total, many with children born in England.[4]

The leadership for the direction of the church in the third quarter of the nineteenth century was still in the hands of a relatively small number of Old Catholic gentry and the small, but significant, convert cohort. As in Australia, the impact of the Irish clergy, with their strong tradition of focusing on parochial community life, gradually became the norm. However, when dioceses were in their early stages of development the governance of the missions was a fluid issue, sometimes provoking unseemly rivalry between the regulars—Benedictine, Jesuits, Dominicans *et al*—and the secular clergy under the local bishops' jurisdiction. In the 1880s the English Benedictine Congregation struggled to define its identity as missionary or monastic (and held the two strands in tension as the true mark of its charism). It seems unlikely that Fr Ambrose Cotham saw the need to make a definitive choice: for the people of Cheltenham he was a mission priest, holding a disparate congregation in unity while mobilising a few in service of the many. For himself, he was a Benedictine monk, counting other Benedictines among his inner social circle and visiting monastic communities as often as he could for spiritual retreats or Congregation business.

324   *The Indomitable Mr Cotham*

At this point in Tasmanian history—1853—the process of overlaying the convict stigma with a respectable public image was at a turning point after the granting of political self-determination. With a reputation deficit of massive proportions the Tasmanian population made a concerted effort to erase the memory of individuals' criminal pasts. Awkward questions about a person's past were avoided or were referred to in coded language: an obituary referring to an 'old colonist' meant the person had arrived free, the absence of the phrase intimated they had not. Even little Alice Burgess, arriving as a 4-year-old child with her convict mother on the *Tasmania* (2), was described as an old colonist at the time of her death. The Cheltenham press were not so correct in their phraseology. The Catholic priests had to read semi-humorous reports every week about their straying (invariably Irish) flock; at best the account was brief. 'Denis Driscol, [*sic*], a genuine native of the Emerald Isle, with a rich Munster brogue, was charged with assault and battery on Mary Regan. The magistrates dismissed the case.'[5] Sometimes every word and blow was given its full force:

> James and Margaret Sullivan, man and wife, living in Rutland-street … were summoned by Margaret Murphy, for an assault. [Mrs Murphy fetched her husband when pushed by Sullivan.] James Sullivan then came back and took hold of complainant's husband by the sleeve of his smock, tore it off, and ran out into the middle of the street shouting 'hooray'. [Cross examined Mrs Murphy admitted] she had a poker in her hand but not until after James Sullivan made a second rush at her. Her husband had no stick or 'shelalah' in his hand. Did not strike either of the defendents [*sic*] but would have done so if they had come near her afterwards. [Eliza Morrison, cross examined by Mr Chessyre] would swear that Mrs Murphy did not strike Sullivan with the poker; she hit at him but missed. Mrs Murphy did not take up a poker until she had been struck down in the kitchen.

'Numerous but Poor' 325

Having heard conflicting witness accounts about pokers and torn off sleeves the magistrates considered the defendants had offered the first provocation and fined each of them 2s 6d.[6]

However, these were relatively minor misdemeanours exacerbated by the awful living conditions in Rutland Street and the neighbourhood of the Lower High Street. H. H. Martyn is renowned in Cheltenham for the quality and scope of the decorative architectural business he founded in 1888. Less well known are Martyn's own philanthropic activities which included forming a social mission to Rutland Street in 1870 with the Revd Mr and Mrs Owen. Years later he described the area:

> Truly the neighbourhood had long been a plague spot, well known, where drunken brawls were frequent and police were shy of interfering ... The state of many homes in that neighbourhood was terrible, and at the time it seemed useless to call the attention of the authorities to it ... Certainly, if a pig had any self-respect it would pity itself in such homes. [Revd] Mr Owen told me that in an experience of London slums for many years he had seen nothing worse. Can you realise a house, one room down, and one up, each about nine feet by seven or eight, the lower floor of which was composed of well-worn bricks, mildew on the walls and damp everywhere? We visited such to find sickness rampant and misery such that Dante would shudder to describe ... One could fill a volume with such cases, and this in one of the wealthiest and most religious towns in our land, few would believe it possible, for fewer went to see it.[7]

Fr Cotham and his assistant priests did go to see it, frequently, although as a duty so regular and mundane it is rarely mentioned in his journal. Hence, on 23 and 24 February 1857 he makes sick calls to one of the McArdles, and on 30 January 1868 the entry is only 'Poor Rut. Barnets, with Mrs Wynyard to Kitty Wells'. It was not frequently enough for the local newspapers who believed the

326   *The Indomitable Mr Cotham*

Catholic clergy could do more to supplement the ineffectual constabulary.

> An Irish Wake in Rutland Street.
>
> On the evenings of Saturday and Sunday, an Irish wake was held in Rutland-street, in consequence of the death of Mary Sullivan, aged 45, and the celebration of which increased the uproar of this usually disorderly neighbourhood to such an extent as to render necessary extra police officers. The corpse was placed on the lid of the coffin, and covered with a white sheet decked with flowers, the face alone being exposed; and upon an adjoining table, the material for the customary saturnalia was placed, consisting of ale, tobacco and pipes. About 40 "raal natives" of the "verminless isle", with their unmistakable cast of countenance, rendered more repulsive by the dingy light of the squalid apartment in which they were all huddled, sat smoking and drinking, occasionally uttering discordant yells mingled with jests and laughter; this was varied by one and another howling over the deceased, and addressing conversation to her. The crowd attracted outside by the noise, were admitted to the room, a few at a time. Of course the police were powerless to prevent a repetition of similar unhallowed orgies, but there are those who might at once repress these exhibitions, and the Rev. Fathers Coltham [*sic*] and Blount, we think, might effect this by exercise of the authority. The deceased was buried on Monday afternoon, in the Cemetery, and followed to the grave by 30 or 40 friends.[8]

An Irish wake is a domestic occasion but the sacrament of baptism is usually celebrated in the church. Nevertheless, the extent of the celebration can be prolonged far beyond an infant's bedtime, as a neighbouring Anglican vicar knew too well:

> Shortly before 11o'clock, last Sunday night, the inhabitants residing near St Pauls Church were aroused by screams proceeding from the uproarious locality of Rutland Street. It seems that two Irish children had been received into the

'Numerous but Poor'

Holy Church, by Baptism, on Sunday, and to commemorate this very important event, the parents had invited an assembly of the 'illegant natives' of Erin, to partake of whiskey toddy, beer, and other beverages which the good Father Matthew plainly saw were the fruitful source of Irish degradation.

Everything was provided to satisfy the cravings of the thirsty Patlanders, and after a few hours spent in this elevating pastime, nothing remained to crown the night's orgies, but the desire to be engaged in one of their characteristic fights. Therefore in the absence of shilelaghs, other articles were pressed into service, such as fire irons, sticks, cups etc. They adjourned into the street and then came 'Tug Of War,' a father might have been seen baitin' his 'broth of a boy', a wife kicking her husband, a daughter displaying her skill with a poker on the head of her mother, amid very unmelodious compliment of oaths, hootings and blasphemy, and the shrill screeches of half-naked spalpeens. Blows were given and exchanged indiscriminately, not one appearing to know what the fight had originated from. The barbarous warfare attracted about 400 spectators, and while it was at its height, the Reverend Mr Lace, curate of St Pauls Church, 'who heard the noise from his residence, No 17, Clarence Square,' with praiseworthy alacrity hastened to be seen to make an effort to quell the disturbance. The moral courage of this minister of Christ soon achieved that which the armed force of 20 policemen would have failed to satisfactorily accomplish.

Bleeding and bruised the combatants became somewhat less infuriating, and more ready to listen to Christian Council, at last the conflict terminated, and the Irish returned to their houses, when the police made an appearance in the street. It was one of the most severe fights in which the Irish residents had ever been engaged. If a beneficial influence could be exerted over an Irish mob by a Protestant Clergyman, what great good might result if the Catholic Priest would exert himself to prevent a recurrence of these scenes.[9]

Ambrose Cotham, well accustomed to the Irish and their ways from his time in Tasmania, might have wondered if his exertions as a convict chaplain had, in fact, been easier than the assorted tasks he was now expected to undertake. A frequent theme of his preaching was unity, and the significance of places of worship. To gather his diverse flock under one roof was a practical aim; to bring them to mutual respect was an aspiration barely conceivable in the year of St Gregory's solemn opening, 1857.

Daniel Evans proved himself a useful bridge in the clash of cultures. St Patrick's Day 1860 was a particularly rowdy time with lengthy newspaper reports covering the so-called Rutland Street Riot. Frs Cotham and Blount followed Evans' suggestion to promote a festive event at St George's Hall to counter the 'unhallowed orgies' which were becoming customary. In return for the closure of some public houses during part of the day Evans and some other 'influential members of the Catholic Communion' provided a tea meeting and concert for three hundred persons of 'every class, grade and sect' a few weeks later. How many came from Rutland Street to join the conviviality was not recorded, but following the loyal toasts and a selection of national songs accompanied by the drum and pipe band of the Rifle Volunteers 'the company were exceedingly amused by the clever execution of several Irish jigs by a "broth of a boy," named Regan, who seemed to enter into the dances with the true energy of an Irishman'. The evening continued with the usual quadrilles and polkas. Although it was difficult to avoid condescension and awkwardness altogether an attempt was being made towards integration and, unsurprisingly, respectability as the clergy 'sought to free their flock from the stigma which might be attached to the whole body of Catholics, by the insubordination of the poorer members, in their uproarious revelries'.[10]

Nevertheless, the residents of Rutland Street and neighbouring terraces were gradually drawn into the life of the mission. By 1874

'Numerous but Poor' 329

the Confraternity of the Blessed Sacrament included Mary Ellen Hurley, Elizabeth Warren, and Catherine Mullins, all from Rutland Street, working alongside their former benefactors, the Lynch Stauntons and Bostocks.[11] Fr Cotham's successor, Aloysius Wilkinson, celebrated their presence and their prominence by placing facing statues of St Augustine of Canterbury and St Patrick in the lower nave after it was completed in 1877, and installing a stained glass window of St Patrick by the South Porch, looking onto the bronze statue of St Peter.[12]

There were earlier Irish immigrants who were not amongst the poorest of the poor. Daniel and Mary O'Keefe were in Cheltenham by 1819 and brought their children to Fr Birdsall for baptism. Daniel had a trade as a plumber and in the mid-1830s the family, with six children, lived in a newly built house in Edward Street, Leckhampton on the southern fringes of Cheltenham. However, the third son, James, born in 1827, seems to have taken a wrong path from a very young age, and was in court for stealing before he was ten. By late 1838 he was serving two months with hard labour in the House of Correction at Northleach with two associates, being 'Rogues and Vagabonds found in a Street, with intent to commit a Felony',[13] but this was only one of several detentions. The magistrates' remarks, that a degree of responsibility attached to his parents for not feeding him properly, so causing him to steal bread, beef, and peas (on separate occasions), was unfair: on another occasion Daniel O'Keefe was commended by the Bench for refusing to sell alcohol (his home was also a local beer house) after licensing hours, although he was badly assaulted for his honesty.[14]

James was incapable of staying at home and out of trouble. He escaped transportation for stealing by being sent instead to Parkhurst Prison. There he learnt a useful trade, shoemaking, and was pardoned on condition that he go to New Zealand as part of the 'Parkhurst Boys' experiment operating between 1842 and 1843. By some means, probably working his passage as a seaman, he returned to England and resumed his former occupations in Cheltenham.

In 1845, still only 18, James was sentenced to ten years' transportation for stealing nearly every brass fitting from an unoccupied house.[15] This time he sailed to Norfolk Island on board the *Mayda*. He was on the island in time to witness the alarming riot of July 1846 and the ensuing executions. A series of repeat offences after transportation brought him close to the fate of these condemned men. These relatively minor offences—having copper nails, a knife, and tobacco in his possession, and malingering—earned him hard labour in chains for short periods but marked him out as a recidivist on a dangerous course. Convict associations bred hardened convicts. The following year he was sent to Tasmania to work initially at the Cascades Probation Station and then at Port Arthur where he continued his pattern of misconduct, which ranged from improper language to concealing files and saws—anything to niggle authority while trying to break free altogether.

Although O'Keefe came within Fr Cotham's circuit of the Hobart stations there is no evidence of them meeting but once in Cheltenham Fr Cotham must have known about the other James from the man's parents. They remained loyal to Catholicism; Daniel died in 1854 without seeing his son again but James was back in Cheltenham before his mother Mary died in December 1859 having received the *Viaticum* from Fr Blount. She knew about his marriage to Sophia Didcote (already pregnant) in the Congregational Church in August 1857, and presumably the Catholic priests knew of it, too. Sophia herself was known to the priests, having been baptised at St Gregory's in 1854 when she was 16; she died in October 1863, a victim of tuberculosis, and the two daughters from the marriage went to live with their maternal grandmother.[16] James disappeared from the area, although whether he continued to work as a journeyman shoemaker (his occupation in the 1861 census) in England or returned, once more, to Australia, is not known.

Notes

1.   Quoted in G. Hart, *A History of Cheltenham* (Gloucester: Alan Sutton, 1981, 2nd impression), p. 203.
2.   A. C. F. Beales, 'The Struggle for the Schools' in G. A. Beck AA (Ed.), *The English Catholics 1850–1950* (London: Burns & Oates, 1950), p. 372.
3.   *Census of Great Britain, 1851: Religious worship and education: Scotland: reports and tables* [1764] H. C. H. Mann, 1854, Vol. LIX, p. XIX. [Accessed online 27.7.2017]
4.   'The number of places of worship belonging to the Roman Catholic in England and Wales appears, from the Census Report on Religious Worship, to be five-hundred and seventy, having accommodation for 186,111 persons. The number of *attendants* on the Census Sunday is estimated at 305,393. The total number persons of this faith in England and Wales cannot be less than 1,000,000, and probably exceeds this number. From the return as to 'birth-place' it appears that as many as 519,959 of the persons resident in England at the time of the Census were born in Ireland: these would be nearly all Roman Catholics; and to them must be added a further number for the children of such persons born since their settlement in England, and also all the English Roman Catholics.' *Census of Great Britain, 1851: Religious worship and education: Scotland: reports and tables* [1764] H. C. H. Mann, 1854, Vol. LIX, p. LXII. [Accessed online 27.7.2017]
5.   *Cheltenham Chronicle,* 3 November 1857, p. 5. Dennis Driscoll's grandsons Francis and John Driscoll and Mary Regan's grandson William Regan, all perished in the First World War; the Driscolls are named on St Gregory's World War I Memorial but the omission of Regan is an unexplained anomaly. All three names appear on the Cheltenham Borough Memorial.
6.   *Ibid.,* 4 December 1860, p. 8.
7.   J. Whitaker, *The Best: a history of H H Martyn and Co: carvers in wood, stone and marble* (Southam, Cheltenham: published by the author, 1985), p. 17, citing an unpublished memoir by Martyn, 1912.
8.   *Cheltenham Mercury,* 6 June 1857, p. 6.
9.   *Ibid.,* 5 December 1857, p. 4. The two baby girls belonged to the Kelleher/Walsh and Kellanan/Lynch/Donaghue families.
10.   *Cheltenham Mercury,* 21 April 1860, p.4, for all references in this section.
11.   The slums of Rutland Street were demolished only in the 1930s and the road renamed Brunswick Street. It bordered St Gregory's School, purchased in 1857.

[12] Equally painful to read is the fracas between William Boodle and James de Lacy Towle, which occurred following the municipal elections in 1857. The ensuing court case was reported at length in the *Cheltenham Examiner*, 5 December 1860, p. 8. The jury gave a verdict against each, for assault and slander respectively; Dr Copeland was called as a witness for his patient, Towle, whom he described as 'a nervous man'. The case was 'bruited about through the whole town', probably with some glee, not least because Towle was awarded damages of one farthing, rather than the £500 he claimed. Towle had hoped to limit local publicity by having the case heard in Middlesex rather than in Gloucester.

[13] See ancestry.com Gloucestershire England Prison Records 1728–1914, p. 1212. [Accessed 27.7.2017]

[14] *Cheltenham Chronicle*, 16 April 1840, p. 3.

[15] *Cheltenham Chronicle and Gloucestershire Advertiser*, 13 March 1845, p. 1. James O'Keefe's criminal career is well documented in Cheltenham newspapers and Australian convict records.

[16] Sophia's death was recorded by Fr Scarisbrick (GRO, D4290 PP 1/7). The two daughters were also baptised at St Gregory's.

28 APPEALS & TENDERS

S INSTRUCTED BY the second church committee meeting George Williams investigated a piece of land in Bayshill, running down to the River Chelt, and offered for £1,400 but the purchase was rejected by the committee in favour of buying the property adjoining the chapel, 10 St James Square. This plot had been bought by Mrs Sarah Neve in 1831 and she lived in the house built for her, presumably for its proximity to Fr Birdsall's chapel. After her death in 1842 the house was held in trust by the Benedictine Fathers Cooper, Scott, and Heptonstall and the income from it was made over to the Chipping Sodbury mission, founded by Mrs Neve in 1838 (her husband had been the Anglican incumbent at Old Sodbury). Fr Cotham knew of Mrs Neve as a subscriber to Bishop Polding's Australasia Mission Fund.

The transfer of ownership to trustees for the Cheltenham mission, Fathers Cotham, Ridgway, and Hodgson, was considered beneficial to both missions at a sale price of £1,000. Less happy about the change of ownership was the last tenant, Mrs Tennyson (Lord Alfred's widowed mother) who, presumably not wanting a Catholic church, however magnificent, built on her doorstep, vacated the property along with an entourage that had included a pet monkey. Acquiring the house did not, in fact, provide a site for the new church; there was only a small garden to the front and rear. It meant, however, that there would be no objection to a Catholic church being built over the entire garden belonging to the old chapel, reaching to within a few feet of 10 St James Square. An early intention was for the clergy to live there and lease the chapel house to a teaching order of brothers when a new school could be provided; in any case it provided a flexible asset for the mission.

The speed of the transfer of the property—detailed proposals were ready by 19 April 1853—suggests the Benedictines had already held talks about plans for the Cheltenham mission

334   *The Indomitable Mr Cotham*

separately from the committee deliberations. James de Lacy Towle acted for both parties without any conflict of interest. The next stage, of raising funds from local subscribers, got underway immediately but promised monies took time to materialise. The architect and building firms responded more quickly. Architect Charles Hansom's plans for St Gregory's have been lost but his written specification dated 10 June 1853[1] gives an idea of how the small chapel with an extensive garden was to be replaced by a large church extending to the edge of the available land.

Three tenders for the proposed building were received by June 1853 but only two were put forward to Hansom for consideration later that month. Thomas Hunt and Sons of Gloucester quoted £2,880 and John Acock of Cheltenham £2,840. George Myers, Pugin's preferred builder and by far the most experienced and prestigious of the three, tendered for £5,400, thereby putting himself beyond financial reach. The first contract was confined to building and roofing the shell of the church, comprising only a nave, side aisles, and transepts, to be finished off by plastering, painting, flooring, glazing, and cleaning down the stonework. A small entrance porch was costed at £110 by Acock. The joint secretaries George Williams and James de Lacy Towle asked Hansom if he could find a way of bringing the costs down further to meet their £2,000 proposed budget. Unsurprisingly, the lower tender from Cheltenham builder John Acock was chosen. In later years Cotham may have wondered if taking a higher tender would have saved him much trouble and been the better economy.

As the Cheltenham mission had no single wealthy patron and was relatively poor as a Catholic district, the net for raising funds was cast widely. In May 1853 an *Appeal to the liberality of Christians of every denomination* (known as the *Catholic Address to Protestants* by the committee) was printed in local newspapers at the same time as advertisements for tenders, and between 18 and 26 May over three hundred and fifty printed circulars were posted. A financial inducement to build a new church was to attract the Catholic gentry who, the committee claimed, had

Appeals & Tenders 335

deserted the town due to the lack of respectable premises for worship. In June advertisements were placed in *The Times*, *The Tablet*, and the *Catholic Standard* by George Williams.

By October 1853 the committee had been promised £1,500 in subscriptions from the summer appeal campaign, the largest single contribution, £600, coming from Fr Cotham himself, followed by £200 from an anonymous convert, and £100 from Williams. The autumn appeal, of 1,000 circulars printed on the reverse with an image of Hansom's drawing of the church, was launched in October 'to our brethren at a distance and to the public at large' on behalf of the 'numerous but poor' Irish Catholics of Cheltenham, 'the poorest of the poor' who comprised two-thirds of the congregation. These circulars were produced by J. R. Jobbins, high class printer of Holborn, London. Unfortunately, the first 1,000 copies received were soiled in some way. Jobbins, replying to James de Lacy Towle's letter of complaint, expressed disbelief that the fault lay with his workshop. He emphasised the care with which each impression was protected by interleaved tissue paper to avoid off-setting fresh ink: he can only think the railway company was to blame by putting a heavy load on top of his package. This was the first of the many small vexations dealt with regularly by the committee, all of them passing through Cotham's hands first.

That the existing chapel was too small was true but to describe it in the circular as 'perhaps without a single exception the most unseemly religious structure in the town' was unfair to the efforts of previous missioners, especially Fr Birdsall. After going on to mention the 'most pressing need' for schoolrooms, the chief motivation for non-Catholics was baldly stated: 'This elegant, wealthy and populous Protestant town seems to demand the erection of a respectable if not stately Edifice.' The Appeal gave an accurate picture of Cheltenham at this time: desperately poor in parts, affluent and strongly Evangelical in others, and above all a young town shaping a still fluid identity.

336   *The Indomitable Mr Cotham*

A third type of appeal was sent to Catholic clergy by individual letters enclosing a print of the proposed church. The clergy were asked to send the small amount of five shillings; those who responded invariably sent postage stamps to that amount.[2] The replies, and other appeals appearing in the Catholic press, make it clear that Catholic churches were being built all over the country drawing on the resources of a relatively small group of worshippers and wealthy patrons. Nevertheless, those who replied wrote encouragingly even when making the point that they had gone without repairs to worn-out shoes to send the donation, or were themselves 'overflowing with debt' owed on their own new churches. Finally, a personal appeal was made to His Eminence the Cardinal Archbishop of Westminster, from Fr Cotham and 'my poor congregation'.

Two of the letters from respondents reminded Cotham that he had continuing associations with Australia. From Fr Bernard Caldwell OSB, now happily on the mission at Cowpen, Northumberland he received the usual apologies along with the five shillings worth of postal stamps. Caldwell added a sardonic observation: 'One would say on seeing your handsome subscription that you had some friendly agent at the gold-diggings. It is really surprising to see the success you have met with even in Cheltenham.'[3] In Caldwell's eyes, Cotham had evidently turned his time in Australia to good financial advantage and returned home a success, unlike himself; the assessment is understandable although not all Cotham's confrères were so good natured about his relative personal wealth. Caldwell's subsequent ministry would not have been predicted by Polding.

> Throughout his long life he was a model of priestly urbanity and priestly zeal. His special predilection was for the music and liturgy of the Church, and in all the missions which he served in his long career he established an excellent tradition of musical taste .... Abbot Larkin, D.D., spoke in feeling terms of the venerable deceased, in whose life he pointed out two characteristic features: simplicity

Appeals & Tenders 337

and fear of God. How rarely do we meet these qualities in
men of the present day.[4]

The impertinent young student had indeed had the makings of
an observant monk.

The contribution from Fr Thomas Ignatius Sisk OC of Mount
St Bernard Abbey, Leicestershire was addressed to Fr William
Cotham. Fr Ambrose wrote on the letter a draft of the reply he
intended to send:

> I remember you well at Stonyhurst in the years '22 and '23.
> I was known there by the name of Little Larry. My brother
> William the Jesuit was called Big Larry. My name is James
> and I am a Benedictine. Sit nomen Domini benedictum. I
> have been 17 years on the mission in Van Diemen's Land—
> Br Luke Levermore of Mount St Bernard's knows me well.[5]

The tone is almost plaintive, that of the 12 year-old little brother
of the future Jesuit who wants to be acknowledged in his own
right: 'My name is James'. The purpose of the brief correspondence—fund raising for a new church—is turned into an opportunity for remembrance of his previous ministry where *he* was well
known as the experienced mentor of Br Luke and, more star-
tlingly, as a reminder of the close relationship with his protector,
William, with whom, presumably, he enjoyed the pun. He may
not have actually sent the reply to Fr Sisk having spontaneously
written down the boyhood memories which came to him from
seeing a Stonyhurst name again.[6]

Occasionally personal appeals were made to individuals such
as Charles Waterton (1782–1865), a naturalist of distinction,
whose scientific merits, unusual among Catholics of his generation, gained him respect and tolerance from his peers. 'Like all
those squires of his generation, to whom political life made no
appeal, he had never suffered from persecution. His contacts with
his neighbours were easy and they were proud of him.'[7] The tone
of his reply to Fr Cotham gives a suggestion of his dislike for

ostentatious show in the practise of his faith, and his own humble piety:

> My dear and Reverend Sir,
>
> I have received the engraving of the new church which you have had the goodness to send me. Long may it prosper.
>
> Please accept my mite, and should you enter the trifle in your book, say it has come from a friend. I always make this stipulation on similar occasions.
>
> In great haste, Believe me Dear Sir, Very respectfully and very truly yours—
>
> Charles Waterton

William Thomson C.C. in Ayr, Scotland was quite carried away by the tone of the appeal. 'I have received your circular regarding the new and beautiful cathedral which you intend getting built in the city of Cheltenham', for which grand undertaking he contributed the customary mite.

Over the winter of 1853 to 1854 fund raising continued slowly. Lady Newburgh of Slindon House near Arundel sent £5, at 90 surely the oldest subscriber, with a note from her housemaid to Cotham, 'her ladyship begs your holy prayers.' Cotham's half-brother 'Tom Shepherd Esq' and the Prior of Ampleforth also sent £5 each. Colonel Graham advanced £50, the 'Pickwick Club 1/-', 'Eyston's French maid 5/-' and 'John Holland 2/-.' Taken overall, the respondents to the appeals cover the spectrum of Catholic sensibilities at this period, from triumphalism to self-effacement, not forgetting the small donations from friendly Protestants such as 'W. Franklin 5/-.'[8]

A year after fund raising began, on Ash Wednesday 1 March 1854, a vestry meeting heard that only £548 16s. 6d. cash was in hand at the bank. Mr Nagle was charged with making a personal application to named persons in the congregation who had yet to pay their promised subscription. Fr Cotham undertook to match whatever the congregation subscribed; when £1,200—half

Appeals & Tenders 339

of the quoted cost of building—had been secured the committee would be in a position to accept a firm contract from the architect. This target was within reach with Cotham's promise of £400 when the outstanding subscriptions of £266 were received. Throughout the building process Fr Cotham regularly gave, or occasionally lent, large sums of money to help the scheme along, a figure probably amounting to half the total cost eventually. This was clearly not gleaned solely from what he had saved from his time in Tasmania or from his government pension. In fact, Cotham in Cheltenham was a man of substantial means. Nevertheless, his successor at St Gregory's captured the spirit of his giving when he said Fr Cotham

> had saved up six hundred pounds when he was in Tasmania, and this sum he gladly contributed towards the new church. It was the first sum contributed and it was all he had. He [Fr Wilkinson] ever thought that generous act obtained the blessing of God upon the work, for it grew and prospered.[9]

Within three weeks of the push for subscriptions the Committee met with Charles Hansom on 27 March to ask for his plans and specification for the first part of the work. Hansom was proud of his own design for Cheltenham and the watercolour he painted gained a prize in the Paris Exhibition of 1855.[10] The design (similar to those provided for St Anne's, Edgehill, Liverpool, 1843, and for Bishop Murphy in Adelaide, 1845) was 'for an early Decorated aisled and clerestoried town church, with central western tower and spire ... reaching its ultimate archeological refinement and enrichment in the St Gregory, Cheltenham, design of 1853'.[11] Despite William Leigh's generous patronage towards the financially struggling new diocese of Adelaide, Hansom's plan was not adopted by Bishop Murphy, but Leigh did use it for the church built on his estate at Woodchester, Gloucestershire, a few miles from Cheltenham.

On 28 March John Acock submitted a revised costing in three parts for the first contract; this included £60 extra for the rise in the price of timber, bringing Acock's estimate to £2,900. He also negotiated first refusal on the second and third contracts when money became available to undertake the work. The contract was duly made on 25 April between Acock and Fr Cotham and Hector Caffieri for the building to be completed by 1 January 1855, on pain of financial penalties.

Foundation work began in the gardens in early May 1854, Provincial Heptonstall laying the foundation stone in a private ceremony; thereafter regular payments of 8 guineas per month were made to Robert Kerridge, Hansom's Clerk of Works. The *Cheltenham Examiner* reported on the various public buildings either being erected or improved at this time, including Cambray Place Baptist Chapel in a 'novel' Italianate style and capable of seating 1,000 and Salem Chapel where an extended gallery would take seating to 1,200. Church-going had become fashionable and competitive and churches were described in terms of taste and elegance. St Gregory's was expected to be 'one of the most stately buildings in the town' with an estimated final cost of £8,000.[12]

The beginning of the work was not an entirely fresh start. Hansom's specification instructed the builder to take down the vestries of the old chapel, keeping doors, windows and grates for possible reuse. The builder was free to salvage the bricks, slates and timber for his own business. The resulting gap in the chapel was to be walled up, except for two access doors between the chapel and new building, with 'the west gable to be built of rubble walling stone in mortar 18 ins thick resting upon the old Chapel wall.' This composite west wall and gable stood some twelve feet inside the present west end of the church, running in front of what is now the baptistry and St Benedict's chapel on either side of the lower nave. At the east end of the building 'the Chancel and [Lady] chapel archways to be blocked up with 18 ins stonework in mortar well bonded to the unworked portions of the jambs'.

Although the east and west ends of the church would look obviously makeshift, instructions for the finish of the body of the church were detailed. 'The interior surface of the walls to be

Appeals & Tenders 341

plastered 3 coats in the best possible manner ... using cow hair in the two first coats and finished with the very best fine grained stucco.' The lightness of the church would be emphasised by the treatment of the roof space.

> The whole of the ceilings to be plastered between the rafters 3 coats on lath nailed on a strip on the side of the rafters the "stuff" to be richer for the ceilings and to have one extra quantity of hair and to be finished with white putty.

The roof timbers were to be exposed to view, knotted and sized, then stained and twice varnished; the doors were to be similarly treated 'with great care by the best painters'. Details for each class of work were provided; the carpenters and joiners were to fix a temporary raised sanctuary area, and the glazier was instructed to use yellow tinted plain cathedral glass with 'extra strong narrow lead (the same as used for stained glass).' Hansom had his eye on the finished design. To give the builder that same vision Hansom suggested looking at a model he had found, and admired, in the town:

> The kind of work for the exterior will be precisely the same, both as to workmanship and materials, as the new church now erecting (All Saints) in the Bath Road ... The whole ... to be most carefully worked in the best stone of the locality, as may be selected by the architect (it will, in all probability, be the same as used for the new church above mentioned).[13]

The expenditure accounts[14] begin in July 1854 with the first payment to John Acock and continue until April 1855 when the final payment of £217 brings his total to £2,335 for completion of the first part of the contract for the nave, aisles, and transepts; refreshments to the workmen for the period starting two months earlier amount to only £1 4s. Further payments made from May 1855 to April 1856 brought Acock's total to £3,484 16s. 4d., more than £500 above his estimate. Nevertheless, **New Year, 1855**

342   *The Indomitable Mr Cotham*

began with a dinner for the workmen on 10 January to celebrate the completion of the first phase of the New Church.

The original plan, to stop when the basic 'box' of the church was complete, was set aside. The committee was joined at this point by Compton-John Hanford and Dr G. F. Copeland, exemplars of old and new Catholicism. Hanford lived with his aunt in St James Square when he was in Cheltenham. He inherited Woollas Hall, Worcestershire—with its Royalist and recusant heritage—from his father in 1854 but retained an interest in the Cheltenham mission until his death in 1860 at the age of 41. With no Catholic background, George Ford Copeland built his own future around that of the new church. The augmented committee was in favour of pushing ahead with Hansom's complete design even though a further £2,000 would be required to meet existing liabilities and build 'the shell of the Chancel, [Lady] Chapel, Choir and one vestry'. Yet again Cotham took it upon himself to provide £1,000, to be repaid out of contributions to the building fund, and the Committee members would provide the other £1,000, being reimbursed with interest if they needed to borrow the money. The confident hope was that 'by zeal and exertions' from the whole congregation the monies would be repaid within three to five years.

The decision to proceed immediately with the third contract was taken before the first two were completed suggesting Fr Cotham had won the enthusiasm and backing of his parishioners. Once again he made it a principle to match whatever money was raised by subscription with a contribution of his own. The workmen were treated to another celebratory meal at the end of the second contract, this time at Mr Melville's London Inn in Charlton Kings

> at which Mr G. A. Williams presided, supported by the Roman Catholic clergymen, and the gentlemen connected with the Chapel. The entertainment was got up in the worthy host's well-known excellent style of catering ... About eighty persons sat down, when a most agreeable evening was spent. Messrs Acock were highly compli-

Appeals & Tenders 343

mented on the liberal and workmanlike manner in which
they had carried out their contract.[15]

Conviviality allowed a toast for 'our Protestant friends, and
thanks for their donations'.[16]

Overlapping with the second contract—interior finishing work
on the nave and aisles—building began in June 1855 and continued until December 1855 on the third contract, again with John
Acock, for the chancel, Lady Chapel, choir room, and sacristy,
estimated at £862. The last task of the year, on 24 December, was
to put canvas stretched on wooden frames over the window
spaces, a temporary arrangement costing £16 5s.

The fourth contract, for finishing works on contract three, was
completed between May 1856 and February 1857, for £400. The
church dimensions at this point were 120 feet by 55 feet, widening
to 65 feet in the transepts. There was seating for 700 people, with
no additional standing room necessary. It was ventilated from
the gables by trap doors operated by pulleys, and lighting and
heating was provided by gas.

That there was, at this juncture, a good working relationship
between Cotham and Acock is suggested by a diary entry for
Thursday 19 June 1856: 'With Acock to St Andrew's Steeple at
Worcester, Powick, Malvern, Stanbrook. Fr President, [Revd]
Sheppherd, Brother Wilfred. Returned on Friday evening.'
Almost all the instalments for sums ranging between £400 and
£50 were paid in cash, as were the payments regularly made to
Charles Hansom; a total of £4,864 17s. 10d. had been handed over
by February 1858. As a reciprocal mark of respect, architect and
builder each donated a small stained glass window from Hardman's studio to the church, the first windows to be ordered, in
March 1855. Charles Hansom's window above the sacristy door
is a design of the monogram 'Maria' against a background of lilies;
John Acock's contribution above the north transept side altar is
a group of three small trefoil windows, 'angels holding scrolls',
again with a Marian theme.

Notes

[1] GRO, D4290 PP 5/1.

[2] During this period, post offices would purchase postal stamps from the public for a charge of three per cent. Advertisements in newspapers indicate this was a widespread practice for sending small payments through the post. Information kindly supplied by Mike Jackson FRPSL of the Great Britain Philatelic Society.

[3] J. B. Caldwell to Cotham, 14 September 1853. Clearly this appeal included a list of subscribers to date and the amounts promised.

[4] *The Tablet*, 16 May 1908, p. 29, obituary.

[5] Ignatius Sisk to Cotham, 22 October 1853. *Sit nomen Domini benedictum* translates as 'Blessed be the name of the Lord'.

[6] Cotham remained attached to schoolboy ways; he could sign off his letters (when appropriate, one hopes), 'Sitting here upon my bottom, yours sincerely, Ambrose Cotham'. PC from Fr Austin Gurr OSB, 23 March 2016, quoting an oral tradition passed on to him by Abbot Sylvester Mooney OSB (1886–1988).

[7] D. Mathew, 'Old Catholics and Converts' in G. A. Beck AA (Ed.), *The English Catholics 1850–1950* (London: Burns & Oates, 1950), p. 229.

[8] GRO D4290 A 3/1 for lists of subscribers.

[9] *Cheltenham Examiner*, 9 May 1883, p. 8.

[10] The impressive painting now hangs in the presbytery of St Gregory's; it was bought at auction by local schoolteacher Basil Gregory and donated to the parish.

[11] B. Andrews, 'The English Benedictine Connection—The Works of Charles Hansom in Australia', *Fabrications*: The Journal of the Society of Architectural Historians, Australia and New Zealand; Vol. 1, Iss. 1, 1989, pp. 38–39.

[12] *Cheltenham Examiner*, 10 May, p. 4, and 31 May 1854, p. 8.

[13] The church is St Luke's, College Road, designed in the Early English style, with a broach spire, by Frederick Ordish. It was originally to be called All Saints, and the congregation was temporarily using a school in Bath Road. See S. T. Blake, *Cheltenham's Churches and Chapels A.D. 773–1883.* (Cheltenham Borough Council Art Gallery and Museum Service, August 1979), pp. 31–32. Among Cotham's papers (DA IV.C.XI) is a handbill printed in 1855 showing in brief the cost of St Luke's, opened in 1854. The site cost £100, Charles Rainger's building costs amounted to £4,394 13s. and John Acock provided the surrounding roads and paving. For this, Revd Close provided a church with 1,100 sittings as well as accommodation for

Appeals & Tenders 345

the neighbouring Cheltenham College.

[14] GRO, D4290 A 3/1.

[15] *Cheltenham Chronicle*, 2 October 1855, p. 2.

[16] J. Goding, *Norman's History of Cheltenham* (London: Longman, Green, Longman, Roberts and Green, 1863), p. 611.

29 CO-WORKER & FRIEND

THE APPEARANCE OF Dr Copeland among the committee members was a crucial development, although not a surprising one given the progress of the Catholic Church throughout the country at this time and the development of Cheltenham. Nevertheless, his wholehearted involvement in the work of St Gregory's must have been due in part to Fr Cotham's personal influence and encouragement. Copeland and Cotham were born within twelve months of each other but their paths converged at St Gregory's from very different starting points.

George Ford Copeland was born in Chigwell, Essex in 1810. He moved to Cheltenham in the mid-1830s, married his first wife, Mary Harris Leacock, and practised as a surgeon in Oriel Place. Mary was born in Barbados, the eldest daughter of the late Mr Joseph Leacock, a plantation owner at Mount Brevitor. Her widowed mother remarried, to Dr Charles Turner Cooke, a well-respected physician in Cheltenham. The marriage therefore gave George an additional financial and professional fillip. His own brother William was an ordained minister of the Church of England and their sister Mary Ann married Samuel Borlase, a landed proprietor in Cornwall. Thus, the Copeland family was well represented in the establishment classes of Victorian England but their church allegiance, at least, was open to change by the middle of the century.

Mary died at the age of 32 in 1842, and William came from Oxford to take the funeral service. The change of circumstances for Dr Copeland, who comes across as a rather pompous and stiff young man, went beyond that of widowerhood. Four years later he married Selina Bacchus in Brighton in January 1846, although she was living with her brother Henry's family in Cheltenham. Also living with them was Selina's best friend Maria Giberne, and it was during a shopping trip to London for Selina's wedding

348   *The Indomitable Mr Cotham*

clothes that Maria was secretly received into the Catholic Church in December 1845. The move was much to her friend's distress and Maria's discomfort as the husband-to-be was opposed to her conversion and it was clear she would not be welcome in his house. Copeland's disapproval justifiably extended to nervousness about the effect on his fiancée's steadiness in the Anglican faith, after Henry Bacchus and his wife Isabella (née Cumming) were received into the Catholic Church in early January 1846.[1] Details of the painful courtship-conversion scenario were relayed to Fr John Henry Newman in Oxford, Maria's lifelong confidante and correspondent. He advised her, 'As to G. C. the less you talk to him the better;—he would find objections in *any* proof; as others do against Scripture'.[2] She had spurned his brother Frank's romantic advances and was a match for anyone in company. Tom Mozley remembered her with some awe:

> In all this goodly array [the Newman set] there was not a grander or more ornamental figure than Maria Rosina Giberne. She was, nay she is, the prima donna of the company. Tall, strong of build, majestic, with aquiline nose and well-formed mouth, dark penetrating eyes, and a luxuriance of glossy black hair, she would command attention anywhere.[3]

Fr Newman suggested to Maria (and Selina, if need arose) that she might find refuge with the Sisters of Mercy in their Handsworth, Birmingham convent. Despite George's continuing opposition Selina was received into the Catholic Church in 1848, Maria keeping Fr Newman informed of her progress. On 6 June 1848 he replied,

> How glad you must be about Mrs Copeland. I wrote to G. Copeland, begging him to convey my congratulations to her, not saying a word about himself. He wrote back kindly, but defending himself against being a Catholic, as if I had urged it.[4]

Co-worker & Friend 349

Two daughters were born to the Copelands before Selina died in October 1850 during childbirth. Again, Fr Newman took a close and prescient interest in Maria Giberne's concerns:

> My dear Miss Giberne, I gave my Mass this morning to dear Mrs Copeland ... It was a great surprise and sorrow to me, as it must have been in a very distressing way to you. But you must thank God, that you have gained a soul to Him. She is now safe—Your work is carried home, and pleads for you in God's sight ... and you have gained a double recompense—the salvation of a dear friend and the reward of a good act.

> As to the children, don't trouble yourself. They are in God's hands—and their baptism will show itself in time to come. Even if they have not Catholic education, they will, through His grace and mercy, be drawn to the dear Mother who received them in infancy into her holy arms, from those of their earthly parent.[5]

In his second widowerhood, St Gregory's became a focus for Dr Copeland's energies after he was finally received into the Catholic Church in 1855. His interest in practising medicine waned after attempts failed early in his career to break into Cheltenham's medical establishment. In his application for one of the posts of surgeon in the new General Hospital and Dispensary, in 1839, he offered his experience as Staff-Assistant Surgeon in the Military Hospital Brussels, House Surgeon St Bartholomew's, London, and occasional surgeon in charge of one of London's largest dispensaries as suitable qualifications. He forbore to mention the career of his eminent uncle, Thomas Copeland FRC (1781–1855), who combined his appointment as surgeon-extraordinary to Queen Victoria with pioneering work in colorectal surgery.

The Daughters of the Cross engaged George in 1864 as the only Catholic doctor in Cheltenham and found him obliging (he visited while ill himself) but his prescription of 'a bottle of quinine mixed with other soothing things' proved ineffective. A few weeks later Sr Aloysia Tixhon consulted a Protestant doctor who not only waived his fee but whose mixture of quinine, camphor, and iron cured her fever. 'Père Cotham sent some good old wine' to speed her recovery.[6] To be fair, at the time there was little hope that Dr Copeland would recover from his own illness. In any case, his move to Cheltenham suggests he was not aiming as high as his uncle. The cultural opportunities of the town proved more attractive to him than medical science. Among other civic good works, he was one of the proposers of a Cheltenham branch of the Archaeological Society (1844), a subscriber to the development of amenities at the Royal Old Wells (1849), and a Director of the Montpellier Gardens Company (1861). Until its closure in 1861 he was, like G. A. Williams, a long-time member of the Cheltenham Literary and Philosophical Institute. Copeland was an ideal Cheltenham townsman: cultured, moneyed, respectable, and above all, while his health lasted, involved. Thomas Copeland FRC died at the end of 1855, leaving a huge fortune of £180,000, with his brother's three children as the main legatees after his widow died within a month of his death. George Copeland's wealth was secured.

In February 1858 Copeland was preparing for confirmation from Bishop Clifford and as a token of gratitude to John Henry Newman, and in memory of his wife's tenth anniversary of reception into the church, he sent Newman a gift. Fr Newman thanked him warmly for the 'valuable ... rare and curious', if obscure, book which was apparently just what he needed for his current line of study. The brief letter was warm and friendly, ending, 'How your handwriting puts me in mind of your brother'.[7] Over the next fifteen years Copeland was the single largest contributor to the church building finances. He paid for the elaborate south porch, with a dedication inscription above the door, as a memorial to his wife Selina. He gave constantly, until the spire was finally completed, and he was one of Fr Cotham's closest associates. The priest dined with him and consulted with him over the accounts. When Mary Elizabeth and her sister Matilda Catherine were married in a double wedding celebration

Co-worker & Friend

at St Gregory's in April 1872, to Henry Charles Brandling of Malvern Wells, and Henry William Berkeley of Spetchley respectively, Cotham assisted the celebrant, the Revd Edward Caswall, a friend of the Copeland brothers from their schooldays in Chigwell. Through the Bacchus/Copeland connection Cotham came into close contact with the Oratorian communities in London and Birmingham and the development of city missions, a pertinent issue in the English Benedictine Congregation's debate about mission and monastic integration.

Edward Caswall, previously ordained in the Church of England, was received into the Catholic Church after the death of his wife and joined Newman's new Congregation of the Oratory in Birmingham. As part of his advance towards Catholicism Caswall visited Ireland to see for himself how the faith was practised among lay people. The experience of witnessing a congregation praying the Rosary was pivotal in changing his opinion about the idolatry, or otherwise, of praying to the Blessed Virgin. In a letter to George Copeland in 1847 he wrote, 'I was perpetually suspecting that in the invocation of the Blessed Virgin there must be some latent spirit of idolatry' but in Dublin his experience was that

> there was too much appearance of love, humility and real religion in the poor men for idolatry to be possible. I knelt down with them till all was over. Every word was in English, and I must say, if ever I saw true praying, it was then.[8]

Copeland at this time had no thoughts of becoming a Catholic but obviously engaged in the debate with his brother and their mutual friends.

George Copeland's brother, the Revd William John Copeland, stayed on as curate of Littlemore after Newman had been received into the Catholic Church. Although he remained an Anglican, and was disappointed as the prospect of corporate reunion between denominations receded, he was a kind friend and loyal supporter of Newman in the face of bitter criticism from others in the Church of England. At Newman's request he edited *Plain and Parochial Sermons* for publication in 1858, the first reissue of Newman's Anglican works. By drawing criticism away from Newman he became a bridge for the acceptance of his early work by both Catholics and Anglicans, as Newman himself acknowledged in a letter written in April 1873:

> You have been of the greatest use to me in the matter of the Sermons, and I only regret you have had so much trouble; but you have not had it for nothing. Unless you had broken the ice I could have republished nothing I had written before 1845–6. The English people would not have borne any alterations—and my own people would have been scandalised had I made none. They murmured a great deal about the new edition of the Sermons, as it was—but since you, not I, published them, nothing could be said about it. After this beginning, I took courage to publish [more].[9]

Fr Cotham's friendship with George Copeland gave him the opportunity for discussions about the development of Fr Newman's position in ecclesiastical and public circles; it is quite possible that he met Newman when the latter visited Copeland, whose brother William was with him, at his home in Bayshill Villas in late June 1870. Writing to his, and Selina Copeland's, friend Sr Pia Maria Giberne on 14 July Newman describes a poignant scene of still-lively minds being hampered by ailing bodies:

> I am very well except when I move about. That tries me. Lately, in execution of long promises, I went from home from Monday to Saturday, visiting Mr Church, my cousin Louisa Deane (whom I had not seen for 26 years), H. Wilberforce, and George Copeland; and was certainly not the better for it. George Copeland, who as you must know, is utterly paralysed except in his head, which is as full of vigorous thought as ever, inquired much after you. I had never seen his daughters before. They are suffering from their Father's long illness. He showed me your first oil painting, which he praised very much.[10]

Dr George Ford Copeland

Dr Copeland was a friend and companion not only for business but also recreation, and Fr Cotham made the most of opportunities for enjoyment. In February 1858 when the former assistant priest Fr Kendal arrived unexpectedly, not having received the telegram that had been sent telling him not to make a visit 'to beg', he and Cotham arranged bookcases together, hence 'all is well'. The following day they walked the eight miles to Gloucester with Copeland, returning by train, perhaps after visiting the building work being undertaken by Fr Leonard Calderbank at St Peter's Catholic Church, close to the railway station. The outing was a success, drawing one of Cotham's favourite comments at the end of the day: '*benè!*'[*sic*]. On the third day of the unwanted visit the two priests dined with Fr Ridgeway and Mr Marshall, again '*benè*'. During the same week Fr Cotham had looked at accounts with Dr Copeland, given alms to the poor, and made visits to the sick, sometimes accompanied by a lady of the parish.

In his friendship with the Copeland family Fr Cotham was brought into personal contact with lay and clerical converts of the 'Second Spring' and the second wave after 1850. In his 1859 visitation report he estimates there were about one hundred converts in his congregation, seventeen having been received in 1858 and about six in each of the two preceding years. Bearing in mind that out of a total Catholic population of thirteen hundred, only five hundred had been Easter communicants in 1858, and that converts were highly observant on this point, at least twenty per cent of adult Sunday Mass attenders were probably converts to Catholicism, bringing their particular expectations and aspirations. There is no figure given for non-practising Catholics, but so-called 'perverts' are optimistically few: a presumed death-bed conversion had 'fallen away' after recovery to good health, and one or two Irish families occasionally attended Protestant churches.

Through Dr Copeland, Fr Cotham was also brought into contact with the Oratorians, the religious order chosen by its most influential advocate; with new and old money; with personal grief and social advancement. All these associations were brought into the fabric of the new building which was taking shape as a symbol of the increasingly visible presence of the Catholic Church in England. Fr Cotham was at his ease here as much as he had been in his northern family home or indeed in colonial Tasmania.

Co-worker & Friend 355

Judith Champ says, 'Nineteenth-century England was unquestionably missionary territory, and the care of the small Catholic flock was only one aspect of the priestly and episcopal task.'[11] To meet these pastoral demands Cotham remained true to the ideals that Bishop Ullathorne put before his diocesan priests in 1853:

> We are missioners, O name, rich with the most noble and generous associations! Our work is that of the apostles … Unless he make himself into a sacrifice, as an apostle would, for the souls of his brethren, he may be a priest, but he is unworthy to call himself a missioner. A missioner is a priest, laborious, patient, not easily discouraged, ingenious by the force of that ardour which the spirit of his position enkindles to meet wants as they arise.[12]

Notes

[1] Their sons John and Francis Stanislaus were ordained priests, the latter with the Oratorians in Birmingham, as was a nephew, Francis du Moulin-Browne.

[2] www.newman.reader.org/works/letters_diaries Vol. XI, p. 111. Newman to Maria Giberne, 12 February 1846.

[3] E. Short, *Newman and his Family* (London: Bloomsbury, 2013), p. 176.

[4] www.newman.reader.org/works/letters_diaries Vol. XII, p. 215. Newman to Maria Giberne 6 June 1848. I am grateful to author Christine Whittemore for drawing my attention to the close friendship that existed between Giberne and Selina Copeland.

[5] *Ibid.*, Vol. XIV, p. 93. Newman to Maria Giberne, 4 October 1850.

[6] L. W. O'Neill DC, *With All My Heart: The Life and Letters of Sr Aloysia* (Privately published, 1977), pp. 123 and 128.

[7] www.newman.reader.org/works/letters_diaries Vol. XVIII, p. 245. Newman to George Copeland, 4 February 1858; the book was *Bibles, Testaments, Psalms and other Books of the Holy Scriptures in English* from the collection of Mr Lea Wilson FSA, brother-in-law of Selina. Only 60 copies were printed.

[8] N. De Flon, *Edward Caswall: Newman's Brother and Friend* (Leominster: Gracewing, 2005), p. 88. Caswall to G. F. Copeland, 15 March 1847.

[9]   www.newman.reader.org/works/letters_diaries Vol. XXVII, p. 293. Newman to W. J. Copeland, 20 February 1873.

[10] *Ibid.,* Vol. XXV, p. 158. Newman to Sr Pia (Maria Giberne) 14 July 1870; also letters from Newman to Mrs J. Mozley, 18 June 1870; R. W. Church, 27 June 1870; Sir Frederic Rogers, 28 June 1870, pp. 146, 149, and 153.

[11] J. Champ, *William Bernard Ullathorne 1806–1889, A Different Kind of Monk* (Leominster: Gracewing, 2006), p. 394.

[12] *Ibid.,* p. 394. Discourse delivered at the conclusion of the first Diocesan Synod of Birmingham, 1853.

30 'A CEREMONIAL OF A VERY GORGEOUS CHARACTER'

T HE YEAR 1857 saw a rush of invoices coming to the committee, especially in the first five months as efforts were made to have the church ready for the solemn opening on 26 May. The essential elements were in place: altar, font, Lady Chapel, and South Porch, but not the ornamentation seen today. There was very little carved work, except for the reredoses, and few statues. Stained glass was confined to the Lady Chapel and chancel; the painted pictures from the old chapel might have been reused as temporary decoration before being auctioned. The incomplete church ended a few feet beyond the South Porch door, with the old chapel backing onto a temporary west wall. The chapel was used as a vestry until the sacristies were completed and it provided a covered way between the priests' house and the new building.[1]

The carving of the high altar frontal and reredos in the chancel, and the altar frontal and reredos in the Lady Chapel, was relatively early work by William Farmer, executed before he set up his successful partnership with William Brindley in London. John Hardman's three windows in the Lady Chapel are in the brightly coloured medieval style of his early work. The two side windows were paid for by Hector Caffieri, in memory of his parents, and by Revd Dunstan Scott OSB of Little Malvern Priory. As the patrons they chose the subjects of the windows: Scott's patronal saints William of Gellone, and the tenth century abbot of Glastonbury, Dunstan, and St Philippe and the Blessed Virgin for the Caffieri parents. The East window in the Lady Chapel, three lights depicting Our Lady of the Immaculate Conception flanked by St Anne and St Elizabeth, was donated by Mrs Elizabeth Brennan, a tenant at 10 St James Square for twelve

358 *The Indomitable Mr Cotham*

months from October 1856, and a long-term patron of the building fund.

In the chancel, Fr James Basil Duck (already transferred from Studley to Liverpool, as if to prove Daniel Evans' point to Bishop Burgess) paid for a side window with lights showing his two patron saints. The main five-light East window showing the Ascension of Our Lord was the gift of John Fitzherbert of Swynnerton Park in Staffordshire, an occasional resident of Cheltenham, one of the many retired landed, military men in the town. Fitzherbert died in 1863 and the family link with the church was broken. The window was praised at the time of its installation but considered 'a very shocking one'[2] by Fr Wilkinson who arranged for it to be replaced by Hardman in 1887, in part exchange, by the present window representing the Assumption of Our Lady. The exchange was taken at a low price as Hardman studios accepted it was one of their inferior productions.

In May the pace of smaller works accelerated as 26 May, the Feast of St Augustine of Canterbury, approached. Twenty-six benches and upholstered kneeling boards, with brass plaques for pew-holders' cards, were provided by Charles Rainger who would gradually replace John Acock as the favoured local builder; forty plain, varnished forms were provided for school children and other members of the congregation in the side aisles. Two wooden screens came from William Marquiss of Bristol, probably intended to block off the unsightly unfinished parts of the church. Carpet was laid in the sanctuary and yards of matting elsewhere. Henry Tidmarsh, trading from Birmingham's Bull-ring, provided one hundred and twenty yards of 'Cocoa Nutt' green baize; his invoice for £23 3s. 5d. is dated 22 May, worryingly close to the opening day.

The work provided to local, regional, and national businesses ranged from the mundane to the highest quality. An invoice from Powell and Brown of Birmingham, for a Benediction canopy, is an example of Catholic and female involvement in the expansion of skilled industry which was part of Birmingham's, and England's, commercial success. Ann Powell, eldest daughter of

'A Ceremonial of a Very Gorgeous Character'

Augustus Pugin and married to his former apprentice-employee, Hardman's nephew and partner William Powell, initially managed the embroidery side of Hardman's workshops. As demand increased for ecclesiastical furnishings she set up her own business, taking into partnership, in 1852, the firm owned by Winefred and Lucy Brown of Birmingham. The canopy was invoiced for £8 15. 6d. and the total amount for vestments was £311 according to a list probably drawn up in 1858 for the Bishop's visitation. 'An exceedingly rich IHS brocaded white silk chasuble with broad and narrow lace, embroidered collar &c' begins the list, costing £25 10s; Richest Red, Purple, Green, and Black Velvet chasubles follow, and so on through the full sets of vestments—copes, hoods, maniples, and stoles—and smaller pieces, the burses, sub-deacons' veils, and five sets of altar apparels in the liturgical colours. In the detailed account book of expenditures there is mention of only two particular items—a white cope for which Casimir Tiesset collected money, and a veil paid for by Fr Blount; in the 1858 inventory every item is individually priced and presumably bought new for the church although apparently not charged to St Gregory's account.

The various press reports covering the solemn opening were comprehensive and complimentary. *The Tablet* used the occasion to feature Cheltenham as 'Number VI' in its series of sketches of the Catholic missions of England. The beginning of the feature is unpromising: 'In one respect we are unfortunate; for Cheltenham is not like Reading or Cambridge; it has no past history.' After a laconic trot through Cheltenham's preceding one hundred years, the writer gathers pace with the arrival of Fr Birdsall in 1809. Birdsall's co-adjutors and successors are listed, including the Revd J. B. Polding in the last quarter of 1827 (in 1857 Archbishop of Sydney), the Revd J. P. Wilson, erroneously described as 'another Australian Bishop' in 1828, and the Revd James Coltham [*sic*], 'that excellent Missioner', in 1853. The chapel at that time was 'an ugly, square, red brick building of rather Methodistical appearance, erected in days long anterior

360   *The Indomitable Mr Cotham*

to Pugin and Hansom'. After an account of the development of the new church and school buildings the writer finishes with figures from Fr Blount's census taken in Lent 1856: the congregation numbered 1,100, annual baptisms amounted to fifty, and Easter communicants numbered above five hundred. The view from London was not likely to please the Cheltenham readership:

> The congregation is partly supported by wealthy Catholics who come to Cheltenham during the season, or to drink its waters. It mainly consists of poor Irish who settle in the town in considerable numbers, and migrate from it in the summer, wandering over the country in search of agricultural employment.[3]

The report in the *Cheltenham Examiner*,[4] reprinted in *The Tablet*, began with a lengthy description of a 'few particulars of the architectural detail' of the building before going on to an account of 'a ceremonial of a very gorgeous character'. The dimensions of the constituent parts are given, and every cornice, capital, and crocket seems to have been noticed and commented on. The overall judgement is that 'the grouping of the several parts is very fine, more especially when viewed from the south-east'. The *Cheltenham Mercury* went into even finer detail, the effusive praise occasionally punctuated with a well-aimed criticism.

> The benches are of the usual height, made of stained deal, with very well-arranged kneeling boards and covered with velvet; but the effect of the arcades is sadly marred by the insertion of a rail which is attached to each bench-end and inserted into the piers, showing an exclusiveness which we were not prepared to find—the side seats being intended for the poor.[5]

On the morning of Tuesday 26 May, Cardinal Wiseman arrived by carriage and four from Spetchley Park, Worcestershire, home of a Catholic branch of the Berkeley family. The Bishop of Clifton, William Clifford, had stayed overnight with Fr Cotham. The *Cheltenham Mercury* was evidently provided with its copy by an

'A Ceremonial of a Very Gorgeous Character' 361

inside source who gave the editor an order of service complete with rubrics, so the newspaper was able to report what took place in the vestry out of sight of the congregation even before the Mass began. A paragraph was needed to cover the action of lighting the incense, involving deacons, sub-deacons, acolytes, censers and navet bearer. The procession from the vestry (the former chapel) into the body of the church was a remarkable sight for the congregation of Catholics, from Cheltenham and other towns, and Protestant visitors. The west end of the church was unfinished, without ornamentation, the wall of the old chapel forming part of the temporary west wall of the new church. Through the functional connecting door the incense bearer, two wax-candle bearers, the cross bearer, the body of clerics, a sub-deacon carrying the New Testament (with the Bishop's maniple between its pages), a deacon, and an assistant priest preceded the Bishop of Clifton 'attired in his gorgeous habiliments'. He was followed by the Archbishop of Westminster, Cardinal Nicholas Wiseman, wearing his cardinal's hat, an ermine tippet, and a crimson robe, 'his train supported by four juveniles in white surplices'.

The list of principal ecclesiastics printed by the *Cheltenham Free Press*[6] worked its way through the bishops, vicars general, provincials, priors, and superiors of religious houses. The Benedictines wore their black robes with polished demeanour, the Dominicans were recognised by their white dresses, sable robes, and tonsured heads, but the Passionists from Broadway, with austere serge habits and closely shaven heads, were the most exotic group, affording a 'remarkable contrast' with the glittering apparel of the prelates. Cotham (SJ) was near the end of the list, which concluded with the Benedictines Blount, Cotham, Bernard, Price, Lynass, Ridgway, Hall, etc, 'altogether about sixty in number'. The occasion brought out the gentry from neighbouring counties, most still accustomed to hearing Mass in their private chapels. Viscount Campden was pre-eminent, followed by various branches of the Berkeleys (though not the Protestant Berkeleys of Berkeley Castle), Monington-Webbe Weston and

362 *The Indomitable Mr Cotham*

his lady, De La Bere Boddenham of Rotherwas, Hornyold of Blackmore Park, two Canning ladies from Hartpury, Biddulph Phillips and his daughter, and Eyston of Overbury. The aspiring George Ford Copeland was not out of his depth among them, though his daughters were still too young to join the congregation; finally the ubiquitous G. A. Williams, Esq. was noted.

Cardinal Wiseman's sermon was delivered from the chancel steps, the splendid pulpit being still unfinished. He spoke for fifty minutes on the text 'The Lord hath reigned' (Psalm 90 v. 1); the substance of his discourse was variously reported, presumably according to the scribes' ability to keep up. The *Cheltenham Mercury* chose to dwell on the allusions to 'the researches of science' which studied geology and fossils to reveal the earth's pre-history, during which period the Lord had also reigned. The *Cheltenham Free Press* decided to stress the references to the philosophies of ancient Egypt and Athens which were doomed to annihilation by the new wisdom of Christianity, served by new buildings such as St Gregory's. The *Cheltenham Examiner* confined its opinions to noting the sermon was 'scripturally historical'. The *Cheltenham Looker-On*, the least sympathetic publication on all matters Catholic, considered the sermon laboured rather than eloquent and carefully constructed to avoid giving offence to the many Protestants attending.[7] All accounts ended with the Cardinal's emollient invitation to the congregation not to judge the Catholic Church by what they may have heard or read, 'but' in the words of the *Cheltenham Mercury* 'by coming from time to time to that place, and hearing the doctrine of their most holy faith'.

One person who remained outside was Robert Cook, waiting for his customer. He was the first victim of the lack of parking space around the church which is fitted tightly onto its site.

> Robert Cook, wheelchair man, was charged with an offence against the bye laws of the Borough, on Tuesday, at the opening of the Roman Catholic Church, by keeping his chair on the footpath, instead of on the carriage way.

> Police-constable Green proved the case. Defendant was
> fined 1s. and expenses 7s.[8]

After the opening ceremony, luncheon was provided by John Churchill at the Plough Hotel in the High Street, presided over by Viscount Campden. He and his wife had stolen a march on Cheltenham, having engaged Charles Hansom to design their domestic chapel in 1854 after making headlines by their conversion to Catholicism. The following year the Viscount endowed the Catholic mission in Chipping Campden, inaugurated by a mission from the Passionist Fathers from Broadway. Though greatly reduced in financial significance, patronage from nobility and gentry added status and pageantry to these occasions and sat comfortably alongside Catholic ceremony. Sixty ticket holders paid a total of ten guineas (tickets would have been variously priced according to the seating arrangements) and sherry, port, stout, and champagne came to £3 17s. For a lesser celebration one hundred and ninety feet of seating (without red covers), tables, and trestles were hired from Gardner and Barnard.

Ambrose Cotham's brother, William Cotham SJ, was similarly engaged in the building boom. While priest in charge of the unostentatious chapel of Our Lady Help of Christians in the Portico district of Prescot he supervised the building of Our Lady Immaculate and St Joseph in the centre of that town. His architect was Joseph Aloysius Hansom, and although the cost was a relatively modest £5,000 his impoverished congregation would have struggled to pay for it but for the generosity of two benefactors. The lack of debt, and the foresight to build large enough not to need further extension in the future, were particular points of satisfaction for William Cotham. The orientation of the church was such that, from a particular spot (and Fr William always made sure visitors stood on that spot) the spire of the Anglican Parish Church appeared to belong to Our Lady's. It was a happy accident he would have enjoyed impressing on his brother. In 1860 he was present at the laying of the foundation stone for Holy Cross Church at St Helens, administered by the Jesuits. The church was built to supplement the inadequate accommodation at St Mary's, Lowe House, one of Fr Cotham SJ's missions. The land for St Mary's had been bequeathed by William Penketh Cotham (related to Dr Lawrence Cotham's branch of the family) in 1797 and was situated on the Hardshaw Hall estate, fronting Cotham Street and Hall Lane. After a gap of some sixty years Henry Walmsley carried out the instructions of Penketh Cotham's legacy.[9]

Although the 1850s and 1860s were a period of intense church building, increased experience did not guarantee trouble-free progress. At Belmont, the employment of Edward Welby Pugin, very young, very gifted, and working on his first independent commission since the death of his famous father, was blighted by problems from an early stage. Fr Provincial Heptonstall lamented the lack of a vigilant overseer, and tried to persuade Fr Ambrose Prest, visiting Hereford from Ampleforth, to extend his stay.

Stanbrook, Worcester

Oct[br] 16 1857

My dear Confrère

Your letter received this morning has dispirited me, made me in fact half melancholy. Alas! that such blunders should have been made at the very commencement of ~~the~~ Building, and we the victims. Cotham was here this morning to whom I read your letter. He understood your observations perfectly and was astonished at such blunders. The particulars you mention were all guarded against in the specifications of the Cheltenham Church. And if the same <u>care had been</u> taken in the Belmont specifications, Maggs and not we must or at any rate ought to repair the blunder at his own expense and if these particulars about the Plinth being so high above the ground &c &c be not in the specifications then Pugin is very much to blame for having the specifications drawn up so losely [*sic*]. We are also to blame, for I am satisfied that with your knowledge and experience on the matter and with that of Father Cotham we might have guarded against these miserable blunders.

'A Ceremonial of a Very Gorgeous Character' 365

> I am very sorry to hear of your being unwell [from chronic bronchitis] for it is clear to me more than ever that your presence in Hereford is very effectual. I hope the President will order all your winter clothing to be forwarded immediately and will assign a <u>liberal allowance</u> to Mr Scarisbrick [Fr William Benedict Scarisbrick OSB] for your board, fire, washing &c so that you may feel yourself perfectly free and under no obligations to Mr Scarisbrick.
>
> Had you been at Hereford three months ago we should probably have saved £100—for I have little confidence in Pugin's estimate for repairs, especially if Maggs ~~is~~ be to treat with us. Pugin himself ought to make the bargain with Maggs, as if he, Pugin, were to stand the loss himself Maggs would then be more lenient and we could hand over the money to Pugin to pay.
>
> I hope then you will be able to make up your mind to remain. Surely the climate in Hereford must be more favourable to you than the climate of Ampleforth or Lancashire. I should like to see Buckley (Catholic Ben[efactor?] the Clerk of Works instead of Pontifex unless you have a high opinion of the latter. Buckley was Clerk of Works at Cheltenham a short time. Cotham speaks very highly of him. He is a thorough good Catholic and a man who can be well trusted. With such a man you would be very seldom required to go up to Belmont. He would walk down to Hereford and keep you well acquainted with what was going on two or three times a week. Buckley was and perhaps still is engaged with the Bodenhams at Rotherwas. On the receipt of this, do write me a line and say how long you will remain.[10]

Cotham and Cheltenham had been fortunate in having Charles Hansom as their architect since he took a close interest in all stages of the work and provided competent clerks of work. However, circumstances could, and did, easily change and Cotham was to have his share of 'miserable blunders'. In the first stage of work, however, he was able to combine the skills gained in Tasmania, and the competence of his architect and builders, in advancing the work in Cheltenham without undue delay or extra costs. His reputation among his Benedictine neighbours was enhanced; he was at that happy point of having past experience and present energy and enthusiasm to enjoy the challenges of his own enterprises and being consulted by those who were struggling with their own. At least he did not have to record, as Cockshoot did, that 'poor Maggs has gone off his head and has gone to the asylum'.[11]

At St Gregory's minor works by Charles Rainger continued from July to November 1857: shortening the benches in the side aisles, providing hat and coat rails in the organ room, and finishing off the parquetry and French polishing in the chancel. The 'richly carved' pulpit, supplied by Lewis and Lane of Birmingham, eventually arrived in time for Christmas; it was sculpted by Richard Boulton, probably while he was still in Birmingham and before his brief stay in Worcester. After he set up his own workshop in Cheltenham in the mid-1860s he became the main provider of stone carving in St Gregory's and in Cheltenham and beyond. Carved from Caen stone, with marble and encaustic tile decoration, the main panel of the pulpit showed Christ seated for the Sermon on the Mount surrounded by twelve apostles; the two side panels contained the figures of St Paul and St Augustine of Canterbury. Two men took four and a half days to pack the parts into ten strong packing cases at the Birmingham workshop; two men travelled to Cheltenham with the load by rail and took twenty-nine days to 'fix' the pulpit onto the foundations prepared by Acock. Mr Lane and Mr Lewis also travelled to Cheltenham to supervise the work personally. The pulpit itself cost £60 and the final bill was for £87 2s. Finally the gilding with gold leaf was completed by John Willis of Cheltenham and invoiced on 22 December. Also in time for Christmas was the arrival from Downside of a confessional box; William Price's bill for fourteen shillings for erecting the box is scribbled on a piece of paper, one

'A Ceremonial of a Very Gorgeous Character'

of the few invoices not prepared on the attractive headed paper used by even the most modest of tradespeople.

The raising of funds continued for more than twenty years after the solemn opening. After the major appeals more prosaic ways were adopted; enticements to spend at church bazaars were an innovation of Fr Wilkinson's rectorship. Subscriptions for the new church were meticulously recorded; for each element of building or furnishing an alphabetical list of names was drawn up. Sometimes whole families were individually recorded: towards general building costs Monsieur Tiesset (Bath Parade) gave £20 and Madame Tiesset £5, Monsieur and Madame Tiesset (Boulogne) £5, the three Tiesset sons—Casimir, Eugene and Charles—each gave ten shillings and their sister Mary £3. Finally, a niece in Guadeloupe—Emma Tiesset—is credited with one guinea. Mlle Sophie Tiesset, one of the stalwarts of the church, gave £25. In subsequent categories for tower, spire, boundary walls and so on, the Tiesset names are repeated, with occasional particular gifts of a crucifix or vestment.

Having come to the building of St Gregory's a little late, George Copeland's munificence made significant parts of the church more easily achievable: he paid £145 each for the organ and the south porch in 1856, and contributed £822 for the Lady Chapel. Copeland gave his money outright. In other cases money was given for a fixed period with interest paid to the donor, and on the expiry date the capital, less interest, remained with the church. Mrs Elizabeth Brennan, for example, made a contract with Cotham and Hector Caffieri, drawn up by James de Lacy Towle, for a five-year loan of £500 with interest of four per cent per annum payable half-yearly; the penalty for non-compliance with the terms of the contract was £1,000. The loan was extended for a further five years until Mrs Brennan herself needed funds and asked for her capital to be repaid. Three hundred pounds was borrowed from Downside College and Fr Cotham lent £200 by liquidating some shares 'set aside to defray the expenses of educating a church student at St Edmund's College at Douai'. He took the occasion to lend further money to pay for new heating apparatus and contribute towards the boundary wall. Whereas Mrs Brennan agreed to four per cent interest (foregoing £1 per annum) in order to be remembered as a benefactor, Fr Cotham stipulated that he was to be paid at five per cent until his capital was repaid. By the time the contract with Mrs Brennan was terminated on 1 February 1867 she had received £206 13s. 4d. in interest, acknowledged by receipts sent from various addresses in Cheltenham and Dublin, showing the interest was meticulously paid throughout the term of the extended loan.

St Gregory's high profile in local newspapers dropped dramatically after the opening ceremonies. The following month a solemn Requiem Mass was celebrated for the soldiers who died in the Crimean War.[12] However, until the next phase of building started the Catholic religion was most frequently referred to in relation to the Cheltenham branch of the Irish Church Missions to the Roman Catholics, a vigorously evangelical organisation, or to the behaviour of the boisterous Irish themselves.

Notes

[1] Only one memorial from the original chapel is extant, and it is probably the only remaining artefact. The memorial placed by her daughter Frances in memory of Annabella Eliza Sartorius in 1849 is now rarely seen being high on a wall in the cleaning cupboard of the Old Priory, adjacent to the church. Annabella, born in London in 1768, was the illegitimate daughter of Sir George Rose (1744–1818), an acquaintance of George III, colleague and confidant of William Pitt the Younger, and long-standing friend of Admiral Nelson. The inscribed marble tablet commemorating Revd Birdsall is a surprising loss from the present church.

[2] DA IV.C.XI, Wilkinson to Fr Provincial Edmund Moore, 18 March 1887.

[3] *The Tablet*, 6 June 1857; Richard Barton Collection now in the author's possession. No page number.

[4] *Cheltenham Examiner*, 27 May 1857, p. 8, and *The Tablet*, 30 May 1857. (GRO D4290 A 3/1; hard copy, p. 339).

[5] *Cheltenham Mercury*, 30 May 1857, p. 8 for all references in the *CM* to the church opening.

'A Ceremonial of a Very Gorgeous Character' 369

6 *Cheltenham Free Press*, 30 May 1857, p. 2.

7 *Cheltenham Looker-On*, 30 May 1857, p. 515.

8 *Cheltenham Examiner*, 3 June 1857, p. 3.

9 A new church was built at Lowe House in 1922 and to commemorate the centenary of Catholic Emancipation a carillon of forty-seven bells was installed in 1929. The Walmsley-Cothams were major contributors to this memorial, including bell thirty-three with the inscription:

Thomas Cotham SJ martyr Invictus 'Domine tu plura pro me passus est' Respice familium tuum humilem
Bertram Walmsley-Cotham

10 AAA RB–263–111; Heptonstall to Prest; 16 October 1857.

11 B. Warde, 'The Foundation of Belmont Abbey', in A. Berry OSB (Ed.), *Belmont Abbey: Celebrating 150 Years* (Leominster: Gracewing, 2012), p. 55.

12 *Cheltenham Examiner*, 17 June 1857, p. 4.

31 'CUM ILLO BENÈ'

FR COTHAM WAS not afraid to take a break from overseeing the building work and the prospect of visits and letters accumulating in his absence did not spoil his enjoyment at being away from business; his journal mixes work and leisure seamlessly. There are no journal entries at all for 1857. In the exercise book used for his Tasmanian journal he found five blank pages and wrote entries for June 1856 followed by a 'recommencement' on 12 February 1858 until 19 March, and yet another recommencement on 12 February 1859 until 23 March (12 February being noted as his 'Birth day').

Fr Cotham made time to visit Downside fairly regularly between 1853 and 1866. The Abbey Guestbook records his arrival for and departure from retreats or community feasts, on one occasion with 'his brother the Jesuit.'

> 1853 14 March Reverends Dr Heptonstall from Coventry and Mr Cotham from Cheltenham came to keep retreat.
> 18 March Revd Mr Cotham left.
>
> 1854 20 June Revd Mr Cotham from Cheltenham came.
> 26 June Revd Mr Cotham left.
>
> 1855 15 January Revd A Cotham of Cheltenham came.
> 20 January Revd A Cotham left.
>
> 1858 27 December [Play night with many guests attending] including J Cotham
> 30 December Dr Heptonstall and Revd Cotham left.
>
> 1860 16 April Revd Cotham [among other guests for the Prior's feast].
> 20 April Revd Cotham left.
>
> 1861 16 April Dom A Cotham came.
> 20 April D. Cotham left.

1865 21 April Revd J Cotham of Cheltenham and his brother the Jesuit came
22 April The Revds Cothams left.

1866 11 May [Cotham at the Prior's feast]
18 May [Cotham leaves].[1]

In 1854 Bishop Willson met up again with Ambrose Cotham during a nine month visit to Europe. During his first month in England he raised concerns, again, with the government about deteriorating conditions on Norfolk Island. The subject was discussed at length when he went to Rome in March 1854. He took the opportunity of celebrating Mass at St Peter's and other Roman churches, and gave particular attention to John Fitzgerald from Tasmania, just approaching his ordination. During John's retreat Bishop Willson visited him at St Eusebio's, and a week later attended his ordination at St John Lateran with Bishop James Gillis, Vicar Apostolic of the Eastern District of Scotland. The following day, Trinity Sunday, Fr John Fitzgerald celebrated his first Mass, the two Bishops being joined for this by Bishop Alexander Goss of Liverpool. The ordination of the first Tasmanian-born priest for the diocese of Hobart, only ten years after Willson had arrived on the island, was a significant occasion for both ordinand and bishop.

Archbishop Polding and Henry Gregory were also in Rome during June and July 1854, in defence of Gregory's report on Polding's behalf. Willson added his censorious opinion of Gregory's role to the debate, and once again went through the Therry affair with Vatican officials. He had a period of illness in July and left Rome in a despondent mood at the end of July, despite having made useful contacts and many representations on behalf of his impoverished diocese.[2]

John Fitzgerald accompanied his bishop for the rest of the latter's time in Europe. They journeyed to England via Douai College where Fr Cotham met them on 18 August, having travelled hard to arrive at 10:30 p.m. the previous evening. Nevertheless, he

'Cum Illo Benè'   373

was eager to take them on a tour of Douai churches in the morning and the Old English College in the afternoon. Cotham's readiness to meet up with Bishop Willson, and renew acquaintance with John, contrasts with the apparent lack of effort to cross paths with Bishop Polding during his visits to England. Even when Polding was joined by a number of Benedictine Fathers—including Cotham's friends Heptonstall, Scott, and Ridgway—for the funeral of Frederick Berkeley at Spetchley Court in 1866, Cotham was not able to cross into the adjoining county to be among them. Before returning home with Fr Fitzgerald, Willson went to Birmingham to visit John Hardman's showrooms and those of Mesdames Powell and Brown, vestment makers, to place orders for his diocese. Ambrose Cotham was soon making similar purchases for Cheltenham and must surely have enjoyed discussing the needs of their respective churches.

In 1856 Fr Cotham took a holiday in the Midlands, again in the company of other Benedictines on the mission like himself:

> Mon 2 [June] To Bromsgrove, Church, to Cougton [*sic*] Fr [Francis] Davis' carriage with Scott, Hep[tonstall]. Slept at Pipers[?]

> Tues 3 Walk to Redditch [Fr Kendal's mission]. Propos: Meeting. Slept Mrs Greens.

> Wed 4 Walk before Breakfast. Beautiful country—Mass etc. Walk to Beily church and Ipsley church. Slept at Mrs Greens.

> Thu 5 Buss to Birmingham. Hardmans etc. Dined with Conors. Chelt.9

The following week Fr Blount went to Downside for Fr Norbert Sweeney's feast day. The weather was fine and Fr Cotham mowed the grass in the Chapel garden, treating 'Bugs with sulpher' in between parish duties and church business with Biddulph Phillips, de Lacy Towle, and Caffieri. Friday 13th was a particularly satisfactory day:

374 *The Indomitable Mr Cotham*

> Work-house Communion to Geoghan and T. to Short. Revd Davis came to dinner. McAlpin's man and Williams fixing Choir and Seraphim. Davis left at ½p4. Blount returned from Downside bringing Revd Antony Bulbeck who stayed the night on his way to Liverpool. Cum illo benè.

After an extempore sermon on confession at the Sunday evening service on 28 February 1858 he was up early the following morning to begin his retreat at the Passionist retreat house in Broadway, fifteen miles north of Cheltenham.

> Monday 1March Started at 5.40 for Broadway on foot; pleasant journey, went by Stanway Church. Got to the Retiro [Retreat] at 10.45. Meditations Lewis of Granada [Venerable Louis of Granada OP, 1504–1588] from beginning to end.
>
> 2 March Rose at 5o'c. Mass, meditations etc, confession benè.
>
> 3 March Rose at 4.30. Offici, meditation. In cab to Evesham 15m from Worcester, on a bend in the banks of the Avon [details about the population, trade and history of Worcester follow]. Mass at Worcester. Walk to Stanbrook. Dined and returned in the evening to Cheltenham.
>
> Thursday, Friday and Saturday usual duties.

The three day retreat-cum-holiday shows Ambrose Cotham at his happiest: plenty of fresh air and exercise, time for prayer and reading, new places to visit and investigate, and a meal with friends. In some regards there was competition among the various religious orders and congregations during this period of resurgence, but in practise personal relationships mitigated tensions. The overlap between Cheltenham and Broadway seems never to have been less than cordial and Cotham was neither isolated as a Religious nor confined to Benedictine spirituality.

Fr Birdsall had bought property in Broadway in the 1820s with the aim of re-founding his dispersed monastery of SS Adrian and Dionysius, Lamspringe, Westphalia. Although the monastery and

'Cum Illo Benè' 375

attached private school were discontinued by 1844, a Catholic mission was established, although it was served only once a month from Cheltenham by Fr Kendal, with Mr Varley acting as a lay reader on the other Sundays. The Passionist Order, originally invited to Woodchester, near Stroud, by William Leigh, was invited to take over the Broadway mission in 1850, at the suggestion of Fr Glassbrook and Fr Kendal. The mission was renamed St Saviour's, and Broadway became the novitiate for the Passionists. Woodchester was taken by the Dominican Friars, more suited to William Leigh's aspirations in their monastic and academic lifestyle, and it, too, became the novitiate for the English Province of that Order.

Broadway was familiar to Cheltonians; it provided a Catholic cemetery for those who could make the arrangements to use it, and those who could afford to, such as Messrs Hanford, Waddy, and G. A. Williams. Caffieri supported both missions, whether Benedictine or Passionist. Caroline Waddy, John Waddy's sister, offered her services as an unpaid school teacher (as a canal shareholder she had an independent income) and with three other ladies living in St Joseph's school house formed a sisterhood aggregated to the Congregation of the Passion. The laity took their opportunities to promote their responsibilities, and profile, within the Church, whether by forming the welcoming party for Cardinal Wiseman to Broadway in 1855, or to turn their status as annuitant spinsters into something more fulfilling.[3]

It undoubtedly cheered Cotham's mood when the sun shone. A constant refrain in his Tasmanian journal was Rain! Rain! Rain! and it is easy to imagine it was a line in a ditty of his own composing which he frequently sang or recited. In February 1860 Fr Anselm Cockshoot wrote to Fr Heptonstall about difficulties with building expenses at Belmont following a recent storm that had done £60 of damage to the roofing. It was a pity, he wrote, Fr Cotham was not there to write one of his poems on the noise and destruction of the storm.[4] He was there, however, in September for the consecration of St Michael's and All Angels. There were many solemn events connected with the expanding numbers of Catholic churches in the decades following 1850. Pugin's example of giving detailed attention not only to architecture but also to furnishings, vestments, and ceremonial presentations set a high standard which others emulated. Bishops, priests, and laity turned out in impressive numbers to each other's celebrations and the novelty of the spectacle was lavishly reported in the local newspapers of each new diocese. The Catholic community in England was close knit and mutually supportive, at least when on public show. Hence, when St Michael and All Angels, Belmont was consecrated in September 1860, Fr Cotham was present as were his faithful parishioners George Arthur Williams, James de Lacy Towle, and Dr Copeland.

While there is no question that Douai was Cotham's true *alma mater*, he embraced Belmont's struggle to create a vision for the future from ambivalent beginnings. On the strength of his presumed knowledge of what constituted a good site for church building he had visited Monmouthshire in the late summer of 1863 with Fr Provincial Heptonstall to view Colonel Vaughan's offer of land near Abergavenny.[5] The site was rejected in favour of one near Hereford; the aim of its major single benefactor, Francis Wegg-Prosser, a Tractarian convert, had obvious parallels with that of Cotham's founding church committee, wanting (and getting) a fine neo-Gothic edifice from which monks would serve the local Catholic people and bring prestige to themselves. Bishop Joseph Brown, in addition to being Bishop of Newport and Menevia and adopting the monastic church as his pro-cathedral, was also a benefactor of Belmont and saw its role primarily as a Benedictine seminary. As personnel moved on so did the ideas.

> It is striking that the founding fathers at Belmont had left within a couple of years of its foundation. Norbert Sweeney, the prior, Benedict Blount, the subprior, Anselm Cockshoot, the bursar, Laurence Shepherd, the junior master, and Benedict Scarisbrick, who like the others was a Canon of Newport and Menevia, had all gone by 1861.[6]

'Cum Illo Benè' 377

Personality clashes were partly to blame during the early years of community formation. Anselm Cockshoot, having put so much effort into the founding of Belmont, was one of the flashpoints for dissension; however, he and Fr Cotham got on well enough, perhaps being similarly resolute during confrontations. When confrères left Belmont they were often still within reach whenever Ambrose Cotham had a day or two to spare. Peter Austin O'Neill, a choir postulant transferred from Douai in 1860 to be organist at Belmont, stayed for longer and eventually attended Fr Cotham in his final illness and as one of his legal executors. Aloysius Wilkinson, Belmont's Professor of Philosophy, left in 1866 for Cheltenham, a far more congenial colleague than the departing Benedict Scarisbrick.

The most zealous portion

In an account of Fr Cotham's life Mrs Mary Ann Monington Webbe-Weston does not have an obvious place to occupy as properly hers. Cotham himself may have excluded her altogether if he had written his own memoirs, or if he had been a man to suffer scruples of conscience. To put her after an account of Cotham's retreats and social visits to his confrères is not to give her parity with them, but to recognise her worth to him as a kind, non-judgemental friend, perhaps the one he knew for longest, after his brothers. She had moved to Bueno House, 10 St James Square, in 1858 following the death of her husband and stayed there until her own death in 1884 at the age of 95, one of the constants in the second half of Fr Cotham's life. He was a considerate landlord to her, and she was a good neighbour to him.

Mary Ann Wright was the youngest daughter of John Wright of Kelvedon Hall, Essex, whose extended family included the firm of Wright and Co., bankers to the Benedictine Order in England in the first part of the nineteenth century, and to most of the 'old' Catholic families. When the firm was bankrupted in the 1840s the effects were catastrophic: 'there is scarcely a Catholic college or chapel in the kingdom which has not had large funds deposited with the bankrupts, who are also trustees for many Catholic charities, and other religious establishments'.[7] Nevertheless, she had impeccable credentials as someone whose family had suffered for its faith. In the wake of the 1789 French Revolution, Dame Constantia Wright of Kelvedon Hall died while under arrest at Grignie, near St Quentin in 1793. Her family's recusant background matched that of Thomas Webbe-Weston whom she married in 1822. Thomas was born at Sarnesfield Court, near Weobley, Herefordshire which he inherited, together with Sutton Place, Surrey on the death of his father in 1824, adding the name Monington to his own. He was a magistrate for the county of Herefordshire and High Sheriff in 1837. During penal times the Weobley area was one of many 'nests of Papists' reviled around the country, and from the sixteenth century until 1835 a Catholic Chapel was maintained at nearby Sarnesfield Court by the Monington family where Mass continued to be celebrated until the 1860s.[8]

Fr Cotham may well have met Mrs Monington before he left Downside for Van Diemen's Land in 1835. Her family was known to Bishop Baines during his time in Bath and Prior Park and Bishop Polding was a visitor to Sarnesfield Court. He asked to be remembered to her in a letter sent to Downside in 1837. He also conveyed information about one of her servants who had arrived in Sydney a few months previously.

> Write to Downside, mon cher [Fr Heptonstall, his cousin] a discreet letter, and tell all my friends they are so deep in my heart they cannot find the way to my pen. The Loughnans and Barnewalls and Bullers. Oh! pray call on Mrs Webb Weston [sic] and give my best wishes. Mention that an elderly person, a servant, I believe, whom I have seen in her house as her servant was at her confession some months since. I saw her on her landing: she was almost broken-hearted about her child, and I told her I would recommend her child to the care of her good mistress.[9]

'*Cum Illo Benè*'

A different slant on the Moningtons' dealings with their servants came from the priest at the Weobley mission. After acknowledging Cotham's request for five shillings worth of stamps, in October 1853, Fr Thomas Rolling asked Cotham *entre nous* if he could have a word with the Moningtons about the frequent turnover of their staff—a situation that had been going on for the past twenty years since they arrived at Sarnesfield. Rolling wrote:

> I consider it no reflection on a servant's character to leave them or to be dismissed by them. Their system of managing servants is very bad although they are religious people themselves. I have been here little more than two years and half yet every servant about the place has been changed 3–4-5 and 6 times and they are now nearly without any at all.

Presumably Rolling heard the grievances from all sides but had felt helpless to remedy a situation which would have quite a serious impact on employment prospects in a small rural community. He blamed the Moningtons as a couple but, once widowed, Mrs Monington had no difficulty keeping her very small domestic staff loyal to her. She repaid the devotion of Mrs Diamond and her daughter Mary, her housekeepers in Cheltenham, by leaving Mary her meagre estate of £190 when she died.[10]

The Monington Webbe-Westons visited Cheltenham numerous times during the 1830s and early 1840s, usually staying at the Clarence Hotel, and no doubt socialising with other Catholic seasonal visitors such as the Vavasours.[11] They were no strangers to St Gregory's mission and made regular subscriptions to the building fund and attended the opening of the church in May 1857. Thomas died later that year in September; the couple had no children and although Mary had a life income of £200 from the Sarnesfield estate, ownership of the property passed to the Salvin family of Croxdale Hall, Yorkshire. Mrs Monington, as Fr Cotham, always called her, moved to the relatively small house in St James Square. It was certainly a noisy, dusty property, with St James GWR Station nearby, and building work in the former garden for a good

380 *The Indomitable Mr Cotham*

part of her tenancy. It can only have been devotion to St Gregory's, or perhaps to Fr Ambrose himself, that brought and kept her there with three domestic servants and occasional visits from her niece Mary Teresa Bedingfield (née Meynall), who was also provided for in Thomas Weston's Will, having become almost like a daughter to the childless Webbe-Westons.

Notes

1   Handwritten notes in W. T. Southerwood Papers, HAA, Tasmania.
2   C. Dowd OP, *Rome in Australia: The Papacy and Conflict in the Australian Catholic Missions, 1834–1884* (Leiden: Boston, Brill, 2008), p. 179.
3   D. Savio (Hamer) CP, *The Passionist Mission to St Saviour's, Broadway 1850–2000* (Altrincham: Privately published, 2000), pp. 3–15.
4   DAA Birt Collection N255; Cockshoot to Heptonstall, 23 February 1860. Quoted in W. T. Southerwood Papers, HAA, Tasmania.
5   B. Whelan OSB, *The Annals of the English Congregation of the Black Monks of St Benedict (1850–1900)*, private publication, 1942 2nd edition, reissued 1971, Vol. 1, p. 43.
6   G. Scott OSB, 'Something of the Struggle for Belmont's Soul, 1859–1909', in A. Berry OSB (Ed.), *Belmont Abbey: Celebrating 150 Years* (Leominster: Gracewing, 2012), p. 79.
7   *The Tablet*, 22 January 1842, p. 8.
8   http://www.belmontabbey.org.uk/page-weobleyandkington.html. [Accessed 27.7.2017]
9   H. N. Birt OSB, *Benedictine Pioneers in Australia* (London: Herbert and Daniels, 2 Vols, 1911), Vol. 1, p. 313.
10   *Cheltenham Looker-On*, 28 June 1884, p. 410: 'June 21 at Bueno House Mary, widow of the late Thomas Mornington Webbe-Weston of Sarnesfield Court, Herefordshire.' Probate for £190 personal estate granted to Mary Diamond spinster of 1 Clare-mount Villas, Henry Road, Gloucester. Mary Diamond (69) and Mary T. Diamond (daughter, 40) were domestic servants in the 1881 Census.
11   *Ibid.*, Arrivals; 9 May 1835, 27 May 1837, 14 July 1838, 12 October 1840, 20 March 1841, 9 April 1842. Departures; 16 May 1835, 4 November 1837, 29 September 1838.

32 SCHOOL REPORT: MAKING GOOD PROGRESS

PROVISIONS FOR THE poorly appointed school were not neglected during the church building work. Fr Blackett, a Capuchin friar struggling to raise funds for the impoverished mission at St Winifride's in Holywell, made the point in his reply to the five shilling appeal, 'I hope that the more wealthy Catholics of Cheltenham will not despise the humble school when compared to the magnificent church which I hope they will now have.' In Cotham's undated notes, perhaps as early as February 1853, his priorities and highest hopes are made plain:

> I cannot but anticipate the happiest results from the establishment of the most excellent institution in Cheltenham of the Sisters of the Sacred Heart. Their residence will immediately adjoin the church—[it] was formerly the Clergy-house, but has been vacated by the Pastors. The assistance we shall receive from the good Religious will be great in every way; and if there is one thing more we would desire for this locality, it would be that one or two of the Brothers of Christian Instruction from Hammersmith might be transferred to it; for <u>the schools</u> are our principal battle-field with sin and heresy, with which this city is so overrun.[1]

Although matters did not materialise as Cotham hoped, a committee of able parishioners under Fr Blount's leadership greatly improved the school situation, moving premises after thirty years at the original site. The first school 'for educating the children of poor Catholics' was opened in April 1827 by Fr Birdsall. It was attached to the Catholic chapel as two upstairs rooms for girls above the presbytery and vestry in Somerset Place. This was essentially what was still in existence when Fr Cotham arrived, with the boys accommodated in a nearby carpenter's

382 *The Indomitable Mr Cotham*

shed. An inspector's report, almost certainly made on the old school premises, shows the need for improvement. It may also explain why the school roll in 1856 was estimated to be thirty-nine boys and thirty-five girls, considerably lower than Cotham's figures given to the 1853 meeting; the removal of the younger boys may well have been made because of the insanitary conditions of the boys' classroom:

> (Boys) The attendance has been diminished by removing the younger boys to the Girls' School, and by an epidemic of which about 30 of the children died. In spite of this calamity, and of irregular attendance, the boys display accurate knowledge of the elementary subjects, and have been taught with care and success.

> (Girls) Mainly an Infant School, without the distinct organization proper to it. The Managers would do well to establish an Infant School, without which more satisfactory results can hardly be obtained.[2]

The earliest plans had recognised that commodious purpose-built premises were needed for the children. John Acock may have had instructions from Fr Cotham when he acquired the former St Paul's National School at auction in 1854. This building, on the corner of Hamilton Place and St Paul's Street North, and built in 1836 for £670, was able to accommodate a school roll of three hundred and seventy. It became redundant in 1854 when Practising Schools, designed by G. F. Bodley and built by Acock and Son 'in a vigorous manner' were opened in the grounds of the prestigious St Paul's Teacher Training College.[3]

Acock renovated the school and sold it to the Catholic mission for £640, of which £336 came from a government grant.[4] The school opened in May 1857 comprising two rooms, each measuring 38 ft 4 in. x 35 ft and having a galleried tier and a stove; the rooms were separated by sliding doors.[5] Thomas and Harriet Crotty were newly married when they took over the new school. They were dedicated to their profession and Thomas was

School Report: Making Good Progress 383

described in March 1859 by Fr Cotham as 'exemplary, efficient and certified'. Harriet's story is familiar: she was 'exemplary, but not quite satisfactory, owing to her having a Family. She presented herself for Examination (result not yet known) last Christmas'. Harriet was successful in gaining a certificate of merit in her examination; she and Thomas also had five children, burying two of them, during the twelve years they were in charge of the school. The male pupil teacher was satisfactory, his female counterpart 'rather backward'. Despite the Crottys' good reputation a fresh attempt was made to bring a congregation of teaching sisters to the town in 1863, for reasons of economy and prestige.

Fr Cotham's report in 1859 demonstrates the slippery nature of school attendance figures.

> Average of Boys 30—Girls & Infants 56. On register Boys 45, Girls 124, total 169. Present at Examination January 1859 Boys 41, Girls 94. At the Night School for Girls about 15.
>
> Number of Children between 3 years & 13 who ought to be at School probably about 200.[6]

The numbers remained unchanged in 1864, only fifty per cent of the register regularly attending.[7] St Gregory's did not run a Sunday School specifically for children, relying on the teachers, with occasional visits from the clergy, and Daughters of the Cross after 1863, to instruct the children in their faith during school hours. The Sunday afternoon instruction was open to all, although adults were usually seen individually in the evenings for instruction prior to being received into the Catholic Church.

> The children attend Mass on Sundays, but many are very remiss in Winter. They recite Prayers before and after each school time. Those who have made first communion approach every month. The others above 7 years of age who are sufficiently instructed about every two months. They repeat the Catechism before every morning. Public

Catechism is given in the Church every Sunday afternoon at 3o'c by the Clergy.[8]

The Cheltenham mission was by no means homogenous. Despite the reputation of Cheltenham as a spa town with a summer 'season' devoted to recreation and fashionable trading, and the growth of its professional class, the majority of the congregation were drawn from the influx of Irish immigrants to the town in the second half of the 1840s. The newcomers from Ireland did not spread themselves evenly among the few urban areas of Gloucestershire but were attracted chiefly to Bristol and Cheltenham. The most pressing need was to provide adequate primary education in the church for which every child was obliged to pay at least one penny per week. When these children and their parents, many of whom did not speak fluent English, were housed in the Union Workhouse they were obliged to attend Protestant services and classes of religious instruction, a situation abhorrent to the Catholic priests who remonstrated with the Board of Guardians but to little effect.

Providing at least adequate schooling was a matter of pride for church congregations. The children of St Gregory's school took their place alongside six thousand Cheltenham youngsters for the celebrations marking the marriage of the Prince of Wales and Princess Alexandra of Denmark in March 1863. Twenty-four schools took part in the procession of Volunteers, Yeomanry, and school children which took over two hours to travel less than two miles from Pittville Gates to the Cheltenham College Playground. At the head of St Gregory's band of two hundred was Fr Cotham, assisted by Fr Scarisbrick, G. A. Williams, Dr Copeland, and Hector Caffieri (and, no doubt, ladies of the congregation to keep an eye on the children), all loyal subjects of the Church and the Crown.

In the printed order for the march[9] St Gregory's contingent is disappointingly half way down the list of participants, behind the Union Workhouse children. But as the schools were split into two columns, in practice Fr Cotham marched at the rear of the

School Report: Making Good Progress 385

first column which was headed by the Anglican minister of St Mary's . On the opposite side of Pittville Park the non-conformist column was led by the Congregational Church; the few children of the Plymouth Brethren brought up the rear. Thus the awkward positioning of the Catholic brigade indicates their ecclesiastical status: neither Established nor Dissenting but proudly present. The *Cheltenham Looker-On* reported that the procession was the highlight of the day's events, towards which Fr Cotham contributed his one guinea with all other upstanding townspeople.[10] It can be imagined that Fr Cotham's high good humour was invaluable on this sort of public occasion, reminiscent of the temperance marches and Queen's birthday levées in which he took part during his time in Tasmania.

The Assistant Priests: Fr Henry Benedict Blount OSB

The first assistant to join Fr Cotham, in July 1854, was 32-year-old Henry Benedict Blount OSB, one of ten children of Edward and Frances Blount from the long established Catholic family of Mawley Hall, Shropshire. He was ordained at Downside in 1849 after becoming the first Benedictine in England to gain an external degree from London University; at Downside he filled the offices of Master of Novices, Prefect of Studies, and pastor of the Downside congregation. Cheltenham was his first mission posting and Cotham apparently found the intelligent young man to be an efficient and trustworthy supporter, despite his inexperience in urban mission conditions. Fr Cotham had been trusted as an educator for student clergy in Tasmania and he gave Blount scope to develop. For the first five months after his arrival the assistant priest conducted every baptism recorded in the register, perhaps the simplest duty to build up his confidence with parishioners. After this initial period he and Fr Cotham shared the workload. They travelled together to Bristol for meetings with Hansom, and Blount negotiated with some of the craftsmen, perhaps overstepping his authority occasionally. The impressive six candlesticks and crucifix for the High Altar were supplied by Walter Evans, a Birmingham 'Manufacturer of Sacred Vessels for the Altar'. In a letter to Cotham he explained that the enamel shields fixed to the candlesticks 'were ordered by the Rev Mr Blount in the Church when we were fixing the size of the Candles and the Cross. They should be fixed about two thirds of the way up the Candles'.[11] He also wrote down his verbal instructions to Blount for cleaning the crucifix by unscrewing the corpus.

However, Blount was undoubtedly an asset to Cotham, taking the lead on some matters of school administration. Together with his management committee, Hector Caffieri, George Copeland, James Healy (a wine merchant), and James de Lacy Towle, he corresponded with the Committee of the Council on Education to satisfy the terms of receiving a government grant of £336 for improvements to St Paul's Street School—and this in the week of the church's solemn opening—having arranged for the builder Charles Rainger, as a professional surveyor in the absence of an architect, to inspect Acock's workmanship. The committee had raised £452 towards the total cost of £788 by the usual method of finding subscribers locally and elsewhere, mostly from among those already subscribing heavily to the church building funds.

Having provided an adequate building Blount went on to seek out the pupils who, though numerous on the streets, were not always visible in school. Writing as the Secretary and Treasurer to the Friends and Supporters of St Gregory's Schools in October 1857, Fr Blount explained that in order to receive government capitation grants each pupil must provide the School Pence. Government policy was unequivocal. A reply to Blount in September 1857 from the Secretary to the Council on Education spelt it out:

> The conditions annexed to the Capitation Grants require that they be allowed for those children only on behalf of whom <u>a parent, or some other person who is legally responsible for maintaining the child</u>, pays a school fee amounting to not less than 3/- in the course of the year for

which the grant is claimed. There can be no uncertainty about the meaning of the underlined words.[12]

Nevertheless, 'the Minute was framed on the principle of encouraging improved practice'[13] so School Managers were not expected to exclude children as long as they were working towards parental responsibility for fees since 'very few things are brought into request by being made permanently gratuitous, and the Education of the poor has been found by experience to be no exception to the common rule.'[14] Notwithstanding the merits of the debate about motivation, in reality a school fee was beyond the means or willingness of many parents to pay. Blount advocated an adoption scheme whereby congregants might 'assist the parents' to keep their child in school. 'Such a plan, I think, will have your approval and ready adhesion, and will probably not merely serve its primary end, but will also produce, what is indeed so desirable, a sympathy between the <u>child adopted</u> and the <u>kind friend</u> <u>adopting</u>.'[15] Blount himself heads the list by 'adopting' two children, followed by the usual names of Tiesset, Caffieri, Wynyard, etc. The mainly Irish names of the children adopted are less prominent in church records: Pat McDonnell, Pat Sullivan 'son of a lame street sweeper (one of three)', the Comerford children, 'the mother a widow'. Blount offered to provide more information about any child since 'it is particularly desirable that a <u>personal</u> interested be felt and cherished'. However, he was not overly sentimental about his little flock; having provided for children already enrolled he wrote that he expected 'A Large Crop of Murphys will come in about December, a Tribe of Donovans ditto, A Collection of Driscolls, Flemings, Sullivans &c &c ditto ditto.'[16]

After the school moved into better premises in 1857, standards gradually improved, although the children lost ground following the disruption of the transition. Her Majesty's Inspectorate gave a favourable report in 1859 on the character and progress of the pupils and the assistance given by pupil teachers. The premises, furniture, and ventilation were deemed excellent, discipline and instruction were good, and some of the boys in the first class were 'well forward in Mathematics, Geography and History. Most of the boys read fluently, but with a provincial accent. Dictation and Grammar may be pushed a little ... Mental Arithmetic is cultivated with some success' in the second class. The girls were not quite so advanced, being very fair or satisfactory in their attainments, although Grammar and Needlework were good. Sadly 'the younger children appear rather stupid'.[17]

In addition to school business Fr Blount had duties at the Union Workhouse and was engaged in the not uncommon argument of the day about the provision of religious services and instruction appropriate to the inmates' faith. In September 1854 he wrote at length to the Poor Law Guardians, taking as his starting point the charge that Mrs Donovan's children had been taken to the Protestant church after attending Mass and were instructed from the 'Protestant Catechism' in the Union School. Blount listed five points to be considered while conceding that the fifth was already granted, that the children be taken to Mass on Sundays, on holidays where possible, and to Sunday afternoon or evening services at the Catholic Chapel in addition to morning Mass. Fr Blount's letter was published in the press and the reply, from the Chairman of the Poor Law Board, was also printed.[18] In essence, Mr Graves agreed with all that Fr Blount said since it was all in compliance with the regulations as practised by the Guardians. Occasionally difficulties arose when the faith of a child could not be ascertained, in the case of very young children or orphans, in which case the State had a duty to assume responsibility for them. If Mr Blount cared to supply copies of the 'Douay' version of the Bible they would be given to the Catholic children. At the time of this correspondence there were only three resident Catholic children, aged 1, 6 and 9, the children of Mrs Donovan. One Catholic man was also in the Union Workhouse.

The Guardians objected to Mr Graves' generous attitude towards what they regarded as Fr Blount's unjustified complaints. The Revd C. B. Trye 'did not see why such a parade should be made on the question'. He thought Catholics should not be

School Report: Making Good Progress 389

allowed out more than once on a Sunday since 'Roman Catholics and Dissenters ought to stand equal' in what was permitted. Mr Leach intervened, 'I am happy to say, as I have said on a former occasion, there is not one Dissenter in the house.' After further conversation it was agreed the Clerk should write to Mr Blount granting all his requests except that Catholics be allowed out more than once on Sundays as that would be 'unusual and irregular'. Fr Blount accepted the Clerk's letter, not because he agreed with all that had been said (the newspaper cutting in the archives at Douai Abbey is annotated with his remarks), but in a spirit of willingness to trust for better understanding in the future. Thus he had the last word in the correspondence, even though nothing had been substantially proven or gained.[19]

Fr Blount was still challenging the Board of Guardians in November 1857, this time on behalf of the two illegitimate daughters of Harriet Jones. Harriet had registered herself as a Protestant when she had been resident in the workhouse, but Blount said this proved nothing. He knew for a fact she had been attended by Fr Cotham at home at the time of her death. It was, Blount said, perfectly understandable that she should 'weakly and criminally' deny her Catholic faith to avoid 'the petty persecutions'[20] when she was in the workhouse, but her sisters and neighbours knew her to be a Catholic. On this occasion Fr Blount's arguments made no impact: the two girls could not be instructed as Catholics despite what their mother had stated about herself, or what their aunts wanted. It did not help Blount's cause that one of the aunts 'appeared before the Board in a beastly state of intoxication, and the Board refused to commit the children to her care, as being an unfit person to take charge of them'.[21]

According to Fr Cotham's 1859 visitation report 'the Catholic poor without exception will not go to the Union Workhouse, nor suffer their children to go; they would, and do, prefer to starve',[22] or keep silent about the shame of it. His report in 1864 was more realistic: there were twelve Catholic residents in the workhouse including four or five children, visited weekly by a priest and

390 *The Indomitable Mr Cotham*

allowed out to Sunday Mass. By contrast, he reckoned only six or eight Catholics were in-patients of the General Hospital each year. When a custodial sentence was unavoidable for young miscreants the priests applied to the court for the boys to be sent to a Catholic reformatory.[23]

It was around such cases as these on behalf of people who would not have made a fuss on their own account that the clergy of all denominations jockeyed for status and prestige among themselves and in the eyes of the newspaper-reading public. In the 1850s it was in the school, the workhouse, and the Lower High Street and St Paul's districts that the Catholic priests met their Irish parishioners. The immigrants to Cheltenham came from a portion of the Irish population that was largely unchurched, with less than thirty per cent Mass attendance in rural Ireland. It was not difficult for the priest to become a dominant authoritarian figure in their lives when the Irish populace was so little regarded generally. Improvement of children's prospects through the school system would gradually raise the status, and contribution, of working class Catholics but shielding destitute individuals from Protestant welfare was also a way of defending Catholic territory. The imperative that 'not one of them should be lost' was a matter of ecclesiastical pride as well as a divine injunction.

Fr Blount was evidently not a strong man. When Cotham spent a week at St Michael's, Belmont in early March 1858 he recorded in his journal 'Mr Blount ill' and 'Dom B sick' on either side of his time away from Cheltenham. In 1860 Fr Blount moved to St Michael's, Belmont as Procurator, but he was caught up in the personnel disputes there and made his own complaints to the Abbot President. In early 1861 he was staying with his family near Cleobury, Shropshire but later in the year he moved to Rotherwas, Herefordshire where the chapel was under the patronage of the Bodenham family. Despite this being an easier and healthier mission than Cheltenham he died on 12 February 1865 aged 43.

School Report: Making Good Progress 391

Notes

[1] For a short time clergy letters were addressed from 10 St James Square after the departure of Mrs Tennyson in 1853. Although the house was 'untenanted for upwards of three years' £50 per annum continued to be paid to Chipping Sodbury. The priests' accommodation returned to 3 Somerset Place when two widowed sisters, Mrs Fitzgerald and Mrs Brennan, took the tenancy from October 1856 until June 1857. See DA VIII.A.Cotham, small accounts book: 'Receipts and Payments on a/c of Bueno House 10 St James' Square commencing May 1853'.

[2] DA VIII.A.Cotham, Inspector's Report initialled FM.

[3] *Cheltenham Examiner*, 31 May 1854, p. 8. St Paul's was founded by Revd H. C. Bromby in 1847. Bromby was appointed Bishop of Tasmania in 1864 with a salary of £1,400 per annum.

[4] The school building was extended and remodelled several times during the nineteenth century, probably to meet government requirements for grants. In 1868 £16 13s. 4d. was subscribed for a 'new room' plus wire over the windows. Additional land was purchased by Fr Cotham in 1872 and an Infants room built for £40 in 1873. In 1876 the average attendance, for an age range of three to thirteen, was one hundred and twelve: thirty-two boys, fifty-three girls and twenty-seven children under five. The school remained far below its maximum capacity of three hundred until the Sisters of St Paul of Charity took over in 1885. By 1899 attendance had risen to two hundred and forty eight. See GRO D4290 A 3/1 especially for Parish Financial Accounts 1857–73.

[5] GRO, D2186/31, Architect's plan 1856.

[6] CDA, Cheltenham Box, Parish Visitation Report, 1858–59.

[7] Many families relied on their children being in work. The Commission on the Employment of Children (1865) 'revealed many cases in Cheltenham of young girls working in the drapery and millinery for twelve hours a day'. G. Hart, *A History of Cheltenham* (Gloucester: Alan Sutton, 1981, 2nd impression), p. 362.

[8] CDA, Cheltenham Box, Parish Visitation Report, 1858–59.

[9] Richard Barton Collection now in author's possession.

[10] *Cheltenham Looker-On*, 7 March 1863, p. 159.

[11] Evans to Cotham, 27 June 1857.

[12] Instruction to Blount, written on Downing Street headed paper, signature indecipherable, 21 September 1857.

[13] *Ibid.*

[14] *Ibid.*

15 DA VIII.A.Cotham, Draft copy document by Blount 'To the Friends and Supporters of St Gregory's Schools', September/October 1857.

16 *Ibid.*

17 *Cheltenham Examiner*, 24 August 1859, p. 4.

18 DA VIII.A.Cotham, *Cheltenham Chronicle*, 12 September 1854, p. 3, and 19 September 1854, p. 3.

19 *Ibid.*, 26 September 1854, p. 3.

20 DA VIII.A.Cotham, copy of Blount's letter; see also *Cheltenham Chronicle*, 24 November 1857, p. 3.

21 *Cheltenham Mercury*, 14 November 1857, p. 8.

22 CDA. Cheltenham Box.

23 See *Cheltenham Mercury*, 19 December 1857, p. 4 for the case of John Sullivan, 12, 'Rev. Mr Blount made a formal application in writing, that Sullivan might be sent to the Roman Catholic Reformatory in Leicestershire'.

33 'MUCH YET REMAINS TO BE DONE'[1]

FOR A BRIEF period after the solemn opening of the church in May 1857 work on the church fabric slowed down. During 1858 the invoices from the previous year continued to come in and be paid but the church was being put to its proper use at last, with mixed results. A rescript was granted from the diocese for the *Via Crucis*—Way of the Cross—to be used as a devotional practice in the church, especially during Lent. A brief fragment of Cotham's journal for 1858 survives; he recommenced it on 12 February, and discontinued it a month later. His birthday spurred him to begin; the conclusion of Bishop Clifford's visit to confer the sacrament of Confirmation on Sunday 14 March was a reasonable place to stop. One hundred and fifty candidates were presented for the sacrament, mainly children, but also recent converts such as Dr George Copeland and his two young daughters, solicitors James Boodle and James de Lacy Towle, Jane de Lacy Towle, and 95-year-old Charlotte Short.[2] Fortunately the candidates shared their sponsors: George Arthur Williams for the adult men, and teachers Thomas Crotty and Sophie Tiesset for most of the children.

A great supporter of the 1832 Reform Act, Boodle was one of the original proprietors of the politically Liberal *Cheltenham Examiner* founded in 1839, but had retired from his solicitor's practice due to ill health and the death of his only son aged 15. He became a generous benefactor of the church but a somewhat difficult character to handle; in giving his money he wanted also to keep a controlling hand on it, calling for diplomacy and sometimes guile to complete the transactions. In his later years he made and remade his Will, 'amounting almost to a monomania'.[3] Both Boodle and de Lacy Towle offered their legal opinions freely to Fr Cotham and negotiated with their professional colleagues to offer him discounted services when he ran into trouble.

Although incomplete, the journal entries for Cheltenham follow the pattern of a full schedule of duties as seen in the Tasmanian equivalent, only with a much greater variety of people to deal with and the continual concern with church building matters. References to Vicar General Wilson, to his old friend Mrs Monington and her niece, recently installed into Beuno House, 10 St James Square, or his confrère Fr Caldwell are all brief and there is rarely a hint as to his pleasure or annoyance with any of them, except for the occasional *Benè* at the end of the day, or 'Nil!' collection money on a Sunday.

> 12th [Friday, February 1858] Revd Wilson spent the night and left at 7.40am for Weobley [Herefordshire]. Vis[ited] Sick. Towle—Caffieri—Gas put into porch, lamps and lighted for the first time.
>
> 13th V Revd Joseph Wilson VG called. Bps Pastoral. Confessional
>
> 14th Sunday—no sermon at 8o/c. Pastoral at 11o/c / Nil!
>
> 17th Rainger to give estimate of Confessionals.
>
> 18th Rt Rev Dr Brown in afternoon.
>
> 19th Stations [of the Cross] first time in N Church. V Poor. Mrs Monington, Miss Meynell about horse and Poor— Danvers Clark ditto
>
> 21st Sermon on Confirmation Evening
>
> 23rd [Revd Thomas Edmund OSB] Caldwell spent the night on his way to Studley Mission
>
> 24th Sick/Calls—ABC Accounts

When Fr Cotham made a new start in the journal the following year, beginning on his 49th birthday, Saturday 12 February 1859, he was busy preparing papers for a formal visitation from the Bishop of Clifton at the end of the following week, while John

'Much yet Remains to be Done'

Marshall was fixing a brass screen in the Organ Chamber to show that work was continuing in the church.

Fr Knight arrived from Kemerton on Friday 18th in time to welcome Bishop Clifford on Saturday at 3 o'clock. Confessions that evening continued until 10 o'clock in readiness for High Mass and Confirmation of one hundred and fifty candidates on Sunday. During the first Mass of the day, at 8 o'clock, the bishop administered Holy Communion to three hundred congregants. Fr Cotham was the celebrant at High Mass at 11 o'clock; Haydn's Mass and Mozart's *Credo* No 2 were sung, as well as the organist Benjamin Joesbury's *Agnus Dei*; several hymns were also sung 'in the course of the morning' but probably not during the Mass. Communion was administered to a few people who had not been present at 8 o'clock (and had not broken the fast from midnight) and then the bishop was vested with cope, pectoral cross, mitre, and crozier before administering the sacrament of Confirmation. His address beforehand was short. Cotham noted in his journal that the bishop 'spoke to the people about completing the church' and attended a meeting of interested parties in the evening. Bishop Clifford took a close interest in the Cheltenham mission from the beginning of his time in office, since his episcopate and the church both dated from 1857, and, of course, he had a personal connection with the Cothams from the time William was chaplain to the Clifford family in Chudleigh.

The following morning, Monday, Bishop Clifford visited the school with Cotham and then took a walk with him, dining with Charles Riddell at 10 St James Square in the evening.[4] A decision was made to call a further meeting on Tuesday before the bishop left Cheltenham so circulars had to be hurriedly sent round the parish. When the meeting convened at midday, after the bishop had made an earlier inspection of the church, the discussion was about making further collections for starting work on the tower and spire, a project which exceeded what had already been achieved in technical, financial, and management terms in Cheltenham, and stretched Cotham's capacities to the limit. However,

Fr Cotham was well supported by faithful parishioners as ever; he and the bishop dined with Hector Caffieri that evening before Clifford left for Clifton at 9:30 p.m. Cotham was satisfied with the day—'Bene'—and closed his journal. His written replies supplied beforehand express general satisfaction with his mission: the fabric of the church was in excellent condition; the school rooms 'as good as new', and the mission house was 'quite sufficient' for the priests' needs.[5] After nearly twenty-five years as a missioner this may have been the most outwardly successful point of his ministry.

Vexatious business soon followed when Benjamin Joesbury gave one month's notice as organist (he was ready for a career in London), necessitating two days spent examining the organ accounts with him and discussing choir matters with Powell, in between making sick calls in the town and worrying about Fr Blount's attack of ill health. But Cotham's focus was on the proposed renewal of building works as he prepared his Sunday sermon on propagation of the faith with particular reference to raising subscriptions for the tower and spire. During that Sunday Fr Cotham received a visit from Mr Middleton, quite possibly the architect John Middleton who was responsible for designing five of Cheltenham's churches which were built during the time St Gregory's was being erected. Although all were intended by Middleton to have spires, only the first—St Mark's—was completed.[6] Significantly, this church had substantial financial backing from its minister, the Revd Mr Griffiths. In any event, the day went well for Cotham.

The following week Cotham had a holiday away from Cheltenham, with his favourite activities: vigorous exercise, socialising, and satisfying his curiosity with new experiences.

> 28th Mon Journey to Hereford. Arrived at 12o/c. Dined at Scarisbrick's. Walked to Rotherwas and examined House & addition; old church. Slept at Farmers.

> March 1st Walk to Bridge Sollers, Byford, Ploughfield, Handley Cross or Top up Point. Dinner at Farmers with Scarisbrick.

'Much yet Remains to be Done'

> 2nd To Weobley. Dined there, to Sarnesfield Court. Church damp.
>
> 3rd Walk to The Homme. At 7o/c to Capt Peploes—Lady Lift, Foxley Credon Hill, Sugis Ferry. Ruckwell common, &c.
>
> Fri 4th To Callow—the Camp. Aconbury. D[ined] at Scarisbricks. Home at 7o/c.

Returning home he found Fr Blount still unwell. As he had predicted, the diary entries became less detailed, noting the times of weekday Mass (8:30 a.m. or 7:40 a.m.), preparing for Lent with sermons on temptation and fasting, and the ever present 'question of the tower'.

The continuation of the building work was by no means guaranteed. Having erected a more than adequate church for worship there was no functional need for a tower and spire. Although highly symbolic in ecclesiastical terms, integral to the architectural design, and a sign of status in society, these parts could be judged an aesthetic ornament that could wait for more prosperous times. The correspondence between Fr Cotham and Robert Biddulph Phillips shows the argument clearly. Phillips had subscribed £10 in November 1853, at that time wanting to remain anonymous in the subscription listings. He took a close interest in the Cheltenham project which ran parallel to his own efforts at Longworth, Herefordshire. In due course he became insistent that St Gregory's should be finished according to Charles Hansom's original plans and since he had developed a warm personal relationship with Cotham, and occasionally visited Cheltenham, he felt able to correspond frankly.

Writing in late September 1859 Phillips alludes to an illness Cotham had suffered during the summer, although his journal for the first part of the year reveals no sign of ill health. Yet even illness could not separate Cotham from his duty towards the projected steeple.

Longworth, Hereford 28 September 1859

Mr dear Fr Cotham

I rejoice exceedingly to hear of your recovery for I was really quite uneasy about you and we cannot at any rate afford to let you climb to heaven <u>at least</u> till you have your steeple to ascend by (tho I hope you may live many years when finished) or I fear no one who came after you wd be equally zealous to raise it and it might not be done at all.

Thank you very much for the particulars of the biddings for the contract which interested me much. Mr Acock does not seem to be so careful in his calculations but some of the others shew that they have calculated very cleverly being almost as you may say <u>neck & neck</u>.

At about the same time as Phillips' insistent letter arrived Fr Cotham received one from James Quin, school master in Hobart. He may have winced as he read 'the Launceston church is falling due to the foundation having sunk … Richmond church has been rebuilt' and groaned as Quin blithely continued 'I have seen an account of your splendid Church in Cheltenham. I suppose it is finished by this time and I hope out of debt'.[7]

In September four tenders were received for the next phase of building. The totals of the four tenders were variously arrived at as the four elements—church, tower, spire, and junction—were given different weighting by each builder. John Acock quoted the highest figure for the spire and the lowest for the tower.[8] On this occasion his was not the cheapest option overall but it was successful, no doubt on the strength of his previous involvement with the committee, although he had been adjudicated a bankrupt at Bristol Bankruptcy Court in June 1859 and a hearing on 31 August was adjourned awaiting further information. There is no suggestion on this occasion that his financial difficulties were connected with St Gregory's but he had various projects running concurrently and his cash flow was precariously balanced. Acock was contracted for the work on 17 October and began immediately by demolishing Fr Birdsall's old chapel. A month after the opening of the church in 1857 the chapel had been put up for

'Much yet Remains to be Done' 399

auction and bought by Mr Cape for £125, with the intention of selling the building materials in lots, but it is not known if he waited for two years before getting his hands on his acquisition.[9] However, the spoil was useful elsewhere:

> The Entente Cordiale. Yesterday men were busily employed carting the earth excavated from the site of the new tower of the Catholic Church to make good the ground in front of its Protestant rival in Clarence Street.[10]

The rival—a mere two hundred yards away—was a temporary iron and wood structure erected to house the congregation of nearby medieval St Mary's Parish Church which had been closed due to its insanitary state. When the flooring had been removed the vaults below were found to be open to the church above, 'so that the effluvia arising from the dead could not but contaminate the air breathed by the living'.[11]

Six weeks after the demolition of the old chapel the foundation stone of the tower was laid on 30 November, without ceremony and attended by 'only a few parties immediately interested in the erection'.[12] Within a week, however, the stone work had already risen four feet above the ground, so speed was obviously valued above another public display, unless there was simply nobody willing to take on the role. Biddulph Phillips looked ahead to the event in his letter of 28 September 1859:

> I certainly intend DV to come to the laying of the stone but I conclude it was a <u>slip of your pen</u> when you talked of my coming to "lay the stone <u>for us</u>" as if <u>I</u> was designated to officiate. Now once for all pray give up that notion which you once hinted before. First—because I am by no means of sufficient position to set aside so real a benefactor as you have on the spot Mr Copeland (and if I had been ever so well I wd not have consented to do so) but secondly my health and unfortunate deafness entirely incapacitate me from occupying any public or prominent position so pray consider this point as <u>settled</u>. No time for more as the post

is starting but remember me kindly to Mrs Monington and Mr Blount. Fr Rollings also sends his kind remembrances.

Enclosed with this letter was a draft appeal circular. Despite their friendship, Phillips' dictation of the wording for yet another fund raising appeal was likely to grate with Cotham who had no trouble writing his own material, and it is very unlikely that his comprehensive draft was used verbatim. Nevertheless, Phillips' anxiety that the church would remain uncompleted, and the pain he felt about an unfinished architectural design, were not unreasonable; there were many examples around the country during this period of truncated projects:

> The Sum of £1500 having been promised by certain parties who are anxious for the completion of this church on condition that the Tower and Spire be completed without further delay and not contracted for separately so as to leave it partially finished only (one of the Gentlemen [Phillips] having stipulated that the £500 which he has offered shall not be paid until its entire completion) the Promoters for the Erection of a new and suitable church for the Catholics of Cheltenham feel persuaded that they shall stand excused before the Congregation in appealing again so soon to their generosity to enable them to bring to a conclusion a good work so zealously begun and so liberally promoted by them which now even only partially completed so far exceeds in beauty and convenience anything which their most sanguine expectations would have previously instilled them to expect.

Phillips does not entirely forget that he is not actually a member of the Cheltenham congregation and allows for the inclusion of somebody else's name, but he is confident of their response to his scheme:

> As the present opportunity is one which if neglected <u>may never again occur</u> however reluctant to make a fresh appeal (the Mbr of the C. mission [written in faint pencil]) feels that he shd be accused of neglecting an obvious duty

'*Much yet Remains to be Done*'

> towards them were he to omit to lay before them an offer so advantageous to their interests, as in all probability, should the noble design (which in all probability if completed would make the Ch. of S. Gregory like the city 'seated on a mountain' the most prominent object on all sides of the approaches in the distant view of their beautiful Town) be now indefinitely postponed, they will have the mortification of reflecting that not only may the present generation pass away and witness their church incomplete but as similar difficulties may occur with those who come after them, the consequence of a lack of energy and want of a little additional self-sacrifice on their parts at the present moment may be, that it may be <u>never completed at all</u>.
>
> As it is the opinion of the Architect that in a work of this magnitude it will take at least 2 years to bring the work to a satisfactory conclusion the subscribers to the undertaking may spread over that period the amount promised towards the work there being sufficient money guaranteed from the above mentioned subscriber to carry on the work for the first 12 months.

Phillips went on to set out in detail how the instalments of the new subscriptions should be paid, to realise as much capital as possible before early spring of 1860.

The keystone for the west porch arch was fixed by Acock on 1 March 1860 and 'after the ceremony had taken place the workmen were supplied with beer to drink success to the undertaking' under the foremanship of Thomas Ford.[13] Work was reported to be progressing steadily in May under the 'unremitting attention of [Cheltenham's] talented townsman Mr Acock',[14] but Biddulph Phillips was still agitated in June about the possibility of incompletion and proposed another inducement to subscribers: the foregoing of the yearly interest on his loan. He admitted the amount was almost inconsequential but he hoped his enthusiasm might count for something. The withholding of his name was a false modesty: Phillips was a member of the Ecclesiological and Oxford Architectural Societies and at the time of writing to Cotham he was engaged in restoring the pre-reformation chapel on his Longworth estate and returning it to public worship, a scheme in which he took a knowledgeable, practical, (and perhaps interfering) interest:

> [19 June 1860] As you know of old, nothing would grieve me so much as to learn that the work had stopped; and tho' what I am going to propose will go very little towards preventing that catastrophe yet it may give a <u>fillip</u> to your meeting if you announce that 'a gentleman' (I must positively not allow you to let my name transpire) who is interested in its continuation has promised you £20 on condition that the work proceeds without interruption to the end of the 2nd contract but that he does not promise it if it is now stopped. Comprenez vous? ...

> My windows are finished and this morning I am informed by Hardman that the case is sent off so I hope to see them up before I go [to Caen]. I shall be much disappointed if they do not turn out well after all my advice and precautions. I am determined to employ E. Pugin to finish the Presbytery at Old Longworth. He was delighted with such a genuine specimen and I hope will take pains to finish it in good character.

According to Phillips, Hansom had estimated that the tower and spire would take at least two years to complete. In the event more than twice as long was needed and elements described in detail in March 1860 were not realised. The fitting of a 'handsome clock' was delayed by nearly eighty years and the elaborate tracery of the West window has never been filled by stained glass. Work on the tower was slow, despite novel approaches:

> Every appliance of art for carrying on the work with rapidity is rendered available, even the very stones being raised in wheelbarrows to the place where they are required, to save the trouble of unloading and of carrying the stone up ladders.[15]

'Much yet Remains to be Done'

There was a series of strikes during the summer for higher wages and shorter hours from the stonemasons, and Acock had competing claims for his attention from St Mark's Church where he had successfully tendered for the contract in June 1860 and was ready to lay the foundation stone only one month later.[16] The following summer there was another 'lengthened suspension in building operations' until Acock set the masons to work again in September[17] and completed the first part of the contract at the end of the year.

In January 1862 Cotham drew up a summary of the building accounts to date in which he separated out his personal contributions to show how the books had been balanced.

Total Expenditure on Church	8,207.3.10
Total Expenditure to 2nd Contract Tower inclusive	2,149.00
	10,176.3.10

General Subscriptions to Church not including Revd J Cotham's £810	5,400.10.0½
General Subscriptions to Tower not including Rev J C's £110	954.10.0½

R B Phillips Esq to Tower	500
James Boodle Esq interest during life	300
Borrowed from Mrs Brennan 4pcent	500
Borrowed from Mrs Holmes, Keenan &c	110
Probable good debts	234
Paid by Rev J Cotham personally	2,177.13.9½
	10,176.3.10

Required to complete the Spire £1300

Small contributions had continued to trickle in ('Mrs Kellanan 10/- for tower' and 'the widow Sullivan 6d for spire') but the year ahead proved to be a difficult one, personally, for pastor and builder. After almost ten years of unremitting fund raising and building the end of Fr Cotham's labours was nowhere in sight and his builder, John Acock was an uncertain businessman.[18] On 28 June the *Chelten-*

ham Mercury reported that work on erecting the spire of St Gregory's church would speedily commence, while the following week it reported on Acock's appearance in the Bristol Bankruptcy Court. Acock claimed that 'within the last 12 months he had business to the extent of £8000. Part of it was on St Gregory's Church Cheltenham. He finished his contract on that building about six months ago … His deficiency [was] now £2140' and there was little or no estate to call on. After a three week adjournment Acock was back in court. His solicitor explained that

> the bankrupt had entered into building speculations beyond his means. During the time the contracts were in progress, however, there had been several strikes, and the bankrupt was not the only person who had been brought there solely owing to the rise in wages, whereby the estimates he formed on entering into the contracts turned out to be entirely fallacious. There was no fraud imputed to him. His Honour agreed and allowed Acock to pass his last examination and take his order of discharge from bankruptcy.[19]

On a visit to Cheltenham, the Provincial, Fr Heptonstall, acknowledged the strain on Cotham and wrote to Dr Clifford in Clifton informing him of a proposed leave of absence:

> 9 October 1862
>
> My dear Lord
>
> Father Cotham, who has had a good share of harassing work with building the Church Tower at Cheltenham, wishes to retire for a time to one of our Houses for <u>spiritual repose</u>. I am willing to acquiesce to his desire & have thought of placing Fr Cuthbert Murphy at Cheltenham to assist Father Scarisbrick during Fr Cotham's absence which may be for a couple of months or longer.

As Fr Cuthbert was coming directly from Douai and had not previously served on the mission he needed 'faculties' from the

'*Much yet Remains to be Done*' 405

Bishop to hear confessions in the diocese, despite having experience as a confessor at the College.

The 'spiritual repose' seems to have been a time of reflection and consultation about whether his future lay in Cheltenham. Meanwhile, at St Michael's, Belmont Fr Anselm Cockshoot was in a similar state of exhaustion. As early as 1859 he had told Fr Prest that 'he was worn out with a year and a half of continued stretch of mind on one subject and was longing for a rest' although all he received at that time was a change of occupation by becoming Procurator for Prior Sweeney.[20] Prest, himself, retired at the end of the year to Ampleforth; his health continued to decline and he died in 1860, not yet sixty. In 1862 Cockshoot was released from his duties by the new Prior, Bede Vaughan, as much for the sake of community harmony as for his own benefit, and his own future was under discussion. He wrote to Fr Provincial Heptonstall:

> St Michael's, Sep. 23 1862
>
> My dear Fr Prov.
>
> I thought Fr Cotham was disengaged, as I understood he was leaving Cheltenham; and moreover that he probably would come into the arrangements ~~for~~ proposed for Abergavenny. With him there would be no difficulty on the score of a maintenance. I expect you at St Michael's.
>
> My best regards to Lady Abbess & Community [Stanbrook], likewise to Fr Short. The Prior, Fr Alphonsus [Morrall, novice master, at Belmont] &c are very anxious for a Missionary Priory at Abergavenny.
>
> Believe me, yrs very sincerely,
>
> Fr A. Cockshoot[21]

Fr Cockshoot had apparently considered asking for a move to Abergavenny, changing his mind with a preference for Cheltenham. The re-establishment of the important mission at Abergavenny had been a project of Bishop Brown's since at least 1856, although sufficient Benedictine manpower to staff it was a constant anxiety.

406   *The Indomitable Mr Cotham*

There is an entry in Cotham's journal on 18 February 1858 that Rt Revd Dr Brown called in the afternoon when the subject may have been appointments for Abergavenny. Fr Provincial Heptonstall assured Bishop Brown that 'the interests of your Diocese and of the Congregation ought never to clash' but he was limited in what he could offer since 'our own resources in the South Province are so miserably slender, and if I were to mention the heavy sums that have been spent on establishing or supporting certain missions you would not be surprised at this state of things'.[22]

If Cotham was indeed coming to the end of his tether and tenure at Cheltenham Fr Cockshoot might be the person to carry forward the initiative. He spent a few months at Cheltenham but the opportunity to replace Fr Cotham, if that was his hope, did not arise. Fr Murphy's visit was not extended and nothing more was said about leaving Cheltenham. While Cotham put in another ten years on St Gregory's church and mission building, Anselm Cockshoot moved onto another heavy posting. He was appointed chaplain to Robert Biddulph Phillips at Longworth but it was not a sinecure. He was appointed Vicar General by Bishop Brown, and continued his involvement with the House Council at Belmont. After Biddulph Phillips died in 1864 Fr Cockshoot became chaplain to the nuns at Bartestree; they benefited hugely from his building, administrative, and pastoral skills, while he worked in partnership once again with Edward Welby Pugin.[23]

Notes

[1]   *Cheltenham Examiner*, 28 December 1864, p. 4.
[2]   Mrs Charlotte Short was able to practise her new faith until her death in the Union Workhouse in March 1862, aged 99. In the same month Fr Cotham buried Bartholomew Connoly of Rutland Street who died aged 103.
[3]   *Cheltenham Examiner*, 10 January 1866, p. 4, obituary. The obituary mentions up to forty Wills.
[4]   Riddell rented rooms at No 10 from October 1857 to October 1858.
[5]   CDA, Cheltenham Box, Parish Visitation Report, 1858–59.

'Much yet Remains to be Done'
407

[6] John Middleton (1820–1885) came to Cheltenham in early 1859. In 1860 he submitted plans for St Mark's Church, which John Acock tendered for at a cost of £2,880. Work began in June 1860 and by the end of 1866 it was completed, with tower, spire, and boundary walls, together with the neighbouring parsonage, Hillfield. The building work seems to have gone forward without undue delays. See B. E. Torode, *John Middleton: Victorian, Provincial Architect* (Zagreb: Accent, 2008), Chapter V.

[7] James Michael Quin to Cotham, 4 April 1859.

[8] The four quotes received were from G. Harrison, Stroud, for £3,085: H. Williams, Bristol, £3,113; J. Acock, Cheltenham, £3,400; and J. Darby, Cheltenham, £3,694.

[9] *Cheltenham Mercury*, 27 June 1857, p. 1–2.

[10] J. Goding, *Norman's History of Cheltenham* (London: Longman, Green, Longman, Roberts and Green, 1863), p. 630, quoting the *Cheltenham Examiner*, 19 October 1859.

[11] *Ibid.*, p. 628.

[12] *Cheltenham Examiner*, 7 December 1859, p. 4.

[13] *Cheltenham Mercury*, 3 March 1860, p. 4.

[14] *Ibid.*, 26 May 1860, p. 4.

[15] *Ibid.*, 10 March 1860. p. 4.

[16] *Cheltenham Examiner*, 20 June, p. 4, and 18 July 1860, p. 4.

[17] *Ibid.*, 14 September 1861, p. 4.

[18] There is a tradition that Fr Cotham made a little hideaway for himself in the tower and when unwanted visitors came looking for him would call down, 'He's not here!'

[19] *Cheltenham Mercury*, 5 July 1862, p. 2, and 26 July 1862, p. 3.

[20] http://www.plantata.org.uk/people.php, obituary material for Anselm Cockshoot.

[21] AAA RB-244–110; Cockshoot to Heptonstall, 23 September 1862.

[22] DA IV.B.1.1; Heptonstall to Brown, 16, and 22 September 1860.

[23] B. Whelan OSB, *The Annals of the English Congregation of the Black Monks of St Benedict (1850–1900)*, private publication, 1942 2nd edition, reissued 1971, Vol. 1, p. 81.

34 'I HOPE YOU WILL WITHSTAND THEIR RASCALITY'

SUBSCRIBERS TO THE church funds who lent money, such as Mrs Brennan and Mrs Keenan, were generally uncomplicatedly open handed in their generosity, but James Boodle took a disproportionate amount of time in arranging his gifts. In 1863 he advanced £500 towards the tower fund, in three instalments, in addition to £300 advanced in 1861. The agreement was that he should be paid four per cent interest on the money during his lifetime at quarterly intervals and at his death the interest would cease and the principal sum would belong to the church absolutely. With each fresh instalment a contract was drawn up and signed by Fr Cotham and Fr Heptonstall, the Provincial. Copies of the agreements are among Cotham's papers but a note added by Heptonstall to the copy of January 1864 throws light on the caution needed in dealing with a rather volatile Mr Boodle:

> Father Cotham told Fr Hep. that the original of the written copy was to be kept in the hands of Mr Williams Snr Librarian and not in the hand of Mr Boodle to prevent difficulties arising. At this period £300 of the above sum of £800 have [sic] been spent on the Tower. With the remaining £500, and the £500 promised by Mr Copeland, it is intended to complete the Spire.

Unfortunately it was not only the getting of money that caused anxiety in 1864. John Acock again fell on hard times and was unable to complete his contract. As a result Fr Cotham became embroiled with disputes on two fronts between rival builders which added considerably to expenditure of time, effort, and money. However, to begin with it seemed the transfer of contractors to complete the spire would be straightforward. Written on

410   *The Indomitable Mr Cotham*

a separate small piece of paper in Cotham's hand is the minute
on what was decided:

> At a meeting held on Wednesday the 4th May [1864]—G
> F Copeland, G A Williams, Revd J Cotham and Charles
> Hansom Esq being present it was resolved that Mr
> Hansom should apply to 4 Builders likely to contract for
> the spire—and that the work should be proceeded with
> and finished so far as to remove the outward scaffolding.

The completion of the spire was to be covered by the third and
fourth contracts. However Hansom had considerable difficulty
finding a builder to take on the project. George Harrison of Kings
Stanton, having been turned down for the first contract, declined
to tender again while Wall and Hook of Stroud were 'so full of
work' they could not oblige. Billings and Son of Cheltenham
replied to Hansom that although they found his calculations for
materials fairly correct, he was greatly deficient in his costings
for scaffolding and hoisting; unsurprisingly, their tender for
£1,200 was not accepted. Bladwell and Ambron were engaged
with contracts for the militia stores in Bath and renovations to
Bath Abbey and so were unable to take work out of their home
city. Messrs Warburton of Manchester answered Hansom's
advertisement in the *Builder* magazine: he considered their
tender high but believed 'they are men who can be depended on'.

Two of the firms putting in a tender—Darby of Cheltenham
(£1,140), and Jones and Sons of Gloucester (£1,100)—made a point
of saying they would be able to complete the fourth tender at a
lesser price if they were awarded both tenders together. For this
reason, and because they were local, Hansom, giving his opinion
to the committee in June, favoured awarding the contracts to one
of these firms, without reference to Samuel and Henry Warburton
of Manchester. Their tender was for £1,100 providing the stone
and scaffolding already on the site became their property for use
in the work. The deadline for completing the third contract was
31 December 1864. Hansom, too, was urging haste:

'I Hope You Will Withstand Their Rascality' 411

> As to the time for commencing, we cannot have a better than the present; if no more time is lost the work may easily be done before Winter weather sets in, or if not, the completion of the four pinnacles wd be all that need stand over till Spring, the <u>spire</u> itself would be completed in good time.

Hansom wrote his letter from Clifton on 18 June, and one of the reasons for urging haste was the heat wave the country was enjoying that summer. For weeks at a time the temperature averaged 80°F deterring people from leaving the 'umbrageous avenues' of Cheltenham to risk being scorched on the exposed beaches of the increasingly favoured seaside resorts.[1]

Despite Hansom's clear preferences the contract was awarded to the Warburton brothers. Although they began work promptly it was not satisfactory. After a personal meeting with the brothers, on 18 August Hansom wrote from Slatter's Railway Hotel in Liverpool to assure Cotham that they intended to follow the architect's instructions and 'to rectify what is complained of— they were much pained to hear that the work so far has not been done as it should be'. The Warburtons suggested the appointment of a Clerk of Works to supervise the bonding of the courses as 'their man', responsible for setting the stone, was the best worker they had and could be trusted to do exactly as he was instructed by the architect. Within four days Alfred Bond was engaged as Clerk of Works with a salary of forty shillings per week.

The progress of the spire was a source of interest to spectators and the local press. It was built without scaffolding until the final forty feet, the building materials being drawn up from the inside to the workmen who worked internally, until the circumference became too small for workmen to work inside it or on the top. At that point—being about eight feet across—iron 'needles' were run through the spire, the ends projecting from small windows to form a foundation for scaffolding from which the workmen could complete the building from the outside. From that stage the spire was built up 'solid' with materials drawn up from the outside. On completion each piece of scaffolding would be drawn back through the windows and lowered to the ground from the inside. By October 1864

> the operations have now assumed a very ticklish appearance; and the position of the workmen appears to a mere looker-on from below one of considerable danger [but] the men are so used to the work as to feel almost as safe in their elevated position as though they were standing on terra firma.[2]

Finally the outside of the spire and tower would be scraped and 'cleaned down' from the top to the bottom to produce an even colouring.

Only one accident was reported during the building work 'though happily unattended with any serious result'.[3] One day in late November 1864 as the light was fading in the afternoon five men were being lowered from the top of the spire by means of a rope attached to a winding drum at the base. When the man on the ground let go the handle while the five were still some twenty feet above the ground the group fell in a heap; only the man at the bottom who cushioned the blow for the others sustained a minor wrist injury himself. 'Numerous reports' of more serious consequences circulated through the town but in fact the incident was notable only for being a rare occurrence during the construction works.

The contract was completed with no days to spare. James Cowley, the general painter, decorator, and handyman for Fr Cotham at this time, painted and gilded two weathercocks and an iron cross, and on 27 December 1864 Charles Hansom with his two senior assistants fixed one of the weathercocks to the wrought iron Greek cross on top of the spire.

The achievement was celebrated in a homely fashion. Not wanting to anticipate success, Fr Cotham went shopping on 27 December; from James Hawarden he bought tea and lump sugar, tobacco and pipes, ginger beer and lemonade. From Garrisons he hired cutlery and china for three dozen people. The following day he bought three dozen loaves of bread, eighteen pounds of

'I Hope You Will Withstand Their Rascality' 413

fruit cake and two tins of dripping cake from Bloodworth the baker. The workmen were given a celebration supper to end the year's work.

The spire of St Gregory's was recognised as an outstanding feature of the church at the time of its construction. It reached some forty feet higher than the nearby St Mary's Parish Church, and four out of the five Anglican churches designed by John Middleton for Cheltenham in the same period were sadly not completed with the towers and spires planned for them. Charles Hansom's design was for a square tower of about eighty feet, a smaller square tower of twenty feet, surmounted by an octagon spire of one hundred and five feet, to be capped by an iron cross and weathercock reaching to a total of two hundred and twelve feet. There were four turrets with pinnacles at the corners of the lower tower, all ornamented. Many subscribers made donations to the cost of the spire although in the 1877 church guidebook payment for the full cost was attributed to George Copeland who donated £1,000 for the purpose. Several Protestants in the town, unable to support the building of the church itself, expressed a willingness to contribute to an illuminated clock on the western face of the tower considering it to be a great convenience for members of the public using the railway station opposite.[4]

With the structure of the spire completed, Richard Lockwood Boulton, based in Worcester at this point, was contracted in March 1865 for the carving and sculptures on the exterior, namely pinnacles and turrets, niches on the parapet, and gables, buttresses, and cornicing on the tower. Three figures had been agreed for statues on the parapet: St Gregory the Great, Pope; St George, Martyr; and St Maurus, Abbot. The cost of the whole works amounted to £85 17s. With further additions of belfry windows, clock face, finial and crockets around the tower door and the fourth statue, of St Augustine of Canterbury, the work completed in the autumn brought the sum to £143, paid in full by November. The statue of St Maurus, probably intended as a tribute to Fr Roger Maurus Cooper who had been so helpful in the transfer of property

414 *The Indomitable Mr Cotham*

from the mission of Chipping Sodbury, was replaced by a statue of St Ambrose of Milan. The reference is obvious but there is no record of who influenced the exchange; in the accounts Fr Cooper donated £100 to the tower fund and £10 for a tower statue, but the identity of the statue is not mentioned.

While outwardly work was progressing satisfactorily, the year 1865 saw a long-drawn out argument between the Building Committee and Warburtons from May to November. Warburtons maintained that the original contract allowed them possession, not merely usage, of any scaffolding already on the site of the tower when they began work. After work ended they claimed the committee was wrongfully detaining the scaffolding (which was, of course, still needed for the carving and sculptures on the spire) and that it was in poorer condition than they had found it. The contract with Warburtons ended in March when their tender for cleaning down the masonry (the fourth contract) was not accepted. In May the builders 'received without prejudice' £114 for work they had been contracted to do; writing to Cobbett and Wheeler, Warburtons' solicitors in Manchester, as a friend of Fr Cotham and not in a professional capacity, James Boodle gave his opinion that Fr Cotham was not obliged to pay this demand but as he was 'anxious to avoid legal proceedings' he was doing so without quibble. As to the dispute about the ownership of the scaffolding used at St Gregory's, Fr Cotham was 'prepared to await the result of a trial.' The letter written two days later by Charles Hansom to Fr Cotham was less temperate:

> Warburtons' conduct is most scandalous and I do not think I ever knew such a gross case before. Of course you must determine whether or not you will go to Law with them—if it comes to a trial it will be sure to be referred— and then you may be saddled with an expensive reference—though I think we should beat them, still there is a chance of losing. I hope you will consult the Committee and then determine to withstand their rascality.

'I Hope You Will Withstand Their Rascality' 415

Fr Cotham did decide to withstand them, up to a point. The firm of T. A. and E. Grundy were engaged as solicitors for the committee in Manchester, instructed by T. and E. Griffiths in Cheltenham acting for St Gregory's. On 5 August Grundy met with Cobbett and Wheeler, the plaintiffs' attorneys, to offer £25 damages. Although they initially said their clients would not settle for less than £50 a compromise was reached and £37 10s. was agreed. However, the second part of the complaint was unresolved and a Memorandum was drawn up agreeing to independent arbitration. The County Surveyor of Worcester, Henry Rowe, was to examine the scaffolding and determine the damage, if any, done to it and the amount of compensation. If the arbitrator found in Warburtons' favour the defendants were to despatch the scaffolding by rail to the plaintiffs and pay all legal costs, taxes, and arbitration fees.

The inspection took place ten weeks later on 18 October. Henry Rowe visited the site of St Gregory's tower and awarded £20 15s. to Warburtons for damage to the scaffolding. This was less than the £25 which they had refused as an informal settlement but they had the satisfaction of claiming costs amounting to £17 19s. 6d. for Samuel Warburton's train, cab, and hotel expenses covering two days' attendance in Cheltenham, plus his own surveyor's costs for accompanying him. Mr Griffiths managed to deduct three guineas from the costs, allowing the Manchester surveyor only one day's fees.

Between August 30 and November 1 St Gregory's Building Committee, in the persons of Fr Cotham and James Hawarden, paid £101 4s. 4d. compensation, and legal and arbitration costs in respect of the spire and scaffolding to three firms of solicitors: Messrs Grundy, Messrs Cobbett and Wheeler, and Messrs Griffiths. The Cheltenham firm, Griffiths, clearly took a personal interest in the case as a sympathetic letter sent to James Boodle on 3 November shows:

> We believe we may now report this unfortunate business concluded. In doing so, allow us to say that we regret the expense which has been entailed on the building commit-

> tee in the conscientious discharge of a public duty, and having experienced from yourself on past occasions acts which it gives us pleasure to remember we shall be happy not to make any professional charge for such services as we may have provided, beyond the repayment of our actual expenses. These amount to £9.5.10 as you will observe from the enclosed statement which we beg to forward.

Although the year closed with Warburtons reunited with the scaffolding, Fr Cotham was still entangled in arguments with John Acock which had been running in tandem with the Warburtons' negotiations. On this occasion the haggling over costs was carried out without the benefit of solicitors and ultimately given to Charles Hansom to adjudicate, as Acock's contract stipulated (as, indeed, had the Warburtons'). When Warburtons estimated the cost of cleaning down the masonry of the tower at £133 in March 1865 Hansom declined their tender 'being in my opinion much above the value of the work'. After the flurry of correspondence which opened legal proceedings with Warburtons at the end of May, Acock agreed with Fr Cotham on 2 June to complete the work, together with new slates on the louvered belfry window for a round figure of £50 which Cotham made clear must not be exceeded. A week later, on 10 June, Acock asked that money be advanced to him each Saturday for materials and labour until he had finished but only two days later he told Fr Cotham 'that the work could not be done for the sum he had stated on 2 inst. and that he thought it might be double the amount'.

In the light of Acock's reputation for giving 'entirely fallacious', though not malicious, estimates Cotham prudently called a halt to the work, 'as he had not the means to go beyond £62.10/-, the total amount placed at his disposal for this part of the work'. A shaky compromise was reached between the two men: work would continue without a fixed amount being agreed. When it stopped on 2 September Acock had received, in advance payments, £117; Acock applied to Cotham for more but was declined having been already overpaid in Cotham's opinion. Instead they

'*I Hope You Will Withstand Their Rascality*'

agreed to go to Hansom for arbitration. In the meantime, 'the sum of £9 was however had by Mr Acock as a loan'. In this sequence of events recorded dispassionately by Charles Hansom as part of his adjudication there is a hint of Fr Cotham's forbearance and sympathy towards a builder who knew his trade, had been with him since the beginning of work on the new church, but was out of his depth in money matters, something which could not be said of Cotham who had learnt financial acumen alongside his pastoral undertakings.

Poor Acock was either tactless or in very straitened circumstances (again) as he could not resist sending in a bill on 7 December for £168 15s. 11d. in which, Hansom caustically noted, 'he again charges £22.8/6d for profit making'. Although the affair with Warburtons had been concluded a month before the consequences still hung infuriatingly over the building work since 'in addition to the sum of £126 paid to Mr Acock, Mr Cotham has to pay to Mr Dutton for the hire of scaffolding for Mr Acock's use, the sum of £1.10/- making in all £127.10/-'.

Hansom met with Fr Cotham and Mr Acock on the afternoon of 4 January 1866 and heard their respective accounts of events. After consideration he submitted his written adjudication on 8 January. He considered £110 was 'amply sufficient' to pay Acock's costs, to which was added £20 for sundry other jobs including, ironically, 'taking down Messrs Warburtons' scaffolding and hauling to Station'. That Acock was prepared to do even this distasteful task suggests remaining goodwill as well as financial hardship. At the end of the lengthy recital Hansom set out the relevant sums: £130 awarded; £127 10s. already paid; £2 10s. owing to Mr Acock. Hansom signed his name without further comment.

John Acock apparently brooded on this outcome and decided to fight for redress in the case of *John Acock v The Rev Father Cottam* [*sic*] brought at Bristol Crown Court in October 1867. Acock felt he was still owed £39 15s. 1d. for 'extra' work unconnected with the contract. A newspaper report briefly summed up the circumstances of the case 'which were of a very complicated character' following the details given in Hansom's adjudication paper. The crux of the matter in this hearing was whether Hansom's decision was binding in all matters connected with the contracts, including 'extras' such as carting the scaffolding to the station. In this the judge found in favour of Fr Cotham with the caveat that 'he had not gone into the merits of the case but had merely considered the question of the award'. Mr Chesshyre on behalf of Acock gave notice of a new trial so the execution of costs was suspended.[5] It was still not a definitive close to the matter but as there is no further mention of the dispute perhaps it was allowed to die away with neither side being recompensed to their own satisfaction. However, relations with most contractors remained cordial and their reputations were enhanced by the association with St Gregory's.

Notes

[1]   *Cheltenham Looker-On*, 13 August 1864, p. 528.
[2]   *Cheltenham Examiner*, 12 October 1864, p. 4.
[3]   *Cheltenham Chronicle*, 6 December 1864, p.5.
[4]   The three clock faces were not, in fact, installed until 1937, using a bequest from Gilbert Dutson Boulton, son of R. L. Boulton. See *Gloucestershire Echo*, 21 August 1937, p. 3.
[5]   *Cheltenham Examiner*, 30 October 1867, p. 2.

35 CELEBRATING THE DIVINE SERVICE

A T TIMES, PERHAPS for most of the time during the second half of the nineteenth century, St Gregory's sounded like and looked like a building site, one of many in Cheltenham. The contemporary newspapers rightly described its outward appearance as impressive and ambitious. The interior was relatively austere until the end of the century—the stained glass, abundant carving, and ornate metalwork were added by Fr Wilkinson year by year—and temporary walls blocked the truncated west end of the church. Nevertheless, the solemn opening of the church on 26 May 1857 was celebrated with dignity and pomp. The *Cheltenham Looker-On*, its focus on high and fashionable society events, admitted 'the scene was altogether such an one as could not fail of inspiring even in the most careless mind a reverential feeling, while to the artistic eye it presented a tableau vivant, such as only such a ceremonial could suggest'.[1]

The music was considered particularly good: Haydn's *Imperial Mass* No. 3, sung by the choir of the Catholic chapel in Bath, with 'superior vocalists'[2] (unfortunately not prominently positioned) and admirably accompanied by the 'clear, sonorous tones swelling and vibrating through the building'[3] of the organ. The instrument had been rebuilt and improved in sound and appearance by Henry Williams of Cheltenham, under specific instructions from George Copeland who paid more than half of the £145 cost. Principal musicians were noticed—Miss Lucy Escott, Miss Dyer, Mr Haigh, Mr Durand of the National Opera, Mr Samuel Moorat, leader of the choir, and Mr Howarth, organist— and the importance of their participation was unquestionable: 'the service of the Mass was most solemn, its effect deriving considerable enhancement from the presence of the ladies and gentlemen just enumerated'.[4] The use of candles, incense and constant 'devotional attitudes and genuflections' completed the spectacle of the service, and everybody would have been disappointed if it had been a less sensual work of art.

Cardinal Wiseman avoided controversy in his sermon but the nature of the opening service was itself a proclamation of Catholic confidence, not only in its novelty—that it was happening at all—but by its parity with the Established Church and profane ceremonial. The choice of music is probably the most anachronistic element from today's standpoint. Having lost the continuity of a widely heard musical tradition since the Reformation and Puritan revolution—and not yet ready to explore the heritage of plainchant or polyphony—the Catholic Church had to fall back on the concert repertoire which their singers and organists knew. In a town such as Cheltenham anything else would have consigned the New Church to social obscurity. Among the congregation were accomplished performers and music teachers, some like Pio Ciancettini dating back to the 1830s, and others such as the Tiesset brothers Charles and Eugene almost ready to begin their professional training in Leipzig.

Nevertheless there was competition among the various churches to recruit and retain accomplished singers so the reputation for good music was never a settled matter. Benjamin Joesbury, who performed so well for the confirmations in 1859 before handing in his notice, used Cheltenham as a stepping stone in his career. He came from Birmingham where his father and grandfather were small-scale metal workers who spent a lifetime making bridles, bits, and spoons. Benjamin, however, was sent to the Brussels Conservatoire to study under C. Duciemien. After an appointment at the Oratory Church in Birmingham he came to Cheltenham in 1857 at the age of 24 to advertise his services as a Professor of Music. By the following year he was calling on his younger sisters Ann and Louisa to support his concert tours as soloists. In April 1858 he produced a Grand Evening Concert at the Assembly Rooms in Cheltenham with an eclectic repertoire

Celebrating the Divine Service 421

which included the premiere of his own oratorio *Judith*, excerpts from Mendelssohn's *Elijah*, and the inevitable selection of secular music. Cheltenham audiences were harder to please than those of the Mechanical Institute in Hobart. The *Cheltenham Looker-On* tried to be even-handed in its criticism; the 'musically educated' were challenged by the demands of the works but the evening was not carried off with the powerfulness expected of *Judith*:

> The materials at his command were altogether inadequate ... there was a levity exhibited by the chorus and occasionally by the principal voices which seriously impaired the seriousness of the music; the whole of which was performed by Mr Joesbury on the piano, in a very beautiful and effective manner ... achieving all that could be achieved by a single instrument for compositions which never can have full justice done them in the absence of an orchestra of 'trained' musicians.[5]

Joesbury's premiere had 'considerable promise' but he had overextended himself; the critic from the *Looker-On* did not tarry for the third act of the concert, the secular selection, which could be heard somewhere in the town on most evenings of the week.

St Gregory's was not unusual in celebrating High Mass in the context of 'a holy concert'. 'Catholic Relief and Emancipation led to the emergence of choirs, independent not just of the congregation but, to some extent, of the clergy as well.'[6] Pope Benedict XIV, in the encyclical *Annus Qui* (1749) permitted the use of tuba, lyres, lutes, and violins 'provided they serve to strengthen and support the voices'.[7] Having opened the way to musical accompaniment the ban on percussion, flutes, horns, trumpets, harps, and guitars and all such theatrical instruments was hardly enforceable. After centuries of Low Masses for the majority of Catholics or High Masses where only trained choirs and soloists sang the Propers, Sequences, or motets, there was literally no place for congregational singing during the celebration of Mass even after it was permissible and desirable to make a demonstration of the Catholic faith. The provision of high quality, theologically sound hymns by the Wesleyan Methodists and reforming Anglicans prompted former Anglican clergymen in particular (Newman, Faber, Caswall, and Oakeley cannot be surpassed) to translate and compose hymns for the Catholic liturgy. It was not until devotional services outside the celebration of Mass became widespread that a context was found for these hymns.

In September 1853 Fr Cotham wrote a particularly courteous letter to John Waddy Esq. (a convert, possibly one of the two from the choir) asking him to take charge of the direction and management of the church choir, which would not be disturbed (unless for good reason) without three months' notice.

> It is also understood that you shall be allowed and paid quarterly all reasonable and proper expenses for tuning and blowing the organ, for providing new music and for donations to the children who are to be instructed in singing to encourage their punctual attendance in the Choir.

Fr Cotham obviously expected professionalism to be exercised with pragmatism, but it was expensive. In 1867 the church expenses totalled £181 12s. 4d., of which £97 11s. 6d. was spent on the choir. Mr Osmond, the organist, was paid £40, the tenor £12 12s., and the alto, bass, and treble £10 each; cleaning and tuning the organ cost £11, new music £1 7s. 6d., and the organ blower took home £2 12s.

The accomplished Fr Blount was delegated to work closely with the choir, aiming to match the one borrowed from Bath for the opening. He struggled, as he tells Bishop Clifford in October 1858:

> My dear Lord
>
> I most reluctantly beg of you a dispensation from the Decree banishing non-Catholics from the Choir: in favour of <u>one</u> of our singers, W J Franklin.
>
> I say most reluctantly because I have thought and schemed and worked to get a Catholic choir but in vain. The reasons I would alledge [*sic*] are:

Celebrating the Divine Service 423

i. The necessity of an attractive choir—all our people who know the place are decidedly of the opinion that the choir must be attractive. Protestants will be lured—an inefficient choir will empty the church.

ii. Our choir can't be attractive with only one male singer and that is what we shall have without Protestants.

iii. Franklin has sung ever since the church was opened. He is a very well-behaved man and much more so than the generality of Catholic amateurs.

iv. Of our original Protestant choir we have converted <u>two</u>. If we send away Franklin, we certainly shall loose [*sic*] even the remotest chance of converting him, if we keep him, he <u>may</u> be drawn into the Church.

v. We shall miss our principal soprano, a Protestant, but if we may retain Franklin the loss won't be so severe, as we shall have <u>one</u> good singer for each part—but without him, we shall be wretched crippled, and most unattractive.

I hope your Lordship will relax so far as to let us retain W. Franklin.[8]

William Franklin, a tenor, was retained and remained loyal: twelve years later with Mr Gilding and Miss Shepperd he was a soloist in Weber's Mass No. 2 on Easter Sunday.[9] To remain 'attractive' St Gregory's was prepared to use Protestant and female singers in a classical concert repertoire. Despite Fr Blount's declared reluctance to use Protestants in the choir, he was advertising for a tenor singer a few months later, with no mention of the applicant's religious affiliation or likelihood of conversion.[10] It was something Fr Cotham had accepted as normal since the days of Mr Reichenberg's sterling work in Tasmania, although the tide of opinion and church discipline gradually turned against the tyranny of organ and prima donna in the performance of settings of the Mass.[11]

The 'principal soprano, a Protestant', referred to in Fr Blount's letter was probably Mrs Smith whom he managed to retain until

424   *The Indomitable Mr Cotham*

Christmas 1859. The occasion of her leave-taking was a 'judiciously selected' concert of secular music, sponsored by Fr Cotham and Fr Blount, and attended by 'a numerous and fashionable audience' of Catholics from the town and neighbourhood.[12] Mrs Smith was joined by sixteen vocalists drawn from St Gregory's Choir and members of the Cheltenham Glee and Madrigal Society. An eclectic mix of 'glees, choruses, madrigals, duets, solos, quartets, etc were executed with considerable taste and skill.'[13] Locke's music to *Macbeth* and the National Anthem concluded the evening's repertoire. This entertainment was unambiguously secular, but the dividing line between sacred and secular music could be remarkably flexible, if it is true that the 'Steersman's Song' from Wagner's *Flying Dutchman* was actually used as an Offertory piece.[14] Fr Cotham may have experienced some aspects of liturgical renewal, in particular the use of Gregorian plainchant, during his visits to Downside and Belmont, but there is nothing to indicate he was dissatisfied with the regime at St Gregory's.

After her first experience of an English Catholic Christmas in 1863, Sr Aloysia Tixhon penned a vivid account to her religious sisters in Liège on 29 December. The simplicity of her language is a relief from the grandiloquence of newspaper reports and the impression she gives is one of freshness and light. The nuns were accompanied through a silent town by three ladies and two young men, for protection, but 'we did not see a soul either going or coming back'. She describes what she found at the church:

> [The Baptistry] was decorated with green garlands and flowers and the font was covered with white roses. All the arches were festooned with greenery, and all the pillars entwined with it. The shrines were filled with flowers; Our Lady's chapel was a mass of white roses; texts and scrolls over the doors, written in large red letters and always decorated with greenery and all lit with numerous gas jets. The whole thing was lovely.

Celebrating the Divine Service

A few minutes before midnight the organ began to play, and there was no other sound in the church; it was as quiet as our own little chapel at home ...

At midnight the Mass began. The choir sang a magnificent Mass by Mozart—but it was not as sweet to me as the singing of our own sisters ...

At the end of Mass, our good Father Scarisbrick had arranged to give us Holy Communion as soon as the crowd had left the church. A few privileged souls profited by the occasion and also partook of the same happiness ...

At eight o'clock Father came to say the two morning Masses for us during which we sang the carols and hymns of <u>Liège</u>. At 11a.m. we assisted at Pontifical High Mass celebrated by Monsignor Collier with great ceremony ... At this Mass all the altar servers wore long purple tunics with scarlet capes and long white surplices. They looked just like little bishops!

Here on solemn feasts and even on Sundays, all the servers wear white stockings and gloves with cloth overshoes, specially for these occasions. I have never seen, neither has any of the sisters, such dignity in worship as here in England. It is for many the beginning of conversion. We have just been asked to pray for a young girl of eighteen, of a very distinguished family in Bath, who having accompanied a Catholic servant to Mass, was so much struck by the majesty of the Liturgy that she asked to receive instructions. She is at the moment persecuted by her family who have left Bath to go and live elsewhere. The Catholics of Bath have written to Cheltenham to ask for prayers for her. I notice with great consolation, how much this work of conversion interests everyone in England, especially the Catholics of some social standing who in this respect, like the primitive Christians, 'have but one heart and one soul'.

We would have liked very much to have some of the lovely flowers they have in the parish church. I have promised the sisters I will beg for some later on.[15]

The profusion of white roses intrigued Sr Aloysia; it may have been an exceptional winter as she remarks 'it was as mild as the month of May' for their midnight walk across town, but the roses are more likely to have come from congregants with hothouses. There is no doubt that the celebration of the liturgy was an opportunity for the Catholic faithful, new and old, to express their devotion, pride and, if necessary, defiance, to their non-Catholic neighbours. For those neighbourly onlookers it was a source of mystery and admiration. The *Cheltenham Looker-On* used snobbery and ridicule to puncture the justifiable complacency of Catholics at these high feasts in its report from Rome for the same Christmas Day 1863:

> Christmas Day in Rome.—Crowding every piazza, palace, and church may be seen a motley crowd of English … A confused babel of languages, amidst which the English loudly prevailed, disturbed the solemnity of the hour and of the occasion. It was Protestant England paying its homage to the splendour of the Catholic rites … The spirit of Christian charity among the Church authorities induce them to show all possible civility on these occasions, but their indulgence is a little tried when a portly East-end dowager, with a bevy of dashing daughters endeavours to explain in a frantic patoise, her determination to occupy a foremost place during the solemnity, on the plea of a Foreign Office passport and an aldermanic husband. Still, from seven o'clock to eleven, when the mass commences, they on and through—they fairly beat back all civil and military authorities. The accents of cockneyism rise even above the clear, thrilling voices of the Papal choir, and the sweet pensive notes of Mustapha and Rossi. Scarcely can the silver trumpets which herald the raising of the Host be heard amid the exclamations of admiration and the excitement of expectation.[16]

St Gregory's did not have many opportunities for fashionable weddings but one was celebrated in October 1867 between Miss Elizabeth Duncan and Lieutenant Constantine Maguire. Once again Dr Collier was the chief celebrant with Fr Cotham and Fr

Celebrating the Divine Service 427

Wilkinson as deacon and sub-deacon respectively. As reported by the local press, the presence of Dr Collier—the Right Revd Dr Collier, Bishop in partibus—gave the church extra éclat on such occasions. The ordinary church choir was able to do justice to the repertoire of Weber's Grand Mass in G, Zingarelli's *Laudate*, with tenor (Mr Franklin) and chorus, and Guglielmi's *Gratias Agimus*. Clara Shepperd took the soprano part, Mr Chattaway, alto, and Mr W. A. Powell, bass, with organ accompaniment by Mr Osmond. The absence of two of these names from the church subscribers' book suggests Mr Franklin was not alone in being a Protestant in the choir.[17]

'Stations [of the Cross] first time in N Church. V. Poor.' Fr Cotham's appraisal of the service celebrated on Friday 19 February 1858 is stark, his feelings unexpressed. As Catholic life normalised during the second half of the nineteenth century devotional practices developed and took strong root among those in the congregation who were not best educated or well seated to appreciate the high culture of the Roman church. The main non-liturgical services inside the church (processions outdoors for Corpus Christi and Marian devotions took a little longer to establish) were the Stations of the Cross, the Forty Hours Devotion, communal recitation of the Rosary and, above all, Benediction, most often celebrated on Thursday and Sunday evenings, and holy days. In the month of May Benediction would be celebrated on Tuesdays and Thursdays, with a sermon or lesson on a Marian theme. According to the 1859 visitation report the Rosary was not prayed publicly in May, but was recited on Mondays, Tuesdays, and Fridays in November, together with the Litany of the Dead. By 1864 the Rosary was prayed every Thursday at Benediction and there were daily devotions and discourses during the month of May. These services provided an opportunity for the laity to sing hymns and pray publicly in the vernacular during an extended time of reflection on the actions of the Holy Mass or meditation on Scripture. In addition, confraternities and sodalities of various types became popular, often affiliated to a particular religious order. These encouraged lay participation in the life of the church community and nurtured opportunities for socialising with fellow Catholics, while also providing opportunities for prayer and singing outside a clergy-led setting.

Neither Cotham's monastic formation nor his experience of the fledging revival of Gregorian plainchant at St Michael's would have greatly influenced liturgical practice at St Gregory's.

> When [Cardinal Wiseman] became the leader of England's re-established hierarchy, [he] laboured most successfully in the work of reparation ... he introduced more frequent celebration of Holy Mass, more frequent Benedictions of the Blessed Sacrament, the adoration of the Forty Hours, and the devotion of Our Lady's Rosary and of the Month of May.[18]

However, while neither Benediction nor the rosary was completely new, after 1850 both became far more important. 'Not only did the absolute number of churches offering Benediction of the Blessed Sacrament and Public Rosary rise at an exhilarating rate, but the *proportion* of churches which catered for both services rose dramatically and inexorably throughout the period.'[19] Cotham's near neighbours, the Passionist Fathers at Broadway, and the Dominican Friars at Woodchester, used these forms of spirituality with great effect during the parish missions they conducted. The occasional visit of a priest was no longer a rarity nor sufficient for the lay faithful. As congregations gathered in larger buildings which were in turn part of a diocesan superstructure, what had been rare became normal and then commonplace, and the new preaching Orders such as the Passionists were invited to visit at regular intervals to renew congregational fervour. The term 'mission' denoted a new phenomenon; Fr Cotham was now, in effect, a stationary priest tied to a building needing constant fund raising, adaptation as spirituality altered, and subsidiary activities to liturgical worship for children and adults.

Celebrating the Divine Service 429

A month after Fr Cotham's private retreat at Broadway in 1859, Fr Goning CP and Fr Morewood OP, from Woodchester Priory, conducted a retreat for St Gregory's. At the end of the fortnight

> the exercises of the Mission concluded with general communion of all the faithful, a grand procession of the Most Blessed Sacrament round the church, and the Forty Hours' Exposition on the high altar on Sunday morning, and in the evening with a most practical sermon on the means of securing the greatest of all graces—the grace of final perseverance—the solemn renewal of the baptismal vows, and the Papal Benediction, which was given by the Very Rev. Father Goning, the superior of the Mission.[20]

Although the enthusiasm generated by an intensive retreat inevitably waned, exposure to the 'mission exercises' had a lasting effect; the poor showing at the inaugural Stations of the Cross a year earlier was gradually overcome. Aside from devotional renewal, the parish mission was an opportune time to introduce a branch of the Young Men's Society to St Gregory's. For the opening meeting the Dominican friars were joined by Fr Bernard O'Loughlin from Broadway (Cotham's equal in zeal) and the usual stalwarts from the congregation—Copeland, Healy, Hanford and Tiesset—in encouraging one hundred young men to enrol as members, according to Very Revd Dr O'Brien's rules and regulations. Fr Blount was appointed as president and Simon Lalor as secretary pro tem. It was yet another delegated duty for young Blount, but a new responsibility for Irishman Simon Lalor from Burton Street, a middle-aged and married working man. The establishment of the Society was anticipated as 'one of the most substantial results of the Mission'[21] aimed at a group likely to lapse in commitment.

The report written in February 1859 by Fr Cotham before the Bishop's Visitation provided full details of the state of St Gregory's. Away from high holy days, Low Mass was celebrated daily, at 8 a.m. or 8:30 a.m. according to the season. Communal prayers before Mass were either the Litany of Jesus or the Litany of the

Blessed Virgin, Psalm 129 'De Profundis' offered for the deceased, and Challoner's preparatory prayer 'And now O God'. After Mass a passage from *Preachers' Meditations* was read. A different set of prayers was used before Low Mass on Sundays, at 8 a.m., and a short instruction or a sermon was given afterwards. At High Mass on Sundays, at 11 a.m., the prayers were followed by the rite of Asperges. The final prayer after Mass was offered for the Queen. The Catechism service held at 3 o'clock on Sundays was the only occasion when English was used throughout: a hymn and simple prayers before the clergy gave instruction and another hymn and the 'Memorare' to close. Unfortunately there is no record of the attendance at this basic service, probably aimed mainly at the young and those preparing for confirmation. It lasted about half an hour, and baptisms took place afterwards. In the evening at 7 o'clock compline was followed by a sermon and Benediction.

The practice of 'visits' to pray privately before the Blessed Sacrament was encouraged by leaving the church unlocked for limited, specified periods. At St Gregory's in 1859 the church was open between 7 a.m. and 9:30 a.m. and 2 p.m. until 4 p.m. Confessions were heard on Saturdays from 2 p.m. to 4:30 pm, and again from 6 p.m. to 9 or 10 p.m. to suit the long working hours of tradespeople, and baptisms and women's churchings were celebrated on Wednesday mornings as necessary. Until the Cheltenham Borough Cemetery, with a Catholic section, was opened in September 1864 prayers for the dead were read over the corpse at home, in the case of poor families.[22] For those able to afford it a Catholic burial service took place at Gloucester, Kemerton, or Broadway.

The activity centred on a Catholic church was intended to be the focus for communal and family occasions, seasonal and personal, to an extent not experienced in England since the Reformation. The authorisation of all devotions and confraternities had to be accounted for; the Society of the Sacred Heart was carried over from Fr Kendal's incumbency, and authorised by Bishop Hendren in 1851. However, the Society of the Living

Celebrating the Divine Service 431

Rosary caused some consternation, its authorisation being undocumented. At the conclusion of the visitation in 1859 Fr Cotham was instructed to construct an aumbry for sacred oils on the sanctuary and a sacrarium for washing sacred vessels in the sacristy while Bishop Clifford went back to Clifton to make enquiries about how he was to rectify the anomalous position of the Living Rosary;[23] at the 1864 visitation it was still one of two named associations, the other being the Altar Society (the Confraternity of the Blessed Sacrament authorised in Cheltenham in 1864). In the development of these closed groups, St Gregory's followed 'the strong tendency for Catholics to wish to separate from those outside its fold [by joining] exclusively Catholic organisations'.[24] Within two decades the influence of English converts was subsumed into a more insular mind-set, as if evangelisation in the context of restoration of liberties had proved too challenging.

Notes

[1]   *Cheltenham Looker-On*, 30 May 1857, p. 515.
[2]   *Ibid.*, p. 515. The choir received £21 for 'expenses'.
[3]   *Ibid.*, p. 515.
[4]   *Cheltenham Examiner*, 27 May 1857, p. 8.
[5]   *Cheltenham Looker-On*, 10 April 1858, p. 350.
[6]   T. E. Muir, *Roman Catholic Church Music in England, 1791–1914: A Handmaid of the Liturgy?* (Abingdon: Routledge, 2016), p. 46. This section on non-liturgical services relies heavily on Dr Muir's work.
[7]   *Ibid.*, p. 46.
[8]   CDA, Cheltenham Box; Blount to Clifford, 28 October 1858. Blount might reasonably expect a sympathetic hearing; J. A. Harding makes the point that three of the four priests with Bishop Clifford in the Pro-Cathedral in 1863 were convert clergymen. *Clifford of Clifton (1823–1893): England's Youngest Catholic Bishop* (Diocese of Clifton, 2011), p. 317.
[9]   *Cheltenham Examiner*, 20 April 1870, p. 8.
[10] *Cheltenham Looker-On*, 16 April 1859, p. 376.
[11] See, for example, correspondence in *The Tablet*, 6 July 1878, p. 11, and 26 September 1885, p. 22.

12   *Cheltenham Mercury*, 7 January 1860, p. 4.

13   *Ibid.*, p. 4.

14   Letter from A Musical Director, 'Protestant Choirs in Catholic Churches', in *The Tablet*, 26 September 1885, p. 22.

15   L. W. O'Neill DC, *With All My Heart: The Life and Letters of Sr Aloysia* (Privately published, 1977), pp. 102–105.

16   *Cheltenham Looker-On*, 9 January 1864, p. 23.

17   *Cheltenham Examiner*, 16 October 1867, p. 4.

18   *The Tablet*, 1 July 1893, p. 5, from a sermon preached by Fr Bridgett on the occasion of the Consecration of England and Wales.

19   M. Heimann, *Catholic Devotion in Victorian England* (Oxford: Clarendon Press, 1995), p. 100.

20   *The Tablet*, 16 April 1859, p. 5.

21   *Ibid.*, p. 5.

22   The first Catholic burial on 12 December was Mary Potts, 'that day buried by Rev. Fr. Cotham.' *Cheltenham Mercury*, 4 December 1869, p. 3.

23   *Ibid.* The Society for the Living Rosary was founded in Lyon in 1826 by Pauline Jaricot, also foundress of the Society for the Propagation of the Faith.

24   M. Heimann, *Catholic Devotion in Victorian England* (Oxford: Clarendon Press, 1995), p. 100.

36 THE CONGREGATION OF THE DAUGHTERS OF THE CROSS OF LIÈGE

ONE OF THE marks of a successfully developing mission was the introduction of a congregation of religious sisters. In England after 1850 the majority of new convents were founded from France or Belgium, usually for the work of education. For non-Catholics, habited nuns were a particularly potent symbol of the Catholic faith: romanticised, demonised, idolised, or simply objects of curiosity. They were 'Roman' and therefore exotic and suspect, but they were also mysteriously (and dangerously) attractive to women from all classes. In practice, they performed good works and were appreciated. For Catholics, they were go-betweens for laity and clergy, set apart by dress and lifestyle yet often doing menial work for no pay among the poorest in society. In Cheltenham, as elsewhere, 'the Sisters' became the bedrock of the Catholic educational system. The first congregation, the Daughters of the Cross of Liège, introduced the town to the existence of their kind, although their educational achievement was limited. Their foreign origins were less objectionable in a relatively cosmopolitan town such as Cheltenham but ironically this worked against them finding a ready place as educators of the poor. The novelty for the Sisters, being the first of their Congregation to work in England, produced their own well-documented account of their arrival in England in November 1863.[1]

The reports in the local press were limited and oblique. The *Cheltenham Looker-On* declined to acknowledge their arrival at all but preferred to run an article that expressed the ambivalence felt towards this new phenomenon by focusing on the establish-

434 *The Indomitable Mr Cotham*

ment of what became the Hospital of St John and St Elizabeth in London:

> The unostentatious, but rapid growth in England of religious communities in connection with the Church of Rome is far greater, and, perhaps, more important, than is generally supposed. The latest addition in the Metropolis is a Convent of Nuns, of the Order of St John of Jerusalem, to which is aggregated a community of the Sisters of Mercy. For their accommodation, a suitable building has been raised in Great Ormond Street, on the site of what was once the French Ambassador's residence during the reign of Louis Quatorze ... the architecture, fittings, etc are in the style of the 14th century, or anterior to the Reformation. In connection with the Convent are the new Church of St John of Jerusalem and the Hospital of St Elizabeth of Hungary ... The Prioress of the Convent, who is the daughter of Admiral Barry, is one of the Sisters of Mercy who followed the British Army to Crimea, and remained there until the peace.

The historical allusions are mixed and muddled; the reference to brave, loyal nurses in Crimea is followed by a sly account of the choir stalls provided for the aristocratic 'Ladies of devotion' who supported the Sisters, one of whom was

> the Marchioness of Londonderry ... a convert. Her father is the Earl of Roden, a nobleman who has made himself somewhat conspicuous by his hostility to that peculiar form of faith, which his eldest daughter has now embraced.[2]

The Congregation of the Daughters of the Cross of Liège, founded in 1833, rapidly recruited sufficient members to establish several houses in Belgium and Germany for staffing schools, both poor and fee paying. A house in India for nursing and education was opened in early 1863 and a foundation in England was seen as a particularly advantageous development for the future of this last venture. For the English foundation Mother Foundress's niece, Sr Aloysia Tixhon, was put in charge of the five sisters who were to be the permanent members of the Cheltenham house. Standing

The Congregation of the Daughters of the Cross of Liège   435

in for the venerable Mother Marie Thérèse Haze, Sr Aloysia wrote over seventy comprehensive letters to her dealing with administrative business, but also full of colourful details about Cheltenham and St Gregory's for the sisters' entertainment during their recreation periods in the mother house.

Fr Scarisbrick, in Cheltenham as assistant priest from 1862 to 1867, dealt with the early negotiations for their arrival. The second of Fr Cotham's assistant priests was probably one of his most uncongenial house companions. Unlike his senior, Fr Scarisbrick had a haughty manner but more damagingly he was also capable of pettiness and a peevish discontent with life around him, including his co-religionists. However, his efforts in helping to establish a convent for the Daughters of the Cross in 1862 to support the school were greatly appreciated by them.[3]

A perennial tendency of correspondence from religious sisters is to gloss over the unedifying aspects of their lives, covering imperfections with a cloak of charity. Sr Aloysia was an astute person, experienced in managing children and women; she saw the vanities and rivalries between men but observed the proprieties of her position and restricted herself to the mildest of hints. She would have realised there was tension between Frs Cotham and Scarisbrick, even without being privy to Fr Scarisbrick's correspondence, so when reading her account of the sisters' gracious introduction to Cheltenham it is instructive to keep in mind the power play in the background. A few weeks after the public display of unity when the Catholic clergy marched at the head of a column of schoolchildren through the town, Fr Scarisbrick sent a blistering letter to Fr President Burchall. 'Scandal' had been caused at the beginning of May, the month traditionally associated with devotion to the Blessed Virgin Mary.

> Cheltenham, May 7/63
>
> My dear Fr President
>
> There has been a fresh scandal in Chelt^m and in obedience to your order I have informed the Provincial of it. I

preached on Dev^n to B. V. on Monday last, the [unclear] of the 'Mass de M.' and again on Sunday morning at 11 o'clock. In the evening of the same day Mr Cotham mounted the pulpit and preached one of the most remarkable sermons that has ever been heard from any Catholic pulpit. He contradicted all that I said—spoke in the most comtemptuous manner of devotion to our Lady—as noways necessary—& spoke of what St Alphonsus, St Bernard, and others had written as mere <u>opinions</u> which we might believe or not as we pleased etc. The Congreg^n (wh. is very devout to the B. V.) is very scandalized and hurt—all talk of their religion being humiliated and disgraced and their own feelings shamefully outraged. There was a sort of meeting on Monday to consider what had best be done and I agreed to write to the President and Provincial. I have sent the Provincial full details by this post. It is a very serious matter and I think ought to be noticed. Some are afraid it will appear in Saturday's paper, as some Protestants when leaving the church were distinctly heard to prophesy that Mr Cotham w^d before long be a Protestant.

You may imagine how painful all this is to me and how difficult my position is becoming.

Dr Collier spoke to him very strongly but produced no effect at all.

I write with the greatest reluctance and not with a view to bring about his removal but only that you and the Provincial may make a record of it.

Mr Copeland and Colonel Graham (No. 8 St James Square) have authorised me to say that they will be quite ready to answer any questions that may be put to them on the subject.

Believe me my dear Fr President, With great respect,

Very obediently yours, Wm Scarisbrick.[4]

The Congregation of the Daughters of the Cross of Liège   437

Fr Cotham was capable of preaching remarkable sermons, enjoyed wordplay and was perhaps too ready to be mischievous towards his rather pompous assistant. He was not, however, unorthodox and knew where the lines were to be drawn between dogma and devotion. His own preaching could be emotive, and personal style naturally coloured the homilist's delivery of doctrine; it has always been the case that people 'might believe or not as we pleased' some of the devotions used to expand liturgical worship. Fr Scarisbrick knew this and was himself being mischievous in fuelling indignation at the impromptu meeting. However, the newspapers did not pick up on the in-house strife, and Fr Cotham did not become a Protestant, and the sisters from Liège were not as naïve as their letters might portray them.

During 1863 Scarisbrick was corresponding with Mme Cleofas J. P. Marisou[5] who wrote from various addresses in Banffshire, north east Scotland. In her accounts of the Sisters' mission to England Sr Lillian O'Neill says that Fr Scarisbrick travelled to Liège to meet the Congregation's co-founders, Mère Marie Thérèse Haze and Canon Habets, although she does not know where the initial introduction came from. In the months leading up to the Sisters' move to Cheltenham Cleofas Marisou acted as the intermediary for correspondence and the necessary arrangements were made with comparative ease.

The superior of the new convent was Sr Cephasie Kearney, born of Irish parents in Jamaica, who spoke fluent French and English; Sr Cyrille spoke English fairly well, Sr Marie Clothilde knew a little, and Srs Noelle and Colette knew none. Shortly before their departure for England Sr Cephasie wrote a letter to Fr Scarisbrick which suggests he was thought to be the priest in charge at Cheltenham.[6] She thanked him for the travel arrangements he had made then addressed the small details so important in women's religious communities, 'about the mattresses': they will use the cocoa-nut fibre mattresses bought for them until they can obtain the straw mattresses required by their Rule. 'Forks, &c' are left to his discretion, preferably the cheapest. 'The iron

438 *The Indomitable Mr Cotham*

bedsteads are <u>without</u> posts and when we have a dormitory for the sisters we manufacture calico walls but we cannot have curtains'. The good ladies of Cheltenham would be hard pressed to meet their simple requirements. Dr Collier had been appointed their Spiritual Director, an excellent and obvious choice given his fluency in French and his previous experience with nuns. As the Congregation was about to start a mission in Bombay Sr Cephasie asked if Fr Scarisbrick knew of any likely candidates to swell the numbers going out. In a postscript she writes:

> We shall follow your suggestions with regard to our travelling costumes. It is very kind of the Revd Father Cotham to meet us at Dover, he will have no difficulty recognising us even in the dark November morning. The Revd Father will certainly have some trouble meeting six nuns and their baggage, but his charity is greater than the trouble may be.

Sr Aloysia wrote the first of her many letters to Mother Foundress the day after arriving in Cheltenham. The sisters docked at Dover on 10 November at 4 o'clock in the morning and were met by Fr Cotham who was 'very sorry to see us in such a state. He immediately decided to change the itinerary'. He made them rest for two hours (all but one had been violently seasick) before taking them to London, prepared to wait until the following day before going on to Cheltenham if necessary. However they revived in London where they had breakfast and took the express train to Cheltenham arriving only four and a half hours later. (Sr Aloysia noted that during their first week in Cheltenham Fr Cotham returned to London on business about the schools.) Sr Aloysia wrote, 'It had been the intention of this good Father for us to have a quiet welcome' but as he had telegrammed the time of their arrival the parishioners were waiting to give them an impressively solemn reception at Lansdown Station.

> Reverend Father Scarisbrick (he who came to Liège and conducted all the correspondence) came forward at the

The Congregation of the Daughters of the Cross of Liège   439

head of the leading members of the Catholic community. There were at least twenty ladies and young girls of the first mark; two noble gentlemen—one a colonel—were at the doors of the two carriages destined for us.

... Although everything [in the house] was done as far as possible in accordance with the rules of holy Poverty, you must be prepared to understand that the word 'comfortable' was invented by the English! Everything here is really very comfortable ... Our beds are iron, painted green with four brass knobs at the ends.

That evening at 7 o'clock the sisters were taken to St Gregory's for what must have been something of an ordeal although St Aloysia described it as 'a great honour'. They joined a large congregation which included Protestants for Solemn Benediction.

The altar and the sanctuary were brilliantly lit by magnificent candelabra. Ten little choir boys carrying censers formed the procession for the priests and Solemn Benediction began. It was sung by a special choir reserved for solemn occasions and I think there can be few to equal it. After the O Salutaris and the Litany of Our Lady, the Te Deum was intoned and sung in several parts. The whole Office lasted an hour and was concluded by Handel's 'Alleluia Chorus' played on the organ. It was a great honour for the poor little sisters in <u>hats</u>(!).

About those <u>hats</u>. Everyone has found our costume very suitable. Father Scarisbrick was very pleased and proud that we managed so well without having to discard the holy habit ... We go out in two styles! When we go to church ... we simply put hats over our bandeaux and guimpes because we like people to see that we are, after all, Religious. But when we go into town we add a little more 'coquetrie'. We take off our bandeaux and guimpes and decorate our hats to hide the fact that we have no 'coiffure'. Then we put scarves over our cloaks and easily pass for women in mourning attire. Especially as we are always accompanied by lay persons on these occasions.

However, these were precautions taken in the very early days of the foundation. The Protestants seemed to lose their apprehensions, about superficial matters at least, quite quickly and regarded the sisters as yet another source of French lessons.

The first week was busy with curious callers—thirteen on one day—to their new home at 4 Bath Place and one from Bishop Clifford a fortnight after their arrival. Although the sisters had been advised to wear hats over their veils and a large cloak when going out to avoid drawing 'the attention of Protestants', it was soon decided they could 'risk' appearing in their habits in public. Sr Aloysia's interest in domestic detail, the mainstay of convent life, gives an insight into the women's sphere in mid nineteenth century Cheltenham. In particular, the sisters find the cost of living in England to be considerably higher than in Belgium. She writes: 'I ask for very ordinary paper costing about five francs a ream, and am sent samples costing thirty francs a ream'; the elegance of Cheltenham and the comfort which the parishioners want to see them enjoying comes at a price beyond their earning power.

The question of who they would teach was also addressed urgently. Although the sisters were prepared to work in the Poor School none of them had a teaching certificate as required by the government for schools receiving a grant, nor were any of the permanent sisters capable enough of leadership in the school. One unnamed young woman whose mother, apparently, was a niece of the Duke of Norfolk, offered to teach English to the sisters and to help in the Poor School where they intended beginning classes on 1 December with a view to taking charge at Christmas. The 'young lady' (a Miss Clifford) proved useful as Sr Cyrille subsequently took and passed the examination for gaining her teaching certificate, Fr Scarisbrick having asked permission from the government for her Belgian certificate to suffice in the meantime. Two local sisters, 'the Misses Curtis who came to Liège and did not impress Sr Cephasie very much are a great help now' and would also join the school team. Within the first month four potential postulants presented themselves to Sr Aloysia.

The Congregation of the Daughters of the Cross of Liège 441

Fr Scarisbrick was in charge of the initiative to find a suitable property to be used as a boarding school, if possible before Sr Aloysia returned to Belgium. Cheltenham already had a reputation for providing a high standard of education for boys and, with Miss Dorothea Beale in charge of the Ladies College, girls' education was being extensively broadened. On the continent the Daughters of the Cross had developed an advanced 'Method of Education' for providing a comprehensive curriculum which could rival that being propounded in Cheltenham's colleges (though not going as far as teaching Latin to girls), but translating that into a viable system for a Catholic girls boarding school was asking too much of the newly arrived sisters. Sr Aloysia expects 'it is unlikely we will have many boarders for a while for most Catholic families have governesses' and families unable to afford a governess were not attracted to Cheltenham. Hence, 'it is the opinion of the Fathers and everyone here that a [Catholic] boarding school is necessary in Cheltenham'.

By the 1860s Cheltenham was moving well away from its Regency reputation as a 'Pleasure Town' and was earnest in promoting its town motto, *Salubritas et Eruditio*.[7] Sr Aloysia picked up on this immediately:

> What is most curious, and singular in England, is the number of students. Cheltenham has been called the town of Colleges because there are so many of them. All the college students wear an elegant cap surmounted by a large square piece, richly embroidered and with different coloured tassels showing to which college they belong. The chief one of these has over 600 students, all lodging in the town and only going to the College for lectures. You can imagine them strolling about outside these times. There are often groups of them outside 4 Bath Place, lying in wait for a chance of catching a glimpse of us, as we never go into town in our habits. We thought it more prudent not to, in a town as Protestant as this one.

However, Cheltenham was not all elegance.

> A veritable plague in England are the beggars. We were warned not to give them anything at the door, not even bread or else we would never have any peace. Ah well, despite our resolution, they soon discovered the weak spot in our defences—our good little portress, Sr Marie Clothilde ... A few days ago Fr Cotham came to say Mass and remarked to Sr Cephasie: 'I see you have already got the beggars' signs on your front gate,' 'And what are those?' asked Sister. 'I'll show you' said Father and taking out a pencil he drew up the following signs. A square meant 'Good here'. A circle meant 'Nothing here'. A circle with a dot in the middle meant 'Here they'll call the police'. Crossed lines meant 'Here you will get bread and cheese'. 'At your gate,' said Father 'there was a square, 'Good here'. We were very amused ... but have not verified whether Father was speaking the truth or merely joking. It is not worth the trouble of putting on our hats to go down to the gate and find out.

By 3 December Sr Aloysia had considered six properties, ranging between £3,500 and £5,000. A seventh option—to buy a plot of land next to the church and to build from scratch—was dismissed because of the length of time it would take to complete, although its total cost of £2,000 and the convenience of its location were in its favour. She missed the expert advice of Canon Habets who had been instrumental in making twenty-two foundations in Belgium and Germany for the congregation over a thirty-year period, but having been in close proximity to him she had learnt what to look for and what to avoid. The property she favoured, Montpellier House, seemed ideal, having three floors and a basement with more rooms than she could put a name to. 'We all said that if we came here, this building would make an ideal little convent, quite separate from the boarding school.' As for the stables big enough for ten horses: 'they could easily be converted into little cells or a dormitory for boarders by linking it by means of a gallery to the main building'.

The Congregation of the Daughters of the Cross of Liège   443

While inspecting the wonderful prospects held out by Montpellier House Sr Aloysia admitted that at present they had only six private pupils; in the Poor School there were seventy little girls who 'devoured us with their eyes in mute longing. Their teacher did not seem to bother with them' (and knew she would soon be redundant). For the private pupils they provided the usual courses in French, piano lessons, and drawing.

> They are not very keen on German up to the present. It is much sought after in other countries but here in Cheltenham they prefer French which is compulsory and which many ladies speak with an elegance that surprises us. They speak very correctly and with an excellent accent—much better than in any other foreign city of my experience. The French teachers in the schools and colleges give private lessons in town. There are also requests for Italian but alas, none of us knows it.

She probably had in mind the stalwarts of St Gregory's, Casimir Tiesset and his sister Sophie, and their nephew Frans Gonez who came to Cheltenham in 1860. The Tiessets had indeed built up a reputation in public and private education and gained respect in the town but it had taken many years of effort and self-advertisement to establish themselves.

Fr Cotham left the daily negotiations about property to Fr Scarisbrick and Colonel William Graham who vied with each other to be considered the special protector and advisor of the Sisters. Sr Aloysia felt the competition acutely, 'The opinion of the Fathers from the beginning has always differed from that of the seculars and I want to keep the good will of both which is happily the case at the moment.' Naturally the priests were in favour of having a new convent close to hand as they would be responsible for all religious duties. For 'the seculars' who would be potential fee-paying parents, the location and amenities of the school were of paramount importance; 'fine and comfortable' were the key attributes they looked for, together with sufficient grounds to ensure privacy. Colonel Graham engineered another visit from Bishop Clifford, a personal friend of his, to settle the matter of which property to choose. As there were plans to build a boys' orphanage near to St Margaret's, the location nearest to the church, he advised taking Montpellier House in a different part of the town. He and the Benedictine Fathers also suggested taking lady boarders as a source of income and a charitable enterprise. 'They say it is a work of growing importance in England where newly converted people often find themselves the only Catholic in the family and are looking for a place where they can serve God.' Or simply live, as Selina Copeland's friend Maria Giberne found, when Fr Newman suggested she could board with Sisters in Handsworth, Birmingham after Dr Copeland made her feel unwelcome.

In the New Year, 1864, as Sr Aloysia was making arrangements to return to Liège, it was decided to give up Montpellier House (the price of house and land having risen to £6,000 during negotiations) and purchase Glenlee Lodge instead for £4,000, with Fr Scarisbrick and Colonel Graham acting, agreeably in tandem for once, for Sr Aloysia. The *Cheltenham Looker-On* reflected the opinion of a portion of the townspeople:

> GLENLEE LODGE, Bays Hill ... has been sold for £4000 to the Roman Catholic Community, for the purpose, it is stated, of establishing therein the Daughters of the Cross, a Sisterhood recently introduced into Cheltenham ... That such a property, situated in one of the most fashionable quarters of Cheltenham, should pass into the possession of a religious community for the purposes so opposite to those with which it has hitherto been identified, must be a matter of sincere regret to those who, like the Looker-On, have been accustomed to associate with such mansions as Glenlee Lodge, a generous hospitality and reciprocations of social enjoyment.

The sisters themselves may have been relieved when 'certain restrictions on the Bays Hill Estate' were found to obstruct the

The Congregation of the Daughters of the Cross of Liège   445

sale. The *Cheltenham Looker-On*, too, was relieved that good works would not interfere with good times.

> We hope, therefore, to see this spacious mansion—now again 'to Let'—ere long tenanted by some such affluent family as that which occupied it last Winter, whose social position and generous hospitalities may contribute to the prosperity of the town.[8]

The equally impressive Montpellier House was purchased instead for the new convent and school, with Sr Cephasie as Superior, without arousing opposition.

Although Sr Aloysia wrote at length, dealing with business and describing for entertainment the disguises the sisters used to allay suspicions in Protestant Cheltenham, their arrival seems not to have been noted in the local newspapers, sceptically or otherwise, apart from the brief negativity regarding Glenlee Lodge. A report carried a few months earlier explains in part Colonel Graham's grounds for solicitousness and assumed expertise in their affairs, besides giving the popular view of how Catholic nuns were meant to behave.

> A CHELTENHAM LADY TAKES THE VEIL. Miss Mary Frances Graham, daughter of Colonel and Mrs Graham of Cheltenham 'took the veil' at Canningon nunnery near Bridgewater on Monday. This establishment … was taken possession of by a number of Benedictine nuns on 15th June [1863]. The following assisted on Monday: Dr Clifford (RC) Bishop of Clifton, Rev Mr Rooker of Bridgewater, Rev Mr Vals of Taunton, Rev Mr Columbier of Clifton, and the Rev Mr Bouvier of Cannington. Mass was celebrated by the Right Rev Dr Clifford after which he preached a sermon, partly addressed to the congregation and in part specially to the new sister, who sat in the gallery facing the altar, and during some portions of the service seemed much affected, her handkerchief being in constant requisition, while her countenance moved those who saw her with sympathy. She was dressed in pure white, and had over her head a long veil, fixed to her head by a wreath of blossoms. On each side of her was a long lighted candle,

446   *The Indomitable Mr Cotham*

trimmed with flowers; and she carried in one hand a rosary from which depended a small gold cross ...

At the conclusion of the sermon the young lady left her seat in the choir and shortly appeared at a small door by the side of the altar. Her new attire was then consecrated by the Bishop, who handed it to her, after her making a solemn and public declaration, in answer to a series of questions put by the Bishop, that by the consent of her parents and herself she was ready to consecrate herself for ever to Almighty God. This was the most touching part of the ceremony. Her answer, to the effect that she wished to immure herself for ever, came tremblingly and feebly, and sounded in strange contrast with the loud voice of the priest, her countenance, otherwise pretty, bearing the same sad look as from the first. The ceremony over, the priest proceeded to bless a bell which had been given by Colonel Graham ... A solemn benediction was passed upon the assembly, after which the proceedings, as far as the public were concerned, ended. Bristol Paper[9]

In this instance the newspaper report needs to be treated with caution. There had indeed been Benedictine connections with Cannington in distant and recent history but Frances Graham was the first novice to join a new foundation of the little known French Congregation of the Blessed Sacrament. Bishop Clifford had arranged for Revd Mother Emilie Pellier, three choir sisters, and a lay sister to make the foundation from their house in Bollene, Vaucluse; the enclosed sisters' sole work was Perpetual Adoration of the Blessed Sacrament, a prayer ministry the bishop particularly wanted for his diocese. Other young women joined Frances Graham in the early years although twenty-five years later it was already an ageing community, but not because of Frances' trembling and feebleness: at the time of the Silver Jubilee celebrations she was the superior, and her three ordained brothers concelebrated the jubilee Mass.[10]

Colonel Graham lived in Cheltenham briefly at 8 St James Square but his main residence was in Bath with his Scottish wife

The Congregation of the Daughters of the Cross of Liège 447

Margaret. Having become a Catholic he evidently made himself useful to Bishop Clifford who probably introduced his daughter to the French sisters. In Cheltenham Sr Aloysia seemed unaware that the colonel was acting as the Bishop's agent in overseeing the establishment of her convent but Fr Scarisbrick might have bristled under his scrutiny. Although it was a minor matter it was an example of the kind of situation occurring throughout the country where regular clergy and secular bishops disputed spheres of authority. In this instance the cordial relationship they enjoyed with Bishop Clifford probably mitigated any resentment the Benedictines might feel.

Sr Aloysia herself was surprised by the number of young women who expressed an interest in joining the novitiate in Liège. By the end of the year two had gone and there were a handful of others preparing to follow, coming to Cheltenham from Ireland and Scotland before travelling onward. From one family, the Curtises from Teignmouth, Devon, Sr Aloysia had hoped that three sisters would enter the Congregation as they all spent time helping the Cheltenham community. The eldest, Selina, did go to Liège in May 1864 and remained with the Daughters of the Cross; her sister Charlotte eventually joined the Franciscan sisters in Chelsea looking after St Elizabeth's Orphanage, while the youngest Amelia spent over forty years as a Benedictine nun at Atherstone, Warwickshire. The attractiveness of the new congregations is apparent and so too is their openness in allowing enquirers to consider alternative religious lifestyles. From Cheltenham, Pauline Caffieri—a daughter of Hector and Marie Caffieri—joined the Daughters of the Cross and moved with them to Chelsea when the Cheltenham house was no longer viable.[11]

Unlike Pauline whose family were lifelong members of the Catholic community there were enquirers such as Miss Constance Smith, 'convert daughter of an Essex clergyman' who wavered while wanting to be persuaded. In practice Sr Aloysia found Constance rather obdurate: she had the opportunity but said she lacked the time to give private lessons; there were too many children for her in the Poor School, and in any case she was tied to her sick relative. Nevertheless, Miss Smith took the trouble to visit and correspond with Fr Newman but was 'very distressed over the advice, or rather the <u>order</u> given her by Father <u>Newman</u>, to spend some time in the world'. Sr Aloysia read a copy of his letter and found it 'very beautiful and very wise' in that he sensibly suggested she spend time away from the sisters and her parents and start again 'with composure of mind and religious calm'.[12] Constance had been taken to see Fr Newman by her cousin who was very close to conversion 'because of his reputation for such direction ... [he] has taken the greatest interest in Constance'. It was all very flattering to the sisters and to Constance although Newman drew the line when Sr Cephasie wanted to join in the correspondence and know what was being discussed. It seems Miss Smith did not take the plunge with the Daughters of the Cross, unlike the postulant from Dublin, Johanna Quin, who passed through Cheltenham on her way to Liège in November 1865; two years later she made early profession of vows so she could join the missionaries in India where she spent the next forty-five years.

The sisters themselves were frustrated by their role in Cheltenham. Their Congregation had established sound methods of education and evangelisation in their management of schools and sodalities on the Continent but in Cheltenham their closest supporters treated them as something of an adornment to the local church, giving them a social standing they could not easily afford nor would have chosen for themselves. Fr Scarisbrick had the delicate task of asking the sisters to take control of the schools for girls and boys while making his opinion plain that they would find it difficult given their lack of qualifications and numbers; if they declined to take the boys a master would have to be appointed, and a single master would be almost as expensive as a master and mistress ('man and wife') so it made sense to take a couple.[13]

The Daughters of the Cross dutifully accepted the change of direction. Montpellier House was well-suited for a girls' boarding school, with occasional lady boarders; with this change the sisters

The Congregation of the Daughters of the Cross of Liège 449

became more remote, geographically and practically, from the hub of the developing community of St Gregory's. Nearly all of their boarders came from outside the county or the country. As early as 1866 the Congregation was considering a request from Fr Lockhard to make a foundation in his London parish where

> the Protestants envy the good schools the Catholics have but without being uneasy about them—quite different from Cheltenham, as the Archbishop's [Manning] secretary also remarked. A little school for poor children could be added but the greatest need, he said, was for the middle classes.

Although nothing came of this opening Sr Aloysia seized the opportunity to make a foundation in Chelsea at Archbishop Manning's request, brokered by James de Lacy Towle. From then on, as the sisters' focus moved to Chelsea and regular communication with Fr Knox of the Oratory, the energy went out of the Cheltenham venture.

The Daughters of the Cross did not accomplish what was hoped of them in education but their arrival as the first religious sisters in Cheltenham was a significant cultural development, opening the way for religious life to become increasingly accepted. In return, they received a surprising number of applicants via Cheltenham who travelled to the mother house in Liège and went on to become full members of the Congregation's missions elsewhere or members of other religious communities. They were pioneers for a generation of independent women who were often able to organise their careers and finances in ways not open to secular women.

Mrs Monington, living in the house which was used as a convent after her death, was privy to the expectations and tensions of these years. She was able to sympathise with Fr Cotham in his difficulties with domestic staff, and would have known it was all the more galling because he blamed his assistant priest for them. In January 1868, when he was 'much occupied' with financial accounts, Fr Cotham also wrote to Mrs Monington

450 *The Indomitable Mr Cotham*

asking her to engage a new housekeeper for the priests' household following a disagreeable episode with a Benedictine visitor. He vented his annoyance in his journal and it is likely Mrs Monington heard about it from him personally.

In early 1868, much to his regret and despite a two pounds wage rise, his housekeeper Margaret Ratcliffe resigned after two valued years as 'a prudent manager'. The previous autumn Fr Fazakerley, from a neighbouring mission to Fr Scarisbrick's new post in Liverpool, had stayed with Fr Cotham after both had attended a jubilee celebration at Stanbrook. Contrary to good manners, the young Benedictine priest had gone into the kitchen to speak with Margaret who, he was 'surprised' to see had not yet left Cotham's employ. 'It is not fair to tamper with my servants', Cotham wrote in his journal, nor for Fr Scarisbrick to offer 'inducements' to their little singer Clara Shepperd to join his congregation.[14] The episode rankled for a week until Fr Cotham found a quotation by Canon Frederick Oakeley (in his *Postscript to Church Music* according to Cotham) to include in his own journal, summing up his distaste for Scarisbrick's behaviour:

> A gentleman who should tempt the servant of another gentleman to leave his situation by the offer of higher wages would, according to the etiquette of the world, be regarded as guilty of a serious breach of social propriety.

His equilibrium restored, Fr Cotham went on to record the funeral of the organ blower, Fred Donovan, a visit to Mrs Stonor, and the fact that the clergy ate game for dinner twice a week during January. Better still, he was no longer obliged to be polite to Fr Scarisbrick at table.

Notes

[1]   Material for this chapter is drawn from *With All My Heart*, unless otherwise noted.

[2]   *Cheltenham Looker-On*, 12 December 1863, p. 798.

[3]   Unfortunately he was not always so kind towards religious sisters. His

The Congregation of the Daughters of the Cross of Liège 451

temperamental weaknesses were most harmful during his term as Bishop of Port-Louis, Mauritius from 1871 to 1887, when he wrangled with the virtuous foundress of the Bon Secours Congregation, Mother Marie-Augustine, and with the island's first Catholic Governor, Sir John Pope Hennessey.

[4] AAA RB-244–173; Scarisbrick to Burchall, 7 May 1863.

[5] Sr O'Neill writes that 'Cleofas paces piously through several letters' but remains a mysterious person. She seems to have entered the Congregation at some earlier point, as well as other communities, always leaving after a short while. She turned her attentions instead to brokering negotiations for foundations (without apparently putting money into them) and was in Scotland in 1863 for that purpose. *With All My Heart*, p. 121.

[6] Sr O'Neill makes the same mistake in her book, describing Scarisbrick as 'Superior of the Benedictines and parish priest of St Gregory's', p. 57. Sr Aloysia realised the error as soon as the sisters disembarked.

[7] *Health and Learning.*

[8] *Cheltenham Looker-On*, 16 January, p. 41, and 27 February 1864, p. 137. The widowed sisters Elizabeth Brennan and Ellen Fitzgerald were based at Glenlee Lodge for a few years in the 1850s, along with a relative Lieutenant General John Woulfe, until his death in 1855.

[9] *Cheltenham Examiner*, 10 September 1863, p. 4.

[10] See *The Tablet*, 25 December 1875, p. 19, 2 June 1888, p. 35, and 30 June 1888, p. 33. The community moved to Park Street, Taunton in 1867. Mother Frances Graham died in 1928 at the age of 85. Her father, a retired Colonel of the Bengal Army, died in March 1888, leaving £34,547.

[11] Pauline Caffieri died on 1 January 1883 at St Wilfred's Convent, Chelsea.

[12] www.newman.reader.org/works/letters_diaries. Visits from Miss Smith 20 September and 4 November 1864, and 15 December 1865, Vol. XXI, pp. 246, 284, Vol. XXII p. 111; Newman to Sr Cephasie, 25 November 1864, Vol. XXI, p. 229.

[13] *With All My Heart*, Scarisbrick to Sr Aloysia, undated letter, pp. 119–20.

[14] Clara Shepperd returned to Cheltenham during her long widowhood and, as Madame Rotunda, was a locally celebrated singer.

37 RELUCTANT GUARANTOR AND LANDLORD

APART FROM THE ever present building work there were other matters to take up Fr Cotham's time and test his patience. During 1869 he became financially entangled with Mr Henry Cookefoye, eventually losing some £200 in bad debts, although none of this is noted in the accounts book for the period.[1] Poor Mr Cookefoye seems to have lost a great deal more. The arrival of Cookefoye coincided with plans for the Daughters of the Cross to make a new foundation in Chelsea, their hopes for a girls boarding school in Cheltenham having failed. Although Cookefoye came independently it is apparent that Fr Cotham saw possibilities in his scheme for attracting boys to a private Catholic school.

On 27 November 1868 a Memorandum of Agreement, confirmed in a handwritten note of 2 February 1869, was drawn up between Fr Cotham and Henry Cookefoye whereby Fr Cotham stood as guarantor for Cookefoye's loan of £200 drawn on the Gloucestershire Banking Company. In the document Cookefoye is described as 'Principal of an Establishment for Private Pupils at Holmesdale Lawn [Lansdown Road] Cheltenham', for which he had signed a lease with Lieutenant-General Singleton in October 1868. As security Fr Cotham was given an inventory of all the goods and plate in the house which he would be at liberty to sell to recover his money should Cookefoye default on the loan.

The scheme was a disaster, although it might never have been a viable proposition: whereas other educational establishments advertised regularly, for example, there are no advertisements in the *Cheltenham Looker-On* for 1869 to alert prospective clients that Cookefoye was open for business. Writing from Chester on 10 November 1869 to Fr Cotham, Henry, 'stricken down with grief and anxiety' explains that he is writing to all his creditors to

454 *The Indomitable Mr Cotham*

tell them that from 'circumstances over which [he] has no control' he has been compelled to give up the school. He had been 'induced' to form the school after receiving six or eight pupils, sons of gentlemen, to be prepared for college or competitive examinations. He had a justifiable hope, he thought, that a reasonable number of other pupils would follow. Since these had not been forthcoming he was now in 'pecuniary difficulties'. He begs forbearance since he had no intention to defraud anyone and solemnly promises to repay, with interest, everything he owes, when he is able.

Cookefoye is described as a 'Tutor' in Woodchester, Gloucestershire when he married in April 1868. Cotham had received a visit from Henry Danvers Clark of Atcombe House, Woodchester just two months before. He may have been one of those who offered inducements to Henry to open a boarding school. The intensely Catholic character of William Leigh's Woodchester estate, complete with Dominican monastery and Franciscan convent, may have led Henry into a miscalculation about the number of pupils he was likely to attract, in a short time, to Cheltenham.

At this point in the letter Mr Cookefoye, 'without money, without effects', realises what a distant prospect this is. 'I can only trust for mercy, for prosecution will profit nothing. I cannot give what I have not.' He sees now that his establishment was a precarious venture and he wants only to be permanently employed by someone else. Enigmatically he writes, 'I had to get quickly away for your interest', perhaps to protect Fr Cotham's promissory note. Nevertheless, Fr Cotham 'would, I think, pity us if you could see us now.' There is no suggestion in the letters that Fr Cotham had been the one to encourage Cookefoye's ambitions but he may have expressed a hope that an establishment with a Catholic Principal would attract the sons of Catholic gentlemen who otherwise would have to go out of the town for their education.

Having appealed for mercy and pity Mr Cookefoye proceeds to list some items 'not on the inventory' which would be useful

Reluctant Guarantor and Landlord

to him. Evidently Cookefoye and his wife had departed Cheltenham in some haste.

> My poor wife left her best skirt, her straw hat, a little hamper with some preserves and Australian mutton, and a set of china the present of a dear friend, and a nightdress, and she begs me to appeal to your goodness to let her have these.

Henry himself then remembers, in precise detail, the items he has 'forgot': his educational tools such as his drawing materials, chemical and physical bottles, and various books. Fr Cotham is entreated to pack these things in a large hamper for transit, ready to be sent to the forwarding address which he will shortly be sent.

Cookefoye received no reply to this letter; two weeks later a similarly worded letter arrived, this time from London, beginning where the previous one ended, with Mr Cookefoye's state of ill health, 'completely knocked up in body and mind, and even yet I am scarcely fit for anything, so weak and unsteady do I feel'. Nevertheless, he has managed to retrieve some paperwork from his few belongings: the fire insurance receipt for Holmesdale Lawn, the lease agreement, and a memorandum of fixtures written by the property agent Mr Sweeting. Cookefoye had provided Fr Cotham with an inventory of the furnishings which he had bought for the house, some of which Sweeting now claimed to belong to the property and not to Cookefoye: certain curtains and chandeliers which could be converted into cash for Cookefoye or his creditors. As for other items, such as the glass spirit lamp and coffee machine (all theoretically now forfeit to Fr Cotham) as they are really not worth much he begs Mr Cotham to send them on to him. The books, magazines, and manuscripts are also valueless to anyone except himself so Fr Cotham is asked to take charge of them until such time as Cookefoye can buy them back.

The letter ends with contrite assurances of gratitude for any favour which can be done for them. The postscript strikes a different note, perhaps hinting at Henry's resilience to teach

456 *The Indomitable Mr Cotham*

another day: 'PS All appurtenances belonging to the double engine, not with the engine itself, will be found in the library amongst the tools. The long brass pipe is the connecting pipe between engine and boiler.'

When Cookefoye fled from Cheltenham he put Holmesdale Lawn 'unreservedly in the hands of Mr Baker', in effect making Fr Cotham responsible for his legal bills. On 13 December Augustus Baker sent Cotham a memorandum of costs, as requested, including £16 5s. 9d. for the 'Cookefoye matter' and this was far from the total amount. Baker informs his friend Fr Cotham, 'I did not charge in our books one half of the attendances and letters—I thought your loss by Cookefoye too great for you to afford to pay full costs. As you will see from the three little bills enclosed I have in most instances charged only costs out of pocket and nominal fees.'

Whether Fr Cotham did take pity on the Cookefoyes is not recorded but Henry's letters arrived while George Wilson was busy with the house clearance from 6 to 13 November ready for T. F. Cossens removals service on the 16th. Finally, in January 1870, exactly a year after guaranteeing Mr Cookefoye's bank loan, Fr Cotham arranged for George Sweeting to take delivery of the goods remaining in his hands to be sold at a discount of twenty-five per cent of the marked costs on the inventory.

Almost overlooked in the correspondence is Henry Cookefoye's wife. Amongst his books is 'a collection of good tracts, catechisms etc [made] with a view to [his] wife's conversion'. She does ask for a few personal possessions, including the 'the curtains in the drawing room which were an especial present to herself'; very likely they had been a wedding present when the Cookefoyes married only a few months before financial troubles hit them. Agnes Mary Relton, from Manchester, was 24 when she married 38 year-old Henry in the spring of 1868 in Cockermouth and she quickly became pregnant. Soon after arriving in Cheltenham, Agnes was confirmed at St Gregory's with ninety-five other candidates on 20 December 1868, sharing Mlle Sophie Tiesset as her sponsor with

Reluctant Guarantor and Landlord 457

half of the group. A daughter, Agnes Mary, was born on 10 July 1869 and baptised in St Gregory's a month later by Fr Cotham, with Bryan Stapleton and Christina Plumer as godparents, neither of whom seems to have been regular congregants at the church. The baby is never mentioned in the correspondence; perhaps she was given to relatives in Cumberland to look after during the chaotic first months after leaving Cheltenham.[2]

Cotham became involved with, and extricated himself from, the Cookefoyes following his own judgement. He inherited another vexatious situation which he tried unsuccessfully to amend for twenty years, only partially succeeding when it was time for him to leave Cheltenham. Although he was without property himself, as missioner for Cheltenham Cotham became trustee for 13 and 14 St James Street, Cheltenham. In 1862 he began a small black accounts book for rent received and expenses paid relating to the two small houses, following extensive building repairs and wall papering. At the end of the book he copied out the conveyance details since the land was first bought in 1806. In 1807 Hugh Reynolds paid £505 for houses standing on a plot measuring 42 ft by 28 ft; if accurate it bears out Fr Birdsall's experience of the high price of land in Cheltenham at that period. These houses were bequeathed by Reynold's widow, on her death in 1848, to Revd William Dunstan Scott OSB and Revd Joseph Wilson OSB 'for the benefit of the Irish poor'. Unfortunately the original state of the houses, and the continuous work needed to keep them habitable, offset the benefits accruing from the rents. Between 1862 and 1867 Cotham recorded £110 16s. 5½d. received in rent, out of which only £16 17s. 3d. was distributed to the 'Destitute Irish Poor'.

St James Street (a coincidental echo of St James Square), at the top end of the High Street, was home to shop keepers and small traders. Samuel Hicks, a fruit dealer, and his wife Mary Ann lived at number 14 with their four small children and paid a regular rent of £1 per month for ten years; number 13 regularly changed hands until it stood empty by 1870. Nevertheless, taxes and rates

458 *The Indomitable Mr Cotham*

increased or were introduced, for sewers and unspecified 'improvement', and repairs were ongoing, from the roof to the well in the garden. Fr Scott grasped the scale of the problem in 1846, two years before Julia Reynolds' death.

> The two houses belonging to Mrs Reynolds were, when I saw them many years ago, in a very wretched state of affairs, and tenants could hardly be found to occupy them ... a little fund of that kind [for the poor Irish] would be useful enough in Cheltenham, but the Houses are in so ruinous a state and in so wretched a place that they will be a continuous plague, and if sold the produce would be but little. I care not to advise on such a matter.[3]

Twenty-five years later Cotham was ready to offload the properties as a liability rather than an asset. Charles Rainger found a cash buyer for the houses: £225 in total, if sold within the week, or he could put them forward for auction with other properties in his portfolio if Cotham preferred. By the time he wrote to Fr Scott, still at Little Malvern, the following month Cotham's proposal was to use the properties as almhouses. Fr Scott 'had not a word to say against it,' as long as Mrs Reynolds' original intentions were honoured. Cotham had suggested his colleague Aloysius Wilkinson as a trustee of the new scheme. The very infirm 80-year-old Scott replied in spidery handwriting,

> You are quite right in putting the property in young and honest names, but they ought to be healthy people. Now, is not Fr Wilkinson frequently ailing and always in delicate health? His name would do well in every way except health. On that account he would hardly be a fit name.

In 1872 this was not a verdict on his assistant priest Cotham wanted to hear. With so much still to be done in Cheltenham no-one could afford to have delicate health, and to be fair to Wilkinson he was Cotham's equal for the next thirty years in dedicating himself to St Gregory's. He was duly appointed a trustee of the Deed of Gift by which Cotham and Fr Wilson

Reluctant Guarantor and Landlord 459

handed over ownership of the St James Street houses, together with Fr Wulstan Richards OSB and Matthew Boyle Williams, one of George Arthur Williams' sons, young and honest names of the next generation and no more delicate than their predecessors.

The two other properties for which Fr Cotham had responsibility gave him more direct satisfaction. Mrs Monington shared some of the maintenance costs for Bueno House, 10 St James Square, but she also had to tolerate a house which was shabby and neglected, despite some new furnishings bought in 1853. A full inventory of furniture was made in October 1857 when Charles Riddell became a tenant for twelve months, prior to Mrs Monington moving in. The five bedrooms naturally reflect the occupants' status; the carpet in the smallest room measured 11 ft by 6 ft, while the main double bedroom had bedside carpeting to a length of thirteen yards. The first floor double drawing room was in effect two rooms, furnished with some fine antique pieces and oil paintings, although the house appraiser noted that various items were damaged or worn. In the hall there was a square clock and a barometer, and another barometer in the hall water closet. The dining room paintings were uninspired coaching scenes, landscapes and ruins, and the soft furnishings tended to be old and dirty, or worn and old. The breakfast room was evidently used as a storeroom for unwanted furniture ('easy chair, covered leather, much worn') including a French bedstead and a quantity of bedding. The library completed the ground floor accommodation which was all provided with gas lighting.

Downstairs in the kitchen almost everything was chipped, cracked or partly broken; the assessor summed up after two pages, 'cooking utensils generally in a bad state'. The same was true of the butler's pantry; fifteen dinner knives were matched with six dinner forks, but pudding knives and forks numbered a dozen. The 'liquor stand, three bottles' had been removed to 3 Somerset House in 1867 when a new dinner service had been bought for Bueno House; the handwriting recording the change is Fr Cotham's. The housekeeping room, scullery, and larder completed the below stairs apartments.

The extent of the work carried out by Mrs Excell in 1860 and Richard Dutton in 1861 indicates how the house had deteriorated in less than thirty years. Mrs Excell, an upholstress employing a number of women, provided new carpets, curtains, bed and sofa covers, and all sorts of fringes, tassels, and leather trimmings to bookcases. The dingy interior of Bueno House was transformed over a twelve month period, for just under £7. Richard Dutton worked on the fabric of the house. The hall, stairs and kitchen were papered and whitened and the chimney pots were repaired and re-sited, suggesting smoke had been an indoor problem. Most of the work, however, was external, partly to improve conditions below stairs and partly to make good problems caused by extending the chancel of the church to within fifteen feet of the house. The ground was excavated to 'make airy' the side of the house and allow light and air into the cellar, and the paving 'sunken by ruts' was taken up and relayed. The window sashes were repaired and the house was repainted back and front. Number ten was clearly considered then, as now, an integral part St Gregory's. A plumber improved various parts of the water closet, pipes and cistern; Ambrose Cotham always had a keen interest in efficient drains. The work, involving a number of craftsmen, cost only £14 5s. and puts into perspective the sum of £10,000 spent on the church, before work on the tower and spire began.

The houses in St James Street and 10 St James Square were sources of revenue for the mission, and the priest in charge had a duty to maintain them adequately. Three Somerset Place was the clergy house, although also used for paying lodgers, and Fr Cotham did not neglect its upkeep. The notebook recording expenses was started in September 1852 detailing the buying of wall paper, carpets and small furnishings, while extensive plumbing work was carried out in November 1858 to excavate, fill and block up the cess pit and replace it with plumbed in water closets. Gas was extended from the church in 1856 and extra ventilation

Reluctant Guarantor and Landlord 461

was installed in 1864. Fr Cotham makes a point of noting when he has purchased items at sales or auctions. James Healy had to sell up his house in 1862, before moving abroad for the sake of his failing health. Cotham spent over £50 at the sale, benefitting his former committee member and restocking Bueno House. From September 1852 to 1 January 1866 he reckoned to have spent £532 15s. 4d. on 3 Somerset Place, offset 'By Lodgers and Boarders with Tuition from 28 September 1853 to 1 January 1866' which brought in £545 9s. 9d. Nothing else is said about these residents; Fr Birdsall had added a third storey to the clergy house to take paying guests and it seems the practice had continued.

Notes

[1] See DA IV.C.XI.2 for all papers relating to Cotham and Henry Cookefoye. The spelling of the surname varies: Cookfoye, and Cook(e) Foy(e) is also used by the family.

[2] The Cookefoyes had two more daughters, Edith Mary, born 1871 and Madeline Ann Mary, born 1872. Henry Cookefoye died in 1881 and his wife in 1909 in Lancashire, although her address was given as Bayswater. She left £1,237, one of her executors being Revd Joseph Aloysius Worsley.

[3] Revd William Dunstan Scott to unnamed Benedictine, 1 November 1846.

38 FAMILY BUSINESS & FINANCIAL ACUMEN

APART FROM RELIGIOUS matters—the state of the Catholic Church in England and abroad, their own experiences as priests of orders which were sometimes mutually acrimonious and territorial, and the challenges of the home mission—the two Cotham brothers shared other concerns. They were intimately involved in their brother's and sister's families. Access to private funds, and the management of Lawrence's share, allowed and made it necessary for William and James to take a personal and financial interest in the education of Lawrence's children. Two nephews and two great nephews were brought over to England for their senior schooling and uncles William and James obviously determined to do their best for the young men. As a member of the Society of Jesus, William was not permitted to own property or manage family finances so James kept the records for him and also for Lawrence in Queensland, Australia. He was allowed to use the money quite freely by William, giving rise to an inflated estimation of his personal wealth.

Isabella Shepherd, formerly Cotham, died in December 1847 and William, her only son in England became her heir, as well as receiving property that had belonged to her sister Mary Ann Pollard. It was after this and other property was liquidated from 1869 onwards in favour of foreign stocks that the Cothams' capital steadily grew. Their wealth came not from the vaunted connections with Hardshaw Hall but from the lesser known maternal side of the family. Isabella's father, James Hall, was a surgeon from Whalley; his marriage to Mary Ann Wharton of Ribchester in 1777 anchored the Cothams in the hinterland of Lancashire rather than the port city of Liverpool where their father practised medicine. In 1848 Fr William Cotham accumulated rural properties in Slaidburn and houses in Manchester from the Hall and Wharton side.[1]

Fr William Cotham SJ, 1806–1895, Fr James Cotham's elder brother.

In an account book with a pasted label on the brown mottled outside cover entitled 'Receipts and Payments on account of the Revd William Cotham's Properties in Lancashire and the Foreign

Family Business & Financial Acumen 465

Stocks' a record was kept of monies invested, collected, and expended from 1862 to 1883. An almost identical notebook turned up among Fr William Cotham's papers,[2] the entries from September 1862 until December 1867 being written in a fair hand that suggest it was copied on a single occasion. There are a few corrections in Fr Cotham's hand and three entries for 1868 written by Fr Cotham complete the book; the remaining pages have been torn out. James Cotham's book starts with an 'Abstract from deeds of <u>property</u> belonging to the Rev. William Cotham; and administered by the Rev. James Cotham'. A page of notes follows headed '1678 Reign of Charles II' concerning land in Bolton by Bowland: Nappy Miredale or Nappy Flats, assigned by Thomas Ayrton to William Godard; and 'the Ring Close' by Godard to William Wilkinson in 1687, the land belonging to Bartholomew Walmsley of Dunkenhalgh. This land amounted to less than two acres and Fr Ambrose chose not to copy the fuller details given in Fr William's notebook relating to property transactions between 1753 and 1828—the Brown Cow Inn at Chatburn, Dugdales Farm, Black Moss Farm and smaller crofts. James Hall of Whalley comes into the property in 1774, shortly before his marriage and adds Manchester property to his portfolio. According to James Cotham the annual rents for all the property amounted to £114 14s. after tax in 1865, when they 'were entrusted to me to administer in education of my Brother Laurence's children'. On the security of the property he advanced money to his brother. The day to day accounts are substantially the same in both books and the following details are taking from Fr James' version.

On the pages following the property details, the serial numbers of one hundred and forty 'Egyptian Viceroys for the year 1865 belonging to the estate of the Rev William Cotham' are painstakingly listed plus a batch of twenty bonds of £100 each invested in the Egyptian Tribute Loan of 1871. The account book is in various hands, mostly as a fair copy with occasional entries in Fr Cotham's own hand. It ends with two pages detailing the work done by Canons Hurworth and O'Neill as 'a friendly and confidential commission' in handling Turkish stocks worth £4,000 for the benefit of two of Fr James Cotham's great-nephews after his death in May 1883. Hence there is some muddle in the book about whose affairs it relates to but on the whole it seems to refer to Fr William Cotham's finances, his share of rental income from shared property, and arrangements made on behalf of Lawrence Cotham and his family in Brisbane, sometimes referred to as 'the Settlement'. Very occasionally Fr James is a beneficiary for a small sum, as in July 1870 for 'Wm C travelling expenses, £1.10s; J.C. ditto £1 4s'. The share of property in and around Manchester was sold on 5 August 1871 for £1,200.

A second account book, a small red notebook with what looks like a postal label on the front, is titled: '**WITH CARE** Numbers of Bonds for Revds William and James Cotham'. However on the inside facing page, numbered '7' with previous pages cut out, thirty-eight bonds totalling £7,000 of the Turkish Egyptian Tribute Loan, 1871 and 1877, are said to belong to the estate of the Revd William Cotham, Preston, Lancashire. This red notebook was probably written during the two years of retirement James spent at St Edmunds, Douai in the mid-1870s. The entries in both books make clear (most of the time) that the estate and money dealt with actually belonged to Fr William Cotham SJ, although Fr James was in charge, keeping a running total of the transactions. Six pages of information about shares is copied out in Cotham's clear hand; the pages are small and the text is not closely written but the sense of it is hard to grasp now, and perhaps was at the time:

> Agreement made 17 Sep 1877. Nominal amount of loan of Egy[n] Tribute Loan £5,378,700. On the extinction of the loan of 1854 the whole of the annual sum applicable to the service of that loan, viz. £99,511 17s. 6d shall be applied as a sinking fund for the loan of 1871.

Nevertheless, he was confident enough to deal in shares:

> 20th January 1879. Bought for the Settlement 30th Instant, 7000 Egyptian Unified 6% @ 49⅞—£3,500 including £8 15s. 0d. commission.

Family Business & Financial Acumen 467

The notebook is completed by fourteen pages of pasted-in newspaper reports from late 1879 to early 1880 relating to Egyptian finances and negotiations engaged in by Messrs Baring and de Blignières to secure the high rates of interest investors had been used to receiving. These cuttings were read and digested as shown by underlining of phrases such as the 'possibility that greedy and litigious claimants may stand out against an equitable arrangement'. Fr Cotham seems to have followed the foreign stock market with informed interest although it is impossible to tell how anxious he was about the safety of the family's investments. Among the heavyweight commentary two small advertisements are pasted in: one for the Bank of Australasia in Threadneedle Street which gave letters of credit and bills in their branches in Australia for the transfer of money, and another promoting 'newly invented acoustics for the relief of deafness ... Conversation Tubes, Auricles, Trumpets to hear in Church &c.'

Was the morality of European investments, especially French and English, in the emerging Egyptian economy of the nineteenth century debated by the Cothams, or by Douai which was similarly involved? The achievement of Egypt's independence from the Ottoman Empire and a race towards Western style modernity was won at the price of becoming a virtual colony of Britain. Transformative schemes pushed through by Ismail Pasha (1803–95) such as agricultural irrigation, nine hundred miles of railways, the building of the Suez Canal by the French, and modern schooling—all dependent on foreign innovation, supplies, and investment—bankrupted Egypt, forcing the country to accept a British military presence in 1882 on the pretext of safeguarding shareholders' interests.[3] Benefitting, for example, from the six per cent interest rate on the Egyptian Tribute Ottoman Loan of 1871 and the Unified Debt Loan of 1876 several thousand pounds worth of shares were bought, occasionally for William Cotham alone or 'the settlement' (Lawrence Cotham) in Queensland.

James Cotham had money of his own; he contributed generously to St Gregory's and left substantial legacies after his death

468   *The Indomitable Mr Cotham*

but there are no separate extant financial records to explain this wealth. The excised first six pages of the red notebook might have explained these holdings further, since it is probable that James invested his Australian pension and other capital in stocks and shares. Whatever level of understanding they had about the effect the national debt would have on Egypt's own economy, the Cothams were meticulous in keeping their account books year by year. It is also incontrovertible that the long term plan was for a large proportion of the stocks to be transferred to the Australian branch of the family, although it was an unwelcome fact to St Edmunds, Douai when the time came for it to happen.

The credit side of the accounts starts modestly with three incoming cash payments for the period: £20 in March 1863 from Revd William Cotham and two payments totalling £50 5s. 11d. against the name 'Nicholas', referring to Mary Ann's son Nicholas Maguire (later Hall), a medical student at King's College, and perhaps mistakenly entered in the wrong column. Thereafter the income until July 1871 comes from property rents. A share of the rent on houses in Kings Street and Cross Street, Manchester yielded £22 half-yearly less tax and three shillings and sixpence deduction for the tenants' dinner each rent day. Other property was owned in and around Gisburne and Chatburne in the so-called Honor of Clitheroe. Repairs and sales of property were put into the hands of Dixon Robinson's firm of solicitors, though not, presumably of Mr Robinson himself who enjoyed the title of 'Gentleman Steward of the Honor of Clitheroe', a position whose residence and office was Clitheroe Castle.

The legal side of managing the properties was handled by Fr Cotham's trusted friend and legal advisor in Cheltenham, Augustus Baker, who did everything from preparing advertisements to travelling to Clitheroe himself only a fortnight before his fourth child was born and baptised. Rents were received from Thomas Scott, Richard Dixon, William Croasdale, and Lord Ribblesdale and the customary tenants' dinner was held at the Brown Cow Inn at Chatburne, owned by the Cothams until it was sold to

Family Business & Financial Acumen 469

William Croasdale in July 1869. Blackmoss and Dugdales Farms were sold to Dixon Robinson for £1,050 in July 1871, and finally two pieces of land in Nappa Flats were sold to John Yorke Esq. in December 1873, bringing to an end the income from property which had long been overtaken in value by dividends and sales of shares which had been steadily accumulated since 1869.

Interest on the Egyptian Bonds begins to appear from September 1869; thereafter there is buying and selling of Peruvian Bonds, Guatemalan Bonds, Honduran Stock, and Egyptian Viceroys and Khedive Loan Bonds, averaging £1,000 per transaction, sometimes specifically for 'the settlement'. The high point for incoming interest was in 1877 when £1,305 8s. was realised.

Looking after the family

Details of the financial dealings are interwoven with entries which explain their practical application. After the preamble pages the first entry of the brown accounts book begins in September 1862 with the following payments:

Account books &c	5/-
Outfit and passage to Brisbane for Master W.C.	£41.9.6
Rev William Cotham to pay St Mary's College, Derby	£32.0.0
Goods sent to Brisbane with Wm. 1863	£10.10.6
Nov 20 Apprenticeship of Wm. In Brisbane	£110.19.11
Aug 13 Hugh's passage from Brisbane to England	£25.00

The notebooks are not merely a record of financial accounting undertaken in Fr William Cotham's name; they are also a summary of the interconnectedness of the brothers. The welfare of the first and second generation of Lawrence and Sarah's family was the concern of all three brothers. Through his nephews and nieces, and their children, Fr Cotham continued to have a possibly unique interest among his Benedictine contemporaries in the future of Australia long after Bishop Polding's vision had failed to materialise. The accounts notebooks coincide with Lawrence Cotham's

470 *The Indomitable Mr Cotham*

move from Tasmania to Queensland when the focus shifts from the establishment of his own career to those of his children.

At the end of the 1850s Lawrence and Sarah Cotham were finalising their arrangements for leaving Tasmania, disposing of their business interests, and providing for the future of their children. They had not suffered badly from the economic depression of the previous decade but financial calamity had hit the Cassidy family after the death of John and his wife. Their only son, Hugh, had continued his family's tradition of generous support for the church, presbytery, and school in Richmond but it seems Hugh did not have his father's business acumen. Fr Dunne, parish priest of Richmond, wrote to Fr Therry, in Sydney, that he had never seen 'so heartrending a spectacle as the departure of the poor Cassidy family' reduced to 'utter destitution'.[4] Dunne opened a subscription to support them, despite his opinion that their ruin had been brought about by neglect and extravagance, and bought Woodburn himself. He enjoyed its use during his lifetime but it was always intended to be *de facto* church property, as specified in his Will.[5] In December 1858 Madame M'Carthy opened a Seminary for Young Catholic Ladies in Launceston, assisted by one of the elder Miss Cothams, Marianne or Isabella. The changes continued into the New Year. In February Lawrence was in court, again, successfully defending himself against selling a damaged boat from his wharf at Restdown Ferry. Two months later his second surviving son, William, sailed for England. The last of Lawrence's livestock and farm implements was auctioned at Glenorchy in April 1860 as he prepared to exchange his small town and rural life for the developing city of Brisbane, Queensland. His choice of the newest settlement on Australia's east coast over Sydney, Melbourne, or Adelaide, suggests his interest lay in the potential it offered rather than the accomplishments already on offer in the older cities.

One of Lawrence's first businesses in Brisbane was the acquisition of a two-year government contract to run the daily mail coach, with extra express journeys when required, between Brisbane and

Family Business & Financial Acumen 471

Ipswich.[6] He also applied to be an assessor of rates for the Municipal Council of Ipswich but his tender was not accepted, in part because he had affronted the councillors by not completing the application form in his own handwriting: they accepted he had a good education but they needed evidence of a 'good hand' as well. For someone who had been self-employed for all his adult life this seems an odd choice of job, unless Lawrence thought it would be a way of prospecting for promising property and commercial opportunities for himself. For the first and only time his wife Sarah advertised in her own right, offering board and residence 'to gentlemen requiring a quiet home in a respectable family'.[7] The Cothams had taken a house in Limestone Street formerly occupied by Mr Cribb, one of the councillors annoyed by Lawrence's proxy application form. Within a year Mrs Cotham was selling up her business (not as a going concern) and advertising the sale of all the household goods. The contrast with their former life in Tasmania, centred on farming and livestock, is marked but not regretted by their children who preferred the pen over the plough.

'Master W. C.' in the first entry of the account book in September 1862 refers to Lawrence's son William; he was the first member of his family to make the journey back to England. The relative frequency of visits thereafter gives the lie to the popular perception of almost total isolation and lack of communication between the two hemispheres. The length of time it took did not deter the passage of people and goods between destinations, even when the journey was made in the hope of seeing a sick relative before death. William was apparently more academically inclined than his elder brother Lawrence. He attended St Mary's Diocesan Seminary (for boys only) in Hobart and gained the prize for geography as a 12 year-old in 1855. At the end of his education there he sailed from Hobart for London in April 1859 on board the *Harrowby* with a number of other young people and a few of their mothers. His uncles had chosen the Jesuit college of Mount St Mary's, Spinkhill, perhaps for its location between Lancashire and Gloucestershire; Fr Cotham had included it in his homecoming itinerary, on 23 July 1851. The three years there were successful for William and he went on to serve his articles in Queensland with Mr F. I. Power of Gympie before qualifying as a solicitor in 1869. William did not marry; his love was for sport—cricket especially, horse racing, rifle shooting, boat racing—both as enthusiastic participant and committee member and he was a popular feisty young man in the town of Maryborough. With two companions he provided 'a startling buggy accident' when the horse bolted, unseating the other men.

> Mr Cotham remained in the vehicle, and indiscreetly taking upon himself to teach the horse, who was rather spirited, a moral lesson, used the whip freely. The whipped steed, accompanied by his mentor, then made a rapid tour of the town ... [Cotham made his escape before the vehicle crashed] the body of the buggy had to be gathered up with a small-tooth garden rake. The evil-minded animal suffered but little from his escapade.[8]

His move to Bundaberg in 1879 was surprising, but taking his chances by going to a sparsely populated district paid off as he was able to establish a reputation for himself in mining matters.[9] Becoming a solicitor made him the first career professional in Lawrence's family and more than that kept him on the right side of the law. Investment in his education had paid dividends. Lawrence and Sarah Cotham's aspirations for their children were founded on their own manual labour and business acumen as well as their readiness to seek new opportunities for the whole family. On the voyage home William carried goods worth ten guineas bought by Ambrose Cotham for his brother's business: there was no disdain for money made from trade.

By 1863 Lawrence was finding his way more confidently in the urban environment and settled on commerce, for a while at least. He was proprietor of a hay and corn store in Mary Street and having registered as a qualified pharmacist in Brisbane opened a chemist and druggist store (which included dispensing horse and cattle medicine) in Stanley Street, South Brisbane. The following year he

Family Business & Financial Acumen

also had a butcher's shop in Sydney Street, later becoming a partner in Walmsley and Cotham butcher's firm in South Brisbane. The nuisance of chasing petty debts from customers and errant employees occasionally spilled over into fisticuffs as on the occasion he assailed Dr Lennox Cunningham and allegedly 'smashed his nasal bone'. Lawrence's defence witness claimed that the doctor had kept up a 'fighting attitude' and had struck the first blow; not for the first time the provocation and threatening behaviour on both sides led to the case being dismissed, without lasting damage to either man's reputation as respectable personages in the community.[10]

Mary Street, Gympie, Queensland, 1868.

Besides providing for livestock, the potential human clientele of Lawrence's pharmacy and the dangers they encountered is vividly summed up in an advertisement from 1866:

> MEDICAL NOTICE. TO HEADS OF FAMILIES, SQUATTERS, AND OTHERS IN THE BUSH. COX'S COMPANION to the FAMILY MEDICINE CHEST, and COMPENDIUM of DOMESTIC MEDICINE, particularly adapted for Heads of Families, Missionaries, and Colonists, with plain Rules for taking the Medicines, to which are

474 *The Indomitable Mr Cotham*

> added Directions for restoring suspended animation, the method of obviating the effects Poisons, a plain description of the Treatment of Fractures and Dislocations, and a concise account of Asiatic or Spasmodic Cholera. Revised and considerably enlarged by R. Davis, Member of the Royal College of Surgeons, assisted by some of the most eminent Physicians and Surgeons of the day. Forty-second edition.
>
> L. COTHAM begs to notify that he has just received a few copies of the above, and that all articles sold and dispensed at his establishment are guaranteed genuine, and imported direct to his order from the first houses in England. Professional gentlemen and the trade supplied at Sydney prices. Stanley-street, South Brisbane.[11]

The orders were being directed via his clerical brothers' agency. Between March 1866 and October 1867 five consignments were sent to Brisbane from Liverpool: drugs bought in Manchester from influential pharmaceutical suppliers such as Woolley and Hodgkinson, druggists' bottles from St Helens, and chemical fittings from Tomlinsons. The total amount of goods totalled little more than £100, a modest sum in light of the later transactions.

The purpose of Lawrence's business activities was to provide for his family materially and socially and part of this involved taking their place among the active Catholics of Brisbane, supporting the fund raising activities to build and maintain churches and schools. As expected, this was the milieu for finding marriage partners. In October 1863 Lawrence's eldest daughter Marianne was the first to marry, to Gustavus Caesar Horstmann, in St Stephen's Church. Her husband had come from Hamburg a few years previously and was to make his reputation as an accomplished accountant in the Auditor-General's office for over twenty-five years before setting up in private practice.

Lawrence's youngest daughter Eleanor received payments of £152 towards her 'Convent pension' at All Hallows, Brisbane from October 1863 to 1865, when she was aged 17 to 19, and a piano

Family Business & Financial Acumen 475

costing £25. A further £100 was sent out to her in 1873; as she did not marry until 1883 when she was 37 Eleanor may have been following a career as a school teacher. The family had even closer links with the Convent. Sarah Cotham, the third daughter, joined the Sisters of Mercy as a novice in November 1864, an event reported in the Tasmanian press:

> A few weeks since, at the Convent of All Hallows, a reception took place. The Right Rev. Dr. Quinn, Roman Catholic Bishop, officiated. The lady received was Miss Sarah Cotham, a daughter of an old and respected colonist of Tasmania, but now a resident in Queensland. This lady was for many years a pupil of the Misses Lavers, at Hobart Town, from whom she received the instruction that has prepared her for the solemn responsibilities of her present position.[12]

As Sr Catherine Mary Aloysius she was sent to work in the Cairncross Orphanage, New Farm in premises which were grossly overcrowded and unhealthy. During an epidemic of whooping cough, measles, and pneumonia among the children Catherine also succumbed; she had been professed only fourteen months and was the first Sister of the Mercy congregation to die in Queensland. The home's chaplain, Fr Robert Dunne (later to become Bishop of Brisbane in 1882) was so affected by the circumstances of her death that he hurried on a move to improved, spacious buildings.[13] The news would have been shocking to her Cotham uncles who were familiar with the 'white martyrdom' of priests who died during the typhoid epidemics in Liverpool in 1840s. Ironically, at the time of Sr Catherine's death Fr William Cotham SJ was visiting the fever hospital in Liverpool, a duty he performed from 1864 to 1872 while stationed at Lowe House, St Helens. After his death *The Stonyhurst Magazine* reminisced that he used to boast how the fever cases fell especially to him 'owing to the fact that his strong constitution was supposed to have rendered him impregnable'.[14]

476 *The Indomitable Mr Cotham*

The eldest nephew, Lawrence Leopold, was making in his own way in the world. In 1861 he married Eliza Chater in Victoria, Eliza's home state, quite possibly being there as a gold prospector. This was Larry, who had seen Uncle James aboard the *Australasia* in 1851, and as a 10-year-old had accompanied Lawrence on a short jaunt to the Victorian goldfields in 1852. The first child, Laura Kate was born and died in 1863; two sons followed, James Ambrose, born in 1866, and Arthur Leopold, in 1868. Lawrence followed the gold rush eight hundred miles north of his parents' home, as far as the Cape River holdings. It was not a place to take family:

> The Cape in 1868 was a decidedly rough locality, there being fully two thousand five hundred men, representing many nationalities, and among them the scum of all the Southern Gold Fields ... Gold was easily obtained and much more easily spent. Dreadful stuff, called whisky, rum and brandy, was sold in shilling drinks, and there was no need to wonder that many of the poor fellows, after the usual spree, became raving maniacs. Picture in your imagination a mob of two hundred or three hundred half-drunk semi-madmen running amok with each other in the brutal fights which were a daily occurrence![15]

Fr Cotham did not need to imagine such scenes after his first-hand experience in Tasmania; thirty years later, after educational opportunities and considerable financial investment, it was not the life his nephews were meant to be pursuing.

The youngest of Lawrence's sons, Hugh, came to England in 1863 when he was 12; unlike his elder brother William he was harder to place in an appropriate school. Details in the accounts book do not appear until October 1865 when he has a new pair of boots for eight shillings and sixpence in preparation for moving to a senior school. For the next four years Hugh appears frequently, beginning with a journey to St Michael's, Belmont where he stayed for two years and needed a cassock, shirts, and skates, as well as pocket money. St Michael's had been founded as a common novitiate for the English Benedictine Congregation and Fr Cotham

Family Business & Financial Acumen

visited as often as possible for refreshment from the rigours of St Gregory's building site. Between 1861 and 1874, during Prior Bede Vaughan's term in office, the college experimented with a 'little seminary' offering secondary education to boys who were not explicitly preparing for monastic or priestly life.

There is nothing to indicate how congenial the seminary setting was for Hugh—life was austere for the monks and probably Spartan for the boys—but he definitely did not have his sights set on further progress at Belmont. At the age of 16 in autumn 1867 he was sent to Mr G. White's school in Kentish Town, London (Mr White probably being an alumnus of Stony-hurst), presumably for training in a professional career. A still-growing boy (although he was never more than 5 ft 2 in.), he needed more shirts, collars, socks, leggings, slippers, and a cap, as well as a suit of clothes for a working lad. Eleven shillings and a penny was paid to Miss Lamont for expenses, presumably to shop for Hugh. He was also given a cricket bat, ball, and wickets costing seventeen shillings and sixpence; cricket became his passion when he eventually returned home. In the middle of July 1868 Hugh travelled to Lille, to enrol at St Edmund's, Douai for a final year of schooling, probably to polish his French language skills. Finally his first, lengthy, visit to England was over and July 1869 was spent preparing for the voyage home. He had a week's holiday in Cheltenham before travelling to Lancashire; a second cabin was booked to accommodate supplies for his father as well as clothes, books, and a stereoscope for himself.

A great deal of time and attention was given to Hugh; having uprooted the family to Queensland his parents may have considered an extended period in England would be more settled for him than the frequent changes they were making in their new home, or they may have seen early signs of waywardness in his character which they hoped a more disciplined approach would correct. While he was away Lawrence and Sarah had steadily prospered in their business enterprises as well as becoming active members of their local Catholic community. Even after the death of their daughter Sarah—Sr Mary Catherine—they continued to support All Hallows Convent in fundraising and social events, and contributed to the development of chapels and churches in the various districts of Brisbane, under the abrasive authority of Bishop Quinn. One evening's entertainment at the convent featured music played on four pianos: Fr Cotham had recorded the shipment of at least three instruments from England, more than enough for family use. In his middle-age Lawrence was even taking an interest in intellectual matters, attending the fortnightly Petrie-terrace Mutual Improvement Society to discuss topics such as the education of the youth of the colony, and 'are the planets inhabited' (answered in the affirmative after an animated and intelligent debate).[16]

Before Hugh arrived home his eldest brother, Lawrence Leopold, died suddenly in early January 1869 while working at the gold diggings in the Gehans Flat, Cape River area of Queensland area 'no doubt of apoplexy' the weather being 'insufferably hot ... the atmosphere positively stifling'. He was 'much esteemed, being a kind-hearted, generous man'; the Catholic burial service was read by a layman in the absence of a priest. Lawrence junior left a widow, Eliza, and two young sons, Arthur Leopold and James Ambrose.[17] Frs William and James Cotham were to take an especial interest in these great-nephews as soon as they were old enough to travel to England. In the meantime, payments for their education with the Christian Brothers in Brisbane were sent from England to their mother and to their uncle Gustavus Horstmann after Eliza married for a second time, to Samuel Finklstein of Maindample, Victoria, in 1877.

On his return to Brisbane Hugh put his education and cricketing prowess to work, most happily when he was honorary secretary to the Alberts Cricket team.[18] Gustavus Horstmann found employment for Hugh, his young brother-in-law, as a junior clerk in the government Auditor General's office where he was the accountant[19] but after five years in employment, and at 23, Hugh was still only one rung above the office messenger boy.

Family Business & Financial Acumen 479

He joined the legal firm of Hart and Flowers as a clerk, where the high point for him was probably being selected to play in the firm's cricket team which fielded a full side against a combined team from other solicitors' offices in Brisbane.[20] Unfortunately there was to be no further career progression for Hugh as his life slowly disintegrated.

When Hugh returned to his family in 1869 it might have seemed as if the worst of times were behind them and he would fill some of the gap left by his late brother. He shared with his father a pugnacious energy which drove them to push against boundaries. Despite the death of his eldest son, Lawrence senior did not lose his appetite for gold mining. By chance or by judgement he had located his family in an area on the brink of a gold rush; the domestic storekeeper was about to become a pioneer again. Lawrence had invested in holdings in the Mary River goldfields—perhaps with the money transferred for 'the settlement' often referred to in the accounts book—and persevered with the other shareholders when their funds ran low and no new backers believed in the seams they were working. No doubt they talked each other into staying with the excavations and Lawrence shared the optimism—dogged and foolhardy—of the prospectors. The sanguine Cotham voice is authentic:

> Mr Cotham, chemist, long resident in South Brisbane, is another of the fortunate party [of lucky shareholders]. In the course of conversation I [the correspondent] have frequently been struck with the decided opionions expressed by Mr Cotham as to the probabilities of his claim turning out well, and this while myself entertaining a high good opinion of the locality.[21]

Lawrence was not reckless and knew how to spread his risks. Although he invested heavily in the Monkland works, he retained his steady, profitable storekeeping for a number of years until he no longer wanted or needed to be bothered with it. In familiar wording he advertised in 1877 to chemists and druggists that 'having embarked in other occupations' he was desirous of

480   *The Indomitable Mr Cotham*

disposing of his pharmacy business on the Monkland on easy
terms, either to sell or let. There were no takers: six months later
he was advertising again for an assistant to live on the premises
and release him from the day to day responsibility.[22]

The goldfields at Gympie, about one hundred miles north of
Brisbane, followed the usual explosive pattern of growth. An
English visitor recorded his impressions of a visit:

> This was in October 1867 and at that time Gympie was an
> uninhabited creek in the heart of the Queensland bush ...
> When I visited it a very few months afterwards, two large
> towns had arisen on this wild and desolate spot, and 7,000
> inhabitants were busily engaged in the work of gold-
> digging ... Each township has its long, narrow, main street,
> winding its unformed, crooked way through the bush, as
> house after house and store after store is quickly run up
> by newly-arrived adventurers. Banks, stores, shanties and
> other buildings of wood and iron, had sprung, as if by
> magic, from the ground; and amongst these you may see
> a circulating library, two or three theatres, and other
> pretentious erections, that one would not expect to find
> in such a truly infant settlement.[23]

In Gympie Lawrence Cotham had money to invest and did not
need to get his hands dirty, though he probably could not resist
it. He seemed to actively seek these infant settlements in order
to exploit their potential and his own contribution to their
development. He readily benefitted from the wealth on offer but
he fulfilled his responsibility of contributing to social improvement. The first Catholic Mass was celebrated in Gympie in
February 1868, in the Brisbane Hotel, by Father Tissot. The
following month, Father Matthew Horan arrived on the newly
established goldfields and assumed his role as parish priest, which
he held for over fifty years until his death in 1923. Initially Fr
Horan pitched a tent on Calton Hill to celebrate Mass while
immediately inviting tenders for the construction of a permanent
timber church building. This building was ready for use by the

Family Business & Financial Acumen 481

end of 1868, but lasted only four years due to the damaging effect of weathering and white ants. Some of the land at Calton Hill was donated to the church by local residents including Patrick Lillis, and other land was bought at auction for the construction of a hardwood church building opened in 1872 by Bishop Quinn. A community of the Sisters of Mercy arrived in 1879 to establish a Catholic school.[24]

The history of Lawrence's experience in Gympie mirrored his beginnings in Richmond, and his involvement in the development of the Catholic Church via his marriage into the Cassidy family. In 1882 his daughter Isabella and Thomas Lillis were married at St Stephen's Church, Brisbane by Dr Cani, the Vicar General, their fathers having become partners in the amalgamated 2 and 3 South Monkland mining companies. When Patrick Lillis died in 1877, Lawrence took his place on the committee of Gympie Hospital; he was now 65 and recognised as one of the wise grey heads of the local community. Apart from her appearance as a lodging house keeper when they first arrived in Brisbane, Sarah Cassidy Cotham does not figure in local press reports, not even alongside her daughters Mrs Marianne Horstmann and Miss Cotham (Isabella or Eleanor) at fund raising bazaars for All Hallows Convent, but given her husband's various occupations, which included living above the shop in some instances, it is likely Sarah managed some of these stores.

There is expenditure in Fr Cotham's red notebook for one year only, from April 1879 to January 1880, probably because the usual brown book was not to hand. This is for a few outgoings to Brisbane to pay for law books and the great nephews' schooling and, more poignantly, money sent to help Cotham's niece in Lancashire. He had written to her on the occasion of her marriage in January 1876, sending a gift £60. A further £25 was sent in May, possibly a gift from Fr William. There is evidence that Mary Ann's daughter Emily Maguire did not have an easy marriage. Her Irish husband, Dr Edward Joseph Renehan, was a surgeon and physician and after marrying they lived in Rochdale. Less happily Uncle

William was assisting her financially in October 1869 when an emergency payment of £15 was sent due to 'Bailiffs in the house', followed by £125 the following month to deal with 'Dr Renehan's insolvency—to secure furniture.' Fr James' shaky handwriting records the payments without comment. Nevertheless, the marriage continued and a daughter, Emily Maria Hilda Josephine, known as Hilda, was born in 1882.[25]

Notes

1. Lancashire Record Office; DDHCL/1/36; transactions made in the manorial court for Slaidburn, part of the Honor of Clitheroe.
2. 'Abstract from deeds of property belonging to Revd Wm Cotham, and administered by Revd James Cotham' Jesuit Archives (Farm Street, London), item 508.
3. K. Armstrong, *Fields of Blood: Religion and the History of Violence* (London: Vintage, 2015), p. 287.
4. Dunne to Therry, 17 June 1861, quoted in W. T. Southerwood, *The Convicts' Friend: Bishop R. W. Willson* (George Town, Tasmania: Stella Maris Books, 1989), p. 238.
5. *Ibid.*, p. 238.
6. *The Courier* (Brisbane), 5 October 1861, p. 2.
7. *Ipswich Herald and General Advertiser*, 26 July 1861, p. 1.
8. *Maryborough Chronicle, Wide Bay and Burnett Advertiser*, 29 January 1881, p. 2.
9. *Gympie Times and Mary River Mining Gazette*, 1 November 1879, p. 3.
10. *The Courier* (Brisbane), 26 February 1866, p. 3.
11. *The Queenslander*, 1 September 1866, p. 1.
12. *Launceston Examiner*, 4 February 1865, p. 2.
13. N. J. Byrne, *Robert Dunne, 1830–1917, Bishop of Brisbane* (University of Queensland Press, 1991), pp. 66–67.
14. *The Stonyhurst Magazine*, April 1895, Vol. V, No. LXXIX, p. 490.
15. W. R. O. Hill, *Forty-five years' experiences in North Queensland 1865–1905: With a few incidents in England 1844 to 1861* (Brisbane: H Pole & Co, 1907), p. 47.
16. *The Brisbane Courier*, 5 June 1865, p. 2.
17. *The Queenslander*, 20 February 1869, p. 7. In her account Marjorie Cotham, the daughter of James Ambrose, states her grandfather Lawrence Leopold 'was a pioneer in North Queensland and at an early age died of typhoid fever.

Family Business & Financial Acumen 483

He was buried in the Cape River Burial Ground, North Queensland.'

[18] *The Brisbane Courier*, 26 September 1883, p. 1.

[19] *Pugh's Almanac and Directory for Queensland 1873* (1874).

[20] *The Brisbane Courier*, 26 March 1881, p. 5.

[21] *Maryborough Chronicle, Wide Bay and Burnett Advertiser*, 9 March 1869, p. 2.

[22] *Gympie Times and Mary River Mining Gazette*, 21 July 1877, p. 2, and *The Brisbane Courier*, 13 February 1878, p. 1. Cotham's pharmaceutical premises were in Caledonian Hill and Mary Street, Gympie (*Pugh's Almanac and Directory for Queensland 1873* (1874).

[23] C. H. Allan, *A Visit to Queensland and Her Goldfields* (London: Chapman and Hall, 1870), pp. 119–20 and 133.

[24] www.stpatsgympie.net.au

[25] Dr Renehan died in 1899, aged 52. Emily died on 2 February 1905 in the Union Workhouse, Dearnley Wardle, Lancashire. Probate was administered six years later to their unmarried daughter Emily Maria Hilda Josephine Renehan for her mother's estate of £1,425. She was married that same year, 1911, to Patrick Walsh.

39 INDEFATIGABLE?

B Y 1868 THE bulk of the construction work on St Gregory's was complete. The mammoth task of raising the steeple, forty-one feet higher than that of the nearby parish church, had been successfully accomplished although the tower at its base remained separate from the body of the church until 1876. Throughout Cotham had been 'indefatigable in seeing that the material and workmanship [were] strictly according to contract.'[1] The building expenditure accounts, subscriptions, and donations relating to the new church were meticulously copied in 1868, not an easy task as there were fifteen years of notes, receipts, and rough copies to collate. Fr Cotham decided to tackle the books in January 1868, as he recorded in his journal, written in an old notebook because he felt he would not persevere with it through the year.

> 13th January: From the 1st inst. been much exercised with accounts. Making up all Church Subscriptions—entering Memo in a/c Book No 1 with Government correspondence in re Returning Allowance, with a little history of why and how we first began this Building of St Gregory's. John Barry[2] at vacations from Hammersmith Training School is writing for me and Dr Collier is kindly auditing the accounts. John has made many errors in adding up. Been up till 1o/c in the morning overhauling the a/cs.

After a page of notes about the domestic incident involving his housekeeper which bothered him a great deal he resumed his accounting, although he would have preferred to be elsewhere. The question arises, why did he choose this point to write up the various accounts? It may have been to keep John Barry busy until the end of his vacation, or he may have felt the bulk of the building work had been completed. If he had any thoughts about moving on from Cheltenham it would not have been surprising, given the unremitting labour of the previous fifteen years, including the vexation of dealing with bankrupt and litigious builders.

> 14th–18th January: Engaged with John Barry with Church a/c all entered and corrected up to this date. Bueno House New a/c Book made up to April and June 1868. New a/c Book for Lancashire and Yorkshire Properties. Poor Book and James St Books made up. Pipes for Heating apparatus Book made up. Rain all the week—no going to St Michael's.

Kept in Cheltenham by the wet weather Fr Cotham wrote a letter to Brisbane, enclosing 'four or six' letters from Hugh, who had probably spent the Christmas vacation with him and needed to be profitably occupied indoors. Cotham also sent a letter to William Gardner 'acknowledging the Receipt of £5 Bank of England Note for Mrs Catherine Day, which came to hand yesterday—went to woman—she had been pawning her clock and drinking'. Mrs Day may have been Gardner's former housekeeper; now sixty, she lodged in Pantile Row, an Irish neighbourhood, and was likewise at a loose end on a wet Sunday.

The interior work of the tower was the next major project but before that there was the annoyance of having to comply with orders from Cheltenham Improvement Commissioners to surrender land in front of the West end (Clarence Street junction) for road widening schemes with a consequent need for new boundary walls. Cotham argued for a review of the plans but the commissioners would not alter the plans. As neither compensation for the land nor a grant towards the new wall was offered by the commissioners, the Congregational Committee felt justified in making a fund raising appeal, even though the amount was for a relatively modest £136, of which £70 had already been promised. The circular which was distributed in 1868, perhaps only to residents and tradespeople in the vicinity, seems aimed at making a point rather than raising £66, a paltry amount in the grand scheme of building:

Indefatigable? 487

COMPLETION OF THE BOUNDARY WALL AND WIDENING OF THE ADJOINING THOROUGHFARES

The Congregational Committee of St Gregory's Church ... having regard to the poverty of the large majority of the Congregation, and the consequent numerous calls upon the benevolence of the minority, do not feel justified in commencing the work until the whole of the requisite Funds are obtained or promised; and they feel bound to appeal to their fellow-townsmen to assist them in carrying out this great public improvement.

The Committee would remind their fellow-townsmen that the Catholics of Cheltenham are giving up to the town a large and valuable piece of accommodation land for the widening of the adjoining much-used and at present dangerous thoroughfares, and without receiving any compensation for it,—and they are about to erect, in the place of the present hoarding, Ornamental Gate-Piers, and a Boundary Wall in all respects similar to the boundary wall in St James' Square. They therefore think they have strong claims for assistance upon the town generally, and especially upon those who will more immediately benefit by the contemplated improvement, and they trust that this appeal will not be made in vain ...

> The Right Rev. Dr. Collier, Somerset Place (President)
> Mr G A Williams, The Library (Vice-President)
> James Hawarden, 134 High Street (Treasurer)
> Augustus M Baker, 9 Oxford Place (Hon. Sec.)
> Healy Thompson, Bayshill
> Robert Walker, MA, 3 Montpellier Parade
> M'Loughlin, High Street
> D Evans, Clarence Street

This Congregational Committee was a short-lived phenomenon at St Gregory's but its personnel show the changing character of the Catholic congregation. Some of the original committee members—Patrick Wybault, Hector Caffieri, and George Cope-land—had died, moved away, or become infirm. In their places a new generation of townsmen came to the fore. Bishop Collier was President, and the ubiquitous George Arthur Williams was Vice President. James Hawarden, Treasurer, was a grocer in the High Street, Charles McLoughlin was a prospering gunsmith originally from Ireland, with premises in the High Street, and Daniel Evans—once a draper in the High Street and active in the congregation during Fr Glassbrook's time—was now in business with his son as a property valuer, appraiser, and auctioneer in nearby St George's Place. Robert Walker MA, belonged to the cohort of Oxford-educated clergymen who were received into the Catholic Church after Newman's conversion in 1845. Being already married at the time, 1846, he struggled to find suitable employment after losing his Anglican living. The final two members were Augustus Mark Baker, Honorary Secretary, and Edward Healy Thompson, both newcomers to Cheltenham. The former became a valued and friendly advisor to Fr Cotham and the latter contributed to national Catholic life by his large and varied literary output. Baker's mother and Healy Thompson had both come under the influence of John Henry Newman and had become Catholics in the mid-1840s but apart from their shared faith there was little else in common between them.

Bishop Collier chose to come to the Cheltenham mission in retirement. Naturally, he took precedence as a prelate on liturgical occasions, but Fr Cotham was fortunate in having Dr Collier living in the clergy house from 1865 to 1870 for practical purposes. After filling the role of prior at Douai, Dr Collier was ordained bishop at the age of 37 and appointed vicar general to the island of Mauritus in 1841. The slaves of the island were just gaining emancipation but over half the population still lived in conditions of oppression and misery. Dr Collier brought over additional priests from France and introduced the Institute of the Blessed Virgin Mary (Loreto Sisters) from Ireland to open schools.

> I could not imagine that a Christian country could fall into such a state of moral degradation. Sometimes, the Europeans do not know much about their religion, but the

Indefatigable? 489

> people here (this large black population) are just like the
> inhabitants of China or Kamtchatka. But how could they
> be otherwise? Nobody has ever taken the slightest interest
> in them. They have been treated like beasts of burden.
> What surprises me even more than their ignorance is that,
> despite their total neglect, they still want to be taught ...
> When I arrived here I found eight priests. I sent three away
> and there are three others that I cannot get rid of. [3]

Having accomplished much in a short space of time Dr Collier
retired from the bishopric of Port Louis, Mauritius in 1847 due
to ill health, no longer being able to withstand the difficult
climatic and travelling conditions which were a trial for most
English priests posted to the island. His experience was exactly
what the Cheltenham mission needed, and Dr Collier himself
needed an outlet for his accumulated wisdom.

> In the wake of Bishop Collier, the management of the local
> Church [in Mauritius] was plain sailing for his successors.
> Collier handed down to them a rich legacy: a diocese
> bursting into bloom: its white, black and coloured com-
> munities virtually all baptised ...; a constellation of
> churches and chapels dotting the territories of eleven
> parishes; a wide network of catholic schools ... ; and, above
> all, the Church-State relationship unfolding within a fairly
> satisfactory framework. [4]

Dr Collier became the President of the St Gregory's Church
Appeal Committee which, from 1863, cast its net across the
country, and beyond, to pay off the debt on the church as it was
thus far completed and to reach the goal of raising a spire which
would surpass any other in the town. The Appeal records were
meticulously kept, each contributor to each section of the church
fabric being individually noted, together with all expenditures,
however trivial. Dr Collier was an expert administrator, diplo-
matic when necessary but not afraid to break fresh ground. Fr
Cotham could not have asked for a better mentor—something
he had conspicuously lacked during his time in Tasmania—but

490   *The Indomitable Mr Cotham*

they might also have shared the experience of finding life in Cheltenham a little tame after the rigours of a colonial mission.

Dr Collier's generosity was not confined to, or exhausted by, his efforts in Cheltenham. While holidaying in **Aberystwyth** he became aware of the spiritual needs not only of local Catholics, but of the increasing numbers of Catholic visitors to the growing seaside resort. Local Catholics, and their bishop, had been trying for twenty years to establish a permanent mission in the town but lacked the financial resources and organisational skills. Dr Collier purchased a suitable site from Sir Pryse Pryse of Gogerddan for a chapel and priest's house and he was invited to celebrate the ceremony of laying the foundation stone on 16 July 1874. 'The mixed gathering' included Protestant clergymen and leading citizens of Aberystwyth and a distinctly '"ecumenical" atmosphere of Christian unity happily prevailed on the occasion.'[5] The stamp of Dr Collier's eirenic influence is clear.

Aged 34, Augustus Baker was the youngest on the committee, at this point a solicitor's managing clerk, and married with one child. He and James Hawarden were brothers-in-law through their wives, Maria Catherine and Lucy Jeffery. Baker's father had been a book-keeper and the three sons started their working lives as clerks in Birmingham. Their mother was widowed after eight years of marriage and with five children to support took over the lodging house her mother had kept in Leamington, Warwickshire. For a time Augustus studied medicine (family tradition said at Heidelberg); he did not qualify as a doctor but his knowledge was sufficient to set him on an unlikely career, as a diplomat, when the opportunity arose. But in 1868 he was a young man willing to do paperwork for the congregation and hopeful of providing a family life that he had not experienced.

If Augustus Baker was to become a man of adventure his co-worker on the committee, Edward Healy Thompson was already an accomplished man of ideas and letters by the time he arrived in Cheltenham, and famous or infamous for the part he played in the war of words contested in print in the aftermath of

Indefatigable? 491

John Henry Newman's conversion. Thompson was a graduate of Emmanuel College, Cambridge and as an Anglican cleric he held a number of curacies until his conversion, with his wife Harriet, to Catholicism in 1846. He wrote his own apologia in *Remarks on certain Anglican Theories of Unity* (1846) and *A few earnest thoughts on the Duty of Communion with the Catholic Church* (1847). He was described to Newman at the time of his conversion as 'really almost a Pupil of yours, having been tutored and instructed by your writings'.[6] In 1851 he was joint editor with James Spencer Northcote of the controversial series of pamphlets, *The Clifton Tracts*.

Thompson's correspondence with Newman began in 1841, about five years after he took Anglican orders; the rapport between the two men developed to the point when Newman saw Thompson as a key ally in his own projects. The hope that Thompson would take the Chair of English at the Catholic University in Dublin eventually came to nothing shortly before Newman himself returned from Dublin. There followed the suggestion, in 1859, that Newman should take on the editorship of the *Rambler* with Thompson as his sub-editor and later that Thompson should become editor of the *Dublin Review*; at all times visible behind the scenes were the controlling hands of Cardinal Wiseman and Bishop Manning. When the *Review* was put under Manning's authority by Wiseman it was with W. G. Ward as editor and E. H. Thompson as sub-editor for the first issue of the New Series in July 1863.

The publication and subsequent reaction in Catholic and Protestant circles to Newman's *Apologia Pro Sua Vita* was reflected in the bitter controversy caused by the stance of the *Review*. Manning and Ward were wary of Newman's encouragement of the publishing aspirations of scholarly English converts, who many felt threatened the discreet approach of Old Catholics, and Newman was unjustly accused of being at odds with Pope Pius IX's condemnation of theological liberalism. Thompson backed Fr Coleridge, one of the editorial staff, who wanted to

492   *The Indomitable Mr Cotham*

devote a whole issue of the *Dublin Review* to a defence of Newman and his Catholic credentials and loyalty. When Ward refused to allow this—interpreted as a shameful personal and intellectual rebuff to Newman—Coleridge and Thompson both resigned from the periodical.

The Healy Thompsons' move to Cheltenham in 1869 was, in effect, a retirement from the politicking of the English Catholic Church. Edward and Harriet continued to use their considerable literary energy, influence, and skill in the service of Catholic publications. Thompson translated many minor works from the Continent to supplement popular Catholic literature alongside his academic periodical pieces. His long writing life, posthumously extended by his wife, is an example of the assimilation by a very English mind to an Ultramontane style of devotion. He positively welcomed the opportunity to widen the communion of saints, canonised and putative, known to English Catholics by translating biographies of St Stanislaw Kostka SJ, Sr Marie Lataste, and Anna Maria Taigi, from Polish, French, and Italian respectively. Like others of his time Thompson was intrigued by the miraculous and visionary phenomena which accompanied Catholic faith. With his broad mind and sympathies he was able to show how a fine balance between simplicity, orthodoxy, and fervour could be personally held by an intellectual while submitting to authority. In correspondence printed in *The Tablet* regarding the silliness or otherwise of writing petitions to Our Lady, in this instance sent to the shrine at Lourdes, he lucidly covers all the salient points:

> The Blessed Virgin is our mother; she was given to us in the person of St. John by our crucified Lord on Calvary; and we treat her with a pious familiarity as such. Our love to her, our confidence in her, cannot be too ardent, too filial, too childlike. If only our "creed" be true, the devotion we show her can have nothing in it of extravagance. So long as we have the example of good and holy Catholics, including priests and religious, the sanction of our Bishops

Indefatigable? 493

> and of our Holy Father the Pope—who, your correspondent may depend upon it, are keen-sighted and sensitive enough to detect error and reprove it—and so long as we have the approval of our Blessed Lady herself, who in this particular instance has testified it by her remarkable answers to the petitions sent her, it is a matter of perfect indifference what Protestants may think.[7]

By the time he wrote the above, in 1885, Thompson had comfortably accommodated his cerebral rigour with an ultramontane outlook but twenty years earlier support of Newman was often seen as a benchmark for judging a Catholic's loyalty to the Pope. Cotham seems never to have experienced this dilemma; his working relationship with George Copeland had grown into friendship and brought him into contact with Newman's inner circle via the Revd William Copeland, at least by report and quite probably through social contact. He would not have subscribed to the charge of a dangerous clash of English versus Roman loyalty supposedly provoked by Newman, the subject of correspondence between Mgr George Talbot in Rome and Archbishop Manning in Westminster. To Talbot's spiteful remark, 'You will have battles to fight, because every Englishman is naturally anti-Roman. To be Roman is to an Englishman an effort. Dr Newman is more English than the English. His spirit mush be crushed', Manning replied,

> What you write about Dr Newman is true. Whether he knows it or not, he has become the centre of those who hold low views about the Holy See, are anti-Roman, cold and silent, to say no more, about the Temporal Power, national, English, critical of Catholic devotions, and always on a lower side. I see much danger of an English Catholicism of which Newman is the highest type ... It is the old Anglican, patristic, literary, Oxford tone transplanted into the Church ... and will deceive many.[8]

494 *The Indomitable Mr Cotham*

Cotham was by no means an academic himself but the transplanted Anglicans had broadened his horizons and his identity as a thorough-going English Roman Catholic.

Ambrose Cotham would have been familiar with Thompson's published work, even from his time in Tasmania, and knew many converts personally, but Thompson's wife introduced him to a new category of Catholic: the intellectual woman. Formal study and the teaching of theology were not open to Catholic women but writing and publishing allowed them a voice. Harriet Diana Healy Thompson, née Calvert, was the daughter of Nicolson Calvert, MP for Hunsden, Hertfordshire, and the Honourable Frances Pery, a celebrated Irish beauty who moved in the Royal 'set'. When Harriet was born in 1811, the youngest of twelve children, her mother was more preoccupied with her elder daughter's honeymoon as she notes in her diary for 25 September 1811: 'This day fortnight I had a very fine little girl. I have had constant charming letters from my dearest Isabella who says she is the happiest of creatures.' However, when Harriet was 8 and old enough to enjoy a children's ball in London she lived up to her mother's expectations.

> Never was anything so admired as Harriet, not for her beauty, but for her dancing, her manners, cleverness, and engaging ways. Lord Grantham told Limerick the next day that she was the delight of the ballroom.

She surpassed herself the following month by astonishing the Persian Ambassdor with her reading skills, an early indication of her love for literature above social accomplishment.[9]

As lay Catholics, Harriet and Edward Healy Thompson worked in close partnership, writing extensively on erudite religious matters and jointly editing the Foreign Periodical Literature section of the *Dublin Review*. Whereas Edward's name appeared frequently in print Harriet's did not; her articles were often attributed to him as he presented them for publication and received payment on her behalf, but there is no doubt that

Indefatigable?

together they made a formidable intellectual double act, and her 'invaluable arts' were recognised by W. G. Ward, her editor on the *Review*. Harriet was also an accomplished (unattributed) author of fiction and although she wrote to proselytise, her books had a lightness of touch that make them entertaining rather than merely didactic. Her earliest novel, *Mount St Lawrence* was first published in 1850 and was judged to be 'full of female insight into domestic Machiavelism'. She received her fullest reviews in the *Rambler* and *The Tablet* but was noticed elsewhere. In the considered opinion of the *Observer*,

> the writer is minutely intimate with the tenets and doctrines of his [*sic*] religion, and explains them most lucidly. For the general reader he possesses other attractions. He writes well, and his knowledge of the human heart, of the prima nobilia of society, is varied, extensive, and profound.[10]

It is unlikely that Fr Cotham read her novels, unless out of politeness, but she may have used him as a model for 'honest, though homely, John Sanders', the foil to her fashionable, foolish characters and the champion of a wise heroine in her last novel, *The Wyndham Family*.[11] John Sanders pays a visit to his sister in London, and her two daughters, Emma and Gertrude. The family observes their Catholic duties in a rather slack manner which John confronts; they meanwhile find him a social embarrassment. His sister confides in her daughter:

> 'Nothing puts John down. He was always like that—afraid of nobody—and would blurt out the truth, and speak his mind upon every occasion.

> One thing strikes me, Emma; the h's are not so bad as I expected. He pronounces them all,—rather faintly, it is true, but that is better than leaving an occasional one quite out.'[12]

John and his and sister discuss their other siblings. Their brother is a pig farmer who keeps his animals uncomfortably close to the house producing a *frousty* atmosphere. Sanders admits

'I do not like it myself, though I am not fastidious and certainly not fashionable, for I live on fresh air, but I must put up with it while I am there; and I shall be mostly out of doors.

And our [related] Australians—do you ever hear from them?'

'I have not heard for a long time,' replied his sister. '... It dropped off—the correspondence, I mean. One hardly knows what to write about to such distant relations'.

'Relations at such a distance, you mean, I suppose,' replied John. 'A sister is hardly a distant relation'.

'But what could I write that could interest her, our lives being so different?' pleaded Mrs Wyndham, in rather an apologetic tone.

'I should have thought every little thing would interest relations at the other side of the globe; at least, I go on that plan'. [Sanders describes their sister's improved social and political standing.]

'Do you think they will return now they have made their fortune?'

'Not they. They are great people there and would be small people here.'[13]

But the final word on Sanders is given to an old friend in Italy:

'No one knows the worth of that man, he does not know it himself; it is hidden from him by his wonderful simplicity, but I believe he stands very high in God's favour—so high that many will marvel when the day comes for the revealing of all secrets.'[14]

Taken as a whole, the novel is either a sustained piece of fictional characterisation or an affectionate portrayal of someone known and respected by Harriet Thompson. The observation about relative smallness and greatness of reputation in Australia and

Indefatigable? 497

England brings to mind the careers enjoyed by the *Anson* staff after 1850.[15]

The work on St Gregory's boundary wall in 1868 was contracted to William Jones of Gloucester, one of Hansom's favoured builders who, unfortunately, had not been accepted for completing the spire. He carried out the work satisfactorily before the winter with only £8 charged for extra costs and he was retained for further work around the tower during the winter months. In January 1869 William Letheren fitted a gate, but it was a functional item costing only £6; he was engaged again, by Fr Wilkinson, before the consecration of the church in 1877 to provide the splendid West end gates which still stand as an example of the work which made his reputation as an ornamental blacksmith.

Between the clock room, in the lower part of the tower, and the so-called belfry section Hansom had designed a stone groined and vaulted ceiling to the clock room which would be visible from the body of the church. This was contracted to Charles Rainger, a builder respected by his peers, thoroughly professional, and known to Fr Cotham over a number of years. He was engaged in November 1870 but was unable to begin work until after the winter. During a site inspection in early March 1871 he was annoyed to find the unglazed belfry windows had let in a large amount of rain water, saturating the new belfry floor and leaking into the clock room below. He had foreseen the risk during the previous autumn but it had been decided (against his better judgement he hints) to leave the belfry windows open to the weather until easier access could be gained when the main work restarted. He writes in March to invite Fr Cotham to examine the floor with him and give him instructions about the remedy. His invoice shows that (belatedly) scaffolding was erected on the outside of the tower to fix glass and shuttering to the window tracery.

It was not only the day-to-day oversight of the building that took Fr Cotham's time. At the beginning of 1871 Cotham wrote to the Provincial, Fr Cuthbert Smith, about progress and finances. They missed each other on the roads between Coventry, Cheltenham, and Hanley so Fr Smith wrote to Cotham about his ideas, which were accepted:

> 13 Jan. Had I met you [at Hanley] I should have made to you the following proposal. As Father Scott will not want the £50 rent from No 10 at least for some years & very likely not at all, and as the Province has made provision for Sodbury by sinking the £1000 for its support—the price which the trustees agreed to accept for No 10—I am hopeful that were I to allow you to appropriate the £50 for some time as the Province offering towards what you have been spending at Cheltenham on the tower you would prefer that arrangement rather than put me to the necessity of contributing the amount at once for which I stood guarantee. The Province monies would be less disturbed by this arrangement and I hope to hear from you that it will be quite convenient and satisfactory to you.

> 23 Janry 1871. Very well, our money matters, then, are settled for the present. It strikes me that with the prospect of being able to fall back on the rent of £50 due to South Province you might venture on an effort to finish the church. Surely someone will come to help us. Is Copeland's generosity towards the church quite exhausted? I hope not. I am glad to hear you propose giving your flock the benefit of a mission next March.

Dr Copeland by this point had been completely paralysed for six years, although mentally lucid. Fr Newman kept Sr Pia Maria Giberne informed of his precarious health:

> We had an alarm a day or two ago that George Copeland had had one, and then a second paralytic stroke; and we thought he was dying. His sister was dying at the same time. Since then we hear that it was a bilious attack, but that he is not out of danger yet.[16]

Undoubtedly Copeland remained committed to the church but Fr Smith's letter reads rather callously and, in the light of the

Indefatigable? 499

work still to be undertaken, unrealistically optimistic about the difference £50 per annum would make.

Rainger kept to his estimate of £252 for the groined ceiling. His invoice for July 1871 includes various extra work including five days for a carpenter to refit book shelves taken down from the priests' house and hoisted into the clock room, together with thirty-seven feet of new shelving. At the same time gas pipes were extended from the house cellar to the clock room for the newly installed gas stove. This level of work strongly suggests that Fr Cotham envisioned a fairly rapid conclusion to the work, when the tower and church would be connected to each other and the whole brought into full use. The shortfall in funds amounting to £310 was divided equally between Fr Cotham and the Provincial, Fr Cuthbert Smith, presumably to bring the slow work to a speedy conclusion. In fact, the connection between the tower and church nave was not made until 1876, by which time Fr Wilkinson was rector; it is unlikely that Fr Cotham ever walked down the whole length of the church nave or saw the clock room used as the choir gallery and organ chamber.

Page 164 of the Subscription and Expenditure Book is given over to a statement added by Fr Cotham himself:

> Paid to St Gregory's by Rev James Cotham three thousand two hundred and eighty pounds from private personal funds, of which sum one thousand and twenty pounds was subscribed as per List of Subscribers page 27 of this Book and given absolutely; But two thousand two hundred and sixty pounds was advanced as a loan without interest, and must be paid to St Edmund's College Douay by the Cheltenham Mission. The whole of the particulars of accounts are in this book and entered and compared with vouchers by the late James Boodle and Mr Crotty. All receipts and vouchers are kept with this Book.

In fact, page twenty-seven lists 'Rev Jas Cotham' as contributing £810 followed by £1 from 'Revd W Cotham'; other entries under Tower and Spire total £200 which leaves his accounting only £10 adrift. The loan is more obscurely accounted for, but he has made his point: as he began the building work with his Tasmanian savings so he winds up the income and expenditure tallies with his personal record of underpinning the whole project, at least until his departure from Cheltenham. Thereafter he expected St Gregory's to manage without him and repay whatever loans were outstanding at his death to St Edmund's, Douai. His intentions towards Douai in 1873 were clear but ten years later the Prior of St Edmund's accused him of disobedient partiality to another Benedictine house.

The expansion of St Gregory's school continued alongside the church building work. A house and garden next to the schools in St Paul's Street North was bought at auction in 1872 together with a corner allotment in Hamilton Place for building an Infant School and playground. The last invoice Fr Cotham wrote in Cheltenham, on 31 October 1873, was for the reimbursement of £480 he had paid for these school plots.

Notes

[1] Undated and unidentified Cheltenham newspaper cutting, but almost certainly c. August 1864. GRO D4290 A 3/1.

[2] John Barry (1846–1925) was educated at Sedgeley Park between January 1863 and August 1866 before going to the short-lived Hammersmith Training College. He was ordained at Ushaw in 1874. The last thirty years of his life were spent at St Mary's, Birkenhead. He was appointed Canon, Provost, and Vicar General of Shrewsbury Diocese, and was especially interested in Catholic education. On 25 January 1868 Fr Cotham noted in his journal, 'John Barry came to take leave nimis omnia.'

[3] A. Nagapen, 'A Century of English Benedictine Apostolate in Mauritius 1819–1916', paper presented to 23rd English Benedictine Congregation History Symposium, 1998. DA, privately published.

[4] *Ibid.*

[5] M. B. Kiely O Carm., B.A, *Our Lady of the Angels and St Winefride, Aberystwyth: A brief chronicle of church and parish, 1857–1957* (Aberystwyth: 1974), p. 5.

Indefatigable?

6   E. L. Badeley to Newman, 3 April 1846. Footnote 4 to Newman's letter of 5 March 1851; Collected Letters.

7   *The Tablet*, 23 May 1885, p. 22.

8   Talbot to Manning, February 1866. Quoted in *Apologia Pro Vita Sua and Six Sermons*, F. M. Turner (Ed.), (New Haven, CT and London: Yale University Press, 2008), Editor's Introduction, pp. 46–47.

9   *An Irish Beauty of the Regency: compiled from "Mes Souvenirs," the unpublished journals of the Hon. Mrs. Calvert, 1789–1822* (John Lane, 1911), pp. 328–329. https://archive.org/details/irishbeautyofreg00calv. Accessed online [27.7.2017]

10   H. H. Thompson, *The Wyndham Family: A Story of Modern Life* (London: Burns & Oates, 2 Vols, 1876). Review extracts are appended to the text of the novel: https://archive.org/details/wyndhamfamilysto01thom; https://archive.org/details/wyndhamfamilysto02thom [Accessed online 27.7.2017]

11   H. H. Thompson, *The Wyndham Family: A Story of Modern Life* (London: Burns & Oates, 2 Vols, 1876).

12   *Ibid.*, Vol. 1, p. 228.

13   *Ibid.*, Vol. 2, pp. 318–319.

14   *Ibid.*, Vol. 2, p. 534.

15   In a similar vein to Harriet Thompson's characterisation is an anecdote related by William Cotham SJ. 'I remember going up for the opening of Farm Street. Father Lythgoe said to me, 'Well, Father Cotham,' says he, 'so you've come.' 'Aye,' said I, 'I've come; and what's more, I've brought something with me.' 'What's that?' says he. 'Why, half a buck, a couple o' ducks, and some cream cheese.' And he said he was mightily glad to see me." House Journal of the British Province of the Society of Jesus, *Letters and Notices*, No. XCIX, April 1895, obituary, p. 132.

16   Newman to Sr Pia Maria Giberne, 10 June 1871. www.newman.reader.org/works/letters_diaries Vol. XXV p. 343.

40 LOOKING BEYOND ST GREGORY'S

By 1873 AMBROSE Cotham's work at St Gregory's was drawing to a close. The invoices were fewer and the accounts books had been completed. His assistant, Fr Aloysius Wilkinson, was poised to take over as senior priest in the mission, and although he always referred to his predecessor in the highest terms the two men were a generation apart in outlook as well as age. Both welcomed the transfer of responsibility. Cotham had concerned himself with the 'erection of a magnificent edifice', dealing in stone, mortar, drains, and gas pipes, to make a statement to outsiders. Wilkinson, urbane and cultivated, would go on to beautify the interior of the church for the whole of his pastorate and nothing delighted him more than its adornment. The subject matter, too, reflected the development of a particular identity. The ancient English Catholic traditions of devotion to Mary, and loyalty to the Pope, were represented, but above all the distinctive Benedictine charism of the church was emphasised by the abundance of Augustine and Benedict imagery used in stained glass, stone carvings, and decorative furnishings.

Fr Robert Aloysius Wilkinson OSB had been assistant priest for the last seven years of Fr Cotham's incumbency, 1866 to 1873, and was his successor as Rector from 1873 to 1905. He praised Fr Cotham's energy and zeal on several occasions and his affection for the older man is evident. Unfortunately, the journal entries for January 1868 say more about Wilkinson's predecessor, Fr Scarisbrick, than about Wilkinson, who is not mentioned by Fr Cotham at all in the surviving papers. The overlapping and subsequent handing over of responsibility for St Gregory's between these co-adjutors (to use Fr Wilkinson's term) was transitional in various respects. Fr Wilkinson belonged to the

504   *The Indomitable Mr Cotham*

modern generation of Benedictines who were grappling—some-times acrimoniously—with their changing identity, from solitary missioners to conventual monastics attached to parishes. Fr Wilkinson was old enough to feel patronised by some of the regulations introduced in the 1880s; Fr Cotham was spared having to make the adjustments.

A signal of the letting-go of responsibility is some increase in Cotham's outside activities, including participation in current political affairs. During his Tasmanian years Cotham often dealt with government officials in connection with his chaplaincy duties but he never passed comment on government policies in his journal. He took the grants on offer and worked within the restraints imposed by his British paymasters. In Cheltenham, however, there are references to party politics which become more explicit as time passes. Cotham's name appeared on a list of voters at the time of the 1855 General Election[1] although he was considered a 'silent voter' by the Tory member of Parlia-ment.[2] In the Registration Court of 1860 Fr Cotham was 'objected to' by the Tories, 'but the clear manner in which he replied to the questions of Mr Taynton, who endeavoured to prove that the rev. gentleman was merely a trustee of the house [10 St James Square] induced the Revising Barrister to allow the vote'.[3]

However, among the unordered jottings, recipes, and ditties on loose pages there is one sustained, undated, piece of writing. It seems to be an imagined address he might have made to a Member of Parliament or a letter he intended to write. Its tone is uncompromisingly antagonistic to what he calls 'The Great Liberal Party' (his own emphasis). Without a date it is impossible to say where this polemic stands in relation to his overt political activity in the early 1870s but it echoes most obviously the denouncement by English Catholics of Whig-Liberal neutrality to the Italian nationalist aggression against the Papal States in the 1860s and the fear that French antagonism would follow. Even without a firm context it is worth reading as a rare example of political writing by Cotham, although it begs the question of

Looking beyond St Gregory's   505

where his own loyalties lay, especially in view of newspaper comments about his local activity.

> I know it is said that faith will remove mountains. But the credulity that believes that a ch —— [a wavy line indicates a break in his train of thought] is so excessive as to exceed in infantine simplicity anything which I supposed to be proposed by the Rt Hon. [*sic*]

> The Rt Hon Gent will pardon me if I say that I regard him as the Red Indian of Debate. By the use of the tomahawk he has cut his way to power and by a recurrence to the [s]calping knife he hopes to prevent the loss of it.[4]

> The tendency of the Great Liberal Party in England, and of all Liberals (they are everywhere the same) is to become democratic, disloyal, revolutionary. The true Liberal has an affected contempt for all merely honorary distinctions. In the great French revolution, titles, armorial bearings, orders of knight-hood, were all swept away, partly as interfering with universal equality and brotherhood, partly as beneath the dignity of a free citizen, and a child of nature. The liberals of those times first abolished the trappings and gew-gaws of rank, then they abolished nobility, then Royalty, then the Church. They next attempted to abolish God. Napoleon reconstructed society by the re-establishment of the Church and the foundation of the Legion of Honour. He who sneers at a nobleman, is generally a genuine snob, who would with pleasure black the same nobleman's shoes in private, if he could thereby obtain the distinction of a nod from him in public. The chief effect of such liberalism of snobbism is to foster the spirit which prompts men to gratify their own base pride and self-complacency by mocking and despising others. The contempt they try to feel for others they cannot help feeling for themselves, and the consequence is an indignant envy and hatred of every superiority whatever. **Catholicism is 'a great school of respect'**, and ~~of~~ one of the grounds of the spiritual <u>opposition, antagonism,</u>

> between Catholicism and Liberalism is that Liberalism is
> a great school of contempt.

From the vehemence of his prose it would seem nothing would induce Cotham to come within spitting distance of a Liberal. How then to account for his presence, with seven hundred men, women, and children, on an excursion train to Ross-on-Wye for the annual outing of Cheltenham's Reform Club in August 1872? Unfortunately 'it rained as though it had never rained before' and the planned dinner in a marquee took place instead in the Corn Exchange. The toast proposed to 'the Bishop and Clergy of all Denominations' was responded to by Fr Cotham and the Revd Flory, 'the first-named gentleman ... meeting with an enthusiastic reception, and speaking briefly by [sic] warmly in support of Liberal principles, and urging all to remain firm to them, and to their member, whose independence and consistency he strongly commended'.[5] After speeches from the President Mr Steele and the Liberal MP Sir Henry Samuelson, tables and benches were cleared for dancing,

> but whether Mr Samuelson quadrilled with Mrs Steele to the music of Old Dan Tucker, or Father Cotham waltzed with Mrs Onley to that of Meet me by Moonlight alone; or the Rev J Flory polkaed with Miss Lenthall to Fly not yet, our informant—the Examiner—does not state.[6]

Fr Cotham's Tory congregants might have been increasingly discomforted to see his name appearing frequently, and satirically, in connection with party politics.

Cheltenham's Liberal Reform Club had come into existence only in 1869, the result of changing the name of the Working Men's Club following the passing of the Second Reform Act in 1867 and the election of Samuelson in 1868. Fr Cotham would not have been a member of the Working Men's Club but he supported its aims. Another of his jottings noted, 'We ought to bear in mind that there is no greater cruelty to the humbler classes than any discouragement of industry or self-reliance', a

Looking beyond St Gregory's 507

sentiment not so far from Samuelson's campaign slogan, 'Working men—have your rights; Support one of yourselves'. The enfranchisement of urban working-class male householders disproportionately benefitted the Catholic and Nonconformist population. Furthermore, Samuelson was in favour of severing the ties between the Church of England and the State, thereby (according to the Tory-supporting *Cheltenham Looker-On*)

> denouncing the existence of the only effectual breakwater which has hitherto served to repel the advancing waves of Roman Catholicism and infidelity, and, anchored behind which, they [the Dissenting ministers who supported him] and the Nonconformists generally throughout the kingdom have been enabled to moor their fragile barques in peace and security.[7]

Samuelson's pro-Catholic standing was further enhanced when he voted against an Enquiry into Roman Catholic Charities in March 1869. Anti-Catholic feeling never went away and at election times it became pronounced. A poster in 1865 produced by the Cheltenham Protestant Electoral Union proclaimed that the Liberal and Conservative candidates, Colonel Berkeley M.P. and Charles Schreiber Esq., had pledged themselves to 'to a firm and uncompromising resistance to the encroachments of the Papacy' by supporting four policies restricting the expansion of Catholic practice in public life, for example in convents, workhouses and prisons.[8] As the 1874 General Election approached, the challenge expected from the newly-enfranchised Catholic voters was interpreted by sections of the Conservative press as yet another wave of papal aggression, co-ordinated by priests following instructions from Archbishop Manning of Westminster. Undeterred by such nonsense Cotham was not afraid to socialise in public with Samuelson and his followers.

Debate over the extension of the vote to women also engaged Fr Cotham's interest at this time. Lydia Becker, from the Manchester Woman's Suffrage Society, spoke at the Corn Exchange in Cheltenham on 'The Franchise as a Protection to Women' and

508 *The Indomitable Mr Cotham*

although Samuelson was absent a number of Nonconformist ministers were on the platform with Fr Cotham alongside them to support Miss Becker.[9] The following year Samuelson did make himself available to hear Rhoda Garrett when she spoke on 'The Electoral Disabilities of Women'. There is, of course, no record of which Catholic ladies were present at these meetings—the presence of Fr Cotham would have reassured them of their respectability—but the absence of Sophie Tiesset or Harriet Healy Thompson would be surprising.

More serious was the charge laid against Cotham by the Tory *Cheltenham Chronicle* in 1872 that he took a view on Catholic education at odds with the hierarchy. The Elementary Education Act of 1870 finally established the desirability of compulsory education, state-funded when necessary for children who could not access voluntary, denominational, schooling. A short period of grace was allowed before building grants for denominational schools ceased; thereafter if there were insufficient places in a voluntary church school a child would be obliged to attend a state-funded school. Education in Christian religion would, naturally, be on the curriculum but not the religious differentiation which segregated schools could offer to strengthen denominational identity. Herbert Vaughan became the champion of Catholic education after his consecration as Bishop of Salford in 1872, and was determined to present a united front against the economic constraints facing voluntary schools. For a priest who had preached vigorously on the importance of unity the allegation of disloyalty to the Church was damaging to his good standing among his flock.

> CATHOLICS AND SECULARISTS.—The newly appointed Bishop of Salford ... denounced the Birmingham Education League as a little, noisy, and domineering sect, who sought to divorce God from knowledge. We commend these words to the Roman Catholics among us (especially Father COTHAM) who have hitherto supported Mr H. B. SAMUELSON in his ardent zeal for a godless education for

Looking beyond St Gregory's 509

> the people. Our member has always voted with Mr DIXON and the Birmingham Leaguers.[10]

Away from Cheltenham, and possible censure from his fellow priests and the congregation at St Gregory's, Cotham regularly took periods of recreation at Benedictine houses but the holiday he took with his brother William in 1873 may have unsettled him, or conversely, settled his mind on a different course for the future. The two priest brothers took the opportunity of travelling together when Fr William was unexpectedly given a mission in Glasgow in 1872. Although he initially felt it was banishment he turned it to good account by taking a tour of the Highlands with James for three weeks in August 1873. The impression the brothers made on others during the Scottish holiday was related in Fr William's obituary notice:

> The two brothers were very similar in manner, habits, and appearance, so that their line of route was afterwards easily traced by frequent allusions to them and inquiries as to who those two venerable priests with rubicund face, long white hair, and loud voice, watching everything that passed, and the observed of all beholders on paddle-box, stage coach, or railway platform, could possibly be.[11]

It is likely that the brothers talked about their respective futures, and that of their youngest brother in Queensland. Although William would return to work in a Jesuit mission in Lancashire in 1874, James took the initiative to move in a quite different direction soon after returning to Gloucestershire.

Notes

[1] *Cheltenham Chronicle*, 24 July 1855, p. 3.
[2] *Cheltenham Mercury*, 25 June 1859, p. 2.
[3] *Ibid.*, 29 September 1860, p. 1.
[4] This sentence is one of Sir James Graham's famous, and frequently repeated, rhetorical flourishes. It was directed against Benjamin Disraeli in June 1859, while Graham was MP for Carlisle.
[5] *Cheltenham Mercury*, 10 August 1872, p. 4.
[6] *Cheltenham Looker-On*, 10 August 1872, p. 508.
[7] *Ibid.,*19 September 1868, p. 958.
[8] CDA, Cheltenham Box, Election Poster, 1865.
[9] *Cheltenham Looker-On*, 4 March 1871, p. 136.
[10] *Cheltenham Chronicle*, 21 November 1872, p. 5.
[11] House Journal of the British Province of the Society of Jesus, *Letters and Notices,* No. XCIX, April 1895, p. 134.

41 RESIGNATION FROM THE CHELTENHAM MISSION

COTHAM'S DIARY ENTRY for 31 October 1873 states baldly, 'Resigned the mission at Cheltenham'. Unlike his predecessor Anselm Glassbrook and his successor Aloysius Wilkinson, Cotham did not receive a testimonial from his congregation to mark his departure (echoing his leaving Tasmania), nor is it mentioned in the local newspapers. It may be that he expressly forbade it, or his resignation may have been clouded by rumours of discontent from the congregation or disapproval from his religious superiors. Two days later Fr Cotham preached on the Feast of All Saints, using Bossuet. By the end of the week he had left Cheltenham for Walsall to stay with Augustus Baker and James McCarten, remaining for a week with each. These two young men were at very different stages of their lives but Cotham would have found rejuvenation in their company and an opportunity to share his plans with men who were facing their own turning points in life.

Augustus and Catherine Baker had brought four of their children to be baptised at St Gregory's in the four years following their marriage. In 1872 they moved to Walsall where another daughter was born in 1873. Catherine died in childbirth the following year, in April, although her son Bernard Joseph Chad lived. So it was with a recent widower that Cotham stayed for a week. The children may have already been taken to Baker's capable mother in London; the eldest, another Augustus, was not yet seven years old. Without the loss of his wife, Augustus Baker would surely have continued as a solicitor's clerk for some years longer. A later family reminiscence described him as 'an eccentric English public servant ... a born wanderer'[1] but it was not until he lost his young family that he gave up settled home life. He may not have been ready to talk about unconventional possibilities with Cotham but unless Baker remarried it was unlikely he would be able to have his very young children at home with him again.

For the two weekends he was in Walsall Fr Cotham preached at Mount St Mary's, the mission of the Revd Dr James McCarten with whom he spent the second week. McCarten was a generation younger; he attended St Edmund's College Douai during the 1840s before going on to Rome for further studies towards his doctorate. He was born in Warwickshire and served in the west Midlands area for the whole of his ministry, moving to Walsall in 1868 where he remained until his death, thirty-seven years later. Although he identified himself with his mission he was 'a cultured man, a ripe scholar and a widely travelled man',[2] and just the sort to share unreserved conversations with Fr Cotham, not only about family and political matters, as Baker did, but also the state of the Benedictine congregation. After Walsall Cotham visited Lichfield Cathedral before staying a few days at New College, Oscott, to which he subscribed £5 and had the honour of being asked to preach on Sunday evening. Cotham's diary breaks off here, 23 November 1873, until, having something of interest to note, he takes it up again seven months later. As before, he had chosen to travel to new places for reinvigoration of his energies. He arrived at Douai in December and spent the next two years there, during which time his spirits rose and sank until he made another move.

Fr Cotham was not transferred to another Benedictine mission after Cheltenham and it seems the initiative to leave came from him. There was talk that he had been forced to retire by bad health, but his activity immediately following his resignation does not suggest a man in seriously poor physical health.[3] He may have been jaded and tired after the building labours at St Gregory's, and his close friend George Copeland had died in July 1873 following a lingering illness, but Fr Cotham was by no means exhausted; on the contrary he left Cheltenham with the idea of going to Australia. A letter from Prior Anselm O'Gorman at

Resignation from the Cheltenham Mission   513

Douai to Fr President Burchall gives a tantalising hint that Fr Cotham's resignation was irregular, or at least questionable. Prior O'Gorman hardly conceals his curiosity about Fr Cotham's standing with the President under the guise of wanting advice on doing the best for his spiritual welfare.

> Yesterday [7 December] I received a letter from Fr Cotham (7 Harrington Square London NW sh^d you wish to know his address) stating that he 'hopes to be at Douai next Thursday to spend three weeks or a month in silent retreat before sailing for Australia'.
>
> Now I should like you to instruct me how we are to receive him. Does he come spontaneously or is he sent? Must we treat him as a guest or as a conventual? As I have heard something of the cause of his retiring from Cheltenham, I should be glad to know if you have any peculiar instructions to give me, for his good and the common good. A few words in reply will be sufficient for my guidance.[4]

There are less than a few words available to know Cotham's intentions at this point. Although no other pioneer missioner had returned to Australia in later life, Cotham had two reasons to be sanguine. Dom Roger Bede Vaughan, Cathedral Prior of St Michael's, Belmont, had gone to Sydney in early 1873 to be Archbishop Polding's co-adjutor bishop. He and his companion Dom Anselm Gillet had known Ambrose Cotham for many years, and one may presume that his impression was favourable. President Burchall had little priest-power to spare from the home mission to bolster Vaughan's team; Cotham had served Cheltenham faithfully, was still active, and could pay his own way. He knew Belmont well enough to fit in with the renewal of monastic observance that Vaughan hoped to instigate in Sydney. If he found conventual life in Sydney problematic (and Archbishop Polding less than well-disposed towards him) he would have a ready welcome in his brother's parish in Queensland, a fall-back position he could facilitate for himself.

When he resumed a personal journal in June 1874 it was to write about the project later referred to as 'the Boulogne affair' that side-tracked him from his primary goal. On 29 June 1874 Fr Cotham travelled the short distance between Douai and Boulogne on important business, examining the property of the 'Cocherie' near Boulogne. On 1 July he recorded, 'Agreed to take it'.

The Douai community, 1874/75. Fr Cotham seated third from left; Prior Anselm O'Gorman, centre; Fr Austin O'Neill, third from right; Fr Wilfrid Raynal, back row, far right.

The property referred to in the journal is La Caucherie (as Cotham comes eventually to spell it correctly). The 'castle' was faithfully reconstructed in the seventeenth century chateau style during the nineteenth century, but the gardens are its glory, having been designed by the landscape architect of Versailles, André le Notre. Cotham had negotiated a lease on it as a House of Education for Douai which was in need of additional accommodation and, an innovative idea, as a retirement house for sick

Resignation from the Cheltenham Mission 515

and aged priests. He stayed with friends in Boulogne, saying Mass at a local church, while spending several days inspecting La Caucherie.

The sixty-fourth General Chapter of the English Benedictine Congregation, comprising President Burchall and twenty-two Capitular Fathers, including Fr Ambrose, convened at Downside from 15 to 27 July 1874. A brief summary written over sixty years later perhaps disguises the length or the tone of the discussion that took place among them concerning Cotham's proposal:

> DOUAI OBTAINS PERMISSION TO OPEN A HOUSE NEAR BOULOGNE. St Edmund's petitioned Chapter that it might be allowed to take a country-house near Boulogne, which should serve as a preparatory school and as a home for sick and aged Fathers. Fr Ambrose Cotham, who was then living in retirement at Douai, was present in Chapter as a Preacher General and told the Fathers that he had already rented a suitable house, for which action he asked pardon of the Chapter. The Fathers granted him pardon and gave their approval to the venture.[5]

At the close of the General Chapter Fr Cotham travelled to Cheltenham, staying with Mrs Monington Webbe-Weston at 10 St James Square on Saturday evening. The following day he celebrated the early first Mass, preached at the 11 o'clock High Mass, and preached again at the evening service. The following week was spent in Lancashire before he returned to Cheltenham for almost a fortnight, during which time he visited Fr Anselm Glassbrook, doubtless for further discussion about La Caucherie. The involvement of Fr Glassbrook at this point is rather surprising. Though their links went back to shared school days in the 1820s at Douai, and though Fr Glassbrook was Cotham's predecessor in Cheltenham during the tumultuous years from 1848 to 1851, Cotham had never mentioned him in his journal, despite a short visit by Glassbrook to Cheltenham in March 1853, at the beginning of the planning for the new church.

Unlike Cotham, whose project of building a magnificent edifice for a prospering town had consumed two decades of his life, Glassbrook had spent his pastorate mostly in poor rural and mining communities in South Wales. In Aberavon and Maesteg he had not only overseen the provision of new church buildings but was remembered as a farmer, doctor, or lawyer as needed by his people.[6] The caustic Bishop Scarisbrick judged him unfairly in his jibe to Prior O'Gorman, 'So you are actually building upon Glassbrook's promises!! I thought he had been found out long ago as a man of words and not of deeds and as like a garden full of weeds.'[7] In 1874 Fr Glassbrook was based at Coedangred, near Monmouth, and he came across the border to Ross-on-Wye, to meet up with his old school friend.

At the end of August Cotham returned to Douai, briefly visiting James de Lacy Towle in London on the way. Besides having discussions at Douai about the General Chapter's approval of the project, he was able to show Fr President, Fr Prior, and Fr Glassbrook the potential benefits of La Caucherie when they made a tour of inspection with him on 8 September. They returned to Douai for final deliberations whilst Fr Cotham remained at the chateau 'in suspense until the letter'.

The letter, when it arrived on 15 September, was a disappointment. The house, Cotham wrote, 'must be given up on account of strength to work it'. His personal indefatigability was not enough in this instance. Fr Cotham returned to Douai the following day and began proceedings to disentangle himself, and St Edmund's, from the lease of La Caucherie. This was not accomplished until the following February when Cotham was finally able to account for £578 18s. paid to 'the Colonel', proprietor of La Caucherie, and his lawyers for the misadventure.

In Mauritius, Bishop Scarisbrick was late getting the news. In September he believed the scheme was still a problematic possibility: 'I hope sincerely the Boulogne house will be a success— your difficulty will be to prevent abuse—everybody will seek to find reason for being there rather than at Douai &c.'[8] At the end

Resignation from the Cheltenham Mission 517

of the year, Scarisbrick complacently summed up his feelings of satisfaction and annoyance that Cotham's plans had been quashed concerning La Caucherie but only after making his superiors look foolish:

> I never quite understood the grounds upon which Cotham's bargain had been accepted—but I took it for granted that <u>he</u> bought it and presented it to the College free of cash. This does not seem to be the case—and he has merely wished to saddle it upon St Edmunds—in which case you have done well to have rejected the proffered loan. But ought not this to have been weighed before you petitioned Chapter to condone Cotham's fault. I had a long justification letter from Giles (entre nous). He seems to think that the Edmundian judgement did not and does not show to advantage in this affair and explains to me why he was in opposition throughout. Now you are all obliged (very late) to come round to his way of thinking.[9]

Cotham met with further disappointment in February 1875 when Fr President Burchall would not allow him to return to Queensland 'notwithstanding the permission given me by the Regimen in the last Chapter'. He did not allow the disappointments to sour personal relations with Douai where he spent the July vacation and provided 'Wine Days'. In his diary for Saturday 11 December he 'wrote out the Memo Book it being two years to the day since I came to Douai'. The two years since his resignation from Cheltenham had not gone according to his plans at all and the Congregation seemed not to know what to do with him. Bishop Scarisbrick was in no doubt that Prior O'Gorman would be better off without him:

> As soon as Cotham is free to go to Australia, I would, if in your place, hurry or at least not oppose his departure—for there is a feeling in England that you are humouring him on account of his money—which of course is a calumny—but rumour only runs on.[10]

518 *The Indomitable Mr Cotham*

That there were ambivalent feelings about Cotham's schemes, and in some quarters outright hostility, is very clear from the series of letters written from Mauritius by Bishop Scarisbrick to Prior O'Gorman at Douai. Their correspondence shows how closely Scarisbrick followed the College's affairs from afar, usually disapproving of what was going on and offering his advice to the Prior who fretted over it. Fr Cotham's former assistant priest had little respect for his elder confrère and despised the financial independence which, he felt, gave his ideas unwarranted consideration. In a letter sent to Douai in February 1876 the Bishop, after grumbling about the great heat of Christmas when roast beef and plum pudding were served for the feast, expressed his concern that the College was 'getting overgrown with infirm and broken-down soldiers'. He congratulated Fr O'Gorman on his approach:

> I am glad to hear you are getting rid of your supernumeraries—they always injure discipline. Be sure you don't take in Cotham. He will send you all into asylums.—Wilkinson (who by the bye is not very sound in upper quarters) is not the man for a leader. I foresee a mess there—& Bishop of Clifton may step in to help himself.[11]

Cotham was making his escape from Douai as Scarisbrick was writing his letter, since he believed it was the College that was going to be the ruin of him and not vice versa.

Notes

1   Augustus Baker's life after 1876 is well documented. See Appendix B.
2   *The Tablet*, 16 December 1905, p. 15.
3   *Clifton Diocesan Year Book*, 1955, 'Parochial item of interest', no page number.
4   AAA RB–249–58; O'Gorman to Burchall, 8 December 1873.
5   J. McCann OSB, *Annals of the English Benedictine Congregation 1850-1901* (Oxford: St Benet's Hall, 1941), p. 127. Basil Whelan OSB adds the detail that the property was also intended to serve as a holiday house for St Edmund's community; *The Annals of the English Congregation of the*

Resignation from the Cheltenham Mission

    Black Monks of St Benedict (1850–1900), private publication, 1942 2nd edition, reissued 1971, Vol. 2, p. 310.

[6]   *The Irish are in Town: Port Talbot Part 1*; www.ballinagree.freeservers.com/ptalbot.html [Accessed online 27.7.2017]

[7]   DA VII.A.3.f; Scarisbrick to O'Gorman, 4 February 1876.

[8]   *Ibid.,* 7 September 1874.

[9]   *Ibid.,* 12 November 1874.

[10] *Ibid.,* 5 February 1875.

[11] *Ibid.,* 4 February 1876.

42 LEAVING DOUAI AGAIN

AT THE END of two years spent mostly at Douai Fr Cotham made preparations to leave. In the first place he put his financial affairs in order, updating his written accounts and transferring funds between banks after 'a confab' with the Community Bursar, and sending instructions to John Waddy, the former choir master at St Gregory's and a bank clerk in Cheltenham. He sent letters to his brother William and his niece Emily Renehan, and as he noted in his accounts book, he sent a long letter to Mrs Monington on 18 January 1876. Among Cotham's papers there are loose notes which almost certainly refer to this letter; they suggest a relaxed confidence in his relationship with Mrs Monington alongside some confusion about his immediate plans about where he intended to go—but to go somewhere appears to be his clear intention. The mixture of banter, doggerel verse, honesty, and affection is probably a fair approximation of what it was like to be in a light-hearted social gathering with him. If Cotham's language seems too effusive it should be remembered that his 'dearest friend' was born in 1789 and was safely twenty-one years his senior. He wrote with Thomas Moore's verses and letters in his memory or at hand but the final, borrowed, line expressed his own feeling exactly:

> Odds pills and boluses! here I am with sciatica! I am made very comfortable here. But all kindnesses do not settle the main point. 'Il me donne des manchettes et je n'ai point de chemise'[1]—To bribe you to write to me immediately on receiving this I will write you an epitaph that will amuse you if you never heard it before

> 'Here lies John Shaw, Attorney at law;
> And when he died, The devil cried,
> Give me your paw, John Shaw,
> Attorney at Law!'

Most sincerely I lament that I did not set out as I had purposed, without enacting the Boulogne affair, since this place has pushed me hard with rheumatism.

Best remembrances to your household and believe in yours most truly. Good by [sic]. God bless you all.

I don't know what your English skies have been doing all this month (I suppose raining, as usual) but here we have had the severest frost till yesterday.

I must leave our friendship to take care of itself, without any looking after, for 6 or 7 months longer.

I think in a fortnight you may count upon seeing me.

I wish, dear friend, you would have a look out in the neighbourhood, for either 2 tolerable rooms or one very excellent, large bedroom for me, where there would be some one merely to bring up my breakfast.

Australia is out of the question for me, till I have got ammunition in my pocket. Take care of yourself, best and dearest friend, and with warm remembrances to our well-beloved N. believe me, Most affectionately yours.' ... [There follows a series of aphorisms, ditties, and anecdotes.]

Cara Maria, vale! At veniet felicius avum, Iando iterum tecum (sim modo dignus) ero.[2]

'Ah, well may we hope, when this short life is gone, To meet in some world of more permanent bliss;
For a smile or a grasp of the hand, hastening on, Is all we enjoy of each other in this.'[3]

'Who trusts in those with whom he deals, Inspires the confidence he feels;
But he who still suspects deceit, Tempts others in their turn to cheat.'

Your last letter was like summer sunshine to me. / I seize the first moment to beg you will accept as many thanks as there are miles between us at this moment for your ready compliance with my request. / Farewell my dearest -, and

Leaving Douai Again 523

believe me to be, as ever, yours affectionately &c. / If wishing you well and happy, and free from all the ills of this life, could in any way bring it about, I should be as good a physician for both your bodies and souls as you could find anywhere.

I am sinking here into a mere vegetable.

On 24 February 1876 he wrote that he had been 'engaged the last days in examining maps and trains for the journey'. In view of his rheumatism and strong antipathy to cold and wet weather the choice of Italy for his journey was sensible. Nevertheless, he remained interested in the College, observing 'Commenced new Building for mill and bakery this week' and paying £25 for a Wine Day on 28 February. Whatever others might say about him, the Benedictine community was his family and his home and he was as immersed in activities for their welfare as he was for his blood relatives.

Although Australia seemed out of the question for Fr Ambrose he had grounds to remain hopeful. The tensions between Irish and Italian mission priests in Queensland came under Bishop Vaughan's scrutiny and were compounded by antagonism towards the autocratic Bishop Quinn of Brisbane. Such difficulties for Vaughan may have been pieces of ammunition in Cotham's armoury. His brother Lawrence had continued to prosper in Queensland and his family was now into the third generation. The difficulties in the Brisbane diocese—money, personnel, factions— were familiar ones and Cotham may have been encouraged by his family to consider joining them as an experienced missioner.

Among his papers is a handbill from the Sisters of Mercy, sanctioned by Archbishop Henry Manning, in which Mother Vincent Whitty asked for public donations to cover the costs of twenty Sisters and teachers who had volunteered for the Queens-land mission.[4] Between November 1870 and January 1872 Bishop Quinn had disbursed over £2,000 to cover the travel expenses of recruits from Ireland but that stream of money had dried up. Fr Cotham's interest in the handbill was probably in the statistics it gave about Queensland's population growth; the paucity of

English clergy was well known, and he was offering to go out, doubtless at his own expense. The handbill also made the point that any 'grown girl' from a workhouse or industrial school trained in domestic skills could be sent out for £1 via the Queensland Emigration Office and the Sisters of Mercy would meet them at the port and house them until a situation was found. Cotham himself had acted as agent for the Queen's Orphan School in Hobart; colonial emigration offered 'rare advantages to the poor' which it seemed judicious to extend to children from the Motherland.

Brief biographies of Fr Cotham's life all say that after leaving Douai in 1876 he spent two years at La Cava in southern Italy.[5] Details about this period are scanty but the inference that he spent two years in monastic seclusion is misleading. The Abbey of the Holy Trinity of Cava de'Tirreni, belonging to the Cassinese Congregation, has the distinction of being the only monastery in the world which has been uninterruptedly occupied by Benedictine monks since its foundation in 1011. However, this occupation covers the period of the suppression of religious houses in Italy promulgated by the law of 7 July 1866. In recognition of the abbey's cultural importance it was declared a national monument and entrusted to the care of the abbot on a temporary basis. In practice this allowed the community to continue its work, especially as an incomparable archive and library, and to maintain the college attached to it.

The election of Abbot Michele Morcaldi in 1878, following a gap of twenty years after the departure of Abbot Onifrio Granata, marked a period of renewal for the abbey and it was in this interim period that Fr Cotham came. The abbey's profound historical significance and contemporary interest would have been an irresistible draw for him but it seems an unlikely place for monastic retirement for someone who never claimed to be a scholar. More appealing to him would have been the abbey's close contact with Frs Rosendo Salvado and Joseph Serra, Spanish Benedictines who left from La Cava to join Bishop Brady's

Leaving Douai Again 525

mission in Western Australia in 1846. Salvado made return visits to Europe and maintained a significant correspondence with Abbot Morcaldi. The link with New Norcia, Western Australia would have provided more than enough common ground between Cotham and the monks of La Cava.

Detailed handbooks for travellers to southern Italy, such as those produced by John Murray and Karl Bædeker, contained instructions for rail travel, donkey hire, and staying in clean and comfortable hotels, and guides such as these were carefully examined by Cotham before departure at the end of February or early March 1876. For an active but rheumatic man of great curiosity it is unsurprising that he chose to base himself at La Cava,

> a favourite summer resort of Neapolitans and strangers, a town consisting of long streets with arcades as at Bologna. On a wooded eminence in the neighbourhood rises the celebrated Benedictine monastery La Trinità della Cava ... This delightful and salubrious valley is admirably adapted for a summer retreat.[6]

Staying at a healthy altitude he avoided the dangers of malaria, and he probably socialised with the well-established English colony in Salerno and Naples. The surrounding area—Sorrento, Amalfi, Paestum, and Pompeii—was easily explored, although his main aim was to regain health and stamina, necessary ammunition for the future, rather than simply pass the time sight-seeing.

The two-year sojourn in La Cava was not a period of total withdrawal from wider society. In Rome the year 1877 was taken up with celebrations for the fiftieth anniversary of the episcopal ordination of Pope Pius IX. Judith Champ has detailed the change in significance Rome had for visitors, Catholic and Protestant, during the course of the nineteenth century. Alongside the perennial appeal of the classical roots of the city, Rome, its catacombs freshly reopened, now attracted both Catholic and Protestant pilgrims who were fired by devotion inspired by the relics of the earliest Christian martyrs. 'The carrying of portable altar stones containing relics by recusant missioners kept alive the association

526 *The Indomitable Mr Cotham*

between relics, martyrdom and the Eucharist in English Catholicism'.[7] The political events of 1870—the unification of Italy when Rome was established as the secular capital, and the loss of papal temporal power—left Catholics to focus their attention more than ever before on the solitary figure of the Holy Father himself, his influence now circumscribed within a strictly spiritual and, moreover, Catholic sphere. Unsurprisingly, attendance at a papal audience became an essential component of any visit by a loyal Catholic to Papal Rome. The large numbers of visitors coming to the city as members of organised parties were handled efficiently by tour operators. Hotels and lodging houses for all classes, and a ticket-only system of timed admissions, allowed many more people to have access to privileged areas.

Successive national delegations visited the Holy City in 1877 to present gifts and loyal addresses to the Pontiff. In May it was the turn of English speaking pilgrims from England, Scotland, and Canada to attend the audience in St Peter's and among the 150 pilgrims and the 300 to 400 English residents of Rome was Fr Cotham. Besides a reception in the Papal rooms the delegation was treated to generous hospitality by leading Catholic lay families headed by the Duke of Norfolk, the Ladies Anne and Margaret Howard, the Dowager Marchioness of Lothian (who died during the celebrations), the Earl and Countess of Denbigh and others, some of whom were related to the twelve bishops in attendance. Fr Cotham was able to reacquaint himself with John Barry, the young seminarian who had helped with the accounts during his Christmas and New Year vacation, 1867 to 1868, and who was now an ordained priest in the Shrewsbury diocese. Among the religious clergy some of the Benedictine contingent were honoured with particular attention.

> The Holy Father, in spite of the many claims upon his sacred person, has deigned to express a wish to receive to special private audience Dom Jerome Vaughan, Dom Wolstan Canon Richards, Dom Romuald Canon Riley, Dom Ambrose Cotham, Dom Basil Hurworth, Dom Placid

Leaving Douai Again 527

Whittle, and Dom Francis Fleming—all members of the English Benedictine Congregation—who will present the Holy Father with an address in the name of the English monks, together with a purse of some £200. Bishop Scarisbrick, OSB, of Port Louis, and Bishop Hedley, OSB, of Newport and Menevia, are also in Rome.[8]

Once again the paths of Fr Cotham and Bishop Scarisbrick crossed, certainly with gracious civility if not warmth.

There was an opportunity for the two of them to meet again later in the year but significantly Fr Cotham was absent from the consecration of St Gregory the Great in Cheltenham on 7 November 1877. Bishop Clifford officiated at that celebration, assisted by Bishops Brown, Collier, Scarisbrick, and Hedley and an array of Benedictines, including James Kendal and Bernard Caldwell. Bishop Scarisbrick preached at the Mass, lamenting the materialism, indifference and dismal corruption of the present age against which the practice of religion was a necessity. His post-luncheon speech was more congratulatory in tone, but he avoided mention of Fr Cotham by name. However, it was an occasion when Cotham was singled out for high praise by others; Bishop Collier described the key point when

> there came to Cheltenham, as Father Wilkinson had said, a man of indomitable energy and he doubted whether there was a man in England who could overcome the difficulties and surmount the apparently insurmountable obstacles, which opposed the laying of the foundations of St Gregory's Church.[9]

Bishop Clifford wished that Fr Cotham, 'a good friend of theirs' could have been present, although he was sure he was there in heart 'and would be unwilling to admit that any, even of the grand churches of Italy, scarcely even St Peter's itself, excelled that church which he had begun in Cheltenham'. The idea was received with cheers and laughter. This was the ninth church the bishop had consecrated in the diocese but he remarked that it had a particular significance for him, since

528 *The Indomitable Mr Cotham*

> he had a kind feeling towards St Gregory's Church, for he
> looked upon it as contemporary with himself. It was a
> quarter of a century since he came into the diocese, and
> the first year of his being there he was present at the first
> opening of St Gregory's.

Whatever his reasons (it may have been only bad weather that deterred him) the absence of Fr Cotham from the consecration of St Gregory's was in no way a sign of disaffection with his Benedictine family. He kept a newspaper cutting describing the ceremony, sent to him from Cheltenham, among his papers. In July 1878 he attended a meeting of the Ampleforth Society, founded three years earlier and numbering eighty members, lay and religious, many of whom had not been educated at the College. In his address to the school after the prize-giving ceremony, Bishop Hedley took as his theme the end to which education was directed, namely the attainment of culture. His words are applicable to Ambrose Cotham himself and to his concern for his extended family:

> The wider our culture, the better we can analyse a great
> idea, and the better we can compare other great ideas with
> it ... The true and precious culture is that which perfects
> the spirit of a man; and the spirit is not bounded in its
> aspirations and its views either by the horizon of the earth
> or the firmament of the heavens ... Culture, as I am now
> using it, means something very high and precious.[10]

Fr Cotham thrived on lofty views, ambitious plans, and wide experience, even if it made him restless and a worrisome colleague at times.

It was not just Ampleforth that drew Cotham's attention, though. He had never lost his interest in Catholic education and now that interest had a very particular focus: once again he found himself needing to take personal responsibility for the needs of Lawrence's family. The few entries in his brown accounts book for 1877 list the interest received from investments, from which £20 was sent to Emily Renehan, and £200 was expended on the

Leaving Douai Again 529

education of his great-nephews James Ambrose and Arthur. Gustavus Horstmann had taken responsibility for their education in Brisbane after their mother Eliza married Samuel Finklstein in 1877. She took nine-year-old Arthur with her to Victoria for a few months, but the thirty pounds sent to her by Cotham was intended to 'fit him out' to rejoin his elder brother. Eliza replied immediately to Fr Cotham, whom she had never met, in April 1878 after receiving the money; she copied two letters, sending one to La Cava and one to Cheltenham to be sure of reaching him. Her eight years of widowhood had been difficult but the second marriage separated her from her boys; now the English great-uncles proposed providing for their higher education in England in due course.

Maindample, Near Mansfield, Victoria, Australia

April 24th 1878

The Revd James Cotham, Cava di Tirrenia, Italy

Dear Sir, Your letter dated Sept 14th 1877 with an enclosed draft of £30 reached me no sooner than April 22nd 1878. Which was forwarded to me by Mr Horstmann. Why so long delayed I cannot tell. On a former occasion I think about two years ago Hugh Cotham by his father's instruction forwarded to me £10.

My dear Arthur is already with his brother at Mr Horstmann's. I received £6 for his outfit and I returned £1. 15 back to Mr Cotham so that £4. 5 was the cost of the outfit and these sums were all that I received on behalf of Arthur. I was delighted some five months ago to receive a few lines from my dear boy James after asking many times. I would rather the children were in England under the supervision of their Uncles, although it is very hard to feel that they would be so far away from me. Yet one certainty that by God's blessing it would be for their future good will enable me to commit them to God and their good Uncles. When they are ready to go away I would certainly like to see them before they depart and the money which I have just received will enable me to do so. God only knows the years of struggle I had and how I suffer in health very much. And my earnest desire and prayer is that both the dear boys may grow up to be good men.

And now I must thank you for your kindness. I pray God to reward you with his divine presence and favour here and with a bright and glorious eternity...

I remain dear Sir, Your aff. Neice,

E Finklstein.[11]

Notes

[1] They provide me with cuffs and I haven't got a shirt.

[2] 'Adieu, Mary, till that day more blest, When, if deserving, I with thee shall rest.' The epitaph by Bishop Lowth on the monument of his daughter Mary at Cuddesden, Oxfordshire, 1768, attracted much admiration and imitation. This early translation is by Lowth's contemporary, the Revd John Duncombe.

[3] Fragment from stanza 4 of 'And doth not a meeting like this' by Thomas Moore (1779–1852), the Irish Minstrel; most of the following lines are also taken from Moore.

[4] DA IV.C.XI.

[5] H. N. Birt OSB, *Obit Book of the English Benedictines: From 1600 to 1912* (Edinburgh: The Mercat Press, 1913), p. 176.

[6] K. Bædeker, *Italy: Handbook for Travellers, Part Third, Southern Italy, Sicily* (Coblenz: Karl Bædeker, 1872 3rd edition), p. 148.

[7] J. Champ, *The English Pilgrimage to Rome: A Dwelling for the Soul* (Leominster: Gracewing, 2000), p. 196.

[8] *The Tablet*, 12 May 1877, pp. 17–18.

[9] *Cheltenham Examiner*, 14 November 1877, p. 3, for all quotations relating to the consecration of St Gregory's.

[10] *The Tablet*, 27 July 1878, p. 19.

[11] Jesuit Archives (Farm Street, London), item 508, 'Abstract from deeds of property belonging to Revd Wm Cotham, and administered by Revd James Cotham'. This single piece of personal correspondence in William Cotham SJ's archive is a tantalising hint of what must have passed between the Cotham brothers over many years.

43 THE FINAL MISSION

DURING THE PERIOD following resignation from Cheltenham and before his retirement from active mission work, 1873 to 1881, the evidence suggests Cotham wanted to initiate a phase of activity of his own choosing. He did not want to be an assistant to a younger man in an urban mission, as Bishop Collier had been to him. Neither his proposals for La Caucherie, which would have involved him closely with St Edmund's, Douai in an experimental enterprise, nor his preference for returning to Australia with the prospect of contact again with the Benedictine enterprise there and with his brother's family, seemed opportune to others. Disappointed in both schemes, and after two years in the warmer climate of Italy, Cotham returned briefly to Downside before going to the Benedictine priory in Bath. He was probably aware by then that he was suffering from cancer and it was reasonable to suppose that he would pass his final years in quiet seclusion. The death of his younger brother in 1881 was further confirmation that the heroic pioneering days were over:

> The scythe of death has again been amongst us and taken from our midst another old, valued, and highly respected colonist, in the person of Mr. Laurence Cotham, chemist, late of Gympie, and father of Mr. William Cotham, solicitor of Bundaberg. Mr. Cotham was a colonist of over 40 years standing, having come to the colony in early life and has brought up a large and numerous family, and had well merited the good-will and respect of all classes of the community.[1]

However, quiet retirement was not congenial to the Cotham temperament and, at his request to go on the mission one last time, Ambrose Cotham was given the remote mission of Bonham in Wiltshire. While there he saw the need to take the mission to

532 *The Indomitable Mr Cotham*

Wincanton and so he came full circle as a 'riding missioner' in the English Benedictine tradition.

Bonham was small but significant as one of only two chapelries in the county, the other being at Wardour in the parish of Tisbury. Bonham House was all that remained of the Stourton family estate which had supported a chaplain since penal times for itself and for the locality. After the Stourtons left in 1804 the Benedictines, recently established at Downside, continued to celebrate Mass in the chapel of the manor house where Catholics from the surrounding areas, including Wincanton, were able to attend. The chaplain lived in the part of the house adjoining the chapel that had not been sold off; in Fr Cotham's case he lived alone. In the 1851 religious census eighty persons were counted at Mass in Bonham on 25 March, recording a relative surge in numbers and conversions. The Catholic school had a roll of thirty-six pupils, which had declined to fifteen by the end of the century.

> It seems [Fr Cotham] may have been concerned about the progress of the school. He appointed a committee of ten men to oversee it: Messrs Simon Creagh, Joseph Shepherd, Joseph Hurden, John Harcourt, Isaiah Farthing, Philip Harcourt, Thomas Hurden, John Heath, Thomas Harcourt and Charles Harcourt. Early in 1881 Miss Holmes, a certificated mistress, took charge of the school. The first government inspection took place on the 11th of October 1881 and was a complete failure. Only three children passed in the three subjects Reading, Writing and Arithmetic.[2]

However, the situation was not entirely gloomy, except for Miss Holmes who was dismissed. In his Advent pastoral letter for 1883 the Bishop of Clifton put two of Fr Cotham's missions in a happy juxtaposition when he noted, 'Extensive improvements have been effected in the beautiful Church of St. Gregory, at Cheltenham, and in the chapel at Bonham'.[3]

Cotham could not resist the opportunity to re-establish a place of worship for the Catholics of Wincanton in their own town. To give the occasion some solemnity his brother William celebrated

The Final Mission   533

the first Mass of the new mission of St Luke in the house of Mr Thomas Clementina, an Italian shopkeeper, in North Street at the end of May 1881. Thereafter Ambrose Cotham travelled the five miles by gig to celebrate Sunday Mass for a few people in Clementina's house. He formed a committee of two from the small congregation—Clementina and Captain John Bradney of Bayford Lodge, the convert son of an Anglican clergyman—and together they resolved to purchase Acorn House in South Street for the purpose of converting a former stable building into a chapel with the house to be used as its presbytery. Captain Bradney contributed £500 and Fr Cotham and Mr Clementina each gave £100. The purchase 'hitherto kept secret having become public property a perfect storm of indignation burst over the heads of the Committee which found a safety valve in letters to a local newspaper'.[4] Nevertheless, the local bank approved the transaction and the modest building, with a frontage facing directly onto a road leading off the High Street, was adapted for worship.

The solemn inauguration of the new mission of St Luke took place on 18 October 1881, its patronal feast. Fr Aidan Gasquet, Prior of Downside, was chief celebrant at the Mass, assisted by Fr Ford playing the organ and by a small choir from Downside. Although many neighbouring priests and lay people attended, Fr Cotham was notably absent, having resigned from the mission because of ill health. The speeches made at the celebration luncheon sparked a correspondence in the local press to which John Bradney and Lord Arundell contributed in defence of Catholic tradition and teaching.[5] Much was made of the persecutions of the sixteenth century, although Arundell admitted both sides had much to regret in the competing histories of Foxe's *Book of Martyrs* and Challoner's *Missionary Priests*. Fr Walsh struggled for some months as Priest-in-charge of the mission in the face of this animosity until in the summer of 1882 the pastoral duties were divided between Benedictines from Downside and Franciscans from Clevedon. At the invitation of the Bishop of Clifton the Discalced Carmelite friars from Kensington took over

534 *The Indomitable Mr Cotham*

the mission, and although they moved into what was 'formerly an old tumble-down house, the residence of a local surgeon, and the crowding of so many cells in this dilapidated building [was] certainly not wholesome'[6] they were able to establish a fully-fledged Priory following monastic observance by early 1885.

John Bradney, with his impeccable English pedigree as a vicar's son who had attended both Eton and Trinity College, Cambridge, had joined the 14th Hussars, and had become a Justice of the Peace in civilian life, was more than equal to building up what Cotham had begun. In 1887 he was begging for funds for the Carmelite friars, unapologetic that this was a rural parish. He wrote to *The Tablet*, intending his letter to be a corrective to common-place assumptions about the material and spiritual needs of industrial England, and to the unwarranted generalisations about very diverse social environments. He spoke out of his Anglican patrimony while hoping for the conversion of England.

> Some Catholics may say these country missions, with only a handful of the faithful, do not want help, and after providing for our own missions if we have anything over we will give it to the struggling missions in the large cities where there are thousands of Catholics composed for the most part of the very poorest of our fellow countrymen. Those who argue thus must remember that these large cities are by no means England, and if they wish for the conversion of the whole kingdom they must aid these little bands of the faithful in the country districts not only by their alms but by their earnest prayers, and they must bear in mind that although bigotry and absurd ideas as to Catholics and their faith may have almost disappeared in these large cities, it is not so in the country, where in the great majority of the counties the same bigotry and absurd ideas as to Catholics and their faith prevail in just the same way as they did fifty or a hundred years ago.[7]

Ambrose Cotham had experienced that bigotry and absurd ignorance about the life and practice of Catholicism across a long

The Final Mission 535

and wide-ranging ministry. Since finishing the work of building a church of major cultural and architectural importance for Cheltenham he had not found an enterprise that would draw on his considerable resources. The final chapter of his ministry, in the rural heart of what had once been recusant England, lasted only a few months. By 1881 his physical strength was spent and industrial cities and rural communities alike were beyond his reach. Many years later the *Downside Review* recalled the last active months of this stalwart, simple man in terms that were affectionate and homely:

> Father Ambrose Cotham, one of the band of Australian Benedictines, and who in his latter days was a neighbour of ours at Bonham, turned vegetarian shortly before his last illness. He started the mission at Wincanton, working it from Bonham. Though he was an old man, he was able after saying Mass on Sunday at Bonham, to drive five miles to Wincanton and say Mass again. His dinner then consisted in a plate of dried onions ('charlottes' as they call them in the neighbourhood), salt and bread.[8]

The span of Fr Cotham's life is easily recognisable is those words: slightly eccentric, never anything but industrious and diligent, and through it all a thorough-going mission priest.

Notes

[1] *Maryborough Chronicle, Wide Bay and Burnett Advertiser*, 13 October 1881, p. 3.

[2] G. Hogarth; private research.

[3] *The Tablet*, 15 December 1883, p. 34.

[4] G. Sweetman, *The History of Wincanton* (London: Williams, 1903), pp. 191-2. http://www.archive.org/details/ historyofwincant00swee. [Accessed online 27.7.2017].

[5] *Western Gazette*, 28 October 1881, p. 8, and 4 November 1881, p. 7.

[6] *The Tablet*, 17 September 1887, p. 22.

[7] *Ibid.*, p. 22.

[8] *Downside Review* XXI, Vol. 2, No 2, 'Odds and Ends' (July 1902).

44 ENFORCED QUIET

AMBROSE COTHAM RETURNED to Bath for a short while but his active days were finally over. He may have made the choice to retire to St Michael's Priory, Belmont, or it may have been pressed on him for its amenities and easiness of access. He had been in the habit of visiting Belmont regularly during his Cheltenham years so he knew it well. It was the newest house in the English Benedictine family, established as a common novitiate for the three communities of the Congregation. In 1882 there were just over thirty young men training for monastic profession and the priesthood with a staff of eight professors; the priory superior was Fr Paul Wilfrid Raynal from Mauritius. The community knew Fr Cotham, too, as a singular character, though their recollections of him are somewhat embroidered.

> It is said of him that having returned to Belmont after many years spent in the wilds of central Australia, he found life in a crowded house intolerable after the bush, and could only sleep in the solitude offered by the top of the Tower.[1]

The tower was not completed during his retirement and it is doubtful if he could have climbed to the top with his infirmity. If he found a crowded house intolerable it would have been because it reminded him too much of the penal institutions he had visited rather than the years supposedly spent in the bush. The Prior of Douai was anxious that Cotham's *alma mater* had been replaced in his affections; having had his proposals spurned by Douai in 1874 he might feel Belmont was more deserving of his attention. The Prior's judgement of Cotham's intentions was wide of the mark, though it is quite likely that Cotham enjoyed keeping him on tenterhooks where money was concerned.

Without a congregation of his own to occupy him, Cotham's interest in the younger generation of his family engaged his mind.

538   *The Indomitable Mr Cotham*

After a three year gap the entries in the brown accounts book resume in January 1881. His handwriting became increasingly spidery and by 1882 the accounts book is written in a different hand although doubtless under his supervision as he spent his final year as an invalid. Regular remittances were sent to Queensland for the great-nephews and nieces he knew by name; £50 was sent 'for the education of Francis Patrick and Mary Lillis, the children of my niece Isabella' although they were still less than ten years old. In January 1881 James Ambrose and his brother Arthur Leopold, aged 15 and 12, arrived in England from Brisbane and were fitted out for Stonyhurst College. It was twelve years since their father had died in the Queensland goldfields. The marriage of their mother to Samuel Finklstein perhaps called into doubt their Catholic upbringing and gave the clerical uncles a particular role to play in their lives, one which their mother preferred over Uncle Horstmann's.

The boys were settled, unsurprisingly, in the north of England. Stonyhurst was tried first but not too successfully. They were both placed in the class called Elements, despite the difference in their ages, reflecting a lack of attainment in key subjects, especially Latin. James was placed in the 2nd Class (out of three) for arithmetic, while Arthur's class number is merely a question mark. Whether because he struggled academically or, more likely, found it too difficult to adapt culturally, Arthur was removed from Stonyhurst in January 1882 after four terms, in favour of St Paulinus College, Catterick, where he did well.[2] His brother stayed at Stonyhurst for less than a year but he had made progress in Elements, being one of the winners at Prize Day.[3] During the summer vacation of 1882 he travelled with Fr William to visit Fr James at Belmont and it might have been as a consequence of this meeting that he chose to go to his Benedictine uncle's *alma mater* in France to continue his education. In November 1882 £23 was paid in advance for his *pension* at Douai College but by the time he arrived there the following August his Uncle James had died.

Enforced Quiet 539

Accounts of Fr Cotham's final illness stress the painful nature of the cancerous tumour which had developed in his thigh; the death certificate suggests it may have been gangrenous at the time of his death.[4] The final invoice sent by Williams' Family and Dispensing Chemists on 9 May shows the attentiveness of Fr Cotham's carers and the limitations of their help. Bottles of soda water and ginger ale were amply provided for his comfort from their shop in Bridge Street, Hereford. The pain caused by lint, an 8 inch probe, and dressing forceps together with many bottles of Sanitas and carbolic oil can be imagined; his old standby—a bottle of eau de cologne— was kindly bought two days before his death. Two of the ordained monks, Basil Hurworth and Peter Austin O'Neill, were assigned to be his close companions and helpers but his personal needs for the last ten months were met by Walter Redding, 18-years-old, and formerly a house servant at Malvern College.

Despite the pain of his terminal illness, Fr Cotham's financial transactions continued until the last week of his life. Deeds of Settlement and Declarations of Trust were drawn up by John Lambe, his solicitor, during February and March 1883 until Cotham was apparently satisfied on 20 March. The negotiations relating to Lawrence Cotham's family in Queensland were complicated and detailed; the Settlement and Trust made individual arrangements for his sister-in-law Sarah Cotham, his nieces and nephews, and their children, but these altered substantially between early February and late March. However, among his papers is a Will dated and signed 10 April, witnessed by Frs O'Connell and Standish of St Michael's. The monies left in this Will are very like the amounts sent to Australia just before his death by the terms of Settlement and Trust, but (perhaps to avoid death duties, or to disassociate his family interests from his religious affiliations) he chose to remove his relatives from the final version of his Will which was witnessed on 27 April, three days before his death, by Mr Lambe and Walter Redding. Between these two signings Prior Raynal wrote to Fr Bede Prest about delicate negotiations in Rome concerning changes in the structure of Benedictine governance. He concluded his letter with what was vividly in his mind: 'What a sad state [Abbot Sweeney] is in! I fear he is no more by this time. Fr Cotham is growing much weaker and his cancer more dreadful. Pray for his Happy Death.'[5]

Mr Lambe itemised the progress of the instructions he was given. The first draft of the Settlement arranged for £750 to be sent in trust to Gustavus Horstmann and Hugh Cotham, his nephew, to be invested for Sarah Cotham's benefit for life, and afterwards to be distributed among her family. According to the second draft Sarah still received £750 (as an outright gift) but a total of £1,520 was divided unequally among the other family members; in the light of later events it is interesting that the largest amount was made to Hugh Cotham and his wife Ann who received £456 each. A total of £2,250 was realised from the sale of 3,000 Egyptian and Turkish Bonds invested in 1871, and £2,070 was dispatched to Australia on 28 April (Sarah Cotham already having received £200).

In the final Will the main bequests were made to the two monastic houses, Douai and Belmont, which housed him first and last. From a total of 10,400 bonds, 7,000 bonds of the Egyptian Unified Loan were allocated to Douai, and 3,400 bonds of the Daira Sanieh to Belmont. Two thousand pounds which Cotham had made available as an interest-free loan to St Gregory's, Cheltenham, was to be divided equally between the Douai and Belmont houses (another £1,000 having been given outright to Cheltenham as his personal subscription). Prior O'Gorman of Douai was disappointed and relieved: it could have been so much more, it could have been even less. The probate court valued Cotham's estate at £7,958 4s. 7d. gross, £7,615 1s. 8d. net. From the estate, St Edmund's, Douai received £4,972 2s. less ten per cent death duties, and St Michael's Priory, £2,390 1s. 2d. less ten per cent death duties, both houses keeping most of their legacies in the form of shareholdings.

There remained a further 4,000 bonds, again divided unequally, for his two great-nephews Arthur and James Ambrose,

Enforced Quiet 541

with 1,800 and 2,200 allocated respectively, to be held in trust by Frs Hurworth and O'Neill until the young men reached twenty-five. Particular gifts, itemised in the solicitor's draft notes, were for £10 each to Canon Richards, Fr Bulbeck, James de Lacy Towle, Fr William Cotham SJ, Doctor—[*sic*, Renehan] and W. Redding. A pencilled note against Walter's name explained the bequest was for '£1 per month gratia in recognition of his care'. Again in pencil a few personal gifts were noted: James was to receive his great-uncle's gold watch, and both boys shared his books. To Brother Joseph he left his silver watch. 'He desired also that those others who had been engaged about him, especially Br Clement, Br Thomas, Fr Basil, Fr Austin, should have some present in token of his thanks to them.'

The bill from John Lambe for £5 1s. 2d. was paid on 26 June. The instructions detailed above are written, informally and neatly, on a separate sheet, showing the alterations and thought behind the final draft. At the bottom are 'Instructions regarding disposal of 3400 Daira Senieh Bonds'. Finally, there are miscellaneous notes: that S. P. Creagh Esq. of Brook House, Stourton, owed Fr Cotham £61; that Fr Cotham owed to St Michael's £63 for (water) ram expenses, and £48 8s. 11d. for board and lodging; and that Fr Wilkinson had been promised £100 which had not been paid. The brief reference to St Gregory's suggests no lingering attachment to that mission. While there he had given everything; now it had to pay its own way and repay what it owed.

The obituary in *The Tablet* after Fr Cotham's death on 1 May was reprinted in Tasmanian newspapers. It emphasised his early years, reminiscent of pre-Emancipation England, when as

> one of the apostles of our convicts in Van Diemen's Land
> ... for 16 years he laboured amongst colonists and convicts,
> visiting all parts of the colony on horseback, with altar-
> stone, chalice, vestments, and all the requisites for Sacrifice
> and Sacraments in his saddle-bags. ... [In retirement at
> Belmont] the pain and the enforced quiet, so irksome to
> his active nature, he bore with edifying patience.[6]

542 *The Indomitable Mr Cotham*

Fr William arrived at St Michael's three days later to celebrate the Solemn Requiem Mass, and his booming voice probably remained steady and defiant in the face of death, as befitted his brother's memory. He also carefully claimed four shillings from James' estate for his cab fare from the railway station on 4 May.

Notes

[1] B. Whelan OSB, *The History of Belmont Abbey* (London: Bloomsbury, 1959), p. 82.

[2] *The Tablet,* 14 March 1885, p. 35. In August 1885 he was one of two successful candidates from the school at the Cambridge University Local Examination. He was back in Queensland by October 1885.

[3] *Ibid.,* 5 August 1882, p. 34.

[4] The bone cancer was probably a secondary tumour, given Fr Cotham's age, so it is likely he had suffered for some time from a primary carcinoma of an internal organ. Medical opinion kindly offered by Dr M. Gompertz, Cheltenham, 2015.

[5] AAA RB–253–59; Raynal to Prest, 16 April 1883.

[6] *The Tablet,* 12 May 1883, p. 38, and *Launceston Examiner* (Tasmania), 26 July 1883, p. 2.

45 THE SPOLIA OF AMBROSE COTHAM'S LIFE

ALTHOUGH QUITE DIFFERENT in substance, the financial arrangements made in the spring of 1883 mirror the spirit of the letter Cotham wrote to Bishop Polding in March 1836. That letter was written with immature audacity: he judged what he saw around him and, risking his Bishop's displeasure, his own reputation, and future prospects he spoke his mind. He did not intend, nor is there in fact, any disobedience or disloyalty on Cotham's part; he simply could not see his way to continuing in the situation he had been placed in. In his mortal illness Cotham worked and reworked his last testament, a declaration of love and loyalty towards his family and the Benedictine community, although it was open to interpretation as obstinate selfishness. The problem lay not in the possession of money—the vow of poverty was not invoked as an obstacle—but in his determination to decide what should happen to it after his death. He did not consider a potential charge of disobedience to be a stumbling block to a holy death.

John Lambe's notes referring to Ambrose Cotham's Will convey something of his client's feelings, together with his wishes concerning the money he had at his disposal. The money allocated to his extended family in Queensland was despatched just before his death, putting it safely out of reach of any dispute. There were no legal grounds for questioning his arrangements, but he was understandably wary of Prior O'Gorman's manoeuvrings even without being privy to the correspondence taking place in the background.

The exchange of letters before and after Fr Cotham's death is not edifying to read but it shows the honest bluntness among the Benedictines and the unsentimental familiarity with which they spoke to and about each other. There is no reason to believe Fr Cotham was any different. The phrase 'but he reserved his rights' is a reminder of the rebuke from President Birdsall at the beginning of Cotham's career, that talk of 'rights' was a presentiment of no little trouble from 'Mr Cotham'. Prior O'Gorman would have said the judgement was prophetic. Fr O'Neill, an intelligent and gentle man, was the go-between, informing senior Benedictines about Cotham's financial deliberations and state of health, and being charged to use his knowledge of both to bring Cotham round to their way of thinking. At the end of Fr Cotham's notebook, 'Receipts and Payments on Account of the Rev William Cotham's Properties in Lancashire and the Foreign Stocks' are two pages written by Canon O'Neill as a record of what was agreed informally between them.

> After the sale and distribution of the £3000 stock recorded on the preceeding page, there remains Turkish stock to the nominal value of £4000, which £4000 the Rev. James Ambrose Cotham, administrator, for and with the general consent of his older brother the Rev. William Cotham, set aside for two great-nephews, James & Arthur Cotham.
>
> During his last illness, the Rev J. A. Cotham, handed over to the Very Rev. Canon P. A. O'Neill and to the Very Reverend Canon H. B. Hurworth, conjointly, not as a formal legal trust, but as a friendly & confidential commission, desiring them to take charge of it, as he had done, with the special directions, viz. 1st that they should not sell out of this Turkish stock, to invest in Government stock, because they were not trustees, but were friends and managers and because the Turkish stock in question, was certain to become more valuable in a few years; 2nd that they should use the dividends for the education of his great nephews aforesaid, 3rd and not give them the capital till they were 25 years old, or at least, settled in some business, or state of life, providing that if either enter the religious state he should receive a smaller share than the one who

The Spolia of Ambrose Cotham's Life 545

would have to make his way in the world, and leaving the division to the discretion of the two managers of the fund.

This arrangement was put in writing by the Rev. J. Cotham in the form of a trust deed, which however was not accepted as such by Canons O'Neill & Hurworth (who were absolutely forbidden by their religious obligations from accepting a formal trust) but merely as a memorandum of Rev. J Cotham's wishes. These wishes were, after his death, submitted to the Rev. William Cotham, the real legal owner of the bonds, who fully assented to the arrangements proposed.

Paying over to Rev. W. Cotham a balance from the Cash dividend of £29.2s.2½d, Canons O'Neill and Hurworth accepted this commission, subject to the will and pleasure of Rev. W. Cotham, who was at liberty to recall it if and when he pleases. The following is the Account from that date. NB the above sum of £29.2s.2½d was paid by Canons O'Neill and Hurworth, as executors to the Will of J. Cotham, as money belonging to the estate of R[ev]. W. Cotham. See preceeding account.

President Burchall wrote to O'Neill from Lancashire, as Cotham's final hour approached; there is a suggestion that he felt Cotham had held on too long to 'money that is said to belong to nephews in Australia':

Woolton, 14 March 1883

Very Rev & dear confrere

I grant you and Father Hurworth permission to act as Trustees in the case you mention. I am glad our poor confrere is at length making over the money that is said to belong to nephews in Australia. With regard to his peculiums, if he will only state to you what he wishes to give or rather what he gives to St Michael's I hope he may be persuaded, when he gets worse and sees that the end is inevitable and approaching, to hand all over to you. I should be truly sorry on his account as also to forestal [*sic*] any

546   *The Indomitable Mr Cotham*

uncharitable remarks that might be made if he kept ~~posses-sion~~ till the last possession of his money. It will be well if you can induce him either to withdraw from the Cheltenham Bank all his shares &c &c or to give you a legal document authorising you to do so at any time. The former is preferable. I trust he will act the part of a good Religious, give up his own will, and let his money go into the proper channels.

If he will hand over everything to you, the less you say to him the better. All of course goes to his monastery with the exception of what he gives to St Michael's.

I agree with you that it is perhaps better that Prior O'Gorman should not write to him. The letter might have a tendency to irritate rather than assuage. May Almighty God grant him the crowning grace of a happy death.

I am my dear confrere,

Yours truly, R. Burchall

Perhaps if you were to allude to the critical situation in France, and to the possibility of our confreres having to leave the country, and to come to England, this might have some effect on him. Another reason for Fr Cotham's giving up everything is the avoidance of succession and legacy duties.

Easy as it was for President Burchall to spell out the Benedictine position, Fr Cotham had never been a man to be easily induced, persuaded, or assuaged in business matters, nor would he, in his simplicity of faith, have feared an unholy death simply because of his financial accounting, which had always been open to scrutiny. After Cotham's death Prior O'Gorman thanked O'Neill, revealing how his state of mind had been considerably agitated by the confusion of prayers and promptings he had sent by post from Rome.

43 Bocca di Leone, Roma. May 9 1883

My dear Fr Austin,

The Spolia of Ambrose Cotham's Life

I must thank you in my own name & that of alma mater for your managing the Cotham Estate. Of course, I should have been more satisfied if he had left all to Douai; but he exercised his rights & to no place sh^d I have preferred him to leave a bequest more willingly than to Belmont. I strongly and heartily approve the arrangement you made about the £1500.

Did not the Pope's blessing arrive in time? I thought he might have lasted another week or so else I sh^d have sent it by telegraph. However it has all ended well. I had almost a suspicious (!) dread that nothing would come of Fr Cotham's spolia[1] as far as Douai was concerned. Tell Fr Prior [Raynal] his documents came <u>most opportunely</u> & will be extremely valuable ...

43 Bocca di Leone, Roma. May 31 1883

My dear Fr Austin,

Just a word to let you know that the council considered your word sufficient for the validity of Fr Cotham's donation <u>before death</u>. Fr Sub Prior, I believe, has written to that effect to Fr Raynal. I intended sending you Fr Sub Prior's letter but in a moment of distraction, & acting in haste I answered and then tore it up ...

3. Did the Papal blessing reach Fr Cotham before death? I asked Fr Cuthbert, but he did not answer. Next time you or he writes I sh^d like an answer to this question. But don't write for that purpose mainly. ...

Love to all. Tell your juniors to be good and pray well and practise conformity to the Will of God and this mania of reforming and extending government will never appear.[2]

Prior O'Gorman had been kept on tenterhooks about the money until the very end, but when a reasonable sum had been secured his concern turned to Fr Cotham's everlasting spiritual welfare. His old soldier really had been a trying subject from start to finish, hence the exhortation to the juniors at Belmont. O'Gorman's business in Rome affecting the future shape of Benedictine life and mission in England was provoking intense debate in the English Benedictine Congregation. It was a particularly trying time for him, advocating the centrality of the mission charism while dealing at a distance with one of his recalcitrant missioners. Contrary to the Continental European trend of governance from centralised authority for resurgent Congregations, monastic revival in England was moving towards autonomous abbeys with responsibility for their own missions, bringing an end to the provincial system. A fresh approach was being taken to life within the monastery—to its liturgy, personal prayer, scholarship, and hospitality—moving away from the concept of the monastery as a training ground from which the priest-monk would be sent out, possibly never to return as a resident.

The venerable Bishop Collier, in retirement at St Osberg's, Coventry could not countenance what Prior Ford of Downside was to propose, 'advocating the abolition of the vow of going on the Mission at all, but to make it optional to every member to stay in his monastery if he chooses. What a radical subversion of our Constitutions!'[3] Ambrose Cotham was spared the debate in which he would have surely sympathised with his 'old colonist' confrère, Bishop Collier, that to be Benedictine was to be mission minded and mission active. Michael Casey, a modern Cistercian author, opposes the unattractive qualities of vanity, verbosity, and rebellion to what he calls St Benedict's triad of humility-silence-obedience.[4] Although it is interesting to consider Ambrose Cotham's authenticity as a Benedictine monk in the light of a modern interpretation of the Rule, ultimately it is an unfair exercise. The pre-eminence of the vow to mission activity had been the lode star of his monastic formation and his subsequent life. To that he had been unwaveringly faithful.

The restructuring of the English Benedictine Congregation was ultimately decided on by Rome. Although absent in person, Cotham's legacy was a subject for discussion at Belmont in January 1891 when the requirements of the Papal Commission

The Spolia of Ambrose Cotham's Life 549

were hammered out. The assets of the two Provinces, in the form of missions and their financial worth, were divided among the three Benedictine families, prior to dissolving the provincial system. Belmont, having been founded as a common novitiate, did not have the historical links with missions enjoyed by the other monasteries and had to be incorporated as a special case. Prior O'Neill made notes which he, as Fr Cotham's executor, presumably understood with greater clarity than they now convey:

> Fr Sumner reads a concrete proposal of division of Mission [relating to Cheltenham].
>
> - Belmont claims £1300 from S. Province
>
> - left by F Cotham to Belmont
>
> He suggests that as Belmont is owed by Cheltenham £1500 ... £200 to each corporation ... the 3 new familiae may take out of the 'commune deposition' ... £200 each—<u>proposed</u> that £1500 (less £100) debt on Chelt. is a debt on the Province, not of the [Cheltenham] Church; and that this was given to St Michael's by Fr Cotham. Prop. by F. Riley, 2nd F. Burge and notify the same to Abbot Moore.
>
> Yes nem. contrad.[5]

Ambrose Cotham would have been prompt to say exactly what he intended and 'draw him up, as off the lines' if any speaker misinterpreted him.

Fr Ambrose's remains lie in the monks' cemetery, overlooked by the tower at Belmont. The cemetery boundary wall, running down to the iron gate, is close by, paid for out of his legacy and proposed beforehand by Cotham as a good use of his money. Other practical uses suggested by him were building a lodge, purchasing land and buying 'the small farm'.[6]

Fr Cotham's grave, Belmont Abbey

In the wider perspective of his whole adult life there is nothing surprising or outrageous in Fr Cotham's final decisions. In Van Diemen's Land from August 1835 to January 1851 Cotham worked in an evolving society where religion was an important

The Spolia of Ambrose Cotham's Life   551

part of social development and moral improvement. As a colonial chaplain he did so in relative isolation from other clergy and almost in separation from his Benedictine superior and confrères. His role as Convict Chaplain, from 1844, coincided with a close working relationship with a diocesan, secular, bishop and mainly secular priests. In Cheltenham, from mid-July 1852 to the end of October 1873, the achievement of building St Gregory's Church was the hub for Cotham's work in establishing schools and ameliorating conditions for Irish immigrants, collaborating with converts and recusant Catholic families, negotiating with his diocesan bishop and Benedictine Provincial, and introducing religious sisters to Cheltenham. The overall impression is that he was able to operate with a high degree of independence in making decisions and taking responsibility for successes and failures, some of the former being in line with national trends while some of the latter were due to personal errors of judgement.

The period after resignation from Cheltenham might have been an unfulfilled period of Cotham's life given the disappointment of his two projects put before General Chapter in 1874. Indeed, he did feel he was 'turning into a vegetable' at Douai from lack of useful occupation. However, in the final two years of his life, in the full knowledge of his mortal illness, Cotham addressed the priorities which had been constant throughout his life: Benedictine identity, mission, and family. As expressed in financial terms, his final choices caused adverse comment among some of his Benedictine brethren and were open to misinterpretation, but they also indicate the strength of Cotham's resolve in maintaining his principles until his final days, and in this he acted with characteristic constancy and integrity.

During the 1880s the English Benedictine Congregation grappled with the overdue task of defining itself in the post-1850 ecclesiastical environment, pitting the work on the mission against the work of the monastery. Though not directly engaged, Ambrose Cotham showed no sign of experiencing an unresolvable tension in the terms of the debate. His provision for Belmont—detailed and practical—displayed an appreciation of the new style of English Benedictine life that was being worked out there. He wanted Belmont to thrive, just as he wanted his extended family to thrive, and for Cotham that meant putting money into the monastery's undertakings. He had been prepared to see through negotiations for a new institution under Douai's patronage at La Caucherie in Boulogne which would have combined a preparatory school and a home for retired and sick monks, the bookends of life on the mission. More attractive to him, though, had been his strong desire to return to Australia.

Family, monastic life, mission, and Australia were the constant threads of his adult life. His capacity for work and his material wealth were put into the service of a broadness of vision and a generosity of heart which were not limited by narrow choices; Cotham believed he could encompass all his commitments without compromising his avowed values.

If the correspondence from Douai lacked warmth, Cheltenham was generous in its remembrance of him. In carrying out his church duties the Revd Father Cotham, a local newspaper reported, had won

> the respect of the town at large, and the affection of those who were brought into personal contact with him. He made himself thoroughly a townsman, taking an interest in the town's concerns and identifying himself with many of its movements.[7]

The same newspaper also reported at length Fr Wilkinson's Sunday homily when he spoke 'in feeling terms' about Fr Cotham's Australian career, alluding to the many stories his predecessor had related about his years in Tasmania. The subsequent building in Cheltenham was carried out with customary 'unflagging efforts and unconquerable zeal'. Fr Wilkinson had taken on the mission of Cheltenham where Cotham had left off. At Wilkinson's funeral it was said of him that a gift of gold to him was the same as a gift to the church since he liked nothing better

The Spolia of Ambrose Cotham's Life   553

than to add to the stained glass, sculpture and ornamentation of St Gregory's. Accordingly when Fr Wilkinson was presented with £350 on his Silver Jubilee in Cheltenham in 1891 (the third of four such Purses he received from parishioners during his pastorate) he knew immediately how it would be spent. 'The special object to which the sum of money then presented would be devoted would be the perpetuation of the memory of his predecessor Fr Cotham by the erection of two memorial windows' in the baptistry.[8]

Fr Cotham had not been pastorally active for at least a year before his death so he did not leave a gap to be filled on the mission. On a personal level the greatest loss was undoubtedly felt by his brother Fr William. Indeed, the latter's obituary notice mentions the drastic effect that was expected to follow James's death:

> Fr Cotham's Benedictine brother predeceased him by several years, though many fell into the mistake of supposing that the death of one would hasten that of the other, so strong was their affection for one another during life.[9]

Fr William did not fall into a decline. Less than a fortnight after his brother's death he attended the customary Broughton Club Day on Whit Tuesday and after the toasts sang God Save the Queen as a solo 'and rendered it with great energy, although he has completed his 77th year'.[10] He soldiered on for another five years before being obliged to retire to Stonyhurst in 1888. For seven years he earnestly prepared himself for his end, permitting himself grumbles as he went, until he reached 'a happy and peaceful'[11] death on 9 February 1895 in his 89th year. He was buried the following Wednesday, the 13th, the day after what would have been his late brother's 85th birthday.

Fr Cotham knew very little about what became of the people he had met during his convict service. Occasionally he would have recognised names in the English newspapers, or received letters from Tasmania. The outcome of their lives after they left Tasmania might have surprised and gratified him. The hapless

Joseph Hay did, in fact, emigrate to Valparaiso, Chile, during an economic boom resulting from the demand for its grain crops from the gold fields of California and Victoria. His son Jose Guillermo was born there in 1848; his second son, Thomas, was born in Guernsey in 1850. His widow Mary returned to Australia with the family after Joseph Hay's death, helped once again by her brother Thomas Lovat; Jose (J. G. Hay) became an early conservationist in New South Wales and Western Australia and a respected amateur naturalist.

John Marabella the 'good cook confict' he met on Maria Island in 1846 became a much-respected butcher in business with his son in Mount Gambier, South Australia. Six Freemasons carried his coffin at his funeral but the obituary in the newspaper could not refer to him as an old colonist.[12]

Little William Butler died, at the age of 73, in 1909 in Cooma, New South Wales. The arrangement made on his behalf when he was in the Orphan School was a success as he stayed close to Fr Walsh's parishes throughout his long life and became a government employee as a police constable. After Margaret Butler married in 1850 at St Joseph's Church, Hobart to John Shakelton, a ticket-of-leave convict, Mary Ann rejoined their mother, but only for four years as Margaret was brutally murdered by Shakelton in 1855. Mary Ann was readmitted to the Orphan School and stayed there until she was fourteen. She moved to New South Wales and married in 1865, at the age of eighteen. The marriage was a good one and she settled close to her brother. The story of their lives, if there had been no others, would have answered Ambrose Cotham's question, *Quid prodest?*

The Spolia of Ambrose Cotham's Life

Notes

1   The term *spolia* as used by Benedictines simply refers to the material left-overs from a monk's life. There are overtones, of course, from the phrase 'the spoils of war'; in Australia it might be called a man's swag.

2   DA VIII.A.O'Neill 2; O'Gorman to O'Neill, 9 May, and 31 May 1883.

3   DA VII.A.3.f; Collier to O'Gorman, Pentecost eve, 1887. Collier was scathing about what he saw as Ford's nonsensical suggestion that monks could stay in the monastery and support themselves by publishing their studies. 'The writers of pious books are already so numerous that they cannot get a sale for their books.'

4   M. Casey OCSO, *Truthful Living: Saint Benedict's Teaching on Humility* (Leominster: Gracewing, 2001), p. 12.

5   DA VIII.A.O'Neill 2.

6   B. Whelan OSB, *The History of Belmont Abbey* (London: Bloomsbury, 1959), p. 82: '[In 1888] there were sundry material improvements to the property of the monastery, which were largely due to the generosity of Dom Ambrose Cotham who had died at Belmont in 1883. Besides helping to pay for the installation of the water-ram ... he also caused the cemetery wall and gates to be built, prior to the cemetery being consecrated and the churchyard cross erected in 1888. Moreover, part of the money he left from his peculium was used to build larger and better farm buildings. Thus the west side of the present farm was built; the wain-house with granary above, and the root-house with haybarn above; and pigsties in the centre. The bricks and tiles of these buildings will be found to be stamped with the souvenir of the Queen's Jubilee.'

7   *Cheltenham Examiner*, 9 May 1883, p. 8.

8   *Cheltenham Looker-On*, 12 December 1891, p. 1139.

9   *Letters and Notices*, No. XCIX, 1895, House Journal of the British Province of the Society of Jesus, p. 134.

10 *The Preston Chronicle*, 19 May 1883, p. 3.

11 *Letters and Notices*, No. XCIX, 1895, House Journal of the British Province of the Society of Jesus, p. 135.

12 *South Australian Register* (Adelaide), 9 September 1873, p. 7.

APPENDIX A: THE LETTER OF MARCH 1836

Launceston,
12th of March 1836
PRIVATE

MY DEAR LORD.—I received your letter dated the 12th of February, this day, the feast of St Gregory the Great, a day of jubilee in our body universally, and particularly so to our kind friends of Downside. It is on the return of these festivals which we were wont to celebrate with religious joy in our College, that we think of the friends whom religion, education and a long habit of intercourse have endeared to us, with whom for years we formed a part in the circle on those occasions, but from whom we are now separated by an immeasurable ocean. Peace be to them.

I now write to you from the town of Launceston where I arrived this morning, after a rather tedious but somewhat romantic journey; for having left Oatlands, where I had stopped for the first night, at six o'clock the following morning, without having breakfasted, in taking a short cut across the country, through the bush, to Ross, I lost myself; and there being no human being visible, or within hearing to direct me in such a mishap, was wandering about high hills and deep valleys till half past four in the afternoon without food, save a little grass which I chewed to moisten my mouth, the heat being great, and my thirst almost intolerable. After a journey of upwards of 50 miles walking up steep hills and rocks where there was scarce any footing, pulling my horse after me, I came fortunately to a cart road which led me to a shepherd's hut, where both I and my good horse received refreshment; and I was happy to find myself within a mile and a half off the house of a friend. I moreover had another romantic adventure this last journey; for in Epping Forest betwixt Campbell Town and Perth, the rains having rendered some parts of the road impassable, I was compelled to go more into the bush and being overtaken by the night, was wandering about for some hours before I heard the friendly voice of a dog in answer to my repeated cooees. I am, however, now arrived quite safe, and just received your letter which had been sent after me from Hobart Town. I am in an Inn without any of kindred feeling around me; your letter, therefore, gave me great pleasure as assuring there was someone at no very great distance who felt an interest in my welfare.

I say Mass here on the Sunday in a large store which belongs to a Protestant; there is no place in which the people can assemble to prepare for the Sacraments. If there was another priest in the country so that I could remain here for a month or two at a time, I would begin to build, and in the meantime instantly take a house, in which I would say prayers every day and give the people an opportunity of going to their duty; at present this is impracticable, living as I do at an Hotel, and my stay being necessarily so short; the people in Hobart Town will not admit the services of Mr Conolly, so that all the duty of the Confessional there devolves upon me, and they all being in such a state of excitement, I cannot remain long away. I have not therefore administered the Sacraments to any here except the infirm; nor do I mean to do so until we can get a proper place for that purpose, where the people can attend without restraint, which would not be the case in a private house; indeed, there is no Catholic person's house here that is suitable. The people here are wealthy, but of the lowest grade in life, the most respectable of those who attend being a District Constable, a Tailor, Publicans etc., etc. Several, indeed, viz., 14 or 15 of the most respectable residents here are Catholics, but they do not for the most even acknowledge themselves as such, but go to Church. They would however all come over with the proper treatment. Mr Conolly has made himself detested here equally as much as in Hobart Town, and has injured our religion by his unchristian conduct. My object in coming down here has

Appendix A: The Letter of March 1836 559

been merely to induce those who have forsaken their religion to return to it and to hold out better days to those who though they acknowledge themselves as Catholics, know no more of their religion than the name. Before such people can approach the Sacraments they must be instructed like children, many have not been to their duty for 30–40 years, and a great many of them have *never* been. I have endeavoured to instruct the people here as well as my short stay amongst them would allow; and I shall inform them next Sunday to prepare to approach the holy Sacraments in the course of 6 weeks when I expect matters will be so arranged by the arrival of another clergyman, that a Priest may be able to come down and reside a month or two on this side, to commence their chapel, and give them at the same time an opportunity of attending their duty.

I applied to the Government for assistance towards the building of a Chapel in Launceston; but no prospects of any immediate assistance. The foundation of the Richmond Chapel is now commenced; nevertheless Government has not secured to us the grant of £300 nor have securities been entered into for the payment of the contractor; he commenced, however, *ex propio motu*. The Governor has been at Launceston for some weeks, otherwise it would have been arranged before now. Mr C will not interest himself about these things; so that I am obliged to return to Hobart Town, whither the Governor has now returned, as soon as possible, to further this matter; what with one thing and another, our religion degraded in every place, the just complaints of the Catholics on every side, without one friend to assist or console me, I am nearly distracted, nearly mad. During Holy Week I shall say prayers every morning in the schoolroom, and attend the Confessional every day that week; and do the same the next week at Richmond. The people do not like going to Mr Conolly's Chapel, nor would many of them attend their duty there if I were to hear confessions in it. I consequently have appointed the schoolroom. Mr Kenny, as far as I have observed or discovered, has conducted himself with great propriety since the time you left; nor have I any fault to find with him, but on the contrary to commend him in everything; his good conduct and attention to the children, and their consequent improvement, have been to me a subject of the greatest consolation, it has been indeed the only beam of sunshine amidst the darkness that surrounded me.

You mention that you have been daily expecting to hear from me; I wrote to you not more than three weeks or a month ago, and, in one or two letters previous to that, informed you of the necessity of a speedy alteration. Mr Conolly's gross misconduct here is a subject upon which I cannot think without pain, and therefore loath to express it upon paper. You were here for a month; you yourself, my Lord, declared that the straightforward line of duty would be his dismissal; nevertheless you left him as Vicar General without my being acquainted in what capacity he stood; and indeed when I was given to understand from you in express terms, that he was only tolerated; that Mr Ullathorne as Vicar General would come down in six weeks or two months at the latest; that he had no power or jurisdiction over me, and nothing to do with me; and that, in a word, everything in the course of two months would be satisfactorily settled. The time you mentioned transpired, three months transpired, I did not even hear from you. When you did write it was nothing to the point to which my anxiety was directed. He still remains here as the highest representative of our Religion, as the person of your confidence, and from the situation he holds from you, as one deserving of commendation and imitation. Great God! How does his conduct answer this situation? He acts with the greatest indifference, with the greatest disregard to its interests, nay, directly against its interests; he is now engaged in another lawsuit to the infamy of his character as a Minister of Religion; he never even thinks of instructing the children, or preparing them for the Sacraments; his conduct instead of being mild when any one by chance applies to him, is unchristian, disgusting; his drunken conduct with Nessward,[1] an old Protestant minister, is a subject now of common conversation; I mentioned to you before that I had seen him several times intoxicated; nay, I do not believe

Appendix A: The Letter of March 1836 561

I could any evening put him, or cause him to put himself into this state, if I were to take wine with him or keep moderate pace with him. I therefore believe these reports which are now common, though I have never seen him in that state in the streets. I attribute his disregard to the interests of Religion and his conduct to the people to this habit of drink. You mention some unpleasant reports of his conduct in my regard; with the exception of his once refusing to let me administer the Holy Communion with his pyx to a poor man from the altar, telling me to make use of my own; and his refusing to lend me an *Ordo Administrandi* when I had lost mine, and which he the following day very kindly lent to me—with these two exceptions, and which were the consequence of a moment's bad temper, he has always acted towards *me* with civility and as a gentlemen; not as a friend, and as one priest should to another, but with civility. But it is on both sides the civility of a policy without much love on either side. I do not know at present how to keep up any understanding with him, since his conduct has become public. I must candidly say I have an opinion of Mr Conolly which I never had of any man yet—it is indescribable. Entre nous, I really have sometimes taken him to have dealings with his Satanic Majesty; nay, really one night when he was *inebriatus*, I thought by what he said, his countenance, and the figure he cut, that he was the devil incarnate; he would never enter into any pious conversation with me; indeed, I do not know what to think of him.

You mentioned that you heard that the people had purchased and furnished a house for me; they have not done so, but would have done so, and made proposals to me to that effect, but I declined them as I am not settled; if some one does not come down from Sydney I cannot in all conscience remain in the Colony; if some one does come down he will in all probability remain at Hobart Town to commence the Chapel, and I could not therefore accept of such a [house], when in all probability I should not answer their expectations in remaining amongst them; to induce me to do so as appearing to remain, for they understood by some means or other that a Priest was not to come from

Sydney, and since they knew if one did not come I would not remain and they would be again, as they thought, left to Conolly, they made me this offer to induce me to stay with them in Hobart Town. I must candidly tell your Lordship that nothing on earth would induce me to remain here much longer, as circumstances are at present. I have fully made up my mind on that score. If a Priest cannot come down in the course of two months, you will hear from me again, when I will explain myself more clearly. I consider it my duty to press once more upon your Lordship the necessity of either coming down yourself or sending Mr Ullathorne or Mr McEncroe or Mr Therry to take the place of Mr Conolly, which would induce him to quit the country. Be assured my dear Lord of my love and obedience, as long as I remain in your Diocese; nothing but the miserable state of affairs here could make me write to you as I have done. I have not any means of attending my own religious duties and cannot therefore minister with the same effect to the salvation of others.

    I remain
    My dear Lord
    Your obedient humble servant,
    J. Cotham
There is a Catholic going to Sydney to-morrow, or rather to-day by whom I shall forward this letter. I wait most anxiously to hear from you.

Notes

[1]   Revd Robert Knopwood.

APPENDIX B: COTHAM'S COMPANIONS AFTER AUSTRALIA AND CHELTENHAM

AFTER AMBROSE COTHAM left his companions in Tasmania, they, too, continued their priestly careers in varying circumstances. Brief obituary notices put their Australian experiences in context and tell what happened next, when they were no longer needed as convict chaplains.

Fr George Hunter

From the obituary in *The Tablet*, 16 January 1869

DEATH OF ARCHDEACON HUNTER. The Roman Catholic Church in Tasmania, says the Hobart Town Mercury, has once again been deprived of one of its most prominent and valued clergymen in the person of the Very Rev. G. Hunter, Archdeacon of the diocese. The deceased gentleman had been a resident of Hobart Town for some 24 years, having arrived in the colony in the year 1844. He was born at Nottingham, in England, on the 21st September, 1825, and his early education was received at Sedgeley Park School in Staffordshire, where he spent several years in diligent study. On the promotion of the late respected Bishop Willson from his office as a missionary priest at Nottingham to the episcopacy of Hobart Town, Mr. Hunter, who was then but eighteen years of age, expressed a wish to accompany him, and the desire having been cheerfully complied with, he came out to Hobart Town in company with that venerable ecclesiastic and the Revs. Messrs. Hall, Bond, and Levermore. On his arrival he recommenced his studies for the church, under the guidance of the Rev. Mr. Cotham, and was appointed a catechist under the imperial

564 *The Indomitable Mr Cotham*

government regulations in September, 1846. He was ordained by Bishop Willson on the 30th of March, 1850. There have been few ministers of any religious communion held in higher respect, not only by adherents of the Church of which he was a member, by those of other creeds, than this sincerely lamented gentleman.[1]

Fr William Bond

On his return to England in 1860, for the sake of his aged father, William Bond was a prison chaplain for a short time in Cornwall before being appointed by Cardinal Wiseman as Rector of St Thomas of Canterbury Church, Fulham, a splendid example of Charles Hansom's Gothic Revival architecture. After retirement due to poor eyesight he remained in Fulham until his death in 1888. His remains were taken back to Chideock by Sir Frederick Weld, Humphrey Weld's son. Lady Weld played the organ for the Requiem Mass and members of the family joined the choir as a mark of respect.[2]

The Cistercians

Fr Luke Levermore

His family originated in Hammersmith, London. His brother George worked as a gardener for the nuns at New Hall, Essex and his widowed sister-in-law lived on the Mount St Bernard, Leicestershire estate of the Cistercian monks: another example of family congregating around the religious community of one of their members. Fr Levermore returned to England in 1853 with Bishop Willson. He spent five years at Mount St Bernard's until taking over the mission at Marple Bridge in the north Midlands. He successfully developed the mission and was evidently well-loved by his parishioners and respected by local people. He died in 1875 at the age of 77; his body was interred at Mount St Bernard's Abbey.[3]

Appendix B: Cotham's Companions after Australia and Cheltenham   565

The Woolfrey brothers

They acquired one hundred acres of land in the Central Coast district of New South Wales after leaving convict service but their hopes of founding a Cistercian monastery were not realised. Both died in Australia: Fr Odilo in 1856, aged 54 and Fr Norbert in 1872, aged 73.

Archbishop Polding expressed his opinion of Norbert Woolfrey in a letter to Rome on 21 January 1861:

> From the mail bag just arrived I have received two letters from Your Eminence. The first speaks of the renewed representations from the Father Superior of the Cistercians concerning Fathers Norbert Woolfrey and Xavier Johnson. In the case of Fr. Johnson I can only repeat what I have already had the honour of conveying to Your Eminence. When he arrived in this colony he was but a lay Brother, with no thought of becoming anything else. We found him well-disposed in character, we educated him right from the very beginnings of a priestly preparation, and he was eventually ordained. All this at the expense of the Diocese, and in my view justice would allot his services to the Diocese. It is no longer necessary, however, to insist on these considerations. I received several months ago a letter from the Fr. Superior in England in which he directly admits that it would perhaps not be good to recall to their monasteries the priests in question, and leaves a decision in the matter to me. I have given all the circumstances my most mature and conscientious consideration and, My Lord, conclude thus: as to Father Woolfrey, I believe it to be in his spiritual interests that he should be returned to the immediate jurisdiction of his monastic superiors. As to Fr. Johnson, however, I am in no doubt that he should remain here. He is already sixty, his health is not good, he is used to the climate and will be able to continue his labours for several more years, whereas the English climate would almost certainly spell an end to his services and his life.

566 *The Indomitable Mr Cotham*

Fr William Johnson

He stayed in Australia, and died in 1872, two months before Fr Norbert, and before his own plans to return to Mount St Bernard could be realised.[4]

John Lewis Harding

From the Bishop of Plymouth's Pastoral Letter, December 1893:

> We cannot close this portion of our pastoral without referring to two other losses, by the deaths of Father George Corbishley... and of a layman, Mr. John Lewis Harding, of Polperro, Cornwall. John Lewis Harding, who on October 12 passed gently away, and well prepared, in his 86th year, was grandson of Sir Harry Trelawny of Trelawne, in Cornwall, who became a Catholic in Rome in 1830; and nephew of Miss Letitia Trelawny, who started the Mission of Sclerder, and through whose generous aid we were in a great measure able to build and, after its fall, to re-erect our Cathedral. Mr. Harding inherited the faith and self-denying spirit of both these relations. In youth he went out with Bishop Polding to Australia, and there laboured for many years as a Catechist. On his return, with failing sight and with small means, he was ceaseless in his almsgiving to the Church and to the poor. He was buried with other members of his family in the Sclerder Cemetery, near Trelawne, and close to the Church, where his heart's love and hopes were ever centred.[5]

The Caldwell Brothers

Thomas Edmund Caldwell born 1819, professed 1839, ordained 1849 in Adelaide, Willunga 1850–2, then convict chaplain in Tasmania 1853–55, returned to England for Weobley 1855, Studley 1858; died 1897. John Bernard Caldwell born 1826, professed 1845, ordained 1850, died 1908. Both brothers were educated at Douai College before moving to Downside. An obituary of Henry Edmund Moore (1824–1899) recorded that he

Appendix B: Cotham's Companions after Australia and Cheltenham 567

had been allowed to go out with Polding because of fears for his life from consumption and returned when his health was restored; no mention was made of friction between the two men.

Fr Daniel Maurus O'Connell OSB

Daniel O'Connell received the Benedictine habit in 1843, made his Solemn Profession of vows in 1845 and was ordained in 1848, Australia's first native-born priest. He was singled out by Polding at the time as 'a very valuable subject', and he did become so, working as the bishop's Secretary at St Mary's Cathedral, Sydney. He was appointed Dean of the Cathedral in 1857 and Rector of St John's, the first Catholic university college in the British Empire. He returned to pastoral work in Tasmania in 1890 and died in Launceston in 1901.[6]

Augustus Mark Baker

Cheltenham has been characterised as a town of incomers for the last two centuries of its modern existence. It was also a town of surprising transition for some of those temporary residents.

Augustus Baker's granddaughter Beatriz de Regil Muse wrote an extensive memoir; the details of Baker's early life, repeated by her mother, Katherine Mary Queadell formerly de Regil née Baker, are sometimes a little inaccurate but the circumstances of the family's later life are vividly evoked. In 1876, 'being at the time at leisure', Baker made use of his medical training and joined Dr Humphry Sandwith's humanitarian team during the Serbian-Ottoman War of 1876 to 1877. Consequently, Baker became Vice Consul at Nish on the Serbian border, was due to be transferred to Khartoum until the Mahdi prevented it, went instead as Acting Consul to Suakim, and eventually became Vice Consul in Vera Cruz, Mexico where his eldest daughter acted as secretary-housekeeper until her marriage. Baker's other children emigrated to Winnipeg, Canada. He died in Vera Cruz in 1891 aged 47; his mother Charlotte died in Mexico in 1894 at the age of 81. An

568 *The Indomitable Mr Cotham*

obituary letter from Čedomilj Mijatović, formerly Serbian Minister in London, appeared in *The Times*, August 1891: 'When Mr. Baker was appointed British Vice-Consul at Nish he made strenuous efforts to develop the commercial relations between England and Serbia. But though we are thankful for the support he never ceased to give to the interests of the Serbian people, we shall cherish sacredly the memory of "Major Baker" chiefly for his admirable services to our wounded during the war.'[7]

Notes

[1] *The Tablet*, 16 January 1869, p. 25.

[2] See Very Rev G. Oliver DD, *History of the Catholic Religion in Devon, Cornwall &c'* (London: Charles Dolman, 1857); *The Hobart Town Daily Mercury* 4 April 1860, p. 3; *The Tasmanian* 14 July 1888, p. 24.

[3] A report of Levermore's death and funeral was copied in *The Mercury* (Hobart), 3 August 1875, p. 3. See also W. T. Southerwood, 'The Land That I Will Show You' in *Tjurunga*, No 8, December 1974, pp. 77–92.

[4] See obituary in *Freeman's Journal* (Sydney), 27 January 1872, p. 7. Online: Sydney Archdiocesan Archives. JBP L61 7, U1418/5–4. Draft in French, trans. BC. The letter of 21 January 1861 is given in Sr M. X. Compton *et al.*, (Eds.), *The Letters of John Bede Polding OSB, 1861–1877, Volume 3* (Sydney: Sisters of the Good Samaritan, 1998), pp. 3–4. Sr M. Gregory Forster, 'Attempts that Failed' in *Tjurunga*, No 8, December 1974, pp. 93–102.

[5] *The Tablet*, 9 December 1893, p. 35.

[6] The foregoing details of O'Connell's life are taken from 'Daniel Vincent Maurus O'Connell OSB: First Australian-born Catholic Priest'; P. J. Wilkinson; *The Swag,* Winter 2013. Reprinted in the *Catholic Weekly*, 21 July 2013.

[7] See the blog maintained by Ben Muse of Juneau, Alaska: 'benmuse.typepad.com/beatriz_de_regil_muse: Beatriz de Regil Muse (1901–1983) and the people she knew'.

APPENDIX C: THE FAMILY LEFT BEHIND

THERE IS NO record of a Will left by Fr William Cotham SJ but his money had been disposed of fifteen years earlier at the time of his brother James's death. More surprisingly there is no mention in his lengthy obituary of his extended family in Australia. He was known only to the four boys who had come to England for their education and it was Fr James Ambrose who had made arrangements for their travel and the shipments of goods. William had no anecdotes to tell about Lawrence's family and he had not seen his youngest brother for over fifty years. Though he had tremendous personal presence he did not have James' level of imaginative sensibility.

> His name was as a household word, and his sturdy figure, high complexion, and white hair, heralded by a corresponding strength and exercise of voice, declared his presence to eye and ear at almost every gathering of Ours [Jesuit Fathers] within a rather wide range of whatever mission was his head-quarters at the time.[1]

The first and some of the second generation of Australian-born Cothams were known to their Lancashire relatives although news about them was probably censored after Lawrence's death. The tenor of their lives cannot be generalised except to say they belong to Australian history and culture. Lawrence Leopold died in the Queensland goldfields, Sr Catherine Mary was the first Australian-born Sister of Mercy to die, and William, a solicitor and keen sportsman, lived a robust bachelor's life before dying young, all three predeceasing Fr Ambrose Cotham. The three surviving nieces, Marianne Horstmann, Isabella Lillis, and Eleanor Geary, made sound marriages (although Godfrey Geary was a long serving Freemason). The marriage of Isabella's daughter, Sarah, to Walter Scott Duff brought the family close to celebrity through her brother-in-law Reg Duff. Walter was a good cricketer (good enough to represent New South Wales) but he was outshone by Reg, an outstanding opening batsman in partnership with Victor Trumper, for New South Wales and Australia. Reg, however, died of an alcohol-related illness aged 33 in 1911.

The Cotham family knew about alcohol abuse from first-hand experience. Hugh Cotham's adult life was blighted and ruined by his inability to resist drink. He did not have a vicious temperament but when drunk he became brutish. The name Cotham appears frequently in the Queensland press during the 1880s and 1890s. Arthur returned from his English education, studied law and was part of Marsland and Marsland's legal firm in Charter's Towers, northern Queensland by 1891, a year after his marriage. As a junior solicitor his name often appears in court proceedings. Unfortunately, his uncle Hugh Cotham's name is featured with similar frequency.

Intimations of Hugh's rashness appeared as soon as he received his uncle's legacy; despatched in late April 1883, by mid-September he was hoping to capitalise on it by an untried line of business. 'Trust Money to Lend, in sums to suit Borrowers, on Freehold Security. H. Cotham, 11 Australian Chambers.'[2] However, Hugh lacked the knowledge and discipline to make it work. The death of his father, brother, and uncle in three succeeding years coincided with his marriage to Ann Barry in February 1881 and the birth of three children by 1885. He kept up his interest in cricket, playing for the Alberts Team and using his administrative skills as Honorary Treasurer. A cricket report in early 1884 shows he was popular and valued: 'It is pleasant to note the name of Hughie Cotham in the Alberts Eleven and every cricketer will be pleased to see that he played a "not out" in the first innings and 19 [the highest scorer] in the second.'[3] Sadly, this was one of the last favourable mentions of Hugh in the press, although his name appeared with shocking frequency for the next fifteen years as his succumbed to alcoholism and violence. His

Appendix C: The Family Left behind 571

wife Ann was seven months pregnant with their third, and last, child Francis Louis, when the first of many newspaper reports on his shadow life was carried by *The Brisbane Courier*:

> ASSAULT ... on the evening in question [Annie Cotham's] husband came home the worse for drink, and demanded more money from her, which, however, she refused to give him, as he only wanted to drink it; he then caught her by the throat, and was attempting to choke her; he also caught her by the arms and dragged her about the house, banging her up against the partitions; one of the neighbours had to come to her rescue; her arms were all black from his violence; her husband had repeatedly assaulted her before, but it was always while he was intoxicated. The accused said he never struck his wife, and expressed his contrition for what occurred, promising to take the pledge. The complainant stated that she did not wish her husband punished, but bound over to keep the peace. The bench ordered the defendant to enter into his own recognisance in the sum of £20 and one surety of £20 to keep the peace for a period of six months.[4]

Eighteen months after the birth of Francis he was again in court.

> The prisoner fainted in the dock, and was removed to be examined by Dr Hare, who gave his opinion that the man was only suffering from the effects of drink ... The wife appeared with her face covered with plaster, and her head bound in linen. From the evidence it appears that the prisoner returned drunk, took off his boot (a hob-nailed one), and threw it at his wife, who had a baby in her arms. He missed his aim, and his wife returned the missile. Cotham then picked up the boot by the toe and belaboured his wife with the heel of it about her head and face. The woman is still under medical treatment. The prisoner said that if the bench would let him off he would leave his wife, and give her a fixed sum weekly for her maintenance. He would not trouble her again. This, of course, the bench declined to do, and he was sentenced to six months'

572   *The Indomitable Mr Cotham*

imprisonment with hard labour. Prisoner was removed to
the cells in a fainting condition.[5]

Thereafter the reports of petty crime, lewd behaviour, and
vagrancy, always precipitated by drunkenness led to repeated gaol
terms; when released he would celebrate in the usual way. His
family may have used their respectability and influence to provide
a break from bad habits. He travelled to England in 1888 but was
back in Queensland by April 1889. The voyage was merely a pause
for the Brisbane courts and brought no benefits for Hugh. By this
time he had left his wife and family and had become a ridiculously
pathetic figure, almost childlike in his wish to be better but
completely unable to help himself become so.

> Hugh Cotham, who was only discharged on Wednesday,
> was again brought up for drunkenness on Thursday. He
> looked very crestfallen, and Mr. Pinnock heaved a heavy sigh
> as he inquired, 'What am I to do with this man?' The
> defendant said that if he were let off he would leave the
> colony. He would have to walk, but he had friends in Gympie
> who would probably assist him. He was remanded for a
> week, and Mr. Pinnock said he would communicate with his
> friends, and would be only too glad to get rid of him.[6]

> Among the names of persons entered on the charge sheet
> at the City Police Court this morning for drunkenness was
> that of Hugh Cotham. Mr. Pinnock has given him every
> chance to reform. On the last occasion when he was before
> the court, charged, of course, with drunkenness, he prom-
> ised most faithfully to leave the colony for at least twelve
> months and to reform. Mr. Pinnock gave him this
> chance—the last one, however. Cotham did not avail
> himself of it, though, in spite of his sincere promises.
> According to Sub-inspector O'Driscoll, Hugh, as soon as
> he was discharged, went straightway and got some money
> under false pretences, and, of course, got drunk with it. He
> took a fit in the court before his name was called yesterday
> morning, and was taken below. He was remanded for a

Appendix C: The Family Left behind   573

week, at the expiration of which he will be sentenced to three months imprisonment as a habitual drunkard.[7]

The offending, fifty offences by 1891, saw him usually brought before Mr Pinnock in court, until he was gaoled for three years for forgery in 1895. His last, farcical, misdemeanour occurred in February 1899: 'Hugh Cotham was fined £1, or fourteen days, for being drunk, while for destroying a policeman's uniform he was fined a shilling, and ordered to pay the damage: 25s.'[8] He died later in the year at the age of 44, leaving debts but no forwarding address. The bare announcement of his death on 28 July in Maryborough Hospital did not appear in *The Brisbane Courier* until 30 September; no family names were added. There are many ironies in Hugh Cotham's story. William and James would have seen many such wasted lives and lost opportunities but it is unlikely they knew how closely their own family was affected.

A letter from Ida Cotham, Hugh and Annie's only daughter, to a newspaper in 1926 omits any mention of her father. Many details are inaccurate, less than forty-five years after Ambrose Cotham's death, but her pride in his memory is evident.

> Sir,—Among the casually mentioned names in your article on the pioneer priests of Australia, was one, Father Cotham. The Rev. James Ambrose Cotham, OSB, came to Australia with Archbishop Polding. He was for a time in Sydney, but later was sent to Tasmania, where he laboured for over 30 years among the colonists. He had numerous hardships to endure—often carrying vestments, altar stone, and requisites for Mass in the saddle pouch. He did most of his travelling on horseback, from which he developed an internal injury. He was invalided back to the monastery of Stonyhurst, where he died. He built the first church at Richmond, Tasmania. One of the Sisters at the convent where I was educated knew him well. Many times he said Mass in their home. He was a grand-uncle of mine. His brother, Rev. William James Cotham, SJ, was for many years attached to Farm-street, London, but never came to Australia. Yours &c,

Ida Cotham,

Pampas, via Toowoomba, Queensland[9]

Fr Cotham's namesake, James Ambrose did not persevere in the monastery, leaving Douai at the end of the summer term, 1888. He had benefited from a good education and followed a career in accountancy but at some point—possibly when he married Charlotte Sawyer, a Protestant, in 1907—there was a rift in the family. He left the Catholic Church and was buried without a religious service in 1953.[10]

James Cotham (Fr Cotham's great nephew from Queensland) seated on the ground, with the novitiate group, 1887/88, Douai.

The last of his generation, Thomas Richard Shepherd lived a quiet, comfortable old age into his ninetieth year, living close to the Benedictine church of St Alban's on Bewsey Street, Warrington with his housekeeper and a maid. A collision with a boy on a bicycle resulted in a broken hip and he died two weeks later

Appendix C: The Family Left behind 575

in August 1908. The details about his extended family were scanty and notices were placed in English and Queensland newspapers. His estate of £28,000 was contested between his next-of-kin, the surviving families of Lawrence Cotham and Mary Ann Maguire, and his heirs-at-law, his father Richard Shepherd's extended family. Respected and experienced lawyer though he was, he had not kept his affairs up to date and contact with the families had been lost. Sarah Duff, née Lillis, in New South Wales, eventually inherited the entire estate in 1910 before her death in 1911; ironically, Thomas Shepherd had remained closest to the family roots in Warrington.

Notes

[1] House Journal of the British Province of the Society of Jesus, *Letters and Notices*, No. XCIX, April 1895, obituary, p. 130.

[2] *The Telegraph* (Brisbane), 18 September 1883, p. 1.

[3] *Queensland Figaro* (Brisbane), 22 March 1884, p. 19.

[4] *The Brisbane Courier*, 10 December 1884 , p. 6.

[5] *Ibid.*, 3 September 1886, p. 5.

[6] *Ibid.*, 24 April 1891, p. 2.

[7] *Ibid.*, 6 May 1891, p. 2.

[8] *Ibid.*, 23 February 1899, p. 4.

[9] *The Catholic Press*, 21 Jan 1926, p. 33. Ida did not marry; she was buried from Rockhampton Catholic Cathedral in 1947.

[10] Neither of James' daughters, Joyce and Marjorie, married. They both followed clerical careers and after their father's death travelled to England more than once. Marjorie's research into her family history brought her into contact with Douai Abbey, Woolhampton, in 1988 via Br Joseph Galvin's research on her behalf. Her biographical essay 'Life and Work of a Pioneer Priest' was published in the *English Catholic Ancestor Journal*, Vol. 2, No. 7, Spring 1989.

BIBLIOGRAPHY

BOOKS

Alexander, A. *Tasmania's Convicts: How Felons built a Free Society.* Crows Nest NSW: Allen and Unwin, 2010.

Allan, C. H. *A Visit to Queensland and her Goldfields.* London: Chapman and Hall, 1870.

Allitt, P. *Catholic Converts: British and American Intellectuals Turn to Rome.* Ithaca: Cornell University Press, 1997.

Armstrong, K. *Fields of Blood: Religion and the History of Violence.* London: Vintage, 2015.

Beck AA, G. A. (Ed.), *The English Catholics 1850–1950.* London: Burns Oates, 1950.

Bence Jones, M. *The Catholic Families.* London: Constable, 1992.

Berry OSB, A. (Ed.), *Belmont Abbey: Celebrating 150 Years.* Leominster: Gracewing, 2012.

Birt OSB, H. N. *Benedictine Pioneers in Australia.* London: Herbert and Daniel, 2 Vols, 1911.

Birt OSB, H. N. *Obit Book of the English Benedictines: From 1600 to 1912.* Edinburgh: The Mercat Press, 1913.

Blake, S.T. *Cheltenham's Churches and Chapels A.D. 773–1883.* Cheltenham Borough Council Art Gallery and Museum Service, August 1979.

Brooke, A. and Brandon, D. *Bound for Botany Bay: British Convict Voyages To Australia.* Kew, The National Archives, 2005.

Byrne, N. J. *Robert Dunne, 1830–1917: Bishop of Brisbane.* University of Queensland Press, 1991

Byrne, F. *A History of the Catholic Church in South Australia.* Adelaide: E. W. Cole, 1896.

Calvert, F. P. *An Irish Beauty of the Regency: compiled from "Mes Souvenirs," the unpublished journals of the Hon. Mrs. Calvert, 1789-1822.* John Lane, 1911

578 *The Indomitable Mr Cotham*

Casey OCSO, M. *Truthful Living: Saint Benedict's Teaching on Humility.* Leominster: Gracewing, 2001.

Champ, J. *The English Pilgrimage to Rome: A Dwelling for the Soul.* Leominster: Gracewing, 2000.

Champ, J. *The Secular Priesthood in England and Wales: History, Mission and Identity.* Oscott Publications, 2016.

Champ, J. *William Bernard Ullathorne 1806 -1889: A Different Kind of Monk.* Leominster: Gracewing, 2006.

Clay, J. *Maconochie's Experiment: How one man's extraordinary vision saved transported convicts from degradation to despair.* London: John Murray, 2001.

Compton, M. X. *et al.* (Eds.), *The letters of John Bede Polding OSB, 1844–60: Volume 1.* Sydney: Sisters of the Good Samaritan, 1994.

Compton, M. X. *et al.* (Eds.), *The letters of John Bede Polding OSB, 1844–60: Volume 2.* Sydney: Sisters of the Good Samaritan, 1996.

Compton, M. X. et al., (Eds.), *The letters of John Bede Polding OSB, 1861–1877: Volume 3.* Sydney: Sisters of the Good Samaritan, 1998.

Cowley, T. and Snowden, D. *Patchwork Prisoners.* Hobart: Research Tasmania, 2013.

Davies, H. *A View of Cheltenham in its Past and Present State.* Cheltenham: H. Davies, Montpellier Library, 1843 4th Edition.

De Flon, N. *Edward Caswall: Newman's Brother and Friend.* Leominster: Gracewing, 2005.

Doyle OSB, F. C. (Ed.), *Tercentenary of St Edmund's Monastery.* London: R. & T. Washbourne Ltd, 1917.

Dowd OP, C. *Rome in Australia: The Papacy in Conflict in the Australian Catholic Missions 1834–1884.* Leiden: Boston, 2008.

Dumont-Durville, M. J. *Voyage au pole sud et dans l'Océanie sur les corvettes l'Astrolabe et la Zélée.* Paris: Gide et Co, 1846.

Dunmore, J. *From Venus to Antartica: The Life of Dumont D'Urville.* Auckland: Exisle Publishing, 2007.

Elliot, S. *Fifty Years of Colonial Life.* Melbourne: T. Smith and Company, 1887.

Bibliography 579

Fitzgerald, P. *Stonyhurst Memories; Or Six Years at School.* London: Richard Bentley & Son, 1895.

Furphy, S. *Edward M. Curr and the Tide of History.* Canberra: ANU Press, 2013.

Gibbs-Smith, C. H. *The Great Exhibition of 1851: A Commemorative Album.* London: HMSO, 1950.

Gilley, S. (Ed,), *Victorian Churches and Churchmen: Essays Presented to Vincent Allan McClelland.* Woodbridge: Boydell Press, 2005.

Gilbert, P. P. *The Restless Prelate.* Leominster: Gracewing, 2006.

Goding, J. *Norman's History of Cheltenham.* London: Longman, Green, Longman, Roberts and Green, 1863.

Hall, M (Ed.), *Gothic Architecture and its Meanings 1550–1830.* Reading: Spire Books Ltd, 2002.

Hamer CP, D. S. *The Passionist Mission to St Saviour's, Broadway 1850–2000.* Altrincham: Privately published, 2000.

Harding, J. A. *Clifford of Clifton (1823–1893): England's Youngest Catholic Bishop.* Diocese of Clifton, 2011.

Harris, S. *Solomon's Noose: The True Story of Her Majesty's Hangman of Hobart.* Melbourne: Melbourne Books, 2015.

Hart, G. *A History of Cheltenham.* Gloucester: Alan Sutton, 1981 2nd impression.

Heimann, M. *Catholic Devotion in Victorian England.* Oxford: Clarendon Press, 1995.

Hill, R. *God's Architect: Pugin and the Making of Romantic Britain.* London: Allen Lane, 2007.

Hill, W. R. O. *Forty-five years' experiences in North Queensland 1865–1905: With a few incidents in England 1844 to 1861.* Brisbane: H Pole & Co, 1907.

Holman, J. *A Voyage Around the World including Travels in Africa, Asia, Australasia, America etc From MDCCCXXVII-MDC-CCXXXII Vol. IV.* London: Smith, Elder and Co, Cornhill, 1835.

Hood OSB, A. *From Repatriation to Revival.* Farnborough: St Michael's Abbey Press, 2014.

Hughes, R. *The Fatal Shore.* London: Collins Harvill, 1987.

Kavanagh, J. and Snowden, D. *Van Diemen's Women: A History of Transportation to Tasmania*. Dublin: The History Press, 2015.

Kelsh, T. *Recollections of the Rt Rev Robert Willson*. Hobart: Davies Bros, 1882.

Keynes, R. D. (Ed.), *Charles Darwin's Beagle Diary*. Cambridge University Press, 2001.

Kiely O Carm., B.A, M. B. *Our Lady of the Angels and St Winefride, Aberystwyth: A brief chronicle of church and parish, 1857–1957*. Aberystwyth, 1974

Madigan, L. (Ed.), *The Devil is a Jackass; William Bernard Ullathorne 1806–1889*. Leomonster: Gracewing, 1995.

McCann OSB, J. *Annals of the English Benedictine Congregation 1850–1901*. Oxford: St Benet's Hall, 1941.

McCoogan, K. *Lady Franklin's Revenge*. London: Bantam Press, 2006.

Mercer, G. *Convert, Scholar, Bishop: William Brownlow 1831–1901*. Downside Abbey Press, 2016.

Muir, T. E. *Roman Catholic Church Music in England, 1791–1914: A Handmaid of the Liturgy?* Abingdon: Routledge, 2016.

Moran, P. F. *The History of the Catholic Church in Australasia*. Sydney: Oceanic Publishing Company, 1896.

O'Brien, E. M. *Life and Letters of Archpriest John Joseph Terry*. Sydney: Angus and Robertson, Vol. 2, 1922.

O'Donoghue, F. *The Bishop of Botany Bay: The Life of John Bede Polding, Australia's First Catholic Archbishop*. Sydney: Angus and Robertson, 1982.

Oliver DD, G. *History of the Catholic Religion in Devon, Cornwall &c*. London: Charles Dolman, 1857.

O'Neill DC, L. W. *With All My Heart: The Life and Letters of Sr Aloysia*. Privately published, 1977.

O'Shaughnessey, P. Inson, G. Ward, R. *The Restless Years: Being Some Impressions of the Origin of Australia*. Australia: Hamlyn House Pty Ltd, 1970.

Piddock, S. *A Space of Their Own: The Archaeology of Nineteenth Century Lunatic Asylums*. Sydney: Springer, 2007.

Bibliography 581

Reynolds, J. *History of Launceston.* South Melbourne: Macmillan of Australia, 1969.

Rosenman, H. (ed.), *An Account in Two Volumes of Two Voyages to the South Seas by Captain (later Rear-admiral) Jules S-C Dumont D'Urville of the French Navy to Australia, New Zealand, Oceania, 1826–1829, in the Corvette Astrolabe and to the Straits of Magellan, Chile, Oceania, South East Asia, Australia, Antarctica, New Zealand and Torres Strait, 1837–1840, in the Corvettes Astrolabe and Zélée: Astrolabe and Zélée, 1837–1840.* Melbourne University, 1987.

Rowe, G. *Illustrated Cheltenham Guide 1845.* Gloucester: Alan Sutton, 1981.

Scott OSB, G. *et al., Douai 1903, Woolhampton 2003: A Centenary History.* Stanbrook Abbey Press, 2003.

Selzer, A. *Governor's Wives in Colonial Australia.* Canberra: National Library of Australia, 2007.

Shakespeare, N. *In Tasmania.* London: The Harvill Press, 2004.

Sherard, R. H. *The White Slaves of England, Being True Pictures of Certain Social Conditions in the Kingdom of England in the Year 1897.* London: James Bowden, 1897.

Short, E. *Newman and his Family.* London: Bloomsbury, 2013.

Snow, S. *The Exile's Return: A Narrative of Samuel Snow Who Was Banished to Van Diemen's Land For Participating In The Patriot War In Upper Canada In 1838.* Cleveland: Snead and Cowels, 1846.

Southerwood, W. T. *The Convicts' Friend: Bishop R. W. Willson.* George Town, Tasmania, Stella Maris Books, 1989.

Sweetman, G. *The History of Wincanton.* London: Williams, 1903.

Tenbus, E. R. *English Catholics and the Education of the Poor, 1847–1902.* Abingdon, Oxon: Routledge, 2016

Thompson, H. H. *The Wyndham Family: A Story of Modern Life.* London: Burns and Oates, 2 Vols, 1876.

Thorpe CP, O. *The First Mission to the Australian Aborigines.* Sydney: Pellegrini and Co, 1950.

Torode, B. E. *John Middleton: Victorian, Provincial Architect.* Zagreb: Accent, 2008.

582 *The Indomitable Mr Cotham*

Turner, N. *A Social History of Catholics in Australia.* North Blackburn: Collins Dove, Vol. 1, 1992.

Ullathorne, W. B. *Memoir of Bishop Willson.* London: Burns & Oates, 1887.

Ward, T. H. *Humphry Sandwith: A Memoir, compiled from autobiographical notes.* London: Cassell & Company Ltd, 1884.

Wentworth, W. C. *A Statistical Account of the British Settlements in Australasia Vol. II.* London: Geo. B Whittaker, 1824, 3rd edition.

West, J. *The History of Tasmania Vol. 1.* Launceston: Henry Dowling, 1852.

Whelan OSB, B. *The Annals of the English Congregation of the Black Monks of St Benedict (1850–1900).* Private publication, 1942, 2nd edition, reissued 1971

Whelan OSB, B. *The History of Belmont Abbey.* London: Bloomsbury, 1959.

Whitaker, J. *The Best: a history of H H Martyn and Co: carvers in wood, stone and marble.* Southam, Cheltenham: published by the author, 1985.

ARTICLES

Andrews, B. 'Pugin's Australian Works—St John the Evangelist's Church, Richmond (Part 1). In: *Newsletter* Pugin Foundation No. 28, (January 2009).

Andrews, B. '"Solemn Chancels and Cross Crowned Spires": Pugin's Antipodean Vision and its Implementation'. In: *Ecclesiology Abroad: Studies in Victorian Architecture and Design*, Vol. 4, Ch. 2, (2012).

Brown, P. L. 'Fyans, Foster (1790–1870)'. In: *Australian Dictionary of Biography, National Centre of Biography*, Australian National University, (1966).

Cotham, M. 'Life and Work of a Pioneer Priest'. In *English Catholic Ancestor Journal*, Vol. 2, No. 7, (Spring 1989).

Cotham, W. SJ. Obituary. In: *Letters and Notices,* House Journal of the British Province of the Society of Jesus No. XCIX, (April 1895), pp. 130–137.

Bibliography 583

Forster, M. G. 'Attempts that Failed'. In: *Tjurunga*, No 8, (December 1974), pp. 93–102.

Gilchrist, C. '"A life of noisy riot, of filth, indecency and profaneness": the convict voice and the bourgeois imagination'. In: *Journal of the Royal Australian Historical Society*, (June 2006).

Knight, D. 'Stonyhurst Civil War'. *The Stonyhurst Magazine* (2003), uncorrected proof copy.

MacFie, P. 'Silent Impact: The Irish Inheritance of Richmond & the Coal River Valley 1840–1970' In: *Irish-Australian Studies, R. Davis (Ed.), 8th Irish Australian Conference*, Crossing Press, (1995), pp. 486 and 489.

McClelland, V. A. '"School or Cloister?" An English Educational Dilemma 1794–1880'. In: *English Benedictine Congregation History Commission Symposium*, (1997), p. 12.

'Memoirs of Distinguished Gregorians. No. II: The Most Reverend John Bede Polding, DD, OSB'. In: *Downside Review*, (April 1881), pp. 166–167.

Miller, E. 'Plantocrats and Rentiers: Cheltenham's Slave-owners'. In: *Cheltenham Local History Society Journal 34*, (2018), pp. 57, and 64–65.

Nagapen, A. 'A Century of English Benedictine Apostolate in Mauritius 1819–1916', paper presented to 23rd EBC History Symposium, (1997).

'Odds and Ends'. In: *Downside Review* XXI, Vol. II No 2, (July 1902).

Petrow, S. *After Arthur: Policing in Van Diemen's Land 1837–1846*, (University of Tasmania, no date).

Ratcliff, E. 'Here I Raise My Ebenezer: Two Transient Architects in Van Diemen's Land and Tasmania'. In: *Tasmanian Historical Research Association, Papers & Proceedings*, Vol. 54 No. 2, (August 2007), p. 87.

The Stonyhurst Magazine, Vol. V, No. LXXIX, (April 1895), p. 490.

Southerwood, W. T. A Benedictine Pioneer In Van Diemen's Land (Tasmania). In: *Australian Catholic Record Vol. L IV1*, (January 1977), pp. 43–62.

584 *The Indomitable Mr Cotham*

Southerwood, W. T. 'Benedictine was first P.P. in Launceston'. In: *New Standard*, (July 1988), pp. 9–10.

Southerwood, W. T. 'The Land That I Will Show You'. In: *Tjurunga*, No. 8, (December 1974), pp. 77–92.

Tuffin, R. 'The Evolution of Convict Labour Management in Van Diemen's Land: Placing the "Penal Peninsula" in a Colonial Context'. In: *Tasmanian Research and Historical Association, Papers and Proceedings*, Vol. 54 No. 2, (August 2007).

Vials, J. 'Endeared to Friends and Pupils Alike: The Tiesset and Gonez Families in Cheltenham, 1836–1884'. In: *Cheltenham Local History Society Journal 29*, (2013), pp. 39–48.

Wilkinson, P. J. 'Daniel Vincent Maurus O'Connell OSB: First Australian-born Catholic Priest'. In: *The Swag*, (Winter 2013). Reprinted in the *Catholic Weekly*, (21 July 2013).

Williams, B. 'The archaeological potential of colonial prison hulks: The Tasmanian case study'. In: *Bulletin of the Australasian Institute for Maritime Archaeology 29*, (2005), pp. 77–86.

THESES

Dean, S. *Our Children, the Orphans*. BA Thesis, University of Tasmania, (2000).

Haynes, E. F. *Edward Swarbreck Hall—Medical Scientist and Social Reformer in Colonial Tasmania* (MA Thesis, UNTAS, 1976).

Wirtenberger, K. *The Jesuits in Jamaica* (1942). Master's Thesis. Paper 426.

UNPUBLISHED ARTICLES

Bentall, C. 'The Sartorius Memorial', (2015).

WEBSITES

https://www.femaleconvicts.org.au for material produced by the Female Convicts Research Centre, Hobart, Tasmania

INDEX OF PERSONAL NAMES

Abbot, Martha *née* Holdich 164, 255

Abbot, Thomas 255

Aberdeen, George Hamilton-Gordon, 4th Earl of Aberdeen 24, 46

Acock, John 334, 339–43, 358, 366, 382, 386, 398, 401–04, 407, 409, 416–18

Aldhouse, Stephen and Mrs Elizabeth *née* Richardson 256–57

Anderson, John Bartholomew OC, Abbot of Mount St Bernard 214

Anstey, Henry Frampton 98

Anstey, Thomas Chisholm 74, 95–8

Appleton, James Francis OSB 14–15

Arthur, Sir George, Lieutenant-Governor of Van Diemen's Land 34, 41, 52, 58, 60

Backhouse, James 106

Baines, Peter Augustine OSB, Bishop of Siga 22, 29, 378

Baker, Augustus Mark 456, 468, 469, 488, 490, 511–12, 567–8

Barry, John 485–6, 500, 526

Batman, John 70

Beale, Dorothea 316–7, 441

Becker, Lydia 507–8

Bedford, William 56, 91, 133

Benson, William 98, 100–04, 139

Berkeley, Hon. Swinburne Fitzhardinge 307, 309

Birdsall, John Augustine OSB, President of the English Benedictine Congregation 21–2, 25, 29, 54, 290, 295–6, 300, 321, 329, 333, 335, 359, 368, 374, 381, 398, 457, 461, 544

Blay, Solomon 92

Blount, Henry Benedict OSB 326, 328, 330, 359–61, 373–4, 376, 381, 385–90

Bond, William Peter 134, 155, 157, 181, 200–04, 230, 242, 245–6, 251, 261, 563–4

Bond, William V and Mrs Nancy 202

Boodle, James 393, 403, 409, 414–15, 499

Booth, Charles O'Hara 174, 180, 201, 205

Boulton, Richard Lockwood 304, 366, 413, 418

Bourke, Sir Richard, Governor of New South Wales 24, 46

Bowden, Amelia 164

Bowden, Dr Edward 162–70, 182, 186, 252–4, 256

Bowden, Phillipa Bull *née* Powell 162–71, 182, 186, 188, 252–6

Boyd, James 207–8

Boyd, Archibald 291

Bradney, John 533–4

Bramston, James Yorke, Bishop, Vicar Apostolic of the London District 21, 22, 33, 39, 60
Brennan, Elizabeth 357–8, 367–8, 391, 403, 409, 451
Brooks, George 185–6
Brown, Mather 63
Brown, Thomas Joseph OSB, Bishop of Newport and Menevia 21, 376, 394, 405–6, 527
Brown, Winefred and Lucy 358–9, 373
Burchall, Richard Placid OSB, Abbot President of the EBC, 272, 282, 435, 513, 515, 517, 545–6,
Burgess, Alice and Robert (siblings) 187–8, 324
Burgess, Esther 187
Burgess, Laurence, Prior of Ampleforth 12
Burgess, Mary 187
Burgess, Murray 200, 231–2, 239
Burgess, Thomas, Bishop of Clifton, 287, 358
Buscombe, James Kestall 42, 121
Bushelle, John and Mrs Elizabeth 75
Butler, Thomas xxi, 56, 77–8, 79, 97–8, 101, 137, 146, 181, 200, 203, 232, 242, 251, 260, 263
Butler, Margaret *See* Shakelton
Butler, Mary Ann 178, 554
Butler, William 177–8, 189, 554
Byron, John, Chief District Constable 109

Caffieri, Hector 309, 312–13, 314, 315, 340, 357, 367, 373, 375, 384, 386, 387, 394, 396, 487
Caffieri, Mary *née* Clowes 312
Caffieri, Pauline 447, 451
Calderbank, James OSB 4, 296
Caldwell, John Bernard OSB 247–8, 336, 394, 527, 566–7
Caldwell, Thomas Edmund OSB 247, 394, 566–7
Campden, Charles George Noel, Viscount, 2nd Earl of Gainsborough 361, 363
Carlyle, Thomas ix
Carolan, Patrick 108–9
Cassidy, Eleanor, *née* Lyons 231
Cassidy, Hugh 189–90
Cassidy, John 33–4, 38, 40, 41–2, 46, 62–3, 98, 120, 122, 181, 226, 231, 263, 470
Cassidy, Sarah *See* Cotham, Sarah (sister-in-law)
Caswall, Fr Edward CO 351, 422
Champ, Judith xxii, 355, 525
Channing, William Ellery 153
Cianchettini, Pio 296, 311
Clementina, Thomas 533
Clifford, Charles 7
Clifford, William, Bishop of Clifton 350, 360, 393–6, 404, 422, 431, 440–7, 527
Close, Francis 291, 292–4, 297, 311, 317, 344
Cockshoot, Thomas Anselm OSB 366, 375–7, 405–6
Collier, William Bernard Allen OSB, Bishop of Port Louis, Mauritius 13, 14, 15, 17, 425–

Index of Personal Names 587

7, 436, 438, 485, 487–90, 527, 531, 548, 555

Connell, Daniel *See* O'Connell

Connell, John and Mrs Maria 76–7

Conolly, Phillip 21, 34–43 *passim*, 49–56 *passim*, 60, 64, 67, 69, 76, 130, 257, 558–62

Cookefoye, Agnes Mary *née* Relton 456

Cookefoye, Henry 453–6, 461

Cooper, Roger Maurus OSB 333, 413–4

Copeland, George Ford, Dr 332, 342, 347–55 *passim*, 362, 367, 376, 384, 386, 393, 399, 409–10, 413, 419, 429, 436, 444, 487, 493, 498, 512

Copeland, Mary Elizabeth 349, 350–1

Copeland, Matilda Catherine 349, 350–1

Copeland, Selina *née* Bacchus 347–52, 355

Copeland, William John 351–2, 493

Corcoran, James Vincent OP 24, 27, 33, 38, 44

Cotham, James Ambrose OSB, immediate family members:

Cotham, Ann née Barry 570–1, 573

Cotham, Arthur Leopold (great-nephew) 476, 478, 529, 538, 540–42, 570

Cotham, Eleanor (niece, 1846–1902) *See* Geary, Eleanor

Cotham, Eliza née Chater, later Finklstein 476, 478, 529–30, 538

Cotham, Hugh (nephew, 1851–1899) 125, 469, 476–9, 486, 529, 540, 570–73

Cotham, Ida (great-niece) 573–4, 575

Cotham, Isabella (niece, 1840–1911) *See* Lillis, Isabella

Cotham, Isabella, née Hall, later Shepherd (mother) 3–4, 8, 18, 275, 463

Cotham, James Ambrose (great-nephew) 476, 478, 482, 529, 538, 540–41, 574

Cotham, Lawrence (brother, 1812–1881) 3–4, 12, 17, 19, 35, 46, 59, 63, 65, 98, 119–26, 154–5, 190, 202, 208, 224, 226, 227, 231–3, 263, 266, 282, 286, 463–81, 523, 529, 539, 569

Cotham, Lawrence (father) 3–4, 8, 364

Cotham, Lawrence Leopold (nephew, 1841–1869) 125, 263, 476, 478, 482, 569

Cotham, Lawrence, of Hardshaw Hall 4–5

Cotham, Marianne Eleanor (niece, 1839–1885) *See* Horstmann, Marianne Eleanor

Cotham, Mary Ann (sister, 1808–1871) *See* Maguire, Mary Ann

Cotham, Sarah (niece, 1844–1868) later Sr Catherine Aloysius SM 125, 475, 478, 569

Cotham, Sarah (sister-in-law) 120, 263, 469–72, 477, 539–40

588   *The Indomitable Mr Cotham*

Cotham, William (nephew, 1843–1882) 125, 263, 469–72, 569

Cotham, William Penketh 9, 364

Cotham, William SJ (brother, 1806–1895) 3–6, 44, 80, 126, 194, 274–9, 305, 318, 337, 363–4, 395, 463–71, 475, 478, 481–2, 501, 509, 521, 529–30, 532, 538, 541, 542, 544–5, 553, 569, 573

Cotham, William SJ (the elder) 4–5, 9

Cotterell, Captain 170, 171

Counsell, Andrew 40

Cowell, James William and Mrs Catherine *née* Pender 71, 74

Cowley, James 412

Crotty, Thomas and Mrs Harriet 382–3, 393, 499

Cuffay, William 266–7

Cullen, Paul, Cardinal, Archbishop of Armagh and of Dublin 275–6

Curr, Edward and Mrs Elizabeth 8, 76, 95

Curr, Edward, Richard, and William (siblings) 8, 95

Curtis, Selina, Charlotte, and Amelia (siblings) 440, 447

D'Urville, Jules Dumont, Captain 83–90 *passim*, 92, 97

Darwin, Charles 57, 134

Davis, Charles Henry OSB, Bishop of Maitland 23, 26, 247, 248

Dawson, Peter and Mrs Anna *née* O'Dell 227–9

De Little, Robert 72–3

Dickenson, Mr 175

Doherty, Fanny 169–70, 233

Donovan, Mrs 388

Dowling, Christopher Vincent OP 21, 139

Doyle, Francis Cuthbert OSB 12–3

Duck, James Basil OSB 286, 300, 358

Duff, Reginald Alexander 570

Duff, Sarah Mary 538, 569, 575

Duff, Walter Scott 570

Dunne, William John xxi, 146, 152, 201, 233, 242, 251, 263, 470

Dutton, Richard 417, 460

Eardley-Wilmot, John Eardley, Lieutenant-Governor of Van Diemen's Land 128–9, 151, 168, 173–4

Eccles, Seth DD 19

Elliot, Sizar 31–3, 45

Ellis, Sir William 163–4

Evans, Daniel 297, 300, 309, 328, 358, 487–8

Ewing, Thomas James 173–4, 256

Excell, Mrs 460

Fairclough, Matthew Charles OSB 12, 15

Farmer, William 304, 357

Finklstein, Samuel 478, 529, 538

Fisher, Clement 24–5, 27, 31–2, 38

Fitzgerald, John 176, 274, 372–3

Fleming, Sir Valentine, Solicitor General 144–5

Index of Personal Names

589

Franklin, Lady Jane *née* Griffin 58, 87, 129
Franklin, Sir John 58, 84–93 *passim*, 96, 128–9, 173–4
Franklin, William 338, 422–3, 427
Fry, Elizabeth 164
Fyans, Foster, Captain and Mrs Elizabeth Alice *née* Cane 176–9

Garrett, James 167
Garrett, Maria Henrietta and Elizabeth (siblings) 160, 167
Garrett, Rhoda 508
Garrett, Robert Stocker and Mrs Martha *née* Bowen 159, 167
Gaskell, Hamer 3
Geary, Eleanor 125, 263, 474–5, 481, 569
Geary, Godfrey 569
Geoghegan, Patrick Bonaventure OFM, Bishop of Adelaide, later of Goulburn 139, 176, 189, 243–4
Gerardot, Jean Baptiste Antoine 4
Giberne, Maria Rosina, later Sr Pia Maria 347–9, 352, 355, 444, 488
Giles, Anna Martha 165
Giles, George and Mrs 164–5, 253
Gipps, Sir George, Governor of New South Wales 91
Glassbrook, Edward Anselm OSB 12, 14, 17, 278, 286, 294, 297–9, 315, 375, 488, 511, 515–6
Goodridge, Henry Edmund 40–1
Gorman, John 25, 33, 38, 45
Goupil, Ernest Auguste 85–8, 92
Graham, Mary Frances, later Mother Frances 445–6, 451

Graham, William, Colonel 338, 436, 443–7, 451
Greenhatch, Mrs 205–6
Gregory, David 285
Gregory, Henry Gregory OSB, Abbot 25, 32, 33, 45, 51, 139, 144–5, 244, 247, 273, 285, 372
Gregory, Sr Mary Scholastica OSB 246

Hackett, James 36, 46
Hall, Edward 12
Hall, Edward Swarbreck, Dr and Mrs Mary *née* Latham 5, 37–8, 43, 76, 142, 162
Hall, James (JAC's grandfather) 8, 277, 463, 465
Hall, Nicholas, formerly Maguire, 277, 468
Hall, William, Vicar General 134, 137, 139, 148, 160, 175, 180, 195, 199, 201, 205–6, 212, 246, 251, 261, 263, 361, 563
Hampton, James Stephen, Comptroller General 200, 216, 252, 253, 254
Hanford, Compton-John 342, 375, 429
Hansom, Charles Francis 304, 334–43 *passim* 360, 363, 365, 385, 397, 402, 410–18 *passim*, 497, 564
Harcourt, Robert 255, 265
Harcourt, Susannah/Sarah *née* Holdich 164, 168, 255, 265
Harding, John Aloysius (Lewis) 30–1, 33, 281, 283, 566

Hardman, John 303–4, 343, 357–9, 373, 402,
Hawarden, James 412, 415, 487–8, 490
Hay, Joseph William 98, 224–6, 554
Haynes, Arthur 71
Healy, James 386, 429, 461
Heptonstall, Thomas Paulinus OSB 272–3, 301, 333, 340, 364, 371–8 *passim*, 404–6, 409
Hislet, George and Mrs Sarah 164
Holdich, Jane *See* Learmonth, Jane
Holdich, Matthew and Mrs Catherine 164
Holdich, Martha *See* Abbot, Martha
Holdich, Susannah/Sarah, *See* Harcourt, Susannah/Sarah
Hombron, Jacques Bernard 84–90 *passim*
Hope, Jonathan and Mrs Amelia *née* Smith 222–4
Horstmann, Gustavus Caesar 474, 478, 529, 538, 540
Horstmann, Marianne Eleanor 125, 263, 474, 481, 569
Hughes, Peter 219–24 passim
Hunter, George 134, 148, 158, 180, 195, 199–201, 205, 215, 238, 251, 261, 563–4
Hunter, Henry 180, 216, 238,
Hurworth, Henry Basil OSB 465, 526, 539, 541, 544–5

Jobbins, John Richard 335
Joesbury, Benjamin 395–6, 420–1

Johnson, William Xavier OC 100, 214, 259, 565–6
Jones, Algernon Burdett 180, 220
Jones, Harriet 389
Jones, William 410, 497

Kearney, Sr Cephasie DC 437
Keating, Jerome 157, 160, 224–5
Kendal, James Nicholas OSB 285, 353, 373, 375, 430, 527
Kenny, John OSB 32–4, 43, 45, 49, 559
King George III xx
Knopwood, Revd Robert 43, 562

Lambe, John 539–41, 543
Lamprière, Thomas James 87
Learmonth, James Allan 255
Learmonth, Jane *née* Holdich 164, 255
LeGrand, Frederick William, Dr 263
Leigh, William Augustine 103, 339, 375, 454,
Letheren, William 497
Levermore, James Luke OC 134, 146, 158, 199, 205–13 *passim*, 214, 251, 261, 337, 563–4, 568
Lewis and Lane, stone carvers 366
Lillis, Isabella 125, 470, 481, 538, 569
Lillis, Patrick 481
Lillis, Sarah Mary *See* Duff, Sarah Mary
Loughnan, John Michael 116, 180, 200, 246, 378
Lowe, George 36, 45–6

Index of Personal Names

Maconochie, Alexander 234, 281
Maggs, Austin 364–6
Maguire, Emily *See* Renehan
Maguire, James 277,
Maguire, Mary Ann *née* Cotham 3–4, 275, 277, 468, 481, 575
Maguire, Nicholas *See* Hall
Maguire, Thomas 275, 277
Manning, Henry, Cardinal, Archbishop of Westminster 315, 449, 491, 493, 507, 523
Marabella, John 209, 554
Marsh, Richard OSB 11
Martini, Antonio and Mrs Mary *née* O'Mara 69–74 passim
Martyn, Herbert Henry 325
Mathew, Theobald 107–8, 111–6 *passim*, 141, 245
McCarten, James Edward DD 511–12
McCarthy, Robert and Mrs Elizabeth, formerly Porter 78–81, 117
McEncroe, John 21, 139, 140–3, 152, 285, 562
Middleton, John 396, 407, 413
Molesworth, Sir William, Bart 128, 221
Monington Webbe-Weston, Mary Anne *née* Wright 362, 377–80, 394, 400, 449–50, 459, 515, 521
Monington Webbe-Weston, Thomas 361, 378, 379
Montgomery, Mrs 109, 166–9 *passim*, 171, 174, 232
Moore, Henry Edmund OSB, Abbot 247–8, 549, 566–7

Morris, William Placid OSB, Bishop 21
Murphy, Francis, Bishop of Adelaide 103, 138, 139, 143, 171, 180, 189, 244, 247, 339
Murphy, Maria 177–8
Murphy, Mary 169–70
Murray, Thomas Joseph Malachy Murray OSB 169–70, 199–200, 216

Neve, Sarah 25–6, 333
Newman, Blessed John Henry OC, Cardinal 282, 292, 348–52, 422, 444, 448, 488, 491–3, 498
Nixon, Francis Russell, Bishop of Tasmania 132–3, 151, 191–2

O'Connell, Daniel Vincent Maurus OSB 77, 146, 567–8
O'Gorman, Edward Anselm OSB 512–18 *passim*, 540, 543–8 *passim*
O'Halloran, Mr 201
O'Keefe, Daniel and Mrs Mary 329–30
O'Keefe, James xi, 236, 329–30
O'Keefe, Sophia *née* Didcote 330, 332
O'Neill, Peter Austin OSB 377, 465, 539, 541, 544–6

Pasha, Ismail 467
Pearce, Edward and Mrs Sarah 164
Perregalli, Mario 71–2

Phillips, Robert Biddulph 304, 362, 373, 397–403 *passim*, 406
Phillips, William Gerard and Mrs Mary *née* Burton 99
Polding, John Bede OSB, Archbishop of Sydney 21–6 *passim*, 29–44, 46, 49–56 *passim*, 60, 64, 74, 75, 77, 96–9, 102, 117, 130–1, 134, 138–46 *passim*, 152, 171, 189, 199, 203, 209, 214, 241, 244–9 *passim*, 252, 257, 258, 261, 273, 276, 304, 333, 336, 359, 372–3, 378, 469, 513, 543, 565–7, 573
Pollard, Mary Ann 3–4, 463
Pope Pius IX 195–7, 294, 491, 525
Powell, Ann *née* Pugin 358–9, 373
Powell, William 396, 427
Powell, William Hardman 359
Power, Margaret 169
Poynter, William, Bishop, Vicar Apostolic of the London District 22, 60
Prest, Richard Ambrose OSB 364, 405, 539
Price, Charles 143
Pugin, Augustus Welby Northmore 44, 131–2, 303–05, 359, 376
Pugin, Edward Welby 364–5, 402, 406

Queen Victoria 271, 349
Quin, Catherine Anastasia 174–5, 189, 211, 225, 245
Quin, James Michael 174–5, 179–81, 211, 225, 245, 398

Quinn, James, Bishop of Brisbane 475, 478, 481, 523

Rainger, Charles 344, 358, 366, 386, 394, 458, 497, 499
Ratcliffe, Margaret 450
Reichenberg, Jane 238
Reichenberg, Joseph 61, 89, 142, 238, 423
Renehan, Dr Edward J 481–3
Renehan, Emily 277, 481–3
Richardson, Elizabeth, Mary, and Sarah (siblings) 164 *See also* Aldhouse
Riddell, Charles 395, 406, 459
Robinson, Dixon 468–9
Rolling, Thomas Austin OSB 379, 400
Roope, George 263
Ross, James 84, 89, 92
Rowe, James Irenaeus 4
Rowe, John Pearson 35–6, 38, 45
Rowe, Mary *née* Lowe 36, 45

Samuelson, Henry MP 506–8
Sartorius, Annabella Eliza *née* Rose 368
Scarisbrick, William Benedict OSB, Bishop of Port Louis, Mauritius 332, 365, 376, 377, 384, 396–7, 404, 425, 435–48, 450–1, 503, 516–8, 527
Scott, William Dunstan OSB 23, 357, 373, 457–8, 498
Serviss, John and Mrs Eliza 164, 256
Shakelton, John and Mrs Margaret *née* Butler 178, 554

Index of Personal Names

Shepherd, John (Cotham half-brother, c 1819-c 1848) 6, 17–18, 202, 275

Shepherd, Richard 6, 17–18, 194, 275, 575

Shepherd, Thomas Maurus OSB 17

Shepherd, Thomas Richard (Cotham half-brother, 1820–1908) 6, 17–18, 202, 275, 338, 574–5

Shepperd, Clara 423, 427, 450–1

Sherwin, Isaac 108–9, 111, 143

Sisk, Thomas Ignatius OC 337

Smith, Thomas Cuthbert OSB 497–9

Sorell, William, Lieutenant-Governor of Van Diemen's Land 58

Spencer, Benedict OSB 25, 32–3, 45, 51, 54, 75

Stevens, C. G., Mr 263, 265

Sullivan, James and Mrs Margaret 324

Sumner, John Charles Bede OSB 24–5, 27, 31, 33, 38, 45, 51, 139, 144

Tennyson, Elizabeth *née* Fytche 333, 391

Therry, John Joseph 21, 42, 47, 56, 64, 67, 69, 73, 74, 77, 78, 85–92 *passim*, 96–98, 102, 130, 137, 141–46, 171, 173–6 *passim,*180

Thompson, Edward Healy 487–8, 490–4

Thompson, Harriet Diana *née* Calvert 491, 492, 494–6, 508

Tiesset, Casimir 316–9, 359, 367, 443

Tiesset, Charles and Eugene (siblings) 367, 420

Tiesset, Sophie 309, 314–7, 367, 393, 443, 456, 508

Tixhon, Sr Aloysia DC 349, 424–6, 434–51

Towle, James de Lacy 304, 309, 314, 319, 332, 334–5, 367, 373, 376, 386, 393, 394, 449, 516, 541

Trumper, Victor 570

Ullathorne, William Bernard OSB, Archbishop of Birmingham 21–2, 34–9, 43, 46, 50–5, 64, 77, 99–101, 128, 130, 142, 189, 195, 213, 221, 241–2, 244, 274, 276, 280–2, 287, 304, 355, 560, 562

Vaughan, Roger William Bede OSB, Archbishop of Sydney 405, 477, 513, 523

Waddy, Caroline 375

Waddy, John 375, 422, 521

Walker, George 106

Walker, Robert 487–8

Wallace, Patrick 91–2

Walsh, Richard 175–8, 189, 245, 281, 554

Warburton, Samuel and Henry 410–11, 414–7

Waterton, Charles 337–8

Watkins, James 55, 60–7, 75, 130

Westwood, William alias 'Jackey Jackey' 223, 230

Wilderspin, Samuel 316

Wilkinson, Fr Robert Aloysius OSB xxi, 22, 287, 315, 329, 339, 358, 367, 377, 419, 427, 458, 465, 497, 499, 503–4, 511, 518, 527, 541, 552–3

Williams, George Arthur 306, 309–12, 318, 333–5, 342, 350, 362, 375–6, 384, 393, 409, 459, 487–8

Willson, Robert William, Bishop of Hobart 78, 116, 117, 129–34, 137–47, 151, 154, 158, 165–71 *passim*, 174–90 *passim*, 191, 195, 199, 205, 213–16, 219–23, 232, 236, 241–49 *passim*, 251–61 *passim*, 274, 280, 303–4, 372–3

Wiseman, Nicholas, Cardinal, Archbishop of Westminster 293–4, 297, 360–2, 375, 420, 428, 491, 564

Woolfrey, Henry Norbert OC 200, 214–5, 251, 258–9, 565

Woolfrey, William Odilo OC 195, 214–6, 251, 259, 565

Wright, Robert and Mrs Sarah 164

Wybault, Patrick Robert 309, 313–4, 319, 487

Lightning Source UK Ltd.
Milton Keynes UK
UKHW011612200119
335715UK00001B/14/P